Shortness of purls p37.

CW01091614

for Julia
Sept 1991
with affection and
admiration

Jonathan.

This book completes the study of the life and political thought of Algernon Sidney (1623–1683), which began with *Algernon Sidney and the English Republic 1623–1677* (1988). In the process it offers a reinterpretation of the major political crisis of Charles II's reign, from 1678 to 1683.

Like its predecessor, the book links political with intellectual history. It describes Sidney's political activity culminating in his famous trial and execution for treason in 1683, and his major political work, the *Discourses Concerning Government*, used as evidence against him at that trial. These are set in the context of the history and the political thought of the crisis in general. This was a period of English history overshadowed by its civil war past, and by its European situation. The crisis hinged, accordingly, on the relationship between present policy and public memory, seen in that European context.

A major theme of the book is the progress of this relationship, and the power of that memory, both in the mind of Algernon Sidney and in the course of Restoration history. It was this which caused the Restoration crisis, and which eventually ended it. It was this also which made it the birthplace, in the works of Sidney, Locke and others, of some of the most influential political writing in English history.

Cambridge Studies in Early Modern British History

ALGERNON SIDNEY
AND THE RESTORATION CRISIS, 1677–1683

Cambridge Studies in Early Modern British History

Series editors

ANTHONY FLETCHER
Professor of Modern History, University of Durham

JOHN GUY
*Richard L. Turner Professor in the Humanities and Professor of
History, University of Rochester, N Y*

and JOHN MORRILL
*Lecturer in History, University of Cambridge, and
Fellow and Tutor of Selwyn College*

This is a series of monographs and studies covering many aspects of the history of
the British Isles between the late fifteenth century and the early eighteenth century. It
includes the work of established scholars and pioneering work by a new generation
of scholars. It includes both reviews and revisions of major topics and books which
open up new historical terrain or which reveal startling new perspectives on familiar
subjects. All the volumes set detailed research into broader perspectives and the
books are intended for the use of students as well as of their teachers.

For a list of titles in the series, see end of book.

ALGERNON SIDNEY
AND THE
RESTORATION CRISIS,
1677–1683

JONATHAN SCOTT

*Fellow and Director of Studies
in History, Downing College, Cambridge*

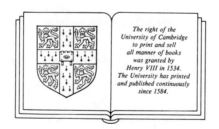

The right of the
University of Cambridge
to print and sell
all manner of books
was granted by
Henry VIII in 1534.
The University has printed
and published continuously
since 1584.

CAMBRIDGE UNIVERSITY PRESS

CAMBRIDGE
NEW YORK   PORT CHESTER
MELBOURNE   SYDNEY

Published by the Press Syndicate of the University of Cambridge
The Pitt Building, Trumpington Street, Cambridge CB2 1RP
40 West 20th Street, New York, NY 10011–4211, USA
10 Stamford Road, Oakleigh, Melbourne 3166, Australia

First published 1991

Printed in Great Britain at
the University Press, Cambridge

British Library cataloguing in publication data

Scott, Jonathan, 1958–
Algernon Sidney and the restoration crisis, 1677–1683. –
(Cambridge studies in early modern British history)
1. England. Politics. Sidney, Algernon, 1623–1683
I. Title
942.06092

Library of Congress cataloguing in publication data

Scott, Jonathan, 1958–
Algernon Sidney and the Restoration crisis, 1677–1683 / Jonathan
Scott.
p.   cm. – (Cambridge studies in early modern British history)
Includes bibliographical references and index.
ISBN 0-521-35291-6
1. Sidney, Algernon, – 1623–1683.   2. Great Britain – History –
Restoration, 1660–1688.   3. Political scientists – Great Britain –
Biography.   4. Politicians – Great Britain – Biography.   I. Title.
II. Series.
DA407.S6S43   1991
941.06′6′092–dc20
[B]   90-2569 CIP

ISBN 0 521 35291 6 hardback

for Stephens and Stephens,
alumni of Butley College, Orford,
and Basil's Lodge, Waihi

And when the Protestants of the Low-Countries were so grievously oppressed by the power of Spain . . . why should they not make use of all the means that God had put into their hands for their deliverance? . . . by resisting they laid the foundation of a most glorious and happy Commonwealth, that hath been, since its first beginning, the strongest pillar of the Protestant Cause now in the world, and a place of refuge unto those who, in all parts of Europe have been oppressed for the name of Christ. (Extract from A. Sidney, *Discourses Concerning Government* (probably ch. 2, section 32), quoted at: *The Trial of Algernon Sidney Esq.* in *Works* (1772), pp. 24–5)

Legal proceedings . . . are to be used when the delinquent submits to the law; and all are just, when he will not . . . if the lusts of those, who are too strong for the tribunals of justice, cannot otherwise be restrained, than by seditions, tumults, and war, those seditions, tumults, and wars are justified by the laws of God and man. (Sidney, *Discourses*, pp. 187–8)

CONTENTS

PREFACE

This is the second of two studies of the seventeenth-century English republican, Algernon Sidney. It is linked both chronologically and thematically to its predecessor, *Algernon Sidney and the English Republic 1623–77* (1988). It is also structurally similar to that work. Each begins with a general, principally analytical section, intended to set the succeeding account of Sidney's activities, and of a major work, in its explanatory context. In the previous book that context was intellectual; the subsequent object was to describe the principal layers of Sidney's intellectual development. Here the context is at once broader in historical, and shorter in chronological scope: it is an examination of the religious and political crisis of 1678–83. The overall objective is, however, the same. It is to complete the account of Algernon Sidney's life and thought, by recreating the contexts which gave them the meaning, and the importance, that Sidney himself attached to them.

As this object has dictated both of these structures, so it has underlain the division into two books itself. In *Sidney and the English Republic* it was possible to achieve the required recontextualisation biographically, without going far beyond the person and ideas of Sidney himself. For the period 1678–83 this has not been possible. One result is that it is not until part two, or chapter 5 of the present work, that the biographical narrative already begun is resumed. This second contextualisation would have been an unacceptable rupture in the midst of a single-volume biography. But it has seemed appropriate to place it at the outset of a second, structurally similar work.

The resulting biographical interruption requires some justification. We would all like to know what happens to Sidney upon his return from exile. But I hope the necessity for part one of the present book will become clear. We cannot understand what Sidney encountered, or what he hoped to achieve, without some preliminary discussion of the situation that confronted him in England. This discussion will be directed to the recovery of a contemporary perspective in which he shared. To begin with, there was neither the wish, nor the intention, to burden this study with a general account of the period. Since it was apparent that the focus of historians on this crisis, and the focus of Sidney himself, were very different, the assumption was that Sidney's involvement in it was both idiosyncratic and peripheral. But this assumption has turned out to be incorrect, on both counts. Instead a very different picture has emerged. It is of Sidney's perspective and concerns far more fundamentally rooted in the nature of the crisis as a whole, as it was seen by all sides, than imagined; of activities taking him remarkably close to the centre of events, and of published opinion; and of political associates who, though they remain obscure in the historiography, were actually at the directing centre of what was going on. As it turns out, Sidney became involved in these events, despite explicit promises to the contrary, because he could not help himself; because this crisis summed up the major themes in his life. And thus he was to be executed, not for being irrelevant to the crisis, but for being at the heart of it, and for giving its deepest concerns voice.

For Sidney, conflict was a way of life. He believed that without it progress was impossible. Readers of this volume, and particularly of its early chapters, may conclude that the author is of the same opinion. Attempts have been made, wherever possible, to cushion the historiographical sword of war. But the author could not find any other way through important points of scholarly contention than by making them clear. He apologises if in this he has imitated the intolerance and bad temper of his subject, and hopes for something other than his end.

One result of the structure of the present volume is that to some extent it stands on its own. Readers interested in Restoration history rather than Algernon Sidney may find some use for it. Nevertheless it has a central theme which can only benefit from prior exposure to the previous work. This is the interrelationship between present and past – in Restoration history, and in the life of Algernon Sidney. From this there has emerged its secondary function: an attempt to give an account of the relationship between the political history, and the political thought, of the crisis of 1678–83.

Like its predecessor then, and as its subject dictates, this book attempts to straddle what remain the substantially separate disciplines of intellectual and political history.[1] Most of the problems it has encountered stem from such historical specialisation, whether of a chronological or of an intradisciplinary variety. One result of the attempt to grapple with them has been a

---

[1] The most important attempt to bridge this barrier for the period under consideration has been Richard Ashcraft's *Revolutionary Politics and John Locke's Two Treatises of Government* (Princeton 1986). Although Ashcraft's work appeared only after most of the writing of this was complete, some attempt has been made to consider and accommodate its findings in chapter 1.

rather ungainly study. Another may be that practitioners of both disciplines will encounter some cause for dissatisfaction. Intellectual historians may find the book methodologically naive, though the author does not believe it to be historically or ideologically so.[2] Political historians may find in its pages a picture of these years which they do not entirely recognise. Most political historians of the crisis have focused on the roles of one or two key individuals – usually the Earl of Shaftesbury – and of a key institution: the House of Commons. The records of both have also been considered in detail here. But they were so only after the examination of over a thousand contemporary books, pamphlets and trials had cast the balance and weighting of this traditional political narrative into doubt. The attempt to marry these two types of evidence: that of the issues of the crisis, and that of its structures or course, lies at the heart of what follows. No one could be more aware than the author of how rough-hewn it is; of how much it stands in need of discussion, and criticism.

Throughout the text, the term 'exclusion crisis' has been avoided, not through any desire to promote historical incomprehension, nor any wish to deny the fact of an attempt made, between 1679 and 1681, to exclude James Duke of York from the succession to the throne. What will be argued is that the exclusion proposal was one result of this crisis, not a cause of it; and that it was never one of the primary issues that fuelled it throughout its duration. Exclusion – or rather, the problem of the succession, to which it (and other proposals) addressed themselves – was one of the several secondary expedients thrown up in the course of a crisis about other things. Their relationship to the (unchanging) primary issues may, and will, be demonstrated. To speak of the 'exclusion crisis' is, therefore, to perpetuate a misstatement of what the crisis was about. This misunderstanding was not shared by contemporaries at any point on the political spectrum. The result has been to give us a relatively superficial view of what was a fundamental upheaval.

In this sense the historiography of the 'exclusion crisis' has come to resemble a tourist, returned from Africa, describing the motions of a rhinoceros horn, in the air, about four feet above the ground. The horn is evidently what interests the person; but the account is sufficiently incomplete to be both incomprehensible, and misleading. The time has come to point out that this horn came into being, was where it was, doing what it was, and was considered as dangerous as it was, only because there was a rhinoceros attached to it. When we ask contemporaries what this crisis was about, what they describe, from all political perspectives, and with consider-

---

[2] For this author's view of the longer term historical and ideological context of this crisis see the review essay 'Radicalism and Restoration: the Shape of the Stuart Experience', *Historical Journal*, 2 (1988).

able emotion, is, as it were, a charging rhinoceros. It was universally recognised, from a previous encounter, even from a distance. It was this terrifying animal which caused the crisis by galloping out of the nation's exceptionally painful past, and through its particularly fragile just-reconstructed present. In the face of this situation, and among the fleeing people and the flying debris, some contemporaries describe one flank; others decribe the other. A few even mention the horn. But the overwhelming majority are fixed on something more general. They describe the return of the beast. So will this book.

The result is two works which, taken together, constitute a single study of Sidney's life and ideas. They are intended to be complimentary, so that information supplied in the first book has not, as far as is possible, been repeated here. *Sidney and the English Republic* identified an eighteenth- and nineteenth-century 'whig myth' of Sidney, to which it attempted to oppose a seventeenth-century 'reality'. The present revisionist thesis is clearly some monstrous offspring of the last. The problem here, however, is not simply retrospective whiggism. It is anachronism; that is to say, retrospective history in general. It is not the problem of treating seventeenth-century politics within the framework of whig party historiography in particular, but within that of party historiography in general.

The result in this book appears, itself, to be of a mixed historiographical character. While its scepticism and anti-anachronism may be seen as revisionist, it has several of the characteristics of whiggism as well. The most important of these is the long view – something seventeenth-century history has lost to its cost. It is only within the context of a perceived century-long struggle, embracing both politics and religion, that the crisis of 1678–83 can be understood. Indeed it is only by combining the insights of revisionism with a century-long view that we can overcome the two principal obstacles to the recovery of a central Restoration reality. Those obstacles are the historiographical dividing line of 1660; and the preoccupation of Restoration historiography with what may be called the shape of the future. The precisely opposite historical reality is the preoccupation, and indeed obsession, of the Restoration period itself with its past. 'The late rebellion', as one contemporary explained, 'need not be remembered, since it is impossible it should be forgotten'.[3]

It is as an experiment conducted under the overwhelming shadow of that past that the Restoration period must be understood. And it is as the key confrontation not only with that past, but with the minotaur at the heart of that labyrinth, that the Restoration crisis began.

---

[3] [Anon] *The Character of a Rebellion, and What England May expect from one* (1681).

ACKNOWLEDGEMENTS

This unruly book has been written in three countries (England, New Zealand and Greece); in three universities (Cambridge, Victoria University of Wellington, and Sheffield); on three different word-processing systems; and at least three times. It has consumed four typists, much timber, and what remained of the author's youth. My first acknowledgement is of victory to the manuscript, which goes into the world after all this, imperfect and unbowed.

That it does so at all, however, owes much to the particular kindness of friends and colleagues. Special thanks are due to John Morrow, who struggled alone but purposefully with an early draft. Colin Davis, Blair Worden, Paul Seaward and Conal Condren all read the final manuscript, furnishing the author with detailed and penetrating criticisms. John Morrill not only did this but perpetrated a near-genocide against the semi-colon population which has greatly added to the stature of those few that remain. I am equally indebted to Mark Goldie, for his example; to Patrick Collinson, for his advice; to Quentin Skinner and John Pocock, for their friendship; and to the Department of History at the University of Sheffield, for being an example in their own right.

Returning to New Zealand reminded me how much I owe to some old teachers and friends, particularly Peter Munz, Miles Fairburn, and Lucie Halberstam. Most of this book was written on the Greek islands of Carpathos (1986) and Samos (1989). For a Pacific islander in love with ancient prudence this was an unforgettable (and, I fear, addictive) experience. To Irene, Nikos, Michaelis, Sophia, Maria and Andreas I offer my humble thanks for furnishing a near-paradise of light, beauty, and peace. I owe no less to my family: Margaret, Rachel, and Kate; and to my wife, Lindsey, who has now seen Algernon off with a patience and *sang-froid* to which he had no title. Finally, greater boldness hath no typist than to venture forth upon the Sheffield mainframe computer, but this is what Heather Dunn did. Only her own talents, the magnificent previous efforts of Kristin Downey, and the generous technical assistance of Paul Leman so emboldened her.

This book is dedicated to Colin Davis and John Morrill, who have given me, through the practice of history, the most precious gift of all.

Part One

THE RESTORATION CRISIS

That which hath been is now,
And that which is to be, hath already been
                                        Eccl. 3.15

❮❮ 1 ❯❯

The shape of the future

Everyone agrees that the Whigs possessed an impressive political
organisation ... Yet on the level of detailed information as to the
operations of this organisation, the evidence remains scanty.
Ashcraft, Revolutionary Politics, p. 172

Of course, this organisation did not appear on the surface. Attempting
to preserve an impression of spontaneity the Whig press was intentionally vague.
J.R. Jones, The First Whigs (1961), p. 168

The Restoration crisis, from 1678 to 1683, was the second of seventeenth-
century England's three crises of popery and arbitrary government. It was
therefore, from the perspective of the historian, linked to both its predecessor of 1638–42 and its successor of 1687–9. What follows is not an
attempt to deny any *historical* links with the latter. Indeed seventeenth-
century England's 'troubles' cannot be understood without considering all
three crises, and the relationship between them. What will be attempted in
the following chapters is the recovery of the perspective on this crisis of
contemporaries themselves. *Contemporaries*, obviously, could not predict
the future. They did not hinge their political interpretations upon prophecy.
But they could, and they did, remember the past. In the Restoration period
they could not forget it. They could be, and to some extent they were, the
prisoners of memory.

Historians, on the other hand, have been more interested in linking the
crisis of 1678–83 with the shape of the future: the future exclusion of James
from the throne; the future birth of parties. In the process they have, it will
be argued, lost touch with the contemporary crisis itself. They have also
gone well beyond what the surviving evidence will allow. It was contemporary perceptions which made the crisis what it was, whatever historians
would later like to make of them. Those perceptions were provoked by the
present, and the reappearance in the present of the most terrible spectres of
the past.

3

1.1 THE RESTORATION

HISTORIOGRAPHY

The historiography of the Restoration period (1660–88), and particularly of its first decade (1660–9), is now changing. Increasing emphasis is being placed on the rootedness of the Restoration Settlement itself, and of the period to which it gave issue, in contemporary preoccupation with the past.[1] In many ways the point is an obvious one. Yet it remains true, particularly for the period 1670–88, that Restoration historiography as a whole has long exhibited two striking, and contrary, characteristics. These have ironically been intertwined.

The first is the division of the century, for the purposes of professional study, at the boundary line of 1660. Thus when Hugh Trevor-Roper wrote that it was 'broken in the middle, irreparably broken, and at the end of it, after the revolutions, men can hardly recognise the beginning',[2] he was accurately describing seventeenth-century historiography, if not history. It remains true that historians working on what may be very loosely termed the first and second halves of the seventeenth-century experience have continued to do so separately; at a different pace, in different style, reaching different conclusions. Historians of the early Stuarts remain linked, professionally and in their historical vision, to the preceding Tudor period. Historians of the Restoration period continue to link it to, and see it as ushering in, something called the 'long eighteenth century'.

From this arises the second notable feature of Restoration historiography. This is the extent to which the period has been studied less in its own right than in terms of its capacity to give birth to, or at least display the origins of, the political structures and sensibilities of the eighteenth century.[3] These two characteristics are linked, and they are of very long standing: as old, indeed, as the study of the seventeenth century itself. To see how, the problem may be stated differently. For much of their existence, both early and later Stuart historiography have been divided by separate but parallel historical imperatives: the quest for the origins of their respective 'revolutions' – 1640–9, and 1688–9.

---

[1] Pre-eminent in this respect is Paul Seaward's superb *The Cavalier Parliament and the Reconstruction of the Old Regime 1661–1667* (Cambridge 1989). See also Ronald Hutton, *The Restoration* (Oxford 1986); Tim Harris, *London Crowds in the Reign of Charles II* (Cambridge 1987); and J. Miller, *Restoration England: The Reign of Charles II* (1985). For an earlier statement of the following arguments see Scott, 'Radicalism and Restoration: The Shape of the Stuart Experience', *Historical Journal*, 31:2 (1988), and 'England's Troubles: Exhuming the Popish Plot' in M. Goldie, T. Harris and P. Seaward (eds.), *The Politics of Religion in Restoration England* (Oxford 1990).

[2] Quoted in M. Finlayson, *Historians, Puritanism and the English Revolution* (Toronto 1984) and Scott, 'Radicalism and Restoration', p. 458.

[3] Scott, 'Radicalism and Restoration'.

For generations, not only the Restoration, but the entire Stuart period was harnessed to the quest for the origins of 'the' English Revolution of 1688, and so of the eighteenth-century world which it created.[4] This is what first established the forward-looking character of Restoration historiography – the quest for the origins of the 'long eighteenth century'.[5] More recently however, and particularly over the last century, early Stuart historians have been no less preoccupied by the search for the origins of 'their' revolution, of the 1640s. The impact of this latter enterprise on historical perceptions of the early Stuart period is now well understood. The word 'revisionism' describes the efforts of the latest generation of historians to correct it. But this impact did not stop there. It also established, and reinforced, the modern historiographical boundary-line of 1660. It is hard to imagine that division persisting as it does if S.R. Gardiner, C.H. Firth, and Godfrey Davies had not ended their accounts in 1660.[6] It is above all the twentieth-century assumption of mid- (rather than late-) century revolution, and of 'revolution' as implying discontinuity, that has underwritten the division of the century into two halves. This universal modern assumption has served as common currency for Hugh Trevor-Roper and Christopher Hill alike.[7]

Finally then, this truncation of the century has simply reinforced the already-established focus of Restoration historiography on the shape of the future. It is for this reason that the Restoration period has continued to be studied as the birthplace of a new era, of the long eighteenth century, rather than as what it was: the second half of the seventeenth century, and a second half peculiarly in the grip of the first. It is thus this layering of two historiographical imperatives, one from the eighteenth to nineteenth centuries, and the other from the nineteenth to the twentieth, that have given us the two chief problems of Restoration historiography: of a period artificially wedded to its future, and artificially severed from its past.

That these should be obstacles to the understanding of any period is understandable enough. In the case of the Restoration period they are fatal.

---

[4] See, for instance, T.B. Macaulay, *The History of England during the Reigns of King William, Queen Anne, and King George I, with an introductory review of the reigns of the Royal brothers Charles and James; in which are to be found the Seeds of the Revolution,* 2 vols. (1844–6); J. McPherson, *A History of Great Britain from the Restoration to the Accession of the House of Hanover* (1775); G.M. Trevelyan, *The English Revolution 1688– 9* (1939).

[5] It is rehearsed again recently by W. Speck's *Reluctant Revolutionaries* (1988); for the discussion of the historiography of the crisis of 1678–83 see below.

[6] I would like to thank Lucie Halberstam, of Victoria University of Wellington, for this point.

[7] See footnote 3 above. Angus MacInnes ('When was the English Revolution?', *History,* 63:221 (1982), 377–8) holds Christopher Hill particularly responsible for establishing the idea of mid-century as a decisive break. While not disagreeing, this argument would suggest that Hill's view formed only one influential contribution to a wider, and older, set of assumptions.

For the political history of the Restoration is the history of a generation living uniquely under the shadow of its past. It appears to be only historians who remain dramatically separated by the interregnum; and only this can account for the remarkable persistence in Restoration histories of claims to uniqueness for events, structures, and issues in the reign of Charles II which are almost xerox copies of events, structures and issues of the early Stuart period.[8] The fact of this historical repetition is hardly surprising; the re-establishment of these features was precisely the purpose of the Restoration settlement itself. Indeed dividing the century at 1660, historians have not only failed to reflect contemporary experience but have ironically inverted it. For it was precisely the shattering impact of the mid-century experience that set contemporaries on their fateful Restoration course; a course not only of continuity, but of repetition.

HISTORY

The Restoration was a deliberate attempt to restore the atmosphere and structures of early Stuart government before they became poisoned by the divisions of Charles I's reign. If the account by the key minister concerned (Clarendon) of those troubles themselves began at 1625, it is hardly surprising that this meant in particular the relatively harmonious reign of James I – by now a halcyon memory. Thus historians who continue to describe the relatively easy-going moral and fiscal laxity of Charles II's court as if it were something unique – in particular uniquely lacking in structure ('a Hobbesian state of nature' is the phrase of one textbook)[9] – exhibit a much shorter memory of Stuart history than that of contemporaries themselves.

The problem is again primarily one of professional boundaries. One historian of the 'long eighteenth century' sees no structure to the Restoration period at all until the 'exclusion crisis' gives birth to the (party) structures of the eighteenth century.[10] But contemporaries did not see themselves as living in a structureless state of chaos. They thought they were living under the restored structures of the Stuart monarchy, and it was inevitable following a major upheaval that they should turn for their models of reconstruction to the past.

The intention behind the Restoration was therefore – like the meaning of the word itself – fundamentally conservative. The lesson of Charles II's reign seems to have been that in giving vent to this psychological impulse the

---

[8] See Finlayson, *English Revolution*, p. 35 and ch. 2 in general.

[9] J.R. Jones, *Country and Court: England 1658–1714* (1978), p. 3. 'It is quite inappropriate to talk of a structure of politics in Restoration England', p. 1.

[10] This was the thesis of J.R. Jones, *The First Whigs* (1961) and is repeated in his *Country and Court*, see for instance, p. 198.

makers of the Restoration period succeeded rather too completely for their own good. For if Charles' court was, to begin with, similar in atmosphere to that of his grandfather, when the honeymoon ended and the (fundamentally negative) Restoration consensus collapsed, the crisis the government endured from 1678–83 was a repeat screening of the crisis of the reign of Charles I. It was fundamentally the same in its causes, its issues, its structures and its course; the only important difference was in its final outcome, a difference which resulted specifically from contemporary recognition of these similarities themselves.

It was the second Stuart crisis of popery and arbitrary government and it began, like the first (1638–42), with mounting concern on these same grounds over royal policy in the same three areas: parliamentary management, foreign policy, and religion. It proceeded via the resurrection of the first popish plot,[11] and an impeachment of the King's first minister (Danby) deliberately modelled on that of the earl of Strafford,[12] and it even called forth a second Scots rebellion before eventually subsiding in the face of a unified chorus of '41 again'. Throughout its duration it was accompanied by a full-scale resurrection of the political literature of the earlier crisis, from republished descriptions of the Irish Massacre of 1641[13] to the republication of Sir Robert Filmer's *Patriarcha*, possibly written as early as 1628.[14] It was indeed this latter work (and not 'exclusion') which became the focal point for the political thought of the crisis as a whole. The Filmerian gauntlet was taken up by both the ablest writers of this period, John Locke and Algernon Sidney, because both well understood the centrality of this resurrected Caroline theory to what was a resurrected Caroline crisis. Both made this quite explicit. In the words of Sidney: 'No authors ... have had impudence enough ... to publish doctrines so contrary to common sense, virtue and humanity, till these times. The production of Laud, Manwaring, Sibthorp ... Filmer, and Heylin, seems to have been reserved as an additional curse to complete the ... misery of our age and country.'[15] Locke echoed the point: 'By whom this doctrine came at first to be broach'd ... and what sad effects it gave rise to, I leave it to Historians to relate, or to the Memory of those who were Contemporaries with Sibthorp and Manwaring to recollect.'[16]

---

[11] On this theme see Caroline Hibbard, *Charles I and the Popish Plot* (North Carolina 1983), esp. pp. 9–10; W. Lamont, *Richard Baxter and the Millennium* (1979), pp. 77, 82–3, 106–7, 330–2.

[12] Antichell Grey, *Debates of the House of Commons 1667–94* (1763), vol. VII, pp. 200–3.

[13] *An Account of the Bloody Massacre in Ireland* (December 1678), reprinted in W. Scott (ed.), *Tracts ... of the Late Lord Somers* (1808–15), vol. VIII, pp. 89–96, was based on Sir John Temple's *Account of the Irish Rebellion* (1646).

[14] See chapter 10, footnote 11.

[15] Algernon Sidney, *Discourses Concerning Government* in *Works* (1772), p. 5.

[16] John Locke, *Two Treatises of Government*, First Treatise, para. 5, ed. P. Laslett (Cam-

The 'exclusion crisis' was not, therefore, it will be suggested, principally about 'exclusion' at all. The real exclusion crisis was in 1688, and ever since then its victors have been redefining the history of the seventeenth century in general, and the Restoration period in particular, in order to give premature birth to themselves. The crisis of 1678–83 was about the rebirth, in the reign of Charles II, of those ugly sisters Popery and Arbitrary Government, as Andrew Marvell's *The Growth of Popery and Arbitrary Government* (1677) pointed out. This piece of Caroline repetition entailed another: the whole battery of public memories and fears which were to paralyse the government of the country for another five years; from 1678 to 1682.

The Restoration, then, succeeded too well, for it restored not only the structures of early Stuart government, but subsequently its fears, divisions and crises. The most important of these fears – because the most politically destructive – was religious, and it is the problem of popery which gives the seventeenth-century English experience its essential unity. This is because, far from being 'broken in the middle', the seventeenth century in Europe as a whole was the century of the victories of the Counter-Reformation. It was a century of disaster for European protestantism, which was reduced in its course to the fringes of the continent, and from 50 per cent to under 20 per cent of its total area.[17]

This was the accomplishment of the two catholic superpowers, Spain in the first half of the century and France in the second. That England and Scotland did not feel themselves peripheral to this process, but actually surrounded by it, owed much to the geographical position of catholic Ireland. It is clear that the anxieties generated by this situation lay at the heart of both Caroline crises, from 1638–42, and 1678–83. In both cases the religious and foreign policies of the crown not only seemed to be failing to stem this disastrous process but actually allying themselves to it. It is striking to find, as late as 1681, a member of the English parliament giving a tearful speech about the fate of Bohemia;[18] and John Miller has remarked on the pervasiveness throughout the 'exclusion crisis' of 'anachronistic' references to events like the Massacre of Paris of 1572, the Gunpowder plot of 1605, and the Irish rebellion of 1641.[19] Needless to say, however, it is not for historians to tell contemporaries what is anachronistic, but rather the other way around. The problem to which these references pointed remained

bridge, 2nd edn, 1967), p. 161. Note also the similarity of the placing of the point in Sidney's and Locke's respective works.

[17] Geoffrey Parker, *Europe in Crisis 1598–1648* (1979), p. 50 (and ch. 2); Scott, 'England's Troubles', pp. 113–15. See J. Miller, *Popery and Politics in England 1660–1688* (Cambridge 1973).

[18] Grey, *Debates*, vol. VIII, p. 328.

[19] Miller, *Popery and Politics*, p. 89.

not only relevant to, but at the centre of, the contemporary crisis. The problem was the Counter-Reformation advance.[20]

The interregnum was indeed to introduce new anxieties into Restoration politics to accompany the old – arbitrary government now meant not only tampering with parliament but keeping a standing army too. But it was above all simply the shattering nature of the experience that underlay the mechanism for repetition. The full course of events, beginning (as the Restoration clergy explained) with the first sin of political disobedience and culminating in the ultimate blasphemy of regicide, had involved far too comprehensive a loss of paradise to be lightly forgotten. It was in vain that one contemporary 'wish[ed] . . . that the years between 1640 and 60 could be raz'd out of the Book of Time, and the memory of this Age'.[21] It fell to the second half of the century to become comprehensively haunted by the first. It was the magnitude of what it had experienced that drove the nation first to seek exit in repetition; and then back into the arms of the same fears again. In short the Restoration is not a 'normal' period, for we are dealing in it with a traumatised patient. Like a road accident victim the nation remained susceptible both to nostalgia on the one hand, and nightmares on the other. The Restoration settlement was an act of nostalgia. By 1678 the nightmare had come.

1.2 THE 'EXCLUSION CRISIS'

HISTORIOGRAPHY

The modern historiography of the 'exclusion crisis' has not entirely ignored its longer-term historical context. The parallel with the crisis of Charles I's reign – the first crisis of popery and arbitrary government – was so universally remarked upon by contemporaries that to ignore it entirely would be impossible.[22] Indeed it was Betty Behrens who remarked, in what remains the best short survey of the pamphlet literature of this period, that 'the similarities between the two situations were so obvious and so consistently proclaimed that the differences were overlooked'.[23] Contemporaries had, in

---

[20] This is why the Earl of Halifax remarked in 1678 that Titus Oates' story 'must be handled as if it were true, whether it were so or no . . . [though it were] vain to hope that it will ever be confessed by those that say still there never was any such thing as the Massacre of Paris, or the Gunpowder Treason in England.' Quoted in F.S. Ronalds, *The Attempted Whig Revolution of 1678–81* (Urbana 1937), p. 18.

[21] *The Loyal Protestants Vindication . . . By a Queen Elizabeth Protestant* (1681), p. 1.

[22] Speck's *Reluctant Revolutionaries* notes this fact about the context for contemporary perceptions (pp. 25–6) but then begins its account at 1660 anyway because this is more 'manageable'.

[23] B. Behrens, 'The Whig Theory of the Constitution in the Reign of Charles II', *Cambridge Historical Journal*, 7:1 (1941), 44.

other words, the utmost difficulty disentangling their present from their past.

What was so obvious to contemporaries, however, and to Behrens, has proved less obvious to historians in general. In most standard accounts the contemporary vision of this crisis has been supplanted by the assumptions, and the interests, of a later age. In religion this has meant the replacement of the genuine crisis situation of the seventeenth century with the incomprehension and distaste for enthusiasm of the eighteenth.[24] The popish plot scare of 1678–81, though in reality, like its predecessor of 1640, at the very heart of the crisis, has thus been portrayed as the baseless effect of credulous hysteria, sustained over the period only by the political impetus and manipulations of the exclusion campaign. This is to mistake cause for effect; the campaign for exclusion, among others, resulted from the much more deeply seated and longer lasting religious crisis, not the other way around.

Politically, ever since the eighteenth century, and still today, two things have interested historians most about the crisis of 1678–83. The first is the dispute it threw up over the succession to the crown: this, reduced in the historiography to 'exclusion', now names the whole crisis. The second is the major historical role it apparently performed in giving rise to the first 'parties' in modern history: the whig and tory parties. These remain the two features of the crisis which every schoolchild can identify. They came together most seminally in J.R. Jones' *The First Whigs* (1961), entrenching an interpretation of the crisis which has never been seriously challenged.[25]

On one level, this double interest in exclusion (the issue) and party formation (the structure), is not surprising. There was, after all, a bill passed by the Commons (though not the Lords), to exclude the Duke of York from the succession. This entered the House of Commons in 1679, was carried to the Lords by its successor in 1680, and lay at the centre of a final deadlock between Charles and his last parliament in 1681. As for the parties, the

---

[24] Scott, 'England's Troubles'.

[25] Accounts of the crisis have, of course, varied enormously in depth and sophistication. To some, most notably Ken Haley's *The First Earl of Shaftesbury* (1968) this author owes a major debt. Almost all, however, have operated within the contours of the traditional interpretation of the crisis established in the eighteenth century, with its focus on Shaftesbury, exclusion, and party formation. In a study of Shaftesbury himself, or Locke, this is to some extent inevitable. Exclusion was certainly a central concern for Shaftesbury, if not for the country as a whole. Other major studies (including Miller's *Popery and Politics*, Plumb's *The Growth of Political Stability*, Harris's *London Crowds* and Speck's *Reluctant Revolutionaries*) treat the crisis in relation to broader themes rather than in its own right. There are, however, at least partial alternatives to this perspective: two are mentioned in note 81 below. And the recently completed doctoral study by Mark Knights ('Politics and Opinion during the Exclusion Crisis 1678–81' Oxford D.Phil. 1989) suggests that a more general change of emphasis may now be taking place. Dr Knights also finds a more limited role for exclusion than has traditionally been assumed. I am grateful to him for letting me see his thesis a few weeks before this book went to press.

labels 'whig' and 'tory' did indeed become attached to groups on the English political scene in the last phase of this crisis (1681–3), and have been with us ever since. The crisis also gave rise to a period of sharp polarisation, in 1680–1, between 'petitioners' and 'abhorrers'. Nevertheless the existence of an exclusion bill does not, without evident demonstration, entitle us to hinge upon it our explanation of the crisis. The appearance, in its last stage, of the words 'whig' and 'tory' do not, without equivalent demonstration, entitle us to assume the appearance of the parties they later named. What is extraordinary is that such demonstration – on both counts – has never been thought necessary, and it has never been provided.[26]

What is clear, instead, is that it is precisely these two features, however peripheral they may have been to the crisis of 1678–83, that serve to link it with the future: with the Glorious Revolution, and the political structures of the eighteenth century which it helped to make possible. In 1688–9 James was indeed excluded from the throne. During the reign of his successor the political structures of British politics were fundamentally changed. One of the most important changes, predicated in turn upon others like the achievement of annual parliaments (from 1689), and triennial elections (from 1694), was the development of the structures of party politics. Before 1689 the preconditions for such a development did not exist. Indeed the subsequent development of English party structures represented the institutionalisation, and so domestication, of precisely those forces of ideology, both religious and political, which the bloody seventeenth century had so conspicuously failed to bring under control. These momentous achievements of William III's reign depended in turn upon others. The most important were a change in the relationship between the British crown and the rest of Europe following from a change in both the national and the religious identity of its wearer. These alterations were not made possible by a domestic 'revolution', since it is not clear that the nation had any greater capacity to solve its troubles domestically in 1688–9 than it had had in 1638–42, or 1678–83. They were the consequence of a successful European invasion, effected by a Dutch Armada five times the size of its Spanish predecessor of a century before.[27]

The crisis of 1678–83 came about precisely because of the inability of the existing domestic structures of politics to cope with the problems at its heart. As such it followed the pattern of its Caroline predecessor. Future chapters will need to call repeated attention to the fact that its participants, in every dimension, had to grapple with *seventeenth*-, not eighteenth-century political realities. Some time ago Geoffrey Holmes, noting the fluid and incomplete process of party formation during the reign of William III,

---

[26] See pp. 12–25 below.
[27] See Jonathan Israel's essay in Israel (ed.), *The Anglo–Dutch Moment* (Cambridge 1991).

concluded that by 1702 'the line separating Tory from Whig had once more become firm and sharp'.[28] The suggestion of this book is that it had become firm and sharp *for the first time*.

'Everyone agrees' then about the existence of the first whig party, though the evidence for such an organisation 'remains scanty'.[29] Under these circumstances what becomes significant is the survival – indeed the robust good health – of the assumption itself. For in fact both key assumptions, concerning the formation of party, and the centrality of exclusion, have always existed independently of historical demonstration. This is because both form part of a mythology of eighteenth-century origins. They compose a retrospective view of what later generations considered significant about the crisis. In the reign of Anne, Robert Harley looked back to these years for the origins of the parties of his own day (though he significantly did not hinge their struggle upon exclusion).[30] Not long after, Henry St John excused Sidney from the (perfectly correct) calumny of republicanism, explaining that he was merely a partisan for that moderate and prophetic bill of exclusion.[31] In fact Harley's retrospective view is not supported by the contemporary evidence; and Bolingbroke's statement of Sidney's position is contradicted by Sidney's own, echoed by Henry Neville, that he could not be an enthusiast for a measure that would simply replace one monarch with another.[32] Yet the structures and causes of 1678–83 were transmuted into those of the eighteenth century with very little protest. And this subsumation of the history of a seventeenth-century crisis to one of eighteenth-century origins has continued unbroken to the present day.

The modern view of the 'exclusion crisis' was arrived at, not through any investigation of the crisis in its own right, but as one contribution to the greatest modern debate about *eighteenth-century* (party) political structures. This debate centred on the work of Sir Lewis Namier. When the Namierite Robert Walcott challenged the notion of party in the reign of Queen Anne, it was natural, within the historiographical framework of 'the long eighteenth century', to show the 'origins' of his alternative 'interest groups' in the reign of Charles II. Walcott's work called forth a hail of criticism, and two of the finest works of the period in J.H. Plumb's *The Growth of Political Stability in England* and Geoffrey Holmes' *British Politics in the age of Anne*. The consensus that Walcott's conclusions for Anne's reign were unsound, combined with the same historiographical

[28] G. Holmes, *British Politics in the Age of Anne* (revised edn 1987), p. 47.
[29] See the quotes at the head of this chapter.
[30] Robert Harley, quoted in Holmes, *British Politics*, p. 53.
[31] Henry St John, Viscount Bolingbroke, *The Works of Lord Bolingbroke*, vol. II (1967), pp. 55–6.
[32] G. Burnet, *History of My Own Time*, 2 vols. (Oxford 1823), vol. I, p. 343; Caroline Robbins (ed.), *Two English Republican Tracts* (Cambridge 1969), p. 9.

parameters, invited J.R. Jones to sweep him out of the reign of Charles II as well. The result was Jones' *The First Whigs*, the function of which was not so much to describe the crisis of 1678–83, as to refute Walcott, by proving the birth of the party in it.[33]

Yet it is fair to say that *The First Whigs* 'proved' relatively little. It contained a series of assertions about 'the first whigs', about Shaftesbury, and about exclusion, which are not adequately documented and which this author believes the contemporary evidence calls into question.[34] To begin with Jones was cautious: '[The] nineteenth century assumed uncritically that the first whigs and tories were parties, indeed the ancestors of those of their own time. Of course, such a view cannot be seriously maintained today.'[35] Inexplicably, however, this caution was abandoned on the same page: 'The first Whigs were, and had to be, a party.'[36] They were drawn together as such by one leader (Shaftesbury), and around one issue (exclusion). It was Shaftesbury who 'made' exclusion the centre of the whole crisis. He did so by manipulating public concern about popery, and by managing his own wide following, both in and outside parliament. According to Jones, 'This concentration on the one issue was a principal reason for (Shaftesbury's) ... greatness and success ... Exclusion appealed to a very large proportion of the nation; almost every section with serious grievances saw in the bill the means to achieving their removal or remedy.'[37] By these means, 'Shaftesbury created the first whigs, the earliest recognisable party. By doing so he divided the nation and called into existence as a counterweight the first tories. Both whigs and tories were unmistakably parties, units far more coherent, disciplined, organised and united than mere aggregates of groups and interests.' In short this 'crisis produced not statutes but parties'.[38]

This author does not wish to prolong this debate here. The suggestion is that it has been historically inappropriate for this crisis to have been treated in the context of it. The debate was about eighteenth-, not seventeenth-century political structures. This is why what is missing from both Jones' and Walcott's accounts of the Restoration crisis is the same thing. It is the moving force behind seventeenth- rather than eighteenth-century political behaviour. It is precisely the destructive force that the later development of party structures was able to bring under control. It is what caused this crisis

[33] R. Walcott, *Eighteenth Century British Politics* (1959); Plumb's work is an extended attack on Walcott's; Professor Jones makes the relationship between his own thesis and that of Walcott clear in both *The First Whigs* and *Country and Court*.
[34] See chapter 3.
[35] Jones, *The First Whigs*, p. 2.
[36] *Ibid.*, p. 2.
[37] *Ibid.*, pp. 6–7.
[38] Jones, *County and Court*, p. 198.

as it had its predecessor. This was the force, not of party organisation, but of public religious and political belief.

It was this, not Shaftesbury's party organisation, which lay beind the political upheaval of 1678 to 1683. In the face of this hurricane, numerous individuals and groups made what political running they could. Among these Shaftesbury was far from the most successful, or important. It was the progress of this belief which underlay all of the successive stages of this crisis (see chapters 2–3 below). The result was not parties but ideology. The Restoration crisis crystallised political belief. This crystallisation took place through the lens of the past, the lens of history. It gave rise to a debate about politics, and religion, which produced some of the most influential political writing in English history. When the words 'whig' and 'tory' appeared, they were coined to identify not 'parties' but polarities of belief; and belief not only about the present, but about that present illuminated through the experience of the past.[39] Both Jones and Walcott share an eighteenth-century high political view of the springs of political action. The debate over parties and interest groups was conducted in these terms. *The First Whigs* in particular notoriously dismissed the entire ideological dimension of this crisis as insubstantial and second rate – a judgement upon which the subsequent relocation of John Locke's *Two Treatises of Government* in this context has been sufficient commentary.[40] In fact it is precisely the lack of attention paid to the ideological dimension of the crisis[41] that has permitted such a profound misunderstanding of its character to persist for so long. It is this which has permitted the non-issue of exclusion to stand, for some centuries, in place of the genuine issues; about which some thousands of books and pamphlets were, and are, most eloquent.

The work that has done most recently to repair this neglect is Richard Ashcraft's *Revolutionary Politics and John Locke's Two Treatises of Government* (1986).[42] It was Ashcraft who first pointed out that, contrary

---

[39] See chapter 2, section 5.

[40] Locke, *Two Treatises*, ed. Laslett, introduction, pp. 33–7 and part 3; Richard Ashcraft, *Revolutionary Politics and John Locke's Two Treatises of Government* (Princeton 1986).

[41] The works of Behrens and Ashcraft, already mentioned, are among the most important exceptions to this generalisation. See also J.G.A. Pocock, *The Machiavellian Moment* (Princeton 1975); Pocock (ed.), *The Political Works of James Harrington* (Cambridge 1977) introduction, ch. 7; *The Ancient Constitution and the Feudal Law* (Cambridge 1987), esp. Retrospect ch. 3; and 'The Varieties of Whiggism from Exclusion to Reform' in Pocock, *Virtue, Commerce and History* (Cambridge 1985). O.W. Furley's Oxford B.Litt. thesis, 'The Origins and Early Development of the Whig Party, with special reference to Shaftesbury and Locke' (1953), summarised its conclusions in 'The Whig Exclusionists: Pamphlet Literature in the Exclusion Campaign 1679–81', *Cambridge Historical Journal*, 13:1 (1957), 19–36.

[42] Ashcraft's book was preceded by two important essays: 'Revolutionary Politics and Locke's Two Treatises of Government: Radicalism and Lockean Political Thought', *Political Theory*, 8:4 (1980); and 'The Two Treatises and the Exclusion Crisis; The Problem of

to the earlier view, the political literature of 1675–85 is remarkable both for its quality and quantity.[43] It produced a galaxy of classics, by Locke, Sidney, Marvell, Neville, Penn, Bethel, Halifax, and Tyrrell, among others. Yet his immersion in the ideology of the crisis did not lead Ashcraft to question either of the other – and more important – earlier assumptions upon which the same view rested: that the central issue was exclusion, and that the pursuit of exclusion gave rise to the central structure: the first parties. Indeed Ashcraft's work seeks to magnify Shaftesbury's importance by 'sketching the dynamics of [a] disciplined and co-operative mass political movement' under his command.[44] While this derives from his focus upon Shaftesbury's client, Locke, yet it is curious for two reasons. The first is Ashcraft's own admission that 'on the level of detailed information ... the evidence' for such party organisation 'remains scanty'.[45] The second is that the ideological focal point of his work, Locke's *Two Treatises of Government*, never mentions exclusion. This was remarked upon as a curiosity by John Dunn, in 1968.[46] And in this, Locke, like Sidney, is not an exception but the rule. The same is true of all the others just mentioned: Penn, Marvell, Bethel, Neville, Tyrrell, and Halifax.

There appears, in short, to be a worrying disjunction between text and context in this crisis. The crisis, we have been told, was about exclusion. Yet none of its major works, not even that of Shaftesbury's own employee, Locke, addressed that 'issue'. The same inattention to the matter in hand is (as we will see) characteristic of most of the pamphlet literature of 1677–83. This was surely one reason behind the sensational recent re-dating of the *Two Treatises* itself from one crisis (1688–9) to another (1678–83). What made the earlier mistake possible was not (as Ashcraft has helped to show), the politically neutral or vague nature of Locke's work. It was our failure to establish the ideological context of the former crisis; its independent identity, separate from the real exclusion crisis of 1688–9. Accordingly Peter Laslett achieved his breakthrough only by establishing that Locke was answering Filmers' *Patriarcha* (published in 1680) rather than Hobbes' *Leviathan*. It was achieved, in short, by scholarly attention to text, rather than context.[47]

In the continued absence of such a context Ashcraft has coped with the problem of Locke by assuming that (while exclusion did indeed lie at the

Lockean Political Theory as Bourgeois Ideology' in R. Ashcraft and J.G.A. Pocock (eds.), *John Locke* (Los Angeles 1980).

[43] Ashcraft and Pocock (eds.), *John Locke*, pp. 34–5.

[44] Ashcraft, *Revolutionary Politics*, pp. ix–xi, 179; Scott, 'Radicalism and Restoration', pp. 464–5.

[45] See quotes at the head of this chapter.

[46] J. Dunn, *The Political Thought of John Locke* (Cambridge 1968), pp. 53–6.

[47] Locke, *Two Treatises*, ed. Laslett, introduction, part 3.

heart of the crisis) after the dissolution of the Oxford parliament in April
1681 the issues changed. Since (unlike Laslett) Ashcraft believes that
Locke's work was written after that date, this explains its focus on different
issues.[48] While there is no reason to question this dating the point is not
crucial. For the fundamental issues did *not* in fact change between 1678 (or
earlier) and 1683. On the contrary, both the political literature and the
practical conduct of the crisis, from the publication of Marvell's *The
Growth of Popery and Arbitrary Government* (November 1677) to the
execution of Sidney (December 1683) exhibit an exceptional continuity, and
consistency.[49] This even applies to the relationship between 'opposition' and
'loyalist' thought itself, as we will see. This consistency within the crisis was
in turn one subsection, or chapter, of a larger whole: a consistency with the
issues, and the political rhetoric, of the entire century.

The political thought of 1681–3 arose, then, not from the latest developments in the crisis, but from the political issues at its core. Those issues
emerged from the nation's present problems seen in the light of its past.
They arose, in this sense, from the political experience of almost a century.
The resulting works of Sidney, Locke and others, were to be so important
partly because they were not only *livres de circonstance* – though they were
certainly that – but because they became *thereby* the distillation of something much greater. It was greater not only in time but in space, since
England's 'troubles' were part of the political and religious troubles of
Europe. They were a chapter, most specifically, in its major early modern
theme: the struggle between the Reformation, and the Counter-Reformation. This was the struggle which linked the French wars of religion with the
English: and the political language of the Reformation with that of the
Counter-Reformation. That authors like Locke and Sidney summarised
both – that they linked themselves, through Filmer, to a debate and a
(natural law) language shared before them by Suarez, Bellarmine, Hotman,
Mornay, Buchanan, Mariana, and Milton – was a natural consequence of
the nature of this crisis itself.[50] So accordingly was the later international
(not simply national) influence of their thought. It was this same European
struggle which linked Algernon Sidney's 'sacrifice' on the scaffold with Sir
Philip Sidney's before it. The 'old cause' for which Sidney offered his life,
and for which God had 'often and wonderfully declared himself', was the
self-defence of protestants against the Counter-Reformation in England,

---

[48] Ashcraft, *Revolutionary Politics*, pp. 312–22.

[49] See Conal Condren, 'Andrew Marvell as Polemicist: His Account of the Growth of Popery,
and Arbitrary Government' in C. Condren and A.D. Cousins, *The Political Identity of
Andrew Marvell* (forthcoming).

[50] Q. Skinner, *The Foundations of Modern Political Thought*, 2 vols. (Cambridge 1978), vol.
II, esp. pp. 156–9 and 174, places Locke in this context; see also J.N. Figgis, 'On Some
Political Theories of the Early Jesuits', *TRHS* n.s. 11 (1897), 89–112.

and in Europe. For English republicans and loyalists alike, the crisis of 1678–83, like its predecessor, was about the 'growth of popery': the European (and domestic) Counter-Reformation advance.[51] The genesis of this 'cause' was not simply Caroline, but Elizabethan. And it was not simply national, but European, for God had declared himself on the battlefield in the Netherlands, and in France, before he had done so in England. It was in this context that Algernon Sidney's insurrection against Charles II, and Sir Philip Sidney's against Philip II, were part of the same struggle. It was the struggle of a beleaguered European religious minority, on the defensive. The Restoration crisis was the latest attempt to defend the Elizabethan (protestant) inheritance under a Stuart monarchy in league with its European enemies. It was this European context which not only underlay all three Stuart crises but which supplied, in the form of a protestant Armada, a lasting resolution of the third (1688–9).

ISSUES: 'EXCLUSION'

The next two chapters will attempt to demonstrate the resulting shape of the crisis, both in theory and in practice. There remains to explain why the traditional picture of the 'exclusion crisis' cannot do so. Let us examine, briefly, each of the two key assumptions in turn: they will be placed in their true context in chapter 3.

Historiographically, 'exclusion' stands at the centre of, and names, this whole crisis. The parliaments of 1679–81 are called the first, second and third 'exclusion' parliaments, whether they were primarily concerned with exclusion or not. The elections to them are similarly the first, second and third 'exclusion' elections, whether they were fought over exclusion or not. The pamphlet literature, broadsides and speeches of this crisis are called 'exclusion pamphlets' whether they mentioned exclusion or not. All have been misnamed, but not only because 'exclusion' did not lie at the centre of any of them. A prior problem is that the terminology of the crisis itself had been changed.

Contemporaries discussing this issue did not refer to 'exclusion', but to 'the succession'.[52] Shaftesbury's 'exclusion' proposal was not an 'issue', but

---

[51] See chapter 2, below, and Scott 'England's Troubles'.
[52] The best-known succession tract is probably Elkanah Settle's *The Character of a Popish Successor, and What We May Expect from Such an One* (21 March 1681) (answered by *The Character of a Rebellion and what England may Expect from One* (1681)). See also, for instance, *A Word Without Doors, Concerning the Bill for Succession* (1679); *A Word Within Doors* (1679); *Great and Weighty Considerations Relating to the D[uke], or Successor to the Crown* (1680); *Great and Weighty Considerations ... Considered* (1680); *A Letter from a Gentleman of Quality ... Relating to the Succession* (1679); *An Answer to a Letter from a Gentleman of Quality ...* (1681); *A True and Exact History of the Succession*

one legislative expedient for dealing with that problem, Halifax's 'limitations' scheme being its principal rival. The succession, in turn, was one of several secondary issues thrown up by a crisis about other much more immediate and fundamental problems. As such it generated little more attention, either in parliament, or in the pamphlet literature, than other secondary issues, whether other specific measures (such as the bill for the relief of protestant consciences) or specific events (such as the murder of Sir Edmundberry Godfrey, or the 'Meal Tub' plot).[53]

This is not terminological hair splitting, for it is partly by the collapsing of such distinctions, and the transformation of its language, that the meaning of the crisis itself has been changed. The 'issue' of *exclusion* – an historiographical invention – links the crisis to the future (the exclusion of James from the throne). For contemporaries, however, the issue of the *succession* carried the unmistakable echo of its Elizabethan past.

Thus, once the crisis was already under way, it was explicitly in the shadow of that past that this (secondary) issue was revived. The Elizabethan arguments of John Hales, Thomas Norton, and Thomas Sackville re-emerged: that the professor of a 'corrupt' and 'foreign religion was barred . . . from the succession by the common law'; that 'the succession was a matter to be settled in Parliament'; that 'a state knit in unity doth continue strong against all force, but being divided [against the Counter-Reformation enemy] is easily destroyed'.[54] These echoes formed part of a crisis saturated, as a whole, with Elizabethan nostalgia and imagery. There were huge public processions on Elizabeth's accession day (17 November): the figure we have for 1679 is 150,000.[55] Pamphleteers paraded their Elizabethan credentials ('by a Queen Elizabeth protestant') and luridly underlined the Marian alternative ('nothing will convince him but French Auxiliaries, and a Stock of Faggots in Smithfield').[56] The alarm of the House of Commons culminated

(1681); *A Brief History of the Succession* (1681); *A Letter on the Subject of the Succession* (1679); *The White Rose, Vindicating the Right of Succession; Pereat Papa, or Reasons why a Popish Successor should not inherit* (1679).

[53] The record of the House of Commons during the crisis is considered in chapter 3; see footnote 50 above. Historians of 'The Meal Tub Crisis' should equally note *The Tryal of Elizabeth Cellier* (1680); *Malice Defeated: A vindication of Elizabeth Cellier* (1680); *Thomas Dangerfield's Answer to Malice Defeated* (1680): *The Tryal and Sentence of Elizabeth Cellier for Writing a scandalous libel called Malice Defeated* (1680): *The Case of Thomas Dangerfield, with some Remarkable Passages [from] the Tryal of Elizabeth Cellier the Popish Midwife* (1680); *To the Praise of Mrs Cellier, the Popish Midwife, on her incomparable book* (1680); *Modesty Triumphing over Impudence, or some notes upon a late Romance published by Elizabeth Cellier* (1680); *The Right Saddle upon the Right Mare* (1681) – an account of Mrs Cellier's tribulations in the pillory.

[54] See M. Levine, *The Early Elizabethan Succession Question 1558–1568* (Stanford 1966), ch. 5 in general, and pp. 42–3, 90, 221–5.

[55] Jones, *The First Whigs*, pp. 112–13; T. Harris, *London Crowds in the Reign of Charles II* (Cambridge 1987).

[56] *The Loyal Protestants Vindication . . . by a Queen Elizabeth Protestant* (1681); *The Great*

in a resurrected Oath of Association, modelled on its Elizabethan predecessor, but widely judged to be less a protection for the Stuart crown than a treasonous declaration against it. Like so much of the activity of this House (October 1680–January 1681), this recalled the attempted revival of the same measure by the long parliament in mid 1641.[57] The similarity of historical circumstances, and the Tudor/Stuart dynastic contrast, were underlined by republications like *The Last Speech and Thanks of Queen Elizabeth of Ever Blessed Memory to Her Last Parliament, after her Delivery from the Popish Plots etc.* [2 Oct. 1601] (1679); and the *Orders ... for repulsing of Foreign Forces ... th[at] should invade us by sea [issued] a little before the Spanish invasion, in the Year 1588* [1681].[58] All of this echoed, in general, the similar Elizabethan nostalgia which had underlain the crisis of Charles I's reign.[59]

The linking of the fate of protestantism and of parliaments in Elizabeth's republished speech was not accidental. For while the Counter-Reformation – 'the popish Plots etc.' – was a constant threat from 1560 to 1680, something else had changed. Under Elizabeth the resources of government, including parliaments, had been employed, however reluctantly, to help counter that threat. Under Charles I, and now Charles II, the government had become a part of the threat itself. When parliaments had attempted to fill the vacant role of *defensor fidei*, they had themselves been attacked by their monarchs and their existence imperilled. Under Elizabeth, therefore, there was a domestic *problem* – the *continuity* of government policy: the succession. Under Charles I and II, the *problem* was government policy itself, and the result was a domestic *crisis*. It was government policy which, in the 1670s, had once again abandoned the Elizabethan watchtower against the Counter-Reformation enemy. It was in this context that Sidney wrote in the *Discourses*:

[Kings] may call parliaments, if there be occasion ... they are placed as sentinels,

---

and Weighty Considerations, Relating to the Duke of York ... Considered, p. 29; see also, e.g. William Bedloe, *A Narrative and Partial Discovery of the Horrid Popish Plot* (1678), p. 1.

[57] *The Act of Parliament of the 27th of Queen Elizabeth, To Preserve the Queen's Person and Protestant Religion and Government, from the Attempts of the Papists, then big with hopes of a Popish Successor* (1679); [Anon] *The Parallel: or The New Specious Association an Old Rebellious Covenant* (1682); [Anon] *The Two Associations, One Subscribed by CLVI members of the House of Commons In the Year 1643, The other seized in the closet of the Earl of Shaftesbury* (1681); J.S.A. Adamson, 'Oliver Cromwell and the Long Parliament' in J.S. Morrill (ed.), *Oliver Cromwell and the English Revolution* (1990), p. 53.

[58] Thomas Diggs, *Englands' Defense. A Treatise concerning Invasion; Or a brief Discourse on what Orders were best for repulsing of Foreign Forces, if at any time they should invade us by Sea in Kent, or elsewhere. Exhibited in writing to the Right Hon. Robert Dudley, Earl of Leicester, a little before the Spanish invasion, in the Year 1588* (1681).

[59] For Elizabethan nostalgia under the early Stuarts, see C. Haigh, *Elizabeth I* (1988), pp. 165–7.

and ought vigilantly to observe the motions of the enemy . . . but if the sentinel fall asleep, neglect his duty, or maliciously endeavour to betray the city, those who are concerned may make use of all other means to know their danger, and to preserve themselves.[60]

That the succession issue should re-emerge during such a crisis was, therefore, in tune both with its wider concerns, and with its historical character. It underlined the continuity of the basic problem – the historical threat. To say that the crisis was *about* the succession, however, is obviously a different matter. In fact it was *about* the present terrifying policies of Charles II, seen in the light of those of Charles I. It was about the growth of popery and arbitrary government. The succession then was a problem; even a serious one. But it did not cause a *crisis*: a breakdown in the normal operations of government. What caused that were the policies of the government themselves.

The Restoration crisis then was not caused by, nor did it centre upon, the issue of the succession, let alone the exclusion proposal for dealing with it. The truth is that none of the three elections from 1679 to 1681 were fought over this issue.[61] Nor was the exclusion proposal the major concern of any of the parliaments of this crisis, even in the House of Commons, let alone Shaftesbury's own House of Lords, which threw it out at the first reading (December 1680). Certainly in relation to the succession a transformation occurred between 1679, when the Commons was equally divided between limitations and exclusion, and November 1680 when the exclusion bill came to receive the unanimous support of the House (*nemine contradicente*) for the first time. This transformation was part of a development which will be described in chapter 3. The result, as far as succession expedients were concerned, was to polarise the two houses of parliament against one another. None of this alters the fact that 95 per cent of the crisis, and of the Commons activity within it, did not concern exclusion at all (or that for most of the crisis parliament itself was out of session).

The political crisis indeed was provoked, as we will see, not from within the parliament, or even from within the country. Traditional accounts have assumed a series of features of the post-1688 political landscape (the centrality of parliament; of the Commons within parliament; and the self-sufficiency of the national context) which are inappropriate to the circumstances of the seventeenth century. Though the central political issue was indeed the *survival* of parliaments (and Protestantism), that fact itself suggests how far that institution was from being the arbiter of the situation. The struggle for its existence had, accordingly, to be waged on a much wider

---

[60] Sidney, *Discourses*, p. 466; see chapter 11 below.
[61] These points will be demonstrated in chapter 2 and (particularly) chapter 3.

front: in France; in London; during periods of parliamentary frustration and suspension.

The pamphlet literature of the crisis tells us the same story. Once again the succession issue makes a remarkably modest appearance to justify the extraordinary claims that have been made for it. Thus Behrens' survey of 'a pamphlet literature, so enormous . . . that it can find no parallel . . . except during the period of the civil wars' was focused not on exclusion and York but on Danby and arbitrary government.[62] Of the 1,450 pamphlets in the major collection for this crisis just acquired by Cambridge University Library, just under 30 focus on the succession; a similar number mention it in the course of dealing with other matters; the remaining 1,400 have their attention turned elsewhere.[63] Sidney and Penn's electoral pamphlet *England's Great Interest in the Choice of this new Parliament* (1679), described by O.W. Furley as a 'whig manifesto'[64] and by David Ogg as 'one of the first clear statements of party doctrine ever put before the English electorate',[65] makes no mention of exclusion, or of the Duke of York. And once again, if 5 per cent of the pamphlet literature, like 5 per cent of the practical conduct of the crisis, was focused on the succession, it is presumably time to ask what the other 95 per cent was about? This is an easy question to answer, since all of the works mentioned, great and small, early in the crisis or late, were addressing the same issues, and the same problem. The issues were popery and arbitrary government; or the threat to protestantism, and to parliaments. The problem was not in the future, but in the present. The problem was government policy, as for the second time this century contemporary confidence in the government collapsed.

STRUCTURES: THE BIRTH OF PARTY

Nor was exclusion the axis around which there emerged the first organised 'parties'. Indeed in the absence of evidence for the existence of such 'parties' what is presently taking its place is the assumption that although such organisation does not 'appear on the surface', it may be taken to be operating out of sight. This is the sibling of its companion argument: that where exclusion is not explicitly mentioned, it may be taken to be *implicit* in published political demands.[66]

Sidney himself used the words 'party' and 'parties' to describe the political

[62] Behrens, 'Whig Theory of the Constitution'.
[63] Cambridge University Library, Sel.2.114–Sel.2.127 (most of the succession tracts are in Sel.2.116); see also Sel.3.245; Sel.3.254; Acton. b.25.391; Acton.b.25.394.
[64] Furley, 'The Origins and Early Development of the Whig Party', p. 90.
[65] David Ogg, *England in the Reign of Charles II*, 2 vols. (Oxford 1955), vol. II, p. 589.
[66] See pp. 58, 73–4 below.

divisions of this period, as of the 1640s.[67] By them he did not mean there were two organised or institutionalised parties, let alone that they developed around the issue of exclusion. He meant to draw rueful attention to a much more complete fragmentation of political life; an illness of the body politic, caused by Stuart misgovernment, for a thinker who continued to seek the Elizabethan and Platonic ideal of organically ordered unity and harmony. Andrew Browning also identified in this period 'parties' which were not 'what . . . by modern standards might be regarded as a . . . party' – such organisations were 'not appropriate to the needs of the seventeenth century'. Rather they were smaller networks of 'interest' primarily based on 'family and local associations'.[68] Keith Feiling too has used the word to describe small-scale associations united less by organisation than by belief.[69] But it was with such faintheartedness specifically in its sights that *The First Whigs* insisted on something more than this: polarities of 'whig' and 'tory' which were 'unmistakably parties, units far more coherent, disciplined, organised, and united than mere aggregates of groups or interests based on family and territorial connections'.[70]

The problem with this claim is not only that no evidence has been presented to support it. It is that there is much evidence against it. There is for instance Burnet, who lamented that what he called 'the Country Party was broken in pieces; for nothing less would satisfy Shaftesbury than . . . exclusion. Halifax would not hear of this, but was as tenacious for a limited power . . . I endeavoured much to reconcile them . . . but in vain.'[71] The French ambassador Barillon commented that 'the interests of those with whom I am in commerce are very different and very opposite.'[72] The Countess Dowager of Sunderland, describing the opponents to the court with whom her son, Sunderland, had to deal, comforted herself that 'One good [thing], they are not all of a mind.'[73] Sidney himself lamented: 'we are here in the strangest confusion that I ever remember to have seene . . .Things are so entangled, that liberty of language is almost lost . . . I do not know three men of a mind, . . . a spirit of [such] giddiness reigns amongst us.'[74]

Similarly, any attempts to explain personal allegiances in this crisis by

[67] e.g. Sidney, 'Letters to Savile', Oct. 1680, in *Works*.
[68] A. Browning, 'Parties and Party Organisation in the Reign of Charles II', *TRHS* 4th ser., 30 (1948), 28–9.
[69] K. Feiling, *A History of the Tory Party 1640–1914* (Oxford 1924).
[70] Jones, *Country and Court*, p. 198.
[71] H.C. Foxcroft (ed.), *A Supplement to Burnet's History of My Own Time* (Oxford 1902), p. 99.
[72] J. Dalrymple, *Memoirs of Great Britain and Ireland*, 2 vols. (1773), vol. II, Appendix, p. 288.
[73] Dorothy Sidney to George Savile, Marquis of Halifax (1680) in B. E. Berry, *Life and Letters of Rachel Wriothesley, Lady Russell* (1819), pp. 132–6.
[74] Sidney, 'Letters to Savile' in *Works*, p. 29 (1679).

party criteria quickly run into difficulty.[75] The notion of a whig party united around 'exclusion' – and of a nation split between proponents and opponents of the measure – must unite Shaftesbury with the courtier Sunderland, who voted for the measure in 1680. It must exclude Halifax, described by Burnet above as one of the leaders of the 'Country Party', and whose limitations scheme Shaftesbury criticised to the King as 'too like a republic'.[76] It must exclude not only other radicals like John Wildman, and Henry Neville[77] but all but two of the 1679 'great Council' (the only exceptions are Shaftesbury and Russell), two-thirds of the Commons, and most of the Lords. It must make the Earl of Essex a tory in 1679, a whig in November 1680, a tory again in December and a proto-republican rebel thereafter.

These problems arise for two obvious reasons. Firstly such a framework doesn't allow for the fluidity of the real crisis – the rapidity with which such secondary expedients, and individual stances in relation to them, changed in response to changing events. Secondly it doesn't allow for the secondary status of the succession issue itself. Thus part of the problem is the attempt to organise an account of a three-to-five-year crisis around an issue which didn't actually feature prominently for more than one or two months of it.

Still more importantly, it involves positing as the focal point for anti-government organisation precisely the secondary expedients by which 'opposition' opinion – as Burnet has reminded us – was divided. Opposition to the court in this crisis was a spectrum of belief, not a party. Shaftesbury, Halifax, Sidney, Penn, and Neville, all participated in the basis of that belief; they were united on the fundamental issues; they all opposed popery and arbitrary government. What they could not agree about however, and would come to acrimonious blows over, was how, with whom, and to what end, to combat them.

Repeated attempts have been made to obscure such divisions – most notably by erasing Halifax and his 'limitations' scheme from the ranks of serious opposition. Such attempts are contradicted by all contemporary accounts, and not least by the Duke of York himself, who took the scheme with deadly seriousness, describing it to the Prince of Orange as 'worse than exclusion'.[78] It is equally contradicted by the record of Halifax himself, who was denouncing popery and arbitrary government in 1672, when Shaftes-

[75] Ashcraft, *Revolutionary Politics*, pp. 178–9.
[76] Haley, *Shaftesbury*, p. 517, and see pp. 530–1.
[77] M. Goldie, 'The Roots of True Whiggism 1688–94' *History of Political Thought*, 1 (1980), 206; Robbins (ed.), *Two English Republican Tracts*, p. 9.
[78] York described 'this limitation project' to both 'his Majesty' and the Prince of Orange as 'Worse . . . than the Bill of Exclusion, and [it] would give a greater shock to the Monarchy by vesting power in the Parliament'. William agreed. Dalrymple, *Memoirs*, Appendix, p. 308; J. Clarke, *Life of James II* vol. I (1816), p. 635; see chapter 6 below.

bury was, in the opinion of many, assisting both.[79] That is why it was to the inclusion of Halifax, not Shaftesbury, that both Charles and James strenuously objected in 1679 when the post-Danby court was reformed.[80]

As in the reign of Charles I, then, the hallmarks of this crisis, in terms of personal and political association, were fragmentation and fluidity. There was no monolithic 'whig' (or any other) party; there were a number of competing factions on both sides. The cohesion that existed between them – and what polarity existed between the sides themselves – was ideological, not organisational. Along this continuum of belief the whole crisis shifted through several stages, in response to a rapidly moving sequence of events. The opponents of government policy were divided, as we will see, not only over the succession, but between numerous secondary issues and tactical goals. And as events transformed the situation, so they frequently transformed the behaviour and immediate objects of those individuals involved.

What united individuals and groups, and shaped the crisis as a whole, was a particular momentum of public belief. It was belief about popery and arbitrary government which produced the Elizabethan processions and the pope-burnings; the parliaments of 1678–81 and the petitioning campaigns of 1679–80. It was this which underlay both 'opposition' and loyalist treason trials (1678–80; 1681–3); both 'opposition' and loyalist pamphleteering. None of these outpourings of public concern, the hinges upon which the crisis turned, focused upon 'exclusion'. What shaped the crisis was the intertwining of public belief with public memory. Like the Restoration settlement, the Restoration crisis unfolded as a dialogue between the present and the past.

In the course of these events, it was Shaftesbury's inflexible focus on 'exclusion' that was the reason for his *failure*, not his 'success'. The truth is that Shaftesbury successively failed to achieve power, in every arena of opposition activity to which he directed his attention, between 1678 and 1682. His pretensions to direct the opposition were eclipsed in the toppling of Danby (by others) in 1678; in his replacement at court (by others) in 1679; in the House of Lords (by Halifax) in November 1680; in the House of Commons between 1680 and 1681; and in the City of London between 1680 and 1682. (All of these claims will be documented in the following chapters.) The dangers of fixing our gaze on this uninterrupted record of failure and mistaking it for a record of the crisis itself are obvious.[81] Shaf-

---

[79] H.C. Foxcroft, *Life and Letters of Sir George Savile*, 2 vols. (1898; repr. 1986), vol. I, pp. 68, 98, 103–4.

[80] *Ibid.*, pp. 146–7: Among Sir William Temple's nominees for the new ministry, it was 'Lord Halifax . . . whom the king . . . kicked at . . . more than any of the rest'.

[81] Two fine antidotes to this tendency remain J.P. Kenyon's *Robert Spencer, Earl of Sunderland 1641–1703* (Cambridge 1958); and Foxcroft's *Life and Letters of Sir George Savile*. Kenyon went on to edit Halifax's *Complete Works* (1969).

tesbury was a frustrated courtier, but he chose the wrong issue to try to force himself back into the court. It was the wrong issue partly because it was peripheral, and by this he marginalised himself from the political situation. His entire career from 1675 to his death in exile in 1682, is one of progressive marginalisation. In the end, as Sidney suggested, for all his unproven boasts about 'ten thousand brisk boys' in Wapping, Shaftesbury died with little more purchase over English politics than the 'Count Tapski of Poland' to whom pamphleteers jeeringly referred.[82]

CONCLUSION

In his *History of England from the Accession of James II* Macaulay pinpointed the origin of the whig and tory parties – 'the parties which have ever since contended, and are still contending, for the government of the nation'. He identified it in the polarisation within the opposition to Charles I that had formed around the *Grand Remonstrance* of December 1641.[83] In the face of similar polarisation, as in other respects, the crisis of 1678–83 would follow the pattern of its predecessor. Yet while agreeing that such polarisation did take place historians of the crisis of 1640–2 would be reluctant to read into it the existence of the whig and tory parties. This is not because Macaulay's point about *origins* (particularly ideological origins) is altogether without force. It is because seventeenth-century politics were not organised in that way. The real situation was both more fluid, and more complex, for these crises involved a *breakdown* in the normal structures of government, not an exhibition of them. Contemporaries faced a malign or untrustworthy government, apparently united with their religious enemies abroad. The result was not parties, but bloodshed.

The crisis of 1678–83 was of this same nature. It began when the greatest fears for the present combined with the most terrible memories of the past. With it came the realisation that the Restoration – an attempt to banish those memories forever – had failed. How had it done so, and why?

[82] e.g. [Anon], *The Last Will and Testament of Anthony King of Poland* (1682).
[83] T.B. Macaulay, *The History of England* (1849), vol. I, p. 106.

2

The shadow of the past

This was the Preludium to the late Rebellion; loud Clamours against
Popery and Arbitrary Government . . .[1]

I believe, it has hardly ever been known, that any one Humor in one and
the same country, has come twice upon the Stage by the same Methods
. . . within the space of Forty Years . . .[2]

It would be somewhat strange, and without all example in story, that a
nation should be twice ruined, twice undone, by the self-same ways and
means.[3]

2.1 INTRODUCTION

The achilles heel of the Restoration lay in the double-edged nature of that
past experience itself. It could be drawn upon for constructive, and for
destructive purposes. And both past and present hinged upon a seventeenth-
century (European) situation which was not entirely under contemporary
English control.

The first crisis of popery and arbitrary government, under Charles I, had
led the nation into an unspeakable series of disasters. The civil wars and
their aftermath had brought with them, by 1659, 'the experience of defeat'
for almost everybody involved. Worst of all, they had resulted in a worse
'popery' (religious sectarianism) and a more overwhelming arbitrary
government (military rule) than anything contemporaries had imagined
possible from the government. The consequent political consensus which
restored the monarchy in 1660 was both negative and conditional (though
no less deeply felt for that). Approval for monarchy as an institution was
not conditional, but approval of this particular version of it – the restored
Stuart regime – certainly was, as 1688–9 would show. It was conditional

---

[1] [Anon] *Fair Warning, or the Burnt Child Dreads the Fire* [1680], p. 1.
[2] [Anon] *An Essay upon the Change of Manners. Being a second Part of the true Protestants
Appeal to the City and Country* (1681), p. 1.
[3] Edward Cooke, *Memorabilia; Or the Most Remarkable Passages and Counsels Collected
out of the Several Declarations and Speeches . . . Made by the King* (1681), p. 101.

upon the future protection of the nation, and particularly its ruling elite, from the twin spectres by which it had been terrorised, not once, but twice. The shape of the Restoration settlement was determined by this fact. The powers of the monarch, of parliament, and of the church, were debated and settled to this end. The Restoration crisis – the collapse of this negative consensus in the face of the return of popery and arbitrary government – represented the failure of the Restoration settlement itself. This was a problem which would not be solved until the second, and successful, restoration of the monarchy of 1688–9. This was a 'glorious revolution' – in the seventeenth-century sense of that word – because at last it restored, and secured, after a century of troubles, what remained salvageable of the Elizabethan church and state. As in 1660 the monarch concerned would have to be imported from the Netherlands. But building upon previous experience, this time the parliamentary convention establishing him would get it right.[4]

This chapter will introduce the genuine issues, and circumstances, by which the Restoration crisis came into being; and the genuine structures which determined its course. The crisis had both short- and long-term contexts, both British and European. The result was that by mid 1678, in the words of David Ogg, 'the Cavalier parliament had become as suspicious of Charles II as the long parliament of his father'.[5]

The revival of popery and arbitrary government in the reign of Charles II brought a revival of the nation's 'late troubles'. Given how much it had loaded onto the Restoration, an attempt to put those troubles behind it forever, this was not a situation that could have come about lightly. 'You cannot but remember' wrote one contemporary, 'with what universal joy did all parties amongst us, even as one man, receive the King at his return ... But behold! how soon our growing hopes were blasted, and all hands at work to hinder any settlement either in Church or State.'[6] And 'sure' cautioned another, '[We] ought now to be very careful of putting to sea again, that have been so dangerously tost in the storm.'[7]

Yet 'put to sea again' the nation did. And in life-threatening weather there was no substitute for seasoned seamanship. The return of the troubles brought with it, from 1678, a remarkable return to political leadership, particularly in the Commons, of men of some experience in such matters.

---

[4] They did so partly by putting religious and political ahead of dynastic suitability, and partly by other adjustments that the rare luxury of two attempts made possible.

[5] For many of the themes in this chapter see Scott, 'England's Troubles'; Ogg, *England in the Reign of Charles II*, vol. II, p. 550.

[6] [Anon] *The Present Great Interest both of King and People* (1680) in W. Scott (ed.), *Tracts ... of the Late Lord Somers* (1825), vol. IX, p. 116.

[7] [Anon] *The Parallel: or, The New Specious Association an old Rebellious Covenant* (1682), p. 14.

Such nautical imagery appealed to a religious island caught, once again, in the tidal rip of the Counter-Reformation. During the crisis readers were regaled with a series of bulletins – 'Letters from Legorn' – concerning the 'Continued Plot aboard the [protestant] Ship Van Herring'. Standing on the deck, once again, was that decorated stalwart of European Protestantism, the English parliament. Yet, as under Charles I, its frantic efforts were being impeded from within: the threat to protestantism also involved a threat to parliaments:

You tell us that whilst the Counsel was warm in searching into this Damnable Design: And making provision for the safety of the Captain and Ships Company, they were unexpectedly Broken up: And that this has been done Divers times: Sir, this greatly amazeth all Sincere Christians that here [sic] of it: Especially because we understand that two great counsels have been quite Dissolved. And the third have not been suffred to sit, since they were chosen.[8]

'Lay popery flat' observed Sir Henry Capel 'and there is an end to arbitrary government.' Once again, now, the two menaces appeared hand in hand. Once again a crisis of protestantism was, or became, a crisis of parliaments. It was the decade of Charles II's 'personal rule', following the fall of Clarendon, that recreated this explosive combination. It was the second half of 1678 that detonated it.

2.2 THE ISSUES

POPERY

What seventeenth-century English people feared was not so much popery as 'the growth of popery'. This had been the focus of their alarm throughout the century. It was by this phrase that they identified a seventeenth-century European phenomenon: the Counter-Reformation advance.[9]

It is hardly appropriate to ask when fears of this revived in the reign of Charles II. For they had never entirely subsided. The King himself kept them firmly on the agenda with his early and repeated attempts to introduce religious toleration for catholics. One of his stated reasons for this was the loyalty that those of the 'old religion' had shown to his father. While this was true, such loyalty was a distinctly double-edged sword. As one of his subjects put it bluntly: 'As to the papists assisting Charles the first in the late wars ... they did as much hurt to his Majesty by the scandal they brought to

[8] *An Answer to the Second Letter from Legorn* [1679/80], p. 14.
[9] My thanks to Robert Latham for this point. See Miller, *Popery and Politics 1660–1688*; Scott, 'Radicalism and Restoration', and 'England's Troubles'.

his party, as they did good by their arms. For they were the cause of that war.'[10]

Two other unstated reasons for the King's attempts in this direction were that Charles disliked religious intolerance in general, and Anglican intolerance in particular; and that he wished to become a catholic himself.[11] In this he reflected most of an adult lifetime spent on the religiously mixed, but predominantly catholic, continent. In such ways, through their exile, both the historical and the European contexts of the popish plot under Charles I were perpetuated into the reign of his successors. A visible symbol of both connections was the Queen Mother Henrietta Maria.

The public perception of a popish threat did not depend on royal policy. What depended upon royal policy was the need to keep it at bay. The threat itself was an axiomatic feature of European history from the later sixteenth century. It was

not unknown to most Persons, nay to every one amongst us, that hath the least observed the former times, how ever since the Reformation there hath been a design carried on by priests and Jesuits, that came from beyond the Seas . . . to subvert the Government, and destroy the Protestant Religion established here in England.[12]

Between the reigns of Elizabeth and Charles II, this concern deepened as the territories of European protestantism were ruthlessly diminished. By the Restoration period there appeared to remain in north-western Europe only the British Isles – the last 'Bullwark of Liberty, Protestantism, and Christian Faith in General, throughout the World: The Main Bank, that hinders the Sea of Rome from over-whelming all Christian Nations'[13] – fortified by the 'outworks of the United Netherlands'.[14]

Charles I had eventually turned his back on this perception. From 1628 'the popish plot' took up residence not only in England, but within the government itself. Counter-Reformation style reforms of the Church and state; an anti-Dutch and pro-Spanish foreign policy; Catholic conversions and papal envoys at court; all of this was too much for the English political elite.[15] When they tried to express their concern through parliaments,

[10] *The Popish Plot, Taken from Several Depositions Made before the Parliament* (1678) in *Somers Tracts*, vol. VIII, p. 59.
[11] I take this to be the meaning of Charles' statement in 1670 that 'he too is persuaded that his realm will never be at peace if liberty of conscience is not accorded to all the principal sects, as he himself desires; and . . . he believes that by giving [this liberty] to others, they will not take it ill accordingly when he also takes it for himself.' PRO Baschet 31/3 no. 125, 4 Aug. 1670; quoted in Scott, *Sidney and the English Republic*, p. 234.
[12] *The Tryals of William Ireland, Thomas Pickering, and John Grove* (Dec. 1678), p. 11.
[13] William Bedloe, *A Narrative and Impartial Discovery of the Horrid Popish Plot* (1679), p. 2.
[14] *The French Intrigues Discovered. With the Methods and Arts to Retrench the Potency of France by Land and Sea* (1681), p. 13; Scott, *Sidney and the English Republic*, pp. 128, 215.
[15] See Scott, 'England's Troubles', part 1.

parliaments themselves became the next casualty. The eventual result of this growth of popery and arbitrary government, this crisis of protestantism, and of parliaments, was the destruction of the government. All seventeenth-century English governments had to take account of this supra-national, European situation, and the anxiety it generated. Neither Charles I nor his sons proved capable of doing so. Eventually it proved necessary for those fortified 'outworks' themselves to rescue their British god-parent for European protestantism.

Following the Restoration, therefore, there was no let-up in this anxiety. Throughout the 1660s parliament reminded the King of the growing 'jealousy and apprehension' of 'your good Subjects ... that the Popish Religion may much increase in this Kingdom', and the 'insolencies of Popish Priests and Jesuits, who declare to all the World, they are in expectation of a plentiful harvest here in England.'[16] As in the 1620s, this anxiety reflected as much continental as domestic developments: the growing power of France, as previously the Habsburg victories of the Thirty Years War. What turned these fears into a domestic crisis were the policies of the English government from 1668–78.

It was of these policies, and what they suggested about the religious sympathies of the court, that public knowledge of James' conversion in the early 1670s became another disturbing symptom. Freed from the restraining hand of Clarendon, from 1668 the King embarked on a high road to disaster. It was above all when he abandoned the protestant Triple Alliance almost as soon as it was concluded, replaced it with an alliance with France, and then helped France invade the United Provinces themselves in 1672, that the Caroline nightmare came flooding back. It was from this action, by which the English King helped to bring 'the protestant Interest in this part of Europe so very near to a final period',[17] that the slide into an actual repetition of the first crisis of popery and arbitrary government began. Where Charles I's alliance with the Counter-Reformation superpower had been passive, Charles II's was active. Where Charles I's religious policy had lessened the gap between protestant and catholic, Charles II's eliminated it. Quite incredibly, in 1670 Charles II signed a treaty not only publicly undertaking support for France and promising to introduce toleration for catholics, but privately promising to convert his country to catholicism, using French troops if necessary. If Charles I had seemed an agent of the Counter-Reformation advance, Charles II was one.

The result was not what historians still call 'the popish plot', as if it were

---

[16] *The Humble Representation and Petition of the Lords and the Commons concerning Romish Priests and Jesuits* (1663), p. 1; *The Speech of Sir Edmund Turner KT, Speaker of the House of Commons, to the Kings most Excellent Majesty* (1666), p. 3.

[17] *An Account of the Reasons which induced Charles II ... to declare War against the States General ... in 1672* (1689), p. 1.

the first that century. It was what contemporaries called 'The plot reviv'd'.[18] Contemporary writers made both the European and the historical contexts of this perception absolutely clear.[19] The plot was 'a design' by 'Foreigners' in general, and those incendiaries of the Counter-Reformation, the 'jesuites', in particular.[20] It involved the Pope, the French King, and a suitable number of 'Irish Persons', thus expressing the full mentality of British Counter-Reformation encirclement.[21] This last stage of the European design was understood to be 'a Work . . . so great, and their Apprehension so glorious, that the most eminent of the Popish Clergy in Europe were engaged in it'.[22] The fear, in short, was of an 'imminent' invasion, led by France, involving Ireland, and resulting in the 'extirpation' of protestantism 'root and branch', by 'fire and sword', in the manner understood to have occurred in Germany, France, Ireland, Bohemia, and Piedmont. In seventeenth-century England contemporaries still considered themselves to be engaged in a 'Holy War . . . not only here, but in Christendom: for Popery or Protestantisme must fall.'[23]

As religious anxieties mounted throughout the 1670s, the country realised that it was slipping back again into a repetition of the crisis of Charles I. Titus Oates, that graduate of a continental Jesuit seminary, constructed his elaborate story from what he had 'read in Sir Hammond L'Estrange's History of Charles the First'.[24] That story, in turn, which broke in August 1678, was an expression, not the cause, of the nation's fears. These had been summed up fully and eloquently beforehand in Marvell's *The Growth of Popery and Arbitrary Government* (1677).

The *general* problem was European. The 'plot' was the Counter-Reformation advance. It was in this context that Halifax explained that the truth or otherwise of Oates' story was irrelevant: It 'must be handled as if it were true, whether it were so or no, though it were vain to hope it will ever be confessed by those that say still there never was any such thing as the Massacre at Paris, or the Gunpowder Treason in England'.[25] There was, explained Sir Henry Capel,

An universal design against the Protestant Party . . . We see France has Fallen upon

---

[18] *The Plot Reviv'd: or a Memorial of the late and present Popish Plots* (1680).
[19] Scott, 'England's Troubles', part 2.
[20] *His Majesties most Gracious Speech . . . to parliament* (21 Oct. 1678), p. 4; *The Tryals of William Ireland, Thomas Pickering and John Grove* (Dec. 1678), esp. 15–16; *The tryals and condemnation of Thomas White, William Harcourt . . . John Fenwick [etc] . . . all Jesuits and Priests* (June 1679).
[21] W. Bedloe, *A Narrative and Impartial Discovery of the Horrid Popish Plot* (1679), p. 14.
[22] *The Popish Plot. Taken out of several Depositions Made and Sworn before the Parliament* (1678), p. 1, reprinted in *Somers Tracts* (1812), vol. VIII.
[23] *Ibid.*, p. 55; *A Speech Made by a True Protestant Gentleman to Incourage the City of London to Petition for the Sitting of Parliament* [1679/80], p. 2.
[24] *The Popish Plot* in *Somers Tracts*, vol. VIII, p. 57.
[25] Quoted in Ronalds, *Attempted Whig Revolution*, p. 18.

the Protestant Party there. The Emperor has martyred them in Hungary, and what has been done in Bohemia, they say, broke the Prince Electors heart . . . Every session of Parliament we are still troubled with popery. In the descent of four kings, still the Parliaments have been troubled with Popery . . . [Now the French King is great] whereas in Queen Elizabeth's time, she would not suffer him to set out a cock-boat.[26]

The *specific* problem, however, was domestic. It was that once again the nation's own government was abandoning its primary duty to protect the country from this menace. And as under Charles I, it wasn't just foreign policy that was involved. This was combined with equally disturbing (and historically resonant) domestic policies, in church and state. Religiously, there were Charles' efforts to introduce liberty of conscience for catholics, what one contemporary called 'the Pope's Mouse-trap to catch the simple'.[27] Politically, Charles had repeated his father's 'arbitrary' rule by other means.

ARBITRARY GOVERNMENT

Alongside popery, 'arbitrary government' made up the second half of the official pathology of seventeenth-century English government. As with its sibling, the threat to which it pointed was seen in European terms; it was consistent across the century; and it was extremely specifically understood.

Historians have written a great deal about 'absolutism' – or even 'the potential for absolutism' in this context.[28] But 'arbitrary government' and absolutism did not mean exactly the same thing. Absolutism was a *type* of government, visible in Europe. 'Arbitrary government', however, was a *way of governing*, sometimes employable by rulers not generally considered legally absolute. It was certainly feared that arbitrary government would lead to continental-style absolutism. If so, other developments, and specifically popery, were suspected to be necessary to that end. But the two expressions remained distinct: one a political means, the other an end; one a way of governing, the other a type of state.

It is necessary to make this point, both to understand the meaning contemporaries attached to the term, and to see its relationship to the companion fear of popery. By 'arbitrary government', seventeenth-century English people usually meant government without the customary participation, or at least consultation, of the political elite assembled in parliament. Such a means of governing might certainly lead to a change in the traditional type of government: to absolutism. But it might also – and this was

[26] Grey, *Debates*, vol. VIII, p. 328.
[27] *Matchiavel Junior: or the Secret Arts of the Jesuites* (1683), pp. 3–4.
[28] J. Miller, 'The Potential for Absolutism in Later Stuart England', *History*, 69 (1984); J. Sommerville, *Politics and Ideology 1603–40* (Cambridge 1986).

the more immediate fear – lead to popery. Indeed attempts to govern arbitrarily came to be regarded as the key indicator that protestantism was in danger. Once again, this was the lesson of the first five years of Charles I's reign. By 1620 in Europe, and by 1628 in England, protestantism was in danger. By 1629, so were parliaments. This was because arbitrary government was understood to be the only means by which popery *could* be introduced in England, over the heads of a protestant political elite. This was the meaning of Capel's remark: 'lay popery flat, and there is an end to arbitrary government'.[29] The latter was considered a necessary means to, and thereby an indicator of, the European design to introduce the former. The phrase 'arbitrary government' then, in 1628 and in 1678, identified a way of governing pursued, it was suspected, 'for the introduction of popery'. This is important because it was by – or in the context of – this European religious problem, that the role of the English parliament itself became a key political issue.

None of this implied the remotest desire on the part of parliaments to *increase* their share in the normal government of the nation. Attendance at parliamentary sessions was both troublesome and expensive and a good monarch did not overburden his subjects with it.[30] What set the alarm bells ringing, however, in this European religious context, was any attempt to circumvent parliaments altogether. Government without the consent of the political elite, assembled in the great council of the realm, could only mean government for the purposes of something to which they would not consent. In the later sixteenth and seventeenth century, that meant popery.

The crises of Charles I's and Charles II's reigns were not, therefore, self-conscious struggles for parliamentary supremacy. They were struggles in which, over the century as a whole, the administratively insufficient institution of parliament was pushed to the political forefront by the need to protect protestantism. This need was created by the repeated association of Britain's Stuart monarchs with the Counter-Reformation powers of Europe. They were struggles, then, for the survival of two endangered species: protestantism, and parliaments; in church and state. And as the threat to one implied the other, so their defence was considered interdependent.

The political threat then, identified by the term 'arbitrary government', was a threat to parliaments. The signals registering this under Charles I had been unambiguous. The King had used his proclamation of 1629 to announce an end to his customary 'love to the use of Parliaments'. And,

The late abuse having driven us out of that course we shall account it presumption for any to prescribe any time unto us for Parliaments the calling, continuing and dissolving of which is always in our own power; and we shall be more inclinable to

---

[29] See footnote 8 above.
[30] Haigh, *Elizabeth I*, pp. 106–9.

meet in Parliaments again, when our people shall see more clearly into our intents and actions.[31]

The result was rule without parliaments as a matter of public policy.

Under Charles II, the situation was both more complicated, and more fragile. The religious and military state of western Europe in the 1670s was even more threatening than in the 1620s. The protestant Netherlands, a part-Elizabethan creation, narrowly escaped annihilation by a Bourbon–Stuart alliance in 1672–3. The attack on the Netherlands was accompanied by an attempt to legalise catholic worship in England. In late 1680, as we will see, the House of Commons looked back to these events as the beginning of the last stage in the European design to destroy protestantism. What further accentuated this fragility was the simple fact of previous national experience of these same problems. This was the double-edged nature of the Restoration inheritance. This both underlay the Restoration yearning for stability, and made it harder to achieve. With the perceived 'growth of popery' then, throughout the 1670s, the truffle-hounds of arbitrary government began to sniff out signs of what they knew must accompany it. By 1678 they had found three.

The first was the style of parliamentary management practised by Charles' chief minister of 1674–8, Danby. This consisted, in part, in the use of government secret service money to buy the attendance of loyal supporters – pensioners – in the House of Commons. The second was the 'standing army' which emerged as a side product of the complicated foreign policy manoeuvres of 1677–8.[32] This added a specifically Cromwellian dimension to the spectre of arbitrary rule. Both of these developments were seen, from 1678–9, as part of a deliberate attempt by Danby to succeed where Strafford had failed: to circumvent parliaments by fraud, and/or force.

By 1679, however, Danby had been unseated and the army was eventually disbanded. These two secondary indicators of arbitrary government fell to one side. What remained the central axis of the crisis was the third. This was the 'arbitrary government' – the parliamentary management – of Charles II himself.

Charles II did not suspend parliaments themselves. He suspended new parliaments. In their place he created the second 'long parliament' of the century, and managed it by adjournments and (particularly) prorogations. By these means, throughout the 1670s, with the court managing a deeply unpopular foreign and domestic policy, parliament was kept in being but largely out of session. Pressure began to build up, and tempers began to fray. Attempts were made by Buckingham, Shaftesbury and others to

---

[31] J.F. Larkin, *Stuart Royal Proclamations vol II: Proclamations of King Charles I 1625–1646* (Oxford 1983), pp. 223, 225–6.
[32] The foreign policy context will be discussed later in this chapter.

declare the parliament dissolved.[33] The explosion came in December 1678, at the height of national alarm about the revived popish plot. Letters were read out in the Commons which revealed that all of these prorogations had been being 'sold' by Charles for an annual pension from the French King. The purpose of this agreement had been to keep England out of the continental military situation. Members of all political persuasions were absolutely stunned. Here was popery, and the Counter-Reformation superpower behind it, funding a second Stuart attempt to 'render parliaments useless'. 'After four or five years [when] we have had nothing but Prorogations and Adjournments of the Parliament without doing anything to purpose . . . [and] can get no Bills of Popery passed',[34] the House had now discovered why.

The revealed letters were from Charles to Louis, and were signed by both the King and Danby. They referred to the anti-French fervour parliament had increasingly demonstrated throughout the decade.[35] They argued that the King could not keep such feeling and the parliaments through which it was expressed, bottled up forever on the sort of salary France was paying. If Louis wanted parliaments of that temper further prorogued he would have to pay something more realistic; something which recognised that it would be years before he could expect to call on them again. Six million livres a year for three years was the sum mentioned.[36]

It was this revelation which triggered the political crisis. 'I wonder', said one member, 'the House sits so silent when they see themselves sold for six millions of livres to the French.' Another wrote:

How clearly does it now appear as if the old Arts of Adjournments and Prorogations had not been sufficient, it is projected now to let a lease of Parliaments to the French for three years; and 'tis reasonably guest they would have been out of humor to grant Supplies when Supplies were gotten from others to destroy them; but how after three years the Parliament should be brought in humor, is not to be supposed: 'tis more probable that the lease would have been renewed.[37]

This was not only arbitrary government, but delivery of the government to a foreign power. The two plots: against protestantism, and against parliaments, now ran together. These letters 'agree . . . with Coleman's Letters' said one member. 'This army was raised for a French War', observed

[33] Jones, *Country and Court*, pp. 191–2.
[34] Grey, *Debates*, vol. VI, p. 355 (19 Dec.).
[35] See footnote 36, and section 2.3 below.
[36] The letters were subsequently published, by order of the House. 'In case the Conditions of Peace shall be accepted, the King expects to have Six Millions of Livres Yearly, for three Years, from the time that this Agreement shall be signed . . . because it will be two, or three years before he can hope to find his Parliament in humor to give him supplies; after having made Peace with France.' *An Explanation of the Lord Treasurers Letter to Mr. Montague . . . March 25th* (1679), p. 4.
[37] *An Examination of the Impartial State of the Case of the Earl of Danby* (1680).

another, 'and so many hundred thousand pounds given for that purpose, and yet we had no War! Money given to disband the army, and that not done! The Popish Plot discovered at that time! And all runs parallel.' 'I hope Gentlemen's eyes are now open, by the design on foot to destroy the Government and our Liberties.'[38]

Parliament's first response was exactly what it had been in 1640: the impeachment of the first minister, amid the widely held belief in his preparedness to use an army to establish the popish despotism feared. 'Now when this great person is on the point to make Parliaments useless, it is treason', concluded one member. 'His crime is great' agreed another, 'and tends to the subversion of the nation, and so it is, when the King shall have no Parliaments.' The vote to impeach Danby was carried on the same day (19 December).[39]

It was thus the coming together of these general religious and political fears, and these specific foreign policy revelations, that set the scene for the domestic crisis. When the impeachment of Danby forced the King to abandon not only his chief minister but his long parliament as well, all the landmarks of Restoration political management duly disappeared. Having, as we will see, been repudiated by Louis XIV as well, the King found himself well out to sea.

Danby's bribery, and his 'standing army', remained important indicators of 'arbitrary government' into 1679. But they were not the most important: the core political issue. That role belonged to the adjournments, prorogations and (soon enough) dissolutions by which the King continued to render his parliaments 'useless' not only up to the eve of the crisis, but throughout it. The crisis became, in its political dimension, a bitter struggle for the being, and voice, of parliaments. It was along the axis of this issue, alongside that of popery, that the events from 1678–83 unfolded. This is as obvious a fact about the practical conduct of the crisis as about its pamphlet literature, and its political thought.

This is what the 95 per cent of the pamphlet collection at Cambridge which does *not* mention exclusion *does* address. This is why Shaftesbury's own *Letter from a Gentleman of Quality* (1675) was not about exclusion, or the Duke of York but about arbitrary government, and Danby.[40] This is why the full title of Marvell's (1677) tract is: *The Growth of Popery and Arbitrary Government in England. More particularly, from the long Prorogation of November 1675.* This is why Henry Neville's *Plato Redivivus*

[38] Grey, *Debates*, vol. VIII, pp. 348–9.
[39] Grey, *Debates*, vol. VIII, pp. 353, 355, 358.
[40] [Shaftesbury], *A Letter from a Gentleman of Quality to his Friend in the Country* (1675). The other most notable thing about this tract, no less than Marvell's, is its historical focus: the problem is the revival of the past, rather than the threat of the future (see for instance pp. 32–4).

(1680) focused, again, not on 'exclusion', but on this second Stuart crisis of parliaments:

Since the parliament of [1614] there has not been one called, (either in that kings reign, or his son's, or since) that has not been dissolved abruptly; whilst the main businesses, and those of most concern to the public, were depending and undecided. And although there has happened in the interim a bloody war, which changed the whole order and . . . polity of England; and [then] . . . by his majesty's happy return . . . the old government is alive again: yet it is very visible that this deadly wound is not healed; but that we are to this day tugging with the same difficulties, managing the same debates in parliament, and giving the same disgusts to the court and hopes to the country, which our ancestors did before the year 1640; whilst the King has been forced to apply the same remedy of dissolution to his last parliaments, that his father used to his four first and King James to his three last . . .[41]

This is why Shaftesbury complained in his speech to the Lords in 1680: 'The prorogations, the dissolutions, the cutting short of Parliaments, not suffering them to have time or opportunity to look into anything, hath showed what reason we have to have confidence in this court.'[42] And this is why Locke's classic polemic of 1681–3, not on behalf of exclusion, but against arbitrary government, listed second and fourth among the four ways by which 'Governments are dissolved from within':

Secondly, When the Prince hinders the Legislature from assembling in its due time, or from acting freely, pursuant to those ends, for which it was constituted [and] . . . Fourthly, the delivery also of the People into the subjection of a Foreign Power . . . by the Prince.[43]

Finally, this is why the loyalist reaction of the same period (1681–3) swung the crisis one hundred and eighty degrees around the same issue, viewed from the same historical perspective. The fear was not of exclusion – which again loyalist literature hardly mentions. It was of the consequences of this second crisis, given the remembered consequences of the first. And the *particular* consequence feared was arbitrary government itself:

Was not a Pretended Conspiracy of the Papists, a Prologue to those sad Catastrophes? Was not there as full a cry then as there is now against Arbitrary Government? . . . Indeed the difference is that the late sad Times were ushered in by a pretended Popish Plot, and the present by a hellish true and real one . . . but its neck being broken, I know not why it should be allowed to be made use of for the carrying on of the same Designs as brought us so lately into Ruin and Destruction, and made us groan under the heaviest Yoak, *and Arbitrary Government*, that ever any Nation was oppressed with.[44]

[41] H. Neville, *Plato Redivivus* (1st published 1680), reprinted in Robbins (ed.), *Two English Republican Tracts*, p. 147. See Pocock's discussion of Neville's tract in *The Political Works of James Harrington*, pp. 133–4.

[42] Shaftesbury, *A Speech Made by a Noble Peer of the Realm* (1681), quoted in Ashcraft, *Revolutionary Politics*, p. 132.

[43] Locke, *Two Treatises*, ed. Laslett, p. 427.

[44] *An Essay Upon the Change of Manners* (1681), p. 1 (my emphasis).

In short, from republican to loyalist, and from 1675 to 1683, what the
political aspect of this crisis hinged upon was not exclusion, but perceptions
and memories of arbitrary government. All the political thought of the crisis
examined from various perspectives by Behrens, Fink, Pocock, Robbins,
Laslett, and Ashcraft, revolves around this issue. This is equally why
Filmer's *Patriarcha*, which argued that parliaments were dependent upon
the King for their being, was republished at this time. All loyalist material
from 1680–3 argued either that the people in parliament were justly subject
to their King; or at least that history had shown that resistance by subjects
resulted in worse arbitrary government (and popery) than any possible
under monarchy. All political writing on the other side argued *against*
absolutism or arbitrary government; or *for* the voice of the people's
representatives in government (and the foundation of legitimate government
in the people's will).

There was, then, no disjunction between the crisis' ideological and its
practical dimensions; between its issues and its course. Nor was there any
change in the fundamental issues between 1678 and 1683. There was,
however, change in the public perception *of* those issues, as we will see.

2.3 THE EUROPEAN CONTEXT 1678

So far, two broad contextual themes have been identified. The first is that
the general context, not only of this crisis but of both the others this century,
was the seventeenth-century European Counter-Reformation advance. It
was this which generated the anxieties – both religious and political – to be
triggered by three British monarchs in turn. The second is that it was by the
royal policies of 1668–78, in reactivating the nightmare of Stuart popery
and arbitrary government, that the domestic preconditions for the second
crisis were created.

It is necessary, finally, to add a third and more specific layer to this
contextualisation. For such anxieties alone, present throughout the 1670s,
were a necessary, not a sufficient condition for political breakdown. This is
because the purely *domestic* political mechanisms did not exist to force a
confrontation with the crown. The major political grievance – arbitrary
government – itself expressed this problem: that the forum through which
such grievances were aired, and redress sought, lay wholly under the power
of the crown.

This was true, at least, so long as the context for English politics remained
purely domestic. In fact, this was rarely the case. What was necessary,
however, to throw the crown into a dependence upon its parliament, no
matter how hostile that body had become, was a decisive intervention from
abroad. Thus the essential preconditions for both English 'revolutions' – in

fact the first and third crises of popery and arbitrary government – were interventions from outside England (by Scots, and Dutch protestant armies).[45] Equivalent interventions (by Monck from Scotland in 1659–60, and the continuing occupation by the Dutch into 1689), were necessary to bring them to an end.

Here, as elsewhere, the second crisis of popery and arbitrary government was no exception to this pattern. Although, as with the others, the necessary preconditions were the European religious context, and the footsteps of royal policy, the final trigger for the crisis was a sudden and devastating intervention from abroad. It was this – and not parliament, or the Earl of Shaftesbury – which destabilised the crown; which created the crisis by delivering it into the hands of its domestic enemies. The story of the crisis of 1678–83 is largely the story of the King's attempts to recover from this situation, and to regain political control.

This intervention – which was necessary both to trigger the crisis and again to end it – has not always been recognised for what it was. For this there are two reasons. One is the general neglect of the European (as opposed to British) context for this century in English history.[46] The exception to this rule for the crisis of 1678–83 is von Ranke, an outsider to the British national historiographical tradition.[47] The other reason is, however, the exceptionally ironic nature of that intervention itself. It came not from a protestant army, but from Louis XIV himself.

The crisis of 1678–81 resulted from, and lasted no longer than, Charles II's rupture with France. It was Louis XIV, not Shaftesbury, who toppled Danby, and it was Louis XIV, not Shaftesbury, who walked away at the end of the crisis with the political spoils. It was as a consequence of this rupture that Charles was forced, for three years, into a quite unaccustomed

---

[45] See C.S.R. Russell, 'The British Context of the English Civil War', *History*, 42 (1987).

[46] (See Scott, 'England's Troubles', part 1.) This neglect is less evident in intellectual than political history, and even for the latter there have always been exceptions. The fact (and the problem) remains that on the whole the professional subdivision of the subject has reflected the modern, rather than early modern, level of nation–state formation. In the case of (what became) Britain, this formation was only *initiated* by the Tudors. It suffered a series of setbacks under the Stuarts, in the face of European (religious) forces which the nation–state could not control. That is why all the major turning points in seventeenth-century English history (1640, 1660, 1688) hinged upon European intervention. The process of statebuilding was only successfully resumed, and spectacularly completed, following the resolution of England's internal troubles from 1689 to 1714. England became Britain, and acquired John Bull, in this period.

[47] The foreign policy context of 1678 has certainly been treated by many historians, notably T.B. Macaulay, David Ogg, and John Kenyon. What distinguishes them from von Ranke, however, is that this context, and the resulting crisis, continues to be viewed from a national rather than a European perspective. There is a difference between considering 'foreign policy' as a political arm of the nation–state, and considering such events and relations from a properly European standpoint. Von Ranke treated this as a crisis in western European, rather than simply English history.

dependence upon a series of parliaments which he could no longer control.[48]
He endured it, however, only as long as Louis decided it was prudent for
him to do so. The crisis came about because, for the first and last time in a
reign which he had voluntarily decided to predicate upon a special relationship with the French King, Charles attempted to turn aside from the obligations of that relationship and exercise the appearances of an independent
foreign policy. While this produced no practical challenge to France's position at the time, it did, in late 1677 produce a dynastic union (between
William of Orange and Mary Stuart) which remained a standing threat for
the future. Louis' response was to spend three years smashing up the
domestic political quiet in England, not only to destroy the architect of that
alliance (Danby), and to render the English government incapable of acting
upon it, but also to make a wider point to Charles about the obligations and
constraints that followed from his special relationship with France. In this
he was entirely successful, and in 1681 Charles gratefully surrendered this
brief and unwanted flirtation with parliament for the renewal of his contract
with the French King. It was the peculiar genius of Charles II that the
purpose of this whole display of independence had been, not the wish for an
independent foreign policy at all, but an attempt within the context of the
existing one to get his salary raised. It was one of the most expensive wage
claims in English history.

The situation in England in 1678 was complicated, and the country left
vulnerable to French intervention, by the fact that the government was
pursuing two different and contradictory foreign policies simultaneously.

The first was the public policy, of which the Stuart–Orange alliance was a
symbol, and its principal architect was not the King but Danby. The marriage, and the treaty by which it was accompanied at the Hague promising
containment of France, was part of the apparently active protestant foreign
policy by which Danby was seeking to rebuild the Anglican loyalism of the
cavalier parliament. The marriage was enormously popular, and a parliament which had been repeatedly prorogued since November 1675 in
exchange for French subsidies was now allowed to meet, in breach of the
(secret) Anglo-French agreement to the contrary, in January 1678.[49] It
responded by voting immediate subsidies for an Anglo-Dutch war against
France, and within a time which amazed observers 20,000 troops were
raised and dispatched to the continent.[50]

As Sidney later pointed out, however, casualties among this army were to

[48] Faced with a 'positively dangerous' level of crown debt as he was: see C.H. Chandaman,
The English Public Revenue 1660–1688 (Oxford 1975), pp. 247–8.
[49] M.E. Houlbrooke, 'Paul Barillon's Embassy in England 1677–88' (M.Phil thesis, Oxford
1971), p. 17.
[50] Kenyon, *Popish Plot*, p. 41; Haley, *The First Earl of Shaftesbury*, p. 437.

be exceedingly light. For while Danby was pursuing this strategy, the King was occupying himself with another. Indeed Charles couldn't have carried this policy through even had he wished to. If necessary the hostage to fortune he had delivered to Paris in the secret treaty of Dover could have been used to immobilise the English government. As it was, Louis found it possible to throw it into three years of chaos by revealing a lesser compact – that of May 1678.

Charles' true political ambitions operated within more circumscribed boundaries. What Charles wanted most from his reign was neither power nor glory (though he was not indifferent to either), but security and ease, and enough money to make his return from his travels both permanent and worthwhile. What his policies sought to capture was this combination: a quiet life at home, and money from abroad. The basic fact of Caroline foreign policy is that throughout his reign Charles used this most secure of royal prerogatives not to project English power abroad, to influence the political or religious balance, but as an extra-parliamentary revenue-raising device. Both his wars (against the Netherlands) were calculated acts of state piracy designed to gain plunder and maximise the increasingly important customs revenue; the first was emboldened by the success of the English Republic's war; the second by the alliance with France. This was equally the *raison d'être* behind the special relationship with France of the 1670s, by which Charles received regular monetary payments from Paris in exchange for using his powers of prorogation to frustrate parliamentary wishes abroad.

To begin with, this policy contributed to both royal aims: domestic quiet and foreign cash. By 1677 however, domestic strains had begun to compare unfavourably with foreign rewards. As his own subjects were becoming increasingly agitated at this treatment and the consequent unimpeded French expansion, Charles' salary was not being increased to take account of this discomfort or its likely ramifications for the future of domestic supply. While his own obligations to France severely limited his room for manoeuvre – basically to putting on pressure to have his pension raised – Charles resolved to co-operate with Danby to try to achieve this at least. He accordingly approved the Stuart–Orange alliance and accompanying treaty – though he made sure the resulting troops were never used – because it seemed to promise him improvement on both fronts. In the short term it brought the government support and renewed harmony at home; in the medium term it could only raise the financial value of British neutrality to France when the nation's war fever had been so starkly illustrated abroad. Charles could, and did, as we have seen, then claim to Louis that he could not keep such feeling, and the parliaments through which it was expressed, bottled up forever on the sort of salary Louis was paying. Charles had been, in short, feeling taken for granted: so during 1678 he attempted to play one part of this political triangle (parliament) off against the other (Louis). The eventual consequence was that both united to destroy his administration.

The more immediate result of this double game was that during 1678, while an English army of 20,000 men languished unemployed on the continent, Charles engaged in a series of tactless negotiations, through Barillon and the Duchess of Portsmouth, with France. These culminated in the secret treaty of 27 May 1678, agreed by the King against the wishes, and without the signatures, of his ministers Danby and Temple. This secured an agreed new (and increased) French subsidy, in exchange for English neutrality and disbandment. With a continental truce completed the English parliament now found it had, not a war abroad, but an army at home, under a monarch now apparently as slow to disband it as he had previously been to use it. In July the Commons registered its alarm by reversing its previous policy and voting £38,000 for the army's disbandment. The money, however, was used to pay arrears and the army stayed in being while the King waited for his first subsidy from France. The widest suspicions now began to be entertained about the use to which the government, and Danby in particular, intended the army to be put – suspicions with some basis in fact if Danby and York's ominous statements of this year are any indication.[51]

Charles had, in fact, been too clever by half, and now, with his own domestic situation in ferment and no money, he was to be punished. Louis seems to have understood both Danby's and the King's foreign intentions well. He had accordingly humoured the King with the financial negotiations leading to the May treaty, in order to neutralise English support for the Prince of Orange until he could use Dutch republican fears to secure a continental settlement. With the triumph of the treaty of Nimuegen in August, the Netherlands was removed from the calculation, and it was no longer necessary to humour Charles. Louis now turned to England, where he had some political scores to settle. Having secured the benefit of the May treaty himself, he now simply refused to pay any of the money promised. Worse than that, however, for the first time in Charles' reign he showed his anger (for the royal consent to the Orange marriage alliance in particular, and Charles' attempts at extortion in general) by ordering payments to English opponents of crown policy instead. Assisted by this money, he turned first to the architect of the Stuart–Orange match himself: the Earl of Danby.

As we have seen, in the tinder-dry atmosphere of late 1678, it was the revelation to the House of Commons on 11 December of Charles' and Danby's letters of negotiation to Louis XIV that precipitated the political

51 Miller, *Popery and Politics*, p. 153; Houlbrooke, 'Barillon's Embassy', pp. 88–9.

breakdown. These concretely connected the threats of popery, and arbitrary government, and forced Charles to abandon both his parliamentary manager, and his long parliament. This was the political trigger for what J.R. Jones called 'the governmental revolution' which followed.

Jones' *The First Whigs* paid little attention to the European context of this 'revolution': 'the Whigs', it reported, 'were relatively uninterested in foreign politics.' These parliamentary revelations were an exceptionally 'astute and skillful' piece of domestic intrigue, managed by Shaftesbury through his 'lieutenants in the commons'.[52] No attempt was made to demonstrate this connection with Shaftesbury, for in fact these events had nothing to do with him. They were the work of those 'French pensioners' upon whom he was to round so furiously in 1680, when they had frustrated his political ambitions in London as well. These people were extremely 'interested in foreign politics', and consequently alive to the opportunities they presented. Their successful destruction of Danby was to usher in a new ministerial regime, presided over by their friends, and Shaftesbury's rivals, Halifax and Sunderland.

Since Sidney was one of these men, these matters will be treated in more detail in chapter 6. For now it need only be noted that the hammer blow came neither from Shaftesbury nor from the House of Commons, nor even from these men themselves. The agent who revealed the letters in the House was Ralph Montagu, an ex-ambassador to Paris. Montagu had personal grievances against Danby, but it was the government of France which gave him the wherewithal to put them into political practice. The letters he revealed were, as we have seen, the negotiations for the May 1678 treaty. They were given him, along with the promise of a large cash reward, by the French ambassador Barillon, as part of the new French policy. On 24 November 1678, Barillon reported to Louis: 'This [project, of destroying Danby, has] obliged me to confide the secret of the treaty of 27 May to Mr de Montaigu and to Mr Algernon Sidney.'[53] Two weeks later Montagu revealed the letters to the House.

It was thus the government of France which toppled Danby, and it was those who co-operated with it in 1678 who helped to precipitate the English political crisis. As a chapter in European history, the crisis was conducted, both now and later, by European means. Thus transpired a second, and cruel irony: that Danby was toppled by royal letters of which he had disapproved, by agents who had meanwhile become real French pensioners themselves. The only justice in the situation was that Louis, having earlier refused to pay the promised stipend to Charles, thereafter refused to pay Montagu as well.

[52] Jones, *The First Whigs*, p. 31.
[53] PRO Baschet MSS no. 141, p. 100.

2.4 THE STRUCTURES

Having argued, in chapter 1, that 'exclusion' was not the central issue, an attempt has been made in this to show what the genuine primary issues were. That the exclusion bill emerged from concern with those issues is obvious enough: exactly what role it played remains to be examined. Similarly, having earlier argued against the existence of parties in this crisis, under the leadership of Shaftesbury or anyone else, it is time, finally, to identify the genuine structures that determined its course.

With structures, as with issues, the key is to abandon our knowledge of the future, for contemporary experience, and memory, of the past. Again the relevant interpretative framework is the first crisis of popery and arbitrary government (1638–42, and particularly 1640–2). This the second one mirrored, though with several minor and one major difference. As with the first crisis the initial spark was religious (anti-popery); and as in 1637–40 it took a foreign entanglement of the crown to expose it to the wrath of its domestic critics.

In late 1678, as in 1640, the King faced not a divided nation, but a near unanimous outpouring of public concern. One reason the notion of institutionalised party tells us little about this crisis is that for so much of its course there was broad public consensus, rather than division. But this brings us to the main difference between these two experiences. In the first, near unanimity in 1640 had given way to polarisation by late 1641, as previous critics of the government (like Edward Hyde) began to feel that the King's opponents were becoming a greater danger to the institutions they sought to protect than the King himself. The original critics of the government became divided, in short, over where the principal threat of 'arbitrary' innovation was coming from. That polarity held, and hardened, through 1641–2, to result in civil war.

The 1678–83 crisis mirrored this experience up to a certain point. It then made a crucial departure which resulted specifically from contemporary recognition of the similarity between the two situations. In its first stage (1678–9) the court, and Danby, faced near-unanimous public outrage. This gave way to a second stage (September 1679–80) in which (as in 1641) an ominous national polarisation set in. This coincided with, and was largely caused by, Charles' year-long prorogation of his newly elected (third) parliament. This both radicalised his opposition, and produced a first appearance of loyalists expressing concern about the implications of this radicalisation. The early stages of this polarisation took place around the petitioning campaign (petitions for parliament to meet) which these continuing prorogations provoked. The two sides thus first appeared (in 1680) as 'petitioners', and 'abhorrers' of those petitions. The polarisation occurred, in short, like every other major development in this crisis, around the central political issue: arbitrary government, still exercised through the prerogative power of prorogation, versus the 'right' of parliaments to meet.

It was at this point that the departure from the previous pattern occurred. As we will see, once it began this radicalisation on one side could not be stopped. Instead it took firm root, under continued provocation, inside the House of Commons as well as outside. This deepening opposition occurred, not in response to the denial of exclusion (by the Lords as well as the King), but in response to the continuing obstructive use by the King of his powers of prorogation and dissolution. It occurred around the axis of arbitrary government.

The result was two-fold. On the one hand, by late 1680 to early 1681, the House of Commons and the City of London had both fallen to a linked leadership much more radical than either Shaftesbury or most of the nation could comfortably tolerate. The speeches and declarations now issuing from both began to remind the majority of contemporaries uncomfortably of another time. This allowed the King to exploit this conjuncture of present concern, with public memory, by a double stroke. He dispensed with the Commons once for all in his reign (the following year (1682) he would also reclaim London). He then issued a *Declaration*, accusing his parliamentary opponents of dangerous and 'arbitrary' conduct, and reminding his subjects of where their last experience of 'arbitrary government' had in fact come from. It had come, of course, not from a royal, but from an out-of-control parliamentary power. It had come from 'the good old cause', to the revival of which loyalist literature now drew unceasing attention. *His Majesty's Declaration* accused the Commons of issuing peremptory orders taking people into custody, for which they had no authority, and of acting 'arbitrarily' both fiscally and judicially. The nub of the matter was historical:

(And) so we assure Ourself That we shall be Assisted by the Loyalty and good Affections of all those who consider the Rise and Progress of the late Troubles ... and desire to protect their Country from a Relapse. And we cannot but remember, that Religion, Liberty and property were all lost and gone when the Monarchy was shaken off, and could never be reviv'd till that was restored.[54]

The beginning of the end of the Restoration crisis came, in short, with an historical reassertion of the necessity of the Restoration. Once again the metamorphosis from one stage of the crisis to another took place around the key issue of arbitrary government. The transformation from opposition to loyalist consensus took place as concern about one sort of arbitrary government was replaced by the memory of another. For 'what is to be got' by

[54] *His Majesty's Declaration ... Touching the Causes and Reasons That Moved Him to Dissolve the Two Last Parliaments* (April 1681), pp. 4–5.

another civil war, wrote one contemporary, 'but certain slavery . . . as you have found by former deplorable Experience'.[55] What did that war achieve? echoed another: not liberty but 'Ruin and destruction, and made us groan under the heaviest Yoak, and Arbitrary Government that ever any Nation was oppressed with.'[56] As Locke and Sidney were writing to oppose the arbitrary government of the crown, contemporaries were remembering another variety.

This public memory was not only of the arbitrary (and particularly military) government of 1646–59, but of its 'popery' as well. The sectarianism of that period (culminating in Quakerism) was widely equated with jesuitism, and held responsible as such for the execution of the King. That the political language of the mid-century religious radicals drew particularly on the natural law theory of the Counter-Reformation did nothing to undermine the comparison.[57] This was another point to be made with vigour by Filmer's *Patriarcha* in 1680.

Thus in its final, as in its earlier phases, the crisis intertwined present fears with public memory. Having begun from this combination, it eventually ended the same way. What must be emphasised here is that the swing to loyalism between 1680 and 1681 did *not* occur because contemporaries stopped believing in the original popish plot. This is made quite clear by the number of loyalist tracts which reiterate their concern on that score. 'All honest men' explained one (in 1681),

[still] believe in the Popish Plot. But it would [now] be more vigourously prosecuted if Commonwealth Protestants [viz, republicans] did not endeavour so visibly to make a hand of it . . . and, having got a real Popish Plot, resolve to make that do the same feat, which, before they did under the bare pretence of one: viz the Alteration and ruin of the government established both in church and State.[58]

The crucial metamorphosis occurred, not because the original fear had diminished, but because it was exceeded by another, both more recent, and more potent.

Fear of the popery and arbitrary government of the crown thus gave way to fear of that of the 'fanatics'. Memory of 1628–40 gave way to that of 1646–59. All of this seems a remarkable contemporary over-reaction, within the context of an historiography which has emphasised the political moderation – the limited goals – of the Commons' 1680–1 campaign. As we will see, however, once again the opinion of contemporaries is to be preferred. The King's *Declaration* struck such a deep public chord because the

[55] *The True Protestants Appeal to the City and Country* (1681), p. 4.
[56] *An Essay Upon the Change of Manners* (1681), p. 1.
[57] Scott, 'Radicalism and Restoration', part 3.
[58] [Anon] *The True Protestants Appeal*, pp. 2–4.

links of the Commons' leadership with the 'good old cause', both past and present, were real.

It is hardly surprising, then, if by 1681–3 the majority of contemporaries had come to equate their two problems. Whether from 'papists' or 'Commonwealthsmen', 'the plot is the same carried on by different parties'.[59] The nation had arrived at 'the opinion', won by hard experience,

That Popery and Phanaticism, are equally dangerous to the Government by Law Established. The Papists, ever since the Reformation, have plotted ... against this Kingdome ... but by God's Providence ... have been always disappointed. The Phanaticks made but one Attempt, and laid aside the Monarchy, Destroyed the Church, and, for almost Twenty Yeares, excercised Arbitrary and Tyrannical Government against Law.[60]

The most remarkable consequence of all this was, and is, the extraordinary symmetry, both of content and language, between the political rhetoric of 1678–80, and that of 1681–3. The 'opposition' rhetoric of 1678–80 described a most 'hellish and bloody' plot, by the jesuits, to introduce popery and arbitrary government, killing the King and overthrowing the existing order in church and state. The practical result was a series of grisly executions for treason – principally of jesuits. The loyalist rhetoric of 1681–3 described a 'Most Horrid and Bloody Plot' by the 'phanaticks' to kill the King, destroy the church, and establish arbitrary government.[61] There followed a second series of executions for the same crime – principally of 'phanaticks'. As we will see in Sidney's case, the trials of this second wave of victims were deliberately and precisely modelled on those of the first.[62]

Throughout this crisis, then, the nation was in the grip of a severe (not only political but) historical logic; a logic of which Sidney became only one of the casualties. It was as if, wrote the Earl of Anglesey, 'the old civil war had now ... transformed itself into a judicial war – men fought with one another in judicial battle';[63] for indeed this was just what was happening. What must be noted behind this consistency of rhetoric is the consistency of its constituency. In both cases we are dealing with a majority of the political nation. The rhetoric was the same partly *because*, in many cases, so were the people expressing it. To a large extent, and with the important exception of some hardliners on both sides, 1678's 'whigs' *were* 1681's 'tories'.[64] This is

---

[59] [Anon] *Advice to the Men of Shaftesbury* (1681), p. 4; Harris, *London Crowds*, pp. 141–4.
[60] Quoted in *Ibid.*, pp. 141–4.
[61] [Anon] *A True and Just Account of a Most Horrid and Bloody Plot conspired against His Most Sacred Majesty* (1683).
[62] Scott, 'England's Troubles', p. 120; see chapter 14 below.
[63] Quoted in von Ranke, *History of England*, vol. IV, p. 159.
[64] This is another, and more literal standpoint from which to view Sir Charles Sedley's remark that whigs and tories were 'much of the same stuff at bottom, since they were so easily converted one into another. I mean self-interest.' Quoted in M. Kishlansky, *Parliamentary Selection* (Cambridge 1986), p. 174.

because the two were not simultaneous 'organisations', taking opposite
standpoints over a particular issue. They were often the same people, using
the same language, to relive two stages of the same historical experience.
That 'whig' and 'tory' later became, under different historical circumstances, the labels for simultaneously existing and permanent party
organisations is both an important and an entirely explicable historical fact.
In this way the political mechanisms of the eighteenth century were built
upon the historical conclusions of the seventeenth. In this crisis, however,
the beliefs the words were eventually coined to describe were not necessarily
even opposed, let alone proof of party organisation. They were consecutive
phases in the nation's thinking about its own history.

The distinction between the two 'sides' in this crisis was, therefore, not
institutionalised, but fluid. It was a polarity, not of organisation, but of
belief. And that belief intertwined ideology with history. That is why the
distinction between opposition and loyalist proved, itself, to be a mark, not
in space, but in time. Unlike the previous crisis of 1640–2, the national
polarisation this time was only temporary. It was located in one phase of the
crisis, bounded by the opposition majority of 1678–9, and the loyalist
majority of 1681–3. It did not persist into civil war.

2.5 CONCLUSION

By claiming something that did not occur, the myth of party in this crisis has
distracted attention from what did. The importance of these events, and the
political writing they generated, arises from their unique character as a
dialogue between the present and the past. The crisis was, or became, not
just a confrontation with present problems, but a meditation upon the entire
seventeenth-century experience. That is partly why it produced some of the
most influential political theory in English and European history. A century
later and beyond, in America, England and France, a remarkable range of
political thinkers and actors would be looking back to the writers of this
crisis for classic statements of their political beliefs.

When the words 'whig' and 'tory' appeared on the scene in 1681, this is
what they were coined to identify. They were markers, not of party, but of
belief. And the beliefs so identified captured this combination of ideology
and history. Each was primarily religious in its significance, and each
referred to one of the past (and foreign) rebellions, by the destabilising
influence of which the English church and state had previously been
destroyed. 'Whig' pointed to the protestant 'fanaticism' of Scotland, behind
the crucial military challenge of 1637–40. (We will see how central this
remembered role of Scotland was to Sidney's thinking throughout the

crisis.) 'Tory', on the other side, pointed to the darkest event in the protestant calendar: the Irish rebellion of 1641.[65]

The difference between 'whigs' and 'tories' in 1681–3 was not what it later became. It was not, as post-1688 whiggism implied, that 'tories' were soft on either popery or arbitrary government. Both 'whig' and 'tory' were polarities of belief, and memory, reacting equally strongly to perceived threats to the English church and state. 'Whiggism' identified the Counter-Reformation threat, allied with a popish and arbitrary crown. This was perceived with sufficient force to carry the country in 1640–1, and in 1678–9 and in 1688–9. These were the three whig 'moments' in seventeenth-century English history. 'Toryism' (that is, loyalism) did not deny this threat, but, by the same conjunction of present and past, identified another, even greater. It had been England's seventeenth-century nightmare that its rebellion against one form of popery and arbitrary government had, principally, served to deliver it into the arms of another. Between 1678 and 1683 that prospect had to be faced again.

[65] See, for instance, *The Character of a Tory* (1681); *The Character of a Modern Whig* (1681); *The Character of a Good Man, neither Whig nor Tory* (1681); *The Whig's Lamentation* (1683); and *The History of Whiggism, or, The Whiggish Plots in the Reign of King Charles the First* (1682).

3

The crisis of parliaments

This is the crisis of parliaments; We shall know by this whether parliaments live or die.

Sir Benjamin Rudyerd (1628)[1]

Now in this Government by Parliaments there hath been found out ways of corruption, and that is when either they sit too long, too seldom, or are too frequently dissolved ... such frequent dissolutions must of necessity ruine us.

J.P[hilolaus], *A Character of Popery and Arbitrary Government* (1679)[2]

We shall accounyt it presumption for any to prescribe any time unto us for Parliaments the calling, continuing and dissolving of which is always in our own power.

Charles I, *Proclamation* (1629)[3]

If it be the undoubted Prerogative of the King to Call, Adjourn, Prorogue, and Dissolve Parliament at his will and Pleasure; it is a high Impudence in any Subject or Assembly of men, to take upon them to advise him (unasked) how and when to execute his Power.

A Well-wisher to the King (1681)[4]

In the last chapter, the various component pieces of the Restoration crisis – its contexts, its issues, and its structures, were discussed in turn. In this chapter they will be put together, in an examination of the crisis itself.

The true shape of the crisis: the interrelationship of structures and issues, of present and past, may best be seen by considering it in its five principal

[1] Quoted in C.S.R. Russell, *The Crisis of Parliaments: English History 1509–1660* (Oxford 1971), frontispiece.
[2] J.P[hilolaus], *A Character of Popery and Arbitrary Government, With a Timely Caveat and Advice to all the Freeholders, Citizens and Burgesses, how they may prevent the same, By choosing Good Members to serve in this New Parliament* [Aug.–Sept. 1679], p. 8.
[3] J.F. Larkin (ed.), *Stuart Royal Proclamations* vol II: *Proclamations of King Charles I 1625–1646* (Oxford 1983), pp. 223–6.
[4] *Reasons Offered by a Well-wisher to the King and Kingdom against Addressing to the King with a petition For the Sitting of the Parliament* (26 January 1681).

stages. These were: the storm against popery and arbitrary government; followed by polarisation; radicalisation; repetition; and reaction. The actual role played in this context by Shaftesbury, and the exclusion bill, will be examined.

3.1 *POPERY AND ARBITRARY GOVERNMENT* (THE FIRST PARLIAMENT, 1679)

Following the attempt by an enraged lower House to impeach Danby, Charles II dissolved his long parliament on 30 December 1678. Given the rupture with France, an army to be paid off, and the ruinous state of royal finances, another had to be called immediately.

It is generally agreed that neither exclusion, nor Shaftesbury and the 'first Whigs', played any role in the resulting elections (January–February 1679). According to *The First Whigs*:

Shaftesbury made Exclusion the central opposition policy in the course of the 1679 session, but it was not an issue during the February elections ... These elections were largely decided by the interplay of local forces, with the revulsion against Danby and his methods of parliamentary management as a background factor. The issues which were to dominate proceedings in the next three parliaments hardly surfaced at all.[5]

In fact, however, the 'issues which were to dominate proceedings in the next three parliaments' and those upon which this election turned, were the same. They were the issues of popery and arbitrary government, given added intensity here by the fact that this was the first general election for eighteen years, and that Danby had attempted to subvert the free political functioning of the body to which the elections themselves were being conducted. In short this election, was, like the next two, about the very being of a parliament which had been prorogued, bribed, cowed by an army, and finally dissolved. It was in this context that Penn and Sidney issued their *Englands Great Interest in the Choice of this New Parliament*. While this made no mention of exclusion, it did focus entirely on the twin general issues, of popery and arbitrary government. In particular it targetted the 'corrupt and arbitrary' practices of the chief minister it held responsible for a deliberate policy of bribing and/or silencing the 'people's representatives' in the Commons. We will examine its demands more precisely in chapter 7.

We must look then at the conduct of the elected parliament itself, and see if Shaftesbury and exclusion really did come to 'dominate [its] proceedings'.

Again *The First Whigs* observes, correctly: 'At the beginning of the session the Duke was hardly mentioned, the House concentrating its attention

---

[5] Jones, *The First Whigs*, pp. 48, 51; *Country and Court*, p. 206.

and attacks on Danby.'[6] The author's impatience with these 'distractions' is, however, made plain: 'The opposition leaders in the commons did not slavishly follow Shaftesbury's lead ... Too much time was given to attacks against Danby ... But [this] ... enabled the opposition to develop the theme that liberties as well as religion were being endangered by a design to establish absolutism by the popish plotters.' Furthermore, as long as attention was directed to these 'innocuous' subjects, 'the House remained united' (the point being that exclusion was later to divide them).[7] Here then we have a House of Commons spending 'too much time' on the issues that really concern them; concerns which are 'innocuous' because they are unanimous. In fact it was these concerns, rather than exclusion, that were to dominate the proceedings, not only of this parliament, as they had the elections to it, but of all its successors. They did so because they were the substance of the crisis itself. And they did so in the Commons, not under the leadership of Shaftesbury, or his client Russell, but that of men who owed their sudden rise to prominence to their relevant political experience (and perspective) acquired in the parliaments of 1640–59. By late 1680, as we will see, Shaftesbury's pretensions to political leadership had been eclipsed in the upper House by Halifax and Essex; in the Commons by Silius Titus, Serjeant Maynard, Col Birch, and Sir William Jones; and in London by their friends and allies.

The first 1679 parliament enjoyed sixty-one sitting days, and the breakdown of how it spent its time tells its own story.[8] Time spent is not, of course, a satisfactory measure in itself of the importance of an issue. But when that time tallies precisely with the prominence of the same issues in the pamphlet literature, then it is significant. In total, twenty-one days of this session were spent on Danby; fifteen on the popish plot (including five on the popish lords); seven on the army and navy; seven on matters of parliamentary privilege combined with concerns about future prorogation; four on various other matters; two on Lauderdale; two on foreign affairs; two and a half on exclusion; and one and a half on the rival scheme of limitations. The centrality of the twin issues of Danby and the popish plot – of popery and arbitrary government – requires no emphasis; what does, perhaps, is the manner in which these problems were approached.

The House's pursuit of the former (for which the remark of Sir Henry Beaumont, that 'If the Treasurer be not suspended in [one] sense, I hope he may be in another', may be taken as a summary of the tone) had to contend

---

[6] *The First Whigs*, pp. 48, 51; *Country and Court*, p. 206.

[7] *The First Whigs*, pp. 48, 51; *Country and Court*, p. 207.

[8] Here and later in the chapter this summary is based upon Grey's *Debates*. While Grey's account is sufficiently detailed to support this kind of analysis the resulting figures should be regarded as approximate.

with the King's attempt to protect him by pardon. This pardon the Commons refused to accept. Its subsequent search for ways to proceed soon arrived at the method of 'Tryal . . . warranted by [the] late precedent . . . [of] Lord Strafford's case.' 'Can any man', it was demanded, 'think that the method of Tryal is altered?' At this point there moved in, to manage the discussions, men who had either actually been involved in Strafford's trial (Serjeant Maynard, Sir Charles Harbord), or had been witnesses to it as members of the 1640 House (Sir Anthony Irby, Sir Henry Ford). The result was that committees were named to draw up proceedings on this basis, in conjunction with the House of Lords. This was a procedure with which the Lords refused to co-operate. An account of Strafford's trial itself quickly appeared.[9]

Discussions of the companion issue, the popish plot, were equally permeated with echoes of the previous crisis. Many of them had already been prefaced by Marvell's *The Growth of Popery and Arbitrary Government*. The standing army was identified as 'a Limb of Popery, set up by this great Minister'. The navy too, was 'one of the branches of the plot. We have a Land-Plot; this is a Sea-Plot'.[10] Extending this line of thought, as Marvell had already done,[11] members were asked how they would feel about a new command 'that it is necessary to give Money to build ships'. An erring cleric was compared by Titus to 'Maynwaring'; in the following session similar references would be made to 'Laud'. The hunt for arbitrary ministers quickly extended to Lauderdale, though it was observed that victims of previous parliamentary addresses had more often been promoted than removed. This led Titus to reflect: 'It may be, that an accusation of the House of Commons is one of the felicities of man.' (It was equally Titus who remarked to a later House that although St Paul 'desired to be dissolved' it was not up to the King to tell him when).

Again this point about addresses echoed Marvell's tract,[12] but again Marvell himself was echoing the previous crisis. It was Walter Yonge in the late 1620s who had complained about 'the frequency with which those questioned in parliament for misdemeanours were promptly released and promoted by the King'.[13] The overarching echo here was of the Commons

---

[9] Grey, *Debates*, vol. VII, pp. 22, 200–23. *An Impartial Account of the Arraignment, Trial and Condemnation of Thomas Late Earl of Strafford 1641* (1679).

[10] Grey, *Debates*, vol. VII, pp. 28, 30.

[11] For ship money and other historical echoes of the same vintage in Marvell, see Conal Condren's 'Andrew Marvell as Polemicist' in C. Condren and A.D. Cousins, *The Political Identity of Andrew Marvell* (forthcoming).

[12] Marvell, *Growth of Popery* (1677; repr. 1971), pp. 51–2: It is 'a Modern Maxime, That no State Minister ought to be punished, but especially upon Parliamentary Applications'.

[13] Richard Cust, 'News and Politics in Early Seventeenth Century England', *Past and Present*, 112 (1986), 86.

debates on the Petition of Right, which had made the same complaint against both Sibthorp and Maynwaring ('a parliamentary complaint against a clergyman seemed the surest way to give him a bishopric').[14] This is the context for Sidney's and Locke's identification of Filmer with 'Sibthorp and Maynwaring' and we will find these same historical echoes in Sidney's and Jones' parliamentary *Vindication* of 1681. The second crisis of parliaments was consciously following the pattern of its predecessor.

As was to be expected, given the nature of the crisis, the lower House showed itself exceptionally concerned to uphold its perception of parliamentary privilege against further royal encroachment. Thus the week-long dispute which began the session, over the appointment of the speaker, arose from the issues at the heart of the crisis, as members showed themselves determined 'not to yield their right' in anything. This was particularly crucial 'Now Popery and foreign fears are upon us! I have ever observed, that Prerogative once gained was never got back again, and our Privileges lost are never restored.' 'I am one of those that have sat here long' observed Mr Garroway, 'and have seen great Miscarriages, Prorogations, and Dissolutions . . . I would not give the King offence, but not part with one hair of our right. If you will not stand to it here, you will have a great many things put upon you.' 'Let every man consider', agreed another, 'the Right of the Commons of England.' To the fears of renewed prorogation or dissolution such intransigence provoked, reassurance was offered: 'That [Short Parliament] called in 1640 sat but three weeks, and the King repented half an hour after he had dissolved it, and then another was called . . . there is no danger . . . though we are sent away.'[15]

Amid all this the Duke of York was first mentioned in the Commons on 27 April. A day had been set aside to consider the succession, in relation to the plot. Even so it took William Russell's intervention in a squabble between Secretary Coventry and Colonel Birch (Coventry: 'I would have Birch let me recriminate what he did in the parliament of 1641, as well as he recriminates on me now') to turn another general debate on the plot to the specific subject of York. Russell was to have to perform the same role repeatedly in future parliaments, to keep the House's minds on the matter. The result was a debate on the relationship (personified by Coleman's letters) between the plot in general, and York in particular. It concluded with a motion that York's religion had given the 'greatest encouragement' to the plot. Russell's appeals for the succession to be considered ('If we do not do something relating to the Succession, we must resolve . . . to be Papists, or burn') were not taken up; but York had now been specifically named by parliamentary address in relation to the religious plot, as Danby

[14] *Ibid.*, pp. 85–8; Derek Hirst, *Authority and Conflict: England 1603–58* (1986), p. 157.
[15] Grey, *Debates*, vol. VII, pp. 407–8, 427.

and Lauderdale had been in relation to the political.[16] The next day the House went back to Danby; the day after to other matters relating to the plot in general.

The court's response to this development was an offer of limitations on the powers of a popish successor. This was debated on the day the royal message was received, but nothing was resolved, and the House turned to other matters. It was two weeks later that both the exclusion and limitations expedients for the succession were raised together in the House, and the case for exclusion developed for the first time. The debate was various and wide ranging. The objection was made to limitations – despite its sponsorship by the King – that 'if you provide thus against the Duke of York, you take away all Royal Power, and make the Government a Commonwealth'. This argument was put to the King by both Shaftesbury and the Duke of York himself. Sir William Coventry argued (intriguingly) on the contrary that the limitations were like those offered by Charles I on the Isle of Wight in 1648, and (in retrospect) neglectfully omitted from the Restoration settlement.[17] (Coventry's point recalls the unsuccessful attempts by Northumberland, Saye and others of the 'Old Lords' to engineer the Restoration on these terms in early 1660).[18] As Professor Jones notes: 'the weightiest speeches in the debate were made against the exclusion proposal and were delivered by former [sic] opposition spokesmen (Capel, Cavendish and Powle) who were now members of the new [great] council'.[19] The implication that these men had, by dint of their membership of the council, sold out their opposition status will hardly do: the council was largely composed of 'opposition' members and Shaftesbury and Russell were members as well. The council lined up 18–2 against exclusion (the two were Shaftesbury and Russell).

Ten days later, an exclusion Bill was introduced and the House went to a division. Although it was carried for a further reading (207–128) a third of the House abstained.[20] And although they have occupied much of our attention here for historiographical reasons, the two succession expedients themselves had occupied a total of between 6 and 7 per cent of the attention of the House. The two principal issues had absorbed the other 93 per cent, and other specific (secondary) concerns arising from them (appointment of the speaker; control of the army and navy) a much higher proportion of that. This is a pattern we will see repeated in the next parliament.

Nevertheless, by the end of the 1679 session *The First Whigs* felt able to discern 'the division of parliament into two sharply hostile factions, the exclusionists or whigs [on the one hand] and the courtiers who were soon to

[16] *Ibid.*, pp. 137–48.   [17] *Ibid.*, pp. 245–57.
[18] This is discussed in I. Ward, 'The English Peerage 1648–60' (Cambridge Ph.D. 1989).
[19] Jones, *Country and Court*, p. 208.
[20] *The First Whigs*, pp. 64–5. These abstention figures are Professor Jones'.

be styled the Tories' on the other.[21] As has been pointed out, these 'tories' included Halifax, identified by Burnet as a leader of the 'Country Party'; Essex, who was to become a republican rebel; and Sunderland, who was nevertheless to vote for exclusion the following year. Indeed the 'tories' were at this stage a very large party, since so little progress had been made on exclusion, and so few people had declared for it. On the other hand, and in another sense, these 'tories' had yet to make a political appearance, for the court was still entirely on the defensive.

Indeed for all the efforts of his new ministry to find a bridge-building solution Charles had, by now, become deeply concerned by the behaviour and tone of his lower House. On 27 May, accordingly, a further singular act of arbitrary government was registered, with its prorogation. This had the (intended) effect, as the subsequent Commons bitterly complained, of erasing all proceedings against Danby, Lauderdale, the Popish Lords in the Tower, the other plot victims, the plot in general, and the Duke of York.

Ten days later the political temperature was raised dramatically by a religious uprising in Scotland. It was a rebellion by protestants against a 'popish' and 'arbitrary' religious tyranny which, to judge by their attacks on Lauderdale, must have commanded the overwhelming sympathy of the lower House. The Scots did nothing to lessen the historical resonance of their action by issuing a *Declaration* calling for the armed defence of the 'True Protestant Religion', and 'the obtaining of a Free and unlimited Parliament ... in order to the Redressing our aforesaid Grievances, for preventing the Imminent Danger of Popery, and Extirpating of Prelacy from amongst us.'[22]

This King succeeded, however, where his father had failed, in quashing this revolt militarily without resummoning parliament. He did so despite a public campaign in London, insisting that this procedure was illegal, and demanding the recall of the two Houses to deal with the crisis.[23] When, thereafter, the still-prorogued parliament was dissolved entirely, a major new provocation was added in line with the original issue underlying the crisis. This was the beginning of a sudden, profound, deepening of the crisis as a whole. For although the King again called new elections, these simply repeated, with more feeling, the pattern of the last ('the same men being', as Sidney put it, 'something sharpened').[24] This being the case, Charles had no intention of allowing the resulting parliament to meet. The consequence was the long prorogation, and the beginning of the national polarisation this would cause.

---

[21] *Ibid.*, pp. 72–3.

[22] *The Declaration of the Rebels Now in Arms in the West of Scotland* (1679). This was followed by a series of reprints of the Solemn League and Covenant, and other Scots declarations of the period 1637–40.

[23] See pp. 151–2 below.

[24] Sidney letter to Henry Savile, 8/18 September 1679 in *Works*, p. 49.

3.2 *POLARISATION* (THE LONG PROROGATION 1679–80)

That the new elections followed exactly the pattern, and issues, of their predecessor, was not accidental. It was a matter of deliberate policy. Electors were advised:

> choose the same Members again that serv'd you faithfully the last time; since in so doing you will both take off that fear of Dissolutions, which is of such fatal consequence in a Parliament, as also oblige them to serve you more cheerfully ever after . . . and do not to be alarmed or troubled at frequent Prorogations or Dissolutions; since if you persist in the same steady course you have already begun, it will but fall more heavily upon the heads of those, that are the contrivers of the Misunderstandings between his Gracious Majesty, and his most faithful subjects.[25]

As this election pamphlet makes clear (it was called *A Character of Popery and Arbitrary Government*), the fundamental issue was the same. But 'dissolutions' had now joined prorogations as evidence of arbitrary government.

> Now in this Government by parliaments there hath been found out ways of corruption and that is when either they sit too long, too seldom, or are too frequently dissolv'd . . . such frequent dissolutions must of necessity ruine us.[26]

Charles' decision to prorogue the new parliament before it could meet – to retrench financially and return, as it were, to government by prorogation – cut the ground from beneath his reforming ministers. While Sunderland chose to gamble on the lot of a courtier, Halifax and Essex resigned, the former to return in the next parliament to champion limitations, the latter to begin the process of radicalisation that would end, alongside Sidney, in rebellion.[27] Over the following sixteen months of parliament-less rule, opinion in the nation began to radicalise, and to divide.

It did so, of course, not over exclusion – which is again hardly mentioned throughout this period – but over the principal issue. How far was it permissible to press against this use of the prerogative – this arbitrary government – for the meeting of the parliament? This was not seen as an abstract matter, but a desperately urgent one, for the salvation of the nation from popery depended on it. It was against this background that there occurred the huge procession in London on 17 November to mark Elizabeth's accession day. *The First Whigs* describes this spectacle as 'a tribute to the quite unprecedented showmanship and capacity for organisation of Shaftesbury and the Whigs'.[28] Once again however, no evidence is

---

[25] Philolaus, *A Character of Popery and Arbitrary Government . . . [and] how [to] prevent the same, by Choosing Good Members to serve in this New Parliament* (1679), p. 5.
[26] *Ibid.*, p. 8.
[27] Foxcroft, *Life and Letters of Sir George Savile*, vol. I, pp. 196–7.
[28] Jones, *First Whigs*, pp. 112–13.

offered for this claim. Nor does there appear to be any. More importantly, it was around this same central issue that the petitioning campaign of 1679–80 developed.

The petitioning campaign marked the first clear national division, between 'petitioners' and 'abhorrers' (of those petitions). 'The petitioning campaign', says Professor Jones again, 'was a sign of the unprecedented efficiency and resolution of Whig organisation.'[29] Once again, however, no evidence is offered for this claim. What, then, were the petitioners demanding? They petitioned, says Professor Jones, 'not merely to demand that Parliament should be allowed to meet in January, but also that it should be permitted to sit until security was obtained for the King's person and the Protestant religion, *thus re-emphasising by implication the need for Exclusion*' (my emphasis). The point is, of course, that this implication is Professor Jones' own. Again, however, the petitions do not mention exclusion. What they summarise, precisely, is the same two general concerns: for protestantism, and for parliaments.[30]

As the records of the subsequent parliament make clear, the petitions had been a straightforward response to the prorogations themselves. They had been 'petitioning for the sitting of the Parliament', and exclusion is never mentioned in connection with them. Moreover the deeply offensive reply registered by the House from the abhorring addresses had been 'That petitioning for sitting of the Parliament was the seed and spawn of Rebellion, and the Principles of 1641'; 'That petitioning for the sitting of the Parliament is like 1641.' To this, as we will see, the next Commons was to attach the utmost importance – 'Next to popery, this matter of petitioning is the greatest point' – and to pursue the abhorrers through the House with a vengeance. The result was a number of expulsions, and the resolution: 'That it is the People's Right to petition for sitting of the Parliament.'[31]

Again, then, the key political development of 1680, the polarisation of the nation into 'petitioners and abhorrers', occurred around the issue of arbitrary government. This polarity, in turn, was registered by contemporaries in terms of the 'Principles of 1641', just as surely as historians have obtruded onto it the principles (and structures) of 1688–9. *The First Whigs'* argument is not assisted at this juncture by its use of the 1681 pamphlet *Vox Populi*. The political issues in 1681 were indeed the same as in 1679–80. But therefore, once again, *Vox Populi* does not mention exclusion. Its full title is *Vox Populi: or the Peoples Claim to their Parliaments Sitting*. It is a classic statement of the opposition's complaint that 'Their Parliaments

[29] *Ibid.*, pp. 115–16.
[30] See below; see also the letter from Mark Knights – who has found both Locke and Sidney's signatures appended to one of the petitions – in the *TLS* 7–13 April 1989.
[31] Grey, *Debates*, vol. VII, pp. 380, 389–91 (and 360–459 in general); vol. VIII, pp. 71–2.

[have been] rendered so insignificant by these frequent Prorogations and Dissolutions.' Its purpose is to muster arguments and statutes to support its central demand: for the people's right to free and unhindered parliaments.[32] As we will see, its message, its purpose, and its concerns, are repeated throughout the 'opposition' literature of 1681.

Similarly the loyalist arguments of the same year exhibit an equal consistency, both among themselves, and with the 'abhorring' responses of 1680. The focal point is the spectre raised by this petitioning agitation, and the radicalisation of London associated with it. It was the spectre of '41 again'. The political choice now lay, between a monarchy (as in 1660) or a commonwealth (as in 1649). And 'pray observe, none [raise the question again] ... but the spawn of those seduced or concerned in the late rebellion.'[33]

Indeed, what was to be most frightening for the court in this year (1680) was not the petitioning campaign in particular, but developments in London in general. That campaign itself was one outgrowth of the fact that, deprived of a focus for national political activity, the radicalising political forces of the country turned themselves in on the capital. By the end of the year, London had become, as Ranke put it, 'a republic by the King's side'.[34]

The first spectacular evidence of this development was the election as Sheriff, in mid 1680, of the republican Slingsby Bethel. *The First Whigs* describes this, again, as a spectacular victory for Shaftesbury and the 'whigs'. No evidence, again, is given for this statement. Abundant evidence, however, exists to contradict it. These elections were a disaster for Shaftesbury, whose own more moderate candidate had been overwhelmingly defeated. Both Shaftesbury and Russell fulminated against those responsible, and with good reason. The politics of the capital, as next of parliament, had moved permanently out of their control.[35]

We thus come to the eve of the meeting of the second parliament, two years into the duration of the crisis, without a single feat of leadership or 'organisation' to lay to Shaftesbury's credit. Yet it was at precisely this point, with the bill of exclusion at last about to command the united assent of the Commons for the first time, that the Earl himself admitted his loss of influence in the lower House. The consequence of the year of prorogations, in hardening hearts and concentrating minds, had been to deliver the House of Commons to a determined and radical leadership of its own. There was

---

[32] *Vox Populi, or The People's Claim to their Parliaments Sitting* (1681).
[33] *A Seasonable Address to both Houses of Parliament concerning the Succession, the Fears of Popery, and Arbitrary Government* (1681) in *Somers Tracts*, vol. XIII, pp. 228–30; see also *The Complaint of Liberty and Property against Arbitrary Government*, pp. 276–81 of the same volume, for the same argument.
[34] Von Ranke, *History of England*, vol. IV, p. 159.
[35] See chapter 8 below.

little room here for a disgruntled ex- (and would-be) courtier like Shaftesbury, particularly after his disastrous showing against Halifax in his own
House.[36] By 25 November 1680, early in the session, a contemporary was
reporting of the lower House:

My Lord Shaftesbury disowns having anything to do in it['s proceedings], and my
Lord Russell. I heard 'twas Montague and the two lawyers Jones and Winnington,
who show their profession ... I fear it will soon appear that those persons who have
now most power [there] would leave the King none ... My Lord Shaftesbury says,
he does no more understand the House of Commons than he does the Court. He
does lose ground.[37]

3.3 RADICALISATION (THE SECOND PARLIAMENT 1680–1)

THE 'GOOD OLD CAUSE'

This report appears to be correct. Before the end of November, decisive
leadership of the House's strategy and procedures had been assumed by four
men, and two in particular. Two of the four were mentioned above: 'the
two lawyers Jones and Winnington'. The other two we have already
encountered in the 1679 House: a third lawyer, Sir John Maynard, veteran
of the trial of the Earl of Strafford; and Colonel Silius Titus.

Titus was a mid-century soldier and radical who had co-authored (with
the 1647 agitator William Sexby) the brilliant pamphlet *Killing Noe Murder*
(1657), a republican call for the assassination of Cromwell.[38] From the
beginning of this crisis he had played a leading role in the Commons, where
he was perhaps the ablest and, certainly, the wittiest speaker. In the process
his old convictions had returned to replace the more recent caution. It was
Titus who replied to a member, counselling the 'safe' course of moderation
in 1678, that while under normal circumstances to ride a horse 'moderately'
was to counsel safety, to ride it moderately when being pursued by bandits
was to offer oneself to be 'knocked on the head'. 'No man advises you to
love your wife and children moderately, or to serve God moderately.'[39] That
there is more than a touch of Sidney in these and other remarks was not, as
we will see, coincidental.

In November 1680 Titus and Sir William Jones took command of an
angry and affronted House. Jones commanded particular respect as 'the

---

[36] Ashcraft wrongly describes Shaftesbury's worsting by Halifax as a piece of 'dramaturgical
nonsense' conjured up by 'Macaulay's imagination'. See Scott, 'Radicalism and Restoration', p. 465.

[37] Dorothy to Henry Sidney 25 Nov. 1680, quoted in Julia Cartwright, *Sacharissa* (1901),
p. 297.

[38] See the discussion in Scott, *Sidney and the English Republic*, pp. 116–17.

[39] Grey, *Debates*, vol. VII, p. 400.

most learned in the laws of England' of his day.[40] He was also – like his friend Sidney – a bitter enemy of Shaftesbury.[41] Contemporary pamphlets, in prose and verse, all confirm this new leadership: 'To manage this [republican] design', reported one, 'a new set of ministers is contrived . . . Sir W[illiam] J[ones] is to be Lord Chief Justice; Col T[itus] to be . . . secretary of State.'[42]

'No freedom of debate was left for you', lamented another,

> When all was Mov'd and Manag'd by a few
> Your leading Maynard Jones and Winnington
> as if all wisdom were in them alone
> [opponents] . . . urg'd all in vain.
> None were of force against the Good Old Cause.[43]

'Maynard in the head' elaborated another,

> In Legal Murder none so deeply read
> Stain'd with the Blood of . . . Brave Strafford.[44]

Readers of the traditional historiography of this crisis could be forgiven surprise at this contemporary association of the leadership of the second 'exclusion' parliament with the 'good old cause'. If the House was in the grip of a party called the 'whigs', whose political object was exclusion, the 'good old cause' could hardly be relevant. It was on this assumption that Professor Jones dismissed Barillon's reports in 1680 on the gathering strength of republicanism in London as a foreigner's misunderstanding of the situation. Barillon was confusing 'the whigs . . . with their nearest continental equivalent . . . the Louvesteiners or Dutch republicans'.[45] In fact, however, Barillon was suffering from no such confusion. Not only had he close contacts with the English republicans concerned (as his Dutch equivalent D'Avaux had with the Louvesteiners) but this republican renaissance was something he had himself helped to create. By the year's end, it was threatening to run out of control. The capital city had, as York lamented, 'set up for a commonwealth'.[46]

---

[40] Barillon to Louis XIV, PRO Baschet no. 147, fols. 402–3; and see note 58 below.

[41] '[Jones] hated Shaftesbury and . . . would not willingly come into the room where he was. His personal virtue and gravity was great, and he could not bear such a flirting wit and libertine as the other was.' North, *Examen*, quoted in Blencowe, *Diary of the Times of Charles II*, p. 71.

[42] *Englands Concern in the Case of HRH James Duke of York . . . to be read by all subjects, whether of Royal or Republican Opinions* (1680) in *Somers Tracts*, vol. VIII, p. 180; see also *A Seasonable Address*, ibid., p. 230.

[43] *A Dialogue between the Ghosts of the two last Parliaments* (1681).

[44] *The Ghost of the Late House of Commons to the New One appointed to meet at Oxford* (1681).

[45] Jones, *The First Whigs*, pp. 150–1.

[46] 'Life of James II 1660–98, written by Himself' in J. MacPherson (ed.), *Original Papers* (1775), p. 112.

In December, accordingly, Barillon at last heeded Charles' pleadings. He warned Louis that the situation had become so serious that the alternative to an immediate resumption of support for the monarch was a restoration of the Republic.[47] It was against the background of this republican revival of 1680 that there emerged from London a further major wave of English republican writing. The connection between the ideological revival and the civic institutions of the City was underlined by the appearance, alongside Neville's *Plato Redivivus* (1680), of Sheriff Slingsby Bethel's Louvestein *The Interest of Princes and States* (1680).[48] The subsequent loyalist reaction developed principally from public perception of this situation. With an appalling historical logic, the revival of popery and arbitrary government was giving way in turn to a revival of the 'good old cause'.

This is not to say that by November 1680 the leaders of the Commons, or the City, were openly declaring themselves to be republicans. That is, however – to public alarm – what some of them had been.[49] It is to make the historiographical point that while the crisis was seen to revolve around exclusion, the 'good old cause' could hardly be relevant to it. But in fact this was the second crisis of popery and arbitrary government; the second crisis of parliaments. It therefore naturally, beyond a certain point, began to throw up the issues, the memory, and the actual personnel, of its predecessor. This crisis quickly developed into an open struggle between the House of Commons on the one hand, and the monarch's prerogatives controlling its being on the other. There were plenty of people on both sides of the polarised nation who remembered that the outcome of the last such struggle had been the destruction, first, of that key prerogative (1641) and, second, of the monarchy altogether.

It was Titus, anticipating Sidney's *Discourses*, who stated openly in the House on 7 January 1681 that 'mankind cannot consist together without a supreme Power, [Sidney had even used the word 'arbitrary'] and that in our Government is the Legislative.'[50] It was 'the Legislative' after all, as Sidney also pointed out in the *Discourses*, who had put Charles on the throne in the first place.[51] (This is again the background to Locke's treatment of 'the

[47] This was the culmination of a long campaign by Charles to get this point across to the ambassador. It was in June 1679 that he first told Barillon that Louis 'must decide whether he wanted a republic or a monarchy in England. If he did not support the royal authority actively ... nothing would prevent parliament from taking over control of foreign affairs and everything else'. J.J. Jusserand, *Recueil des Instructions Données Aux Ambassadeurs et Ministres de France*, vol. XXV *Angleterre* (Paris 1929), p. 271. See Barillon's report to the King, PRO Baschet no. 143, p. 291.
[48] See the discussion in Scott, *Sidney and the English Republic*, ch. 13, pp. 215–16.
[49] See chapter 8 below.   [50] Grey, *Debates*, vol. VIII, p. 278.
[51] This is the burden of Sidney's repeated accusations against Charles of 'ingratitude', and of usurping powers 'contrary to his institution'. See, for instance *Discourses*, pp. 379–80; and chapter 11 below.

legislative' in the Second Treatise). These facts deeply influenced public perceptions of this crisis. After the experience of 1640–60, no one underestimated parliament's capacity for construction or destruction in the struggle for its own existence.[52] In 1642 it had called an army into being to defend itself against the arbitrary government of the King. In 1660 it had called the King back to rescue itself from the arbitrary government of the army. Now the whole situation had been re-opened.

The second crisis of parliaments, and its progress, thus led to a revival of the 'old cause', because it *was* the 'old cause'. It was to rescue their martyrs from anything so dangerous that whig historians converted the partisans of this struggle into 'exclusionists'. Thus severed from their past, they could become innocent victims of Stuart tyranny, and prophets of the future, at the same time.

Once again, however, we must prefer the perception of contemporaries, on both sides of the political spectrum. For the association of Jones, Titus and others with the remnants of the 'good old cause' was a practical fact. A radicalised House of Commons had now reconvened in a radicalised city. The city had supported the House throughout 1680 with the petitioning campaign. With the resumption of parliament itself this co-operation was extended and intensified. It was to try and break this most historically disturbing of connections that Charles moved the following session to Oxford in 1681.

The first independent exercise of power by the new House was the trial and destruction of Lord Stafford in December 1680. This was a deliberately grandiose and public display of muscle by the Commons, and it was registered as such by the King, who swore (and duly exacted) vengeance.[53] The trial was presided over by Sir William Jones as Lord Chief Justice. Following his conviction, Stafford was handed over to Slingsby Bethel, who promptly issued a warrant for his execution, and accompanied his victim to the scaffold. A close friend of both Jones and Bethel was Algernon Sidney. Barillon reported, in late 1680:

Mr Algernon Sidney is a man of great views and very high designs, which tend to the establishment of a republic. He is in the party of the independents and other sectaries . . . [who] were masters during the late troubles . . . they are strong in London . . . Mr Sidney . . . is intimate with Mr Jones, who is a man of the greatest knowledge in the laws of England, and will be chancellor if the party opposed to the court shall gain the superiority . . . and it is through the intrigues of the sieur Algernon Sidney that one of the two sheriffs, named Bethel, has been elected . . .[54]

---

[52] A point made in a different context recently by Mark Kishlansky, *Parliamentary Selection*, p. 136.
[53] Against Sidney, among others, see below. *The Tryal of William Viscount Stafford for High Treason* (1681); Kenyon, *The Popish Plot*, pp. 231–2.
[54] PRO Baschet no. 147, pp. 402–3.

Sidney's earlier association with Bethel in the Netherlands was described in *Algernon Sidney and the English Republic*. He had more recently become intimate with Jones, both through his political and legal activities, and through their shared relationship with the Pelham family. In 1681, Sidney would join with Jones, Titus, and that veteran of the Putney Debates, John Wildman, to pen the Commons' official reply to the King's *Declaration*: the *Just and Modest Vindication of the Proceedings of the Two Last Parliaments*. Sidney's personal association with Wildman would continue until 1683. When, in that year, Sidney objected to the procedures being adopted at his own trial, he was referred to those used earlier against Stafford – 'I do not doubt but you remember it. And Sir William Jones, against whose judgement, I believe, you will not object, was attorney at that time.'[55]

THE RECORD OF THE HOUSE

The 1680–1 House sat for a similar period (sixty-two sitting days, as opposed to sixty-one) to its predecessor. The only well-known aspect of the session relates to the exclusion bill. Indeed the central drama of Professor Jones' account: the passing of the bill of exclusion in November; its being carried from Commons to Lords (by Russell) 'with a shout'; and its nemesis there under Halifax's oratory, is perhaps the best-known episode of the whole crisis. The equation of the concerns of the Commons with exclusion is so complete that once this exercise has been played out the parliament is taken to have no further purpose; although it sat for almost two more months. 'But exclusion could not be [re-]introduced during the session, so that although they voted menacing resolutions against anyone advising the King to dissolve or prorogue, the whigs welcomed the end of the second Exclusion parliament.'[56] By this stage, then, the reading of the parliament's intentions has progressed from assuming 'implicit' meaning in preference to that which is explicit, to assuming the exact contrary to what is being stated by them.

In truth, as we have seen, this matter of the prorogation and dissolution of parliaments was itself the fundamental political issue. Consequently, when the news of impending dissolution came finally on 9 January the House convened in an uproar to vote it treason.[57] Once again, the record of the whole session tells a different, and illuminating story.

As far as the bill of exclusion is concerned – and it occupied the same secondary role in this parliament as it had in the last – a transformation had certainly taken place over the period of the long prorogation. It had now

[55] *The Trial of Algernon Sidney* in *Works* (1772), pp. 12–16; see chapter 13 below.
[56] Jones, *Country and Court*, p. 212.
[57] Grey, *Debates*, vol. VIII, p. 285.

come to enjoy the unanimous support of the Commons (though not the Lords) for the first time. It had fallen into line with the other mainstream expressions of concern about popery and arbitrary government – such as Danby, the popish lords, the army, and so on. This is the state of unanimity – *nemine contradicente* – which *The First Whigs* considered as denoting 'innocuous issues' in 1679. Let us examine how this came to be the case.

For the irony is, the exclusion bill achieved this status only when it became detached from the single-issue strategy of Shaftesbury and Russell. It was only when it became one part of a much broader strategy, under the new leadership, and *in line with the main issues of the crisis*, that it achieved this level of backing *for the first time*. Thus it was, as we have seen, in November 1680, when this transformation occurred, that Dorothy Sidney recorded Shaftesbury's loss of influence in the lower House. It was now in the power of men who she feared would 'leave the King none'. Both Anti-chell Grey and Sir William Temple recorded that it was the intervention of Sir William Jones (rather than Russell) on its behalf which brought the House unanimously behind the exclusion bill for the first time.[58] According to Professor Jones, the 'self interest [of these men] is obvious'; they had no positive political strategy, only a spiteful 'dislike of Shaftesbury'.[59]

To understand what had happened to exclusion, we need again to see it in the context of the record of the whole House. The parliament had reassembled on 21 October (1680). The first two days were spent on routine procedural business, to which Serjeant Maynard brought his usual flair for precedent ('I was in the Chair of the Committee of Elections in the Long Parliament in 1641, and the course was this. . .').[60] The House then turned, through a debate on the King's message, to the matters of greatest concern. These were the obstructions received in the prosecution of the plot (including the contrivance of the 'Presbyterian Plot . . . or Conspirators in a Meal Tub') and the obstructions received to the sitting of the Parliament (including the vindication of the right of petitioning, and the pursuit of the abhorrers).

The house spent the next five days heatedly discussing these matters, sometimes alternately, sometimes intertwining the two. It sought to address the root problem, of the 'so many interruptions' and 'the late prorogations' of parliaments, while pursuing the abhorrers who (like Danby) served as the only symbols of that obstruction accessible for punishment. The anger of the House showed in both the discussion itself: 'The King, in his letter to the Convention from Breda, said he looked upon the Parliament as a vital part

[58] *Ibid.*, vol. VII, p. 451; Blencowe (ed.), *Diary of the Times of Charles II*, vol. II, pp. 70–1.
[59] Jones, *The First Whigs*, pp. 151–3.
[60] Grey, *Debates*, vol. VII, p. 351.

of the Nation . . . We know the Kings opinion [now]' – and in the resulting resolutions; in particular:

That it is . . . the undoubted Right of Subjects of England, to petition the King for the calling and sitting of Parliaments, . . . [and] that to traduce such Petitioning . . . as tumultuous and seditious, [these were the exact words – tumult and sedition – that Sidney was to defend in the *Discourses*] is to betray the Liberty of the Subject, and contributes to the design of subverting the ancient legal Constitution of this Kingdom, and introducing arbitrary power.[61]

This was followed by resolutions for the condign punishment of those who had countered the petitioning by likening it to the conduct of 1641: for 'If this doctrine be preached, 'That petitioning for the sitting of the parliament is like 1641', what will become of us that made the vote the other day, 'That it is the People's Right to petition for the sitting of Parliament, etc'?[62]

It was after these resolutions, and on the fifth day of the continuing debate, intertwining these general concerns of 'Popery [and] this matter of petitioning', that on 30 November the subject of exclusion was first raised. Moreover it was raised in the same manner, and by the same person, as in the previous parliament. It was in the course of the continuing debate on the plot in general that William Russell intervened to try to turn the House's attention to the specific subject of the exclusion bill, and he asked for a day to be set for its consideration. His appeal was lost, however, in the continuing general hubbub: that progress in the prosecution of the plot had been obstructed by dissolutions, abhorring, and so on.[63] One of those called to testify against the abhorrers was Sidney's future plotting colleague and envoy, Aaron Smith. Justice Wythens, reported Smith, 'At the Rainbow Coffee-house did declare, That petitioning for the sitting of the Parliament was the seed and spawn of Rebellion, and the principles of 1641.'[64]

The next initiative, however, came from Titus, and this was effective. After recommending his own pet project, a bill for the relief of protestant consciences (to receive the same amount of attention in this House as the exclusion bill), Titus took up the mood of the *general* discussion. He proposed that the House make its point about the unlawfulness of 'the late interruptions, prorogations etc.' by basing the proceedings of this session precisely on those of the last. As we have seen, this had been exactly the thinking behind the elections to this House in August–September 1679: that 'you persist in the same steady course . . . choose the same members again . . . since in so doing . . . you will take off that fear of Dissolutions'. Titus now argued: 'When the World shall see Parliaments go on where they left off, it will put them by that way of proceeding [prorogation, dissolution

61 *Ibid.*, vol. VII, pp. 368–70.   62 *Ibid.*, pp. 390–1.
63 *Ibid.*, pp. 391–3.   64 *Ibid.*, p. 389.

etc]. Therefore I desire that the Journals of the two last Parliaments may be inspected.' The order was accordingly given.[65]

The next day (1 November) was entirely devoted to the House's pursuit of the abhorrers. The day after, the journals of the previous House were read, as had been ordered. This gave rise to yet another instalment of the continuing debate about the prosecution of the plot. Once again Russell impatiently intervened to try to bring the House round to the subject of the Duke of York in particular. 'There was a motion made the last Parliament ... [concerning] the Duke of York being a Papist, and [that] his hopes of coming such to the Crown, hath given the greatest countenance and encouragement to the present Designs and the Conspiracies ... I move therefore [in accordance with Titus' proposal of continuity with the previous House] that you will vote the same thing now'. Titus responded with 'Pray see in the journals what the vote was.'[66]

Under the patronage of Titus and Jones the vote of the previous House was now read, and passed *nemine contradicente* for the first time. At the same time, *every other resolution of the previous House* was now read in turn, and also passed *nemine contradicente*. The exclusion bill passed the Commons and was carried to the Lords, under these circumstances: it had become attached to the mainstream of the Commons' grievances for the first time.

If we now look at the record of this session as a whole, it is easy to see what had and what had not changed about the role of exclusion within it since 1679. The point has been made that the duration of this parliament was extremely similar to the last. Despite some inevitable change of detail resulting from the progress of events, the underlying pattern of its concerns is exceptionally consistent. Once again the biggest two blocks of discussion stemmed directly from the same two general issues: popery, and parliaments. Between nine and ten days were spent on continuing discussion of the popish plot (as against nine in the last parliament); and the biggest block – eleven days – spent on means and measures for the punishment of the 'abhorrers'. If we add to these eleven days the further six consequently spent dealing out punishments to named individuals, we find a total of seventeen days spent on this: comparable to the twenty-one spent on Danby in the previous House. This had been the greatest category there as well; for the underlying issue, and crimes, were the same: arbitrary government and the obstruction of the free meeting of parliaments. Similarly, if we add to the nine to ten days on the plot in general, the further nine spent on the trial of Lord Stafford, we again get a similar total (eighteen) to that spent on the plot plus the popish lords in the previous House (fourteen).

---

[65] *Ibid.*, pp. 392–3.   [66] *Ibid.*, p. 395.

Moreover, looking at the record of the house in its entirety, we find an even more remarkable similarity. This was not just because the same problems persisted, but was an outgrowth of the nature of the key political issue itself. The Commons itself had voted *deliberately* to make its proceedings in the second session mirror those of the first. Accordingly, not only did direct prosecution of the two basic issues, the popish plot and attempts to obstruct parliament, again account for the bulk of the attention of this house. They accounted, together (seventeen plus eighteen days respectively) for exactly the same number of days (thirty-five out of sixty-two; as compared with thirty-five out of sixty-one in 1679). The places of lesser issues also followed a strikingly similar pattern: two days spent on foreign affairs (the same as previously); two and a half condemning another minister (Halifax; similar to the two spent on Lauderdale previously); four and a half spent on exclusion – with the briefest mention of limitations (similar to the four spent on both previously). Six days were spent on various other minor issues (four previously); six on the King's speech (the equivalent of the seven spent on the row over the King's appointment of the speaker previously); and finally four days spent on the new project of liberty of conscience for protestant dissenters (replacing the now defunct issue of the standing army, on which seven days had previously been spent).

Within the quite striking consistency of this general pattern it is easy to see what has changed in relation to exclusion – and what has not. In the Commons it was no longer a question of limitations versus exclusion; support for the former has collapsed into the latter. Four and a half days spent discussing the two together in the last parliament (one and a half on limitations, two on exclusion) has become four and a half days simply on exclusion in this one. What has happened, in relation to the succession – a secondary issue – is that the Commons and the Lords have polarised respectively around a different choice of the two expedients.

This is not to deny that the rejection of the now unanimous exclusion proposal by the Lords, as well as the King, caused fury within the Commons. Indeed it simply hardened the conviction of the House that the measure was essential. Members particularly lamented Halifax's role in this reverse: said Sir Henry Capel: 'When I consider his Birth, Quality and Father . . . his parts and wit so beyond other men. I have [previously] been silent to hear him fighting our Battles in the Lord's House.' Halifax had gone, concluded Titus grimly, 'from being the best Freeholder in England to be the Worst Earl in Court. From him I expect persecution most, who was once amongst us.'[67]

Thus when they were invited by the King to reconsider the bill, the House

[67] *Ibid.*, vol. VIII, pp. 280–3.

refused (on 7 January) 'The thing had been thoroughly debated and settled, and why we should withdraw from it, I know not.' Once again Jones and Titus in particular spoke in favour of this policy, and the result was that a second vote was taken unanimously reaffirming the first.[68]

It was the adoption of this measure – which the King would not accept – into this general Commons strategy of repetition and intransigence, which helped to render the crisis insoluble. But this is hardly the same as to say that it had caused it in the first place. It is not true, of course, as demonstrated by the Commons in the previous session, and the Lords in this, that in the exclusion bill everybody with 'serious grievances' perceived a solution to the crisis. In the opinon of Halifax and the Lords, it was only in 'limitations' that such a solution was possible. But the exclusion bill, among others, had now become part of a larger Commons strategy, a managed confrontation, by which the lower House would accept no further interruption of its demands. To explain how this strategy had come into being, and the thinking upon which this confrontation rested, we need to look, not at Shaftesbury, or at exclusion, but at its managers: Jones, and Titus.

That this was a dangerous stance to adopt was apparent, not least, to the lower House itself. But a deep conviction had now taken hold that they had little choice. In the face of these repeated interruptions, which had now been going on for over five years, the Commons must now stand firm. That way, as they explained to the King in their *Address* of 28 November,

even if the subtle [arts] . . . of that Party and Design should yet prevail either to elude or totally obstruct the faithful Endeavours of Us Your Commons for a happy settlement of this Kingdom, We shall have this remaining comfort, that We have freed our Selves from the Guilt of that Blood and Desolation which is like to ensue.[69]

In fact, however, the faith of the managers of this strategy did not lie, as they assured his Majesty, in the King and God. Jones and Titus, Sidney and their accomplices, were a good deal harder headed than that. It lay in an historically tried and tested accompanying strategy of financial strangulation. As the last such crisis had demonstrated, against an intransigent crown financial desperation was the only hope a House of Commons had. And the problem for Charles was that these hopes were being held by a group of people with their hands not only on the Commons itself, but on both major sources of extra-parliamentary revenue. These were the City of London, and the coffers of the French King.

As we will see, it was nothing to do with exclusion that allowed Charles eventually to break this deadlock and dismiss the House. It was the long

---

[68] *Ibid.*, pp. 260, 268–70, 284–5.
[69] *The Humble Address of the Commons in Parliament Assembled Presented to His Majesty Monday 28th day of Nov 1680*, p. 85.

delayed, and pleaded for, restoration of funds by the French King. This was granted only when Barillon urgently confirmed the gravity of the political situation Charles was facing. As we shall see, the King's subsequent *Declaration*, justifying his dismissal of his last two Parliaments to the nation, made it painfully clear that it was in this (financial) sense that the Crown had been held to ransom by an exceedingly tender portion of its anatomy.

The purpose of this account, so far, has been to explain how the exclusion bill, along with all the other resolutions of the previous House, had come to represent not just the dangers of popery, but the struggle for parliaments as well. That is how exclusion came to eclipse limitations in the Commons, though it never changed the secondary status of either. Thus for all Russell's efforts, the House still couldn't be persuaded to spend more than four and a half days, or 7 per cent of their time on it, and when it was defeated in the Lords, the Commons – while taking due offence, in accordance with the larger issue of 'obstructions' and 'interruptions' – nevertheless got on with their other and principal business. The one exception to this generalisation was Russell himself, who continued to bring the House back to the issue (for instance on 18 December and 6 and 7 January).[70] But in general, under the direction of Jones, Titus, Maynard and other veterans of the first long parliament (like Sir Henry Capel and William Harbord), the House of Commons spent the rest of the session probing, in various directions, the increasingly serious implications of the situation they were in.

The menace was not only the threat to the being of parliaments, but what lay behind it: the threat of popery. The result of 'the late interruptions' was that this menace was now apprehended more urgently than ever. 'Consider how restless the spirit of Popery has been ever since the Reformation.' As usual the two causes, of protestantism and of parliaments, were seen as intertwined. Harbord reminded the House, 'Ever since King James' time Popery has been increased when the Parliament was dissolved, and suppressed while they have been sitting.'[71] 'I have sat here many years', said Sir Henry Capel, 'and I find that every Session of Parliament we are still troubled with Popery. In the descent of four Kings [sic], still the Parliaments have been troubled with Popery.' 'The old English Government has been' said one member, 'to keep up a good Correspondance betwixt the King and his people; the King living upon his Rents, and frequent Parliaments *petitioning* [my emphasis] and offering the King presents; and the King had his subjects purses freely; and all this must naturally fall upon us, if we suppress Popery.'[72] 'No man that knows anything', continued another, 'but might be

[70] Grey, *Debates*, vol. VIII, pp. 188–9, 255, 261–2.
[71] *Ibid.*, vol. VII, p. 380.
[72] *Ibid.*, pp. 360, 362.

large upon the growth of Popery; and I shall show you the progress the Papists have made, since the dissolution of Parliament . . . When the good Patriots in the Long Parliament were out-voted in many things, yet they kept up the Protestant Religion.' 'The springs of all [grievances]' explained another, from the 1670 stop of the Exchequer onwards, 'is from France and Popery, and nothing else. [Yet when we try to mend it, it is] buzzed around by ill men. Let the king have care of the Parliament; they will pull down the Crown . . . and the actions of 1641 [are] thrown amongst us.'[73]

Equally predictably, the English plot had also now developed a sinister Irish dimension. The House was informed by the Lords that '[there is a] horrid and treasonable Plot and Conspiracy carried on by those of the Popish Religion of Ireland, for massacring the English.' Dozens of grisly pamphlets appeared, detailing the threat.[74] The result was a series of urgent speeches, again by veterans of the long parliament of Charles I, some of which were exceptionally risky in their tone. The House heard from Colonel Birch how the toleration granted by Charles I to the papists had led to 'that dismal time . . . in Ireland . . . that bloody Massacre in October 1641'. Serjeant Maynard asked 'Shall we be led like Ox to the Slaughter? . . . can we believe but they who have so embroiled their hands formerly in Blood, have still the same design?' Sir Henry Capel recounted:

A Parliament met in 1640, and the Massacre was in 41, countenanced by Papists in the Court; and now you have '41 out and explained. It is far from me to justify the Miscarriages of that time to the Kings Death; [but] there were provocations on each side.[75]

The discussions returned to Strafford and to Laud. One of the articles against Laud, it was remembered, 'was for dissolving the [short] Parliament of 1640'. Minds wandered to 'Rich[ard] II's time'.[76] From all of these concerns, a number of practical measures emerged. One was the bill for the relief of protestant consciences (for the better solidarity of protestants against papists); another bill (on the same basis) for the naturalisation of protestant aliens; and another for disarming papists and banishing them, first from London, and then from the whole Kingdom. They included Sir William Jones' revival of the Elizabethan Oath of Association, to protect protestantism, His Majesty's person, and the protestant succession, by force (sanctioned by the House of Commons alone) if necessary. Elizabeth's councillors, observed Jones ruefully, 'took great care to keep out Popery . . . [and] I hope they will do so now; but since they are not of the same

---

[73] *Ibid.*, pp. 361–2.
[74] *Ibid.*, p. 251; many of these Irish popish plot *Narratives* and *Informations* are collected in the Cambridge University Library Sel.2.117; see also Sel.3.245, and Acton b 25.391.
[75] Grey, *Debates*, vol. VIII, pp. 132, 135–6, 140.
[76] *Ibid.*, p. 167.

disposition now, as they were then, I fear it. I wish they were.'[77] Jones reminded members not to put their faith in words alone: 'Proclamations have been [made] against Papists, in the late King's time and this, without effect.'[78]

As the tone of these debates suggests, the House had by now come to face remarkably squarely that it was back in the situation which had previously led to the civil wars. It was agreed that it must be resolved, 'or we must come to blood.' Some members publicly buckled on their armour, declaring themselves ready to defend their religion again by force if there was no other way.[79] Unfortunately for the Commons however, the resolution of the crisis, peaceful or otherwise, did not depend solely upon itself. It was under these circumstances, and in this atmosphere, that on 8 January 1681 the House was dissolved again.

3.4 REPETITION (THE THIRD PARLIAMENT 1681)

The immediate result was another election, but this time with a difference. For unbeknown to the House – though not, as we will see, unsuspected – the result of Barillon's warning had been, after a three-year hiatus, an agreement by Louis to resume his special relationship with the English King.[80] The reason for this decision was not, as we will see, any feeling of loyalty to Charles, but the consideration that a restored English Republic would be dangerous to the interests of France. Charles seized upon this opportunity with relief. Once again parliament could be kept out of session, in exchange for French extra-parliamentary funding, and this would be the case for the rest of reign. We know now that what enabled Charles to subsist quite prosperously from 1681 to 1685 was a buoyant customs revenue.[81] Charles didn't know this in early 1681. What turned the crisis, for him, by returning him to the pre-crisis situation, and giving him the confidence to play the last parliament as the pure piece of political theatre it was, was the resumption of his special relationship with France.

Following the January dissolution, a petition was presented to the King by sixteen peers, led by the Earl of Essex. Again this did not mention exclusion. Instead it drew his majesty's attention to two issues of the utmost urgency. The first was the appalling 'dangers that threaten the whole Kingdom, from the mischievous and wicked plots of the papists' – plots now in Ireland, as well as England. The second was that 'to our unspeakable grief

---

[77] *Ibid.*, p. 135.
[78] *Ibid.*, pp. 205, 258, 263.
[79] *Ibid.*, pp. 264, 404–10.
[80] Houlbrooke, 'Barillon's Embassy', pp. 79–80; Kenyon, *Sunderland*, p. 78; Jones, *Country and Court*, p. 214.
[81] C.H. Chandaman, *The English Public Revenue 1660–88* (Oxford 1975), pp. 31, 35, 61.

and sorrow, the [last] parliament . . . [was again] . . . prorogued and dissolved before it could perfect what was intended for our security'. The petition ended with a defence of petitioning for the meeting of a parliament; and a denunciation of the 'abhorrers'.[82]

Unsurprisingly, this did not cause a reversal of royal policy. It did attract a loyalist reply. This compared the petition rather precisely to that presented to Charles I by twelve peers, led by the Earl of Bedford, in September 1640. This had similarly appealed to his majesty concerning the urgent dangers threatening the kingdom in church and state: the popish innovators in England, the dangers from forces raised in Ireland, and so on. Charles I, the pamphlet concluded pointedly, had heard that petition: and everybody knew what had happened to *him*.[83]

Charles had called the next parliament to Oxford, in itself a potent piece of historical symbolism. The keynote of the elections, as of the session which followed, was not only continuity, but deliberate repetition. Once again electors were counselled to re-elect the same members. The result was a House, as Sidney put it, 'like unto the last'.[84] When it reconvened in April, the previous speaker, Sir William Williams, accepted his re-election on the same principle: 'Apprehending this choice proceeds from the Example you have from your Countries by your own Elections, making this Parliament, as much as in you and them lies, the same with the last; therefore you have the same Speaker.'[85]

Equally consistently, *The First Whigs* described these elections as the greatest testimony yet to 'whig electoral organisation': 'Shaftesbury's hold on the nation remained as strong as ever.'[86] Once again, no evidence for these statements is offered. Instead, there is the admission that 'Of course this organisation did not appear on the surface. Attempting to preserve an impression of spontaneity, the whig press was intentionally vague as to the origin of the [electoral] addresses.'

What, then, did the addresses actually say? According to *The First Whigs*, one set of draft 'instructions' to electors '*obviously* [my emphasis] served as a model for the addresses presented all over the country. These instructions, of course, began with Exclusion'. Where did this draft come from? It comes from the Shaftesbury papers. What did the actual *printed* addresses from the rest of the nation say? They, it is admitted, were much more 'general and ambiguously worded', for 'other safeguards were demanded against arbi-

---

[82] Reprinted in *Somers Tracts* (1812), vol. VIII, pp. 282–3.

[83] *A Letter to a Noble Peer of the Realm [Essex] about his late Speech and Petition to His Majesty* (1681), *ibid.*, pp. 285–6.

[84] Sidney, 'Letter to Savile' in *Works*, p. 3. (This letter is falsely dated 1678/9.)

[85] *The Speech of the Hon William Williams . . . upon the Electing of him Speaker* (21 March 1680).

[86] Jones, *The First Whigs*, pp. 160–8.

trary government besides Exclusion'.[87] What were these other safeguards? They were the demand for frequent parliaments; for free elections; for the right to petition for parliaments; for the punishment of those abhorring such petitions; and for the continued investigation of the popish plot. In short they were the demands of the previous parliament itself, and of the whole crisis by which its concerns had been actuated. They were also the demands of the opposition pamphlet literature of 1681 in general.

The Oxford session lasted only seven days. It deliberately took up where its predecessors had left off. Sir William Jones, who had achieved clear pre-eminence among the leaders of the House by the end of the previous session, dominated the discussion in this. As before, the bills of the previous parliament, exclusion among them, were obstinately revived. As before, the discussion in general focused not on any particular bill, but on the two great themes: the popish plot, and above all the continuing interruptions of parliaments. 'Consider how many interruptions Parliaments have had of late, in the greatest businesses, by Prorogations and Dissolutions'. 'This confirms me in the opinion of the design some men have to depress the honour of this House'. 'The greatest Arbitrary power that can be used in England, is to cow a Parliament ... Danby ... [and] after him ... new Ministers of State ... shuffle and cut the cards again, and will dissolve and prorogue Parliaments, till they can get one for their turn; and in this condition we are.'[88]

The principal distinction between this parliament and the last was, however, in atmosphere. There was a palpable increase in tension. This had been heightened, rather than decreased, by the move from 'republican' London to loyalist Oxford. Verbal were now replaced by physical expressions by MPs of their willingness to defend the 'old cause' in the old way. Parliamentarians arrived in Oxford armed.[89]

Unlike previous parliaments however, this one was not given time to proceed far with any of these matters, either general concerns or particular bills. Observing – and subsequently publishing – their deliberate refusal to be diverted from the course of their predecessors, the King finally dissolved them for good on 28 March. His powers of dissolution and prorogation had indeed turned out to be, not only the central issue in the crisis, but its principal arbiter as well.

---

[87] *Ibid.*, pp. 168–70.
[88] Grey, *Debates*, vol. VIII, pp. 301, 306, 310.
[89] Stephen College was the first to suffer for this symbolic rupture of the public peace. See Mark Goldie, 'Danby, the Bishops and the Whigs' in Goldie, Harris and Seaward (eds.), *The Politics of Religion*, p. 99.

3.5 REACTION

Immediately thereafter, as we have seen, the King issued his own *Declaration Touching the Reasons That Moved Him to Dissolve The Two Last Parliaments* (1681). These 'Reasons' centred, once again, *not* on the Commons insistence on exclusion, but on its own increasingly, and dangerously, 'arbitrary' conduct. In particular the *Declaration* pointed with indignation to the Commons' attempts to 'disable Us' (the crown), passing resolutions to the effect that anyone advancing money upon 'the Branches of the King's Revenue, arising by Customs, Excise, or Hearth-Money, shall be adjudged to hinder the Sitting of Parliaments'.[90]

As we saw in chapter 2, it was this *Declaration*, with its inversion of the accusation of arbitrary government, that became the focus for the loyalist reaction. It was met by a flood of loyalist addresses from all over the country. 'If', wrote one indignant 'well-wisher to the King',

it be the undoubted Prerogative of the King to Call, Adjourn, Prorogue, and Dissolve Parliaments at his will and Pleasure; it is a high Impudence in any Subject, or Assembly of men, to take upon them to Advise him (unasked) how and when to execute his Power.[91]

This should be compared with the earlier *Proclamation* of Charles I, of 1629, setting out the reasons for his abandonment of his 'use of parliaments':

the late abuse having driven us out of that course we shall accouynt it presumption for any to prescribe any time unto us for Parliaments the calling continuing and dissolving of which is always in our own power.[92]

The same parallel was not lost on the Commons. In Sidney, Jones and Titus' extraordinary reply to the *Declaration*, the *Just and Modest Vindication of the Proceedings of the Two Last Parliaments* (1681), it was called upon in the most explicit terms. After denying that the powers of prorogation and dissolution lay solely in the King, the *Vindication* explained that the experience 'of our ancestors' had led them to provide against Princes who had

through defect of age, experience, or understanding . . . or by passion [and] private interest . . . be[en] so far misled as not to assemble parliaments, when the public affairs require it; or to declare them dissolved before the ends of their meeting were accomplished.[93]

---

[90] *His Majesties Declaration*, p. 5.
[91] *Reasons Offered by a Well-Wisher to the King and Kingdom* (1681).
[92] Larkin (ed.), *Stuart Proclamations*, vol. II, pp. 223–6.
[93] *A Just and Modest Vindication of the Proceedings of the Two Last Parliaments* (1681), reprinted in *State Tracts in the Reign of Charles II*, vol. IV, Appendix, no. XV.

It would not have escaped any readers who was the last King 'so misled'. The *Vindication* then came to the point:

The first Declaration of this sort which I ever met with, being that which was published in 1628[9] . . . was so far from answering the ends of its coming out, that it filled the whole Kingdom with jealousies, and was one of the first sad causes of the ensuing unhappy war.[94]

This was, and was meant to be, a threat.

This historical context, then, was recognised, and drawn upon, by both sides. This was the second crisis of popery and arbitrary government; the second crisis of parliaments. It was this recognition which underlay the loyalist reaction itself, with its hundreds of warnings of, and parallels with, '41 again'. It was the same recognition which lay behind the publication of Filmer's *Patriarcha* in 1680. But the same warning was being made from the opposite perspective by the other side. The cause of protestantism, and of parliaments, was the 'old cause'. When a hardened minority took up arms on its behalf there were a remarkable number of civil war veterans amongst them.

From 1681–3, as we will see, the thinking of this minority followed from this situation. In this period there appeared some of the finest ideological expressions of the cause. Works like *Vox Populi*, *A Dialogue at Oxford*, the *Just and Modest Vindication*, Locke's *Two Treatises*, and Sidney's *Discourses*, did not argue the case for exclusion. All argued the central issue of the parliamentary cause. This was, most specifically, the 'Peoples Right to their Parliaments Sitting', but more generally, the people's rights in their government in general, in the face of arbitrary power. All of these arguments were directed, as they had been from the beginning of the crisis, against Charles, not James. A monarch who would not govern for his people, or allow their legitimate political voice to be heard, had separated himself from the end of his own institution, and could justly be overthrown. This view was underlined by the institution of this King, in fact if not theory, by the parliament itself in 1660.

The same political logic, and the same historical perspective, governed the practical proceedings of this group. If the King could not be brought to resummon parliament voluntarily, he would have to be brought to it by force. This was not to be embarked upon lightly, but eventually the royal reaction, both political and religious, left its victims little choice. Not only protestantism and parliaments, but lives, liberties and estates, came to depend upon it.

For the rebels, history showed how this task could be accomplished. Eleven years after haughtily insisting on that key royal prerogative, Charles I

---

[94] *Ibid.*, p. cxxxvi.

had been made to surrender it, permanently. The instrument of this remarkable deliverance was a protestant rebellion in Scotland. This had served up the King to the protestant outrage of his own subjects. It was for organising a rebellion in Scotland that Sidney was arrested and tried in 1683.

4

Retrospect

Only two years after Sidney's execution, James II came to the throne. Within four years he had confirmed every fear which had lain behind the earlier concern over the succession. This led to a crisis which enabled his actual exclusion from the throne (along with his heirs) through the agency of a Dutch invasion.

It is hardly surprising, given the historical significance of this event, that historians writing in its aftermath should find its anticipation in the exclusion bill the most important and significant aspect of the earlier crisis. It is less surprising still, given the appearance in 1681 of the labels whig and tory, and the consequent temptation to construct a prototype 'whig party' around the prophetic cause of exclusion. This had the further attraction of separating the first 'whigs' – the flag carriers of a future political age – from a damaging truth about their role. This was that they had been what the court and, by 1681, the majority of the nation were saying they were: dangerous, radical, and embarked again on the cause that had led to the civil war.

There followed the tremendous historiographical weight which this has placed on a fairly brief period of the nation's history. The years 1678–81 became the birthplace of not only the political structures of the eighteenth century, but those of much of the western world. These were claims of such significance that historians could not, and have not, seen a great deal else in this crisis. It is this perception, maintained over three centuries, which has kept this traditional interpretation in place; and which has kept historians from seeing that too many of these claims are simply not grounded in evidence.

It is this weight of the future which the preceding account has attempted to lift from our perspective on the crisis. Inevitably this has involved a good deal of negative argument. While this has been necessary, it has only been useful as one means toward a more positive end. That end has been to bring an alternative vision of the crisis into view: that of contemporaries themselves.

The means to this end has been simple enough. It has been to base an account of the crisis on what contemporaries themselves were saying, rather than on what they can be taken to be implying. It has been to look at a wide range of evidence – particularly parliamentary proceedings and pamphlet literature – over a long period of time. Doubtless this has resulted in a certain literal-mindedness, productive of its own mistakes. But it also produces a different view of the crisis; one of which historians surely need to take account. What is most striking about the evidence is how consistent this view is, both over time (and a much greater period of time than simply the crisis itself), and across the range both of political opinion and of types of documentation. In the face of this consistency it is surely better to abandon the perspective of the historiography, directed to the future – the future threat of James, his future exclusion, the future structures of party – in favour of the perspective of contemporaries, anchored as it was in the past.

Despite all this, it remains perfectly possible to insist that there was an 'exclusion crisis'. The role of the exclusion bill between November 1680 and April 1681 would obviously provide the core of such an account. It might be assumed, and it has been, that concern about the religion of York, rather than the foreign, political and religious policies of the government, underlay the growing apprehension of the 1670s; the outbreak of the crisis itself in 1678; and its first two years from 1679–80. A reputable account would need to admit that this is not what the bulk of the sources tell us, but argue that a certain amount of reading between the lines is necessary. Contemporaries could not always be open about their ultimate objects – despite the breakdown of censorship again in 1679 (this accounts for the huge pamphlet literature). It would also need to admit that exclusion has nothing to tell us about the flip side of the crisis: the second threat of popery and arbitrary government of 1681–3.

Between November 1680 and April 1681 such an account would, however, find some primary material upon which to base itself. Perhaps the strongest would be something like the Commons' *Address to His Majesty* of 28 November 1680, following the loss of the exclusion bill. This complained about the rejection of the '*one Remedy* of these *great Evils*, without which (in our Judgements) all others will prove vain and fruitless'.[1]

What this certainly tells us is that, under circumstances already described, the exclusion bill lay at the heart of a deadlock between the Commons and the crown at this moment. It also demonstrates a unanimous determination on the part of the lower House not to surrender a demand which it knew was unacceptable to the King. If we take this statement in isolation within this document, and if we take this document in isolation within the whole

[1] *The Humble Address of the Commons in Parliament Assembled, Presented to His Majesty, Monday 28th day of November 1680*, in Cambridge University Library, Sel.2.117.

crisis, we may certainly persuade ourselves that the exclusion bill lay at the heart of this whole situation.

What the previous three chapters have attempted to do is paint in the three contexts: that of the crisis as a whole (1678–83); that of the 1670s as a whole; and that of the century as a whole, that tell us why we should not do so. To do so is to ignore most of the evidence that explains to us what the crisis was about. The overwhelming majority of contemporary documents and accounts, opposition and loyalist, from whatever year we care to name, fix their gaze elsewhere. According to those, the issues are clear. They were a revival of popery and arbitrary government in the reign of Charles II. Of this problem York's religion, like Henrietta Maria's before it, was a symptom, not a cause. The problem, and the evidence for it, lay in present, not future, government policy. And the progress of the crisis, through all its stages, hinged not on exclusion, but on the relationship between this present perception, and memories of the past.

If we return to the Commons *Address* of November 1680, we find it reproduces exactly this perspective. The bitter allusion to the lost exclusion bill occurs as one sentence in a sixteen-page diatribe. This diatribe is an attempt to explain to his majesty why, until nearly a decade of the obstruction and betrayal of parliament has ended, he must not expect any financial co-operation from the House. The whole of this explanation is focused on two issues – popery and arbitrary government, in this reign, not the next.

Eight pages are spent reminding the King of the 'Attempts of the Popish Party, for many years last past ... not only within this, but other your Majesties Kingdoms, to introduce the Romish, and utterly to extirpate the true Protestant religion'.[2] As usual this design is set in its full European (not just British) context. Its progress in Britain is traced step by step, as it had been by Marvell, from the terrors and deceptions of the Anglo-French relationship of the 1670s. Its principal agents are the 'Great swarms of ... Jesuits' who have repaired to the kingdom in fond expectation of a plentiful harvest. And a key instrument in this progress has been that,

After some time ... [these Jesuits] became able to influence matters of State and Government ... the continuance or Prorogation of Parliaments has been accommodated to serve the[ir] purposes ... Ministers of England [Shaftesbury included] were made Instruments ... to make War upon a Protestant State ... to advance and augment the dreadful Power of the French King ... and to press upon that State ... the public exercise of the Roman Catholic Religion ... [and] When in the next Parliament the house of Commons were prepared to bring to a legal Tryal the principal Conspirators in this Plot, that Parliament was first Prorogued, and then Dissolved. The Interval between the Calling and Sitting of this Parliament was so long, that now they conceive hopes of Covering all their past Crimes, and gaining a reasonable time and advantages of practising them more effectually.[3]

[2] *Ibid.*, p. 76.   [3] *Ibid.*, pp. 77–82.

The idea of an 'exclusion crisis' will remain arguable for as long as there was an exclusion bill, and, at a certain point in the crisis, a direct confrontation over it. What the preceding account has attempted to recover is the context of that confrontation, and of the whole crisis. What it suggests is that the crisis itself was not about the exclusion bill at all. It was the second crisis of popery and arbitrary government; a struggle for the being of protestantism, and of parliaments.

What does not seem to be possible however, at least with the present state of the evidence, is the idea of a Shaftesburian (or any other) 'whig party'. Here we encounter the distinction between some evidence and none at all. What we do know is that Shaftesbury himself, with his client Russell in the Commons, did indeed set his sights upon exclusion; that he drew up electoral addresses and lists of MPs who might be expected to 'vote the right way'; that he wished to be manager of the crisis and manipulate public concern (about popery and arbitrary government) to this end; that accordingly he, with Russell, sought power not only in both Houses of parliament but outside it, in London and elsewhere. We also know that he failed in all of these places in turn. The exclusion bill certainly did eventually pass the Commons, *nemine contradicente*; but only as it passed out of Shaftesbury's control, as part of a wider strategy; and when the focus of parliamentary anger had fixed itself more securely than ever on Charles (rather than James).

For those who wish, then, for whatever reason, to extrapolate backwards in time from the names of the first parties (1681–3) to the things (1679–83), their existence needs to be demonstrated rather than assumed. If such a 'party' were found, it would certainly not be the Shaftesburian monolith that has been imagined. And it is in the nature of this crisis, and of seventeenth-century politics in general, that such proof will not be easy. Even the clearest products of organisation in this period do not lend themselves naturally to interpretation of this kind. A part of one contribution to the petitioning campaign, recently found by Mark Knights, contains 16,000 signatures. This number itself is indicative of the breadth, and range, of anti-court sentiment at this time. These signatures included clients of Shaftesbury's, like John Locke; and of Sidney's, like Slingsby Bethel. Bethel was shortly to invoke Shaftesbury's bitterest wrath and indignation by defeating his candidate for the shrievalty. Did these people all belong to one party? If so, who was its leader? And where is the evidence that this was the case?

The advantages of a different perspective on the crisis are not simply evidential. They are also more generally historical. It is not only that we have more to learn by seeing the crisis as contemporaries themselves saw it. It is also that this view of the crisis fits in so well with what we know about the Restoration period in general. We know that contemporaries were not clairvoyants. We know that they were living under the shadow of the bloodiest and most shocking domestic upheaval, not only in English, but in recent European history. How understandable was it then, that the breathtaking irresponsibility of their monarch, in recreating the public perceptions that had destroyed his father, should plunge them not only into a second major crisis, but into the terrors of that past?

Charles has often, and rightly, been congratulated for the skill with which he extracted himself from the consequences of this situation, once it had eventuated. He didn't panic; he didn't surrender key prerogatives; and (contrary to common belief) in general he showed his customary flexibility. When the chips were down, he showed that he could heed the lessons of history. But it is a pity that he didn't heed them sooner. Until 1667 he had Clarendon doing that job for him.[4] Thereafter, and until the crisis itself had brought him to his senses, the entire nation fell a victim, not only to his irresponsibility, but to his dishonesty and duplicity. By 1678 he had so many foreign policies going on simultaneously that he was strangled by them.

All of this makes, or should make, this crisis particularly interesting to historians. Here we have the past rising from its grave, and making new history. 'I am sure you are all good Historians' wrote Edward Cooke hopefully (in 1681) 'and [to understand the crisis] need only resort to the Record of your own Memories.' Observing that it would be, within such a short time, 'without all example in story, that a Nation should be twice ruined, twice undone by the self same way and means, the same Fears and Jealousies', Cooke counselled as an antidote large doses of Machiavelli:

an Author much studied of late in this Kingdom . . . and . . . in History . . . a master . . . [who showed] that the true reason . . . [for] the destruction of States and Empires is, because their Governors have not observed the same Mischiefs heretofore in Story . . . which . . . if they had done, they might easily have preserved themselves.[5]

On the authorial side at least, this was counsel of which Sidney (and Henry Neville) could scarcely have disapproved.

Whatever the merits or demerits of this view of the crisis, we are now in a position to appreciate Sidney's conduct and writing within it. Contemporaries did not, to his chagrin, share all of Sidney's beliefs. But what we have been recovering is a perspective which crossed the political and religious spectrum. It transcended ideology, because it was a property of the nation's history. It was the fruit of a common experience, whether first or second hand: that of the generation which had lived through the civil war.

---

[4] One major theme of Paul Seaward's *The Cavalier Parliament* (1989).
[5] Edward Cooke, *Memorabilia* (1681), p. 101. Cooke took these passages from a speech given by Clarendon in the House of Lords on 19 May 1662. See *Journal of the House of Lords*, vol. XI, p. 476. My thanks to Paul Seaward for this most interesting piece of information.

Part Two

THE SHADOW OF THE PAST

[H]e had lived 16 or 17 years beyond the sea in France and Italy after ye King was restored, and seem'd resolved never to come back, but his father being very old he pretends a desire for to see him, and he obtained an Intercession from ye Court of France, and upon his promise not to meddle with ye Government he was suffered to come over.

Gilbert Burnet, Add. MS 63, 057, vol. II, p. 138

Family politics 1677–83

my desir of being ... somme service unto my old father perswaded me to ask leave to comme over ... but [he] ... being dead within six weekes after my arrivall, I have noe other businesse heare then to cleare somme small contests that are growne between one of my brothers and me concerning that which he hath left me, and, if it please God to give [me] successe ... have [only] ... the desire of retiring from hence, without any thought of ever returning ... carrying with me ... sufficient to purchase a convenient habitation in Gascony, not farre from Bordeaux, where I may in quiet finish thoes days that God hath appointed for me.[1]

Sidney to Benjamin Furly, 29 November 1677

5.1 INTRODUCTION

After eighteen years on the continent, seventeen of them in exile, Sidney landed in England in late September 1677. He may have arrived at the Castle at Dover, of which he had been commander almost thirty years before. From the Kentish coast there was not far to travel to Penshurst, where his father was to die five and a half weeks later.

Sidney seems to have returned alone, though doubtless accompanied by the usual 'domesticks'. Despite the later reference to a daughter, to marry his 'valet' from Nerac, Joseph Ducasse, there is no evidence that such a person travelled with him now.[2] Ducasse himself, however, was to join Sidney's household in London three years later, in 1680/81. And there remains at least the possibility that his wife, Marie, had the relationship with Algernon of which Vernon's later letter spoke.

In 1682 a satirical *Elegy* was published on the death of the republican Thomas Merry. In a fictional death-bed scene Merry convoked his three friends: 'The Noble Peer/With Tap in Side[;] the Salamanca Seer/In his Geneva Cassack[; the] Colonel/With Cobs, with Scabs, with Cloak, with Sword most fell'.[3] As the first two are unmistakably Shaftesbury and Oates,

---

[1] J. Forster (ed.), *Original Letters of Locke, Shaftesbury, and Sidney* (1830), pp. 79–80.
[2] See Scott, *Sidney and the English Republic*, ch. 14, section 4.
[3] [Anon] *An Elegy on the Death of Thomas Merry Esq.* (1682).

so the third is certainly Sidney. His war wounds were as publicly appreci-
ated a physical identifier as the extra-curricular plumbing of Count Tapski.
It was Burnet who recorded in this period: 'Sidney was a man of great
Courage, of which as he had given eminent proofs in ye Civill Wars, so he
carried ye marks of it in many parts of his body.'[4] A royalist ballad, following his execution, had Sidney saying grandly: 'View my Hack'd Limbs . . .
each honourable wound The Pride and Glory of my numerous Scars, in
Hells best Cause the old republic Wars.'[5]

To each of his friends, Merry distributed a part of his worldly goods.
When it came to Sidney he said:

> To thee my colonel . . . I give my Arms and Armour . . . [and] Into thy hands I do
> commit my spouse, whose Life I sav'd, yet ne'r read Aristotle . . . She's as Blithe, as
> Brisk and Debonair, as she she thou hast of Danish Race and Hair.[6]

Aside from the reference to Aristotle, which rather strengthens the identification with Sidney (as we will see, he was donning the persona of a
'philosopher' in these years)[7] – what is intriguing here is the last line. To
whomsoever this refers, an illegitimate daughter begotten while Sidney was
ambassador in Denmark (1659/60) would be the right age to be marrying
Ducasse in this period. It is therefore just possible that, having left such a
person in the care of Ducasse in Nerac, when it became clear in 1680 that
Sidney's stay in London would be prolonged, both of them came over to
join him there.

So much for the speculation. What is clear is that in 1677– and later –
Sidney intended his return to be temporary. In this his *Apology* agrees with
the letter he wrote to Furly in November of that year. Later the *Apology*
complained:

> My father dyed within a few weeks after my coming over; and when I prepared
> myself to return into Guascony, there to passe the remaining part of my life, I was
> hindered by the earl of Leicester my brother, who questioned all that my father had
> given me for my subsistence; and by a long and tedious suitte in chancery, detained
> me in England, until I was made a prisoner.[8]

Sidney may indeed, as we will see, have returned to France in 1680–1 to
purchase a property there, and Ducasse (with whomsoever) may have
accompanied him back from that trip.[9]

Once again, therefore, and as the next chapter will particularly remind us,
it is necessary to reverse the traditional national perspective on these last
seven years of Sidney's life. The longer preceding period in France was not
simply a hiatus, pending a permanent return 'home', though permanent it

4 Burnet BM Add. MS 63,058 II, p. 137.
5 [Anon] *Algernon Sidney's Farewell* (1684).
6 See footnote 3.   7 See pp. 163–4 below.
8 Sidney, *Apology*, p. 4.   9 See pp. 271–2 below.

became, for reasons of which Sidney cannot entirely have approved. There are obvious reasons, and not simply his political conduct, for continuing to see Sidney's real 'home' in this period as in France. The nation that would posthumously clasp a fictionalised Algernon to its bosom would exile and then martyr the real person first. In the interim he had been stripped, by statute, of all the personal possessions he had left behind. Moreover Sidney was to be executed, as we will see, as a foreign *agent provocateur*, who had imported into an English crisis the most dangerous possible continental thinking about rebellion. It was not, as England's (and Sidney's own) history had shown, that the English were incapable of rebellion. But such rebellions only came about through the extremest combinations of circumstances; and it was a major consequence of the mid-century upheaval that the majority of the nation had become peculiarly querulous about the possibility of a repetition. There have, after all, been no major domestic military upheavals in England from that time to this day.[10]

What Sidney brought to this situation, however, was not only a far more robust approach to the institution of monarchy. He imported the practices, not only the attitudes, of the aristocratic *frondeur*. At their heart lay an entirely natural preparedness to use force – frequently if necessary – to keep the monarchy in check. These attitudes were not simply French – they were European; and they stemmed (as the quote on p. vii of this book suggests) from a particular reading of the last century and a half of European history. One result was, in the *Discourses*, one of the most belligerent English calls to arms of the entire century. What made the *Discourses* unique within English political theory was its preparedness to explicitly justify 'civil wars', 'tumults' and 'rebellions' – both the words, and the things.[11]

These attitudes were accompanied by an exceedingly incomplete – that is to say, equally European – view of where the boundaries between nation states lay. Since at the time of Sidney's return Charles II was labouring under a similar misunderstanding, no one proved more capable than Sidney of exploiting it. Both in politics, and in Sidney's own life, England had become a limb of the main European drama, centred in France. And as Charles II was to discover, there was nothing like one returned French exile, assisted by France herself, to destabilise the rule of another.

Over the next seven years, in short, we will find Sidney more than seconding the prescient Charles' earlier description of 'the dangerous intentions . . . [of this] most opinionated republican in his realm, [who] might do much harm'.[12] Much of the evidence of this is, as we would expect, partially

---

[10] The nearest exception being Monmouth's rebellion; the exception that proves the rule. For like the successful 'revolution' of 1688 it was triggered only by a continental invasion.
[11] See chapter 11 below.
[12] Scott, *Sidney and the English Republic*, pp. 234–5.

hidden, but there is more than enough to piece together the story. By 1683, with Sidney goading his English colleagues with copies of Mariana, and *bon mots* from the rebelling academies of France, the government decided it had had enough. It was for thus confirming every aspect of the King's earlier better judgement about allowing him into the country in the first place that a dignified and geriatric Sidney was eventually to mount the scaffold. As Charles put it:

Algernon Sidney had, on his return to England, promised him to behave blamelessly towards him; how was he to spare men who would not have spared him had he fallen into their hands?[13]

All of this sets up the central problem, or theme, of the rest of this book. Sidney returned to England temporarily (his initial pass was for six months) following elaborate and (almost certainly) sincere promises to stay out of trouble.[14] He considered his active political life to be over, and he was deeply grateful for the conjunction of personal favours which had made this visit possible. What happened?

To this question there is a short and a long answer. The short answer is that Sidney had been making these promises for the future. He had not reckoned, any more than the nation had, on being so suddenly overwhelmed by the past. It is the past upon which exiles particularly subsist; and as his conversations with his friend Jean-Baptiste Lantin in Paris had made clear, inside Sidney it still burned with a peculiar intensity. As he had put it in the *Court Maxims*: 'But God kept a lamp still burning in the House of David.'[15] It was when these embers, inside Sidney himself, were ignited across the whole country, that he could not keep himself from entering, and fanning, the flames.

The long answer begins with this chapter. For the political crisis to come still lay a year away. Almost immediately upon his return, however, Sidney found himself faced with a family and legal 'exclusion crisis' that was to last the rest of his life.[16] The first year of this, in particular, was to absorb him to the point of producing his first (though not last) sojourn in prison. It was on this family and legal, rather than the political front, that Sidney's dangerous English past first returned to claim him.

Both of the major legal disputes involved will be treated in full here. They were the dispute over his father's will; and the revival of his moribund entanglement with Strangford. These struggles not only preceded, but pro-

[13] Quoted in von Ranke, *History of England*, vol. IV, p. 188.
[14] Scott, *Sidney and the English Republic*, p. 246.
[15] *Ibid.*, p. 8 and (for Sidney's conversations with Lantin), pp. 24, 105, 113, 247–9; Sidney, *Court Maxims*, p. 200.
[16] Scott, *Sidney and the English Republic*, pp. 67–72; and, for the biographical, family, and legal backgrounds to the rest of this chapter, see chs. 4 (in particular) and 7.

vided a constant background to, his later political activities and writings. They became a personal, alongside the political, struggle for the recovery of the lost liberties, both individual and national, by which Sidney became engulfed.

5.2 THE LEICESTER INHERITANCE

INTRODUCTION

As usual, the excerpt from Sidney's *Apology* quoted above contains a mixture of fact and fiction. Ewald's summary: 'The only legacy bequeathed him by the Earl of Leicester was the trifling sum of five thousand one hundred pounds. And even this small sum was disputed by his eldest brother, who questioned Algernon's right to the property'[17] in fact faces two objections. The first is that in 1677 (as opposed to 1877) £5,100 was not a 'trifling sum'. The second is that in fact Sidney was left substantially over twice this amount, as the complicated picture now available through the legal documentation shows. Indeed, as the picture is unravelled, we will have reason to spare a thought for Philip, whose contestation of the Earl's will as it stood – grossly unfavourable to him as it was – was inevitable. If Algernon felt that, given the 'irrational' custom of primogeniture, the cards of life had been stacked against him from the beginning, Philip had equal reason to feel, given the same custom, that he had been singularly unfortunate in God's choice of a younger brother (and father).

The resulting chancery suits became as long and bloodthirsty as they did, partly because, for reasons with which some readers will be familiar, Algernon himself refused to compromise with Philip out of court. Instead he chose to pursue his precise legal rights in the matter to the (literally) bitter end. Indeed he did so with all the assiduity of a hunting dog that refuses to release its prey until the death certificate has been signed, stamped and published in the local newspapers. This quality won him the case, but no popularity among his relatives. This was the role of Sidney the avenging barrister which led one of them to wonder in 1681 why 'nobody shoots him'. His eventual furious rounding on his younger brother Henry, in 1682,[18] followed Henry's final weary abandonment of his brother's five-year long personal crusade just as the bite was beginning to tell against his harassed victim.

Feeling that life had never given him anything that he hadn't wrested by his own efforts, his own virtue, Sidney had no intention of relaxing that effort now. This was a crucial moment. In the wake of his father's death, his

[17] A. Ewald, *Algernon Sydney*, vol. II, p. 37.
[18] Scott, *Sidney and the English Republic*, pp. 235–8.

share of the inheritance came to represent everything that was left to him from the dreams and the effort of his pre-1660 world.[19] This was the world which the Restoration had destroyed; and with which his father's death had now severed the principal connection. Sidney's legal crusade was partly an attempt to redeem seventeen years spent in exile, suffering exactly the dependence – the loss of liberty – that he had previously worked so hard to guard himself against. The practical object was to use the money so gained, the delayed fruit of those efforts, to end that dependence by financing a habitation in France. This was understandable enough since neither of his siblings were political exiles whose employment prospects had been ruined, and who had been dependent on a paternal stipend which would now end.

Yet neither was the point of this crusade primarily financial. This became clear when Sidney spent most of the inheritance trying to regain the rest. It was also an attempt to prove, in the courts, the paternal regard which had given that whole earlier sequence of effort meaning, and of which the inheritance now remained the only concrete expression. Neither colleagues nor opponents in this enterprise – and one of these colleagues was our old friend Sir William Jones – properly understood what was at stake here, or how deeply this need went. For it was necessary for Sidney to prove that regard, above all, to himself. This was a syndrome, in relation to the past, which readily transferred itself to the political sphere, with even more destructive results.

THE SETTLEMENT

The purpose of Sidney's letter to Furly in November (already quoted) had been to 'receave [Furly's] advice and assistance' for the investment of 'a considerable summe of money'.[20] This money Algernon had already collected from his father, aside from what was in contention with Philip. It is to the details of the estate settlement that we must now turn.

The basis of the Leicester will lay in the marriage settlement made for the eldest son Philip in 1645. By this, Algernon's father, the Earl of Leicester, had secured to Philip the estate and title, but reserved to himself the right to charge the estate with anything up to £29,000, to be paid before possession could be taken. Between 1660 and 1677, far from lessening the estrangement from his father, Philip had increased it by refusing to co-operate over the development of Leicester Fields in 1672. The improvements to Leicester Fields (present-day Leicester Square) involved the construction of several major buildings and 'faire houses', for the protection of their outlay on which the builders required 42-year leases. These accordingly required the

---

[19] *Ibid.*, ch. 4.
[20] Forster (ed.), *Letters of Locke*, pp. 79–80.

signature of Lisle, the prospective heir, as well as Leicester, and this he unwisely refused. Explaining in a letter that he and his family had received nothing from the Earl for 'thirty years' but one suit of clothes for his son, Philip stated that he would now 'unwillingly lett goe any slender hold I retaine upon my naturall or legall rightes'.[21]

Leicester had first registered his intentions towards Algernon with a codicil to his will of March 1667 which bequeathed him £10,000.[22] This arrangement was later overridden by other codicils, but the amount involved remained the basis of Sidney's final settlement. By April 1671, as we have seen,[23] both Algernon and Henry had been left, instead, £5,000 each (£2,000 each of which was on Leicester house; the other £3,000 each on the Sidney lands in Kent and Sussex), plus half each of the Earl's personal estate (originally intended for Lisle): all his 'Goods, Chattles, Household stuff . . . plate and moveables', everything, that is, but the land and buildings (themselves charged with the other legacies).[24]

By 1673, Leicester had made a further rearrangement and substituted for Algernon's half of the personal estate a further legacy of £5,000; this not charged to the estate but available in ready cash on five bonds of £1,000 each, all specified within the codicil concerned. He almost certainly did this in the belief that Sidney now intended to stay in France permanently, and so to make it readily available and portable for him; this was not to punish him but rather according to an assumed valuation of half the personal estate at £5,000 which would make all three codicils since 1667 consistent in value. Henry on the other hand was now left with all the Earl's personal goods, not necessarily as a special mark of favour but because with Robert dead (1668), Philip in disgrace, and Algernon in exile there was nobody else to leave it to. In addition the family estate was charged with annuities of £150 each for Henry and Algernon, with smaller amounts for other people.[25]

Thus Ewald's figure of £5,100 probably refers to the (first) £5,000 portion of Sidney's legacy, charged to the estate (Leicester House, and the Kent and Sussex lands) which was dependent upon Philip's preparedness to pay, and which thus became the subject of the Chancery litigation. What it doesn't take into account is either the £150 annuity (also subject to the litigation) or the other £5,000 in cash bonds which Sidney collected immediately in November (this was the 'considerable summe' – no 'trifling sum' – referred to in his letter to Furly).

Nor, however, was this all. The Earl's charging the estate with £5,000

---

[21] PRO Chancery C10 195/28, Answer of Executors to Leicester 9 July 1678; Add. MS 32,680 f.17, 2 March.
[22] Kent Archives Office, Maidstone, De Lisle MS U1475 F32/4.
[23] Scott, *Sidney and the English Republic*, p. 236.
[24] De Lisle MS U1475 F32/4.
[25] PRO Chancery C5 515/25; C10 195/28.

each for Algernon and Henry, plus £4,000 for the payment of debts and other legacies, left up to a further £15,000 legally chargeable under the 1646 settlement should the Earl wish it. He did not take a final decision about this until a mere three days before his death. This was at Penshurst where he was attended, it is important to note, by Algernon and Henry, though not by Philip. To understand the arrangement made it is necessary to know also that in January 1673 Leicester had agreed to Lisle's inheritance of Leicester House (the family's London house) 'provided [that should the Earl wish it] persons who the Earl may appoint may enjoy the profits of Leicester fields and Swan close for 60 yrs, the persons not being more than three in number'.[26]

The Earl now decided both to enforce this provision (on behalf of his younger sons), *and* to use the weight of the full remaining amount chargeable, to try to force Philip to confirm the disputed leases on these properties. Thus on 31 October 1677, a final codicil was drawn up in which the dying Earl (or whoever was holding the pen for him) ordered that the further £15,000 must be raised by Philip in full, of which £9,000 was to be paid to 'Henry Sidney ... on condition [however] that if [Philip] should within 6 months after his death confirm the leases and convey the rents [of those properties: Swan Close and Leicester Fields] to Henry and Algernon for their lives ... then the said deed [for £9,000] should be of no effect'.[27]

Thus the will in its final shape offered each brother different prospects, and in general two possible outcomes, hinging on a choice to be made by Philip. In reality it was designed to give Philip little choice. Provided he made the only sensible decision, it left little difference between Algernon's and Henry's inheritances respectively. Either way its effect on Philip was devastating. His 'choice' involved either

(1) Confirming the leases: in which case he had then to raise lump-sum payments totalling £20,000 (in addition to the loss of Leicester's personal effects to Henry and the £5,000 cash to Algernon, something over which he had no control), plus to Algernon and Henry additionally half the resulting rents of Leicester Fields and Swan Close each for life, and £150 annuity each for life. That was the soft option.

(2) Alternatively, should he fail to confirm the leases in six months, he would have to raise £29,000, with the same losses, rents, and annuities. The immediate beneficiary of this situation would be Henry, to the tune of £9,000.

On the other side, the final shape of part of Algernon's inheritance was left as dependent, negatively, on Philip's choice as Henry's was positively. Either way Algernon would get the £5,000 plus £5,000 plus £150 per year;

[26] De Lisle MS U1475 E71/2.
[27] PRO Chancery C10 195/28: The document is paraphrased here.

but providing the leases were confirmed he would also get half the substantial rents for the buildings for life as well. In that case Henry would similarly get £5,000, plus the Earl's personal estate, plus the same annuity and rents. Should Philip refuse to co-operate however, regardless of the cost to himself, Henry would reap the benefit of the £9,000 penalty,[28] but Algernon's (as well as Henry's) share of the building rents would be jeopardised.

The final settlement had one other crucial feature. Leicester made Algernon and Henry its executors (with a third: Thomas Pelham). It was the function of the executors to ensure that the terms of the will were met before Philip came into possession of the estate. He thus put enforcement of these terms into the hands of their principal beneficiaries. This also *potentially* covered Algernon's vulnerability in the final settlement relative to Henry, should Philip make the wrong decision. He could attempt to protect himself by holding Henry privately to an agreed joint executive policy, backed by the power of the £9,000 to produce an out-of-court settlement. It was this in particular that made co-operation with Henry so essential for Algernon, and why the eventual breakdown of that co-operation in 1682 was to produce such outrage.

Either way, Philip was left isolated and hamstrung; excluded from the estate subject to his paying his younger brothers a quite stupendous amount of money (£20,000 or £29,000, plus rents and annuities). The nature of his initial offer (£4,000 in total) shows that his mind wasn't even operating on this level, let alone intending to make a full settlement. When the offer was refused he set himself to challenge the entire will, as the only way forward. Meanwhile he refused to pay anything.

Accordingly six months passed by. Philip then found himself owing not £20,000 but £29,000, and Algernon found his claim to the rents of Leicester Fields and Swan Close facing a precarious future, subject to the co-operation of Henry. From this newly complicated situation it fell to the executors to try and extract something, and Sidney soon moved into the driver's seat, determined to extract everything (his rents included).

THE STRUGGLE FOR THE INHERITANCE

It is hardly the case therefore that in November 1677 Algernon found himself destitute and compelled to fight for what little had been left him. On

[28] It is not clear why the penalty was attached to Henry only, rather than split evenly between himself and Algernon, as would seem logical in terms of the rest of the will. This may reflect Henry's particular involvement in the final codicil, or may have been the quite arbitrary product of some circumstance such as who was available on a certain day (Sidney may have been at Leicester House in London: see below). It seems clear that Leicester framed the codicil in order to give Philip (as he saw it) no choice but to obey, and never expected it to be invoked.

the contrary, the Earl's demise left the executors Algernon and Henry in de facto possession of the entire estate pending Philip's performance of the crushing de jure terms of the will. Accordingly Henry 'entered into and possessed himself of the Barony house of Penshurst'[29] while Algernon took over Leicester House in London, where he was to live for the next four years (it was from there that he wrote to Furly in November).

At the same time, as Algernon helped himself to the £5,000 in 'ready money' in London, Henry actioned at Penshurst his liberal interpretation of what constituted the Earl's 'movables' and 'personal estate'. This involved not only helping himself to everything that wasn't fixed to the ground but cutting down some things that were: to wit, the sale of 'a pcell of timber to Sr Charles Biggerstaffe'.[30] To Philip's outrage at these depredations Henry answered that the felling had begun before the Earl's death (i.e., by implication, with his permission), 'and none after . . . though some might have been on the morning of his death day'.[31]

We must spare a thought then for the fragile Earl; his last sighs lost in an upstairs bedroom at Penshurst amid the hewing and crashing of timber. This is a no less Gothic alternative to the death-bed scene already offered by Algernon (see my *Algernon Sidney and the English Republic*, p. 237). At worst it may be a metaphor for the conduct of the executors in this period in general. There was nothing Philip could do but begin filing a series of Chancery actions against the trustees and executors seeking a court order that would control their actions, while simultaneously questioning the 'equity' of the settlement as a whole. His first complaint was filed on 8 December; a second and third followed on 26 January and 3 April 1678.[32] When these complained that 'the great house called Leicester house . . . is worth £700 a year and the said Algernon Sidney should be accountable for it', Algernon replied that '[He and Henry] coming to Towne soone after their said fathers death to put in execution his said will and testament did observe that £4,000 of their money was charged on Leicester House and so finding the house empty did make use thereof as they hope was lawful.'[33] The court issued a decree in support of this interpretation of the matter. Subsequently it was only when 'According unto the sayd decree the £2,000 and £2,000 charged upon Leicester house was payd on the 21st of Nov An: 1681 [that] possession of the house [was] deliverd' by Algernon to Philip.

It is not necessary to trace every step of the subsequent battle through Chancery. This culminated (in law, if not in practice) in the great victory won by Algernon's 'The Case of Algernon and Henry Sidney . . . referred to Sir William Jones' in mid-to-late 1680.[34] This was, as we have seen, at just

[29] PRO Chancery C10 195/28.   [30] *Ibid.*   [31] *Ibid.*
[32] C5 515/25; C10 195/28.   [33] C10 195/28.
[34] The dating of this decision is suggested (though not confirmed) by the comment of Dorothy

the time when Sidney's political partnership with Jones was coming to dangerous fruition. But Sidney's legal association with Jones also predated 'The Case', for as we will see it was he (with Sir Francis Pemberton) who managed Algernon's other Chancery business against Viscount Strangford. Here the decision of the doubtless entirely impartial Attorney General enforced the letter of the Earl's will against Philip, and required his performance of its terms by 'the last day of Michaelmas 1681'. But the payment of £4,000 mentioned above that released Leicester House was in fact Philip's only response by that time. Sidney was now required to live somewhere else, and as his surrender of Leicester House (November 1681) coincides with the beginning of an eighteen-month period in which he disappeared from view in London and worked on the *Discourses*, it seems likely that much of that work was written at the remaining available 'executor's residence', Penshurst. The likelihood is much increased by the fact that throughout this period the house was otherwise unoccupied: Henry spent almost the whole of 1680–3 at The Hague. This introduces the further possibility that during the writing process he had access to his father's library and his commonplace books, a possibility of importance for reasons already discussed.[35] Thus by late 1681 Sidney had discovered that it was easier to win a settlement in law than to secure its enforcement; and having now lost Leicester House he complained that this settlement was necessary as he had spent most of that part of the legacy he had received (£5,000 in 1677 and £2,000 in 1681) on legal fees to recover the rest.[36] Indeed in a sense Sidney's serious problems only began at this point, in late 1681/early 1682. Because although he had made all the legal running to date, his doing so had been dependent on the co-operation of his co-executor Henry. Now this proved his achilles heel.

In his later bitter expostulations on this subject Algernon claimed that from the moment of his father's death 'Alg: Sydney in all things joined with Henry, because he knew it was the will of his father, that he should doe soe, though in many respects, very prejudiciall unto himself.' This cannot be sustained: Sidney joined with his brother because their co-operation was the single necessary pre-requisite for the following through of their unassailable position in law.

Typically it had been Algernon who assumed management of this joint

---

Sidney on 1 July 1680: 'Sir William Jones . . . says . . . that my brother's business could not be determined otherwise than it is, after he had taken so many fees of my brother Leicester.' Berry, *The Life and Letters of Lady Russell*, p. 122.

[35] Scott, *Sidney and the English Republic*, pp. 55–8.

[36] This seems to have been an exaggeration: he had also both sent money to Furly and purchased his small property in Gascony; but the point can be accepted that he certainly needed at least the remaining £3,000, and preferably the annuity and rents as well, before he could satisfactorily return to France.

executor's policy, with all the work that this entailed. The wording of all the relevant legal documents (under the name of both men) establishes his authorship, with the exception that proves the rule of the few months at the beginning of 1678 when Sidney was unfortunately indisposed (see 'The Strangford estate, pp. 99–103 below) and Henry managed one major answer. Throughout this period 1677–82, therefore, it was Algernon who turned the progressive twists and turns of the suit into an increasingly absorbing private obsession, with the slightly dim Henry signing the necessary documents, but becoming increasingly detached, principally by his role from 1679–84 as Sunderland and Temple's ambassador to the Prince of Orange.

To see exactly how the situation finally broke down, we need to return to the situation between the three brothers as it stood in 1678. This found Algernon, as we have seen, in possession of Leicester House, and £5,000; and seeking £5,000 more (£2,000 charged on Leicester House; £3,000 on the Kent and Sussex lands), plus an annuity of £150 a year, and half the rents of Leicester Fields and Swan Close for life. Then at the beginning of May 1678, as Philip refused to confirm the leases on Leicester Fields and the six months expired, the terms of the settlement and the balance between the co-executors changed. Philip now became liable to pay Henry not £5,000 but £14,000 (plus his annuity); by the same token Algernon's share of the rents from Leicester Fields was thrown into jeopardy. The cheerful Henry seems never to have seriously expected his brother to pay him £14,000 (and on this score one cannot help feeling grateful that for whatever reason the Earl at the last moment attached this clause to Henry and not Algernon), but the legal threat of such a large sum could be used to extract from Philip a satisfactory out-of-court settlement for *both* brothers concerning the buildings and the rents. This accordingly became Algernon's strategy: with Henry's approval he became determined to use the £9,000 penalty to extract a satisfactory settlement for both of them in line with the original (pre-May 1678) terms of the will. For himself that meant his share of the building rents as well as the lump sum and annuity to which the amended settlement entitled him anyway. The principle behind this policy was defensible: the original terms expressed the true will of his father toward both brothers. The practice however was vulnerable: it relied on Henry's continued preparedness to allow what was now legally his £9,000 to be used in this way.

What happened was this. Algernon successfully directed the settlement to its legal confirmation against Philip in 1680. Philip then owed him £5,000 plus £150 per year, and Henry £14,000 plus £150 a year; his payment of the £4,000 charged on Leicester House in 1681 lowered these lump sums to £3,000 and £12,000 respectively. The crunch for Algernon now became to maintain Henry's preparedness to use the extra £9,000 owed to him to secure instead the building rents for life for both of them. At this juncture Philip did what one would expect: he approached Henry separately and sought a private deal. The test of executor solidarity had come.

Henry dutifully 'told Alg Sydney, of somme overture of treaty that had bin made unto him by the E of Leicester wheareupon he desird his advice'. Sidney replied 'with somme caution' but advised that Henry should offer to settle for the payment to each of them of 'the £3000 and £3000 with the annuityes and the arreares of them, the leases confirmed unto the builders [at Leicester Fields] and they sufferd to receave the rents for their lives unlesse the E of Leicester rather chose to give a compensation [for the rents] in mony Alg: offering to take £1,500 for his part, of which he gave a note unto Henry as a help unto his memory'.[37]

In short (predictably) Algernon took a hard line, insisting on the full original settlement. Predictably, too, Philip was not impressed. Then in early 1682 Algernon 'was informed that Hen: Sydney contrary to the trust reposed in him by the late Earle Robert, and his word given unto Alg: Sydney, had made an agreement with the now Earle [Philip] comprehending his own concernements, which being satisfied he was to give up the deed for the £9000, charged upon the estate to oblige the now Earle to confirm the builder's leases and secure the enjoyment of the rents of the new buildings unto Alg. Sidney [sic] as well as himself'.[38]

'By this meanes' concluded Sidney, 'Alg: Sydney who had not as yet complained of all the losses brought upon him by the abovesayd frauds is deprived of all means of recovering that which the late Earle his father gave him for his subsistance ... after having lost somme and spent much of his legacy in his long attendance upon the suite ...'

ALGERNON VERSUS HENRY SIDNEY 1682–3

The result was Algernon's initiation of the further Chancery suit, this time against Henry (and Gilbert Spencer), which was discussed in *Algernon Sidney and the English Republic* (chapter 14). In fact, as we have seen, Sidney had not been 'deprived ... of all ... his father gave him' by Henry's defection, but rather only his share of the building rents (valued here by himself at £1,500). He had already received £7,000, and legal proceedings for the recovery of the remaining £3,000 and the arrears of the annuity were still in progress. Yet it is indicative of Sidney's whole attitude to the legal settlement that he should not only spend one half of his legacy to recover the other half, but that five years later the last 10 per cent of it should come to represent 'all ... his father gave him' simply because it was the only part that Philip looked able to legally avoid paying. Throughout this period

---

[37] De Lisle MS U1475 L5.   [38] *Ibid.*

Sidney had been preoccupied with the money from the settlement not principally because he needed it, but because it was the concrete representation of his father's wishes and regard for him (in contradistinction to those for Philip). Now this remaining legacy represented (and might end up costing) the whole settlement not by any financial logic, but because it was the remainder of the money '*his father gave him for his subsistance*' [my emphasis]. His father intended him to have it; he attached such an enormous penalty to the six-month clause specifically to ensure that he got it; it was now Henry's clear moral duty to use that penalty to carry that intention through.

But Algernon had no case in law; Henry could do as he wished. The reasons for his defection are easy enough to understand. It was not a ruse to take the £9,000 for himself: he could probably have got more by sticking with Algernon than by coming to terms alone with Philip. It was because the obsession in this matter was Algernon's, not his. This legal crusade had been going on for five years, upsetting the entire extended family. Now that the legal case had been decided, Henry wanted to bring it to a satisfactory end as soon as possible: given the shape of the final settlement (exceedingly generous to both younger brothers) he presumably thought it no more urgent that Algernon should get his last 10 per cent than that Philip, who had been excluded from his inheritance for five years, should finally be allowed into it. There was, among the executors, a mismatch between the one who had the drive to push the settlement to the limit (Algernon), and the one who had the means to do so (Henry), and in the fifth year of the struggle their alliance collapsed.

Thus it was that Sidney was deprived of all means of recovering the last part of his inheritance: the rents of Leicester Fields, or £1,500 in lieu. He was traumatised by this 'betrayal', and the case against Henry displays paranoia. Sidney was left, familiarly, with only one friend in the family: the memory of the dead father in whose shadow the whole enterprise had been launched. Here the spectre of his father overshadowed his private recollections in the same way that the English Republic did his political ones. The anti-*Patriarcha Discourses* was written throughout this year (1682) under the shadow of both, and the memory of the decade – the 1650s – in which they had united to give Sidney real power.

Meanwhile, regular proceedings against Philip to recover the remainder of what he owed Sidney under the 1680 settlement continued. Payment of a further £1,000 reduced the amount concerned to £2,000, plus the annuity and arrears. On 23 April 1683 an affidavit was granted licensing Sidney to be 'lett into and have possession of [some part of Philip's estate] . . . in order to raise what is due to him according to the decree with interest'.[39]

[39] PRO C41/24 p. 1030.

Only two weeks later, however, Algernon was arrested for treason and sent to the tower. During his time in prison, reported a local diarist:[40] 'Mr Henry Sidney his brother carryed to him with great respects and prudence, and is well reported of all men for it. His brother the Earl of Leicester with whom he had very great differences about an annuity of £2,000 [sic] did not come visit him but sent him £1,000 of it, because he could no longer hold up the cudgells.'

The estate of a traitor was forfeit to the crown, unless the King himself chose to grant it to one of his subjects. In his last letter, to an unidentified friend, possibly Henry Neville, a fortnight before his execution, Sidney wrote:

[Our friendship was such that] I . . . doe not think that any thing could break it, but that which is now shortly to ensue – For want of a better way of expressing it, when I made my will in March last I gave you all I had except some small legacyes. That is now cutt off and whatsoever is [usable?] can be saved only by one that is like to obtaine somme favour [at court]. I knowe none so likely as my brother Harry and he having indeed behaved himself well unto me, since I am in prison, I have given it unto him, and send you only as a token one bill for £1,376 upon a very honest merchant in London, and tow bills of exchange from Holland for £507 . . . If a few dayes of life remaine unto me I may perhaps gather up a littell more. Pray doe not in this mistake me: I doe not think to endeare my memory unto you, though I would leave forty times as much, but such things as are usuall amongst men, must be sufferd to passe.[41]

Thus in a few months Sidney's mind had been turned from the pursuit of his father's will, to the construction of his own.

5.3 THE STRANGFORD ESTATE

The other legal visitation from Sidney's past concerned the estates of Lord Strangford.[42] This struck with initially even more devastating consequences. It was to end earlier however, and with a conspicuous display of virtuosity in Chancery procedure by Sidney which must have made Strangford nostalgic for the 1650s.

Given the untidiness with which Sidney's earlier involvement with Strangford had been terminated there was perhaps an inevitability about the two men falling again to legal blows after Sidney's return to England. We have seen Sidney's claim from Italy that the Strangfords owed him several thousand pounds and had made a prey of his possessions at Sterry, and his consequent refusal to surrender control of the estate until it was dissolved in his absence by Parliament in 1665. Yet it is possible that Sidney now had no

[40] Dr Williams Library, London: Roger Morrice's Entering Book, vol. I, p. 398.
[41] Lewes Record Office, Glynde Place Archives no. 794, letter 10, 22 Nov., pp. 1–2.
[42] Scott, *Sidney and the English Republic*, chs. 4, 7.

wish to stir up that old hornet's nest again, and only came to re-assert his claims when he heard that Strangford (whose remarkable thirst for litigation had not been slaked) was about to do the same against him.

It was on 10 December 1677 that Sidney wrote to Strangford requesting that he restore to him the legal papers taken at Sterry, 'with an ebony cabinet and somme other littell things belonging to me'. In addition he added:

I had reason to hope you would . . . pay me at least the mony remaining due unto me under Mr Smily his name, that which I disbursed in keeping you, and your family at Sterry, the valewe of the cattell, corne and other provision imployed for the maintenance of it, in my absence, and such other summes as without dispute you knewe to be due unto me, and could not but be amazed to heare about a fortnight agoe, that instead of this, you did pretend that severall great summes were due unto you from me, of which I should shortly hear from you . . .[43]

Sidney closed with a brisk demand for a 'just and reasonable compensation for the sayd summes', and added hopefully, 'I presume you have heard my father hath by his will given you tow thousand pounds, and will take such care concerning it, as shall be requisite'.[44]

Strangford's eventual reply was shattering. Early in 1678 (but after 3 April, the date of Sidney's last letter of this period to Furly) he joined with tenants of his estates who were still owed money (including John Symonds and Thomas Andrews) to bring an action for £5,500 debt against Sidney at common law. And as Sidney's subsequent Chancery complaint put it (June 1678): 'the Ld Strangford insistinge . . . on speciall Bayle Wherein your orator [Sidney] could not give them satisfaction hee your said orator was comitted Prisoner to the Kings Bench Prison where your Orator still remaines a Prisoner'.[45]

Within six months of his return Sidney had been thrown from Leicester House into debtor's prison, and there he remained until he could secure a Chancery injunction for his release. This is part of the reason for his disappearance from the historical records from April to August 1678, and the reason why the management of the inheritance dispute passed temporarily to Henry in the same period.

We will never know how much substance lay behind Strangford's charges, though it can be shown that some of them were malicious nonsense. An example is the fact that the £5,500 included the £1,200 mortgage to Thanet (*Sidney and the English Republic*, p. 122), for which Sidney was

---

[43] A copy of this letter is in the De Lisle MS U1500 C2/4, wrongly dated 1679; the true date is made clear by Sidney's mention of the letter in his chancery bill C7 327/50 (June 1678).

[44] *Ibid*. Strangford's response was to become a party to the general litigation concerning the will, demanding much more: cf C6 82/52, C7 317/62 (Strangford's bill of complaint), and C6 28/56.

[45] PRO Chancery, C7 327/50.

able to produce a document bearing Strangford's own signature as authorisation. Strangford's response, that Sidney had tricked him into signing a document he did not understand, was hardly adequate (as Sidney would have put it) in reason or law. Strangford's action too may be best interpreted as a pre-emptive strike against what the letter had led him to expect from Sidney. If so it was to prove an expensive one for both of them.

Sidney's response, from his new accommodation in the King's Bench, was to lodge a complaint in Chancery seeking a Chancery injunction to halt the proceedings at common law. This he was able to do by claiming that Strangford's raid on Sterry in 1660 had removed all the legal documents by which he (Sidney) could have proved his case at common law. The equity jurisdiction of Chancery was intended for just such cases, where the documents or witnesses required as proofs in common law were not available. The managers of his complaint (by whom it is signed) were Francis Pemberton and Sir William Jones. Chancery accordingly granted the injunction, which by staying the proceedings automatically released Sidney from prison. Chancery now assumed jurisdiction of the case, and an order was produced requiring Strangford to produce the documents in question. He replied, predictably, that no such documents existed. But the initiative had now been gained by Sidney, within an arena of law in which he had become a masterful operator. Strangford spent the next two years vainly struggling to regain it.

In his bill of complaint Sidney rehearsed his entire involvement with Strangford from the 1640s to the (bitterly recounted) parliamentary act of 1665; he included an itemised schedule of Strangford's debts at the time of taking up the Trust. The upshot – and in quantity of paper involved the case between Sidney and Strangford far outweighs the dispute over the Leicester inheritance – was the claim by Sidney that contrary to the common-law case's assertions Strangford owed *him* between £5,000 and £6,000.

The importance of the initiative in Chancery stemmed from the fact that each bill of complaint commanded an answer, within its own terms, by a certain time, subject to physical arrest upon failure to comply. Strangford replied to Sidney's bill on 16 November (1678)[46] but had meanwhile tried to regain the initiative by presenting his own complaint on 16 October.[47] Sidney responded in mid January 1679 by objecting to the terms of Strangford's complaint on grounds of insufficient documentation,[48] while presenting his own second complaint (16 January), objecting to Strangford's answer to his first, and calling for more documentation for that as well. Strangford found himself subpoenaed by the court[49] to reply (at enormous

[46] C7 327/50.   [47] C6 82/69.
[48] PRO Chancery Affidavits, Hillary 1678 (January 17 1678/9), p. 46.
[49] PRO Chancery Decrees and Orders, Michaelmas 1678, p. 207.

length and expense, on 27 February)[50] to Sidney's second complaint before
Sidney had replied to his first.

Clearly enjoying himself, Sidney now objected to the second answer, and
a series of court orders between March and May 1679 attempted to come to
grips with these competing claims.[51] These climaxed on 24 May when the
standard 'Com[mission] of rebellion' awarded against Sidney for his refusal
to answer Strangford's (first) complaint was judged to be 'very irregular',
'after two ord[er]s for staying proceedings on [Strangford's] bill [un]till [he]
had answered [Sidney's complaint against his second answer] touching
writeings made by [him] to [Sidney]'.[52] Sidney could not, however, maintain
these delays forever and in the same week, while Strangford went away to
prepare yet another answer, Sidney himself received through his lawyer 'Mr
Whitelock' (son of Bulstrode?), the order of the court to answer as well.
Even so he continued to avoid doing so until a second decree on 28 June[53]
gave him two weeks to produce something or the Sergeant at Arms would
take him into custody.

By this time the case had been running for a year. During this period
Strangford had produced one complaint and three answers, running in total
into hundreds of pages; and Sidney, rather emblematically, had produced
three complaints and no answers at all. When his answer finally came on 5
July 1679 it was less than a page long.

This makes clear why he had delayed it as long as possible. Sidney's
answer ignored Strangford's thrice-reiterated life story and employed a legal
device which squashed his case like a fly; though only (and this is the point)
at the cost of squashing his own. He was not required to respond to
Strangford's charges, he observed drily, because of 'an act made in the 21st
year of king James [called] *An Act for Limittacons of Acc[tio]ns*'. This
stipulated that a bill of complaint must be presented within six years of its
cause.

Strangford's case had been derailed from common law to Chancery. He
had then been the subject of numerous court orders which had made him
spend a fortune on answers that his opponent had never had any intention
of reciprocating. He had now been finished off with a coup de grace which
was legally unassailable.

Further salt was applied to the wound by the report of Edward Lowe, one
of the clerks of chancery, on 15 July. This upheld for Sidney 'the first
Except[i]on ... As allsoe ... the second Exception ... As allsoe ... the 3d

---

[50] C6 82/60; see also the reply of Symonds C7 327/50.
[51] PRO Chancery Decrees and Orders, 1678, Michaelmas, pp. 223, 260, 276; Easter, pp. 307,
314, 315, 317.
[52] *Ibid.*, p. 315.
[53] Decrees and Orders, 1678, Trinity, p. 431.

and 4th, 5th, and 6th Exceptions [sic] . . . As allsoe the seventh Exception' made by Sidney to Strangford's last answer. Strangford was ordered by the court to produce one more (17 April 1680)[54] before the matter could be quietly laid to rest.

[54] PRO Chancery C7 357/50.

$\twoheadleftarrow$ *6* $\twoheadrightarrow$

European politics 1678–80

[The object of Charles II and the Prince of Orange] had been to take into their own hands the decision of European affairs. As matters turned out, their decision was far more dependent on the union of Louis XIV with the aristocracy in Holland and the opposition . . . in England.

Leopold von Ranke (1875)[1]

just at the moment my most intimate liaison is with Mr. Algernon Sidney; he is the man in England who seems to me to have the greatest understanding of affairs; he has great relations with the rest of the Republican Party; And nobody in my opinion is more capable of rendering service than him.

Barillon to Louis XIV, 6 Oct. 1678.[2]

6.1 STUART AND ORANGE REVIVED

In this chapter we find Algernon Sidney and Charles II reading opposite ends of the same political map. The map is of Europe, centred on France particularly, with offshoots in the Low Countries and the British Isles. It is the geographical ensemble which registers naturally with both returned exiles. The man holding the map is the French ambassador, Barillon.

Sidney's relationship with Barillon, and the European world of which it formed a part, will be the subject of this chapter. It is somewhat artificial however to separate these relationships from their domestic context. Nor did they end in 1681: as we will see, the European dimension of Sidney's activities continued for as long as he did. Nevertheless, as in the last chapter, it is important to illustrate the internal logic of these involvements here; while remembering that they formed one part of a strategy to be set out in full in the chapters to come.

No subject caused Sidney's whig admirers more pain than his involvement with the European dimension of this crisis.[3] For they attributed to his situation both attitudes and circumstances that were theirs and not his.

---

[1] Von Ranke, *History of England*, vol. IV, p. 561.
[2] Paris, Ministère des Affaires Etrangères, Corresp. Politique, Angleterre, XLI.
[3] See Scott, *Sidney and the English Republic*, pp. 4–5.

Their attitudes took as their starting point a national political structure, and a solidarity against France, which were achievements of Stuart displacement, in 1688. Those working for such displacement in 1678 had to do it under Stuart, not later, conditions.

As an outgrowth of the crown's own European entanglements, the Restoration crisis bequeathed some version of those to everybody effectively involved. It was those who, in later whig terms, got their hands dirty, by working with foreigners like Barillon, who produced the results in this period. For Sidney in particular it was both natural and unavoidable, even aside from the policies of Charles II, that he should see England in the context of the greater political and religious situation in Europe.

What most electrifyingly recharged a major theme from Sidney's own past was Danby's Stuart–Orange marriage alliance of November 1677. Within a month of his return to England, this re-established the Stuart–Orange union of 'interest' which had been the focus of his *Court Maxims*. Soon enough, as we will see, Sidney was quoting chapter and verse from the *Maxims* in a second attempt to influence French participation in this situation. Written in the Netherlands in 1665–6, the *Court Maxims* had traced the history of this union of 'interest' from the beginning of Stuart rule in England in 1603.[4] Its promotion by the Stuarts was, he argued, an axiomatic strategy for the destruction of its 'irreconcileable contrary': the republican interest of both England and the United Provinces. This chapter will be largely concerned to recount the revival of this 'interest' – the linked causes of English and Dutch republicanism – a revival which was partly a consequence of the Stuart–Orange match. Sidney's interest analysis had itself been borrowed from Dutch republican ideology, of which it formed a primary component. In 1677, on the eve of the Stuart–Orange match, the Dutch republicans or Louvesteiners remained in control of the trading capital of the United Provinces (Amsterdam) and locked in a struggle for control of Dutch foreign policy with the Prince of Orange at the Hague.

The Anglo–Dutch republican revival of 1678–81, in which Sidney was intimately involved, was to be spectacularly successful. It is to the political results of this situation that von Ranke refers in the quote at the head of this chapter. The fact of this success owed less, perhaps, to the efforts of the republicans themselves than to the fact that they had the backing of the most powerful nation in Europe. Underwritten by the indefatigable efforts of three French ambassadors: Barillon in England, and d'Estrades and d'Avaux in the United Provinces, by 1680 the republicans and their allies had done a good deal more than simply render Stuart–Orange foreign policy redundant. They now part-controlled London as well as Amsterdam;

[4] *Ibid.*, pp. 205–6; For a modern treatment of the same subject see Pieter Geyl, *Orange and Stuart* (1969).

they had helped to create a major political crisis in England; and they were effectively exploiting it to put both financial and political pressure on the King. While Sidney put the arguments of the *Court Maxims* to Barillon, one of the London Sheriffs, Slingsby Bethel, issued them in print (*The Interests of Princes and States* (1680)). At the same time, their allies, Titus and Jones (the former also a recipient of French funding) co-ordinated the parliamentary end of a united political and religious strategy.

It was these developments, rather than exclusion, which preoccupied – and terrified – all the major participants in the international dimension of this crisis. They included Charles II, the Prince of Orange, and the Duke of York. And these were developments which were only brought under control when Charles finally recovered from this group the active support of the French King. Nevertheless this is a story – of the revival of the 'old cause', in England as well as in the Low Countries – which has been almost entirely absent from the English historiography of this crisis.[5]

One reason for this situation – the neglect of the European context for this century of English history, by an historiography whose parameters remain anachronistically national – was touched upon in chapter 2. That is why only von Ranke, a continental historian equipped with his doctrine of 'the primacy of foreign affairs', has painted it from its properly European perspective. Retrospective national pride – still popular in politics – is a great distorter of history: the 'glorious revolution' turns out to mean that the country was successfully invaded. The Restoration crisis was a chapter in European history, during which England was a plaything of the French King.

The second reason however, is still more important, and has been more all-embracing. Whig historians, after all, did not hesitate to call attention to the dependence of Charles II upon France, though they refrained from mentioning the same fact about his opponents. The second reason stems from the triumph, or the beginning, in 1688–9, of the whig cause itself.

For it is above all in face of the perception of William of Orange as the *saviour* of English liberties, that Sidney's own opposite perception – of no less than an 'irreconcileable contrariety' between the two – is difficult to recover. It is the assumptions of this historical tradition that make his remark to Barillon in 1682, that he 'feared the Prince of Orange more than the Duke of York', difficult to understand.[6] The same goes for the remark of his close friend John Hampden jnr in mid 1680, when informed of an Anglo–Dutch [government] league: 'This will all be turned against us . . . I am afraid this will fool the Parliament . . . we shall have the Prince of

---

[5] An exception is J. Ralph's unusually complex and complete treatment of the crisis in *History of England* (1744).
[6] PRO Baschet no. 150, fol. 261 (1981).

Orange with an army here.'[7] This perception greatly offended Dorothy Sidney, whose son Sunderland and brother Henry Sidney were negotiating for the league.[8] 'These are good Englishmen and Protestants!' She exclaimed; 'They are so mad they know not what they say'.[9] Yet Hampden can scarcely be described as 'mad' when 'the Prince of Orange with an army here' is exactly what he lived to see, eight years later.

For participants in this strategy, and this perception, the events of 1688–9 were not a victory, but a shattering (and permanent) defeat. For the second time in the century, Stuart displacement was achieved, but this time for the benefit of monarchy, rather than republicanism. Following the return of England's 'troubles', what the invasion of 1688 made possible was a second Restoration; not a second revolution. The domestic result was not a popular uprising – it was a second Interregnum and a second Convention parliament, learning from the experiences of the first. And the settlement which emerged was, from both Dutch and English sides, explicitly anti-republican.[10] William intervened in the third and final crisis of the Stuart monarchy specifically to rescue his inheritance from the Dutch-style republicanism he imagined, and the English-style republicanism the nation remembered, to have been the consequence of the first. If the basis for such a concern in 1688 seems improbable, it is partly because the story of the English republican renaissance of 1678–81 has not been told. We are accordingly recovering here the efforts, and the political logic, not of the whigs – the 'winners' of 1688 – but of one contingent of the losers. That this is not easy derives from two further circumstances.

One is the myth of the 'glorious revolution' as universally satisfying: until recently this led, at the other end of the spectrum, to a shading out of the importance of Jacobitism as well.[11] Several recent works have now drawn attention to the fact that the amorphous tradition of post-1688 'whiggism' concealed within its name distinct and opposed radical groupings who were to be bitterly disappointed by 1688, and whose political legacy – of republicanism rather than whiggism – was to find fruit not in England at all, but in America.[12]

[7] Countess of Sunderland to Lord Halifax, June 1680, reprinted in Berry (ed.), *Life and Letters of Lady Russell*, p. 118.
[8] All of which illustrates the welter of Sidneys and Sidney relations tied up in those affairs – a fact pointed out by Walcott (*British Politics*, pp. 78–9) and too quickly dismissed by a number of his opponents.　　　　　　　　　　　　　　　　　　[9] See note 7.
[10] J.R. Western, *Monarchy and Revolution* (1972), pp. 207, 302; J.P. Kenyon, *Revolution Principles* (Cambridge 1977), p. 9.
[11] Now see E. Cruikshanks, *Ideology and Conspiracy: Aspects of Jacobitism* (Edinburgh 1982); B. Lenman, *The Jacobite Risings in Britain 1689–1746* (1980); and P. Hopkins, 'Aspects of Jacobite Conspiracy in England in the Reign of William III' (University of Cambridge PhD thesis, 1981).
[12] Mark Goldie's 'The Roots of True Whiggism', *History of Political Thought*, 1:2 (1980) was

The other problem is the inherent difficulty of recovering the history of republicanism in a country where it was a remarkably brief and unpopular failure. The phrase 'the rump parliament' sums up perfectly the inglorious place it holds in the history of the nation. England's republicans – participants in that experiment – influenced the entire western world; but they remain better known outside the country than in it. Republican thinking and practice still run contrary to established political tradition.[13]

As early as 1679, England's foremost 'authority' on the United Provinces, Sir William Temple, was deliberately minimising for English consumption the importance of a republican element in the States General which operated not only separately from, but within a tradition of 'irreconcileable contrariety' to the Stadtholder.[14] English foreign policy consequently assumed that the Netherlands operated like a heavily limited and federated principality, under the overall leadership of the Stadtholder, particularly in foreign affairs. It was on the basis of this entirely false assumption that the alliance between Mary and William was made in 1677. It was because of this assumption was so mistaken that the makers of the alliance were subsequently to have events taken out of their hands.

6.2 ANGLO–DUTCH REPUBLICANISM REVIVED

REPUBLICAN PERCEPTIONS

In the United Provinces, the effect of the Stuart–Orange match was instantaneous. It re-ignited 'the war of Parties in Holland'.[15] In August 1678 the Dutch republicans took their revenge by destroying the Stadtholder's foreign policy in the States General. In its place they concluded the treaty of Nimuegen with France. As an English contemporary remarked: the Stuart–Orange match had reactivated 'the suspicion of the states party in Holland that there was a plot against their liberties . . . they had therefore foresaken the [Stuart–Orange] coalition against France'.[16] This treaty amounted to a

a particularly important contribution to this subject – though it might have helped to point out that what was called 'true whiggism' for propagandistic purposes was not whiggism at all, but republican legs venturing abroad in whig trousers. Pocock made this point more recently: 'this whig canon was in fact a republican canon' (*Virtue, Commerce and History*, p. 88). Kenyon's *Revolution Principles* first explored a number of these themes; Ashcraft's *Revolutionary Politics* succeeds in dissociating Locke also from the distasteful events of 1688–9.

[13] It was entirely in line with this traditional perspective that Margaret Thatcher's attempt to steal the thunder at the French revolution celebrations on 14 July 1989 should have referred to the (monarchical) revolution of 1688. It took President Mitterand, a republican, to remind her of its predecessor of 1649.

[14] Sidney, 'Letters to Savile' in *Works*, pp. 50–1 (and see below).

[15] J. Ralph, *The History of England*, vol. 1 (1744), p. 488.

[16] Quoted in Haley, *Shaftesbury*, p. 502.

declaration that under present circumstances the States General considered Louis XIV less of a danger to their liberties than the Stadtholder. It was concluded 'almost over [the] dead body' of the Prince himself, who vainly attempted to destroy it with a post-treaty military attack.[17] From William's point of view it destroyed the (military) point of the Stuart–Orange match altogether, and it was only by his risky adventure to England ten years later that he was able to reclaim it.

Having rendered his continental military opposition impotent, Louis now turned to England where, as has been explained (in chapter 2), he had some political scores to settle. The situation there was more complicated. There was no equivalent 'republican opposition', and Barillon was to establish a range of contacts with opposition figures whose 'interests' he described as 'very different and very opposite'.[18] There was at their centre, however, a group of republicans – products of the civil war and interregnum – with longstanding Anglo–Dutch experience, perspective and ties. Their identical perception of the Stuart–Orange match made them the most natural allies of Barillon's enterprise in England. Foremost among them was Sidney himself. It was by this stroke of *fortuna* that in late 1678 Sidney found himself, as Barillon's testimony at the head of this chapter suggests, the most valued English contact of the French King. Historical attention to Sidney's relationship with Barillon has focused on the exchange of money between them. Following his orders, Barillon was to hand over to Sidney 500 guineas between December 1678 and March 1679, and the same amount again a year later.[19] That Sidney should have accepted it is hardly remarkable, given that he had asked Louis for a hundred times as much twelve years earlier. Accepting the external support of hostile great powers was rule one in the Frondeur's handbook.[20]

In Sidney's case, other circumstances also applied. He had never been squeamish about political means. His interest was in results, and his politics were, in practice and in theory, a sceptical politics of ends. Secondly, his cause had never been national, but was European. Finally, Sidney's relationship with France, like his relationships in London, and with the leaders of the House of Commons, was part of a strategy of financial strangulation of the crown. In this sense, the alternative receipt of French money was not incidental, but basic, to the relationship.

Even so, money was not, particularly in the early stages, the most valuable commodity which Sidney received from Barillon. That was informa-

---

[17] Kenyon, *Sunderland*, pp. 37–8.
[18] Dalrymple, *Memoirs*, Appendix, p. 288.
[19] *Ibid.*, p. 315; PRO Baschet no. 142, pp. 192, 317.
[20] Witness, for instance, the conduct of Condé during the Frondes, and his relations with Spain.

tion. Needless to say, this was a favour which Algernon reciprocated at length. Not surprisingly, Barillon found Sidney's analysis of English politics – expressed in interest language, and related to the continental context from which both men had just departed – to be peculiarly convincing. He was soon repeating Sidney's opinions verbatim back to his King as an objective analysis of the situation. It was an analysis which set this second crisis firmly in the context of the first.

This was, thus, an exchange of information which enhanced Sidney's power as it flowed in both directions. It was from Barillon, in turn, that in the course of 1678 Sidney learned more than enough to confirm his own analysis of the political situation. His initial assumptions were those of the *Court Maxims*: that whatever Danby said, and whatever the Prince of Orange thought, from the English side the Stuart–Orange alliance was built around the object of securing power and money at home, rather than military action abroad. This was an axiom of Sidney's republican theory, but it was also correct. As early as 18 April (1678) Barillon had written to Louis: 'The high treasurers' aim is to procure money and he would willingly increase his masters authority.' Although Danby's chosen instrument to this end was parliament, as early as April 1677 he had foreshadowed the possibility of using the army to raise (war) finance if parliamentary co-operation broke down.[21] If it was the crown's rather than Danby's religious inclinations that were popish, it was the equipment of arbitrary government Danby was erecting that made those inclinations so threatening. And it was to Barillon himself that Charles confided that his primary object in the match had not been foreign, but domestic. It was to pacify his parliament, and to dissociate the Prince from his domestic enemies, from those who 'seek a pretence to rise against me, and who would endeavour to get the Prince of Orange on their side'.[22] In short, while William's object in the alliance had indeed been military and anti-French, Charles' had not; and it was only by eliminating the Stuart component of the relationship in 1688 that William was able to redeem its original purposes.

Such information Barillon was now able to pass on to his English contacts. The most spectacular such indiscretion, as we have seen, was the 'secret of the treaty of 27 May', which Barillon reported he had 'confided ... to Mr de Montaigu and to Mr Algernon Sidney'.[23] The purpose of this divulgence was to convince Sidney, if he needed convincing, that no serious action against France had ever been intended. Given the conduct of the King, the purposes of Danby's sham foreign policy could only have been domestic. In fact Sidney needed no convincing on this score. Nevertheless,

[21] Dalrymple, *Memoirs*, Appendix, p. 143.
[22] Miller, *Popery and Politics*, p. 147.
[23] Dalrymple, *Memoirs*, Appendix, p. 127.

such revelations did give him specific information with which to convince others, and 'insinuate . . . to his friends' (particularly 'those who wish to maintain the army by reason of their animosity towards France') that they were only adding so much weight to their own chains.[24] Thus it was that Burnet recorded:

I first knew [Algernon Sidney] in ye year 78, when ye Parliament was pushing ye King into a war with France, and he opposed it with so much violence, yt it was thought he was a pensioner of France; and this suspition was encreased by his being so much with ye french Ambassador; but he said to me yt he knew ye court had no mind to make a war with France and yt they only intended to raise an Army and get a great deal of money to make themselves Masters at home.[25]

What Sidney was attempting to achieve (Stuart displacement) was in effect what William was forced to, ten years later. But Sidney wanted to achieve it to the benefit of republicanism, not monarchy. It was not only that he believed, as both the *Maxims* and the *Discourses* make clear, that monarchy was by its nature preoccupied with domestic objectives. It was private interest government, bent on the subordination of the governed to their parasitic governors. It was also that monarchy was, partly for this reason, militarily incapable. The contrast between the English Republic's and Charles' wars against the Dutch made the point. Therefore, nothing was to be hoped for the service of protestantism, at home or abroad, until the control of policy lay in different hands. Until then, nothing mattered but the achievement of that end. Money given to the King would only compound the problem; money withheld, and indeed diverted, became the opposition counter-strategy.

Thus as early as January 1678 Sidney wrote to Furly:

True it is, that the King in his speech yesterday to the Parliament did speak of [war against France] as a thing not to be avoided, and yet . . . his demands for the carrying it on having been soe vast . . . [and] the thing itself not [as] pleasing to the Parliament and people, as was believed . . . some . . . doe think that all will end in a good peace.[26]

The assumption – to be ably confirmed by Barillon – was that Danby's foreign policy was simply the latest in a line of ruses to augment the financial independence of the crown. As Sidney had put in the *Maxims*: 'a body opprest by disease nourishes not itself but the disease by taking meat'; or in the *Discourses*: that such money would simply enable him to 'gain so many to his particular service, as are sufficient to keep the rest in subjection'.[27]

[24] PRO Baschet no. 141, p. 100.
[25] BL Add. MS 63,057, vol. II, p. 138.
[26] Forster (ed.), *Letters of Locke*, p. 83.
[27] Sidney, *Discourses*, p. 298; *Court Maxims*, p. 14.

The same analysis was a feature of other republican writing at this time. Neville's *Plato Redivivus* confirmed that the strategy had been 'in fine, by offering them [parliament] a war with the French, to . . . lay them asleep, and get a good store of money.' Like Sidney, Neville believed that no foreign policy venture against France, or on behalf of protestantism in Europe, 'will signify anything . . . till our government be . . . new modelled'. Meanwhile he too advised parliament 'against giving of money towards new wars or alliances; that fine wheedle having lost them enough already.'[28]

From these assumptions and perceptions followed the strategy of the King's opponents. The impeachment of Danby was a good start; but both the situation and the King's record were so dire that the only acceptable solution became, eventually, a form of parliamentary supremacy. This is what both Titus and Sidney meant by locating an undivided sovereignty in the 'legislative'. On a *general* level this was to be achieved by whatever means came to hand; and it was in character for Sidney to attempt to use French power to sponsor a transformation of which France would be the principal victim. (It was equally in character, as we will see, for Barillon to see that that is what he was doing.) For Sidney, having just arrived from France, saw in this remarkable Anglo–French rupture an unprecedented second opportunity for Stuart displacement. The *particular* means to this end was the reverse, or contrary, of Danby's strategy. This was to starve the crown of finance, both within parliament and outside it, until, like Charles I, it was brought to dependence upon the Commons.

The object became, in time, more specific than this. It became to force the crown to surrender the royal prerogative at the heart of the political crisis: that of summoning, proroguing and dissolving parliaments. This monarch, after all, owed his political being to parliament; not the other way round. Sidney was to lay particular and angry emphasis on this fact, and its financial basis, in the *Discourses*. The Restoration had been the work of a:

parliament full of lewd young men chosen by a furious people in spite to the puritans, whose severity had disgusted them . . . Many knew not what they did when they annulled the triennial act; voted the militia to be in the King; [and] gave him the excise, customs and chimney money; made the act for corporations, by which the greatest part of the nation was brought under the power of the worst men in it, drunk or sober passed the five mile act and that for uniformity in the church . . . [this] emboldened the court to think of making parliament to be the instrument of our slavery, which had in all ages been the firmest pillar of our liberty. There might have been perhaps a possibility of preventing this pernicious mischief in the constitution of our government. But our brave ancestors could never think their posterity would degenerate into such baseness as to sell themselves and their country.[29]

[28] H. Neville, *Plato Redivivus* (1680), in Robbins (ed.), *Two Republican Tracts*, pp. 143–4. In these and some other matters, and despite some important differences between them, there is a good deal of identity between Neville's work and Sidney's *Discourses*.
[29] Sidney, *Discourses*, p. 503.

It was these terrible mistakes that Sidney now set himself to try to undo. In the process,

> how great soever the danger of [trusting in parliament] may be, it is less than to put all into the hands of one man, and his ministers. The hazard of being ruined by those who must perish with us is not so much to be feared, as by one who may enrich and strengthen himself by our destruction ... it were to be wished, that our security were more certain; but this being, under God, the best anchor we have, it deserves to be preserved with all care, till one of a more unquestionable strength is framed by the consent of the nation.[30]

THE FALL OF DANBY

From the beginning of 1678, Sidney had watched the Dutch republican revival, through to its triumph at Nimuegen in August, with excitement. In Paris he had noted:

> that the States seeme very averse to the continuance of the warre, either through the secret negociations with the French, [or] antient and new jealousies of the tow Houses of Stewart and Nassau.[31]

On 9 August he wrote to Furly:

> That which hath fallen out of late at Nimueghen, is as I presume ... well understood by you ... [and] you knowe we weare ... confident [here] it would be done ... The greatest businesses now in Europe depend upon your neighbour's [France's] resolutions; for if they adheare to the treaty signed, I am confident the peace will be general ... and noe man ... can expresse the troubles that will arise if the contrary fall out. We ... doe not see what is likely to bring in the contrary.[32]

Following Nimuegen, Barillon set his sights 'contre l'armée et contre le grand Trésurier'.[33] On 6 October he made the report to Louis of 'Mr Algernon Sidney ... [of] the Republican Party ... nobody ... is more capable of rendering service than him.'[34] Employing information from Barillon, Sidney contributed to the successful campaign to persuade the House of Commons that it had been giving its money under false pretences. By later in the year the House had reversed its previous stance and voted, in a state of high alarm, for the army to be disbanded.[35] The focus shifted from Europe to popery and arbitrary government at home.

As for Danby, it was in late November that Barillon reported divulging the secret treaty to Sidney and Montagu. On 20 November, Danby noted in a private memorial that Sidney, Montagu and others were planning an attack on him through parliament. He recorded that Sidney's nephew 'Lord Halifax was most bitter against me', and that Sidney had been passing

---

[30] *Ibid.*, p. 503.
[32] *Ibid.*, pp. 87–8.
[34] See note 1 above.
[31] Forster, *Letters of Locke*, p. 85.
[33] PRO Baschet no. 141, p. 87.
[35] Kenyon, *The Popish Plot*, p. 47.

information concerning the intrigue to another nephew, Sunderland.[36] Four days later, Barillon wrote to Louis: 'I am careful not to appear to have dealings with milord Halifax, but Mr. Sidney who I see more freely makes known to him what we desire.'[37] At the end of December the ambassador was to refer back to 'Mr. Montague ... Mr Harbord, [and] Algernon Sidney ... From all of whom I ... received great help in the affair of the Earl of Danby.' It was presumably for these services that shortly afterwards the payment to Sidney of 500 guineas was recorded.[38]

Montagu's subsequent exposure of the correspondence relating to the May treaty (on 10 December) not only ended the Caroline career of Danby himself, but also that of the 'long parliament' upon which the entire restored regime had been based. From this heap of political rubble there emerged, in the following year, three new ministers to dominate the reconstructed government. They were Sidney's two nephews: Halifax and Sunderland; and his cousin, the Earl of Essex.

Over the next two years (1679–80), Sidney's efforts in relation to the European context of the crisis were aimed in three directions. He attempted to use his influence within the new ministry to counteract that of Sir William Temple and prevent the emergence of an Orangist foreign policy. When that failed, he used his contacts both in London and Amsterdam to sabotage the policy which emerged. Secondly, as this implies, he re-built his links with the reviving forces, not only of English, but of Dutch republicanism; and, through the latter, with the French ambassador to the United Provinces, D'Avaux. Finally, he cultivated his relationship with Barillon, and ultimately made through it, for the second time in his life, a republican political bid for the support of the French King. In this enterprise he became the direct competitor of Charles II himself.

THE ORANGE CARD

For the first six months of 1679, Sidney remained on close terms with all three of the new ministers, Halifax, Sunderland, and Essex. The most alarming among these, to both Charles and James, was Halifax. He was exceptionally able; his opposition credentials were impeccable; and he was rumoured to be a republican. When Charles eventually established a joint limitations strategy with Halifax, York became deeply worried. Doubtless overwhelmed by the calamity that had befallen him, his brother now appeared (politically speaking) to be playing with matches. Like all the participants in the international dimension of this crisis – Barillon,

---

[36] A. Browning, *Thomas Osborne, First Earl of Danby*, 3 vols. (1951), vol. II, p. 9.
[37] PRO Baschet no 141, p. 87.
[38] *Ibid*, no. 142, pp. 192, 317; Dalrymple, *Memoirs*, Appendix, p. 315.

D'Avaux, Louis XIV, Charles II, Sidney and William – James invisaged only two possible outcomes, republicanism, or monarchy. Thus in June 1679, when we might have expected him to be worrying about exclusion, he was instead writing to William:

[the King] has yet the fleet, the garrisons, his guards, Ireland and Scotland firm to him, so that if he will stand by himself, he may yet be King ... [but] I ... believe, that whensoever he shews he will no longer be used as he has been ... there will be a rebellion.[39]

York had first acquainted William in late 1678 'that all things look as they did in the beginning of the late rebellion.' By early 1679, with the King's establishment of his Great Council, to include the full spectrum of opposition opinion, the Duke reported (perhaps thinking of the republican Council of State): 'the new modell things are put into is the very same [as] it was in the time of the Commonwealth.'[40] Thus it was that a few months later William was acquainted by the same hand with the limitations scheme: 'a thing so prejudicial to all the royal family ... [that it] would draw after it the ruin of the Monarchy.'[41] Charles was similarly earbashed, James

aquainting his Majesty he thought this limitation project wors, if possible, than the Bill of Exclusion, and would give a greater shock to the Monarchy by vesting the power in the Parliament ... to drop the Government more gently into a Commonwealth, [and] that Algernon Sidney and his partie had express'd as much.[42]

James retained this view throughout the crisis, and repeated it in late 1680, when his nerves had been further frayed by the genuine republican successes in London ('This looks as if London would be set up for a commonwealth'); 'Algernon Sidney and the ablest of the republican Party said that if a bill of limitation was once got, they should from that moment, think themselves sure of a republic.'[43]

In fact there is little evidence associating Sidney specifically with the limitations proposal, or with its rival. He was more interested in ways of deepening the crisis than in measures for resolving it. But it was certainly Halifax, rather than Shaftesbury, with whom he associated in this year, and the limitations scheme certainly did receive the backing of other members of Sidney's London republican community, including John Wildman and Neville.

William was entirely persuaded by James' reasoning. He accordingly wrote to secretary Jenkins,

intreat[ing] you to represent this in my name to the King, and to beg of his Majesty

[39] Dalrymple, *Memoirs*, Appendix, p. 221.
[40] Ronalds, *The Attempted Whig Revolution*, pp. 19,83.
[41] Dalrymple, *Memoirs*, Appendix, p. 308.
[42] Clarke, *Life of James II*, p. 635.
[43] McPherson, *Original Papers*, pp. 111, 112.

on my part, that he will not consent to a thing so prejudical to all those who have the honour to be of his family ... [for] though they spread it about that this ... would be of no consequence to Kings of the Protestant religion, it must not be imagined, that if they had once taken away from the crown such considerable prerogatives as are talked of, they would ever return again.[44]

(This may be compared with the Commons speech quoted in chapter 3: 'I have ever observed, that Prerogative once gained was never got back again, and our Priviledges lost are never restored'.)

At the same time, attention was falling on the resumption of communications between the republicans in London and those in Amsterdam. In April 1679, a pamphlet noted the reappearance of that 'three fold cord ... the interest of a republic in Holland, England and Scotland'.[45] It parodied the 'Louvesteiners, venting their oracles against the house of Orange and Court of England' and observed how their British counterparts 'trace the old method of 1640 again'. On 17 October, the Duke of York again wrote to the Prince:

I had not time in my last to let you know a piece of intelligence I had ... that there is a private correspondence between some parliament men ... and some of those [that] are called here the Louvestein party in Holland, which I am sure cannot be to your advantage ... you would do well to look ... after it where you are, for believe me the Presbyterians and other republicans [sic] here have as little kindness for you as [for] the rest of our family.[46]

Meanwhile, from the middle of 1679, Algernon had been applying himself to matters of foreign policy. Here the situation suddenly began to echo 1678. Following upon the dissolution of his 1679 parliament, and from the beginning of a renewed eighteen-month spell of government-by-prorogation, Charles set about repeating a remarkably well worn foreign policy duet. On the one hand, what remained of his ministry – this time led by Sunderland – was to attempt to revive Danby's protestant foreign policy of 1677–8.[47] Its object was a Stuart–Orange league – possibly also involving Spain – the public object of which would be the containment of France.

The true object, however, was once again different. It was partly to appeal to a House of Commons, which had yet to be allowed to meet. Its other purpose however, equally reminiscently, was to raise the value to Louis of an Anglo-French royal rapprochement. Thus, under storm clouds of *dejà vu*, between July and October a simultaneous secret effort was made

---

[44] Dalrymple, *Memoirs*, Appendix, p. 307.
[45] [Anon] *A Letter from Amsterdam to A Friend in England* (April 1679), in *Somers Tracts*, vol. IX, pp. 86–9.
[46] Dalrymple, *Memoirs*, Appendix, p. v; York wrongly ascribed this correspondence to Shaftesbury and some 'men of his faction'. As the equation of republicanism and presbyterianism suggests, sectarian distinctions were not James' speciality.
[47] Kenyon, *Sunderland*, pp. 35–8.

by Charles, the Duchess of Portsmouth, and Sunderland, to patch things up with Louis, and agree a new pension.[48]

The thinking behind this outrageous return to form by the King was reasonable enough. It was that he couldn't get into any more trouble than he was already in; but he could, if either of these gambits succeeded, and preferably the French, considerably increase his room for manoeuvre. It was, after all, by the successful playing of this French card that the King eventually saved himself in late 1680–1. The attraction of these policies for his ministers was, however, a good deal less obvious. Nothing better illustrates the hardened nerves of a gambler than Sunderland's conduct of both halves of this policy. In the event, although a sum was settled (1,000,000 livres a year for three years) petulance on one side, and arrogance on the other, was to preclude a settlement that would have to wait until 1681. In November 1679 Sunderland was glad to break off negotiations which reminded him uncomfortably of the fate of Danby.[49]

While Sidney's reaction to the public face of this 'foreign policy' can be imagined, the situation was intriguingly complicated by his family relationships with all of those concerned. The overseer of the matter was his nephew Sunderland. The chief architect of these renewed Orangist meanderings was Sir William Temple, son of his close friend, and Sidney client, Sir John. And the envoy appointed by Sunderland to travel to the Hague and negotiate with William was none other than Algernon's own brother Henry. Their preparations amounted, however, to an expensive refitting of the *Titanic*. For the only effect of this reactivation of the Stuart–Orange alliance was the reactivation of its Dutch, French and English opposition in turn.

On 10 July, Sidney wrote sarcastically to Henry Savile:

> I long since found that the design of sending H Sydney into Holland, was like the rest of Sir William Temple's projects, a matter of great depth, and kept so close, that not one of them would speak to me of it; but this day was a se'nnight a gentleman came to see me, took a letter out of his pocket, newly come from Holland, wherein the whole end of his negotiation, is set out very plainly ... [and is] no more, than under pretence of guaranty to draw Holland and Spain into a league with England, which may help the prince of Orange with an occasion of breaking the peace lately made; which I believe will take effect, if the French can be persuaded to sleep three months, and take no notice of it, if the Louvestein party in Holland ... can be brought to believe the prince of Orange thinks of advancing no interest but the public good of the country; and if our house of commons can be so well satisfied with the management of the last business in Flanders, as to be willing to raise a new army under the same conduct.[50]

Having uncovered Temple's scheme, Sidney now took both Sunderland

[48] Dalrymple, *Memoirs*, Appendix, pp. 237, 242.
[49] Kenyon, *Sunderland*, pp. 35–8.
[50] Sidney, 'Letters to Savile' in *Works*, p. 46.

and Henry aside for some political advice. He told them that the proposed alliance would certainly fail in the face of the alliance between the Dutch republicans and D'Avaux. Its only effect would be to 'raise the party in Holland that is least for the Prince of Orange, and cast it into a [further] dependance upon France'. This would, however, be preferable to its success, 'a league that would certainly have produced a rupture of the peace, renewed the war all over Europe, exposed Flanders to be lost the first year (which this must have done; it being as certain, the assistances expected from hence would have failed, as that it hath not in itself that which is necessary for its defence)'.[51]

'This', recorded Sidney to Savile, 'and a great deal more on the like subject was told the Lord Sunderland, and Mr H Sydney before he went; but Sir William, who was taken for the oracle of those parts, assured them, that there was no such thing as a party in Holland inclined to oppose the prince of Orange; that all was submitted unto his authority, and united in desiring such an alliance with us . . . and that the French who had made the peace [of Nimuegen] for fear of us, would by the same reason more exactly keep it . . . I should think him bewitched, that doth not see there are as many falsities, as to matter of fact, and mistakes in judgement in this matter, as there are words; but I see no intention of receding from such counsels, nor remedy for the mischiefs they bring upon us.'[52]

Having failed at the English end of the negotiation, however, Sidney and his republican colleagues in London now made sure it was sabotaged at the other. This they had to do twice, since following the failure of Henry's first mission the project was to be revived in 1680.

When Henry arrived in the United Provinces in August 1679 he found Algernon had been right. He reported that Amsterdam was 'mightily inclined to France. Monsieur d'Estrades [Algernon's old friend from 1665] and Monsieur d'Avaux gain vastly, and I was told I should never do my business here.'[53] Accordingly his offers were dismissed. When he returned to England in October his sister Dorothy reported that 'He lays much upon the English Fanatics, who say we are not to be relied upon.'[54] Accordingly, when the mission was revived again in mid 1680, Dorothy wrote again (to Halifax):

My brother [Henry] says that from this city [London] did come letters to the states of Holland to persuade them not to make a league with us; for we were in so ill condition by the division amongst ourselves, if they quitted France for us they were

[51] *Ibid.*, pp. 50–1.
[52] *Ibid.*, pp. 50–1.
[53] C. Blencowe (ed.), *Diary of the Times of Charles II* (1843), p. 65; Ogg, *The Reign of Charles II*, vol. II, p. 546.
[54] Berry, *Life and Letters of Lady Russell*, p. 158.

ruined . . . It is certain the mutineers are out of their wits, and may be ashamed of the lies they have told.[55]

Once again, however, it was this reading of the situation which carried the day in the Netherlands, and so once again 'Mr [Henry] Sidney's offers were dismiss'd.'[56]

As John Kenyon observed:

Sunderland, in spite of [Algernon] Sidney's warnings, failed to appreciate the strength of the liaison between the Dutch republicans and Louis' ambassador at the Hague, d'Avaux. And he did not realise that his skittish pourparlers, first with Louis, then with William, tended to drive Holland and France closer together, each in mutual fear of the other's making an alliance with England first.[57]

What neither Henry nor Dorothy may have known is that chief among these 'mutineers' was Algernon himself. Indeed taking this chapter together with the last, we may be in a position to offer Sidney the title of the most fractious sibling of the seventeenth century. Observant readers will have noticed the similarity between the reasoning of these letters from London and Algernon's own earlier reasoning to Sunderland and Henry. And they will remember that from mid 1680 London was succumbing to the charms of old Louvesteiners like Sidney and Bethel. But it is the *Memoirs* of D'Avaux that inform us that 'One of the most considerable republicans in Holland had an intimate correspondence with the leading men in the English parliament; and [with] Colonel Sidney, a famous republican, who was afterwards beheaded.'[58]

Through this connection, D'Avaux contacted Sidney himself. By means of this 'considerable republican'

[he] signified to Colonel Sidney . . . that so long as the prince of Orange remained so powerful in the States General, nothing could be more prejudicial to the parliament of England, and the republic of Holland, than to allow the King of Great Britain, to make an alliance with the Prince of Orange, for it was certainly intended to hurt the common liberty; that the grandeur and power of the French Monarch, the pretext for this union, could not possibly be more hurtful to either state, than such an alliance . . . Colonel Sidney wrote to his friend, that he was strongly convinced by the reasons advanced, and that he had likewise communicated them with success, to the majority of the parliament.[59]

Although this section of D'Avaux's memoirs could refer to 1679 or 1680, the latter date seems more likely. The 'leading men in the English parliament', with whom Sidney was on such close terms, were almost certainly Titus, Jones and others. For following the revival of the alliance project in

[55] *Ibid.*, p. 117.
[56] J. Ralph, *The History of England*, vol. 1 (1744), p. 488.
[57] Kenyon, *Sunderland*, pp. 37–8.
[58] *Negotiations of Count d'Avaux*, 4 vols. (1756), vol. I, p. 9.
[59] *Ibid.*, p. 9.

the second half of 1680, it was the formidable financial combination of London and the Lower House that flatly refused to accept it:

The Colonel and his friends were so thoroughly gained, that after a negotiation of three months, the city of London, and the leading members in Parliament, positively refused to furnish such supplies as were necessary for the King of England, to support an alliance with the States General.[60]

THE REPUBLICAN CARD (1679–80)

'The Colonel and his friends' had not simply been 'gained' by the French ambassador. They were attempting to use their contacts with Barillon, with D'Avaux, with the Dutch republicans, in the City and in the House of Commons, to subject the crown to financial and political strangulation. What eventually prevented this, as we have seen, was only the defection of France. As opposition financial pressure began to tell, it thus became an urgent priority to prevent this development.

Accordingly, when Sidney replied to D'Avaux in mid 1680, having voiced his concurrence with their common object, he took the opportunity to warn the ambassador:

that the French King began to give powerful succour to the King of England; that he had sent him lately a considerable sum of money; and that if the King of England, by the assistance of his Christian Majesty, should be able to do without his parliament, in that case, he would become absolute sovereign; and this would oblige them to make an alliance with the States General.[61]

At the same time (26 July 1680), he communicated the same anxiety about French intentions to Savile, complaining about a King who

perhaps doth not always know his own mind, or thinks it a part of his greatness to vex as many as he can ... Those that he sent lately hither, spake of nothing so much as *la gloire de leur Maître*, though perhaps there were more of true glory in the steadiness of a little good common sense, than in all the vanities and whimsies their heads are filled with. But if you find some inconvenience in being obliged ... to comply with them where you are, even we that are afar off from that fire, are so much scorched by it that we expect not trouble but ruin from it.[62]

It was doubtless in the context of this same concern that Sidney reapplied himself to Barillon in the following months. In September the ambassador reported: 'Je suis rentre dans un grand commerce avec le Sieur de Sydney.'[63]

For a glimpse of the precise objects of the strategy of which these consultations formed a part, we are again indebted to d'Avaux. He recorded:

The famous [Dutch] republican ... who wrote to Colonel Sidney, sent me likewise another piece of intelligence which he had of him; that the Parliament of England

---

[60] *Ibid.*, pp. 9–10.   [61] *Ibid.*, pp. 62–3.
[62] Sidney, 'Letters to Savile' in *Works*, p. 56.
[63] Barillon, PRO 31/3, Baschet no. 146, p. 304.

would not come to a reconciliation with the King of England, but upon these terms.
(i) That his Britannic Majesty should renounce all right to prorogue his Parliament by his sole authority; because they pretended this was a power usurped for some years.
(ii) That his Majesty should also give up to Parliament the right of choosing general officers by sea and land.
(iii) And that he should likewise grant them the liberty of naming commissioners for the management of the treasury, and payment of the army.
I know not whether the Prince of Orange was fully apprised of all these designs of the house of commons, which aimed at the intire subversion of the royal authority of a crown to which he aspired.[64]

The centrality of the first demand – which also recalls Sidney's bitterness about the 'annulling' of the triennial act – requires no emphasis. The other two are very like the limitations scheme sponsored (to 'howls of outrage' from York in Edinburgh) by Sidney's friend Essex in the Lords in December 1680.[65] The demand was that Charles surrender to parliament control, firstly over its own being; and secondly over much of the apparatus of the state.

At the same time, finally, Sidney was using his relationship with Barillon to bid directly – against Charles – for French backing for a restoration of the Republic. Like Charles' own counter-manoeuvres, this was not as improbable as it now sounds. As Sidney in effect pointed out, as an absolute monarch Louis had no interest in allowing others to be so. His securest Dutch allies were republicans; why should not the same be true in England?

Barillon's other English contacts (and financial beneficiaries) included Sidney's friends John Hampden jnr and Colonel Titus. They aso included Sir Roger Hill, Sidney's running mate in Amersham from 1679–81. Barillon described Hill as a former 'officer dans les troupes de Cromwel, il est republicquain [sic] et forte vehement contre la cour'.[66] In the Commons, similarly, Barillon noted another close friend of Sidney's in these years, *Col. 'Ingoldsbi [qui] a este Colonel du temps de Cromwell, et l'une des juges du feu Roy'*. During the petitioning campaign of 1680, Barillon recorded among the presenters of a petition in January *'Desborough fils d'un maj-gen sous Cromwell . . . Ierton fils de Henry Ierton . . . Chrispe neveu et heretier [heir] de le regicide R. Wilson, Smith captaine de cavalry sous Cromwell . . .'* and others.[67] He might equally have noted the ex-rumper Colonel Mildmay, who was to support Sidney's electoral petition to the House in December

[64] *Negotiations of Count d'Avaux*, pp. 62–3.
[65] Kenyon, *Sunderland*, p. 68.
[66] PRO 31/3, Baschet no. 142, p. 192; no. 146, p. 243; Dalrymple, *Memoirs*, Appendix, p. 317.
[67] *Ibid.*, p. 316; Baschet no. 146, p. 243; Paris, Ministère des Affaires Etrangères, Correspondence Angleterre no. 137, Supplement 1679–80, p. 150. This point is also made by Houlbrooke, 'Barillon's Embassy', pp. 81–2.

1680, and who presented a petition from Essex. He was confronted by the King with the warning to 'remember forty-one', to which he is said to have responded 'Sir, I remember sixty.'[68]

When the Scots rebelled in 1679, Sidney's excitement was echoed by Barillon, who informed Louis of the similarity of the situation to '*Les troubles d'Ecosse . . . en 1638 . . . Les presbyteriens des deux Royaumes aut de grandes intelligences ensembles.*'[69] When the five popish lords were sent to the tower in December 1678, Barillon reported that this was how proceedings against Strafford had begun in 1640.[70] And in both the growing co-operation between the City and the House of Commons from 1678–9 to 1681, and the decision of the Commons from 1679 to publish its proceedings, Barillon reported strong parallels with the situation from 1640–2.[71]

Of Sidney himself and his associates, Barillon provided a series of illuminating descriptions. The group with which he was said to 'maintain great liaisons' was variously the 'independents and other sectaries', 'the independents and republicans', 'those who want a republic.' 'The most considerable among them' explained Barillon, 'were in the past wars and would like to make another . . . they hope that what has happened [once] can happen again.'[72]

This 'party', he recorded in 1680,

were masters during the late troubles . . . they are strong in London . . . the Duke of Buckingham . . . believes himself at the[ir] head . . . but at the bottom Doctor Owen is the patriarch of the sectaries . . . Mr Pen is chief of the Quakers . . . [and] . . . Mr Sidney . . . is intimate with Mr. [William] Jones, who is a man of the greatest knowledge in the laws of England, and will be chancellor if the party opposed to the court shall gain the superiority.[73]

Barillon described Sidney as having 'the principal credit among the independents'; an opinion which we will see echoed elsewhere. 'He was . . . considerable during . . . the first wars and is a natural enemy to the court . . . a man of great views and very high designs, which tend to the establishment of a republic.' Sidney, he added, 'is not attached to Mr Monmouth, but pretends to make a figure by himself.'[74]

When Sidney, for the reasons discussed, spent a good deal of time with Sunderland between June and August 1679, Barillon reassured Louis:

Mr [Algernon] Sidney has . . . for some time been suspected of being gained by Lord Sunderland; but he always appeared to me to have the same sentiments, and not to

[68] Ronalds, *The Attempted Whig Revolution*, p. 79.
[69] Baschet no 142, pp. 192, 229; no. 143, pp. 263–4.
[70] *Ibid.*, no. 141, pp. 115, 117.
[71] Houlbrooke, 'Barillon's Embassy', p. 82.
[72] Baschet no. 142, pp. 192, 229; no. 144, p. 29.
[73] *Ibid.*, no. 147, pp. 402–3; Dalrymple, *Memoirs*, Appendix, p. 287.
[74] Baschet no. 143, p. 369; no. 146, p. 245.

have changed maxims. He ... is ... intimate with those who are most opposite to the court in parliament ... he is very favourably disposed to what your majesty may desire; and is not willing that England and the States-general should make a league. He is upon bad terms with his brother, who is in Holland, and laughs at the court's making use of him as a negotiator. I believe he is a man who would be very useful, if the affairs of England should be brought to extremities.[75]

For all of these reasons, Sidney felt himself to be, for the second time since the Restoration, the eminently qualified individual to put the case for a republican solution to the French King.[76] At the same time, however, Barillon was receiving, and conveying, the counter-arguments of Charles II. For the second time, again, what is extraordinary about this exchange, and these opponents, is the political assumptions and language they shared. Sidney and the King were products of the same generation; of the same experience of exile, in the same countries (France and the Netherlands); possessed of the same scepticism; the same desire for liberty of conscience; the same interest in trade; the same European perspective. It was more than anything else the passing of their generation, marked forever by the experience of the civil war, which made way for the peaceful political transformations of 1688–1714. To achieve the 'revolution' of 1688–9, it would be necessary to sweep both Stuarts and republicans aside.

Now their counter-proposals to Barillon spoke the same political language, and assumed the same political alternatives. These may have reflected their shared (Franco/Dutch) experience, for the alternatives were monarchy and republicanism, and the language was interest theory. It was in mid 1679, following the Scots rebellion and the prorogation of the new parliament, that Charles instructed Barillon to tell Louis that he must decide whether he wanted an English monarchy, or a republic. The point he made about the latter, a government of the people, was that the inclination of the people was passionately anti-French. Barillon registered the point and wrote to Louis that 'I do not think a republic in England would be in the interests of France; one saw by experience how powerful the nation became under such a united government.'[77]

In this remarkable exchange, both Charles and Barillon echo the assumptions of Sidney's own republican interest theory. Here Charles offered monarchy to Louis precisely to achieve the frustration of foreign endeavour – the 'contrariety' to public interest – which was the basis of Sidney's republicanism. Barillon agreed, equating a united 'republican public interest' with effective foreign power, as Sidney did. Once again therefore, as in 1665–6, the obstacle Sidney faced was not any weakness in his own case;

[75] *Ibid.*, no. 143, p. 369.
[76] Scott, *Sidney and the English Republic*, pp. 181–4.
[77] Jusserand, *Recueil des Instructions*, p. 271.

either practical or theoretical. Rather it was the opposite. For France, as earlier for De Witt, what made a revival of the English Republic unacceptable was its own previous military success. That achievement, for Sidney, had been the most formative experience of his political life. Now it was his perpetual obstacle.

Thrown back again to the situation of the *Court Maxims*, Sidney did not, however, accept defeat. He applied himself to Barillon with counter-arguments in the same interest language. These repeated the core theory of the *Court Maxims* with a precision which makes them important corroborating evidence for Sidney's authorship of that tract. They also read like an explicit attempt to pre-empt the eventual settlement of 1688–9. Several of Barillon's London contacts had been applying such arguments to him 'for some time'; but 'Mr Sidney . . . talks to me with the most force and the most openness in this matter.'[78] Sidney and his friends wished Barillon to

understand that is an old error to believe that it is against the interest of France to suffer England to become a Republick; they endeavour to prove [that] . . . the union of England and the United Provinces, under a Protestant King, authorised as the Prince of Orange would be, is much less conformable to the true interest of France than a Republick, which would be more occupied with trade than any other thing, and would believe, as Cromwell did, that it should gain rather at the expense of Spain than of France; they add, that the interest of England as a Republick, and that of Holland governed as it is, could not easily agree, wheras the Prince of Orange can re-unite in his person the power of the States General and of England together. In fine they establish for a fundamental principle that the House of Stuart and that of Orange are inseperably united, that their common interest engages them to augment their power in England and in Holland, and that it is the interest of France to maintain the liberties and priviledges of both nations, and to endeavour rather . . . the ruin of those that would oppress them: they even believe that the safety of the Catholick religion might be established in England, if people were not afraid that a Catholick Prince would be in a position to change the government and laws; and they observe by the example of Holland how much the condition of the Catholicks in Holland is better than in England.

All of this is vintage Sidney: the basic arguments of the *Court Maxims*, adapted as they had been in 1670 for Turenne. Even the offer of a liberty of conscience so broad as to include Catholics has survived into a time when, with Sidney's approbation, numerous priests and Jesuits have recently been executed for treason. The distinction between the threat of the Counter-Reformation, and the ideal of liberty of religious worship for all, remained as clear in Sidney's mind as it had always been. The only entirely opportunistic – not to say dishonest – part of the argument is the implication that the Republic would follow Cromwell in opposing Spain. Both Sidney and Bethel, author of *The World's Mistake in Oliver Cromwell* (1668), knew better than that.[79]

[78] Dalrymple, *Memoirs*, Appendix, p. 313 (for the following passage).
[79] Scott, *Sidney and the English Republic*, pp. 124–6 and chs. 12–14.

6.3 CONCLUSION

The importance of these transactions for the biographer of Sidney is obvious enough. But their importance for the history of this period should also be clear. It is too easy to assume, in the aftermath of 1688 and the historiographical perspective it has bequeathed, that these efforts and perceptions were incoherent, immoral, unimportant, or any combination of the three. But they were none of these. On the contrary, Sidney's political logic, and his assumptions, were (in their own terms) entirely correct. They made him dangerous enough to help pull down one government, and rather too dangerous to be put in charge of another. As von Ranke reminds us, it was the participants in this perception, the opponents of the Stuart–Orange alliance, who determined events in this period. We have been taught, on the contrary, that it was the prophets of 1688: the Earl of Shaftesbury, the exclusion bill, the House of Commons, which moved this crisis. In fact it was a last fling of some of those who would be vanquished by 1688 – particularly the French, and the republicans. In this respect, Shaftesbury's denunciation of Sidney in 1680 as a 'French pensioner, and my Lord of Sunderland's spy'[80] registered the anger of political impotence.

Finally, what has been drawn in here is the European context for a more specific aspect of this crisis. That aspect was the last chapter – practical as well as ideological – of the seventeenth-century English republican experience. The circumstances of this republican revival were both historical – as part of a more general revival of the past; and European – as part of a revival of republicanism in two countries. During the English crisis that followed, with French support, the capital city became a republican bastion; it produced new and important works of republican theory; it formed a powerful alliance with the leadership of a radicalised House of Commons; it influenced foreign policy; and it caused, accordingly, an urgent debate about republicanism among the ambassadors and heads of State involved. By late 1680, as von Ranke put it: 'It seemed to foreigners that the city was, as it were, a political republic by the King's side.'[81]

Throughout this situation, Sidney's hopes were resting on the same historical foundation as his frustrations. This was the precocious power and achievement of the English Republic itself. It may above all have been this, rather than any of the circumstances of the present, which prevented the Restoration crisis from becoming what he wished for: a Restoration of the Republic.

---

[80] Dorothy Sidney, quoted in Berry, *Life and Letters of Lady Russell*, pp. 128, 131.
[81] Von Ranke, *History of England*, vol. IV, p. 159.

7

Domestic politics 1678–9

it has long been the practise of the Popish and Arbitrary Party, that the King should call frequent, short, and useless Parliaments.[1]

7.1 INTRODUCTION

In 1678, as in 1640, the struggle against popery and arbitrary government was the struggle for protestantism, and for parliaments. On this the whole nation was agreed: both 'conservatives' and 'radicals'; both the architects and the victims of the Restoration settlement. It was the breadth of this political consensus which gave the crises of both of these years such force.

Now again however, as from 1640–2, the unfolding of the crisis itself was to test the limits of this consensus, and to end it. It did so because, as in 1660, the consensus was negative: agreement that the nation was in danger did not equal agreement about how it should be saved. For Sidney, the struggle for protestantism involved, indeed hinged on, the struggle for liberty of conscience. For others it was the King's attempts to introduce liberty of conscience that had provided the first evidence that protestantism was in danger. For Sidney the struggle for parliaments involved, indeed hinged on, the struggle for parliamentary sovereignty. For others it was parliamentary sovereignty which had given England its harshest experience of arbitrary government itself. In the end Sidney would die a sacrifice, not so much to the arbitrary power of Charles II, as to the nation's memory of his own.

Sidney's involvement with the first phase of the domestic crisis (1678–9) centred upon two sets of relationships. The first was with the quite extraordinary network of his close relations who, as we have seen, dominated the court after Danby's demise. Since Sidney had himself helped to bring about that demise, in liaison with members of this group, we have already come across some of these names. The post-Danby court was to be dominated by two nephews of Sidney (Halifax and Sunderland) and one cousin (Essex).

---

[1] *A Letter from a Gentleman of Quality to his Friend* (1681), quoted in *His Majesties Declaration Defended: In a Letter to a Friend* (1681), p. 4.

126

They surrounded themselves with clients and members of the same family network, equally well known, and/or related to Sidney (William Temple; William Coventry; Henry Savile; Henry Sidney; Sir William Jones).

The other set of relationships was political and religious in character rather than familial and aristocratic. This was the no less extensive network of Sidney's nonconformist and republican friends in and around London. The best-documented early relationship within this group was with William Penn, and it was in partnership with Penn that Sidney attempted from early 1679 to get himself elected to parliament. Eventually, as the crisis radicalised, Sidney's friendship with Penn ended, but his involvement with the political core of this community grew. By 1680–1 it had become a significant personal power base, linked to both the government of London and the leadership of the House of Commons. After the abandonment of parliaments and the beginning of religious persecution in 1681 it was from this community that plans for insurrection grew.

Both of these groups had links outside the country, and so each has bequeathed us an important set of Sidney's letters: to (Halifax's brother) Henry Savile in Paris, and (Penn's friend) Benjamin Furly in Rotterdam. It is from these letters that much of our information about Sidney's relationships and activities in this period comes. The extent of Sidney's links with both of these groups is a reminder of two aspects of the political circumstances of these years: not only how well connected Sidney was in 1679, but how small this political world in London was. Within the community of aristocratic high politics Sidney was related to everybody because everybody was related to one another. Moreover these already claustrophobic parameters were pulled tighter between 1678 and 1683. Although when government was functioning normally it depended upon the localities, when it entered a period of crisis, as 1640–2 had shown, the shape and outcome of the struggle centred increasingly on London. In the 1640s the eventual result had been the republican government form of a city state. Once again by 1680 the principal danger to the monarchy had become the fact that it had lost control of London. Between 1680 and 1683, as in the 1640s, the principal political battleground became the crown's efforts to recapture its own capital city. Once again this was the struggle into which Sidney would become absorbed.

Finally the extent of his personal connections, at court, in London, and among the diplomatic community, had one obvious consequence for Sidney. They made it even more difficult than it already was for him to remain aloof from events. Many of his early activities, in relation both to the European situation and the court, began in this grey area between personal and political involvement.

In this respect, the electoral contests beginning in January 1679 are significant, for the decision to stand for parliament is a declaration of political intent of an undeniably public character. Somehow, since Sidney's promises to the King two years earlier, a good deal of relaxation had taken place on both sides. When informed of his election for Amersham in August 1679 Charles remarked rather cryptically that 'he did believe Mr Algernon Sydney would prove an honest man'.[2] There was of course nothing inherently sinister about this shift from informal to formal political involvement; rather perhaps the reverse. But these early activities proved to be the thin end of the wedge, and as the course of the crisis itself first polarised the country, and then closed down the legitimate channels for protest, Sidney proved one of those willing to follow the logic of his involvement to its illegitimate conclusion. It is hardly surprising if, after losing control of his House of Commons and his capital city (again) for three years, Charles finally repented of his earlier lenience and decided to bring down the axe on this 'most opinionated republican in his realm'. It was a decision which echoed, by way of retrospective confirmation, the earlier fate of Sir Henry Vane.

7.2 THE QUAKER CONNECTION

Between 1679 and 1681 Sidney mounted five election campaigns. In a period which saw only three general elections, this record was achieved by adding a by-election, and by standing for two seats in one contest simultaneously. Thereafter Sidney petitioned the House four times, once after each result, and finished his life in fierce litigation with the innkeepers of Amersham concerning payment for liquor consumed in the last attempt. It is possible in elections to know how much the campaign cost, or who voted for whom. In Sidney's case we know how much was drunk, what, and by whom. As a whole these campaigns yielded, not a parliamentary seat, but some remarkable recipes for cocktails.

It is a pleasant irony therefore that what equally characterised these events, and a number of these innkeepers, was their strong involvement with quakerism. Both of the first two attempts, in Guildford (Surrey) and Bramber (Sussex), were joint campaigns by Sidney and William Penn. Both seats lay in the part of south-eastern England dominated by the landholdings of the Sidneys in Kent and Sussex, the Percys at Petworth, the Pelhams at Halland (Thomas Pelham was married to Algernon's sister Lucy) and close to Penn's Sussex house at Worminghurst. The remaining three contests took

<hr>

[2] Letter, Ralph Montagu to Henry Sidney, 11 Aug., Blencowe (ed.), *Diary of the Times of Charles II*, pp. 70–1.

place in Amersham (Buckinghamshire), a strongly quaker borough dominated by Penn's close friend Isaac Pennington.[3]

For Sidney at least, as we will see, this quaker community was not a closed denominational unit. It formed one part of the larger community of 'independents and other sectaries' already identified by Barillon. Sidney gave an exaggerated picture of its extent when he spoke of 'above a million men, that go under the name of nonconformists'; and of 'an act for the banishing of the papists ... penned ... so well by the industry of the bishops, that if the commons should pass it without amendment, all the nonconformists of London would be driven out of town and all the shops shut up'.[4] Sidney's campaigns in Amersham, as we will see, were managed by baptists, republicans and other sympathetic members of this London community, alongside the quakers.

Particular light, however, is thrown on Sidney's relations with the quakers by his partnership with Penn, and his correspondence with Furly. It was probably through their shared relationship with Furly that Sidney's friendship with Penn began. In early 1678 Sidney wrote to Furly of his pleasure at the new friendship his introduction had given him occasion to begin; in August he continued 'I think in a few dayes to see our friend WP in his owne house and shortly after to return again hither.'[5] It was partly through Penn that Sidney became involved with his quaker and other nonconformist merchant friends in London: John Swinton, John Osgood, Gerard Roberts, and Penn's partner in the famous jury case of 1670, William Meade, a wealthy London cloth-merchant.[6]

These connections are important, not only because they remind us, from Furly to Penn, of Sidney's attraction to politically active quakers. They also remind us, yet again, of the general connections between this long-persecuted English community and its Dutch counterparts over the channel. It was to this Dutch (Louvestein) community that letters went from Sidney and his friends in London to frustrate royal policy. It was with the French ambassadors, both in London and Amsterdam, that such policies were co-ordinated, and to whom hopes were offered, under a republican government, of Dutch-style toleration for catholics in London. It was to this Dutch community and its economic achievements that the English community and state were urged to look by Sidney, Penn, Wolsely, Locke, and Bethel. And it was to the same Dutch haven that members of this London

---

[3] H.E. Wildes, *William Penn* (New York 1975), pp. 115–16; M.M. Dunn emphasises the extent of Penn's Amersham contacts in *Politics and Conscience*, p. 37.
[4] Sidney, 'Letters to Savile' in *Works*, pp. 29, 54.
[5] Forster (ed.), *Letters of Locke*, p. 88.
[6] H. Barbour and A. Roberts (eds.), *Early Quaker Writings 1650–1700* (Michigan 1973); Dunn, *Politics and Conscience*, p. 13.

community fled when things became politically dangerous. It was for this reason that Furly's friends in this period would include not only Sidney and Penn, but Locke.[7]

This relationship is of particular historical importance, in several respects. It is so religiously, for obvious reasons. It is so ideologically, because English political theorists of such stature were involved, and both Locke and Sidney would produce or perfect political work in the Netherlands itself. And it is so economically, because this was the period when London, now the largest city in Europe, stood poised to replace Amsterdam as the principal European entrepot for world trade. So much of importance in seventeenth-century British history: in politics, religion, agriculture, and trade, amounted to imitation of the Dutch achievement by its larger neighbour; and we find consistent exhortations to just such imitation in the writings of Sidney, Bethel, Penn, Wolsely and Locke (among others). We will see in the next chapter what happened when Bethel attempted to introduce into London's municipal arrangements some of the Dutch-style frugality which he considered the necessary precondition for 'the Rise and Glory of a Trading City'.[8]

It should not surprise us therefore that we find, in Sidney's correspondence with Furly, just this idiosyncratic combination of religion, politics, finance and trade. Its nineteenth-century editor, who had expected the first two elements but not the others, was embarassed. 'The Patriot', he observed darkly, 'seems to have been not inattentive to affairs of his private fortune.'[9] Nor are the connections always obvious – as when Sidney wrote in April 1678:

Your Friends [the quakers] seem to have succeeded well the last weeke, before the Com[ittee] of the House of Commons, as to being distinguished from Papists ... never the lesse I finde many Parliament men very bitter upon them in private conversations, as I think without knowing why, and therefore perhaps the more I desire you to let me know ... your opinion as to the present wayes of imploying money, for my father hath left me somme at interest, which I call in ... and if I live upon the maine stock, it will soone comme to nothing.[10]

In addition to requesting financial advice, Sidney ordered trade goods as well. He asked Furly to send him 'the best and warmest Indian gowne that you can finde, which I presume will be had at Amsterdam' and some of 'that spirate of cinamon that you sent me once into France'.[11] This shopping list gradually extended to horses, purchased by Sidney through Furly for his friend Essex. In addition he solicited Furly's help in investing the money of others:

---

[7] See Scott, *Sidney and the English Republic*, ch. 13.
[8] See chapter 8 below.
[9] Forster (ed.), *Letters of Locke*, Preface, p. cxv.
[10] *Ibid.*, pp. 84–8.   [11] *Ibid.*, p. 88.

A friend of mine, seeing the uncertainty of things, is desirous to place four or five thousand pounds beyond seas ... John Swinton proposeth the imploying of it in exchange, but I desire to know your opinion upon that point.[12]

Such fluctuation and uncertainty was the keynote of the world of commerce, as of politics. Thus Sidney echoed his political views when he spoke of 'the bungling and dissimulation that is too much in fashion ... you know their [sic] are upon the Exchange men of many parties, interests, and principles, soe as one may prevaile one day, and another the next.'[13] He also became, for Furly, in a typical act of epistolary relativism, a merchant himself. It was thus that he discussed his own affairs:

A friend ... hath lately sent me a parcell of French wines, and twenty pieces of brandy, which I am told would be worth above fifty pounds the tunne in a moneth, if we should have a warre, but not knowing what will be the end of the business now in agitation, I chose rather to take forty pounds a tunne yesterday, then to expect a better market.[14]

And Furly's:

I hear you have a huge proportion of grain come in your hands, and as farre as I can guesse, unless you have a probability of being further supplied from the Balticke, things can hardly goe so as to hinder you from gaining much by keeping it, for I think none can comme from England or Germany, soe as if there be a warre the advantage must be very great.[15]

Sidney invested some of his own money overseas with Furly, and some within this quaker financial community in London. There were predictable consequences. In January 1679 – the month of his first election campaign with Penn – he complained bitterly to Furly:

Gerard Roberts, whoe was to have payed me £297.10s the 16th of April last, hast dealt very vilely with me, and Will Mead, and John Osgood, whoe have the management of his businesse, not at all better, and to say the truth, I having foreborne to trouble him for my money at Will: Penn's desire ... [but one] could not find more nigling, shifting, cavilling, and, indeed, downright lying and knavery from the men of the worst repute in London, than I doe from all three of them, and particularly Mead and Osgood are much more inclinable to cast unjust reproaches upon Will: Penn, then to doe me the justice he adviseth, which, together, with what is suspected of John Swinton ... will much impaire the credite those of your profession have hitherto had.[16]

Students of Sidney's French experience will recognise an unmistakable odour of gunshot and partridge feathers about this outburst. Its effect was

---

[12] *Ibid.*, pp. 92–3. [13] *Ibid.*, p. 91.
[14] *Ibid.*, p. 92. [15] *Ibid.*, p. 92.
[16] *Ibid.*, p. 89: It is not completely clear here whether Sidney means Furly's religious or mercantile 'profession'. The former seems likely; profession of faith is a more seventeenth-century use of the word; the story is being related about quakers to a quaker; and it is not clear that the mercantile profession had a significant reputation for honesty at any time.

to remain with him to the eve of his execution in 1683 when he wrote in his
Apology:

I believe that the people of God in England have, in theis late yeares, generally grown
faint. Somme, through feare, have deflected from the integrity of their principles.
Some have too deeply plunged themselves in worldly cares, and soe as they might
enjoy their trades and wealth, have less regarded the treasure that is layd up in
heaven. But I think there are very many who have kept their garments unspotted;
and hope that God will deliver them and the nation for their sakes.[17]

The clear survivor of such disturbances, in 1678 at least, was Sidney's
relationship with Penn. About this, and the electoral partnership into which
it issued, some historians have expressed puzzlement. Mary Dunn
concluded:

Just why [Penn] worked so hard for Algernon Sidney is something of a mystery. He
had known the Sidneys for many years, and he shared some of Algernon's
experimental republican principles. But W P did not share Algernon's enthusiasm for
rebellion against tyrants nor his eagerness for a warlike state.[18]

Yet it is not clear why we need expect identity in details of theory
unrelated to the basis of their practical co-operation. That basis was liberty
of conscience, the point of which was toleration of variety in matters indifferent, for the purpose of bringing men together. To accept this was to be
what Penn called 'Men of large principles ... as will Inviolably maintain
Civil Rights for all that will live soberly and civilly'; dogmatic protestants
were as bad as papists: 'such Partial men don't love England, but a Sect'.[19]
On his side, Sidney did not share Penn's pacifism, but their point of identity
was 'large principles' for the good of 'England', not the theological terrain
of a sect. What is surely more noticeable, and what is genuinely striking, is
the fundamental *identity*, both in principles and language, between Penn's
and Sidney's political theory.

Indeed beside Milton's, no political theory is more like Sidney's than
Penn's. (The aspect of Sidney's theory both lack is the same: its Machiavel-
lianism.) Penn shares with Sidney his political language (interest theory; in
both its international and national versions), most of his sources, and most
of his religious and political ideas. Throughout Penn's work we can hear
Sidney's *Court Maxims* in particular, something that should not surprise us
given their common connection with Furly, and their common education at
Saumur.

Like Sidney, Penn defined true religion as a matter of practice and conduct, not 'profession' (hence the unimportance of the fact that Sidney was
not a quaker). We can hear the *Maxims* in Penn's argument that:

[17] Sidney, *Apology*, p. 31.
[18] M.M. Dunn, *Politics and Conscience*, pp. 32–4; (ed.), *The Papers of William Penn*, p. 546.
[19] Philanglus [Penn], *Englands Great Interest* (1679), pp. 1–3.

the government of conscience belongs to God, and cannot be delegated to another, because no other can be infallible. Christ's kingdom is a spiritual kingdom; worship at the command of the magistrate is not the spiritual worship which God requires.[20]

Like Sidney and Milton, Penn used the same source – Matthew Paris – for his assertions that the Saxons were a free people, and that 'the conquest is no conquest; the Normans adopted Saxon law'. Like them both (and Locke) Grotius was his source for natural law theory and the conclusion that 'Liberty and Property' are a man's 'Natural and Civil Rights'.[21] In his discussion of history since 1066 Penn used many of the same illustrations as Sidney, emphasising the absurdity of tying religion to government decree by reference to the frequent changes of official religion under the Tudors and Stuarts, and invoking the same old scapegoats in 'Empson and Dudley'. Penn's theory was based on the same basic distinction between the government of men (will), and law (contract), the former opening the road to tyranny.[22]

The closeness of Penn and Sidney's interest theory has been discussed in more detail elsewhere.[23] In 1675 Penn had written of the need to govern 'on a ballance [that addictive Polybian/Harringtonian word, adapted yet again], as near as possible, of the severall Religious interests'. This is the same advice we found Sidney offering Charles II in 1670: via Penn it found its way to James again in 1687. In 1679, in *One Project*, there developed the claim that 'Civil Interest is the foundation of Government' in general. It is again interesting, in this year of contact with Sidney and Furly, to find Penn defining this 'Civil Interest' in true Dutch style, like Bethel and Locke, as not simply the maintenance of liberty and property, but their increase. 'Civil Interest is a Legal Endeavour to keep Rights, or augment honest Profits . . . men join together to protect their civil interest, civil rights – where each is sure of his own, he is happy to make a contribution to the whole.'

For an illustration of the 'power of a United Civil Interest' Penn begged his reader to look at the Netherlands.[24] In 1675 Penn had argued that 'toleration was good for commerce and trade . . . [and] affirmed that the greatness and prosperity of Holland were due to religious toleration'.[25] When dissenters are persecuted, argued Penn, 'This oppression causes Poverty and destruction among industrious trading people who are great contributors to the King's revenue by their traffick: which Consequence,

---

[20] Penn, *The Great Case of Liberty of Conscience once more Briefly Debated and Defended* (1671), quoted in C.E. Whiting, *Studies in English Puritanism 1660–1688* (London 1968), pp. 139–40.
[21] Penn, *England's Present Interest Considered* (1675) in *Works* (1756), vol. I, pp. 676, 701–2.
[22] *Ibid.*, pp. 687, 694–5; vol. II, p. 482.
[23] Scott, *Sidney and the English Republic*, ch. 13, pp. 209–10; 216–17.
[24] Penn, *Works*, vol. I, pp. 682–3, 685–6.   [25] Whiting, *Puritanism*, p. 140.

how far it may consist with the Credit and Interest of the Government, I leave to better judgements.'[26] Everything about the King's policies suggests that Charles himself was firmly persuaded by this argument.

It was thus natural that Sidney and Penn's shared religious and political concerns should have issued into a joint practical exercise in which Penn, who could not stand for public office because he could not take oaths, joined forces to work for Sidney, who could do so. Nevertheless, nimble exploiter of political patronage though Penn had always been, such open electioneering by a leading quaker was new, and it resulted in the politicisation of the quaker communities at Guildford and Amersham. This sent a ripple through the quaker community in general, and exposed the sect to the crackdown against dissent that came with the loyalist reaction of 1681–5. For this reason the whole episode has been condemned by some historians. According to C.E. Whiting, Penn's electioneering for Sidney 'caused much searching of the heart amongst many of the Quakers . . . [and] . . . did them a great deal of harm. The Conventicle Act was enforced with rigour in many places because the Quakers and others had taken the opposition side in the elections.'[27]

About this two things must be said. The first is that we do indeed see Sidney here in a familiar role: as the *agent provocateur*, eliminating the distinction between religious and political dissent, rejecting religious quietism. He was now pursuing that role in practice as previously (in the *Court Maxims*) in theory. On the other hand, Whiting's judgement is a retrospective one, and the dividing line between politics and religion was not as clear in this period. Penn, the political theorist, had always demonstrated that the religious liberty he sought was a political issue and had to be won by political means; it was thanks to the efforts of himself, Sidney and patrons like Halifax and Shaftesbury that this goal came closer to realisation in 1679–81 than at any time since 1660. Later too, under James, Penn has been criticised by historians for the company his dedication to this object led him to keep ('collaborator' is a favoured term).[28] This is the high-minded objection of the armchair critic, removed from the circumstances in which he operated; it also overlooks the single-minded greatness by which Penn eventually enrolled himself in the history, not of gestures, but of results.

---

[26] Penn, *Works*, vol. I, p. 693.
[27] Whiting, *Puritanism*, pp. 175–6.
[28] J.H. Plumb, *The Growth of Political Stability in England 1675–1725* (1967), p. 41.

7.3 THE FIRST ELECTION: GUILDFORD JANUARY–
FEBRUARY 1679

[Choose rather] a stranger ... recommended by an unquestionable Hand, than a
Neighbour Ill-affected to your Interest.[29]

It is not so exactly true to say that Sidney stood for Guildford in this
election, as that he attempted to, and was subjected to a series of comic
rebuffs.

The King's sudden dissolution of his long parliament exposed the crown
to a series of elections beyond its political experience or its capacity to
control. The result was high excitement and a certain level of chaos. By 19
March the parliament had received twenty-eight petitions contesting
individual results; by May the number had grown to fifty, many of these
debating the nature of the franchise in each seat.[30] As the crisis progressed,
Houses were dissolved and new elections called before many of these could
be heard, the number of petitions and the confusion surrounding them
multiplied. It was into this melting pot that sometime in January 1679
Sidney and Penn took the plunge. On 28 January a correspondent reported:
'Amongst many others who endeavour to be chosen, Major Wildman, Mr
Nevil, Colonel Sallawaie and Algernon Sidney are mentioned – men well
known for their Commonwealth principles'.[31] Already, in short, the lid of
1660 was lifting to reveal the remnants of 1659 beneath.

One attraction of Guildford for Sidney was almost certainly the identity
of the incumbent, Thomas Dalmahoy, Lauderdale's principal apologist in
the Commons. Sidney's letters to Savile make it clear that 'Latherdale', the
tormentor of Scots dissent, had been selected as the next pillar of the
Restoration regime for destruction after Danby. It was indeed for an
intemperate attack on Lauderdale in the House that Savile himself had been
ordered out of the King's sight 'forever' in May 1678.[32]

The best-known feature of this first Sidney/Penn campaign is its
manifesto, *England's Great Interest in the Choice of This New Parliament*
(1679). This directed itself squarely to the primary issues in the crisis,
popery and arbitrary government, in this reign, not the next.

Thus of the five demands it put forward three were: the removal of
'corrupt and arbitrary' ministers and counsellors; the defeat and punishment of 'pensioners' of the previous parliament (Dalmahoy presumably
included); and the securing of the 'Ancient laws' by new ones 'such as relate
to *frequent parliaments* [my emphasis], the only true check on arbitrary

---

[29] Philanglus, *England's Great Interest*, p. 3.
[31] HMC Ormonde 36.7, p. 311.
[30] Plumb, *Political Stability*, p. 41.
[32] Haley, *Shaftesbury*, p. 448.

ministers'. This was underpinned by a statement of the true 'fundamental rights of the Commons of England', of the correct relationship between legislative and executive power, and of the 'Property' that parliaments were elected to represent, in respect of which 'every man is a sort of little Soveraign to himself'. It was these concerns, rather than exclusion, that lay at the heart of the political thought of this period, receiving classic treatment in the *Two Treatises* of Locke.[33]

The remaining two demands predictably centred on the other key concern: popery. It placed the equally universal demand that the plot be pursued ('the Trojan Horse with an Army in the belly of it'), alongside Sidney and Penn's particular concern with the ease of protestant consciences. This was supported by a ringing rebuke against protestant persecution: true christians are good men, not opiniated men, and to hate popery but practise persecution yourself is to 'hate the papists, but not Popery'. Finally these two threads, political and religious, were brought together thus: 'that Principle which introduced Implicit Faith and Blind Obedience in Religion, will also introduce Implicit Faith and Blind Obedience in Government ... This is that fatal Mischief Popery brings with it to Civil Society.' Sidney was to repeat this point in the *Discourses* against Filmer's statement that in politics 'an implicit faith is given to the meanest artificer'. The pamphlet ended on a highly practical note: advising electors in Guildford to rather choose a 'Stranger ... if recommended by an unquestionable Hand, than a Neighbour Ill-affected to your Interest'.[34]

The authorities in Guildford, however, seem to have cocked their municipal ear to a different sort of pamphlet, and a different kind of electoral advice. Another contribution to the same election was *An Impartial Survey of such as are not, and such as are, fitly Qualified for Candidates for the approaching Parliament*.[35] This listed among 'those that are not': 'Presbyterians, Independents, Anabaptists, Rumpers, Pensioners, Worcester-Fight Men, Papists, Quakers, Levellers, Brownists, and Fifth-Monarchy Men'. This was followed by the witty *A More Exact and Necessary Catalogue of Pensioners in the Long Parliament Than is Yet Extant*,[36] playing upon the now double meaning of 'long parliament'. Shifting attention from Charles' institution of this name to its more famous predecessor, it listed

[33] Philanglus, *England's Great Interest*, pp. 1–3.
[34] *Ibid.*, pp. 1–3; on this pamphlet and its authorship see my *Sidney and the English Republic*, ch. 13, and also William Hull, *William Penn* (New York 1937), p. 214. The identification of 'Philanglus' here with Penn has led (for instance in the Cambridge University Library catalogue) to the attribution to him of other works using the same pseudonym like *The Protestants Remonstrance Against Pope and Presbyter* (1681), which he certainly didn't write.
[35] *An Impartial Survey* (1679), pp. 1–2.
[36] Both of these tracts may be found in the Cambridge University Library Sel.2.118.

among the 'pensioners' of the latter 'Algernon Sidney, Governor of Dover Castle'. In the event the loyal Corporation of Guildford showed no inclination to welcome an interloping 'Rumper and Independent' assisted by 'Quakers' as their MP.

Election to Guildford lay in those, it was eventually determined, who were paying scot and lot – who numbered about 170. Sidney informed the Mayor of his intention to stand and desired him to inform the Corporation, to which the Mayor replied 'that both himselfe and they were engaged to Mr Delmahoy, and that it was the Custome of the Towne, for the Electors to vote as the Magistrates [who were the Mayor and Aldermen] did'.[37]

Sidney was deeply unimpressed by this intelligence, but he required the co-operation of the magistrates on one point: 'that he heard Mr Delmahoy's Party had given out, that he was incapable of being chosen a Burgesse for that Towne, because he was no Freeman; to prevent which Objection, he did tender himselfe to [the Mayor], and desire he might be made Free of the Towne of Guilford'.

The Mayor equivocated and promised to confer with his associates. He also equivocated about the date of the election while promising to give 'the Colonell . . . timely Notice thereof'. According to Sidney he subsequently called a snap election 'the next Day [1 March] at 9, which was Markett Day, and never knowne before'.

The result was that when Sidney presented himself for election 'the Recorder . . . asked if he was a Freeman; and being answered no; he, in the Court House, where the Election was, openly declared before the Electors, he could not be chosen, although he had Plurality of Voices'. Among other simultaneous indignities 'severall of those, that would have poled for the Colonell, were laughed at and affronted, and refused their Pole, because they did not pronounce the Colonell's Name right' and

One Mr Penn, a Quaker, appearing for the Colonell, was called into the Court . . . and told by the Recorder he was a Jesuite (an Affront to the Colonell) to whom the Recorder would have tendred Oathes (at that Time contrary to Law) and at last the Mayor turned him out of the Court, and forbid him to appeare amongst the Colonell's Party, to the great Discouragement of them; and more particularly to such as were of the same Perswasion with Mr Penn; amongst which Party, the Colonell had severall Voices.[38]

The evening of this humiliation Penn wrote to Sidney advising him on his petition to the House and offering his lobbying services in support.

the Conjuncture considerd; thy Qualifications, and Alliance, and his Ungratefulness to the House . . . all may amount to an unfair Election . . . I offer to waite presently

[37] Henning (ed.), *House of Commons*, p. 410; Collins (ed.), *Letters and Memorials*, vol. II, p. 153.
[38] *Ibid.*, p. 153.

upon the Duke of Buckingham, Earl of Shaftesbury, Lord Essex, Lord Halifax, Lord Hollis, Lord Grey etc. to use their utmost Interest . . . I hope the Disapointment so strainge . . . does not move thee; thou (as thy Frends) had a conscientious Regard to England; and to be putt aside, by such base Ways, is really a Suffering for Righteousness; thou hast embarqu't thy self with them, that seek, and love, and chuse the best Thing: and Number is not Weight with Thee . . . it looks not a fair and clear Election . . . thy selfe so often putt by, a Thing not refused to one of thy Condition.[39]

Sidney's petition was referred to the Committee of Priviledges and Elections on 28 March, but not reported before the prorogation on 27 May. He thus remained confined to the role of observer, based in Leicester House, and staying abreast of developments at court and in parliament through his contacts in each. But the experience at Guildford hadn't been wasted; it was built on in Sidney and Penn's next election attempt, and it seems to have rather rattled those involved. At the next contest in August Delmahoy took the opportunity to retire, and it was reported that nevertheless the municipal authorities of that loyal borough had called their second snap election in a row.[40]

7.4 THE SAVILE CONNECTION APRIL–OCTOBER 1679

I continue to give you an account of what I hear because these irregular motions are often the forerunners of great matters; and as they denote the temper of a nation, they give good grounds for guessing what it will end in. (Sidney to Savile 5 May 1679.)[41]

INTRODUCTION

We know of Sidney's view of events between March, when the new parliament met, and July, when it was dissolved, from thirteen letters he wrote to Henry Savile. These have been widely used by historians, but biographers of Sidney have been disappointed by the (relative) caution with which they express his views. As Sidney explained to Furly on 23 March:

I am not like your other correspondents, soe busy in hunting after mony that I could not have leisure to write to you of other matters, but the truth is, letters are soe often opened, that noe man in his senses will write anything that is not fit for the publike view, and that which is soe, every man sees in the publike papers.[42]

Yet the truth is that these letters are extremely revealing, read with Sidney's background and preoccupations in mind. Indeed on a number of

[39] Dunn, *Penn Papers*, p. 547.
[40] *Commons Journal* (1679), p. 578; E. Lipson, 'The Elections to the Exclusion Parliaments 1678–81', *English Historical Review*, 28 (1913), 60.
[41] Sidney, 'Letters to Savile' in *Works*, p. 28.
[42] Forster, *Letters of Locke*, p. 94.

occasions, as in the *Discourses*, where a similar policy of caution was attempted, Sidney is frank to the point of riskiness. Where this is not the case it is not just what he says but what he chooses to speak about, and at what length, that make his reading of the events of this period clear.

When Savile was posted to Paris in March 1679, Sidney determined to express his continuing gratitude to him for facilitating his return to England by furnishing regular news from London 'lest others should . . . leave you in the dark, as my friends did me when I was abroad . . . You [were] so much afore-hand in obliging me when I most wanted a friend, that I cannot hope in the long time to pay my debt . . . but you may be sure of all that is in my reach.'[43]

This posting made the irreverent Savile a 'courtier'; a fact about which Sidney teased him. It attached him, more to the point, to the whole family network which combined to dominate the high politics of 1679. This was to be Shaftesbury's first deep frustration of this crisis; that Danby had finally been destroyed, by friends of Halifax and Sunderland, not himself, to usher in a new era dominated by this Spencer–Savile–Sidney network, not himself. This was not because Halifax was less 'radical': it was Shaftesbury who inveighed against Halifax's limitations scheme 'as much more prejudicial to the crown, then the exclusion of one heir'. It was Halifax, not Shaftesbury, as Haley pointed out, who remarked that 'no man would take the son of his coachman to be his driver'. And it was the Duke of York who looked upon the limitations scheme accordingly, as the project of 'a man yt in his heart hated all kingly government'.[44]

By every test of both practice and theory in fact, Halifax was the habitual critic of the court in 1678 (and distrusted there accordingly), and Shaftesbury the professional courtier. Within the context of this crisis of popery and arbitrary government, Halifax wished to pursue both causes – the resurrection of parliament from the manipulations of the crown, and the prosecution of popery – he continued to do this even from 1682–4, with nothing but personal conviction to support him.[45] As a sceptic and pragmatist he did so by holding power and fixing it to a realistic strategy which would achieve both objects: the strategy of limitations, realistic because despite the protests of Orange and York the King had made it clear he would accept this. Shaftesbury, seeking personal office and Halifax's displacement, confined himself to a strategy that cast him in the role of wrecker – wrecker not only of his own career but, partially perhaps, of the parliamentary cause. This was a disaster which Halifax, for all his 'personal' success, was powerless to prevent, and upon which he was to have some

[43] Sidney, 'Letters to Savile', in *Works*, pp. 11, 17.
[44] Ronalds, *Whig Revolution*, p. 122; Burnet, BL Add MS. 63,057 vol. II, p. 8.
[45] See Barillon, PRO Baschet no. 151 (1682), pp. 8, 17, 45; no. 157 (1684), p. 185.

years to reflect. It is hardly surprising that he concluded that a republic, though abstractly speaking the best form of government, required good men; and good men were in short supply.

SIDNEY AND HALIFAX

Algernon Sidney ... plied Hallifax much ... [though he] grew to hate him out of measure when he went into ye Court ... Hallifax did use him in extremity like one yt remembered ye old friendship more than ye late Injuries. (Burnet)[46]

All of this helps us to understand why Sidney spent a good deal of time in 1679 not only writing to Savile, but cultivating his brother Halifax. Eventually this friendship, like all Sidney's others including that with Penn, would end in tears. By 1681 his feelings about Halifax echoed those we have already heard from Titus, and for the same reason. Fellow sceptic and pragmatist though Sidney was, he had, in the end, little of the Earl's flexibility when it came to the question of the rights of the Commons, a subject upon which his political experience had invested him with extreme opinions. Nevertheless Sidney's original relationship with Halifax is worth pausing over, for what it tells us not only about this year, but about the shared intellectual make-up of both men.

When John Kenyon described Halifax as that rare thing, a political writer who was also a politician, he correctly put his finger on one source of the Earl's intellectual scepticism.[47] But he could also have put alongside him in that respect Henry Vane, Henry Neville, and Algernon Sidney. What Sidney in particular shared with Halifax was a very great deal: social status, family connection, temperament, intellect, huguenot background and education, religious and political goals, and much of their political thought.

All of this resulted in a shared protestant–international perspective, so that we have seen Halifax remarking, as the grand-nephew of Sir Philip Sidney might have done, 'that the plot must be [investigated] ... though it were vain to hope it will ever be confessed by those that say still there never was any such thing as the ... Massacre at Paris'.[48] Both men agreed on the principal religious and political issues. Both were long-time critics of popery (in Penn's wider definition, as intolerance; it is in this sense that Danby's regime was 'popish' and 'superstitious'). From 1679–81 it was Halifax who promoted Sidney's and Penn's goal of protestant toleration in the lords.

It is therefore not surprising that the practical co-operation of both men grew from a common opposition to Danby. Their shared objection was not simply to his Cavalier intolerance of both religious and political dissent, and

---

[46] BL Add MS 63,057, vol. II, p. 138.
[47] Halifax, *Works*, ed. Kenyon, Introduction.
[48] Ronalds, *Whig Revolution*, p. 18.

his tampering with parliament for the enhancement of the power of the crown. It was also philosophical. Halifax's speech in the House in 1673 ridiculing Danby's Test Act had done so on identical (sceptical) grounds to Sidney's criticism of the oath in the republican parliament of 1649. The point was echoed by Penn: 'Neither in private . . . nor . . . public transactions, have men adhered to their oaths, but their interests. He that is a knave was never made honest by an oath.' (Compare Sidney: 'a snare to any honest man, but every knave will slip through it'.)[49] What all three men shared, in short, was a specifically protestant scepticism, for which we should again look to the common reference point of Saumur (attended by Sidney and Penn, and where Halifax sent his eldest son to be educated) and to the scholarship of Mornay and Daillé. We should not be surprised, then, to find the interest language used by Sidney and Penn at the centre of Halifax's political thought as well.[50]

A host of specific coincidences between Sidney's and Halifax's political writing were first noticed by Halifax's excellent nineteenth-century biographer, Hilda Foxcroft. Those to which she drew attention[51] stem partly from these more general connections of background, education and intellect. Like Sidney, Halifax was an aristocratic intellectual who was born to the world of politics but drifted between its practical and speculative involvements as the former impelled him. Like Sidney he was a great practitioner of 'retirements' followed by re-entries onto the 'stage of the world'. According to Burnet Halifax had a 'vast wit' but was not externally 'flashy, as ye Duke of Buckingham.'[52] His religion was devoid of external ceremony, so that he was reputed to be an atheist, but he was 'not so Atheistical as ye world takes him to be'. Instead his religion was founded on 'great notions of an exact Morality'[53] – just the description Burnet gives us of Sidney's faith. Halifax protested to Burnet that his faith was entirely underestimated just because he could not believe everything the clergy told him, or 'digest Iron as ye Ostrich'.[54]

If thus in religion Halifax's scepticism left him with a faith like Sidney's own, it is that much less surprising that in politics, according to Burnet again, he was 'full of commonwealth notions . . . and studied to infuse into some a zeal for a commonwealth. And to these he pretended, that he preferred limitations to an exclusion; because the one kept up the monarchy still, only passing over one person; wheras the other brought us really into a Commonwealth, as soon as we had a popish king over us'.[55]

[49] Hull, *William Penn*, p. 215; Scott, *Sidney and the English Republic*, p. 93, note 5.
[50] Scott, *Sidney and the English Republic*, p. 217.
[51] Foxcroft, *Life and Letters of Sir George Savile*, vol. II, pp. 279, 285–6, 288–9, 292, 294–5, 293, 338, 397.
[52] Burnet Add MS. 63,057, p. 7.   [53] *Ibid.*, p. 8.   [54] *Ibid.*, p. 8.
[55] Halifax, *Works*, p. 12; Burnet, *Own Time*, pp. 201–2.

According to Burnet, Halifax 'had ye highest notions of publick liberty, and of ye obligations yt lay on Princes to consider themselves only as great officers for ye good of ye people, of any man I ever knew.' But in particular 'he has read ye Roman Authors much and delights mightily in them'.[56] This is significant because the one important aspect of Sidney's thought which Penn does not share, but Halifax does, is his use of Machiavelli.

Thus echoing Sidney's *Discourses*, Halifax insisted upon this key tenet of Machiavelli's book of the same name:

[that] in all constitutions ... there will ever be some matter of strife and contention; and ... men's passions and interests will raise them from the most inconsiderable causes ... [but] These strugglings, which are natural to all mixed governments, while they are kept from growing into convulsions, do by a mutual agitation from the several parts rather support and strengthen than weaken or maim the constitution; and the whole frame ... cometh to be the better and closer knit by being thus exercised ... Our Government is like our climate ... There are winds which are sometimes loud and unquiet, and yet with all the trouble they give us, we owe a great part of our health unto them; they clear the air, which else would be like a standing pool.[57]

This was allied, in Halifax's writing, as in Sidney's *Discourses*, with the belief 'that constitutions were not immutable and should be adapted to changing circumstances'.[58] As Kenyon pointed out, this was a conclusion drawn from practical experience, 'not [just] abstract theory' – that is partly why Machiavelli, Sidney, Vane, and Halifax all stressed the same point.

The key echoes between Sidney's and Halifax's writing noted by Foxcroft relate to their use of the concepts of liberty, reason and virtue; that is, to their shared humanism, or perhaps, their classical republicanism. Halifax also shared that common conception of English foreign policy held by Sidney and his father before him:

[that England had been] a perpetual umpire of two great contending powers ... a piece of greatness which was peculiar to us ... it being our safety as well as glory to maintain it ... [Now] instead of weighing in a wise balance the power of either crown, it looketh as if we had learnt only to weigh the pensions, and take the heaviest.[59]

Similarly, he shared Sidney's view of the decline of the modern nobility:

The original Gentleman is almost lost in strictness; when posterity doth not still further adorn by their virtue the escutcheon their ancestors first got for them by their merit, they deserve that penalty of being deprived of it ... [and] men of quality in their several degrees must either restore themselves to a better opinion, both for morality and diligence, or else quality itself will be in danger of being extinguished.[60]

There is a similar identity in their descriptions of the political state of France, a country both knew well: 'Let us look upon the most glittering

56 Burnet Add MS. 63,057, p. 7.   57 Halifax, *Works*, p. 63.
58 *Ibid.*, p. 13.   59 *Ibid.*, p. 87.   60 *Ibid.*, p. 162.

outside of unbounded authority, and upon a nearer enquiry we shall find nothing but poor and miserable deformity within' (Halifax).[61] 'The beauty of it is false and painted. There is a rich and haughty king . . . But the whole body of that state is full of boils, wounds, and putrid sores' (Sidney).[62] In *Character of a Trimmer* Halifax observed that the King of France gives 'at least an outward . . . [even] when he when he refuseth a real worship to the laws'; the same point was made by Sidney in the *Discourses*. Foxcroft wondered about Halifax when Sidney wrote in the *Discourses*:

Not long since a person of the highest quality and no less famous for learning and wit, having observed the state . . . to which [England] has been reduced, since the year sixty, as is thought very much by the advice and example of France, said, that they were now taking a most cruel vengeance upon us for all the overthrows received from our ancestors.[63]

We are certainly right to wonder about Sidney when, a few months after his trial, Halifax wrote against recent judicial excesses: 'Westminster Hall might be said to stand upon its head . . . when the reason of him that pleads is visibly too strong for those who are to judge and give sentence'.[64] And we might reasonably imagine Halifax talking to Sidney himself when he remarked:

It is not a sound way of arguing to say that if it can be made out that the form of a Commonwealth will best suit with the interest of a nation [exactly what Sidney was telling Barillon in 1679], it must for that reason of necessity prevail. I will not deny but that interest will not lie is a right maxim . . . [but the operation of a Commonwealth] maketh it so long before they can see their interest, that for the most part it is too late for them to pursue it.[65]

But if Halifax had this reservation about the theory expressed in Sidney's *Court Maxims*, he nevertheless agreed that whatever powers were claimed for Princes 'the world hath an interest . . . there is a natural Reason of State, grounded upon the good of mankind, that in all changes and revolutions still preserveth its original right of saving a nation, when the letter of the law perhaps would destroy it.'[66]

The final significance of all of these similarities is that what Halifax's political thought connects with is the specifically French (sceptical humanist) background of Sidney's own: the thought of Mornay, Daillé, Du Rohan and de La Rochefoucauld. It is with Halifax alone among Sidney's English colleagues in this period that we can imagine him continuing the recently abandoned dialogue with de La Rochefoucauld. The point is important: this is partly why Halifax, no less than Sidney, was to attract the later attentions of Montesquieu and Rousseau.

[61] Foxcroft, *Savile*, p. 297.
[63] Quoted in Foxcroft, *Savile*, pp. 334–5.
[65] Halifax, *Works*, p. 157.
[62] *Ibid.*, p. 297.
[64] *Ibid.*, pp. 285–6.
[66] *Ibid.*, p. 60.

How much more of a direct kind we are entitled to make of such similarities is not clear. But as one reads Foxcroft's catalogue of particular similarities between the *Discourses* and Halifax's works (mostly written between 1684 and 1688) it is worth at least bearing in mind what remains the great unsolved mystery of Sidney's political thought. How did the manuscript of the *Discourses*, confiscated by the crown as evidence of treason, find its way from a hostile state in 1683 to a sympathetic publisher in 1697–8? One of the several possibilities centres upon the only person who was a senior government minister at the time of Sidney's execution, still an active political presence after 1688, and remained nevertheless sufficiently sympathetic to Sidney and his political thought to seek their preservation. It was certainly Halifax in 1683 who mitigated the rigours of Sidney's imprisonment, and delivered his (as usual, insufficiently penitent) petition for mercy to the King. Finally and most importantly it was Halifax's signature which headed the order to seize the manuscript itself[67] – he was therefore in a good position to take an interest in its disposal.

THE SAVILE LETTERS

Predictably, Sidney's letters to both Furly and Savile in late March and early April were preoccupied with the fall of Danby; and 'I believe the next work will be concerning Lauderdale, and that never men weare less pitied in their fall, than they will be'.[68]

You will have heard from all hands what temper the [new] house of commons appears to be of, and that the Earl of Danby hath accomplished his promise of bringing it into an entire subjection unto the king's will, as well as ... paying his majesty's debts, encreasing his treasure, and rendering him considerable among his neighbouring princes; which are verified in leaving twenty two shillings in the exchequer, two and forty hundred thousand pounds of passive debt, and the revenue anticipated for almost a year and a half. Notwithstanding all this the lords Berkeley, Frecheville, and others of the learned, think he hath behaved himself so well, as to deserve no punishment ... Essex and Halifax differing something in opinion from them.[69]

Sidney reported the Commons' intransigence in the face of the royal pardon for Danby, and their insistence on a bill of attainder; and continued that 'The next important point likely to be pursued is, to prosecute the last week's vote, that all forces now in England, except the trained bands, were

[67] D. Milne, 'The Rye House Plot and Its Consequences until 1685' (London PhD 1948), p. 167.
[68] Forster, *Letters*, pp. 94–5; Sidney, *Letters to Savile*, pp. 5–6. Lauderdale was attacked by Shaftesbury in the House on 25 March: 'In England popery was to have brought in slavery; in Scotland, slavery went before and popery was to follow'. Haley, *Shaftesbury*, pp. 510–11.
[69] Sidney, 'Letters to Savile' in *Works*, p. 6.

kept up contrary to law.'[70] Thereafter he turned to Ireland, and an old enemy: the man who had been appointed by Charles I to replace his father:

The duke of Ormonde's miscarriages are so extreme, and his favour to the Irish so apparent, that few believe he can continue in the government of Ireland. Some speak of three justices and a good commander of the army, wholly fixed upon an English interest; but if a lieutenant be sent, I believe it will be Essex or Halifax.[71]

This letter closed with an account of the plot, and attempts to suborn Bedloe from testifying against the popish lords. He added: 'That you may see the good humor we are in, I here inclosed send you a piece of poetry given unto me by a friend of yours' (later identified as Halifax). '[A]nd if you have not seen another, which is the speech of Hodge the clown . . . I will endeavour to send it unto you.'[72]

Sidney subsequently copied Hodge's speech out for Savile. A few lines will give its flavour:

> [Hodge] saw the Goatish king in his Alcove
> With secret scenes of his incestuous Love;
> To whom he spoke:
> 'Cease, cease, O Charles, thus to pollute our Isle;
> Return, return to thy long wisht Exile . . .[73]

Again the accent of this none too moderate versifying is on rescinding the decision of 1660.

In the next letter we find Sunderland added to make up the family triumvirate and we are reminded of Sidney's attempted use of Sunderland at this time as a counterweight to Temple's (Orangist) influence on foreign policy: 'We have every day foolish alarms from the French fleet, and I find no body but the Lord Sunderland and myself believe not one word of it.' The principal news of this letter however was the King's surprise formation of his 'great council . . . consisting of fifteen officers of the crown, ten lords, and five commoners'. Kenyon described this experiment as a device to detach the principal opposition leaders from the Lords and Commons.[74] This may well be correct, but it was also an attempt by Charles to create a smaller copy of parliament embracing the full range of its opinions (in 1679 principally opposition) which would be easier to manage than the real thing. It was the attempted bridging device of a King with no experience in the management of new parliaments and with his own parliamentary manager languishing in the Tower. In the end the momentum of the crisis destroyed this attempt at containment.

Sidney reported the King's promises in relation to this council:

[70] *Ibid.*, p. 6.   [71] *Ibid.*, p. 6.   [72] *Ibid.*, p. 6.
[73] The poem has been attributed, presumably falsely, to Marvell: *The Speech of Hodge the Clown from the top of the Mountain* (1679), p. 1.
[74] Kenyon, *Sunderland*, pp. 25–6.

That he would have no first or principal minister ... but that in all things he would follow and rely upon their advice ... all that I have yet spoken to seem much pleased; though it might have been wished, that some of those that are chosen had been left out. A friend of yours and mine [Sunderland] is as far as I can understand, the author of all this;[75] and if he and two more [Halifax and Essex] can well agree amongst themselves, I believe they will have the management of almost all busines-ses, and may bring much honour to themselves, and good to our nation.[76]

One of those Sidney would have wished 'left out' was Ormonde, about whom he opined hopefully again: 'I find men's hearts much set upon taking the government of Ireland out of ... Ormonde's hands. If a lieutenant be named, I believe it will be Essex or Halifax.'[77]

As we have seen, Sidney's interests remained centred so far on the replace-ment of the Restoration triumvirate of Danby/Lauderdale/Ormonde with that of his friends and relations: Essex/Halifax/Sunderland; along with the continuing issues of the plot ('popery') and royal finances and the army ('arbitrary government'). In the next letter he reiterated the same themes, putting the arguments for the illegality of Danby's pardon at greater length, and reporting further attacks on the government of Scotland and Ireland. One attacker in this case was Arlington, who said 'that though this council seemed in some degree to be reformed, no good could reasonably be expec-ted, as long as one continued in it, who did by such violences and other undue ways advance arbitrary power in Scotland, and one that had masses said for him in Ireland.'[78] It helps to put the better-known roles of Shaf-tesbury and Buckingham in this year into perspective to be reminded that one effect of the eclipse of Danby was a partial re-activation of 'the Cabal'.

Sidney updated for Savile parliament's prosecution of the plot. He reported that the change in ministers had been followed by a change in judges; and the address of parliament that 'all the sea-ports, places of strength, and command of ships may be put into trusty hands'.

I believe it will then be debated, whether such an association shall be entered into as was appointed in Queen Elizabeth's time; or an act made, that this parliament should not determine in such a time as should be limited, though the king should die.[79]

Exactly this proposal for the prolongation of parliaments was to feature in the limitations scheme sponsored by Halifax and Essex in the following month. We have already seen the resurfacing of this idea of an Elizabethan association from Sidney's friend Jones in late 1680. Sidney continued:

Shaftesbury and Halifax are eminent in pleading for indulgence to tender-con-scienced protestants, and severity against papists ... Yesterday was appointed extra-

---

[75] In fact the authorship of the Council remains contested – like much else – between Sunder-land and Temple.
[76] Sidney, 'Letters to Savile' in *Works*, p. 16.
[77] *Ibid.*, p. 17.   [78] *Ibid.*, p. 24.   [79] *Ibid.*, 27–8.

ordinary by the house of commons, to consider the succession of the crown in relation to popery, upon the debate of which secretary Coventry . . . is said to have reproached Birch, that his discourses savoured of the years 1640 and 1641 . . . unto which Birch replied . . . taxing Coventry of [sic] having broken his word to the parliament twice the last year, in relation to a war promised . . . upon France . . . and concluded, he was as fit to be turned out of the council as any one that had been so.[80]

It was at this point (in late April) that Charles first put forward to the council, and subsequently to parliament, his offer of limitations on the power of a popish successor. These, reported Sidney on 5 May, involved 'the king's yielding that the parliament should not end with his life, or [should] be revived by his death, if it chanced to be dissolved in his life-time, and [should] have the nomination of all officers, both civil and military, if his successor proved to be a papist'. In this proposal the King may have taken the advice of the Sunderland/Essex/Halifax group on the council. In the event Shaftesbury was the only councillor of note to oppose the plan as 'too like a republic'. This was the final parting of the ways between Halifax and Shaftesbury. Despite the similarity of some of their objectives Shaftesbury had always wished to preserve and to use royal power to achieve them, Halifax to limit it (particularly in relation to parliament) for the same end.

Although Sidney's personal relationships tied him to Halifax rather than Shaftesbury in 1679[81] it would be missing the point to say that he supported limitations over exclusion, or vice versa. These matters were secondary (tactical) considerations, alongside the principal issues. He may, like Neville (and as York insisted) have supported limitations – he is certainly on record as saying that it made no difference to him whether York or Monmouth were King, an explicit criticism of the rationale behind exclusion. Yet he came, after late 1680, to support the Commons demand for exclusion, along with its other demands, not because of the nature of the proposal but because of what he considered the right of the House to insist on any measures it thought necessary in the face of a malignant and intransigent court. He came to support it, in other words, for the same reasons, and in the same context, as his friends Titus and Jones (and it was dealt with in the *Just and Modest Vindication* accordingly, as a secondary issue).

Another instructive model here may be the Earl of Essex, with whom Sidney's relationship developed and deepened throughout this period. Essex supported limitations (with Halifax) in 1679, exclusion (with Titus and Jones) by late 1680, and a draconian scheme of limitations again by December 1680 to January 1681. His objects were consistent but the passage of events meant that his strategic perceptions changed.

[80] *Ibid.*, pp. 22–4.
[81] His one surviving letter to Halifax is dated 16 April of this year: Foxcroft, *Savile*, appendix to ch. 6, p. 204.

This view is reinforced by the *Discourses*. What interests Sidney there is not any particular proposed solution to the crisis but the sheer fact of it, as a harbinger of greater things. Thus what we find in the *Discourses* is not the advocation of either expedient, but, firstly the point that it is a characteristic of monarchy that it lays itself open to dangerous crises of this kind, and secondly an insistence upon the right of the 'people' in parliament to resolve such crises as they see fit. After reporting the Commons' reception of the limitations scheme (on 5 May), and canvassing the 'various counsels' proposed instead, Sidney remarked that he could see difficulties in all of the proposals and concluded: 'But when I have said what I can upon this business, I must confess I do not know three men of a mind, and that a spirit of giddiness reigns amongst us, far beyond any I have ever observed in my life.'[82]

Thus whatever the merits or demerits of the exclusion proposal in itself, what Sidney liked about the bill was equally clear. It was that it

> asserts the power of parliament to dispose of the succession, as best conduced to the good of the kingdom, which had been often exercised [in the past] ... This pleaseth the city so well, that a petition is framing there, which will be presented in two days, signed by one hundred thousand men [sic], to give thanks unto the parliament for their vigorous proceeding ... and promising to assist them in so doing with their lives and fortunes.[83]

His interest, in short, was not so much in the proposal itself, but in the 'vigour' with which it gave parliament occasion to insist on rights of a distinctly dubious character. Nor should the historical significance of these references to the support of the city, and its willingness to press the Commons through petitioning, be lost, particularly given their ominous inflation of the currency of debate to 'lives and fortunes'. Only one activity required expenditure in this combination. Republicans like Neville settled for one specific proposal – in this case limitations – on the grounds that the civil war had been such a tragedy that nothing justified its repetition. For Sidney however, on the contrary, there were 'ways of dying worse than the sword', and forms of peace 'no more to be valued, than that which men have in the grave'.[84]

Subsequent letters of Sidney's continued the narrative of the two key prosecutions – of the popish plot, and Danby (or of popery, and arbitrary government). Details of the former recounted particularly the contributions of Sir William Waller, and Sir William Jones.[85] But at this point the hint of menace already detected in these letters was suddenly excited and amplified by two developments.

[82] Sidney, 'Letters to Savile', in *Works*, p. 28.   [83] *Ibid.*, p. 33.
[84] Sidney, *Discourses*, pp. 132, 224; Scott, *Sidney and the English Republic*, pp. 31–3.
[85] *Ibid.*, pp. 29, 34.

The first was the King's prorogation of the new parliament on 27 May. The question to which Sidney had no answer at this stage was whether this resulted from the advice of his friends or had occurred in spite of it. Whatever the answer the political implications were clear; and there is again undeniable menace at the end of Sidney's response:

No man will avow having been the king's counsellor in this business . . . [which] fills men with many ill humors; the parliament-men go down discontented, and are like by their reports to add unto the discontent of the countries [sic], which are already very great; and the fears from the papists at home, and their friends abroad, being added thereunto, they begin to look more than formerly unto the means of preserving themselves.[86]

As if to confirm these words, the second development was much more serious. On 7 June, news reached London of a rebellion in Scotland.

THE SCOTS REBELLION

Throughout May Sidney had been watching Scottish affairs closely, and as early as 5 May his general commentaries on the misgovernment of Lauderdale (and Ormonde) had matured into the prediction that 'Scotland . . . is every day likely to be in arms.'[87] On 12 May he reported to Savile the murder of the Archbishop of St Andrews:

It is not known who [the murderers] are . . . but Latherdale [sic] is graciously pleased to lay it upon the non-conformists, and hath thereupon caused a very severe proclamation to be issued against them; but others believe it was upon a private quarrel with some gentlemen, that by fraud and power the prelate had thrown out of their estates, he having been most remarkable for outrageous covetousness, besides other episcopal qualities.[88]

Indeed Lauderdale did institute vicious retribution against nonconformists following this murder, and it was partly these measures that provoked the rebellion of the following month. In the first week of June Sidney had also been closely following another case of resistance to Lauderdale's 'arbitrary government'.

There hath been a suit of law in Scotland, between the earl of Argyle, and one Maclaine, a great man in the Highlands, and the earl (as is said by the favour of Duke Latherdale), hath obtained a decree for the lands in question . . . to be put into execution . . . and fire and sword to be used in case they find resistance; as probably they will, Maclaine resolving he will not be turned out of his ancient inheritance by a trick in law, and a decree from corrupt judges. This man being head of a numerous and stout people, helped by the fastness and poverty of their country, may perhaps make good what he proposeth to himself . . . [and] he hath already entered into Argyle's country with 800 or 1000 men.[89]

---

[86] *Ibid.*, p. 34.   [87] *Ibid.*, p. 29.   [88] *Ibid.*, pp. 31–2.
[89] *Ibid.*, pp. 34–5; for the dispute between Argyll and the Macleans see P. Hopkins, *Glencoe and the End of the Highland Wars* (Edinburgh 1986), pp. 65–7 and ch. 2 in general.

Here is a classic Sidney theme: encroachment by 'arbitrary' royal power against the independent 'ancient nobility' and 'stout' northern resistance thereto. We should also perhaps note the parallel between Maclaine's attitude to his 'inheritance' and Sidney's to his own. But what is most abundantly clear from these letters is that by early June Sidney had been willing a Scots rebellion for months.

There is little mystery about why, for in every respect Sidney's interpretation of the unfolding events of this year betrays a preoccupation with the precedent of those of 1637–42. In the first Caroline crisis of popery and arbitrary government the essential military challenge that had made parliament's own heroic resistance possible had come from Scotland. And in 1641, just when the force of that resistance threatened to flag, it received a second terrible reinforcement from Ireland. Sidney added to Savile in the same letter:

Ireland [also] is in extreme disorder, by the Duke of Ormonde's negligence, and favour to the Irish. Douglas' regiment thinking to use the same licentiousness at Kinsale, as it had been accustomed to in France, gives great distaste, and apprehensions of such works as began almost by the same ways in 1641.[90]

It can thus readily be imagined with what excitement Sidney greeted the news on 9 June that rebellion had actually broken out. He wrote to Savile on that day: 'No man doubts the truth of the news brought hither by an express . . . that the conventicle-men of Glasgow are in arms . . . the discourses I have heard very often of late, of those who every day expected some such thing, persuades me to believe it is not fallen out by chance.'

A week later he continued:

The Scotch news . . . doth still possess the minds of all men here . . . The last week we heard of nothing but raising of great forces to subdue these rebels . . . but [then] . . . the lord Grey gave up his commission, Mr Thynne refused to take any; Cavendish doth not raise any men upon his, and Garrett swears he will not be at a penny charge to raise a man.[91]

Here we find inserted the next piece in the jigsaw of 1637–42 wish-fulfillment. What made the last Scots rebellion invincible was the reluctance of the English army, under Sidney's uncle Northumberland, to fight – on behalf of 'popery and arbitrary government' – against them. Sidney continued:

Whilst ways were sought to remove these difficulties, the Scotch lords that are here endeavoured to persuade [the King that] in as much as these men having been driven into a necessity of taking arms, by the extreme pressure suffered from those that did abuse the authority his majesty had trusted them with, the people being eased of those burthens, the persons removed that had caused them, and such men placed in

90 Sidney, 'Letters to Savile' in *Works*, p. 36.
91 *Ibid.*, p. 38.

the government, as were acceptable to the nation, they durst undertake that all may be composed without blood.[92]

More to the point, continued Sidney:

in the year 1641 acts of parliament were made in both kingdoms, making it treason for any person belonging unto either to make war upon or invade the other, without the consent of parliament ... no man can doubt but [that] remains in force; and whosoever marcheth against Scotland incurs the penalties of treason denounced by it ... the parliament then [in 1641] finding they had upon the like pretence engaged against Scotland in 1638 and 1639, made this act expressly to ... take care that England should never be again engaged against Scotland, without the consent of parliament.[93]

Strangely enough however, the King did not share Sidney's touching determination to have his conduct in this crisis ruled by the legislation of 1641. Sidney relayed with disgust his (reported) reply to the Scots lords (Hamilton and others):

[the King defended his prerogative on] three points he would not suffer to be touched: 1st ... he having a right of disposing of all places ... 2dly, ... it belonging to him to prevent all conspiracies, he might secure and imprison suspected persons; and that there was no such thing as a Habeas Corpus in Scotland, nor should be as long as he liv'd: 3dly ... That ... he might raise such forces as he pleased, quarter them where he thought fit, and employ them as occasion should require. To which Lockhart replied, that the *places* in question ... had ever been chosen by the people ... And as to ... conspiracies and rebellions, he thought he could prove, that what his majesty did assert did neither agree with the laws of Scotland, nor any other law, nor the ends for which ... government was constituted.[94]

Nothing daunted by this brief preview of the *Discourses*, his majesty dispatched Monmouth with a force to Scotland. Nothing daunted either (and exercising in his turn the prerogative of hope) Sidney announced that the expedition remained mortally handicapped by 'the little probability yet appearing of the parliament's being any ways engageable in it'.[95] At the same time he reviewed hopefully

The forces of these conventicle-men, or, as they call themselves, the Western army ... Some say, they have 14000 or 15000 men ... [and] between two and three thousand horse, well armed and mounted [this is an exact parallel of Sidney's account of the forces of the English Republic to Lantin] ... that a brother of the earl of Galloway was coming to them ... with above four hundred horse and foot, and that they have parties of good strength in several other places.[96]

Finally Sidney reported that under the impetus of these events there was once more:

a certain petition preparing in London to be presented unto the king ... taking notice of the army having been raised upon pretence of the French war, kept up by

[92] *Ibid.*, pp. 34–5.   [93] *Ibid.*, p. 39.   [94] *Ibid.*, p. 42.
[95] *Ibid.*, p. 41.   [96] *Ibid.*, p. 42.

Danby's means contrary to an act of parliament, as a standing army ... [and] the acts of parliament made in England and Scotland, making it treason for subjects of either kingdom to invade the other ... and shewing the dangerous consequences of forcing the protestants of [these] kingdom[s] to imbrue their hands in each others blood ... [and] desiring his majesty to ... compose things there, suffer parliament to meet the 14th of August, bring Danby and others to their trials, [and] perfect the disbanding of the army.[97]

It need hardly be pointed out that the contents of this petition read exactly as if Sidney had composed it himself; nor to detail again the historical resonance of the fact that it leaves the causes of the Scots, parliament, and the city of London, firmly intertwined. Once again the arbiter of all is to be parliament, and parliamentary legislation. It would be interesting to know who in the city Sidney had these discussions and (probably) framed these petitions with.

The very next day, however, this petition too, and all Sidney's hopes, were dashed by the defeat of the rebels at Bothwell Bridge.

Some letters say, two thousand are killed upon the place; but my Lord Sunderland tells me there is only some hundreds slain, many taken, and the whole party dissipated and destroyed ... the Scotch lords have been so wise as to leave their countrymen to be cut in pieces ... I find mens judgements various as to [what will happen now] ... Some did think that they being a poor people, brought unto despair by the most violent persecution, pitied by all both in England and Scotland ... were to be spared ... Others, who look upon it as a fine thing to kill a great many men, and believe monarchies are best kept up by terror ... say there is no other way of suppressing old rebellions, or preventing new ones, than by force and rigour; looking upon Caligula as a great statesman, and *oderint dum metuant* as a good maxim ... [and] thereunto the prisoners are used most cruelly, and it is said, that at least forty of them shall be put into the boots my Lord of Latherdale hath brought into fashion.[98]

Sidney's sympathy for the persecuted and tortured Scots ('my Lord of Latherdale's boots' make a mournful drumbeat through the remainder of this correspondence) stands in conspicuous contrast to his attitude to the catholic priests who were being executed at this time. After detailing the continuing investigations into the plot, and the fact that at their executions the priests 'confessed nothing', he remarked coldly:

Those who use to extol all that relates to Rome, admire the constancy of the five priests executed last week, but we simple people find no more in it, than that the papists ... have found ways of reconciling falshood in the utmost degree with the hopes of salvation ... [and] have made men die with lies in their mouths.[99]

This is a sharp reminder of the nature of the age of which this crisis (like the last) formed a part: of the bloody religious wars in Europe. This age spanned, and characterised, most of the early modern period, and Sidney's

[97] *Ibid.*, p. 43.　　[98] *Ibid.*, pp. 43–4.　　[99] *Ibid.*, p. 45.

attitudes, thought, and experience were archetypal products of it. Concerning the legal proceedings that resulted, the earl of Anglesey observed 'that the old civil war had now, as it were, transformed itself into a judicial war; men fought with one another in judicial battle – for what was right troubled neither grand nor petty juries'.[100] The biographers who waxed piously over the injustice of Sidney's trial would have done well to remember this aspect of the struggle in which he was engaged, how little quarter he had given in his turn, and that his own trial was modelled on these, which he accepted.

For Sidney two lessons emerged from the Scots crisis. Firstly it was a vivid demonstration of the fragility of the political situation and with luck (and good management) it could be expected to recur. It was also necessary to learn the lessons of this episode; and he can hardly be accused of not doing so, when his attempt to repeat it in 1683 featured Monmouth as rebel general. Secondly the major difference between this outbreak and its historical predecessor was that in this case the King had been able to take care of it without re-summoning parliament. Sidney thus became newly determined to target both the crown's extra-parliamentary armed forces and its extra-parliamentary revenue for destruction. When the next crisis came parliament, 'under God the best anchor we have', had to be enabled to become its arbiter.

Thus when in mid July the prorogued parliament was dissolved and a new one called for October Sidney's reaction was two-fold. On the one hand he had been living since late May with the uncomfortable knowledge that the King's chief ministers at the time of the prorogation had been his friends Sunderland, Halifax, and Essex.[101] From this point onward his relations with both Halifax and Sunderland, while they remained personally friendly, became politically more distant. As Sidney wrote to Savile on 10 July:

now the parliament is prorogued I hear little more than I shall do when I am dead. The truth is, some of our friends being newly grown men of business, are so politic and secret, that a man who sees it can hardly bear laughing; but none is so ingenuous as to be content men should do it, except the lord Halifax, who is sometimes free enough with his companions to begin.[102]

Moreover Sidney was not slow to point out to Savile the implications:

This business [the dissolution] is wholly imputed unto your two friends [Sunderland and Halifax] and the other that ever joins with them [Essex] . . . and . . . they begin to be spoken of all over England in the same manner as Danby, and I fear may be impeached in the next parliament upon this point, and the war in Scotland, as is said, contrary to an act of parliament in the year 1641.[103]

[100] Von Ranke, *History of England*, vol. IV, p. 159.
[101] See Haley, *Shaftesbury*, pp. 522, 525–6; Kenyon, *Sunderland*, p. 21.
[102] *Ibid.*, p. 46.
[103] Sidney, 'Letters to Savile' in *Works*, pp. 47–8.

The ambiguous personal dilemma in which this left Sidney was summarised in a letter to Savile after the following elections, in late October:

nothing can be assured . . . unless it be that as I and my principles are out of fashion,
my inclinations going one way, my friendship and [family] alliance with those that
are like to give occasion for the greatest contests drawing another, I shall be equally
disliked and suspected by both parties, and thereby become the most inconsiderable
member of the house.[104]

This 'polarisation' within himself was to be a pointer to the political
situation to come. But given his increasing identification of his own cause
with that of parliament, the dissolution of July also provided Sidney with an
important new opportunity:

The new parliament is to meet on the 7th of October: there will be as great canvassing of places as ever, people believing this parliament was dissolved only in hopes of
having one that would be less careful of the public interest. All men that wish well
unto it, think it necessary to imploy all their industry in endeavouring to make it
better in that sense; and many believe they will effect it; [and] though some probably
will grow weary of the expenses of elections . . . the ways of preventing them as yet
are not settled.[105]

[104] *Ibid.*, p. 50.   [105] *Ibid.*, p. 48.

8

The Mutinous City 1679–81

8.1 THE SECOND ELECTION: BRAMBER AND AMERSHAM JULY–SEPTEMBER 1679

Given this second opportunity, Sidney and Penn were to produce a major improvement in the techniques, and extension of the range, of the 1679 electoral effort. There was a correspondingly spectacular result: 'the most remarkable', said William Harrington, of the whole election.[1]

The lessons of Guildford had been learned, and they were applied on a number of levels. More care was necessary in the selection of seats, particularly the avoidance of boroughs in the grip of a hostile municipal corporation. It was equally preferable to run in two seats rather than one. By the beginning of the last week of July, Sidney's agents were at work in both Bramber and Amersham.

In both seats the franchise lay with all the 'burgesses and inhabitants', though there was room for argument about exactly what this meant. Bramber had no municipal institutions. In both boroughs the constable acted as returning officer, and both the seats had traditionally fallen under the sway of a local great family. In Bramber this was the Gorings of Highden; in Amersham (since 1637) the Drakes of Shardeloe. But the informality of such gentlemen's agreements – plus the attraction of two seats apiece – made them vulnerable to outside penetration at a time of political crisis. This crisis and its flurry of elections shook a number of seats out of a nineteen-year slumber. At Amersham Drake was to suffer the shock of an eighteen-month displacement from parliament and the expense of three contests with their attendant petitions to the House (the first of which he was to lose). He was 'sufficiently alarmed by the radical irruption to go to the expense of building a market-hall in the most conspicuous position in the town'.[2] As for Bramber, a biographer of Penn remarked rather charmingly that 'In making the choice [of seat, Sidney] and Penn displayed a lack of political knowledge, for

---

[1] Sir Wm Fitzherbert MS, HMC 13th Report p. 19; Harrington was Shaftesbury's cousin and electoral agent – see Henning, *House of Commons*, p. 138.

[2] *Ibid.*, pp. 419, 137–8.

Bramber was notoriously corrupt.'[3] This time the two carpetbaggers had done their research.

Bramber lay adjacent to the lands of Sidney's brother-in-law Sir John Pelham; and to Penn's own house at Worminghurst. Amersham was the nearest thing in England to a quaker borough, its quaker 'interest' shared between two powerful local families closely connected to Penn: the Penningtons and the Childs. Penn's own marriage certificate was signed by Giles Child, Isaac Pennington, and three others of the Pennington family.[4]

Two of Sidney's three electoral managers in Amersham were to be Giles Child himself (a wealthy clothier) and Edward· Halford, an important London merchant connected to the Childs by marriage.[5] The third was Colonel Henry Danvers, a religious radical well known to historians and an old republican colleague of Sidney's from the Rump parliament. Danvers was a General Baptist who had still in the 1670s been 'writing at great length about adult baptism and the 1000 years rule of the Saints'. His connection with the Sidney/Penn electoral enterprise may be readily comprehended from the focus of all of his writings against the civil magistrate's powers of religious compulsion.[6] The same point had been laboured in print by Sidney's running-mate in Bramber, Sir Charles Wolsely, a survivor of the same period. This re-appearance around Sidney of fellow-survivors from 1640–60 was a growing feature of his activities from this point onward.

Campaigning in both seats had begun in earnest by late July, and Sidney made a number of trips between the two. He was out of London from 16 July until the beginning of September, with the exception of a two-day visit back there from 31 July to 1 August. 'It seems' wrote Gilbert Spencer to Henry Sidney, 'he [Algernon] had a great desire to be a Member, and therefore Penn and Sir John Fagg, and such men, made him interest in several places; and the design, as I find since, was to get Woosley in [in Bramber], if he got in anywhere else'.[7] Spencer's correspondence arose from the fact that, at an early stage in the Bramber campaign, a startling development had taken place. Algernon's brother Henry, clearly feeling there was insufficient existing sibling rivalry, threw his name into the ring for the same seat.

As mentioned by Spencer, Sidney and Penn had another ally in Bramber: that other Sussex worthy Sir John Fagg. This proved, however, to be a

---

[3] Wildes, *William Penn*, p. 116.
[4] M.M. and R.S. Dunn (eds.), *Papers of William Penn*, 2 vols. (1981–2), vol. I, p. 239.
[5] PRO Chancery C6 244/2 – see the Answer of James Child 30 Jan; Henning, *Commons*, p. 138.
[6] See for instance *Certain Quaeries Concerning Liberty of Conscience* (1649), quoted in A. Woolrych, *Commonwealth to Protectorate* (Oxford 1982), pp. 215–16; also R. Greaves, *Deliver Us from Evil: The Radical Underground 1660–63* (1987), p. 7 and thereafter.
[7] Blencowe (ed.), *Charles II*, p. 115.

liability in terms of the Pelham connection, since Sir John Pelham's only specific interest in the contest became to thwart his rival Fagg's 'aspiration to represent the county'.[8] Thus when Henry entered the same contest, and Pelham found his Sidney alliance split two ways, Fagg's involvement proved decisive to Algernon's (and Wolsely's) cost.

Penn began his electoral approach to Bramber by writing to Pelham requesting support for Sidney in late July. Pelham replied on 25 July that 'I doe find that the difficulty will be much greater to gett your friend chosen than . . . Sir John Fagg or you apprehend'. He discoursed on the strength of the Goring interest before adding that 'Ther is another thing now . . . wch renders it in some kind indecent . . . that my brother Harry Sydney is now proposed ther to stand, so that till I have some assurance that this report is groundlesse I must beg your excuse for [not] appearing ther.' Finally Pelham's irritation on another ground became clear: 'If Sr John Fagg had bin here as I with others did expect our farther proceedings in this might have bin carryed on with the more unanimity and certainty.'[9]

Undeterred, Penn wrote to Sidney from Fagg's house at Wiston four days later suggesting a personal follow up to this approach.

Sir John Fagg has been a most zealous, and, he believes, a successfull Friend to thee . . . [and] upon a serious consideration of the Matter, it is agreed that thou [should] comst down with all Speed; but that thou takest Hall-land [Pelhams seat] in thy Way, and bringest Sir John Pelham with thee, which he ought the less to scruple, because his haveing no Interest, can be no objection to his Appearing with thee; the commonest Civility, that can be is all desired.[10]

As the letter continues we find that another old friend of Sidney's had involved himself on his behalf:

The Burrough has kindled at thy Name, and takes it well . . . Sir John Temple is at Work dayly . . . Sir John Pelham sent me Word, he heard that his brother, Henry Sidney, would be proposed to that Burrough . . . and till he was sure to the contrary, it would not be decent for him to appear; of that thou canst best inform him. That Day you come to Bramber, Sir John Fagg will meet you both; and that Night you may lie at Wiston, and then, when thou pleasest, with us at Worminghurst. Sir John Temple has that Opinion of thy good Reasons to perswade, as well as Quality to influence the Electors, that . . . the Business will prosper.[11]

This was the first Algernon had heard of Henry's candidacy and, of course, he was furious. Henry was in the Netherlands and his campaign was being run in his absence by his steward Spencer. If Spencer is to be believed Henry put his name forward without knowing that Algernon himself was involved. Spencer wrote to Henry after the contest: '[Algernon] seems to be mightily disgusted because you should stand at Bramber, where he intended

[8] Henning, *Commons*, p. 419.   [9] Dunn (ed.), *Penn Papers*, p. 531.
[10] *Ibid.*, p. 533.   [11] *Ibid.*, p. 554.

once to stand, which I have taken upon me to answer to Sir Jo. Pelham, that you knew nothing of it'. Sunderland too wrote to Henry on 19 August: 'My uncle Algernon is a Parliament man [for Amersham], and had thoughts of standing in Sussex, and is very angry with you for pretending to anything he had a mind to.'[12]

According to Spencer, Penn subsequently (and after Sidney's victory in Amersham),

> wrote to Sir Jo. Pelham that your [Henry's] standing at Bramber would make a greater feud between you and your brother than is between you [both] and the elder; unless, for an expedient, your interest and Sir Jo. Pelham's credit were engaged for that worthy patriot, C[harles] W[olsely]: whether this were only cunning in Penn, or true in your brother, I cannot well say; but I believe you have most cause to take the matter ill from him, who, after he knew you stood, should have turned by and put in a stranger.[13]

Unable to remonstrate with Henry in person, there was little Sidney could do about his candidature. It greatly complicated the situation at Bramber, but meanwhile the election at Amersham was to be held three weeks earlier, and it was to that which Sidney turned his attention first.

Three days after Penn's letter to him of 29 July, Sidney wrote Savile a note from London explaining his movements: '[I have] bin out of towne, ever since I writ last [16 July] till within theis last tow days. My first journey was to Althrope [Althorp – Sunderland's house], the next for a Parlmt S[e]lection [in Amersham] and I am now going into Sussex without any other designe or businesse then to be a littell longer from London.'[14] As the 'business' outlined in Penn's letter makes clear, this was hardly a frank account.

Concerning the circumstances of his first coming to Amersham, Sidney stated later in a chancery case that in 'the middle of September [in fact July] 1679', being then in Northamptonshire, he 'had notice given him that several of the burgesses' of Amersham Co. Bucks being dissatisfied with one Sir Wm Drake who had served them as burgess in parliament hitherto, were 'very desirous that he should do so, and that the major part of the electors were so too'.[15] This claim should obviously be taken with a grain of salt, but it is interesting for its suggestion that the target was not simply Amersham in general but Drake in particular. Sidney thus, with 'three or four of his friends', repaired to Amersham.

---

[12] Blencowe (ed.), *Charles II*, p. 115.
[13] *Ibid.*, p. 116.
[14] This is the one letter from Sidney to Savile which has not been printed; Chatsworth, Devonshire MSS, Halifax Papers, Savile Correspondence, 1 August [1679]. 'I should put more valewe upon my letters than I knowe they can deserve, if I made an excuse for the intermission of them . . .'
[15] PRO Chancery C6 244/2, Sidney's Bill of Complaint.

The four friends with whom Sidney travelled to Amersham fifteen months later for the subsequent by-election were Lord Howard, Sir William Waller, Henry Ingoldsby and Richard Nelthorp. On this occasion one of them was probably Danvers, and another may have been Sidney's 'running mate' in the seat, Sir Roger Hill. Hill, as we have seen, was another recipient of money from Barillon, who described him as a republican and 'fort vehement contre la cour'.[16] Most of what we know about the subsequent campaign derives from the electoral appeals in which it was to result.

These came from both Sidney and Drake, since there had been a double return. One had been taken by the traditional 'long poll' of all the inhabitants, in which Drake's strength lay; the result was an indenture bearing forty-four signatures, in favour of Hill and Drake. The other return questioned only those inhabitants paying scot and lot – in confirmation of which narrower franchise Sidney petitioned the House – and the result was a second indenture bearing twenty-three signatures, in favour of Hill and Sidney. The outcome on 7 August therefore was that Hill was elected unopposed; and Sidney and Drake only provisionally, to await the decision of the House on the franchise. In his subsequent petition, however, Sidney claimed a victory even by the long poll, according to two other returns: one 'taken by Humphry Gardiner (who took it by the appointment of Francis Child Constable, and had taken all the Polls that had been within Thirty years past)', and the other 'taken by Mr Henry Danvers perfectly agreeing with it, whereby it did appear, that all the Householders being admitted, he had 74, and Sir William had but 64 voices'.[17]

Drake's appeal accused Sidney of both bribery and slander. The unlikely medium for the bribery was one 'Richard Norwood Overseer of the Poor', who was accused of handing out money and, in one case 'a Suit of Clothes' to those who voted for Sidney. Algernon replied that this was nonsense; rather, 'being to return to London' after the election, 'many poor people came about his Coach begging of him; and he being told it was a thing decent and customary to give something to them, did first appoint Five pounds, and afterwards Five pounds more [this was a man who had to supplement the initial payment to his own executioner] to be given to them, which accordingly was put into the hands of Richard Norwood Overseer of the Poor to be distributed . . . ' This account was confirmed by Norwood and his son, and is similarly confirmed by the practice of other elections in this period, involving figures of well-known probity like Sir Ralph Verney.[18]

[16] Barillon, PRO 31/3, Baschet Corresp. 146, p. 243.
[17] Henning, *Commons*, p. 138; *The Case of Algernon Sidney*, BL Casebook ref. 105e.60(7), p. 1; Buckinghamshire Record Office (Aylesbury) D/Dr/12/38; D. Hirst, *The Representative of The People?* (1975), pp. 132–3.
[18] *The Case of Algernon Sidney*, p. 2; E. Lipson, 'The Elections to the Exclusion Parliaments', *EHR* 28 (1913), 80–1.

As for the other charge, 'It was also said that some of those who were for Mr Sidney had scandalized Sir William, saying, he was a Papist and a Pensioner.' To this Sidney replied:

As to the reproachful Language against Sir William Drake . . . he cannot rule other men's Tongues; that he no wayes approves of the Licence usually taken in such Cases by using ill Language; that Sir William must suffer that as well as others . . . [and] he could have proved such Language was then and still is used of him-self every day by Sir William himself and others, his Friends and Agents, which neither he nor they, as he believes, will undertake to make good.[19]

Despite the provisionality of the result Sidney's feat in displacing Drake in Amersham caused a public sensation. Indeed most accounts speak of his election as a confirmed certainty, and he seems himself to have been confident of the result. Shaftesbury's cousin William Harrington wrote to George Treby on 19 August:

The most remarkable thing about the elections is the success of Colonel Sydney at Amersham where he was brought in by the activity of two or three persons, though he was wholly unknown there, and he defeated Sir William Drake, an inhabitant and lord of the place.[20]

Treby heard from another correspondent too that 'At Amersham, Algernon Sydney is chosen and Sir Roger Hill.'[21] Many of Henry Sidney's correspondents informed him of the result, most amusingly Henry Savile on 28 August: 'Colonel Algernon is I hear, chosen a Member of Parliament; I did not think I should ever have so good a reason to wish to be so too, as to hear how he will behave himself.'[22] Ralph Montagu wrote cryptically:

Youre brother Algernon is already chosen, but upon a double return so that I shall have an opportunity of shewing my respect to him when his election comes to be disputed. The king when he heard he was elected, said he did believe Mr Algernon Sydney would prove an honest man. If Mr Henry comes into the house and proves like his brother, I am afraid I shall not be of his majesty's opinion.[23]

The result in Amersham now made it possible for Sidney to transfer his 'interest' at Bramber to Wolsely. He now took up residence with Penn and joined the campaign. As Spencer bitterly recounted:

this added to the trouble and your charge, for he [Algernon] having been there about eight days before the election, and given money to some in the town, and made his learned speech with thanks for their good will to him, and recommended to them that gent. [Wolsely], and left ten or twelve guineas to thank them as was pretended, and left instructions and promises with some of that party of £10 a man, which works powerfully under hand. Those promises on the one hand, and Mr Gorings frequent treats and drinkings on the other, made us spend more than we should, to keep our party firm.[24]

[19] *The Case of Algernon Sidney*, p. 2.   [20] HMC Fitzherbert, 13th Rep. p. 19.
[21] *Ibid.*, p. 18.   [22] Blencowe, *Charles II*, p. 103.
[23] *Ibid.*, pp. 69–71.   [24] *Ibid.*, p. 116.

The purpose of Spencer's letter, it need hardly be pointed out, was to justify the level of his own expenditure – some £300. 'It is not to be imagined' he continued, 'what those fellows, their wives, and children will devour in a day and a night, and what extraordinary reckonings the taverns and alehouses make, who, being Burgers, are not to be disputed with on that point.' They were not to be disputed with at least, as Algernon was subsequently to demonstrate, until the election was over (and lost). Nevertheless Henry got his seat, with some help from Pelham, who 'sent over half a buck, with which we treated bravely', and the heroic actions of Spencer himself 'in kissing of old women, and drinking wine with handfulls of sugar, and great glasses of burnt brandy, three things much against the stomach'.[25]

Wolsely was less fortunate, and on 2 December Algernon's sister Dorothy wrote disapprovingly: 'I dare say by what Montague has told me Mr Algernon has been a good while at Pen's, and not gone to Halland [Pelham's]. Penn did what he could to help Fagg and hinder my brother Pelham, who had not one gentleman against him.'[26] Sidney's and Penn's efforts had ruffled a good many feathers, but only in Amersham did they have a political toehold to show for it.

For this to bear fruit parliament had only to meet, but it was precisely this that was to become the major political issue in the next year. September 1679 began a decisive new stage in this crisis: that of the long prorogation, which was to last until October 1680. Sidney wrote to Savile on 8 September,

At my return [to London] I found mens minds more disturbed than ever I remember them to have been, so that there is no extremity of disorder to be imagined, which we might not probably have fallen into if the king had died, or which may not yet reasonably be feared if he should relapse ... Though the parliament is like to signify little, people are busy in bringing those in, who are of their own mind ... many believe the house will be composed as the last was, or as some think, of a more harsh humor, the same men being something sharpened ... Your friend the Lord Latherdale is more powerful than ever in Scotland ... I know not how much your friends and mine do grow at court, nor whether the gains they expect to make there, will countervail those they loose in the nation ... [but] two of them [Sunderland and Halifax], who were ... as well esteemed as any men I know are now as ill spoken of as any; and the asperity [Halifax] ... shewed against the papists, is now most bitterly retorted upon him.[27]

On 15 October the King announced the prorogation of the new parliament until 26 January. On 26 October Sidney wrote:

I am not able to give so much as a guess, whether the parliament will sit the 26th of January or not, and though I think myself in all respects well chosen, am uncertain

[25] *Ibid.*, p. 123.   [26] Add. MS 32,680 f284.
[27] Sidney, 'Letters to Savile' in *Works*, pp. 49–50.

whether I shall be of it or not, there being a double return; and nothing can be assured, until the question arising thereof be determined.

Thus the result of Sidney's efforts remained in suspension, and there it was to remain for more than a year. In the interlude, in common with many others, he responded to this renewed executive obstruction of parliament by turning himself to another sphere of action, and electoral activity, altogether. In 1680, the high point of polarisation came with the republican capture of London.

8.2 THE 'MUTINOUS CITY'

The humor of the citty [is] the same as it was 40 years ago. (John Verney, May 1681)[28]

This looks as if London would set up for a Commonwealth. (James, Duke of York, 1680)[29]

Sidney's activities over the next eighteen months must be pieced together from more than usually fragmented sources. With the restriction of legitimate political activity, much of what was occurring was driven underground. The broad outlines, however, are perfectly clear, and a number of them have already been discussed. Sidney had a power base in London, and in 1679–80 he began to use it. The deepening of his personal involvement, and the radicalisation of the parliamentary cause, occurred together. By 1680–1 he was a key link between the leaders of the House of Commons, and the City government. It was from this situation that there emerged, in 1681, Sidney and Jones' *Just and Modest Vindication*, the beginning of his *Discourses*, and eventually plans for this community's armed self-defence.

London first made its presence felt during the prorogation by its petitioning campaign. As we have seen from Sidney's letter to Savile in the last chapter, this link between the City and the Commons through petitioning was already being established while the previous House was still in session. Its historical significance, remarked upon by Barillon, was clear to all concerned; and when the petitioning became a major civic movement the political nation began to divide in alarm.

Since the 1679 petitions quoted by Sidney sound so remarkably as if he himself had composed them, it would be surprising if he were not involved with the 1679–80 campaign. We no longer need to guess in this matter, since Mark Knights has found both Sidney's and Locke's signatures, among 16,000 others, appended to a petition presented to the King on 13 January

---

[28] *Ibid.*, p. 4; Bucks R/O M11/35, quoted in Knights, 'Politics and Opinion during the Exclusion Crisis', p. 18.
[29] MacPherson (ed.), *Original Papers* (1775), p. 112.

1680. Other signatories included Slingsby Bethel and his fellow sheriff-to-be, Henry Cornish. The petition reminded the King that 'there hath been and still is, a most Damnable and Hellish Popish Plot', and requested him to summon parliament.[30]

Charles' response to this was to further prorogue the house, and then issue a proclamation outlawing 'tumultuous and seditious' petitioning. This didn't stop the petitions, but it did produce the first counter-address, condemning the petitioning as the 'seed and spawn of rebellion', and 'the principles of 1641'. A co-presenter of the first 'abhorring' address was Sir George Jeffreys, with whom Sidney would have a final personal confrontation in 1683. What particularly disturbed Jeffreys then, as we will see, was Sidney's extraordinary justification, in the *Discourses*, of both 'tumults' and 'seditions'. In the case of an incorrigible tyrant, Sidney had explained, 'something more is to be done than petitioning'.[31]

We first hear of Sidney in 1680 through the letters of his sister Dorothy, first to Henry Sidney, and then to her son-in-law Halifax. He had clearly decided to age in the most angular and least compromising fashion possible, and his relatives continued to suffer the consequences. On 19 February Dorothy complained that

Mr Algernon never goes to [the Pelhams at] Halland, though they have sought him, so that I have wondered at it often. All the women went to see him; the married Pelham and the two sisters[,] and the men did; but he has used them so abominably they are ashamed of it.

It was at about this time that Dorothy reported that Lady Harvey 'wonders nobody shoots him'.[32]

What these relations found impossible about Algernon – a cantankerous lack of attention to social form – was quite deliberate. It was part of a general haughty disdain for outward ceremony – social, political and religious – in favour of internal 'principles'. As he grew older, Sidney became less and less prepared to condescend to the frippery and vanity of a Restoration world where youth and 'lewdness' were in, and his 'principles . . . out of fashion'. In 1680 he devoted himself, with Bethel, to a successful attempt to re-introduce the austerity of these principles into local government – with unfortunate effects that we will shortly notice. Thereafter he turned, more satisfactorily, to recording them on paper for posterity. As he did so he donned increasingly the persona of the platonic philosopher – studying, living frugally, still in the world but with at least one limb beyond it. This made his subsequent elevation to protestant sainthood a slightly shorter

---

[30] Dr Knights announced his find in a letter to the *TLS* on 7–13 April 1989; I am grateful to him for corresponding with me about it.

[31] Sidney, *Discourses*, p. 314.

[32] Blencowe (ed.), *Charles II*, vol. I, pp. 278, 303.

journey. It also made his abandonment of this *vita contemplativa* for a final
bout of the *vita activa* in 1683 that much more impressive: the point about
platonic philosophers was, after all, that they (and not kings) should be
kings.

On 27 March Dorothy reported: 'Our brother Algernon is very ill of a
cough; he eats nothing but water-gruel. I do not see him but I have sent to
him twice.' This expression of concern produced a response: on 6 April she
wrote that 'our brother Algernon has been once with me; how far he will
proceed I know not; I gave him a very civil reception; though we were alone
a great part of the time, we did not say a word of any difference that has
been. He looks very ill.'[33]

Ten days later she continued:

My brother Algernon, upon my sending to know how he did when he was ill, has
come to me three times, and I believe will continue it, for he seems very well pleased
with it. We have not said one word of any difference, and I never contradict him
when he says such things as that Sir William Coventry is no more an able man than a
handsome man.[34]

At the same time Dorothy complained bitterly of the 'unseasonable
factiousness' of some of her acquaintance, and their 'particular malicious-
ness to my son' (Sunderland). Among these 'Tom Pelham is, but you shall
never hear it ... or else he would not be such a slave to his father in law's
humors.'[35] His father-in-law, yet another of Algernon's relations – was Sir
William Jones.

We have already heard Barillon reporting this year on the 'intimacy'
between Sidney and Jones; and on the responsibility of Sidney's 'intrigues'
for Bethel's election to the shrievalty in July. We have also seen his association of Sidney with the 'party of the independents and other sectaries ...
those who want a republic ... of the same party is Mr Pen, who is Chief of
the Quakers'.[36] In the same month that Dorothy reported 'Mr Algernon is
busy; about what, God knows. Last night he was called out of my chamber;
I asked, by whom? and my man said, a Quaker.'[37]

At the same time, and two weeks before the shrievalty election, Dorothy
gleefully related to Halifax:

[Something] that has taken well pleases me, [and] that I believe is true – my Lord
Shaftesbury's and Mr Algernon's quarrel, who has heard Shaftesbury say he is a
French pensioner and my Lord Sunderland's spy ... this is like to go as high as
tongues can ... my brother [Algernon] is suspected to be in with the Duke of
Buckingham; today he was with [John] Wildman; how far that is a sign of it, I know
not; but it is one good, they are not all of a mind.[38]

[33] *Ibid.*, vol. II, p. 25.   [34] *Ibid.*, p. 40.   [35] *Ibid.*, pp. 261–2.
[36] PRO 31/3 Baschet Corresp. 144, p. 28; 146, p. 245; 147, pp. 402–3.
[37] Berry, *Life and Letters of Lady Russell* (1819), pp. 132–4.
[38] *Ibid.*, pp. 128, 131.

That the public boiling over of this acrimony at this time was related to Sidney and Shaftesbury's fierce rival politicking for the shrievalty is clear. Having begged the electors 'not to choose fanatics',[39] and campaigned on behalf of his client Sir William Russell, on 29 July Shaftesbury was to see his efforts overwhelmed. 'There were', reported a contemporary, 'a greate Party in ye Citty for makeing Slingsby Bethell and Mr Cornish Sheriffs, in opposition to Sr Wm Rusell, Mr Box and Mr Nicholson three persons of more moderate tempers'.[40] To add insult to injury the result was a landslide, with Bethel and Cornish more than a thousand votes each clear of their nearest rivals.[41] Somewhat bewildered by these sectarian divisions, Dorothy Sidney reported: 'my Lord Russell said he was sorry [Bethel] was chosen, for he was as great a Commonwealthsman as Algernon Sidney. I wonder what his Lordship is if he is not so too, and goes so far towards it.'[42]

This election caused not only despondency in the 'moderate' camp, but a wider public sensation. Bethel was to find himself thrust, none too gently, into the national limelight, carrying his past in tow. Secretary Leoline Jenkins wrote to Henry Sidney:

The losing of the day in the election of the new Sheriffs in London is, it must be confessed, a disreputation to the loyal party ... but the Sheriffs can do the Government no great harm that can be foreseen ... The country gentlemen [he wrote hopefully] have an indignation at the proceedings of the city, and do look upon their election as a parallel line drawn to that of 1641–2.[43]

To begin with, Lady Rachel Russell too attempted to look on the bright side: 'Bethell has dined at Capt-Hall, and professed he did not find courtiers such bugbears as some would have them; so that possibly it is hoped in time he may understand himself.'[44] This was not, however, to be the case. Burnet wrote:

Bethel was a man of knowledge, and had writ a very judicious book of princes: but as he was a known republican in principle, so he was a sullen and wilful man; and turned from the ordinary way of a Sheriffs living into the extreme of sordidness, which was very unacceptable to the body of citizens, and proved a great prejudice to the party ... The setting up Bethel gave a great colour to this jealousy [at court]; for it was said he had expressed his approving the late King's death in very indecent terms.[45]

---

[39] *Ibid.*, pp. 28–9.

[40] Marginal note on a contemporary pamphlet in Cambridge University Library Sel.2.118: Philo-Patris, *A Seasonable Address to the ... City of London upon their Present Electing of Sherifs* (1680): 'This came out when there were a greate Party in ye Citty for makeing Slingsby Bethell & Mr Cornish Sheriffs, in opposition to Sr Wm Russell, Mr Box and Mr Nicholson three persons of more moderate tempers.' The writer was probably Ralph Verney.

[41] *The Proceedings of the Guild-Hall in London on Thursday July 29th 1680* (1680).

[42] Berry, *Life and Letters of Lady Russell*, pp. 132–4.

[43] Blencowe (ed.), *Charles II*, vol. II, p. 87.

[44] Berry, *Life and Letters of Lady Russell*, p. 40.   [45] Burnet, *Own Time*, pp. 242–3.

Bethel's 'sordid' way of living was his replacement of the pomp and feasting of the shrievalty with a conspicuously puritan, Dutch- (and Sidney-) style frugality. This offence, however, was only part of a wider problem: Bethel's whole election, as Jenkins had suggested, had confirmed fears about the return of a previous age. And as it turned out, even the 'citizens' own temporary enthusiasm for the principles of that age did not survive this confrontation with its culinary preferences. Culture shock quickly followed cultural revolution.

An early pamphlet reacting to Bethel's victory warned of what was to come. It foreshadowed in the process the axis upon which the crisis was to turn – the achilles heel of republicanism in the matter of arbitrary government. There was now, it remonstrated, genuine cause to fear another

> Rebellion . . . [and] the [English] know upon experience that they shall all then be rifled of their Plate, Pewter, and Brass, their Pigsties and Henroosts robb'd, and their Daughters ravisht . . . And as our late unnatural Wars begat such Taxes and Impositions, as England never heard of before, so another like War will revive the same.[46]

By early 1681, attacks on Bethel personally had reached the point where, while Sidney composed his *Vindication of the Two Last Parliaments*, his colleague published a *Vindication* of himself. *The Vindication of Slingsby Bethel Esq; one of the Sheriffs of London . . . Against the several Slanders cast upon him* (1681) makes clear that a number of these slanders would have applied more precisely to his patron, Sidney.

One was that he had been 'a soldier in the Parlmt army', to which Bethel countered that he had been in Hamburg until 1649. The next, however, was 'That being at Hambourgh at such time as the late King's Death was resolved of in England, I did there say, That rather than he should want an Executioner, I would come thence to perform the Office.' This Bethel denied to the point of warning that he was instituting legal action. What is interesting is the obvious closeness of the story to the legends about Sidney in Copenhagen. The next 'slanders', built on the same theme: that Bethel had been 'one of the late king's judges' and in particular that he had been 'one of those in vizards' on the late King's scaffold.[47] This last image expressed public concerns so picturesquely that no denials would dislodge it. Hereafter Bethel was doomed to be a legend in his lifetime, the Sheriff who had been 'one of those in vizards'. Merciless satires on this subject continued for years.[48]

---

[46] *Goodman Country: To His Worship the City of London* (1680), p. 3.

[47] Slingsby Bethel, *The Vindication of Slingsby Bethel Esq* (1681), pp. 2–3.

[48] See e.g. *The Last Words and Sayings of The True Protestant Elm-Board* (1682) – a conversation between an 'Elm-Board' and Dr Gilbert Burnet – followed by *A Sober Vindication of the Reverend Dr and the Harmless Board* (1682); *More Last Words . . . of the . . . Protestant Elm-Board* (1682); and *Notes Conferred, or a Dialogue Betwixt the Groaning Board, and a Jesuite* (1682).

It is against this interpretation of his past that Bethel tackled the citizen's complaints about his conduct in the present. The first was that 'I live in a Garret, and keep no House'. The self-justification provoked by this vile accusation reveals that Bethel had indeed revived certain 'ancient laws' limiting the shrievalty's obligation to entertainment: 'and I think no Laws are more properly called wholesome, than those which prohibit the excess of feasting'.[49] This thought led the Sheriff to expound for several pages on the wholesomeness of frugality, and on 'how great an Enemie this great expence of time, in Luxurious Eating and Drinking is, to that sober Industry, which is the rise and glory of a Trading City'.[50] A more explicit association of puritan manners with the rise of capitalism could hardly have been conjured up by Max Weber himself. All of this led a loyalist reply to redouble public warnings against dining with Bethel: 'you will be offered nothing to eat but paragraphs'.[51]

We will find Howard warning Monmouth of much the same hazard to be run at Sidney's table in 1683. We are reminded even more forcibly of Sidney's writings – specifically the *Court Maxims* and *Englands Great Choice*, his election manifesto written with Penn – by a second hostile reply to Bethel's tract, Bethel having been

telling us it is *a Maxim, That those that are most saving of their own Estates, will be most careful of the People's*; thereby unhandsomly insinuating that a Parliament-Man is only a kind of Pad-lock, for securing the People's Money ... But pray, Mr Bethel come no more among us with your sordid *Maxims*, 'tis well known, that we have better Maxims of our own.[52]

This last image, of the padlock, sounds rather like a reply to *A Dialogue at Oxford*, published in the same year (1681), which had accused its loyalist participant of speaking as if 'by the Constitution of our Government, a Parliament had only been designed to be a Conduit-Pipe for the Peoples purses to run out at.'[53]

The *Dialogue at Oxford* was, like Sidney and Jones' *Justification*, a classic statement of the parliamentary cause of this year. It featured the familiar relation of the popish plot from the time of crown's relations with France in 1670, alongside its central political cause: the rights, and the being of parliament. It identified as the key problem the 'late Prorogations and Dissolutions', which had not only rendered parliaments unable to tackle the

[49] *The Vindication of Slingsby Bethel*, p. 5, and pp. 5–8.
[50] *Ibid.*, pp. 5–8.
[51] *Animadversions on the late Vindication of Slingsby Bethel Esq* (1681) (by a loyal citizen), p. 3.
[52] *A Seasonable Answer to a Late Pamphlet entitled The Vindication of Slingsby Bethel Esq* (10 July 1681), p. 5.
[53] *A Dialogue at Oxford between a Tutor and a Gentleman, Formerly his Pupil, Concerning Government* (1681), p. 15.

plot but 'strikes at the very Root and Being of Parliaments themselves'.[54] In turn it asserted not only the people's present right to petition for a parliament, but the footsteps of 'our wise Ancestors in modelling our Government' to that end. The original constitution had always made provision for 'frequent meetings of the States', but 'experience' showing that 'Princes not caring to have ... male – administration ... look't into ... that *Tacit* principle of having frequent Parliaments, was literally explain'd by subsequent Statutes made in the time of Edward the 3d, and ascertain'd to them having Annual ones'.[55] Not only that, but:

> there are wise and learned men (and who upon a good occasion may be spoke with) that do conceive there is a Statute made in the time of Richard the Second, and now in being, though not in Print, which provides, that no Parliament shall be dismist till all the Petitions are answered, which I think comes home to the point; Bills in those days, many times appearing in the form of Petitions: as not long since we had an excellent Law made, called the Petition of Right, subsequent to this Statute.[56]

Doubtless chief among these 'wise learned men' of English law was Sir William Jones. All of this is certainly very close to Sidney and Jones' *Vindication*. What makes the *Dialogue* more than usually interesting for the biographer of Sidney, however, is the number of striking echoes it contains, not only from the works of 1681, but from both his *Discourses* and *Court Maxims*. It is not only the content but the form of the latter it shares: a parliamentary–loyalist dialogue.[57] The very title of the tract, *A Dialogue at Oxford ... Concerning Government*, brings both Sidney's works to mind, along with the fact that Neville's *Plato Redivivus* was first published in 1680 under a very similar title. Such similarities help to tune us into the voice of the religious and political community by which these writings were being produced, and with which Sidney was deeply involved. This voice was, as Pocock has recently reminded us,

---

[54] *Ibid.*, pp. 13, 16.

[55] *Ibid.*, pp. 8–9.

[56] *Ibid.*, p. 10.

[57] The close coincidences of content between the *Dialogue* and both Sidney's major works cover a range of sources and particular points. Most fundamental to Sidney's thought is the *Dialogue*'s statement (pp. 2–3) that: 'I will allow you that Government in general is the Ordinance of God, and of Divine Right, for without it, there could be no such things, as humane Societies in the World, which makes St Paul in the 13th to the Romans, affirm as much of all Powers, none excepted, but then as to the ... different species of Government, God Almighty has left no standing Ordinance, whereby to prefer to command one kind above another, and it's absurd to think he should, except we do Imagine that there ought to be exactly the same frame of Government throughout the whole World, notwithstanding the variety and difference of climates, of Interests and Inclinations of People in particular Nations, and that all, who differ from us in their Policies (as all do more or less) do therein violate God's ordinance, which is equally ridiculous and uncharitable. Therefore the particular kinds of Government, must have another and lower Fountain to flow from, which can be no other than humane.' This point, made in exactly this language, is a major feature of both the *Court Maxims* and (particularly) the *Discourses*.

a link with something older and more urban than Harrington: a London-based radicalism looking back through the lens of the Good Old Cause to the Agitators and Levellers of 1647, of whom John Wildman was a living if battered reminder. This had its own political language, as old as the Levellers, in which natural rights and historic birthrights merged in ... a claim to the effect that frequent or annual parliaments were rooted in medieval or Anglo-Saxon antiquity ... an ancient constitutionalism more radical that Petyt's or Atwood's, closer to the concerns of the more violent [radicals] ... and serving to link them with their Commonwealth antecedents.[58]

It was to the republican section of the same community that a loyalist pamphleteer referred, somewhat less charitably, in 1681:

Tis too well known, [the dispositions of] ... the greatest of these two noblemen [Buckingham] ... [and of] Major W[ildman], and H[enry] N[eville], as notorious for the same perfections, and their love of a monarchy and hatred of a commonwealth; nor did A[lgernon] S[idney] want his share in the consultation, a stout asserter of prerogative, as witnessed by his and others [e.g. Bethell] living out of this kingdom ever since the king's restoration, until they saw some likelihood of a change ... [where] they concluded to take hold of this opportunity for the carrying on of some long-hatched designs of their own ... pray observe ... none [are involved] but the spawn of those seduced or concerned in the late rebellion.[59]

The point has already been made that the republican renaissance in London in 1680–1 expressed itself both in political action and in publication. The quote above is rare, for its linking of Sidney in this period with his cousin and old rump colleague Henry Neville, one of the major authors of this period. We know, however, that they had at least two close friends in common (Wildman and John Hampden jnr) and there is a serious possibility that the final letter of Sidney's life, written to his 'dear[est] friend and kinsman', was to Neville.[60]

It also expressed itself in dangerous talk. When the time came later for a settling of scores, the government was pleased to receive the information of John Fitzgerald, of

sev[era]ll treasonable expressions he ... heard [in 1680] from Coll: Englesby [Ingoldsby – another ex-Rumper], Major Wildman, Coll Sydney and others ... Coll Henry Englishby [sic] ... said in my company and the Quakers that, notwithstanding the last Parliament at Westminster was prorogued and dissolved and all the other discouragement England met with from their King ... England will be England still

---

[58] Pocock, *Virtue Commerce and History*, p. 226. See also the same author's 'The History of British Political Thought: The Creation of a Center', *Journal of British Studies* 24:3 (1985), 306.

[59] [Anon; falsely attributed to Halifax] *A Seasonable Address to both Houses of Parliament Concerning the Succession, the Fears of Popery, and Arbitrary Government* in W. Scott (ed.), *Somers Tracts VIII* (1812), pp. 227–30. 'Major ' is here identified as Major Walcot the Rye House Plotter – another false attribution in my view, corrected above to 'Wildman'. The latter was well known in this context in 1681; the former (if at all) only later.

[60] Robbins, *Two English Republican Tracts*, pp. 15–18; M. Ashley, *John Wildman: Plotter and Postmaster* (1947), p. 217.

and ever and Englishmen will lose their lives and fortunes, before they lost their properties and liberties ... Much after the same manner have I heard Major Wildman, Col Sidnie and others speak treasonable expressions, as I shall more amply declare.[61]

Ingoldsby, who had saved his neck in 1660 by capturing Lambert, had clearly become tired of it again, and allowed this London atmosphere to go to his head. He was quoted further as saying that York, Lauderdale, and Ormonde were the three great enemies 'these nations hath', and that Strafford had lost his head for the same in 1641.[62] The information is made credible not only by its content, which echoes a variety of Sidney's expressed concerns, but also by Sidney's known association with both Wildman and Ingoldsby (not to mention 'the Quaker') in this year (1680). Ingoldsby was one of the four to accompany him to Amersham in December.

During 1680 and 1681, the combination of such talk, publication and action percolated to a treasonous crescendo. Ingoldsby was not the only one who let the atmosphere go to his head, as Sidney's *Vindication*, or his republican proposals made to Barillon in this same year (1680) make clear. But what allowed this atmosphere – this whole situation – to develop, was above all the judicial protection offered by the City of London. It was in this respect that the elections to the shrievalty had been crucial.

The two major areas in which the government of the City found itself able to influence the present situation were judicial and financial. We have already seen how, financially, the City and the House of Commons cooperated at the end of 1680 to attempt to force the crown to accept the Commons' demands. We know that Sidney was involved with this not only because of his close relations with both leaders in the City (Bethel) and the House (Jones), but because D'Avaux reported him as a leader of the whole enterprise.[63] We have seen too that when he had dispensed with parliaments altogether Charles' *Declaration* fixed upon this financial blackmail as a key example of his opponents' 1640s-like arbitrary behaviour.

Over the whole period, however, the rather more important powers wielded by the City were judicial. This is because, with this civil war being fought, as Anglesey put it, through the courts, control of the courts was critical. One of Bethel's key powers as Sheriff, should he choose to use it (and as we will see, he did) was the ability to control and supervise the selection of London juries. By dint of this apparently humble power, over the next two years London erected both a high wall against the intrusion of the royal will, and a formidable political instrument for the destruction of its enemies. In the absence of a republican government over the whole

[61] PRO State Papers 44 nos. 81–2; CSPD 1682, pp. 65–6.
[62] *Ibid.*, pp. 656.
[63] See pp. 119–20.

country, in short, the government of London turned the judiciary into an instrument of executive power. Needless to say, Sidney, alongside Bethel, was deeply involved with this.

Thus when the crown attempted to try political opponents in London the juries brought in *ignoramus* bills. The most famous example is Shaftesbury, but an earlier and equally well-known case at the time was that of Stephen College, the 'protestant joiner'. (College was later shifted to loyalist Oxford and tried and executed there; an early sign of what was to come.) Following this frustration of royal wishes, a loyalist pamphlet parodied a letter from College:

Return my thanks in the lowest and most prostitute manner to Sheriff Bethel (whom next to Alg[ernon] Syd[ney] I esteem as the chief patron of our Cause) for his True Protestant Ignoramus Jury, which so honestly discharg'd their Conscience ... And thou knowest who teacheth when he holds forth, That for a few to be Perjur'd for the benefit of the Nation, and True Protestancy, is ... a piece of Service becoming the Godly Party and the favourers of the Good Old Cause.[64]

The naming of Sidney as 'the chief patron' of these goings-on is of course significant, particularly since it agrees with Barillon. Barillon added, on 28 September 1681:

I have found Algernon Sidney strongly determined to reject any sort of accommodation with the court ... He is more important than he has ever been among the independents, and I believe that he will be able to render great services if Parliament reassembles.[65]

Similarly, as we have seen, when the Commons wished to make a demonstration of its power, the public trial of Stafford was conducted by Jones and the execution supervised by Bethel. On the scaffold Stafford delivered a last speech remarkedly anticipatory of Sidney's own. It 'ended by begging God not to avenge his innocent blood on the nation or on those who were the cause of his death'. He also begged the Sheriff to quiet the jeering of the crowd, to which, with a frugality even of pity, Bethel replied: 'Sir, we have orders to stop nobody's breath but yours.'[66]

It was not necessary for God to avenge Stafford's death, however, since the King, having sat powerless through the whole trial, had already icily vowed to do so. Once again, in his subsequent May *Declaration* Charles pointed to the House's legal, alongside its financial, arbitrary and tyrannical conduct. As the royalist 'Tutor' put it (quoting from the *Declaration*) in *A Dialogue at Oxford*:

Well! but were there not Arbitrary Orders made, for taking Persons into Custody,

---

[64] *A Letter Written from the Tower by Mr Stephen Colledge (the Protestant Joyner) to Dick Janeway's wife* (July 1681), p. 1.
[65] Barillon to Louis XIV, PRO 31/3 Baschet no. 150, p. 261.
[66] Ronalds, *Whig Revolution*, p. 143.

for matters that had no Relation to priviledges of Parliament, and strange illegal
Votes, declaring divers eminent persons to be enemies to the State, without process
of Law, or hearing their defence, of having any proofs made against them[?][67]

The most persistent and harsh of these measures had of course been
against the 'abhorrers'. Of these, Sidney had reported with satisfaction to
Henry Savile in October 1680, near the beginning of the new session:

Sir Robert Howard desired the house to proceed cautiously therein, his majesty
having by proclamation declared such petitions to be contrary to law. Notwithstanding which admonition, the house did vote *nemine contradicente* That it was,
and had ever been the right of the subjects of England to petition his majesty for the
meeting and sitting of parliaments until all petitions were heard and grievances were
redressed . . . [and they] appointed a committee to examine who had been guilty of
obstructing such petitions, and therein betraying their country. There are six or
seven members of the house of commons said to have declared themselves detesters
and abhorrers of such petitions, who, as is thought, will be turned out . . . without
other ceremony.[68]

From all of these developments a number of important consequences
followed, not only for the nation, but for Sidney himself. The first was that
the crown really did lose control of its capital, for two years, with very
important consequences. The City really did become 'a republic by the
King's side'. The capital was turned into a radical redoubt from the interior
of which plans, actions, talk and publication of an increasingly treasonous
variety were able to develop into a political culture. In the face of this
situation the court was almost powerless. It was, however, storing up
trouble of a very precise kind in the future, for all those involved. This was a
political game being played for high stakes, and Charles personally never
forgot the humiliation he suffered or what it revealed to him about the
enemies he faced. Nobody tried and sentenced to die between 1681 and
1683 was pardoned, and for the rest of his reign the King displayed a quite
unprecedented firmness of approach.

The loyalist reaction which eventually allowed the King to put an end to
this situation began, as we have seen, in response to these developments
themselves. It was the revival of the 'good old cause', in London and in
parliament, that captured the attention of the nation and that turned the
crisis around. Charles' first step out of this morass was his removal of
parliament to Oxford. The second and decisive move, however, had to wait
until the middle of 1682. This was a literal (and illegal) storming of the
London shrievalty, that allowed the crown to take the judicial institutions of
London back into its grasp.[69]

It was at this moment that the rubber-band of radicalism, which had been

[67] *A Dialogue at Oxford . . . Concerning Government* (1681), p. 15.
[68] Sidney, 'Letters to Savile' in *Works*, p. 53.   [69] See pp. 272–3 below.

stretched out to its full length over the previous two years, snapped back painfully on to those holding it. Suddenly all judicial protection was removed. But worse than that, considerably worse, it was made clear that the political judiciary of Sheriff Bethel – 'Mr Bethell was the first yt begun to return the Juryes himself'[70] – would now be maintained, to destroy its creators. It is hardly surprising if among the chief to suffer was Sidney who, in addition to all his other activities, had been threatening the crown in print, with impunity, as recently as 1681. As one contemporary put it, 'Sidney was lost' in 1683, because his fate was a precisely organised act of political revenge. He was tried before an 'abhorrer' (to whom he objected), by a politically selected jury *à la Bethel* (to which he objected), by the rules and procedures of Stafford's trial *à la Jones* (to which he objected). He objected to all of these things because he knew exactly what they meant, and what was happening to him. His trial is famous partly because he fought it as the piece of single-handed political combat it was. And he fought it from previous experience on the other side.[71]

It has been necessary to anticipate our story here, in order to properly explain the practical, before we examine the theoretical achievement to which Sidney contributed in these years. The republican capture of London, and its eventual partnership with a 'sharpened' lower House, was the high-water mark of the radicalisation set in train by the long prorogation of 1679–80. It was of the profoundest political importance, and rightly became the centre of the nation's, as well as the government's, attention. Its effects considerably outlived the subsequent loyalist reaction, and the City had to be wrested from its citizens in 1682 by force. The whole adventure resulted in some of the most important political thought English writers have ever produced, which would outlast even their own century. But the price to be paid was this: that such a profound impact did these events and developments have on contemporaries, that they would even outlast themselves; they lasted for long enough to destroy those held responsible for them.

8.3 AMERSHAM REVISITED, DECEMBER 1680

THE MEETING OF THE PARLIAMENT, 1680

The long prorogation came to an end when the parliament elected in August 1679 was finally allowed to meet, on 21 October 1680. A week before, Sidney had written to Furly:

---

[70] Before 1680, London juries were usually returned by secondaries, or in Middlesex by the under-sheriff. 'Mr Bethell was the first yt begun to return the Juryes himself, Mr Shute after him did the like.' Under-sheriff Sir Peter Rich's testimony to the Lords Committee in 1688, *Journal of the House of Lords* (1688), p. 281.

[71] All of this will be covered in detail in chapter 13 below.

We are here in the strangest confusion that I ever remember to have seen in English businesse. There never was more intrigues, and less truth ... The approaching Sessions of Parliament is like to be very turbulent, and none lesse than a Prophet, can tell what will be the issue of it.[72]

Within a week of its meeting, this tone of tense expectation had given way to a deep involvement in the proceedings. Sidney wrote to Savile:

We are in a busy time, and how empty soever any man's head hath formerly been, the variety of reports concerning things in agitation do so fill it, at least with an imagination of contributing something to other men's inventions, that they have little leisure to do anything else.[73]

For obvious reasons, Sidney chose to be no more specific in the mail about the identity of these 'other men', or their 'inventions'. What we can piece together from other sources has already been described. But the meeting of the parliament also brought suddenly to the fore a matter of more direct personal concern to Sidney. In the same letter to Savile, a week into the session, Sidney reported:

On Monday ... the committees were named, and a multitude of petitions concerning elections presented, and referred to that of priviledges and elections ... The Lord Halifax brought in a bill for the speedy discovery and conviction of papists, and ease of non-conformists, but so contrived, that both parties are almost equally incensed against him for it ... [and] I could have wished, that intending to oblige above a million of men, that go under the name of non-conformists, he had been pleased to consult with one of that number, concerning the ways of doing it.[74]

Sidney's electoral petition was read within five days of the opening of the session, on 25 October, Drake's not until 3 November. Both were referred to a Committee which reported on 11 December.[75] The feeling that Sidney had, in this parliament, the requisite friends in high places, was soon enough confirmed.

Of the Committee's two recommendations, the first was a key victory for Sidney, and this concerned the franchise. Despite Drake's indignant claim that this 'pretence [was] ... contrary to all former usage, [and] ... a meer surprize upon the Inhabitants', the Committee resolved that in future in Amersham 'only those inhabitants who pay scot and lot have right of electing'. When this recommendation was challenged in the House, Sir William Jones ended the debate by intervening in its favour. A narrower franchise was essential, he explained, since otherwise beggars and almsmen would vote, 'and how, you know'.[76] The matter was resolved without division.

---

[72] Forster (ed.), *Letters of Locke*, p. 88.
[73] Chatsworth, Devonshire MSS, Halifax Papers E.18.
[74] *Ibid.*
[75] *Commons Journal* 1679–81, pp. 638, 646.
[76] *Ibid*; see note 17 above; Grey, *Debates*, vol. VIII, pp. 127–8.

This is an important reminder of a point that this author and others have made elsewhere,[77] that in the seventeenth century radicalism and popularity were not the same thing. Radicalism was a minority creed, favoured by urban professionals and intellectuals, and the effort to secure its effects in government had always to be unpopular, as the short-lived history of the Republic had shown. The Restoration was popular; the Republic was not. Drake's strength lay in the long poll because the support of the majority of the inhabitants was easily seized by a local magnate upon whose benevolence the welfare of the parish's poorer members depended.

The second resolution of the Committee, however, was that the elections of both Drake and Sidney must be considered void, and a new one called. Although the resolutions concerning both the franchise and Drake's non-election were accepted without contradiction, the motion to void Sidney's election went to a division, to be lost 191/83. The tellers in Sidney's favour were Col. Mildmay, another survivor of the Rump parliament, and 'Mr Bremen', another republican. Writs were issued calling a by-election in Amersham for the following week: 18 December.[78]

ALCOHOL ABUSE IN A QUAKER BOROUGH: AN EXCLUSIVE REPORT

What we know of this by-election stems entirely from a subsequent chancery action against Sidney by certain 'burgesses and Inkeepers' of Amersham concerning the payment of election-night debts. Despite Gilbert Spencer's dictum that being 'burgers' the innkeepers were not to be challenged on this point, by 1682, with no seat in parliament and no further elections in prospect Sidney had clearly decided to the contrary. The liquid expense of five campaigns in three years cannot have been easy to bear; nevertheless the whole case throws Sidney's frugality into harsher relief. Between them, and in addition to their financial strategy, Bethel and Sidney seem to have been pursuing a policy of famine and drought. In a world where political truth had to be backed up by hard liquor, Sidney offered wisdom, experience and a just proportion of light ale. The result proved the limits of the people of Amersham's thirst for knowledge.[79]

According to Sidney's later Bill of Complaint (1682), immediately following the writ for the by-election:

severall of the burgesses [of Amersham] came to [me] and were very desirous [that I should stand] ... and taking notice that [I] had been at some charge at the last

[77] Scott, 'Radicalism and Restoration', pp. 465–6.
[78] *Commons Journal* 1679–81, p. 646.
[79] All quotations to follow come from PRO Chancery MSS C6 244/2. They have, where necessary, been paraphrased to omit repetitive legal formulae. In particular, Sidney referred to himself in the third person throughout (as 'your orator').

election [claimed that I] ... should be freely chosen ... and it should not cost ... one farthing if I should appear.

Accordingly,

On December 17th [the day before the election] [I] with three or four of [my] acquaintance repaired to Amersham ... about 10pm and suddenly about 10 of the burgesses came to [me] whom [I] entertained at the house of John Cheeseman, Inneholder, where [I] lodged that night ... [And] being informed that several of the burgesses were at the house of William haly Inneholder with some of [my] friends did send one of [my] servants ... to provide entertainment for [them] and such burgesses as paid scot and lot until the election was over.

In short the House seemed to have ruled with effect on the qualification for drinking, as well as for voting. The identity of one of Sidney's 'friends' emerges:

The next day [18 December] being the day for the election the Ld [William] Howard and [I] rising very early ... enquire[d] what quantity of beer and ale was drunk of both houses ... [and were] informed ... that there was not above 20s in drink spent before ... and £10 during, all the election. Which being over [I] about 3 o'clock on Dec 18th, having earnest occasion to return speedily to London went the same day from Amersham to Uxbridge Co. Middlesex and being in such hast[e] would not stay to settle the accounts of Cheeseman and Hayly but ... delivered a bag of money to John Tanner ... and Giles Child a victualler ... in which was £50 or so ... being much more than was sufficient, Cheeseman and Hayly being the only ones [I] gave order to provide any thing.

Sidney's understanding of this matter does not seem to have been very widely shared. Instead Cheeseman, Hayly and others claimed that he had authorised them to provide for 'all persons whatsoever who should come into their houses, and Giles Child, James Child, Andrewe Burrowes ... Thomas Petite of Amersham victuallers and Dudley Pennard mercer ... do likewise pretend they received the same order'.

The result was a shot in the arm for the economy of Amersham. Sidney complained that Cheeseman paid himself for 'sugar and brandy and several other things ... for which there was no necessary occasion'; and Hayly presented him with an unpaid bill for over £30 for 'meat and drink and great quantities of syder brandy sugar spices tobacco and many other things which [I] never desired'. And although all the innkeepers concerned knew 'there were not above fourscore who had the right to vote they entertained many hundreds with beer, ale, brandy, syder, etc'. According to Hayly, however,

about three or four days before [Sidney] came to the burrough a servant [of Sidney's] repaired to [my] house with several electors and called for half a crowne or three shillings of drinke, and ordered that from thenceforth until the election should be over [I] should make much of and entertaine all [Sidney's] friends and burgesses who should come to the house ... in the same way as [I] had in the previous election.

Hayly thus kept open house at Sidney's expense until 17 December, when 'upon this account [he] did particularly lodge at his house Sir Wm Waller, Sir Henry Ingoldsby and one Mr Nolthroppe [Richard Nelthorp] ... with several of their servants all of whome arrived about 7 or 8 that night ... with [Sidney and] ... did also entertaine in his stables 4 coach horse and several saddle horses belonging to the said gent[s] and their retinue and on the day of the election did entertaine these gentlemen with dinner with their servants and attendants, and one Captaine Ward who came to the burrough with [Sidney]'.

Sidney, Howard, Waller, Ingoldsby and Nelthorp had thus travelled to Amersham together, the former two staying at Cheeseman's; the latter three at Hayly's. Consequently Hayly charged to Sidney 7 barrels of beer (£7); 7lb of tobacco (56s); 50 gallons of 'syder' (£5); bread, meat and cheese (£12); brandy and syrupp of cloves (44s); 1 sack and 1 claret (3s 6d); hay and corne and shoeing for horses (6s). His agent had tendered his bill for £31 to Sidney in London who had told him it was too much 'and therefore should not pay itt' but said he would pay a lesser account. Hayly recklessly moderated it to £29 3d but this was still too much.[80]

James Child similarly confirmed that three or four days before the election 'Giles Child [as Sidney's agent] ordered the inkeepers to give entertainment from then until the election was over.' Cheeseman confirmed that Sidney and Howard 'with several of their servants' had lodged at his house on 17 December. Both Child and Cheeseman had been paid from the £50 so only Burrowes and Pennard joined Hayly in listing what they had supplied on Sidney's behalf. Sidney's 'friends and burgesses' at Burrowes' house had dispatched 5 barrels of beer, 5lb of tobacco, 18 gallons of fine cider, 30 gallons of burnt cider, and a large quantity of fish, meat, bread, butter, and cheese.

Unlike the others Pennard, owner of a coffee house, had been a stranger to Sidney in the 1679 election. But his friends and agents 'did endeavour still to preserve [Sidney's] interest in the said Borrough' in order for the by-election, and did 'by much persuasion by setting forth [to me Sidney's] greate pts and abilities for pformeing the Busines of a Burgesse in Parliamt persuade [me] to vote for him in the second election, by which means I came to be connected with [Sidney] and this vexatious suit'.

Like the others Pennard had entertained 'several of the electors ... and friends' at his house several days prior to the election 'where they were then consulting and debating the management of [it] ... on the behalfe of [Sidney] for sev[era]ll howers' in which time they dispatched 7 qts of 'Wrum'

[80] By the standards of the electoral contests of this period, these sums were small. It was not uncommon for candidates to spend over a thousand pounds. See Kishlansky, *Parliamentary Selection*, pp. 194–6.

and half a gallon of coffee. Pennard confessed he had no direction to charge this supply to Sidney other than that of the drinkers themselves.

The next day, however, following Sidney's own arrival in the borough, Pennard received order from Messrs Tanner and Davis, agents of Sidney, to entertain his 'friends, agents [sic], servants, burgesses' at Sidney's expense. That night he provided 3 gallons of coffee, 10 gallons of 'Wrum'; 23 gallons of cicera 'to witt Cider mixed with the Juice of Black cherries and boyled with spice and sweetened with sugar', and 1lb of tobacco. The next (election) day he dispensed a further 7 gallons of coffee, 23 and a half gallons of rum, 28 gallons of cicera, 1 gallon of brandy, 2lb of tobacco, and 1 shilling of horsemeat. And far from abusing the provisions of Sidney's order Pennard was 'abused and like to be beaten' and several windows were broken and stones thrown into the house by strangers wishing vainly to join the party.

As one of five houses acting for Sidney in one of his three campaigns in a borough with fewer than fifty eligible voters this level of consumption is truly impressive. What makes it even more so is that thus buoyed into Amersham on a river of beer (12 barrels), brandy (21 gallons), cicera (51 gallons), cider (163 gallons), rum (37 gallons), and tobacco (23 lb) Sidney still lost the election.

'Despite the clear ruling on the franchise, there is no evidence that it was followed. Drake was returned by both constables and the inhabitants at the by-election, and before any decision could be reached on Sidney's [resulting] petition, parliament was [again] dissolved.' An indenture recording the choice of 'the honerable Algernon Sidney Esq' by a list of burgesses including Pennard, Hayly, the Childs and others survives in the Sidney papers, dated 18 December, and sealed in the presence of Ingoldsby, Hill, Waller, and Nelthorp, but it is not clear what authority this carried. Sidney's petition reached the house only two days later (20 December); he was becoming a practised petitioner, and this was probably the reason for his hasty departure for London on the day of the election. Despite orders to do so on 20, 21, 23 December and 4 January however, when parliament was dissolved again on 10 January Sidney's petition still hadn't been heard.[81] He now found himself facing yet another election.

[81] *Commons Journal* 1679–81, pp. 686, 687, 692, 699.

The Vindication *of parliaments 1681–3*

9.1 1681

THE CHANGING OF THE GUARD

As the previous two chapters have suggested, by 1681 a certain changing of the guard had taken place among Sidney's political associates. This was another result of the process of polarisation, and of radicalisation. By 1681 he was keeping more dangerous company altogether.

Among the Lords, the major casualty was Halifax. His crime was, as we have seen,[1] that he had sided with the King, and frustrated the wishes of the Commons. When Sidney wrote to Savile again on 3 February 1681, he apologised for not having related events in December and January when parliament was in session:

The truth is, some of your friends, and mine, were so entangled in business then upon the stage, that I could say nothing to the purpose, without mentioning them; and the parts they had taken upon themselves were such as I was unwilling to relate ... The result of all this is that the Lord Sunderland is out of his place and the council ... Essex is also put out of the council and lieutenancy of Hertfordshire, upon presenting a petition from the Lords [this was Essex's 'inflammatory' petition against the re-siting of the new parliament at Oxford]. The Lord Halifax is gone to ruminate upon these matters at Rufford.[2]

The close relationship which would emerge from this situation and deepen over the next two years was with Essex. Sidney had remained on good terms with him throughout the period – he was buying horses for him through Furly in mid 1680.[3] Essex was an attractive, capable and morally upright individual whose earlier ministerial career Burnet held up as a model.[4] He shared important aspects of that career with Sidney, having been both an ambassador to Sweden, and Lord Lieutenant of Ireland from 1672 to 1677. In view of the close interest displayed by Sidney in the matter,

---

[1] See chapter 3 above, p. 68.
[2] Sidney, 'Letters to Savile' in *Works*, p. 3.
[3] Forster (ed.), *Letters of Locke*, pp. 96–8.
[4] Burnet, Own Time, pp. 97–9; *DNB* Arthur Capel, Earl of Essex.

179

we should take seriously the suggestion of Essex's involvement in moves to unseat Ormonde during 1680.[5] But it was between 1681 and 1683 that Sidney's relationship with Essex became a key to the political conduct of both men. Burnet described Essex's extraordinary political transformation under Sidney's influence in those years with apprehension and alarm.[6] In this, the family connection between them played a crucial role. Sidney must have first met Essex in 1653, when, as the young husband of his cousin Elizabeth Percy, he had to come to live, alongside Algernon himself, at the Northumberland household at Petworth.[7]

Providing a counterpoint to Essex was another lord of precisely opposite probity and moral fibre: Lord Howard. As we have seen, Sidney's relationship with Howard also went back at least to 1680. There was no family relationship here, but there was a shared historical experience of sufficient potency to fill in for it: Howard had been a rare titled member of the Rump parliament. He had also, under rather different circumstances, intrigued in the Netherlands with De Witt. His early career had, however, given important signs of a lack of promise: he was the only Rump member to be expelled for corruption.[8]

Sidney was not unmindful of this fact, but he had reached the stage of the political situation where past failings could be compensated for by present zeal. As Burnet put it:

Howard and [Sidney] were of a mind as to a Commonwealth and agreed in their aversion to ye King as well as to Monarchy in generall: and Sidney was so much taken with Howard's submission and going up as high as he did, yt tho, as he told me himself, he knew he had once been a knave, yet he came not only to trust himself entirely to him but he Imposed [him] on Essex [too].[9]

When Howard was arrested and sent to the Tower in 1681, it was Sidney who put up the money to bail him out. There survives among the Sidney papers note of 'a mortgage . . . made by the Lord Howard of Esgrigg to Coll Algernoon Sidney of the Mannor of Tollesbury in Essex . . . for £300' which probably dates from this period.[10] According to Burnet again 'Algernon Sidney took [Howard's] concerns and his family so to heart, and managed everything relating to him with that zeal and that care, that none but a monster of ingratitude could have made him the return that he did after-

[5] Kenyon, *Popish Plot*, pp. 197, 203–4.
[6] Burnet Add. MS 63,057, vol. II, p. 138; see chapter 12, pp. 278–80 below.
[7] HMC 9th Rep. p. 22, Salisbury MSS, p. 428; Sanford and Townshend, *The Great Govern-ing Families of England* (1865), vol. I, p. 220, quoted in Ian Ward 'The English Peerage 1648–60; Government, Authority and Estates', Cambridge PhD 1989, p. 167, notes 2–3.
[8] Worden, *Rump Parliament*, p. 85; Haley, *Shaftesbury*, p. 650; K.D.H. Haley, *William of Orange and the English Opposition 1672–4* (1953), pp. 35–6; Ward, 'The English Peerage 1648–60', pp. 22–4.
[9] Burnet Add. MS 63,057, vol. II, p. 138.
[10] Kent AO, Maidstone: De Lisle MS U1475 E99, 1 March 1688.

wards.'[11] At Sidney's trial Howard was quoted by a witness as having 'said he was in the Tower two years ago, and [Sidney], he believed, saved his life'.[12] It must have weighed fairly heavily with Howard that he was, eventually, to perform the opposite service.

Among Sidney's other associates we have noticed Sir William Waller, the obsessive priest-and-crucifix hunter of this period, with Richard Nelthorp, and Henry Ingoldsby. There were also Sir William Jones, Colonel Titus, John Wildman, Slingsby Bethel, and John Hampden jnr. (Some of these relationships will be discussed further in chapter 12.) Sidney's sister Dorothy reported in 1680, after Sidney and Shaftesbury's row, on

the great endeavours of those who have designs that can never be compassed, but by the whole nation being in a flame. I have told you how my Lord Shaftesbury and Mr Algernoon have railed at one another; now messages pass between them, I believe by Mr Hampden, but that I do not know ... [Algernon] says he does not go to him, because he tells lies of him and his friends; but he undertakes to know Shaftesbury's mind; he says he professes to have no design for the Duke of Monmouth: then you may imagine what he pretends to Mr Bethell to be for.[13]

When Sidney wrote to Savile of election results for the Oxford parliament, on 10 February, he reported particularly, 'Sir William Waller and Poultney were this day chosen at Westminster without any opposition. Col Titus and Sir Thomas Proby were with the same facility chosen knights of Huntingtonshire; Hambden the elder, and Wharton, of Buckinghamshire ...'[14] Another associate of the years 1681–3 was Gilbert Hollis, the Earl of Clare.

Alongside Halifax, the other great casualty of the same period among Sidney's friendships was William Penn. As the tenor of the crisis had become more violent, Penn had turned aside from it to channel the ideals for which he had fought the 1679 election campaigns into a project for the founding of a new colony. The rift between them – of which we know through a letter from Penn to Sidney in October 1681 – found its occasion in the proposed constitution of Pennsylvania, in which Sidney had taken a critical interest.

Sidney was not the ideal person to assist Penn with the constructive side of his enterprise; specific constitutions were not his speciality. Sidney's writing was concerned with general principles of government; he was sceptical about particulars. Thus Penn recalled 'the discourse we had at my house about my drawing Constitutions, not as proposals, but as if fixt to the hand ... [and] to which the rest were to comply, it they would be Concerned with me'. Unfortunately, at this stage concrete specifics were what Penn's enterprise required. Yet, he recorded:

[11] Burnet, *Own Time*, p. 281.   [12] *Trial* in Sidney, *Works*, p. 42.
[13] Berry, *Life and Letters of Lady Russell*, p. 136.
[14] Sidney, 'Letters to Savile', in *Works*, p. 4.

thy [Sidney's] objections were presently complyed with both by my [Penn's] verball
denyall [that] ... such ... words ... were imposed, and not yet free ... for debate,
and also [I] took my Pen and immediately alter'd the Termes, so as they Cor-
responded (and truly I thought more properly) with thy objection & sense. Upon this
thou didst draw a draught as to the Frame of the Government[,] gave it me to read,
[and] we discourst it, with a considerable agreement] it was [afterwards] Called for
back by thee, to finish and polish. I suspended proceeding in the Business of the
Government ever since (that being to be done after other Matters) instead of any
further Conference about it.[15]

Despite this level of agreement, however, from the rest of the letter we
find that Sidney's criticisms of Penn's proposed Frame of Government to
others had been intemperate and wounding. The last phrase of Penn's letter
may have been by way of explanation for a lack of further consultation
which Sidney wrongly took as rejection of his advice. What seems clear is
that Sidney's insistence on 'ruling' others – the psychological twin of his
refusal to be ruled – kept him friends like Howard, and lost him others of
greater originality and worth.

Concerning the extent of Sidney's contribution to the constitution of
Pennsylvania, we have no information other than what this letter provides.
Yet much ink has flowed on this subject. For 130 years biographers of
Sidney and Penn have perpetuated a civil war of which Penn, at least, would
have disapproved. This was waged between the view that Sidney was something like sole author of the constitution, and its opposite (repeated in the
most recent assessment by the Dunns) that Penn's 'remarks more plausibly
demonstrate that Sidney had little or no influence in that effort'.[16] It is
difficult to understand how either of these extremes of opinion have been
maintained, when Penn's letter lends them so little support.

Since Penn's remarks leave the matter unclear, firm opinions on either
side are best avoided. What the letter does seem to indicate is that Sidney
was a serious influence on the initial formulation of the constitution, but
that the final draft was, particularly on the powers of the Governor (Penn)
himself, some distance from Sidney's desires. On the eve of Penn's first
expedition to the colony such powers had become a financial and practical
necessity, demanded by the investors, and were criticised (on similar
grounds) by Benjamin Furly as well. Having found, however, the compro-
mises necessary for construction beyond him, Sidney demonstrated his
uncompromising capacity for destruction in their place. Penn wrote to him,
deeply hurt:

There are many things [that] make a man's life uneasy in the world ... but scarcely
one equall to ... the ... Injustice of Friends. I have been askt by severall since I came
to town if Coll Sydney and I were fallen out, and when I ... laught at it; they told me

---

[15] Penn to Sidney, October 1681 in Dunn (ed.), *Penn Papers*, p. 125.
[16] *Ibid.*, p. 124.

I was mistaken, and ... [that] he had used me very ill to severall persons, if not Companys; saying, I had a good County but the basest laws in the world ... and that the Turk was not more absolute than I ... I meet with this sort of language in the Mouths of Severall; I shall not yet believe it ... but if it be true, I shall be sorry we were ever so well acquainted, or that I have given so much occasion to them that hate us to laugh at me for more true friendship and steady kindness than I have been guilty of to any man I know liveing.[17]

THE END OF PARLIAMENTS

Following the dissolution of the parliament, and the calling of its successor to Oxford, Sidney wrote to Savile (on 3 February):

The fruits expected from the last parliament having been lost by little under-hand bargains, and, as some say, the king and parliament equally betrayed ... men's minds seem to be filled with ... many jealousies. Some think, the writs for calling the parliament are ... void, as being without the advice of council ... or that if it should meet at Oxford, its acts would be void ... for want of the freedom of voting, which is essential unto it. Others say ... that [men] ought to think themselves safe, when [the king] is safe, *though their danger be from him*. I know not what this will produce, but I never saw men's minds more heated than at present; and cannot think that portends less evil than the comet.[18]

The rest of this letter proceeds very much in the manner of the *Discourses* (begun this year), from sustained sarcasm on the subject of government ministers, to an undeniable tone of political threat.

His majesty ... resolves to reform his court, that all shall be of one mind. Mr Seymour ... brings his two friends Conway and Ranelagh [sic] into the management of business; and the first of these being as eminent for finesse of wit, quickness and easiness in state affairs, as the other in the excellency of all moral virtues, things cannot but go well ... [so] that England will keep up its reputation of being, as the cardinal Pallavicini says, the mother and nurse of the best wits in the world, when all foreign ministers shall come to treat with Jenkins and Conway, who will be taken for patterns of the genius of the nation ... Civil and military affairs thus being settled, treasures flowing in unto us on all sides, and all foreign princes, concerned in our affairs, being sure unto us, we need not fear a few discontented lords, a mutinous city, or murmuring counties.[19]

Sidney's own final election attempt at Amersham was held on 29 January. The candidates were Drake, Hill, Sidney, and William Cheyne, who had last stood in the seat in February 1679. Once again Drake 'disregarded the recent [franchise] decision and polled the inhabitant householders ... He and Cheyne were returned [by the constables, though] on the scot and lot franchise Sidney and Hill had the majority.' On the long poll the results

[17] Penn to Sidney, October 1681 in Dunn (ed.), *Penn Papers*, p. 125.
[18] Sidney, 'Letters to Savile' in *Works*, p. 3 (my emphasis).
[19] *Ibid.*

were: Cheyney 77, Drake 73, Hill 41, Sidney 33; on the short poll: Hill 40, Sidney 37, Drake 28, Cheyney 27.[20] Sidney wrote to Savile (3 Feb):

[the] parliament ... will probably be like unto the last; but it is thought many officers will be prevailed with to make false returns. I hear of no election passed, but that of Amersham. Of those who by the last parliament were there judged capable of giving their voices, Sir Robert Hill had forty; Mr Sydney seven and thirty ... Drake twenty eight ... Cheyney twenty nine; but the constables have been pleased to return the two latter.[21]

Once again both Sidney and Hill petitioned the House at Oxford, which met on 22 March. The petitions were referred to committee on 24 March, but once again the House was dissolved before it could make a decision.

All of this might have tried the patience of a saint, but Sidney was not one. If he now found himself driven to contemplate less-than-parliamentary means of combatting this continued arbitrary government, it cannot be said that he hadn't attempted all parliamentary means first. The first step on this post-parliamentary road was an appeal to 'the people'.

9.2 'A JUST AND MODEST VINDICATION OF THE PROCEEDINGS OF THE TWO LAST PARLIAMENTS' (1681)

INTRODUCTION

On 18 April the King issued his declaration justifying the dismissal of the last two parliaments. As we have seen, this became the focus for the loyalist reaction, with its clever appeal to public memory: it was answered by a flood of loyalist addresses from all over the country. In their wake Burnet remarked that 'in their cups the old valour and the swaggerings of the cavaliers seemed to be revived'.[22]

Given the pivotal nature of the declaration, it is understandable that a similar level of importance was attached by the Commons to a reply. According to one (hostile) account:

it was generally agreed by the heads of the discontented Party, that this Declaration must be answer'd, and that with all the ingredients of malice which the ablest amongst them could squeeze into it. Accordingly, upon the first appearance of it in Print, five several Pens of their Cabal were set to work; and the product of each having been examin'd, a certain person of Quality appears to have carried the majority of Votes ... a man cut out to carry on vigorously the designs of the Phanatique Party, which are manifestly in this paper.[23]

This last remark is a reference to that answer's evident part-republican-

---

[20] Henning, *Commons*, pp. 137–8; Sidney, 'Letters to Savile', in *Works*, p. 3.
[21] *Ibid.*
[22] Burnet, *Own Time*, pp. 276–7.
[23] [Anon] *His Majesties Declaration Defended: In a Letter to a Friend* (1681), p. 11.

ism: the 'Phanatique' of 'Quality' was Sidney himself. The answer was *A Just and Modest Vindication of the Proceedings of the Two Last Parliaments*, which Burnet called 'the best writ paper in all that time'.[24]

The exceptional lucidity of the *Vindication* as a political statement has long been recognised. In addition to Burnet's judgment that 'it was by much ye best writ piece yt came out in all these Embroilments'[25] Ralph called it 'certainly the most judicious and important of all that the Party ever set forth: nor is the state of the Controversy between the two Factions to be understood without it'.[26] Behrens too named its author as the most persuasive 'whig' polemicist of the period.[27] For all these accolades, the tract itself has never been given the detailed examination its stature commands. This reflects partly the neglect of the political thought of this period in general, and partly perhaps the belief that opposition polemics written after the last 'exclusion' parliament came too late to be important. In fact most of the best 'opposition' writing belongs to this period, and it is precisely the timing of the *Vindication* that make it the fullest and most mature statement we have of the Commons' cause. By 1681, moreover, the cause of 'parliaments' against arbitrary government was increasingly obviously the 'good old cause'.

For it was again to this same central issue, consistent since Marvell's *The Growth of Popery and Arbitrary Government* (1677), that the *Vindication* applied itself. This should hardly surprise us, since the accusation of arbitrary government had been the focus of the King's declaration itself. The response was a *Vindication* of the rights of the people in parliament to political expression free from the obstructions, manipulations, prorogations and dissolutions of the crown.

In this it echoed, not surprisingly given its authorship, *The Humble Petition and Address of the . . . City of London* (1681), presented to the King at the same time. This insisted that since 'one of the most effectual means the [popish plotters] . . . proposed to accomplish their Designs was by the frequent Adjourning, Proroguing, or Dissolving of Your Parliaments We [could not but be] . . . surprized with Astonishment at the untimely Dissolution of Your late Parliaments, before . . . they could fully pursue the Discovery and Suppression of the said Designs'.[28] The same issue lay at the heart of *A Dialogue at Oxford* (1681), and *Vox Populi* (1681), both of which consistently use language almost identical to the *Vindication*. The complaint of 'the people' was that

---

[24] Burnet, *Own Time*, pp. 276–7.
[25] Burnet, B L, Add. MS 63,057, vol. II, p. 116.
[26] J. Ralph, *History of England* (1744), quoted in Behrens (see note 27).
[27] Behrens, 'Whig Constitution', 59.
[28] *The Humble Petition and Address of the . . . City of London* (1681), p. 5.

Their parliaments . . . [are] rendered so insignificant by these frequent Prorogations and Dissolutions . . . that not to suffer Parliaments to sit to answer the great ends for which they were Instituted, is expressly contrary to the Common Law, and so consequently to the Law of God as well as the Law of Nature, and thereby Violence is offered to the Government itself, and Infringement of the People's fundamental Rights and Liberties.[29]

It is this language and this issue, of course, which provides the context for Locke's *Two Treatises*, and Sidney's *Discourses Concerning Government*. What parliaments demanded from 1678–81, what the petitioning movement demanded in 1680, what these tracts demanded in 1681, and what the major works of political literature to emerge throughout the period demanded was not exclusion but the people's 'rights to their parliaments sitting' – their fundamental [political] rights and liberties' – a demand grounded in 'the great ends for which . . . [Government is] Instituted', the people's good.

While the general importance of the *Vindication* in this context is clear, our interest in it here is more specific. An examination of the tract alongside Sidney's 'Letters to Savile' and *Discourses* helps to confirm the claim, first made by Burnet, that Sidney was its principal author. This claim seems to have been forgotten by scholars and Sidney biographers until Blair Worden recently re-directed our attention to it.[30]

Authorship of the tract has conventionally been attributed by bibliographers to Sidney's friend Sir William Jones. This will have assisted its neglect, since the pivotal role played by Jones (and Titus) in this crisis has not been generally recognised. Burnet's claim can now be considered more carefully, by comparing the original manuscript of his *History* with the published version. In the manuscript Burnet wrote of the *Vindication*: 'It was beleived to be penn'd by Major Wildman, and digested by Jones. But many things were put into it by Colonel Sydney, and some few by Mr Titus.'[31] In the published *History* this became: 'An answer was writ . . . with great spirit and true judgement. It was at first penned by Sidney. But a new draft was made by Somers and corrected by Jones.'[32]

Between the two versions, claim to primary authorship thus moves from Wildman to Sidney, possibly when Burnet became surer of his information (this would support the change in wording from 'It was believed to be penn'd by . . . Wildman', to 'It was . . . penned by Sidney'). Secondly, only

29 [Anon] *Vox Populi*, pp. 1–5.
30 A.B. Worden, 'The Commonwealth Kidney of Algernon Sidney', *JBS* 24 (1985), p. 15; see the discussion of Robert Ferguson's rival claim to authorship in James Ferguson, *Robert Ferguson the Plotter* (1887), p. 57. Ferguson's claim, unsupported either by other testimony, or by the style and content of the *Vindication* itself, should be taken as evidence of the quality rather than origin of the tract.
31 Burnet, BL, Add. MS 63,057, vol. II, p. 116.
32 Burnet, *Own Time*, p. 276.

two names appear in both versions – Sidney and Jones – and of these only Sidney is given primary authorship, with Jones consistently allocated responsibility for a second draft. From Burnet, therefore, Sidney emerges with the strongest claim to primary authorship, with secondary help from the legal expert Jones. This is both how Sidney himself wrote, and exactly how the tract reads, and it is to the illustration of this probability that the following discussion of the text will be directed.

The *Discourses* shows that at its best Sidney's writing possessed a peculiar style and force. It also shows that he needed help or editorship to moderate claims and length, to eliminate repetition and over-statement. We know that Sidney himself knew this; that the *Discourses* never received such revision only because he was arrested before it was finished. We know that he intended to submit the manuscript for comment to 'friends' before publication – and in 1681, for the *Vindication*, Jones would have been the obvious one (he died in 1682). It seems very likely that this is how the *Vindication* was written. If so, it is the only finished political work of Sidney's (though not solely his) that we have, and that was published in his lifetime. This would be appropriate enough since it summed up the 'old cause', the cause of a lifetime. The final point about Burnet's attributions is that we know that Sidney, Wildman, Jones and Titus were working together at this time, inside the House and outside it. For all of these reasons the *Vindication* is important, not just as a rare surviving work of Sidney's own, but as the most important statement we have of the parliamentary cause, from the men at its heart.

THE TEXT OF THE 'VINDICATION'

Blair Worden has drawn attention to one textual connection between the *Vindication* and the *Discourses* which helped to reinforce the idea of Sidney's authorship. This concerns Sidney's claim in the *Discourses* that crown lands were a public trust rather than a private patrimony, and could not be alienated by the monarch without the consent of the public council of parliament. According to the *Discourses*,

The king . . . [cannot] dispose if it [his land], because it is annexed to the office, and not alienable by the person. This is not only to be found in regular mixed monarchies (as in Sweden, where the grants made by the last kings have been lately rescinded by the general assembly of estates, as contrary to law) but even in the most absolute, as in France, where the present King, who has stretched his power to the utmost, had lately acknowledged, that he cannot do it . . . that the demesnes of the crown cannot be alienated . . . [and] all the grants made within the last fifteen years have been annulled.[33]

[33] Sidney, *Discourses*, p. 437.

According to the *Vindication*:

The king of Sweden, within these few months has, by the advice of the states, resumed all the lands which his predecessors had in many years before granted from the crown ... and Tacitus observes, that the first of the [Roman emperors] who looked upon the public treasure as his own, was Claudius, the weakest and most sottish of them all. The present king of France did within these twelve years, by the consent of his several parliaments, resume all the demesnes of the crown's which had been granted away ... That haughty monarch, as much power as he pretends to, not being ashamed to own that he wanted the power, to make such alienations ...[34]

What adds further considerable weight to the many coincidences between the two passages are Sidney's own years in Sweden and France; and his frequent references to Tacitus, Claudius, and the 'sottish' Roman emperors in the *Discourses* as well. It is also worth noting how the references to time correspond: the *Vindication*, written in April–May 1681, says of Sweden 'within these few months' and of France 'within these twelve years'; this section of the *Discourses* (p. 437), almost certainly written in March–April 1683, says of Sweden 'lately' and of France 'within the last fifteen years'.

This is only one of a clear procession of Sidney's footprints running through the tract. There are countless coincidences of both style and content between it and Sidney's writing elsewhere, particularly of this period. It also contains passages – sometimes whole pages – which seem suddenly the work of another hand. The dominant tone is, however, Sidney's own, with two important consequences. The first is that, as always, and as with the *Discourses*, despite a visible attempt at self-restraint the tract becomes permeated with both republicanism, and with political menace. Given the context, this constitutes another typical Sidnean victory for belief over intention – one serving to confirm rather than refute the King's own allegations. If there is any reliable hallmark of Sidney's writing, this is it, and it helps to confirm the status of his eventual execution as the culmination of a lifetime's work. The second consequence is that the tract's content further belies the characterisation of the political thought of this crisis as superficial; the *Vindication* advances a coherent philosophy of government, as well as a fundamental challenge to the government now in being.

One of the rhetorical devices most recurrent in the *Vindication*, the *Discourses*, and Sidney's writing in general, is his frequent appeal to 'the wisdom of our ancestors'. In the *Discourses*, as discussion gives way to threat, this becomes 'the courage of our ancestors'. Another, admittedly widespread at this time, is the teleological habit of describing and judging things by reference to their ends. All of these characteristics appear in a close echo of the *Discourses* at the very outset of the *Vindication*:

[34] *A Just and Modest Vindication of the Proceedings of the Two Last Parliaments* (1681), reprinted in *State Tracts in the Reign of Charles II*, vol. IV, Appendix no. XV, p. cxlviii.

It is not to be denied, but that our kings have ... been entrusted with the power of calling and declaring the Dissolutions of Parliaments. But, lest through defect of age, experience, or understanding they should ... mistake our constitution or by passion [and] private interest ... be so far misled as not to assemble parliaments, when the public affairs require it; or to declare them dissolved before the ends of their meeting were accomplished: the wisdom of our ancestors has provided by divers statutes, both for the holding of parliaments annually, and that they should not be prorogued or dissolved till all the petitions and bills before them were answered and redressed. The constitution had been equally imperfect and destructive of itself, had [these matters] been left to the choice of the Prince.[35]

If the subject and style of this passage are strongly redolent both of Sidney in particular, and of the issue at the heart of this crisis in general, they are equally reminiscent of anti-absolutist argument in the early-Stuart period. It cannot have escaped many contemporaries which King was last 'so far misled as not to assemble parliaments' or when. The statute enjoining annual parliaments to which Sidney here refers (4. Ed. III c.14) was a favourite of Edward Coke's for use in exactly this way in that period. We have recently been reminded that this demand for annual parliaments preceded Charles I's coming to the throne, featuring in a widely circulated manuscript tract written in the second half of James' reign.[36]

We have seen, too, that in a letter to Henry Savile on 3 February of this year Sidney had said: 'Some think, the writs for calling the parliament are themselves void, as being without the advice of council.' The *Vindication* says: 'parliaments are never called without the advice of council, and the usage of all ages [another characteristic Sidney expression] has been never to send them away without the same advice'.[37]

The way the argument then develops is notable, for it is a quiet but definite shelving of the fiction of blaming the King's advisers – a feature of the rhetoric of this crisis as it had been of the last. Again, we have already seen Sidney's remarks in his letter to Savile in February: 'Others say ... [men] ought to think themselves safe, where [the King] is safe, though their danger be from him.'[38] The *Vindication* elaborates:

To forsake this safe method, is to expose the king personally to the reflections and censures of the whole nation ... Our laws have taken care to make the king always dear to his people ... by wisely preventing him from appearing as author of any thing which may be unacceptable to them ... It is therefore that he doth not execute any considerable act of royal power, till it be first debated and resolved in council ... but we know not whom to charge with advising this last Dissolution: it was a work

---

[35] *Ibid.*, p. cxxxiv.
[36] Sommerville, *Politics and Ideology*, p. 104; P. Croft 'Annual Parliaments and the Long Parliament', *BIHR*, 59 (1986), 155–71; quoted in R. Cust and A. Hughes (eds.), *Conflict in Early Stuart England: Studies in Religion and Politics 1603–42* (1989), p. 18.
[37] *Vindication*, p. cxxxv; 'Letters to Savile' in *Works*, p. 3.
[38] *Ibid.*

of darkness; and if we are not misinformed, the privy-council was as much surprized at it as the nation.[39]

The *Vindication* then turns to the related matter of who to hold responsible for the King's *Declaration* itself. At this point, as we have also seen, it makes the ancestry of its own cause explicit, and issues what amounts to a threat:

The first *Declaration* of this sort which I ever met with, being that which was published in 1629 ... was so far from answering the ends of its coming out, that it filled the whole kingdom with jealousies [compare Sidney to Savile on 3 February: 'mens minds seem to be filled with many jealousies'] and was one of the first sad causes of the ensuing unhappy war.[40]

Its subsequent note of any ministers or advisers that were involved, that they 'cannot blame us for hoping one day to see justice done upon such counsellors', recalls again the *Discourses*' reminiscences about the ship-money judges and its remark: 'I leave it to the reader to consider, how many in our days may expect vengeance for the like crimes.' The *Declaration* itself the *Vindication* finds to be riddled with 'Gallicisms which ... shew the writer to have been of another nation, or at least so much taken up for the interests of France ... [as to use] form[s] of speech peculiar to the French, and unknown to any other nation. The reader (who understands that language) will observe many more of this kind ...'[41] There were few people better placed by personal experience than Sidney to make this remark, and again it invites comparison with the *Discourses*:

This is the languge of French lackeys, valet-de-chambres, taylors, and others like them ... who when they fly to England for fear of a well earned gally, gibbett, or wheel, are ready to say 'Il faut que le roi soit absolu, autrement il n'est point roi.'[42]

There is another parallel – on the same topic – from Sidney's *Court Maxims*, according to which:

The king of France well understands ... ye power of money ... in our Court, and has disbursed large sums ... to his great advantage. There's nothing so secret in our court, but by the next post 'tis known at Paris.[43]

According to the *Vindication*:

Let us then no longer wonder, that the time of dissolving our Parliaments, is known at Paris sooner than at London ... the reasons now given for it, were formed there too.[44]

Moreover, according to the *Vindication*,

This Declaration was not communicated to the privy council till Friday the 8th of April ... but M Barillon, the French ambassador, did not only read it to a gentleman

---

[39] *Vindication*, p. cxxxv.   [40] *Ibid.*, p. cxxxvi.
[41] *Ibid.*, p. cxxxvii.   [42] Sidney, *Discourses*, p. 248.
[43] Sidney, *Court Maxims*, p. 149.   [44] *Vindication*, p. cxxxvii.

the 5th of April, but advised with him about it, and demanded his opinion of it, which his excellency will the better remember, because of the great liberty which the person took in ridiculing it to his face.[45]

(It was in late 1680 that Barillon 'rentre dans un grande commerce avec le Sieur de Sydney', and in August 1681 that he described him as more important than ever.)[46]

Echoes of Sidney's electoral observations in the Savile letters are visible in the *Vindication*'s claim that:

the court never did yet dissolve a parliament abruptly . . . but they found the next parliament more averse, and to insist upon the same things with greater eagerness than the former. English spirits resent no affronts so highly as those which are done to their representatives; and the court will . . . find the effects of that resentment in the next election.[47]

Equally so is the particular attention he paid in those letters to the King's breaking his promise of April 1679 to be advised by his Council:

[Other] Declarations since . . . signify as little: we will only remember [that of] 20th of April 1679 . . . wherein his majesty . . . professes his resolution . . . to be advised by . . . his council, in all his weighty and important affairs . . . [and] every man must acknowledge, that either his majesty has utterly forgotten this public and solemn promise, or else that nothing weighty and important has happened from that time to this very day.[48]

The memory of the *Vindication* on this subject eventually proves a little more capacious, and ominous:

For surely this Declaration . . . will make but few converts . . . because the people have been so often deceived by former Declarations . . . They have not yet forgotten the Declaration from Breda, though others forgot it so soon, and do not spare to say, that if the same diligence . . . had been made use of in that affair, which ha[s] been since exercised directly contrary to the design of it . . . all of his majesty's subjects would now have enjoyed the fruits of it, and would now have been extolling a prince so careful to keep sacred his promises to his people.[49]

Sidney's hand is unmistakably visible in the *Vindication*'s criticism of the recently completed Spanish alliance:

if the present king of Spain should imitate his great grandfather Philip the second, and oppress any of his subjects, as cruelly as he did those of the Low Countries, and so force them to a necessary self-defence; we have renounced the policy of our ancestors, who thought it their interest and duty to succour the distressed.[50]

This is a key passage, for it identifies not only Sidney's authorship (it is not

---

[45] *Ibid.*, p. cxxvii.
[46] PRO Baschet no. 146, p. 304.
[47] *Vindication*, p. cxxxviii.
[48] Sidney, 'Letters to Savile' in *Works*, pp. 14, 47–8.
[49] *Vindication*, pp. cxxxvii–cxxxix.
[50] *Ibid.*

difficult to remember which ancestor he has in mind here) but the grounds
for his belief in the legitimacy of armed resistance. This is the same 'necessary self-defence' – the 'self-defence of protestants' – that Sidney defended
from the Tower to John Hampden jnr in 1683; 'Somme may say the protestants of Holland . . . weare guilty of treason in bearing armes against their
princes, but [that] is ridiculous . . . when it is certaine, they sought noe more
then the security of their own lives.'[51] It must be compared most particularly
with the *Discourses*:

> And when the Protestants of the Low Countries were so grievously oppressed by the
> Power of Spain, under the proud, cruel, and savage . . . Duke of Alva, why should
> they not make use of all the means that God had put into their hands for their
> deliverance? . . . By resisting they laid the foundation of . . . a most glorious and
> happy commonwealth . . . the strongest pillar of the Protestant cause now in the
> world, and a place of refuge unto all those who in all parts of Europe have been
> oppressed for the name of Christ.[52]

It is because this was Sidney's cause: 'the protestant cause' – the century-
long struggle against the Counter-Reformation – that the *Vindication*
echoes the contents, as well as the title, of Sir Philip Sidney's friend Du
Plessis Mornay's *Vindiciae Contra Tyrannos*. Like that work, and the *Discourses*, it was a vindication of the right of self-defence of protestants in that
cause.[53]

The *Vindication*'s treatment of English history equally echoes that of the
Discourses – not least, once again, in its menace. It praises Henry V as a
'wise and brave prince' (it was from Henry V's death that Sidney dated the
'general impairing of our government' in the *Discourses* (pp. 506–8)), and
Elizabeth (also praised in the *Discourses* as approving acts of parliament by
the handful). It contrasts their reigns with the 'unfortunate' [sic] experiences
of 'Edward 2, R[ichard] 2. and Hen[ry] 6. [which] ought to serve as land
marks, to warn succeeding kings from preferring secret councils to the
wisdom of their parliaments'. The *Discourses* invoked the same cautionary
examples, as did *Vox Populi*.[54] The blatantly intimidatory nature of these
references drew the attention of the loyalist *Seasonable Address* (1681)
which noted: 'These things, and the frequent mentioning the fates of
Edward II, Richard II, and Henry VI, cannot but alarm his majesty.'[55]

Vox Populi had asked: 'if Empson and Dudley in Henry the Eights time

---

[51] Sidney to Hampden, 6 October 1683, Letter 4, East Sussex Record Office, Glynde Place
     Archives, no. 794.
[52] Sidney, *Discourses*, ch. 2, sect. 32; 'Trial' in *Works*, pp. 24–5.
[53] See Scott, *Sidney and the English Republic*, ch. 3; Mornay's *Vindiciae* was published in
     English eight years later as [Junius Brutus] *Vinidicae Contra Tyrannos: A Defence of
     Liberty against Tyrants* (1689).
[54] Sidney, *Discourses*, pp. 506, 257; *Vox Populi*, p. 14.
[55] Scott (ed.), *Somers Tracts*, vol. VIII, p. 234.

... were Hanged ... then what shall become of those [in our time who have done worse]?' The *Vindication* observed that 'no names [are] remembered with greater detestation than those of Empson and Dudley ... [who] were punished as traitors in the reign of [Hen. 8]'. Sidney's *Discourses* repeated: 'Empson and Dudley were charged with treason for subverting the laws of the land, and executed as traitors.'[56]

We can similarly hear an echo of both the *Discourses* and the *Court Maxims* in the *Vindication*'s demand that the King 'deliver up to justice those wicked wretches, who have infected him with the fatal notion, that the interest of his people are not only distinct [from] but opposite to his'. This is equally like Locke, who wrote in the *Two Treatises* of 'Those who speak as if the Prince had a distinct and separate interest from ... the community ... [whose] flattery, taught princes to have separate interests from their people'.[57]

The *Vindication*'s argument concerning exclusion was that parliaments have the right and power to nominate any successor they wish: as the *Discourses* was to put it: 'the institution of a kingdom is the act of a free nation'. It referred to the case of 'Henry of Bourbon, who, though accomplished in all the virtues required in a prince, was by the general assembly of the estates at Blois, declared incapable of succession to the crown of France, for being a protestant.' Sidney's *Discourses* makes the same claims for parliamentary power at length, and refers again to the case of 'Henry of Bourbon [who] was without controversy the next heir; but neither the nobility nor the people ... would admit him to the crown, till he had given them satisfaction ... by abjuring his religion.'[58]

The *Vindication* accuses York personally of 'all imaginable excesses of cruelty' in Scotland, and 'exalting the prerogative ... beyond its due bounds'; it then makes the connection with Charles I by remarking that he was 'bred up in such principles of politics, as made him in love with arbitrary power'. It observes that 'The duke with the papists might then make such a peace, as the Romans ... once in our desolated country, by the slaughter of all the inhabitants able to make war ... This is the way to have such a peace as the Spaniards, for the propogation of the gospel, made in the West Indies.'[59] Sidney's *Discourses* repeats:

This peace is in every wilderness ... Our ancestors the Britons observed [such a] ... peace, which the Romans established ... consist[ing] in the most wretched slavery and solitude ... This is the peace the Spaniards settled in their dominions of the West Indies.[60]

[56] *Vox Populi*, pp. 15–16; *Discourses*, pp. 393, 488.
[57] *Vindication*, p. clvi; Locke, *Two Treatises*, ch. 8, p. 3.
[58] *Vindication*, p. clviii; *Discourses*, pp. 255, 254.
[59] *Vindication*, p. clviii.
[60] *Vindication*, p. clviii; *Discourses*, pp. 132–3.

Finally Sidney's distinctive style and readiness to envisage a military outcome are apparent in the *Vindication*'s typically menacing conclusion on
this subject:

But as it is not to be imagined that any nation that hath virtue, courage, and strength
equal unto the English, will so tamely expect their ruin, so the passing a bill to
exclude him may avoid, but cannot . . . establish a war . . . if there must be a war, let
it be under the authority of law . . . against a banished excluded pretender . . . The
whole people will be an Army for that purpose, and every heart and hand will be
prepared to maintain [it].[61]

The first and last lines of this passage reappear constantly throughout the
Discourses.

Other parallels of style and content between the *Vindication* and the
Discourses include both figures of speech ('But if such as delight in these
cavils . . .'; 'But, to silence the most malicious . . .') and characteristics of
form: the (admittedly common enough) listing of arguments by number for
instance. Parallels of content include both sources ('Bracton tells us . . .'),
and the use – shared by *Vox Populi* – of the same three key statutes to define
'the law of the land, that is, the law and custom of parliament': 4. Ed. III;
25. Ed. III; and 36. Ed. III.[62]

Yet it is towards the end of the *Vindication* that we encounter the most
startling footprint of all of Sidney's involvement. So far this chapter has
argued that for all its 'constitutional' veneer the *Vindication* betrays its true
authorship in two ways. The first is that it bristles with remarks about the
monarch and monarchy, and parliamentary power, which convey a political
attitude that can only be described as republican. The second is that it
contains a series of statements about the Declaration of Breda, the fate of
Edward II and Richard II, the desire for 'vengeance', the precedent of
Charles I, the legitimacy of 'necessary self-defence', and the nation's readiness for 'war', which are blatantly intimidatory. These are both – as we will
see in the next chapter – characteristics of the *Discourses*, where they are
taken much further. But in this context there was one rhetorical device
peculiar to Sidney which allowed him to take his argument where no (seventeenth-century) English writer had gone before.

This was Sidney's habitual readiness to take on board terms of political
abuse and, by subjecting the words to scrutiny, defend them against their
users. A key example of this occurs in the *Discourses*, as we will see, in
relation to the word 'rebellion'. Towards the end of the *Vindication* just
such a rhetorical opportunity arises, and no considerations of prudence can
dissuade Sidney from taking it. This was the King's *Declaration*'s claim that
its opponents – and this means the leaders of 'the Two Last Parliaments' in

---

[61] *Vindication*, p. clviii–clix.
[62] *Vindication*, p. clxiii; *Vox Populi*, pp. 6–7; Sidney, *Discourses*, pp. 346, 395.

the Commons – were actuated by 'Common-wealth principles'. Sidney cannot resist both accepting the charge and defending the fact. The result is an impassioned defence of such principles against the new-fangled innovation of 'arbitrary government'. Seldom have the bases of Sidney's (in this sense conservative) political perspective, and of his indignation at the modern political world, been laid so bare. In the process the *Discourses'* familiar catalogue of republics: Rome, Venice, Genoa, Switzerland, the United Provinces, all find their way into the argument, along with much of the rest of its historical, political and geographical terrain. According to the *Vindication*:

[Our ancestors thought] the liberty and welfare of a great nation was of too much importance to be suffered to depend upon the will of one man ... if they mean by these lovers of Common-wealth principles, men passionately devoted to the public good and to the common service of their country; who believe that kings were instituted for the good of the people, and government ordained for the sake of those that are to be governed ... [then] every wise and honest man will be proud to be ranked in that number. And if a Common-wealth signifies the common good, in which sense it hath in all ages been used by all authors, and which Bodin puts upon it when he ... calls [France] a republic, no good man will be ashamed of it ... It is strange how the word should so change its signification with us in the space of twenty years. All monarchies in the world that are not purely barbarous and tyrannical, have ever been called Commonwealths. Rome itself altered not that name, when it fell under the sword of the Caesars. The proudest and cruellest of the emperors disdained it not. And in our days, it doth not only belong in Venice, Genoa, Switzerland, and the United Provinces ... but to Germany, Spain, France, Sweden, Poland, and all the kingdoms of Europe. May it not therefore be apprehended that our present ministers, who have so much decried this word so well known to our laws, so often used by our best writers, and by all our kings, until this day, are enemies to the thing. And that they who make it a brand of infamy to be of Common-wealth principles ... do intend no other than the hurt and mischief of that people? Can they in plainer terms declare their fondness of their beloved arbitrary power, and their design to set it up, by subverting our antient legal monarchy, instituted for the benefit of the Commonwealth ... Let the nation then to whom the appeal is made, judge who are the men that endeavour to poison the people, and who they are that are guilty of designing innovation ...[63]

It is hardly surprising, after this magnificent tirade, that the nation 'to whom the appeal is made' seems to have judged that the King's accusation was correct. All of this passage reappears, in one form or another, in the *Discourses*.

It is of course possible to argue, as earlier writers did of the *Discourses* itself, that this is not republican; that there is nothing here contrary to what Behrens identified as the cardinal 'whig' concept: 'mixed monarchy'. But as this was a superficial judgement of the *Discourses* – Sidney states this once but the whole book contradicts him – so we should not take the *Vindication* at face value either.

[63] *Vindication*, pp. clxviii–clxix.

It has already been shown how central much of this thinking was to the 'opposition' side of the crisis as a whole, particularly from 1680. Here we find much of the republican *Discourses*, and its author, at the heart of the key statement issued by the 'parliamentary' cause in mid 1681. This was the high point of that cause's radicalisation – the 'good old cause' – issued by the commons leadership just as they had lost their last parliament and the wave of reaction was beginning to break over their heads. Both inside the House and out, what was becoming apparent about that cause was that by 1681, as in 1641, the struggle for parliaments – for parliamentary government – no longer meant 'mixed monarchy' at all, but parliamentary supremacy. This is what the cry of '41 again' was all about. Where a King bent on 'arbitrary government' had control of the sitting of parliaments, there was no alternative.

We have seen Titus within the house, and Sidney outside it, making this clear. It is hardly surprising therefore that following the publication of the *Vindication* – which must have confirmed his worst fears – Charles remarked to Barillon that to restore order he would have to 'cut off a few heads'.[64] It took him two years to recover the control of London necessary to do so. When, thereafter, the principal author of this tract faced just this fate – having written another to furnish the crown with evidence – Charles 'said that Algernon Sidney had, on his return to England, promised him to behave blamelessly towards him; how was he to spare men who would not have spared him had he fallen into their hands?'[65]

Given that Charles was correct about Sidney's promises, why have historians been so reluctant to see the crown's side of this matter? The answer is that whig historians painted this crisis not as what it was – the second struggle for parliaments, which shaded off naturally, following the first, into republicanism and insurrection. They painted it simply as a justified attempt to anticipate the events of 1688 by excluding James from the throne. By such criteria, the execution of leading 'whigs' in 1683 was a piece of outrageous over-reaction which rightly made its victims martyrs (to the 1688/whig cause). Yet Sidney's cause, as he would make clear on the scaffold, was not that of 1688 but the 'old cause' (of protestantism and parliaments) for which he had been in arms, one way or another, since 1643. By 1681 the loyalist majority of the nation shared this opinion: that the central issue was not whether the nation would have exclusion, but whether it would have a republic or a monarchy.

The stage was thus set for the last stage in the 'opposition' side of this drama, following the suspension of parliaments altogether. This raised the stakes to a point where most people threw in their hands. Those who did

[64] Von Ranke, *History of England*, vol. IV, p. 188.
[65] *Ibid.*

not either felt they had exposed themselves already to the point of no return, or had experience of the first crisis of parliaments which gave an unstoppable historical momentum to the second. Even so – and Sidney may have fitted both categories – people showed themselves highly reluctant to take up arms. What forced them to contemplate such a step was the aggressive and vengeful advance of the court itself. Against this there seemed no other protection: no choice but self-defence. It was under these circumstances, and in order to exploit them, that Sidney's *Discourses* was written.

Part Three

THE OLD CAUSE

Discourses *(1) First principles*

there is work enough for four or five years, to make out what is mentioned in those
scraps of paper. (Sidney, on the *Discourses* at his trial (*Works*, pp. 44–5))

[I]t is the fundamental right of every nation to be governed by such laws, in such
manner, and by such persons, as they think most conducing to their own good.
(Sidney, *Discourses Concerning Government*, p. 462)

God has left it to every nation ... as their fundamental right, to be governed in such
a manner, by such persons, and such laws ... as they may judge to be best for them
... This became a[n eighteenth century] truism. (J.C.D. Clark, *English Society
1688–1832*, p. 176)

10.1 INTRODUCTORY CONSIDERATIONS

DATING AND AUTHENTICITY

Sidney probably began his *Discourses Concerning Government* a few
months after completing the *Vindication*, in the second half of 1681. He
was still writing it almost two years and 508 pages later when he was
arrested in May 1683. We must thank the strong arm of the law both for
saving the manuscript and for applying some limit to its length.

That it was written in the order that we have it is suggested by the topical
references discussed by Dr Worden;[1] by its polemical structure as a
paragraph-by-paragraph refutation of Filmer's *Patriarcha*; and by the
gradually mounting crescendo of its insurrectionary content. The litmus test
of the latter reveals a beginning on a par with much of the *Vindication*, but
eventually leaving even its elementary caution behind. The spectre which
hangs over the whole book is arbitrary government – encapsulated by
Sidney's repeated references to Caligula and Nero – and the quality which
Sidney champions in its stead is liberty – 'civil and spiritual' – the heart of
the 'good old cause'.

---

[1] See Blair Worden's definitive discussion of the dating of the *Discourses* in 'Commonwealth
Kidney', Appendix pp. 38–40. The dating of the early section to 1681 is supported by
Sidney's reference to his friend Jones on p. 7; Jones died suddenly in April 1682.

Dr Worden's scholarship has also recently cast into focus our grounds for concern over the authenticity of the text.[2] This has led John Pocock, for one, to seek some assurance on this matter.[3] In the absence of the original manuscript, no absolute assurance is possible, though something less entire is. Dr Worden himself following his most detailed discussion of the text has come to the view that if it was tampered with at all, by John Toland or anyone else, it was so only superficially. It remains after all an unfinished, repetitive, unedited sort of work.[4]

This author supports this view, but would wish to state it more strongly. Hundreds of echoes, specific and general, from the *Court Maxims*, Sidney's letters, and the *Vindication*, effectively remove any doubt about the *Discourses* authorship. A number of these have been, and will be, noted in this book, as they were in the previous one. These are combined with the *Discourses* biographical content which has also been used throughout this study. There remains the possibility that a superficial editing has taken place; that small parts of the text have been added or removed;[5] but on balance even this seems unlikely.

POLEMIC AND PRACTICE

Sidney wrote this text under the shadow of the loyalist reaction. This, and the responses of Sidney and his friends to it, has a practical history which will be covered in detail in chapter 12. Because the writing of the text covered such a long period, it spanned a number of phases in this history. It was begun early in the first phase, following the abandonment of parliaments. The beginning of the second phase, ushered in by the storming of London in mid 1682, probably came about midway through this book. And the progress of the third, comprising Sidney's own insurrectionary efforts, lies behind the last, substantial, part of the writing. The footsteps of these phases can, as we will see, be seen in the text. But one context united them, and the *Discourses* as a whole. This was the reaction itself: the onset of royal persecution and revenge, both religious, and political. This effectively restored the context of Sidney's *Court Maxims*. The insurrectionary message of both the *Discourses* and the *Court Maxims* accordingly is the same; as we will see, there is substantial repetition between them. The *Discourses* then, was a contribution to that old cause of Sidney's, the practical shape of which will be described in detail hereafter. This was the self-defence of

---

[2] Edmund Ludlow, *A Voyce from the Watchtower*, ed. A.B. (1977), Introduction pp. 26–8; Worden, 'Commonwealth Kidney', Appendix. See Scott, *Sidney and the English Republic*, pp. 168–70.

[3] Pocock, *Virtue, Commerce and History*, p. 232; *Ancient Constitution*, p. 348.

[4] Worden, 'Commonwealth Kidney', Appendix.

[5] *Ibid.* Note, finally, Sidney's own admission of authorship in 1683: see pp. 314–15 below.

protestants against persecution, both religious (popery) and political (arbitrary government). It was an attempt to convince people that they had a right to such self-defence from nature; independently of any political obligation; and to plead with them, practically, to exercise it.

In *Sidney and the English Republic* a good deal was said about the intellectual context of the *Discourses*. It is not the purpose of the next two chapters to repeat any of that information – about the *Discourses* itself, or its family, political or intellectual background.[6] The intention of these chapters is to move from that discussion of themes to the text itself, to examine it as a whole, and as it was written.[7] The purpose of this is twofold.

The first is to convey some sense of the *Discourses* itself, its style and its content. There will be extensive quotation from the text to this end. For a work that was to be, in the eighteenth century, one of the most influential works of political theory ever written, and yet has been out of print in England since 1772, in France since 1796, and in America since 1810, no excuse for this seems necessary. The second object is to understand how and why the work was produced, in its immediate political (as opposed to its longer-term biographical) context. For this we need to consider both its practical and its polemical intention, and the relationship between the two.

I have said that the practical intention, as with the *Court Maxims*, was to argue for insurrection. In this role, the *Discourses* was to provide what may be the only explicit defence of rebellion, both the word and the thing, in seventeenth-century English political thought. On these grounds it can be argued that the spectacular book-launching provided by Sidney's execution, to which some historians have solely attributed the posthumous influence of his work, arose naturally from the content of the book itself, and was well-earned.

The polemical intention of the *Discourses* was to refute Sir Robert Filmer's *Patriarcha*. This served both as a stylistic vehicle through which to

---

[6] See Scott, *Sidney and the English Republic*, ch. 2 in particular.

[7] This involves a deliberate eschewal of any extensive engagement with the secondary literature relating to the *Discourses* (for which see Scott, *Sidney and the English Republic*, ch. 2). The purpose here is to understand what Sidney himself thought and wrote, not what has been thought and written about him. Important discussions of the *Discourses* are to be found in: C. Robbins, '*Discourses Concerning Government*: Textbook of Revolution', *WMQ*, 3rd series 4 (1947); C. Robbins, *The Eighteenth Century Commonwealthsman* (Cambridge, Mass. 1959); Z. Fink, *The Classical Republicans* (Evanston, Ill. 1945); Worden, 'Commonwealth Kidney'; J.H.M. Salmon, *The French Religious Wars in English Political Thought* (Oxford 1959); J. Conniff, 'Reason and History in Early Whig Thought: The Case of Algernon Sidney', *JHI*, 43:3 (1982). See also G. Schochet, *Patriarchalism in Political Thought* (Oxford 1975); J. Daly, *Sir Robert Filmer and English Political Thought* (Toronto 1979); F. Raab, *The English Face of Machiavelli* (1964); Pocock, *The Ancient Constitution*; G.H. Sabine, *A History of Political Theory* (1948), ch. 25; Kenyon, *Revolution Principles*; G.P. Gooch, *Political Thought in England from Bacon to Halifax* (Oxford 1946).

project, and a rhetorical device by which to disguise, its primary practical intention. On the former level *Patriarcha* was ideal, an apparently simplistic and extreme absolutist mirror in which Sidney's equally extreme anti-absolutist views could be reflected in all their starkness. This aspect of Filmer probably attracted Locke as well. On the latter score, however, *Patriarcha* became a liability. While enabling Sidney – as he indignantly pointed out at his trial – to steer most of his discussion toward 'general principles' and away from contemporary affairs, Filmer's work conjured up such a powerful accumulation of righteous indignation in Sidney that the effect of this was largely cancelled out. In the end, as the government said, the practical intention was made extraordinarily clear.

This is not to say that Sidney had no interest in the business of answering Filmer for its own sake. Every sentence makes it clear that he considered this essential. But it is to suggest that the way to understand the *Discourses* as it was written is to bear the intertwining of these intentions in mind. It is *Patriarcha* which entirely dictates the *Discourses*' formal structure. It pro-vides the test-pattern through which the message emerges. This message cannot be unlocked therefore without reading the *Discourses* as Sidney wrote it, with *Patriarcha* in hand. Having done so, however, the contours of Sidney's primary message – the justification of a line of conduct in response to external events – become increasingly clear. On this score we can detect in the *Discourses* the march of those events themselves, and as they increase in their urgency and menace, so does Sidney.

In all of these respects, and others, the *Discourses* is not unlike the *Vindication*. It is as if, having cut his teeth on the King's proclamation, Sidney settled on Filmer as the next and more substantial court-offering for refutation. It served equally as the next vehicle to take him further down the same insurrectionary road. Accordingly the *Discourses* takes up – on a more abstract plane – where the *Vindication* left off. But while it covers much of the same ground, it goes very much further, and this is not a road along which Sidney proves able to return.

THE PRACTICAL OBJECT

As Sidney's previous work had been a *Vindication of the Proceedings of the Two Last Parliaments*, so the writing of the *Discourses* formed a bridge between the end of parliaments in Charles II's reign and the end of Sidney himself. It is too easy to assume in retrospect that progress over this bridge was inevitable; this was not, however, the way Sidney saw things. The key to sharing his perspective is, as usual, to desert our knowledge of his future, for his vision of the past.

It has been argued in the last two chapters, as in this book as a whole, that for the opponents of 'popery and arbitrary government' the events of 1678–83 constituted both the second popish plot crisis, and the second Stuart crisis of parliaments. It was along the axis of the perception that the opposition effort in the crisis moved through its various stages: from the prosecution of Danby (and popery) in 1679, through the petitioning movement and the prosecution of the abhorrers (and popery) in 1680, to the *Vindication of the ... Two Last Parliaments* in 1681. Throughout this process the stimulus of arbitrary government came in the form of the prorogations and dissolutions by which parliament had been 'rendered inconsiderable' in the reign of Charles II. We have seen how throughout the crisis Sidney looked to parliament in general, and the House of Commons in particular, as the crucial focus for resistance to this double menace. He did so not because parliament was perfect, or because it possessed contemporary powers commensurate with this expectation, but because in the previous crisis of popery and arbitrary government it was only parliament which had proved capable of providing the crucial (and semi-legitimate) focus of resistance to Charles I.

The events of 1679–81 made it clear that despite the temporary success of Danby's fall this struggle for parliaments was far from won. Yet the history of the struggle itself gave strong reason for hope. For by comparing the King's proclamation of 1681 with that of 1629, the authors of the *Vindication* made their vision of the situation clear. The experience of Charles I showed that rule-without-parliament was easy to declare; it was more difficult to maintain. When he set to work on the *Discourses* Sidney believed he had time, and history, on his side. To telescope the time scale rather, if monarchy could be restored, and thereafter arbitrary government, then so in time could resistance to tyranny, and parliamentary victory.

To understand Sidney's hopes for this period – and so the intention of the *Discourses* – we need only to remember what it was that had made Charles I's personal rule untenable. Attempts by the English crown to rule without parliament were secure only as long as the crown could avoid the financial imperative of war. In this respect, in most circumstances, the facts of British geography were on the crown's side. In only one case did the English share a land border with another kingdom which had, therefore, a unique capacity to pose a military challenge. It was thus a Scots rebellion and invasion which had proved Charles I's undoing, which had turned a haughty King who had dismissed his parliaments indefinitely and issued a *Proclamation* justifying the fact into a captive and victim of the indignation this had provoked. It was for attempting to organise a rebellion in Scotland that Sidney was ultimately brought to the scaffold.

The *Discourses* is in part another vindication – this time against Filmer – of the people's right to order their own political affairs through their representatives. But it also seeks to provide a means to this end. There is no evidence that Sidney and his colleagues were self-deluded enough to believe they could take control of the nation's government by a simple insurrection. Many of the alehouse plotting anecdotes which have dominated our view of 1683 suggest this but they disguise a harder-headed, or more sober strategic perception. By this historical reading – and a feature of the plotting of these years is the number of old civil war soldiers it involved – if the government in London could or should not simply be seized by force, it could be forced to re-summon and submit to parliament by a sufficient military challenge. When the legitimate representatives of the people had thereby regained control of their own destiny, then they could provide for the future of the nation; remoulding the constitution if necessary, Sidney insisted, to eliminate the threats of popery and arbitrary government once and for all.

Sidney's *Discourses*, as well as the evidence to be discussed in subsequent chapters, make it clear that this is the scenario Sidney had in mind. When he began writing the *Discourses*, in the second half of 1681, his principal concern was to emphasise principles – the people's *right* to govern themselves. From approximately the middle of the book however – behind which we may vaguely assume the events of mid 1682 – the emphasis changes. We now find an alternating insistence on two not particularly consistent themes. The first is the right, and the duty, of the people to revolt against absolutism; and the second is the absolute sovereignty of parliaments. These intertwine in the claim that in times of emergency parliaments can and must be summoned by the people or their representatives by force; and that they may be so summoned by any person – 'those who best see the danger' – and by any means.

From this there followed the next claim, repeatedly emphasised, that in their political capacity (through their representatives) 'the people' may alter the existing constitution, or make an entirely new one to correct present defects, as they wish. This is the most theoretically interesting aspect of the *Discourses* – Sidney's politics of change, his insistence that such alteration is not only necessary in times of emergency, but necessary as a constant feature of political life. Only states that embrace change can grow and respond as times change; only by this means can such emergencies themselves be avoided.

It seems that when he began writing, Sidney regarded an eventual forced summoning of parliament as both essential and inevitable. It was not, however, an immediate prospect. There was plenty of time to begin a large book explaining the people's rights in this matter. What changed this time-is-on-my-side stance was the increasingly aggressive onslaught of the court. By the time the *Discourses* itself had been used to arrest its author, he had indeed begun urgent steps to force this development immediately, and by any means. The repeated justifications which we find of this line of conduct, particularly in the last third of the book, are partly Sidney's justifications of it to himself. As with the *Court Maxims* then, this insurrection in theory was part of the same thing going on in practice. Sidney was neither a fool, nor a martyr. He was a rebel with a cause, and an acute sense of history. He was also, unlike many of his colleagues, in both 1665–6 and 1683, prepared to let his beliefs be the author of his actions.

This is the clear story told by the *Discourses* itself. While beginning his discussion with 'principles', the reliable perversity of Filmer's own soon have Sidney mounting a series of increasingly strident republican diatribes. As these give way to an obvious and developing emphasis on the legitimacy of rebellion – beginning with the provocative claim that there is nothing inherently unjust in 'sedition, tumult and war' – Sidney can no longer confine himself to historical examples and begins, despite his promises to the contrary, to refer by analogy and name to the rulers of the present day. Finally this refrain becomes so insistent that almost every chapter, at whatever point it had begun in Filmer's text, arrives at the same insurrectionary conclusion in Sidney's.

It is impossible to dissent in this respect from the verdict of the book's first reviewer, Judge Jeffreys. Jeffreys concluded that its object was 'to stir up the people to rebellion'; that it 'contains all the malice, and revenge and treason, that mankind can be guilty of . . .

it fixes the sole power in parliament and the people; so that he carries on the design still, for their debates at their meetings [in 1683] were to that purpose. And such doctrines as these suit with their debates; for there a general insurrection was designed, and that was discoursed of in this book and encouraged . . . there he gives many instances in story; and from foreign nations he comes home to the English, and tells you how all the rebellions in latter ages have been headed; and tells you the parliament is the head, or the nobility and gentry that compose it; and when the king fails in his duty, the People may call it.[8]

All of this is true enough.

THE POLEMICAL OBJECT

That whosoever wrote those papers they were but a small part of a Polemicall Discourse in answer to a booke written abt 30 yeares agoe upon generall propositions applyed to noe time or any particular case. (Sidney, Petition to the King (25 November 1683))[9]

In his role as a diplomat Sidney had difficulty overcoming his earlier training as a commander of cavalry. The same qualities characterise his

[8] *Trial* in Sidney, *Works*, pp. 51, 58.
[9] Sidney, 'To the King's Most Excellent Majesty the humble Petition of Algernon Sidney esq', Longleat, Bath MSS, Whitelocke Papers, vol. XX, f.176.

contest with Filmer, the last undoubtedly military encounter into which Colonel Sidney was to gallop. The unusual bellicosity of the *Discourses'* content is fully at one with its tone.

Thus we may contrast the tone of another opponent of the same book (James Tyrell), who said of Filmer: 'I honour his memory as a Person of genteel learning and very ingenious' – with Sidney's description of him as the 'vile . . . brutally ignorant and maliciously contentious [author of] the utmost degree of impudent madness, to which perhaps any man in the World has ever arrived'; his opinions 'if he were alive . . . would deserve to be answered with stones rather than words'.[10] In this respect the *Discourses* was less a polemic than a verbal artillery bombardment proceeding from an apparently limitless supply of ammunition. Every one word of Filmer's receives twelve – a veritable hail of stones – back from Sidney. Every utterance in *Patriarcha* is systematically wrestled to the ground.

Filmer's *Patriarcha* was a work of political absolutism written under Charles I, possibly as early as 1628, possibly as late as 1642.[11] Sidney's decision to answer it, like that of Locke, was a recognition of the centrality of this resurrected Caroline theory to what was a resurrected Caroline crisis. In this way the polarities of the political debate of 1681–3 carried over, or repeated, those of the crisis of the reign of Charles I. That is why the best survey of the latter, J.P. Sommerville's *Politics and Ideology in England 1603–40*, is also the best introduction to the ideological ground covered by the Filmer vs Sidney/Locke confrontation.

Sommerville divides the political thought of his period into two camps, absolutist and anti-absolutist. Within the former he identifies two principal strands of argument, patriarchalism and designation theory, a variant of natural law theory. Far from being original, Sommerville finds Filmer to be an orthodox patriarchalist using ideas common before 1640, and expressed by Hadrian Saravia in England as early as 1593. On the other side, Sommerville divides anti-absolutist thought into three types: immemorialism; classical (particularly Ciceronian and Tacitean) theory; and most importantly 'a certain type of natural law thinking' – exactly the 'type' later used by Sidney and Locke.[12]

Filmer's *Patriarcha* has been called the only work he wrote positively – that is, not as an appreciation of, or an attack upon, somebody else's

---

[10] James Tyrell, *Bibliotheca Politica* (1718), Preface p. vi; Sidney, *Discourses*, pp. 4, 27.

[11] For the argument for 1628 see Richard Tuck 'A New Date for Filmer's *Patriarcha*', *Historical Journal* 29:1 (1986). Note, however, the tract *The Power of Kings . . . Learnedly Asserted by Sir Robert Filmer, Kt. With a Preface of a Friend: Giving an Account of the Author and his Works* (1680) dates all Filmer's works, describing *Patriarcha* as 'written about the year 1642 and never Published till of late'. The content of Filmer's work makes clear only that it was written against opposition to Charles I and before the outbreak of war.

[12] Sommerville, *Politics and Ideology 1603–40*, chs. 1–2.

ideas.[13] But in fact most of this book is simply a series of polemics against the three strands of anti-absolutist argument Sommerville has identified: natural law theory (which he associates with the Jesuitism of Bellarmine and Suarez); Tacitean and Ciceronian republicanism (which he associates with Machiavelli, and counters by attacking the Roman Republic and exalting the Empire); and immemorialism (which he associates with the parliamentary critics of Charles I, and attacks by challenging the antiquity of parliaments). Sidney's and Locke's replies are reassertions, in the face of Filmer's attacks, of one or more of these three types of anti-absolutist argument in turn. The principal difference between them is that Locke chooses to mount his challenge on the ground of natural law theory alone; the result is an incomplete refutation but a coherent theory. Sidney, conversely, determined to refute Filmer's every line, reasserts every one of the three theories Filmer had attacked. The result is a typically Sidneian victory of completeness over consistency. Where the natural law argument, for instance, renders the immemorialism redundant, Sidney, having noted the fact, cannot resist making the case for the latter anyway.

From this two things follow. The first concerns the nature of the *Discourses* itself. Positively speaking, Filmer's work is a piece of patriarchal absolutism typical of the reign of Charles I. This is what Sidney believed, associating Filmer with Heylin, Sibthorp, Mainwaring and Laud as one of the 'partisans of absolute monarchy'.[14] Locke made the same point; negatively however, since the content of Filmer's work was largely dictated by the theories he was attacking (and which he described as the 'foundation of popular sedition').[15] And since the same is true of Sidney's reply, the result in Sidney's *Discourses* is a reassertion of the full spectrum of anti-absolutist arguments from the reign of Charles I with some accretions – particularly a fully developed classical republicanism – from the period 1640–66. Ideologically, therefore, the *Discourses* may be described as a work of anti-absolutist and republican theory; combining natural law, classical, and immemorialist argument, not simply to answer Filmer but to re-lay in the process the 'foundation' for the 'popular sedition' Filmer had written to destroy. In Sidney's case there also is a further point. Filmer attacked, specifically, the natural law theory of Grotius; the classical republicanism of Machiavelli; and the ancient constitutionalism of Sir Edward Coke.[16] Sidney, steeped in all three through his family background, used the *Discourses* to reassert them all. In the process, as we will see, he

---

[13] Filmer, *Patriarcha*, ed. P. Laslett (1949), Introduction.

[14] Sidney, *Discourses*, pp. 5–6.

[15] Filmer, *Patriarcha*, ed. Laslett, p. 54.

[16] (See chapter 11 below). These theories are discussed in that order – see Filmer, *Patriarcha* (1680), chs. 1, 2 and 3 respectively.

combined Machiavelli and Grotius in particular to produce a justification of rebellion that was new.

The second point is of wider importance. If this second crisis of protestantism and parliaments was a resurrection of the first, it is not surprising that we should find in its ideological centrepiece – the debate between Filmer and his opponents – a resurrection of the absolutist/anti-absolutist positions of the reign of Charles I. Yet through the medium of this resurrection the crisis of 1678–83 laid the basis for the ideological polarities – party and otherwise – of eighteenth-century political thought as well. When H.T. Dickinson wanted to describe the origins of the latter he began with the opposing theories of Filmer on the one hand, and Sidney and Locke on the other.[17] For it was this exchange that set the terms for much of eighteenth-century political thought.

In their confrontation with Filmer, therefore, Sidney and Locke proved the most important lightning rods by which a sixteenth- and early-seventeenth-century political view of the world was transmitted more or less intact to the eighteenth century, where it proved all-conquering. The importance of the *Discourses* lies principally in its role in this exchange. The importance of that transmission itself can hardly be overestimated.

THE IMPORTANCE OF THE 'DISCOURSES'

The debate between Filmer and his opponents is of great significance because it helped set the terms for the thought of the eighteenth century, not only in England, but in Europe, America and still in much of the western world today.

No two works did more to shape the political vocabularies and sensibilities of the eighteenth century than Sidney's *Discourses* and Locke's *Two Treatises*. In England Sidney's work was more influential than Locke's in the first half of the century and equally so in France and America in the second. The rapidity with which basic utterances from Sidney's *Discourses* (which had been treason in 1683) became 'truisms' soon after is illustrated by the quotes at the head of this chapter. By the late eighteenth century much of the *Discourses* spanned the entire political spectrum. As it furnished inspiration for French republicans from Rousseau to Robespierre, even Burke took as his starting point Sidney's conclusion about the inevitability of change; the question was not whether there should be change, but whether it was good or bad. Burke's statement that 'circumstances are infinite, are infinitely combined, are variable and transient; he who does not take them into consideration is not erroneous but stark mad; A statesman, never losing

---

[17] H.T. Dickinson, *Liberty and Property* (1977), ch. 1.

sight of right principles, is to be guided by circumstances'[18] could have been lifted directly from the *Discourses* itself. At the beginning of the century, Sidney's work had been the fullest and the classic expression of what Dickinson called the 'Whig theory of liberty, based on the social contract, the natural rights of man, and the ultimate sovereignty of the people'.[19] By the century's end – as Rousseau himself remarked – Filmer's side of the argument had been so completely eclipsed that there was nothing else.[20] As the career of Bolingbroke suggests, much of the *Discourses* stood as common assumption for whig and tory alike.

Sidney did not create this situation, but his book became an important part of it. And his thought still sits securely at the centre of modern political discourse. Deeply rooted on both sides of the Atlantic by the late eighteenth century,[21] Sidney's aggressive rhetoric of liberty seems presently to be triumphing over still more of the globe. Framed in the shadow of its opponent, Sidney's ideology was strident, militant and competitive. It offered the stark choice between liberty and progress, or slavery and decline. Liberty begat industry, increase, the expansion of knowledge, of moral good, and (not least) of military power. Absolutism, the negation of self-rule, produced degeneration, demoralisation, poverty and collapse. If this was rhetoric rather than reality, the rhetoric remains.

The *Discourses* was influential partly for its sheer lack of originality. By summing up, with heedless thoroughness, the ideology of an age, it furnished the raw materials for another age in turn. The age it summarised was the Early Modern: the two centuries from 1500–1700 that were the era of European statebuilding, and of the European religious wars. They marked the polarisation of political thought into absolutist and anti-absolutist camps: Sidney's *Discourses* furnished a complete summary of this process from Machiavelli, through Hotman, Bodin and Grotius, Vane, Harrington and Locke. This summary of Early Modern thought – itself built from the remnants of its medieval and classical predecessors – helped to furnish the basis for modern political thought in turn.

The *Discourses* was not influential, however, only for its completeness, or for the conservatism such completeness implies. What gained Sidney the admiration of men like Montesquieu and Rousseau, Franklin and Jefferson,

---

[18] Quoted in Dickinson, *Liberty and Property*, p. 305.

[19] *Ibid.*, pp. 57, and 59–79.

[20] In *A Discourse on Political Economy* Rousseau described *Patriarcha* as 'a work to which two celebrated writers [Sidney and Locke] have done too much honour in writing books to refute it'. See Rousseau, *The Social Contract and Discourse*, ed. G.D.H. Cole (1973), pp. 93, 120.

[21] Thomas Jefferson described Sidney (alongside Locke) as one of the two principal sources for the American understanding of liberty. Thomas Jefferson, *Writings* (New York, 1984), p. 479.

Shelley and Keats, Coleridge and Byron, Neibuhr and Gladstone, was not simply the content of his theory but the way it was expressed. For all of its faults – primarily its length and its repetition – the *Discourses* contains numerous examples of the greatest talent Sidney had. The essential accompaniment to Sidney the self-publicist was Sidney the prose stylist; the imperiously high moral tone that made him famous was equipped to succeed principally by the power and the force of his writing. Indeed – as his admirers never tired of pointing out – the quality conferred upon his ideas by his means of expressing them was not only power but 'nobility' – a quality of unique value to an early modern theorist of rebellion.

Sidney, then, expressed his ideas in a classic style, with a force and power uniquely his own. And he reinforced the power of his words with deeds. But was there anything *original* about his thought rather than simply characterful about his style? There is no need to believe so; its importance stands independently of (and to some extent counter to) its originality. Hobbes was more original, and, for that reason, less influential. Even so, whether or not we wish to call it originality – a ghostly quality anyway – three things marked out Sidney's use of the political languages he employed from that of others.

The first was his discussion of change: his insistence on its inevitability, and desirability. There is no more important aspect of the intellectual transition from the early modern world to the modern. The second was connected to this: Sidney's conception of the state. This was neither medieval, nor modern, but decidedly early modern: a product of the era of statebuilding. Sidney regarded the state as a, and perhaps the, key moving and shaping force in human life: religious, moral and material. Thus the dynamic role he accorded the state, part of an exceptionally dynamic political vision, is that of a moulder of its citizens; even, in a sense, a moulder of time. The *Discourses* sets itself against a limited, negative, Augustinian view of government – that it is simply an instrument for the containment of sin. What it delivers instead is a lecture on the rights, and the duties, of positive creative political architecture.

The third point of interest is, not surprisingly, Sidney's treatment of rebellion. Building on Machiavelli and Grotius, Sidney produced a defence of rebellion which is original both in the form of the argument and in the frankness with which it is expressed. Since it was as a theorist of rebellion that Sidney became best known – and since this was the primary intention of the book – this will be carefully examined.

Having said all this, a final simple but important point must be made. It is that a detailed explication of Sidney's text fully justifies itself. For there is at its core a sustaining political vision which is clear, unrelenting, and powerful. It is, for that reason, a great work. The attempt to come to terms with it, and to understand it, has guided all of this author's endeavours. If we can understand this political vision we will not come closer than that to understanding Sidney himself. It was to the beliefs set out here that he devoted his life (and death). It is above all, therefore, to an attempt to recapture that vision that the following discussion of the text is devoted.

THE TEXT

Though it is divided, like its two most important sources Machiavelli's *Discourses*, and Grotius' *De Jure Belli ac Pacis*, into three books ('chapters'), and within them into many sections, what overall shape the *Discourses* possesses derives principally from the shape and content of Filmer's own work. Since that work was itself a relatively shapeless refutation of other things, the result is a limited coherence of form that is responsible for most of the *Discourses'* repetition. Nevertheless the progress of Filmer's own work combined with Sidney's increasingly discursive responses to the same allow us to see a development within the *Discourses*, and a series of dominant concerns applying to different sections of the book. For convenience of discussion, and on this basis, I have divided the text into four sections. It must be emphasised that these divisions are arbitrary. They are not formal divisions within the book itself, and the matters they treat are usually touched upon to some degree throughout the work. But it is necessary to impose this framework to convey the meaning, while avoiding the pitfalls, of Sidney's text.

The first of these four phases of the *Discourses* comprises Sidney's answer to Filmer's patriarchalism, and to Filmer's attack on natural law theory (*Patriarcha*, ch. 1, and ch. 2 sections 5–10); that is to say Sidney's own attack on patriarchalism, and his reassertion of natural law theory in its place. This is the subject of the *Discourses*, ch. 1, and ch. 2 sections 1–10 (pp. 1–109); with the same themes repeated particularly in ch. 2 sections 16, 20, and 31; and ch. 3 section 33.

The second (*Discourses*, ch. 2 sections 11–29, pp. 110–248) marks a sudden departure in length, for Filmer's attacks on the classical republics (*Patriarcha*, ch. 2 sections 11–16, pp. 54–71) so enrage Sidney that he takes 18 sections to Filmer's 6 and 138 pages to Filmer's 17 to adequately reply. In the process he goes well beyond Filmer's simple assertions on the subject and sketches a complete typology of republics and republican terms, as well as a comprehensive argument for the superiority of republics in general over the 'government of princes'.

In the third phase of the text (*Discourses*, ch. 2 section 30 – ch. 3 section

14, pp. 248–400) Sidney presents a range of arguments against absolutism and begins to sound more insistently the call to resistance. In this section in particular we encounter substantial repetition from the *Court Maxims*.

Finally in the last phase (*Discourses*, ch. 3 sections 15–45) Sidney allows Filmer to lead him into his ancient constitutionalist history of the Anglo-Saxons; and thereafter he joins to the growing demand for rebellion a series of claims for the absolute sovereignty of parliament.

The remainder of this chapter will discuss the first of these four parts; the next will examine the other three.

10.2 PART ONE: PRINCIPLES: INHERITANCE VERSUS LIBERTY, REASON, AND VIRTUE (ch. 1, ch. 2, sections 1–10, 16, 20, 31, ch. 3, section 33)

THEOLOGICAL ASSUMPTIONS: THE CONSEQUENCES OF THE FALL

God is our Lord by right of creation, and our only Lord, because he only has created us. If any other were equal to him in wisdom, power, goodness, and beneficence to us, he might challenge the same duty from us. If growing out of ourselves, receiving being from none, depending upon no providence, we were offered the protection of a wisdom subject to no error, a goodness that could never fail, and a power that nothing could resist, it were reasonable for us to ... submit ourselves to him ... But what right can from hence accrue to a mortal creature like to one of us, from whom we have received nothing, and who stands in need of help as much as we?[22]

As with Filmer himself, all of Sidney's political assumptions – his view of relationships between men – stem from prior assumptions about man's relationship with God. As he said to Lantin in Paris in 1677, 'political science, or the study of the world of men, is second only to Theology, or the study of God'. This means that one cannot, without blasphemy or idolatry, make categorical statements concerning men's relations to one another, without first taking into account their prior relationship to God. God is the creator, the first mover, so man's relationship to him is first in time, as well as in moral, political, and religious importance. Filmer commits both blasphemy and idolatry by investing the power that belongs only to God as creator in a mortal man.

Filmer's view of this relationship is orthodoxly Augustinian, overlain by the Fall and the fact of sin – overlain, in other words, by the fact of a separation from God which cannot be bridged in this life. Because of the Fall, man is both morally and actually incapable of self-government. He can only be ruled by an authority sanctioned by God himself outside and prior

[22] Sidney, *Discourses*, pp. 106–7.

to human history. God created the means for government – in the patriarchal authority of Adam – the moment he created man. Only after the Fall did that government become necessary, and its function was to curb sin.

Sidney is as aware of the Fall, and sin, as Filmer, in some senses more so. But the separation of man from God is not complete. Although all people are sinful, and 'nothing in this world is perfect', all people are also endowed with reason, a fragment of the nature of God. Within every individual the reasonable and sinful parts of their nature compete. The drama of the Fall is replayed within every lifetime, and the ultimate object of this drama is the reunion of each individual with God. It is reason that endows humans both with the capacity for self-government, and with the capacity to know and rediscover God.

For Sidney, as for Locke, people are naturally equal – not actually, but morally, in their relationship to God. They are also naturally free – in their relationship to one another, not in their relationship to God. The absolute obedience Filmer demands for his patriarchal ruler – the reputed father of his subjects – is owed only to their real creator, God. When Filmer begins his book with an assault on 'The Tenet of the Natural Liberty of The People', which he identifies as 'the first principle . . . [supporting] the whole Fabrick of this vast Engine of Popular sedition', Sidney replies by accusing him of 'having declared war against mankind, [by] endevouring to over-throw the principle of liberty in which God created us'.[23] When Filmer reminds what he takes to be a credulous and sinful populace that it was 'liberty' that caused the Fall, Sidney replies, just as Locke does, that this 'liberty asserted is not a licentiousness of doing what is pleasing to every one against the command of God, but an exemption from all *human* laws to which they have not given their assent'.[24]

Much of this ground is familiar, both from chapter 2 of the previous book and from the vast literature on Locke, whose natural law theory assumptions and argument here are identical – and identically indebted to Grotius. There is thus no need to map it out again in detail. What must be stressed here is the way in which, in the seventeenth century, when most political theory remained a branch of theology, the diverging shapes of these theories took their trajectories from differing theological assumptions. Both Filmer and Sidney argue rationally from differing premises about man's relation-ship with God from creation, and the numerous doubtful historical claims in which both indulge serve as illustrations rather than proofs of these premises.

For Sidney, as for Milton, political liberty represents the God-given

---

[23] Sidney, *Discourses*, p. 3.
[24] Sidney, *Discourses*, p. 3; Locke, *Two Treatises*, ed. Laslett, pp. 288–9, makes the same point.

opportunity for fallen mankind to rule itself in accordance with reason rather than sin, and so in accordance with the nature of God rather than that of the devil. As Sidney wrote (following Vane) in the *Court Maxims*, all politics takes its root from 'the contrariety of principles, that is between God and the devil'. The grant of liberty – while it always carried with it the opportunity for sin which Filmer fears – is nevertheless the necessary premise for a life of self-government, both personal and political, in accordance with reason rather than passion and sin. It is for this reason that Sidney states that societies founded on 'good principles' (liberty, reason, and the consequent virtue) will progress, that is, change in a positive direction. This change Sidney conceives of not primarily as temporal and material but moral and religious, motion upwards for men towards 'the nature from which they are fallen', towards God. For Filmer, who takes the Fall as the basic premise of political life, no such motion is possible.

Conversely for Sidney, Filmer's denial of liberty not only denies this opportunity – and so 'all that in this life deserves to be cared for', and nothing less – but by subjecting everyone regardless of their various moral or political capacities to the rule of one man, Filmer is subjecting them to the perpetual rule of sin. For everyone knows no men have feared the laws of God and man less than absolute monarchs, and a glance at Caligula and Nero emphasises the point. It is on this ground that Filmer is the political spokesman of the devil, and when Sidney levels this accusation it is not simply a rhetorical device. Government in accordance with liberty results in the progressive acquisition by society of goodness, virtue, and knowledge; everything that is good for men – a movement towards God, whose nature is goodness. This motion represents, in turn, a return by God's creatures towards their original nature, the nature from which they have fallen. At the very least, it allows individuals possessed of these qualifications for eternal life to separate themselves from the sin of others. The denial of such liberty results in slavery, misery, degredation and vice – a movement away from the nature of God. And so this question of 'whether we are freemen or slaves . . . [is] the difference between the best government and the worst'.[25]

In a sense what is at work here is the willingness of Sidney, like Locke, Milton, and Vane, to treat the Fall as a metaphysical proposition – a moral challenge – rather than a finished historical event. This explains both the attraction of all of these people to Platonic metaphysics and their use of the concept of the state of nature – of people dwelling in liberty and equality under the law of nature (God's law) – this is an obvious analogy for the pre-lapsarian state. This is why Filmer, for whom politics begins with the Fall and not before, vilifies this concept as a wicked fiction which has never

[25] *Ibid.*, p. 22.

existed in history and which is designed to give sinful mankind a liberty that will destroy it. One theory begins before the Fall when all the options are open – it then treats the Fall as a problem to be faced, understood and grappled with. This is exactly the terrain investigated with such grandeur by Milton's poetry. The other begins with the Fall itself and all that implies – the result is a much narrower range of options and a much simpler theory. For Filmer the City of God and the City of Man are categorically separate; for Sidney and Milton (as for Plato) they are fundamentally intertwined.

In Filmer's theory, the Fall as an historical *fait accompli* not only renders men incapable of creating legitimate political authority; in political terms it renders them morally uniform as well. Since on this score (and I mean politically, rather than privately, which is for Filmer the proper realm for piety) there is no moral difference between men, then the necessary restraint of liberty that is the function of political authority may as well come from the will of one man as the will of all; there is no difference, given that the authority for this government comes from God, not man. Indeed the sinfulness of men is such, argues Filmer, that it is better that they be restrained by the will of one man than the will of many, since the will of many simply results in a multiplication of wickedness. As Sidney illustrates the consequences of absolutism by reference to Caligula, Filmer illustrates the consequences of the rule of many by reference to the 'Blood . . . suckt up with Spunges' in the marketplaces of Athens and Rome.[26] Thus although Filmer expresses his confidence that Princes will rule as fathers of their people (and Sidney asks if the behaviour of Nero and Caligula proceeded from a surfeit of 'fatherly kindness'?) he in fact implies that the quality of government is irrelevant, and he states that the means of coming to government are also irrelevant to his argument. The latter admission – of which Sidney makes much – is in a sense surprising given Filmer's insistence that modern Kings be accounted the literal descendants of Adam. But the relevant phrase here is 'be accounted' – for *Patriarcha* is not a political history, but a political meditation on human sin. As an extrapolation from the Fall, what matters in *Patriarcha* is not the quality, or the *human* origin of government, but the fact of it: the fact of the restraint of sin. This is why *Patriarcha* was written: not to prove the descent of government from Adam, but to defend the fact of government, against theories by which it was threatened.

For Filmer then, fallen man cannot redeem himself in the world, by politics or any other means. Politics is simply a negative (but vital) holding operation authorised by God for the restraint of sin. If (as is undoubtedly true) the instruments of its exercise are themselves fallen – be they one or many – then they will sometimes govern wickedly. Such suffering is simply

---

[26] Filmer, *Patriarcha* (1680), pp. 61–2; see also pp. 55–6.

part of the condition of fallen and wicked mankind, and against it there is no remedy but 'crying to God in that day'.[27] Attempts to remedy the situation simply result in the replacement of one tyrant with many. Filmer settles for the mechanism of primogeniture inheritance not because it produces virtue and good government – these are Sidney's concerns, and the grounds upon which he opposes this mechanism – but because the quality and human origin of government are relatively unimportant alongside the fact of it. What matters for the fact of government is its unargued and unbroken transmission by a simple rule unopen to question or 'tumult'. It is above all the moral flatness of this theory that Sidney cannot bear.

It is basically on the grounds of this moral flatness that Sidney fights Filmer from trench to trench and sentence to sentence from the beginning of the book to (almost) the end. For Sidney men (rather than God) establish political government not just (negatively) to contain sin but (positively) to 'seek their own good; for [even] the will is ever drawn by some real good, or the appearance of it'. What Sidney is saying is that given the liberty and the knowledge (to distinguish 'real good' from 'the appearance of it' – the imagery here is straightforwardly Platonic) men will naturally seek to redeem the tragedy of the Fall and return to the nature from which they are fallen. 'This is that which man seeks by all the regular or irregular motions of his mind. Reason and passion, vice and virtue, do herein concur, though they differ vastly in the objects *in which each of them think this good to consist.*'[28] This is a claim of great importance: that the difference between reason and passion, between the good and bad parts of the human soul, is a difference not between fixed components of good and evil (the consequence of the Fall) but a *difference of human knowledge.* This is again Platonic: virtue is knowledge; as Plato said in the *Protagoras*: 'no man voluntarily pursues evil, or that which he thinks to be evil. To prefer evil to good is not in man's nature.'[29] Sin is an effect of ignorance – of separation in this respect from the all-knowing God – and by the acquisition of knowledge it can be overcome.

The implications of this assumption for Sidney's theory are all-important. The assumption itself – shared by Milton and Vane – underlay the *Court Maxims'* statement that liberty and good government resulted in the progressive banishment of darkness and the acquisition of moral knowledge. The problem is not man's nature itself – that is the creation of God in His image – it is the separation of man from what Sidney called 'the law of his creation' by the Fall and its consequences. That separation – the work of the devil – entails ignorance: ignorance of God and his ways. That is why Sidney takes the purpose of Filmer's book – an instrument of the devil – to

[27] *Ibid.*   [28] Sidney, *Discourses*, p. 37.
[29] Plato, *Protagoras* in *The Portable Plato*, p. 113.

be the safeguarding and perpetuation of human ignorance. The first bedrock of absolute monarchy is to keep the people in darkness and ignorance; to deny them the use of reason and substitute that with an 'implicit faith' which, in religion as in politics, is the mark of the devil.

I have been sometimes apt to wonder [said Sidney], how things of this nature could enter into the head of any man . . . But [then] . . . I considered, that a people from all ages in love with liberty . . . could never be brought to resign [it] . . . unless they were made to believe, that in conscience they ought to do it . . . that there was a law set to all mankind, which none might transgress, and which put the examination of [such] matters out of their power. This is our author's work. By this it will appear whose throne he seeks to advance, and whose servant he is, while he pretends to serve the king. And that it may be evident he hath made use of means suitable to the ends proposed for the service of his great master, I hope to shew, that he hath not used one argument that is not false, nor cited one author whom he hath not perverted and abused. [M]y work is so to lay open these snares, that [even] the most simple may not be taken in [by] them.[30]

For Sidney therefore the moral and religious status of man in this life is not set by the Fall; it is improvable, though all attempts at such improvement have to contend with the consequences of the Fall. That improvement is to be achieved by the acquisition of knowledge; specifically knowledge of good, or of the nature of God, by His creatures who have fallen from the law of their creation. The effect of that knowledge is to lessen the separation between man and God, to lessen the chasm opened up by the Fall. While this effort can never be completed in this life – 'that is reserved to complete the felicity of the next' – it is both achievable within the parameters of this fallen world, and it is natural for man to seek this movement from his Fall, and toward his original nature. Every individual life is thus a moral drama; a moral effort to bridge the consequences of the Fall. For Sidney politics is a moral science with *the* crucial role to play in this drama for every person in the care of the state. By denying this role to the state, and by denying its members the crucial equipment given them by God to achieve it (liberty, reason and virtue) Filmer denies people the chance to improve themselves, and condemns them to an eternity of wickedness and sin. Everyone knows that Paradise was Lost. The critical political question remains for Sidney (as for Milton) how far it may be Regained. This is a great weight to put on politics and political theory in general, and this is one reason why Sidney's (like Milton's) exchanges with political opponents were so acrimonious. It is a reminder of what was thought to be at stake; these difference had been the subject not simply of debate, but of civil war.

The misery of man proceeds from his being separated from God; his separation is wrought by corruption; his restitution therefore to felicity and integrity, can only be brought about by his reunion to the good from which he is fallen . . . If Plato

[30] Sidney, *Discourses*, p. 2.

therefore deserve credit ... [no man can] perform the part of a good magistrate, unless he have the knowledge of God, or bring a people to justice, unless he bring them to the knowledge of God, who is the root of all justice and goodness.[31]

Monarchy may be natural to beasts, says Sidney, but it is not so to man, for as man's *original* nature is reason, so that remains his *fundamental* nature still. Monarchy cannot be natural to man because 'nothing can be universally natural to him that is not rational'. Nothing indeed can be universal – that is, unchanging – unless it is rooted like reason in the only unchanging being: God.

In Sidney's dynamic world, divided between the choices of good and evil (the Fall is not over; the choice is constantly replayed), between progress (toward God) or regression (away from Him), political government is given the major responsibility for deciding the direction of man. Government – what Sidney calls political science – is the mechanism by which the half-understood gropings of men towards separate goods may be collected together and guided truly on behalf of all (the public good) towards God. The responsibility of good government is to fix itself on a foundation of 'good principles' – liberty, reason, and virtue – which 'having root in God [are] subject to no change' – and so to climb upon what Plato called 'the wheel' of progress; of positive change in a contingent world; of moral and religious advance.

10.3 POLITICAL ARCHITECTURE

[Men] are rough pieces of timber or stone, which it is necessary to cleave, saw, or cut: this is the work of a skilful builder, and he only is capable of erecting a great fabric, who is so. Magistrates are political architects. (*Discourses*, p. 64.)

According to Sidney then, Filmer's 'doctrine, and the questions arising from it, seem so far to concern all mankind, that, besides the influence on our future life, they may be said to comprehend all that in this world deserves to be cared for'.[32] In reply, Sidney states at the outset what he considers to be the function of government: it is not to restrain the sin of, but to *increase the good of* mankind.

[In the opinion of] they, who have hitherto been esteemed the best and wisest of men ... such only deserved to be called good men, who endeavoured to be good to mankind ... And, inasmuch as that good consists in a felicity of estate, and perfection of person, they highly valued such as had endeavoured to make men better, wiser, and happier. This they understood to be the end for which men entered into societies ...[33]

But

If we believe Sir Robert, all this is mistaken ... [men] are not to inquire what

---

[31] *Ibid.*, pp. 63–4.   [32] *Ibid.*, p. 1.   [33] *Ibid.*

conduces to their own good; . . . we are not to live to him [God], nor to ourselves, but to [a] master he hath set over us . . . no limits can be set to the power of the person [concerned] . . . we are not to examine, whether he or she be young or old, virtuous or vicious, sober-minded or stark-mad . . . a praise to those that do well, and a terror to those that do evil, or [vice-versa], it concerns us not; for the king must not lose his right, nor have his power diminished, on any account.[34]

On his own account Sidney begins, as we have seen, by stridently defending the liberty Filmer 'endeavours to overthrow'. This owes nothing, he replies, to the subtlety of 'school divines' in general, or that of the papists Bellarmine and Suarez in particular. '[T]he common notions of liberty, are not from school divines, but from nature.' As such they are oblivious to reason,

written in the heart of every man, [and] denied by none, but such as were degenerated into beasts . . . Thus did Euclid lay down certain axioms, which none could deny that did not renounce common sense . . . And they may with as much reason be accused of paganism, who say that . . . two halves make the whole, or that a straight line is the shortest way from point to point . . . [or] he might as well have joined the puritans with the Turks, because they all think that one and one makes two.[35]

At an early stage, given the purpose of *Patriarcha*, the debate shifts from these principles to their practical application, and as usual Sidney is far from shying from the challenge. Those who hold these opinions, said Filmer, 'allowed to the people a liberty of opposing their princes'. This is 'a desperate opinion'. 'But why' challenges Sidney, 'is this a desperate opinion? If disagreements happen between king and people, why is it a more desperate opinion to think the king should be subject to the censures of the people, than the people subject to the will of the king? Is the king for the people, or the people for the king?'[36] Again what is unusual here is not the content of this theory – it is vintage huguenot, more than a century old; it is the strident manner of the challenge.

To Filmer's contention that the people have an 'implicit faith' in their governors and should 'not . . . meddle with mysteries of state' Sidney replies that such 'implicit faith . . . [is] the foundation of papal power . . . [and] can stand no longer than [Roman Catholics] . . . can be persuaded to submit their consciences to the word of priests . . . [instead of setting their reason to] the necessity of searching the scriptures, in order to know whether the things that are told them are true or false.' As for refusing to meddle with 'mysteries of state' 'who will live in a house that yields no defence against the extremities of the weather, because the mason or carpenter assures him it is a very good house?'[37] As with doctors and lawyers, so with politicians,

34 *Ibid.*, p. 2.   35 *Ibid.*, pp. 3–4.
36 *Ibid.*, pp. 4–5, 6.   37 *Ibid.*, p. 6.

it is up to the employers of these people to judge their performance and retain or dismiss them accordingly. Just the same point was made by Silius Titus in the House of Commons on 14 April 1679. After employing another of Sidney's favourite analogies (the physician) Titus came to a version of this one: 'Suppose I build me a house, and I give my steward money to buy bolts and bars, and he go away with my money and buy none; shall I therefore take a resolution to have none, and expose my throat to be cut?'[38]

What then gives 'every prince . . . [the] wisdom to understand these profound secrets of state better than other men? . . . We see princes of all sorts; they are born as other men . . . wise or foolish, good or bad, valiant or cowardly.' If the latter, their 'judgement is as little to be relied on, as that of the poorest peasant'.[39] This is good humanistic common-sense, and no one has ever

had impudence enough to deny such evident truth . . . or to publish doctrines so contrary to common sense, virtue, and humanity, till these times. The production of Laud, Manwaring, Sibthorp, Hobbes, Filmer, and Heylin, seems to have been reserved as an additional curse to complete the shame and misery of our age and country.[40]

Similarly, to Filmer's objection that if 'by the law of God, the power be immediately in the people, God is the author of a democracy' Sidney replies: 'And why not, as well as of a tyranny? Is there anything in it repugnant to the being of God? Is there more reason to impute to God Caligula's monarchy, than the democracy of Athens?' In short it is not the form of government but its quality that is important; its goodness or otherwise; its closeness or 'repugnan[ce] to the being of God.' To this end 'God . . . having given to all men, in some degree, a capacity of judging what is good for themselves, he hath granted to all likewise a liberty of inventing such forms as please them best.'[41] The people themselves are, by their reason, the 'only fit judges of the performance of the ends of the institution', and 'the multitude that institutes, may also abrogate' and amend government as they wish. Only thus may those for whose good governments are instituted keep them to that purpose, and improve them as the consequent improvement of their own 'wisdom, industry, and experience' permit.

And we may as reasonably affirm, that mankind are forever obliged to use no other clothes than leather breeches, like Adam, to live in hollow trees, and eat acorns, or to seek after the model of his house for a habitation, and to use no arms except such as were known to the patriarchs, as to think all nations forever obliged to be governed, as they governed their families.[42]

Nature, in other words, has been given by God for the good and use of man; reason is the pattern for its use; and as 'God has not only declared in

[38] Grey, *Debates*, vol. VII, p. 113.   [39] Sidney, *Discourses*, pp. 5–8.
[40] *Ibid*., p. 5.   [41] *Ibid*., p. 13.   [42] *Ibid*., pp. 14–15.

scripture, but written in the heart of every man, that it is better to be clothed, than to go naked, to live in a house, than to live in the fields . . . and to prefer the benefits of society, before a savage and barbarous solitude', so He has given men the means, in reason, 'to frame such societies . . . to establish such laws' and to improve them in time accordingly.[43]

When Filmer turns to the first outline of his patriarchal theory from scripture, Sidney does not simply reply that scriptural prescription is irrelevant in a matter which God has left to the free choice of man. In addition he chooses to argue in detail on Filmer's own ground – to show that *Patriarcha* is also a tissue of perversions of what scripture actually contains. And here again the difference in their assumptions is clear. For Filmer the object is to demonstrate the legitimacy of a single form of government by (its divine) origin; for Sidney the point is not form but effect; not origin but quality. '[W]e are not therefore so much to inquire after that which is most antient, as that which is best . . . the authority of custom as well as law . . . consists only in its rectitude.' The only question about government is 'whether it be good or bad [or indeed] . . . so good, that nothing better could be added to it, which never was'. On this score Sidney argues:

I desire it may be considered, that we have but three ways of distinguishing between good and evil. 1. When God by his word reveals it to us. 2. When by his deeds he declares it; because that which he does is good, as that which he says is true. 3. By the light of reason, which is good, inasmuch as it is from God.[44]

On the first point scripture contains no 'explicit word for that continuance of power in the eldest'; we must therefore 'conclude it to be left to our liberty. For it agrees not with the goodness of God to leave us in perpetual ignorance of his will in a matter of so great importance.' Sidney repeats the *Court Maxims*' point – a basic maxim of natural law theory, made by Suarez – that there is a fundamental distinction anyway between paternal and political power. Moreover if the patriarchs were fathers they were not kings; the first king was Nimrod, 'Noah's accursed son'. And as 'this kingdom of Nimrod was an usurpation, void of all right . . . [so its] progress was suitable to its institution, and that which was begun in wickedness, was carried on with . . . pride, cruelty, injustice, madness . . . [and] the utmost fury.'[45] This shows that Nimrod had 'set himself up against God, and all that is good', and this is as good a guide to the relationship between God and monarchy as any. Moreover – continuing to pursue Filmer on his own terms – as for his 'pretended paternal right . . . to regality, if there be anything in it, [it] is divisible or indivisible . . . if divisible, it is extinguished' by division into the multitude; if indivisible then it must have devolved, to

[43] *Ibid.*, p. 14.   [44] *Ibid.*, p. 27.   [45] *Ibid.*, p. 18.

this day, to one man. 'This is the man we are to seek out . . . [but] I know not where to find him . . . [and] Those that call themselves kings in all other nations, set themselves up against God and man.'[46]

As for the second point – the 'dispensations of his providence' – Sidney demonstrates that they 'have gone contrary to this pretended law' of patriarchal monarchy. This leaves the third: the 'light of reason', and

If there be any precept, that by the light of nature we can in matters of this kind look upon as certain, it is, that the government of a people should be given to him that can best perform the duties of it . . . If there were a man, who in wisdom, valour, justice, and purity, surpassed all others, he might be called a king by nature; because he is best able to bear the weight of so great a charge . . . But if this right do not belong to him that is truly the eldest, nothing can be more absurd than a fantastical pretence [that it does] . . . [B]efore a man be admitted to practise physic, or set up a trade, it is his own skill that makes him a doctor or an artificer . . . An ass will not leave off his stupidity, though he be covered with scarlet . . . And it is hard to imagine a more violent inversion of the laws of God and nature, than to raise him to the throne, whom nature intended for the chain; or to make them slaves to slaves, whom God endowed with the virtues required in kings.[47]

It is not difficult to detect, behind this theme, upon which the *Discourses* bestows much of its length, Sidney's self-opinion, in relation to two aspects of his personal experience: his experience of 'the eldest' in his own family; and his experience of government under the Republic. It was after reading this passage that Sir William Temple remarked sourly: 'I, that knew him very well, can assure you, that he looked upon himself to be that very man, so qualified to govern the rest of all mankind.'[48]

The Grecians, among others who followed the light of reason, knew no other original title to the government of a nation than that wisdom, valour, and justice, which was beneficial to the people . . . [For] if governments . . . are instituted by men according to their own inclinations, they do therein seek their own good . . . This is not accomplished simply by setting one, a few, or more men in the administration of powers, but by placing the authority in those who may rightly perform their office. This is not every man's work; valour, integrity, wisdom, industry, experience, and skill, are required for the management of those civil and military affairs that necessarily fall under the care of chief magistrates. He or they therefore may reasonably be advanced above their equals, who are most fit to perform the[ir] duties . . . in order to the public good, for which they were instituted.[49]

Conversely, Sidney makes much of Filmer's admission (in effect) that his argument from origins was analogical rather than literal, that it matters not how rulers come by their power. Sidney could not sufficiently admire the title 'father by usurpation'. According to Filmer 'the fraud of his wife' was a sufficient title for Tiberius, and 'a wet blanket laid over his face' sufficed to 'invest Caligula with the same. But if there be any such thing as right or

[46] *Ibid.*, p. 24.   [47] *Ibid.*, pp. 28, 33.
[48] Burnet, *Own Time*, pp. 341–2.   [49] Sidney, *Discourses*, p. 37.

wrong . . . these extravagances can have no effect of right . . . No right is to be acknowledged in any, but such as is conferred upon them by those . . . concerned in the exercise of power, upon such conditions as best please themselves.'[50] Moreover political obedience depends not only on the rightness of that power's institution, but equally its exercise:

the same obedience is equally due to all, whilst . . . they do the work of God for our Good; and if they depart from it no one of them has a better title than the other to our obedience . . . Magistrates are distinguished from other men, by the power with which the laws invests them for the public good; he that cannot or will not procure that good, destroys his own being, and becomes like to other men.[51]

This argument, again running closely parallel to Locke's, equally echoes the *Vindication* and begins to point clearly towards Charles II. This withdrawal of obedience, says Sidney, extends equally to those who were indeed (as in 1660)

by the people's consent, duly advanced to legitimate power; [but] having sworn to administer it . . . for the good of those who gave it, turn all to their own pleasure or profit, without any care of the public . . . This may be liable to hard censures; but those, who use them most gently, must confess, that such an extreme deviation from the end of their institution annuls it; and the wound thereby given to the natural and original rights of those nations cannot be cured, unless they resume their liberties . . . and return to the antient custom of choosing those to be magistrates, who for their virtues best deserve to be preferred . . . to perform the great end of providing for the public safety.[52]

At the beginning of his second chapter, Filmer argued that Aristotle had shown that kingdoms grew from families, and had called kingship the 'first and divinest' form of government.[53] In fact this is quite misleading, since Aristotle's *Politics* had discussed the family in order to distinguish it from the polis, as a separate (and private rather than public) structure. Moreover Aristotle had said, as we have just seen Sidney paraphrase, that a natural king must be 'the first and divinest' among men – not that kingship was the first and divinest among governments. By this he meant – as Sidney indignantly pointed out – that no man ought to be king unless he were 'the first and divinest' in natural ability, and in the absence of such a person there should be no king at all. In the process of pointing out these errors, Sidney spent some time explaining the political theories of both Aristotle 'and his master Plato'; in particular their view that the necessary qualification for political office was virtue (rather than birth).

It was from encounters like these that Sidney was led to complain about Filmer's 'custom' of 'tak[ing] pieces of passages from good books, and turn[ing] them directly against the plain meaning of the authors, expressed

---

[50] *Ibid.*, p. 38.   [51] *Ibid.*, pp. 38–40.
[52] *Ibid.*, p. 40.   [53] Filmer, *Patriarcha* (1680), pp. 27–8.

in the whole scope and design of their writings'.[54] Another writer in this category was Filmer's supposed principal (non-scriptural) source, Bodin. The whole shape of Bodin's essentially Aristotelian enterprise is changed in Filmer's work, only to be resurrected in the *Discourses* itself. This is so not least in relation to the matter just discussed, where Aristotle's distinction between the political community and the family is scrupulously maintained by Bodin. In general, aside from Grotius, who was heavily indebted to Bodin himself, there is no closer model for the humanist intellectual style of the *Discourses* than Bodin's *Six Books of the Commonwealth* – a work we have seen Sidney quoting in his support in the *Vindication*. The distinctive balance struck by Bodin between humanist relativism and natural law universals was to be maintained into the seventeenth century by Grotius and Sidney, and (partly through them) into the eighteenth by Montesquieu.

Sidney's explanation of Plato and Aristotle then led him into a repetition of the discussion of natural (as opposed to artificial) inequalities noted in the *Court Maxims*.[55] In the process he made it clear that this whole preference for men of virtue – the belief that 'it is ever good to be governed by the wisest and best' is as fundamental to the spirit of the Greeks' rational and moral philosophy as Filmer's (basically medieval) concern with genetic inheritance is foreign to it. He closes with a favourite metaphor of Plato's own: '[In short] If the nature of man be reason ... it were not only a deviation from reason, but a most desperate and mischievous madness, for a company going to the Indies, to give the guidance of their ship to the son of the best pilot in the world.'[56] Overtones of Halifax here.

According to Sidney, moreover, 'as the work of a magistrate ... is the highest, noblest, and most difficult, that can be committed to the charge of a man, a more excellent virtue is required in the person who is to be advanced to it, than in any other.' What exactly is this work then?

In the answer he gives to this question we find that Sidney's role for the state goes far beyond that of pilot or guide; politics is a constructive science, a form of architecture, in which the state becomes the builder and moulder of men. This vital aspect of Sidney's theory must be emphasised against the alternative possible laissez-faire interpretation, in which 'liberty' means liberty from rather than through the state. There is indeed both a positive and a negative sense of liberty in Sidney's thought. But the negative meaning – that liberty involves an 'independency from' the will of others – is more accessible to the modern mind. Equally central to Sidney's own experience was the coercive side of liberty – that people must be made free. The struggle against will, and for reason, was hard, both in the self and in the

---

[54] Sidney, *Discourses*, p. 312.
[55] *Ibid.*, pp. 60–1; Scott, *Sidney and the English Republic*, p. 192.
[56] *Ibid.*, p. 61.

community. For Sidney the whole point of politics lay in the positive potential of the state as a coercive moral instrument, for the (if necessary, compul-
sory) political and religious betterment of its members. A 'good'
government was not a popular one but one that brought its members closer
to the nature of God. It was this belief – shared by Sidney, Milton, and Vane
alike – that lay at the heart of the political experiment of 1649–53; and it
was in Sidney's view for this reason that the 'furious people, in spite to the
puritans' had opted in 1660 for the softer option of monarchy instead. For
all its rhetoric Sidney's primary political allegiance – as he made perfectly
clear on the scaffold – was not to 'the people' but to God. When he uses the
phrase 'public good' we need to pay more attention to his understanding of
the second word, than our understanding of the first.

Thus, argued Sidney, it is impossible for men to attain the good they seek,
independently of political structures:

The weakness in which we are born, renders us unable to attain [that] good of
ourselves; we want help in all things, especially in the greatest. The fierce barbarity
of a loose multitude, bound by no law, and regulated by no discipline, is wholly
repugnant to [this good] ... The first step towards the cure of this pestilent evil, is
for many to join in one body, that every one may be protected by the united force of
all. [The next is that] ... the various talents that men possess, [must] by good
discipline be rendered useful to the whole, as the meanest piece of wood or stone,
being placed by a wise architect, conduces to the beauty of the most glorious
building ... [Men] are rough pieces of timber or stone, which it is necessary to
cleave, saw or cut: this is the work of a skilful builder, and he only is capable of
erecting a great fabric, who is so. Magistrates are political architects; and they only
can perform the work incumbent on them, who excel in political virtues.[57]

Sidney speaks in the same way when he refers to the most successful of all
states: Rome. The Romans began as a 'fierce people . . . composed of unruly
shepherds, herdsmen, fugitive slaves and outlawed persons'; but their
'boisterous humor [was] gradually tempered by discipline [again the key
word] under Romulus', and 'a new race grew up capable of liberty'.[58] In
short it is not the raw materials of the state that are important; it is the
quality of the political architecture.

Two things should be noticed here: the key word discipline, mentioned
three times (and its instrument, law); and the strength of the imagery Sidney
used (cleave, saw, cut) to describe the moulding of the state's citizens. How
did Sidney see this 'moulding' coming about?

Like his republican colleagues, Sidney saw the soul as both reasonable
and passionate, capable of both virtue and sin. By freely joining (for their
own protection) a public body restrained by law, and governed by reason
and virtue, individuals joined an apparatus for the restraint of the passion-

----

[57] *Ibid.*, p. 64.   [58] *Ibid.*, pp. 59–61.

ate part of their nature and their (consequently self) government by reason. The result was a diminution of sin – of evil, ignorance and distance from God; and an increase in good (the 'public good') and a movement towards God. By co-operating in this collective exercise of (in theory at least) self-discipline, people enjoyed this collective benefit of self-improvement. It was the sole purpose of politics – of political architecture – to provide this apparatus and make these benefits possible. And Sidney believed that the benefits concerned were incalculable. The simple restraint of vice through public discipline invited a limitless increase in virtue, knowledge, power, felicity, wealth, and truth. At the same time, by bringing a people closer to God, it laid the basis for far greater and more lasting benefits in the world to come.

Political societies, in other words, were the means by which God's creatures used His gift of reason to erect a collective apparatus of self-improvement, in accordance with His wishes.

[I]nasmuch as [God] ... did endow [men] ... with understanding to provide for themselves, and by the invention of arts and sciences, to be beneficial to each other, he shewed, that they ought to make use of that understanding in forming governments, according to their own convenience, and such occasions as should arise, as well as in other matters ... If a faculty [reason] as well as liberty was left to every one ... [to] practise such things ... in the matters of least importance, it were absurd to imagine, that the political science, which of all others is the most abstruse and variable according to accidents and circumstances, should have been perfectly known to them who had no use of it; and that their descendants are obliged to add nothing to what they practised.[59]

Filmer, on the other hand, by peddling the irrational political mechanism of inheritance, 'as far as in him lies, endeavours to take from us the use of reason, and extinguishing the light of it, to make us live like the worst of beasts, that we may be fit subjects to absolute monarchy'.[60]

[59] *Ibid.*, p. 98.   [60] *Ibid.*, p. 99.

⇜ 11 ⇝

Discourses *(2) Rebellion, tumult and war*

Rebellion, being nothing but a renewed war ... of itself is neither good nor evil, more than any other war; but is just or unjust, according to the cause or manner of it. (Sidney, *Discourses*, p. 457)

he is a fool who knows not, that swords were given to men, that none might be slaves, but such as know not how to use them. (Sidney, *Discourses*, pp. 291–2)

11.1 PART TWO: PRACTICE: COMMONWEALTHS VERSUS MONARCHIES (ch. 2, sections 11–29, pp. 110–248)

THE REPLY TO FILMER: PART I

In the last section of the previous chapter we discussed the building materials for Sidney's political architecture (liberty, reason, and virtue), and the purpose of the resulting construction, that of other human arts and sciences – the good and improvement of man. In this section we will see this schema of principles pushed into practice, and in the process what Sidney took to be the consequences of their absence, as well as their presence. 'The bestial barbarity in which many nations, especially of Africa, America, and Asia, now live, shows what human nature is, if it be not improved by art and discipline.'[1]

This is the first section in which Sidney departs significantly from Filmer's text to mount an independent course of instruction of his own. Filmer's attack on the classical republics leads Sidney into an extended lecture on commonwealths which is a clear amplification of the *Vindication*'s harangue on the same topic. This includes the heart of the *Discourses*' 1650s 'classical republican' theory and involves an irrefutable clarification of Sidney's own political stance. While elsewhere Filmer's extreme absolutism allowed Sidney to claim that it was only 'absolute monarchy ... that I dispute against, professing much veneration for that which is mixed, regulated by law, and directed to the public good', this section reveals that Sidney's principles lead in practice to a crisp distinction between republics

---

[1] Sidney, *Discourses*, p. 304.

and monarchies and to a championship of the government of 'popular assemblies' against the 'government of princes'. Once again we should be aware of the relevance of this distinction to Sidney's analysis of the political circumstances of 1681–3.

Although we can attribute the length and character of this section to the nature of Sidney's own political interests, the subject is nevertheless Filmer's choice. It is Filmer who finally turns (in ch. 2, section 10 of *Patriarcha*, pp. 50–3), from a general attack on the notion of popular government, to a specific attack on the classical popular states. He condemns their turbulence and instability ('the Blood hath been suckt up in the Market Places with Spunges'), their seditions, faction, and violence, and concludes that there is 'no Tyranny . . . [like] the Tyranny of a Multitude'. This wickedness and disorder Filmer takes to be an 'unavoidable adjunct of Democracie', since democracy represents the will of most people, and most people are wicked. The fewer people, and the less 'the people' in general are involved in matters of government the better. It is the Roman Republic that bears the brunt of this attack. Much of Filmer's argument hinges on the accusation of instability, and this culminates in the claim that even the longest lasting Republic (Rome) lasted only 480 years, whereas the Assyrian and Babylonian monarchies lasted 1,200 and 1,495 years respectively.[2] To this Sidney replies, in effect, that this is no more a cause for congratulation than 1,200 years of toothache. What matters, again, is not longevity, but value: that something endures interminably does not make it a good thing.

It is a valuable function of the *Court Maxims* that we know that the classical republics in general, and Rome in particular, were important to Sidney's theory independently of Filmer. But we need to be aware of just how centrally the content of the *Discourses* was being dictated by Filmer, both the natural law theory of the previous section and the classical republicanism of this. Even the crisp distinction between monarchies and popular governments – also a feature of the *Court Maxims* – was here assisted by Filmer's own claim that mixed monarchy was a contradiction in terms, that there were only governments of the people (democracies), or governments of one man (monarchies). Sidney disagreed and replied lamenting the ignorance of those who understood neither the several species of government' nor the 'various tempers of nations'; 'there never was a good government in the world, that did not consist of the three simple species'. Here too he remained much closer to Bodin's relativistic (and so equally lengthy) treatment of this subject than Filmer, Bodin's concept of indivisible sovereignty (which Sidney in fact shared) notwithstanding.[3]

[2] Filmer, *Patriarcha*, pp. 61–2, 69–70, 70–3.
[3] Sidney, *Discourses*, p. 138. Sidney agreed with Bodin that sovereignty was indivisible, but

Sidney's reply hinges from the beginning on establishing a necessary connection between political success and moral good. Because popular governments depend upon the virtue and bravery of the body of their citizens they cultivate it; because monarchy does not, it does not do so. This latter argument would be developed, in the next section in particular, into a repeat of the *Court Maxims'* claim that on the contrary absolute monarchy depends upon the weakness and depravity of its subject populace – and so cultivates that. The effect in this section is (as usual) to tackle Filmer head on by reasserting, and indeed further emphasising, the Machiavellian picture Filmer is himself attacking. Consequently Sidney holds out the choice between flourishing amid turbulent liberty; or dying of starvation and moral degradation in perfect peace.

Sidney's is a powerful argument because it links the appeal of moral rectitude with that of competitive success. It convinces because it pictures popular governments at the head of a great and perpetually increasing pool of human resource – the basis of any state's power. This line of argument established, Sidney can then ridicule Filmer's quite different preoccupation with longevity over value. Indeed Sidney's argument becomes unassailable precisely because its posited moral objectivity is so fundamentally subjective – there is no obvious reference point from which it can be disproved. If Filmer could show that all nations in the world were governed by monarchies, says Sidney at one stage, this would prove not that monarchies are good but that mankind has renounced the use of reason.

Our author's judgement, as well as inclinations to virtue, are manifested in the preference he gives to the manners of the Assyrians ... before the Grecians and Romans. Whereas the first were never remarkable for any thing, but pride, lewdness, treachery, cruelty, cowardice, madness, and hatred to all that is good ... the others excelled in wisdom, valour, and all the virtues that deserve imitation ... And I think no example can be alleged of a free people, that has ever been conquered by an absolute monarch, unless he did incomparibly surpass them in riches and strength. On the other hand, many great kings have been overthrown by small republics: and the success being constantly the same, it cannot be attributed to fortune, but must necessarily be the production of virtue and good order. Machiavel, discoursing of these matters, finds virtue to be so essentially necessary to the establishment and preservation of liberty, that he thinks it impossible for a corrupted people to set up a good government, or for a tyranny to be introduced, if they be virtuous; and makes this conclusion, 'that where ... the body of the people, is not corrupted, tumults and disorders do no hurt; and where it is corrupted, good laws do no good': which being confirmed by reason and experience, I think no wise man has ever contradicted him.[4]

Sidney next quarrels with Filmer's attribution of the word 'order' to

---

followed Grotius in arguing that even so the type of state through which it was exercised could be mixed. See Scott, *Sidney and the English Republic*, p. 190.

[4] Sidney, *Discourses*, pp. 109–10.

absolute monarchy. Again Sidney takes this word to be value-laden; in politics it means 'good order' (it can hardly mean 'bad order'). Thus political order

principally consists in appointing to every one his right place, office, or work; [wheras Filmer] . . . lays the whole weight of government upon one person, who very often does neither deserve, nor is able to bear the least part of it . . . Our author's next work is to show, that stability is the effect of this good order. But . . . stability is . . . only worthy of praise, when it is in that which is good. No man delights in sickness or pain, because it is long or incurable; nor in slavery or misery, because it is perpetual . . . He must therefore prove, that the stability he boasts of is in things that are good . . . [and] we might leave him here with as little fear that any man [will] remove this obstacle, as that he himself should rise out of his grave, and do it: but I hope [in addition] to prove, that of all things under the sun, there is none more mutable and unstable than absolute monarchy.[5]

We have already seen that for Sidney only those principles rooted in God can have any permanence in a mutable world. 'Nothing can be called stable, that is not so in principle and practice . . . if there be any stability in man, it must be in virtue . . . for in weakness, folly and madness there can be none.' Accordingly a form of government where 'the succession goes to the next in blood, without distinction of age, sex, and personal qualities' is unstable in its very foundation – and it should be noted that this point applies to any hereditary monarchy, not just absolute monarchy. It is later extended to encompass elective monarchy as well.

This would be the case, though it were . . . an even wager, whether the person would be fit or unfit . . . But experience shewing, that, among many millions of men, there is hardly one that possesses the qualities required in a king, it is so many to one, that he, upon whom the lot shall fall, will not be the man we seek, in whose person or government there can be such a stability as is asserted.[6]

This claim established, there remains only to traverse the histories of the world to prove it, which Sidney duly does, touching upon the Hebrews, English, French, Romans: 'Tiberius . . . being stifled, the government went on with much uniformity and stability. Caligula, Claudius, Nero, Galba, Otho, Vitellius, regularly and constantly did all the mischief they could . . .'[7]

Sidney takes the opportunity to mention how rules for both private and public inheritance differ all over the world. There is thus no universal principle involved. This makes hereditary monarchies inherently unstable, prone to frequent disputes and 'bloody contests for the crown'. The personal/legal and political background to these remarks requires no emphasis:

The like may be said of all the kingdoms in the world: they may have their ebbings and flowings according to the virtues and vices of princes . . . but can never have any stability, because there is, and can be, none in them . . . [and] there is another ground of perpetual fluctuation in absolute monarchies . . . that cannot be restrained by law

---

[5] *Ibid.*, p. 111.   [6] *Ibid.*, p. 112.   [7] *Ibid.*, p. 114.

... [and] that is, the impulse of ministers, favourites, wives, or whores, who frequently govern all things according to their own passions or interests ... I might draw too much envy on myself, if I should take upon me to cite all the examples of this kind that are found in modern histories.[8]

From monarchies Sidney turns to republics, and wonders (on Filmer's behalf) 'how a few of those giddy Greeks came to overthrow those vast armies of the Persians ... and seldom found any other difficulty than what did arise from their own countrymen'.[9]

[And] I desire it may be considered, whether ... stability be wanting in Venice; whether Tuscany be in a better condition to defend itself since it fell under the power of the house of Medici ... whether it were an easy work to conquer Switzerland: whether the Hollanders are of greater strength since the recovery of their liberty, or when they groaned under the yoke of Spain; and lastly, whether the entire conquest of Scotland and Ireland, the victories obtained against the Hollander when they were at the height of their power, and the reputation to which England did rise in less than five years after 1648, be good marks of the instability, disorder or weakness of free nations ...[10]

Having thus laid his republican cards on the table – and note how specifically military his emphasis is – Sidney then turns to Filmer's *bête noir*: republican Rome. In the several chapters which follow Sidney uses Livy to argue, like Machiavelli before him, that 'all that was ever desirable, or worthy of praise or imitation in Rome, proceeded from its liberty, grew up, and perished with it ... [unless the people had] been more worthily employed by the Tarquins in cleansing jakes and common sewers, than in acquiring the dominion of the best part of mankind'.[11] To this Livian picture of Roman virtue, and particularly military virtue, Sidney contrasts the account of Tacitus, 'who well describes the state of the empire, when the power was absolutely in the hands of one'.[12]

But if this virtue, and the glorious effects of it, did begin with liberty, it also expired with the same. [Under the Emperors] the best men ... were gleaned up by the proscriptions, or circumvented ... by false and frivolous accusations. Mankind is inclined to vice, and the way to virtue is so hard, that it wants encouragement; but when all honours, advantages, and preferments, are given to vice, and despised virtue finds no other reward but hatred, persecution and death, there are few who will follow it.

To Filmer's accusations, therefore, of constant innovation and tumult in the Roman Republic Sidney replies not only that 'no change of magistracy ... brings any manner of prejudice, as long as it is done by those who have a right of doing it ... according to times, and other circumstances'; but also that it is impossible to found a state without the need for change, since 'men

---

[8] *Ibid.*, pp. 115–16.   [9] *Ibid.*, p. 116.
[10] *Ibid.*, p. 118.   [11] *Ibid.*, p. 119.
[12] *Ibid.*, p. 120 (and for the passage following).

can hardly at once forsee all that may happen in many ages'. Changes are, therefore, not only inevitable but necessary, and are chiefly achieved 'by means of these tumults which our author ignorantly blames'.[13] Following this Machiavellian line of thought Sidney responds to Filmer's statement that Rome enjoyed its longest peace under Augustus:

Peace is [only] to be sought by states that are constituted for it ... or perhaps it might simply deserve praise, if mankind were so formed, that a people intending hurt to no-one could preserve themselves. But the world being so far of another temper, that no nation can be safe without valour and strength, those governments only deserve to be commended, which by discipline and exercise increase both, and the Roman above all, that excelled in both ... [Furthermore] That peace only is to be valued, which is accompanied with justice ... which was wholly wanting during the reign of Augustus and his successors.[14]

In short, peace, like stability and longevity, has no absolute, but only a relative value, a fact of which Filmer seems unaware.

To Filmer's imputation of 'corruption and venality to commonwealths', Sidney replies with a suitably amazed demonstration to the contrary. In the course of it the *Court Maxims*' republican assumption of a private vs public interest dichotomy reappears. If 'False witnesses and accusers ... whores, players, fidlers, with other such vermin' are natural to courts, it is because

the[se] ... vices may be profitable to private men; but they can never be so to the government, if it be popular or mixed. No people was ever the better for that which renders them weak or base. And a duly created magistracy, governing a nation with their consent, can have no interest distinct from that of the public, or desire to diminish the strength of the people, which is their own, and by which they subsist. On the other side, the absolute monarch, who governs for himself, and chiefly seeks his own preservation, looks upon the strength and bravery of his subjects as the root of his greatest danger, and frequently desires to render them weak, base, [and] corrupt ... that they may neither dare to attempt the breaking of the yoke he lays upon them, nor trust one another in any generous design for the recovery of their liberty.[15]

Thus both 'all popular and well-mixed governments' on the one hand, and all 'absolute monarchies' or 'tyrannies' on the other, 'have their continuance from contrary ... principle[s] in nature suitable to their original. All tyrannies have had their beginnings in corruption; all popular governments in wisdom, goodness and virtue; and both must maintain themselves by the same means.' Popular governments thus may fall into corruption; but absolute monarchy is rooted in it.[16]

Sidney then explains that the genus of popular government contains many species; Filmer's dreaded 'democracy' is only one of them. Having described the 'three simple [Aristotelian] species' from some mixture of which all good

[13] *Ibid.*, pp. 123–4.   [14] *Ibid.*, p. 133.
[15] *Ibid.*, p. 156; see also pp. 216–17.   [16] *Ibid.*, pp. 156–7, 160.

governments are composed, Sidney then begins to discuss the types in more detail. He does so in the course of demonstrating his next claim against Filmer: 'that mixed and popular governments preserve peace, and manage wars, better than absolute monarchies'. In the event not much is said about 'preserving peace'. What follows is a series of chapters on Sidney's special interest: the republican prosecution of war. These are the first significant departures from Filmer's own text, and they are obviously heavily indebted, both to his own experience, and to his reading of Machiavelli.

[In] a popular or mixed government every man is concerned; every one has a part, according to his quality or merit; all changes are prejudicial to all ... the body of the people is the public defence, and every man is armed and disciplined; the advantages of good success are communicated to all, and every one bears a part in the losses. This makes men generous and industrious and fills their hearts with love to their country. This, and the desire of that praise which is the reward of virtue, raised the Romans among the rest of mankind; and wherever the same ways are taken, they will in a great measure have the same effects ... The same order that made men valiant and industrious in the service of their country in the first ages would have the same effect, if it were now in being. Men would have the same love to the public as the Spartans and Romans had, if there were the same reason for it. We need no other proof of this than what we have seen in our own country, where, in a few years, good discipline, and a just encouragement given to those who did well, produced more examples of pure, complete, incorruptible, and invincible virtue, than Rome or Greece could ever boast.[17]

In absolute monarchies on the other hand, where private interest reigns in the government, it reigns among the people and the soldiers too. To fight for the state is to fight for somebody else; to win is to add weight to your own chains. This leads to the dependence of kingdoms upon mercenaries, concerning the well-rehearsed dangers of which Sidney quotes both Machiavelli and Guicciardini.

From this point Sidney widens the discussions to explain the different types of 'Commonwealths ... [as they] seek peace or war, according to the variety of their constitutions'. This is necessary because 'our author without distinction has generally blamed them all ... [although] the constitutions of commonwealths have been so various, according to the different temper of nations and times, that if some of them seem to have been principally constituted for war, others have much delighted in peace'. This section repeats the *Vindication*'s claim that 'commonwealth' means here all varieties of government short of absolutism (for the common good), but the political schema itself is borrowed directly from Machiavelli's *Discorsi*.

Before Sidney, James Harrington had borrowed Machiavelli's distinction between republics for expansion and those for preservation. Sidney however introduces his own subdivision within these, adopting the new criteria of trade – presumably a reflection of his own Dutch and English republican experience. Thus according to Sidney there are four basic types of commonwealth: those designed for war for conquest (Rome and Israel); war for defence (Sparta); war and trade (Carthage – mentioned in the same context in the *Court Maxims*); and peace and trade (Venice). He also introduces one entirely new category: that of federated republics (Switzerland and the United Provinces), again reflecting his own experience. This last is of some importance, for it was taken up – with acknowledgement to Sidney – by Montesquieu, who developed it at some length in *The Spirit of the Laws*, and was subsequently credited with inventing the concept for the benefit of the United States of America. *The Spirit of the Laws*, which contains many footprints of Sidney's work in general (and, like that work itself, of Aristotle, Machiavelli, Bodin, and Grotius), shows particular signs of having absorbed this section of the *Discourses* carefully.[18]

Sidney praises all these republics for their common 'love to the public' before coming down categorically in favour of those designed for war for conquest. The Venetians he criticises for the 'mortal error' of their 'too great inclinations ... to peace', and remarks that their reliance on mercenary soldiers has forced them 'very often to buy peace on ignominious and prejudicial conditions'. At various points he makes it clear that his favoured model republics are Israel and Rome; the latter pre-eminent among republics which have prospered without direct divine aid. Sidney's vigorously argued conclusion then is 'that is the best government which best provides for war'.[19] He is so emphatic on this point that for the only time in the *Discourses* he allows this value to override the distinction between republican and absolute governments itself: '[A]ll governments, whether monarchical or popular, absolute or limited, deserve praise or blame as they are well or ill constituted for making war.' In many ways this unqualified bellicosity is the touchstone of Sidney's political thought.

This represents a decision to develop this aspect of Machiavelli's thought – at the expense of the cult of Venice – in a way that separates Sidney from all the major English republicans except Nedham.[20] But it is clear that the level of military emphasis in Sidney's republicanism is uniquely his own; not even Nedham matches it. One source tending to produce this perspective, shared by Machiavelli, Nedham, and Sidney, was Livy; and Livy's *History* is almost as fundamental a source for Sidney's *Discourses* as it was for Machiavelli's. But it's clear also that this reflects Sidney's practical experience, not only as a military commander and governor, but as a senior

---

[18] Montesquieu, *The Spirit of the Laws*, pp. 237–9; R. Shackleton, *Montesquieu: A Critical Biography* (Oxford 1961), pp. 276–7 and note 5.
[19] *Ibid.*, pp. 174, 178.
[20] Scott, *Sidney and the English Republic*, ch. 2 section 3; see also ch. 6 section 3.

member and military administrator within a government the most spectacular accomplishments of which were military. By the time of the *Discourses* these accomplishments had been polished by nostalgia into precious stones.

This military posture also, however, links up with a second key characteristic of Sidney's thought: his insistence on dynamism and change. Once again this takes its beginning from Machiavelli, whose *Discorsi* are the source for Sidney's statement that 'If [a power] . . . does not grow, it must pine and perish; for in this world nothing is permanent: that which does not grow better will grow worse.'[21] Once again, however, Sidney develops this insight into the full-blown argument for the necessity of change to which we will be returning later in this chapter. In a world of flux, the key to success is dynamism and change – that makes Sidney's emphasis on arms absolutely necessary. In a world of limited resources, and so of political competition, arms must provide the cutting edge for change. We have already seen the basis for this view in Sidney's portrayal of politics – in opposition to the stasis of Filmer's vision – as a form of progressive architecture. Thus:

The whelp of a lion newly born has neither strength nor fierceness. He that builds a city, and does not intend it should increase, committs as great an absurdity, as if he should desire his child might ever continue under the same weakness, in which he is born . . . This increase also is useless, or perhaps hurtful, if it be not in strength, as well as in riches, or number; for everyone is apt to seize upon ill guarded treasures . . . [Accordingly] when a people multiplies, as they will always do in a good climate under a good government, such an enlargement of their territory, as is necessary for their subsistence, can be aquired only by war.[22]

In short the object of (good) government is increase – of moral and religious capacity, of status and power, of the numbers of people themselves, and the fact of increase necessitates war.

Both the dynamic/progressive assumption of this theory, and its military edge, are features of other English republican writing to a lesser degree. This is in part, again, a result of the nature – and the brevity – of the English republican experience. Yet it is Sidney's thought as a whole that produces by far the fullest and most strident expression of the two combined, and their implications.

Nor does this point – that arms are the cutting edge for change – exhaust their importance for Sidney's theory. For his next excursion from Filmer's text is on a different but related subject, altogether more central to the purpose of the book. It is the first instalment of Sidney's justification of rebellion. Although it begins, like the last, with Machiavelli, the theorist who eventually provides the key concept is Grotius. And although throughout this section Sidney's chapters had been increasing in length, the

[21] *Ibid.*, pp. 30–5; Machiavelli, *Discourses*, book 1, ch. 6.
[22] Sidney, *Discourses*, pp. 178–9.

chapter in question is over twice the length of any so far. The key concept is that of just war.

The occasion for Sidney's argument on this subject came from Filmer's criticism of republics for their frequent 'seditions, tumults and wars'. As with the *Vindication* on 'commonwealth principles' or the *Discourses* later encounter with the word 'rebellion', Sidney's response is not to deny the charge but to ask whether 'seditions, tumults and wars' are indeed, or always, a bad thing. The provocation involved is not lessened by his own insertion of the word 'civil' before 'wars'.

At first glance this seems straightforwardly Machiavellian, and Filmer is almost certainly himself here attacking Machiavelli's famous praise for the 'tumults' of Rome as an invigorating mechanism. This is not, however, how Sidney chooses to develop the point.

He begins by asserting, characteristically enough, that 'It is vain to seek a government in all points free from a possibility of *civil* wars, tumults and seditions: that is a blessing denied to this life, and reserved to complete the felicity of the next.' What must be asked therefore is not whether there be seditions, tumults and wars in a state, but whether those seditions, tumults and wars be good or bad, just or unjust, necessary or unnecessary. If, in other words, the effect of a 'sedition' is to finish the life of a bad government and begin the life of a good one, then it is a 'good' thing, and smiled upon by all good men (and God). We can see here just what a potent and dangerous revolution ideology followed from this bogus assumption of moral objectivity – something we have seen to be characteristic of the whole of the *Discourses* so far. It was exactly this type of theory – and its consequences – which terrified Hobbes. But Sidney appears quite exceptional in the explicit nature of its statement.

It may seem strange to some that I mention seditions, tumults, and wars upon just occasions; but I can find no reason to retract the term. [Nor, it has to be said, could Charles II find any reason to retract Sidney's death sentence the following year.] God, intending that men should live justly with one another, does certainly intend, that [justice should be enforced] . . . and the law that forbids injuries were of no use, if no penalty, might be inflicted on those who do not obey it. If injustice therefore be evil, and injuries forbidden, they are also to be punished; and the law instituted for this prevention must necessarily intend *the avenging of such as cannot be prevented* [my emphasis].[23]

Leaving aside for the moment this noteworthy intrusion of vengeance – and all the time here the *Discourses* is moving closer to the *Court Maxims* –

[23] *Ibid.*, p. 187.

this association of 'civil wars, tumults, and seditions' with 'justice' fore-shadows Sidney's recourse to the Grotian concept of just war. According to Grotius 'just wars' are made 'for the protection of the innocent' against those who cannot be held in check by judicial processes. It is therefore particularly interesting that at this same time we find Henry Neville recom-mending these same two sources on this same subject. Neville wrote:

wherever any two co-ordinate powers do differ, and there be no power on earth to reconcile them otherwise, nor any umpire; they will, in fact, fall together by the ears. What can be done in this case justly, look into your own countryman, Machiavel, and into Grotius; who in his book *De Jure Belli ac Pacis*, treated of such matters long before our wars.[24]

Grotius had applied the concept (in *The Law of War and Peace*) principally to international affairs, where the power of states stood outside the jurisdiction of the particular positive laws of any one of them.[25] The crucial adaptation made by Sidney was to re-apply this concept from external to internal affairs – and to the *civil* war in which he had himself been involved. Thus he was able to paint civil war/tumult/sedition as sometimes necessary to 'protect the innocent' against the absolutist monarch who placed his 'will' outside the jurisdiction of the positive laws of his own country (as Filmer insisted was necessary). It is one of the deeply interesting parallels between Sidney's and Locke's answer to this same book that they use this same argument – from the same (Grotian) source – though they phrased and structured it rather differently.

This is where Locke got his idea of the 'Right of War', though he is much more careful about describing the (limited) circumstances under which it came into effect. These are, in effect, outside political society – both before its creation or after its dissolution – because the existence of such a right at other times would make society ungovernable. Sidney, however, makes no such qualifications. This right applies at all times. As 'the sword of war' was given by God 'to protect the people against the violence of foreigners', 'the sword of justice is put into the[ir] hands' for protection against internal injury. In both cases

The ways of preventing or punishing injuries are judicial or extrajudicial. Judicial proceedings are of force against those who submit or may be brought to trial; but are of no effect against those who resist, and are of such power that they cannot be restrained. It were absurd ... and impious to think, that he, who had added treachery to his other crimes, and usurped a power above the law, should be protected by the enormity of his wickedness. Legal proceedings therefore are to be used when the delinquent submits to the law; and *all are just* [my emphasis], when he will not be kept in force by the legal.[26]

---

[24] Neville, *Plato Redivivus* in Robbins (ed.), *Two English Republican Tracts*, pp. 148–9.
[25] See Scott, *Sidney and the English Republic*, p. 20.
[26] Sidney, *Discourses*, p. 187.

Like war then, a 'tumult' is simply the 'trial by force, to which men come, when other ways are ineffectual'. And in conclusion:

If the laws of God and men are therefore of no effect, when the magistracy is left at liberty to break them, and if the lusts of those, who are too strong for the tribunals of justice, cannot otherwise be restrained, than by seditions, tumults, and war, those *seditions, tumults, and wars, are justified by the laws of God and man* [my emphasis].[27]

Men who delight in cavils may ask, who shall be the judge of these occasions? and whether I intend to give the people the decision of their own case? [But] . . . when the contest is between the magistrate and the people . . . [whichever] party, to which the determination is referred, must be the judge of his own case. [There remains only to ask then] . . . whether the magistrate should depend upon the judgement of the people, or the people on that of the magistrate; [a question answered by asking for whose benefit political society is established].[28]

[Thus] whoever condemns all seditions, tumults, and wars, raised against such princes, must say that none are wicked, or seek the ruin of their people, which is absurd, for Caligula wished the people had but one neck that he might cut it off at a blow. Nero set the city on fire. *And we have known such as have been worse than either of them* [my emphasis].[29]

By this stage – its theoretical basis having been laid out clearly – the insurrectionary message of the *Discourses* has become perfectly explicit. It is Charles II 'who has added treachery to this other crimes, and usurped a power above the law'. Once again we need only remember the contemporary English context to see how dangerous this open defence of 'seditions . . . and civil wars, raised against princes' – from a participant in the last one – was. But such princes:

must either be suffered to continue in the free exercise of their rage . . . or must be restrained by a . . . judicial, or extrajudicial way. They who disallow the extrajudicial, do as little like the judicial . . . [Filmer] will not hear of bringing a supreme magistrate before a judicial tribunal [either] . . . This is to license the undaunted practice of any injustice and wickedness without restraint . . . [in summary] Extrajudicial proceedings, by sedition, tumult or war, *must take place*, when the persons concerned are of such power, that they cannot be brought under the judicial. They who deny this deny all help against an usurping tyrant, *or the perfidiousness of a lawfully created magistrate, who adds the crimes of ingratitude and treachery to usurpation* [of powers contrary to his institution] [my emphasis].[30]

Thus Sidney progresses from 'may' to 'must', and from Kings of 'our' experience in general to the case of Charles II (as prefaced in the *Vindication*) in particular. By means of these extrapolations from Grotius, arrived at via Machiavelli, Sidney lays the basis for a defence of rebellion that is both plausible and exceptional. As justifications of 'sedition, tumult, and war' go – and I'm not aware of any others in this century, written in settled

27 *Ibid.*, p. 188.   28 *Ibid.*, p. 192.
29 *Ibid.*, p. 193.   30 *Ibid.*, pp. 193–4.

times – it possesses a lucidity, frankness and force which make Sidney's later importance as a revolution theorist in Europe and America entirely understandable.

THE REPLY TO FILMER: PART II

Following this considerable achievement, Sidney returns to Machiavelli again to pursue the refutation of Filmer in Machiavellian terms. Once again having it both ways, Sidney both denies that republics are worse than monarchies for 'seditions, tumults and wars', and then argues that even if they were, 'Civil wars and tumults are not the greatest evils that befal nations.'[31] By this route he eventually arrives – as a man of his political experience might well – at the Machiavellian argument that such wars are in fact a sign of political vitality.

It is ill, that men should kill one another in seditions, tumults and wars; but it is worse, to bring nations to such misery, weakness, and baseness, as to have neither strength nor courage to contend for anything; to have left nothing worth defending, and to give the name of peace to desolation. [When the cities of Greece and Italy] . . . were free, they loved their country, and were always ready to fight in its defence . . . They sometimes killed one another; but their enemies never got any thing but burying-places within their territories . . . [Now] Instead of many turbulent, contentious cities, they have a few scattered, silent cottages . . . [where they] enjoy the quiet and peaceable estate of a wilderness. Again, there is a way of killing worse than that of the sword . . . by taking from men the means of living, bring some to perish through want, drive others out of the country, and . . . dissuade men from marriage, by taking from them all ways of supporting their families . . .[32]

This last sentence is almost certainly a commentary by Sidney on his own life.

[P]opular . . . governments [on the other hand] have always applied themselves to increase the number, strength, power, riches, and courage of their people . . . This may sometimes give occasion to tumults and wars . . . [but] unless a tyrant arise [like Cromwell] they soon recover, and, for the most part, rise up in greater glory and prosperity than before.

This 'increase' was a natural effect of popular governments because they were based on the principle of liberty; of self-government; of 'every man finding his own good comprehended in that of the public . . . This was a [natural] encouragement to industry'.[33]

Most of the rest of this section is spent by Sidney in a familiar rehearsal of other matters under the general theme of commonwealths versus monarchies. Its most notable feature is the continually increasing intrusion of references, both implicit and explicit, to Sidney's own time. This begins with a lengthy rehearsal of the frequent bloody disputes over the succession to which monarchies are prone. It continues on the subject of their equal

---

[31] Ibid., ch. 16, p. 223.   [32] Ibid., pp. 223–5.   [33] Ibid., p. 233.

susceptibility to 'venality and corruption', when Sidney asks his readers to
consider

whether bawds, whores, thieves, buffoons, parasites, and such vile wretches as are
naturally mercenary, have not more power at Whitehall, Versailles, the Vatican, and
the Escurial, than Venice, Amsterdam, and Switzerland; whether Hyde, Arlington,
Danby, their graces of Cleveland and Portsmouth, Sunderland, Jenkins, or Chif-
finch, could probably have attained such power as they have among us, if it had been
disposed of by the sufferages of the parliament and people.[34]

In a chapter on the 'mischiefs and cruelties proceeding from tyranny'
Sidney observed of 'king James' (cited as an example of moderate principles
by Filmer) that 'by overthrowing justice, which is the rule of civil and moral
action, and perverting the gospel, which is the light of the spiritual man, he
left nothing unattempted that he durst attempt, by which he might bring the
most extensive and universal evils upon our nation that any can suffer'.
After describing the attempts of tyrants in general to eradicate religion and
virtue he observed ruefully that 'I wish I could say . . . they lived only in past
ages'. This chapter repeats the *Court Maxims*' claim that tyrants 'consider
nations, as graziers do their herds and flocks, according to the profit that
can be made of them . . . they must be delivered up to the slaughter, when he
finds a good market'.[35] Under a tyrant the nation is:

composed of good and evil, the first will always be averse to the evil government, the
others endeavouring to uphold it . . . If the best prove to be the strongest, he must
perish. And knowing himself to be supported only by the worst, he will always
destroy as many of his enemies as he can . . . justice is perverted, military discipline
neglected, the public treasures exhausted . . . there is no end of their devices and
tricks to gain supplies. To this end swarms of spies, informers, and false witnesses
are sent out to circumvent the richest and most eminent men; the tribunals filled with
court-parasites that no man may escape . . . [This is] so straight a way to universal
ruin, that no state can prevent it, unless that course be interrupted[; for which
purpose the people must] examine whether his government be such as renders him
grateful or odious to them; and whether he pursues the public interest, or, for the
advancement of his own authority, [an interest] contrary to that of his own people.[36]

Finally in this confrontation of popular with monarchical government,
Sidney allows himself to come from ancient examples to the contemporary
contrast at the heart of his own thinking. This produces the extended
comparisons, quoted in *Sidney and the English Republic*, between the
wisdom, justice, integrity, and power of England's government after 1649,
with that after 1660; in short between 'the glory and reputation not long
since gained, with the condition into which we are of late fallen'.[37] Similarly
to the ancient illustrations of monarchical incapacity at war:

we may add some examples of our own . . . in the year 1639, and 1640, the kings

[34] *Ibid.*, p. 227.   [35] *Ibid.*, p. 231.
[36] *Ibid.*, pp. 232–3.   [37] *Ibid.*, p. 238.

army, though very numerous, excellently armed and mounted, and, in appearance, able to conquer many such kingdoms as Scotland, being under the conduct of courtiers, and affected as men usually are towards those that use them ill, and seek to destroy them, they could never resist a wretched army conducted by Leven; but were shamefully beaten at Newburn, and left the northern counties to be ravaged by them.[38]

Beneath these stark comparisons lay a perpetual cause, immune to Sidney's relativism: the general principle of government that dictated a state's progressive or regressive direction through time:

It is absurd to impute this to the change of times; for time changes nothing; and nothing was changed in those times, but the government, and that changed all things. This is not accidental, but according to the rules given to nature by God, imposing on all things a necessity of perpetually following their causes ... As a man begets a man, and a beast a beast, that society of men which constitutes a government upon the foundation of justice, virtue, and the common good, will always have men to promote those ends; and that which intends the advancement of one man's desires and vanity, will abound in those that foment them. All men follow that which seems advantageous to themselves. Such as are bred under a good discipline, and see that all benefits, procured to their country by virtuous actions, redound to the honour and advantage of themselves ... contract from their infancy a love to the public, and look upon the common concernments as their own. When they have learned to be virtuous, and see that virtue is in esteem, they seek no other preferments than such as may be obtained that way; and no country ever wanted great numbers of excellent men, where this method was established. On the other side, when it is evident, that the best are despised, hated, or marked out for destruction; that all things are calculated to the honour or advantage of one man, who is often the worst ... and his favour gained only by a most obsequious respect, or ... servile obedience all application to virtuous actions will cease.[39]

11.2 PART THREE: ARGUMENTS AGAINST ABSOLUTISM
(ch. 1, section 30–ch. 3, section 14, pp. 248–400; Filmer ch. 2, section 16–ch. 3, section 8, pp. 70–101)

[I]f kings ... will neither judge nor be judged, and there be no power to redress public grievances or private injuries, every man has recourse to force, as if he lived in a wood, where there is no law; and that force is generally mortal to those who provoke it. No guards can preserve a hated prince from the vengeance of one resolute hand.[40]

INTRODUCTION

In this section Sidney moves, following Filmer, from a tit-for-tat comparison of popular states with monarchies, to the question of what constitutes the legitimate power of monarchs. Here Filmer argues his case for absolutism;

---

[38] *Ibid.*, p. 240.   [39] *Ibid.*, p. 236.   [40] *Ibid.*, p. 257.

in particular, following his own interpretation of Bodin, for the freeing of monarchs from accountability to any other earthly power, and for their status as the sole authors of positive law.[41] In the process Filmer, like Bodin, attacks a variety of doctrines standing in the way of this conclusion: those of the mixed state, of the right of the people *in extremis* to judge or depose their sovereign, and in particular the (to Filmer, hopelessly confused) notion that the kingdom is governed by the laws, rather than by the King himself, who is simply an agent for their application. According to Filmer, this is like saying 'that the Carpenters Rule builds an House, and not the Carpenter; for the Law is but the Rule or Instrument of the Ruler'.[42] The function of the positive law – which the King may follow, 'mitigate . . . or suspend' as he sees fit – is to restrain the multitude, not the King. The King is above the law, and may protect his subjects from the potential tyranny of the law. The law is not above the King, to protect his subjects from the potential tyranny of the King. Filmer follows his doctrine of non-resistance with a corollary of absolute obedience, to the point of saying (quite unlike Bodin) that even if the King orders something blatantly against the law of God, he must be obeyed. The sin is then the King's, not the subject's.

Sidney's response to this can well be imagined, and much of it develops territory already broached in the previous two sections. What is most significant about this part of the *Discourses* is that by shifting the focus from the historical practice of commonwealths to a description and defence of absolutism, Filmer brings the debate to centre on the political problem of Sidney's own time, and so increasingly to the practical object of Sidney's own work. By denying the legitimacy of any resistance to absolutism he gives Sidney the opportunity to argue the opposite; and by his extreme subordination of religious and moral considerations to the imperative of political obedience he gives Sidney the opportunity to argue an equally extreme reversal of these priorities.

One result is that throughout this third quarter of Sidney's work we encounter a steadily increasing number of references to contemporary affairs, and a steadily escalating drumbeat of direct political menace and threat. This reflects, as I have said, developments within the political as well as the polemical context of this section of the work. Secondly, and as a consequence, this section contains increasingly frequent echoes of both Sidney's earlier works: the *Court Maxims*, and the *Vindication*:

[T]hey who admit of no participants in power, and acknowledge no rule but their own will, set up an interest in themselves against that of their people, lose their affections, which is their most important treasure, and incur their hatred, from whence results their greatest danger . . . This is the state of things that pleases Filmer . . . who for the introduction of the same among us, recommend[s] such an elevation

[41] Filmer, *Patriarcha*, p. 94.   [42] *Ibid.*, pp. 70–2, 88–94.

of the sovereign majesty, as is most contrary to the laws of God and men, abhorred by all generous nations, and especially by our ancestors, who thought nothing too dear to be hazarded in the defence of themselves and us from it.[43]

THE GOTHIC POLITY

According to Filmer 'if the king admits the people to be his companions, he leaves to be king'. This Sidney describes (as in the *Vindication*) as the 'language of French lackeys, valet-de-chambres, taylors ... who fly to England for fear of a well-deserved gally, gibbet, or wheel'. On the contrary, while the people may admit a king to government 'It seems absurd to speak of kings admitting the nobility or people ... for though there may be, and are, nations without kings, no man can conceive a king without a people'. Secondly 'It is strange, that he, who frequently cites Aristotle and Plato, should unluckily acknowledge such only to be kings as they call tyrants.' Finally, however, the principal burden of Sidney's argument involves an illustration from scripture, history, and the state of contemporary Europe that whatever Filmer's extreme claims in theory 'The practice of most nations ... has been ... directly contrary to the[m].' It was pointless to say that only absolute kings were kings if in fact almost no kings were absolute.[44]

Predictably the burden of Sidney's discussion of scripture falls on the same two texts – 1 Samuel 8, and Deuteronomy 17 – used so extensively in the *Court Maxims*. As for modern Europe, 'whoever understands the affairs of Germany [for instance], knows that the present emperors, notwithstanding their haughty title, have a power limited as in the days of Tacitus'. This is the beginning of Sidney's (in origin, Tacitean) theory of the 'Gothic polity' or Gothic balance, which was to form such an important part of his theory. This had been made famous in the previous century by Francois Hotman's anti-absolutist *Francogallia*. The formula quoted above about a king being inconceivable without his people was equally a monarchomach commonplace. Although elsewhere Sidney, like Milton, used Hotman's own source for the theory directly (Tacitus' *Germania*), there is nothing in his use of it here to challenge the probability that he lifted it directly from Hotman.

'All the kingdoms peopled from the north observed the same rules.' In France 'Hottoman, a lawyer of that time and nation, famous for his learning, integrity, and judgement, having diligently examined the antient law and histories of that kingdom', showed that until recently the same had existed there.[45] 'This golden chain' was broken only in the late fifteenth century: 'Lewis the eleventh of France was one of the first', as the accounts of Philip de Comines (Hotman's source for this claim) and Mezeray showed.

---

[43] *Discourses*, pp. 262, 400.   [44] *Ibid.*, pp. 248–9.   [45] *Ibid.*, pp. 252–3.

Elsewhere Buchanan had showed how 'James the third of Scotland' had followed his example. The same ancient liberties had fallen victim to modern 'kingcraft' in Spain and England (not least under James I).[46] The previous free state of England was sufficiently illustrated by the response meted out to the 'lewd extravagances of Edward the second, and Richard the second'.[47] 'If it be said' accordingly:

> that kings have now found out more easy ways of doing what they please, and securing themselves, I answer, that . . . it is not yet time for such as tread in the same steps to boast of their success . . . if in this corrupted age, the treachery and perjury of princes be more common than formerly, and . . . their parties are stronger than formerly, this rather shews, that the balance of power is broken . . . [than] what this will produce. While the ancient constitutions of our northern kingdoms remained entire, such as contested with their princes sought only to reform their governments . . . but they may not be so modest, when they see the very nature of their government changed, and the foundations overthrown . . . [I]t is not improbable, but that when men see there is no medium between tyranny and popularity, they who would have been contented with the reformation of their government may proceed farther, and have recourse to force, where there is no help in the law. This will be a hard work in those places where virtue is wholly abolished; but the difficulty will lie on the other side, if any sparks of that remain.[48]

Sidney can hardly be accused here of making the practical drift of his thinking unclear.

J.H. Salmon has identified Sidney as 'one of the first Englishmen to express the legend of the Gothic constitution',[49] and this element in his writing was taken up and amplified by followers like Molesworth, who published the first English translation of Hotman's *Francogallia* in 1711. Yet in doing so Sidney was only following the example of mid-century writers like Milton and Nathaniel Bacon, both of whom had used Tacitus (and Hotman) to trace English liberties back to their Germanic origins.[50] Harrington too used the same concept of the Gothic polity, though in his case only to criticise it as imperfect.

More to the point perhaps, in European rather than simply English terms (always the correct context for Sidney's thought), this was a mainstream line of anti-absolutist argument by the time Filmer wrote. Sidney employed it here partly because Filmer was himself attacking it (and, in particular, Buchanan) for that reason. Furthermore Filmer's model for much of this

[46] *Ibid.*, pp. 252–3, 243, 255.
[47] *Ibid.*, p. 257.
[48] *Ibid.*, p. 262.
[49] Salmon, *The French Religious Wars in English Political Thought*, p. 160.
[50] Nathaniel Bacon, *A Historical and Political Discourse of the Laws and Government of England* (1682 [1st pub. 1649]), p. 2; Scott, *Sidney and the English Republic*, p. 107; cf. Marchamont Nedham, *The Case of the Commonwealth of England, Stated*, ed. P.A. Knachel (Virginia 1968), pp. 115–16 .

section – Bodin – had himself framed his theory partly as a response to the claims of the monarchomachs in general and those of Hotman in particular.[51] Sidney's answer to Filmer accordingly reasserted a range of monarchomach arguments, and especially those of Hotman.

THE 'COURT MAXIMS' REVISITED

Sidney's discussion of scripture in this section – in particular the text 1 Samuel 8–10 – was equally provoked by Filmer, who used the text himself to argue that God's harsh prescription for the Israelites was to be understood as a description of monarchy in its natural form, rather than a warning against it. Since the text did not mention the (in fact Greek) word tyranny, this description could not be understood to imply anything other than legitimate kingship; and there was no legitimate response available against such government but 'Crying and praying unto God in that day'.

In fact this was a tendentious and deliberate mis-reading of the text, not unlike that earlier of Aristotle's *Politics*. Once again Sidney was driven to explain laboriously what the text actually said, and in what context. This led him to repeat at length this whole section of the *Court Maxims*, with its description of 'the folly and wickedness of the [Israelite] people, who chose rather to subject themselves to the irregular will of a man, than to be governed by God, and his law'.[52] And this – and the drift of this part of Filmer's work in general – leads Sidney to increasing revisitations of the *Maxims* in general, and its core interest argument in particular. Once again the private interest of a monarch and 'the public good of their subjects . . . have been always thought to comprehend the most irreconcileable contrariety'.[53] Once again the root of this contrariety at the heart of human politics lies in the contrary principles at the heart of human life (good and evil). 'As no man can serve two masters, no man can pursue two contrary interests.'[54]

The matter would not be much altered, [even] if . . . in the time of Saul, all nations were governed by tyrants . . . for though [people] might not think of a good government at the first, nothing can oblige men to continue under one that is bad, when they discover the evils of it, and know how to mend it. And [even] though no condition [limiting royal power] had been reserved [in the original contract], the public good, which is the end of all government, had been sufficient to abrogate all that should tend to the contrary.[55]

In short even could a contract for tyranny or absolutism be found, 'the

---

[51] Bodin, *Six Books of the Commonwealth*, book 2, chs. 4–5.
[52] Sidney, *Discourses*, p. 279 (and 271–91, 300–6 in general); Filmer, *Patriarcha*, pp. 80–1.
[53] Sidney, *Discourses*, p. 348.
[54] *Ibid.*, p. 304 (and 298).
[55] *Ibid.*, p. 304.

folly and turpitude of the thing would be a sufficient evidence of the madness of those that made it, and utterly destroy the contents of it' – a common
enough natural law theory argument (used, for instance, by Matthew Kel-
lison before 1640).[56] As the nature of God is goodness, so it is the business
of man, so far as he is able, to seek out that which is good – in politics, the
public good:

Men were sent into the world rude and ignorant, and if they might not have used
their natural faculties to find out that which is good for themselves, all must have
been condemned to continue in the ignorance of our first fathers, and to make no use
of their understanding to the ends for which it was given.

On the contrary nothing could oblige men to continue to tolerate a
government that was not good, or good for them. Such a government was fit
only for

slaves by nature ... [that] have neither the understanding nor courage that is
required for ... [self] government ... [that] can neither desire the good they do not
know, nor enjoy it if it were bestowed on them ... But such nations as are naturally
strong, stout, and of good understanding, whose vigour remains unbroken, manners
uncorrupted, reputation unblemished, and increasing in numbers; who want neither
men to make up armies to defend themselves against foreign *or domestic* enemies
[my emphasis], nor leaders to head them, do ordinarily set limits to their patience.
They know how to preserve their liberty, or to vindicate the violation of it; and the
more patient they have been, the more inflexible they are when they resolve to be so
no longer. Those who are so foolish as to put them upon such courses, do to their
cost find there is a difference between lions and asses; and he is a fool who knows
not, that swords were given to men, that none might be slaves, but such as know not
how to use them.[57]

This fighting talk was much enjoyed by eighteenth-century admirers and
is exactly like that Sidney employed in practice, in 1683, to push his foot-
dragging plotting colleagues into action. It arose increasingly naturally, at
this point in the text, from the continuing re-excavation of the content of the
Court Maxims. Eventually Sidney pushed the *Maxims'* central theme, of
contrariety, into what is clearly an extremely interesting commentary on the
period 1678–81.

When a magistrate ... sets up an interest ... in himself, repugnant to the good of the
public, for which he is made to be what he is ... These contrary ends certainly divide
the nation into parties; and while every one endeavours to advance that to which he
is addicted, occasions of hatred for injuries every day done, or thought to be done
... must necessarily arise. This creates a most ... irreconcileable enmity ... The
people think it the greatest of all crimes, to convert that power to their hurt, which
was instituted for their good ... that *the injustice is aggravated by perjury and
ingratitude* [my emphasis] ... and [that moreover] the magistrate gives the name of
sedition or rebellion to whatever they do for the preservation of themselves, and

---

[56] Sommerville, *Politics and Ideology 1603–40*, p. 71.
[57] Sidney, *Discourses*, pp. 291–2.

their own rights. When men's spirits are thus prepared, a small matter sets them on fire ... and when any occasion, whether foreign or domestic, arises, in which the magistrate stands in need of the people's assistance, they, whose affections are alienated, not only shew an unwillingness to serve him with their persons and estates ... [but] fear that by delivering him from his distress, they strengthen their enemy, and enable him to oppress them.[58]

This piece of wishful thinking sums up both Sidney's interpretation of the events of 1637–40, and his hopes of the present situation. Charles II has aggravated the misuse of his power by 'perjury and ingratitude' – perjury for breaking the promises made at Breda; ingratitude for abusing his power to destroy the very institution (parliament) from which he received it in the first place. Charles is equally 'the magistrate' who in 1679–80 gave 'the name of sedition or rebellion to whatever they do for their preservation' – petitioning for the meeting of the parliament. From 'when men's spirits are thus prepared ...' the rest of the passage illustrates Sidney's hopes of re-creating a military emergency in Scotland to which the King's alienated subjects would prove no more willing to respond than they had been under the same circumstances in 1639. Meanwhile:

as no man, or number of men, is willingly subject to those who seek their ruin, such as fall into so great a misfortune, continue no longer under it than force, fear, or necessity, may be able to oblige them. But as such a necessity can hardly lie longer upon a great people, than till the evil be fully ... comprehended, and their virtue, strength, and power, be united to expel it, the ill magistrate ... will endeavour to prevent that union, and diminish that strength ... And as truth, faithful dealing ... and integrity of manners, are bonds of union ... he will always use tricks, artifices, cavils, and all means possible ... by corrupting the youth, and seducing such as can be brought to lewdness and debauchery, [to] bring the people to such a pass, that they may neither care nor dare to vindicate their rights, and that those who would do it, may so far suspect each other, as not to confer upon, much less join in any action tending to the public deliverance.

This last passage is probably the rumination of a frustrated plotter on problems being encountered in the present design. Once again, as in 1659, and 1665–6, these problems hinged on deep 'divisions' between the plotters themselves. The coincidence of content at this point between the *Discourses* and the *Court Maxims* owes a great deal to the coincidence of practical context.

It is entirely on cue, then, that at this juncture, as in the *Court Maxims*, Sidney sets about disposing of Christian objections to the use of armed force. As Filmer quotes the Church Fathers on this subject, Sidney answers this argument exactly as in the *Maxims*: by returning to the relativism of Daillé:

Au[gu]stin, Ambrose, or Tertullian ... were excellent men, but living in another

[58] *Ibid.*, pp. 379–80.

time, under a very different government, and applying themselves to other matters, they had no knowledge at all of those that concern us ... we, who do not renounce use of the civil or military sword, who have a part in the government, and think it our duty to apply ourselves to public cares ... [must not] lay them aside, because the ancient christians, every hour expecting death, did not trouble themselves with them.[59]

Provoked by this thought Sidney suddenly abandons (temporarily) any pretence of speaking hypothetically, and produces a startling confirmation of the topicality of his message:

Our ancestors were born free, and ... they left us that liberty entire ... the happiness of those that enjoy the like, and the shameful misery under which they lie, who have suffered themselves to be forced or cheated out of it, may persuade, and the justice of the cause encourage us, to think nothing too dear to be hazarded in defence of it ... the king is under the law ... and we all know how to proceed against those, who, being under the law, offend against it: for the law is not made in vain. *In this case something more is to be done than petitioning* [my emphasis].[60]

Returning to *Patriarcha*, Sidney then proceeds to dispose of Filmer's (equally predictable) next gambit: St Paul's Epistle to the Romans. This recalls (among others) the pro-parliamentary pamphleteers of 1642–3.[61] The manner in which he does so is both ingenious and characteristic. According to Sidney, St Paul, comanding us to be subject to the higher powers, requires us to ask ourselves who the higher powers are. Since St Paul is the apostle of God, the higher powers turn out to be, not any powers, but those who do the work of God for our good. 'The apostle, farther explaining himself, and shewing, who may be accounted a magistrate ... informs us: "Rulers are not a terror to good works, but to the evil ... do that which is good ... for he is the minister of God, a revenger to execute wrath upon him that doth evil." He therefore is only the minister of God, who is not a terror to good works, but to evil.' From this it follows that what St Paul is actually saying is that men should be obedient to republican powers – who govern for [the public] good; and wilfully disobedient to absolute monarchs and tyrants, who do the opposite. '[T]he apostle comanding our obedience to the minister of God for our good, commands us not to be obedient to the minister of the devil to our hurt; for we cannot serve two masters.'[62]

It is simply by extension of the same view of obedience that Sidney makes his next point – which particularly struck William Gladstone – that 'that

[59] *Ibid.*, pp. 308, 310, 312.
[60] *Ibid.*, pp. 312, 314.
[61] See, for instance, Jeremiah Burroughes, *A Briefe answer to Doctor Ferne's Book* [1643], quoted in A. Sharpe (ed.), *Political Ideas of the English Civil Wars 1641–1649* (1983), pp. 74–6.
[62] Sidney, *Discourses*, pp. 317, 328.

which is not just is not law, and that which is not law is not to be obeyed'. Quoting Tertullian – who has apparently suddenly resumed contemporary relevance – Sidney remarks that 'The sanction . . . that deserves the name of a law . . . derives not its excellency from antiquity, or from the dignity of the legislators, but from an intrinsic equity and justice'; and the stoic Seneca serves to develop (prophetically enough) the same idea: 'he that will suffer himself to be compelled [to do evil] knows not how to die'.[63] Once again this chapter winds its way to a familiar conclusion: that as ministers of evil and injustice 'many emperors and kings of the greatest nations in the world . . . have been so utterly deprived of all power, that they have been imprisoned, deposed . . . killed, drawn through the streets, cut in pieces, thrown into rivers, and indeed suffered all that could be suffered by the vilest slaves'.[64]

Accordingly whether the magistrate be called king, duke, marquis, emperor, sultan, 'the name . . . is no way essential to the thing . . . The same obedience is equally due to all, whilst . . . they do the work of God for our good: and if they depart from it, no one of them has a better title than the other to our obedience.' Filmer's instruction that subjects must obey even sinful commands was indeed an edict of the devil; for where did it leave the distinction between good and evil, and where did it leave the command of St Peter 'that it is better to obey God than man'?[65] This question leads Sidney to locate Filmer's doctrines in their original historical context:

God, having required th[e sabbath] day to be set apart for his service and worship, man cannot dispense with the obligation, unless he can abrogate the law of God. Perhaps . . . I may be told, that this savours too much of puritanism and calvinism. But I shall take the reproach, till some better patrons than Laud, and his creatures, may be found for the other opinion. By the advice and instigation of these men, from about the year 1630, to 1640, sports and revelings, which ended, for the most part, in drunkenness and lewdness, were not only permitted on that day, but injoined. And though this did advance human authority, in derogation to the divine . . . [some men], resolving rather to obey the laws of God than the commands of men, could not be brought to pass the Lord's day in that manner.[66]

'Unjust commands' then, like unjust laws, were not to be obeyed; and

If any man ask, who shall be judge of that rectitude or pravity that either authorizes or destroys a law? I answer, that as this consists not in formalities and niceties, but in evident and substantial truths, there is no need of any other tribunal, than that of common sense, and the light of nature . . . the meanest understanding, if free from passion, may surely know.

And it was precisely this freedom from passion that it was the function of good political order to achieve, so far as the 'condition of mankind' allowed

[63] *Ibid.*, p. 329.   [64] *Ibid.*, p. 330.
[65] *Ibid.*, pp. 333, 382; Filmer, *Patriarcha*, p. 98.
[66] Sidney, *Discourses*, p. 383.

– for even 'the best men can never wholly divest themselves of passions and affections.' Governments

must be founded upon that eternal principle of reason and truth ... and not ... the depraved will of man, which, fluctuating according to the different interests, humors and passions ... one day abrogates what has been enacted the other ... [Thus] Laws and constitutions ought to be weighed, and whilst all due reverence is paid to such as are good, every nation may ... retain in itself a power of changing or abolishing all such as are not so ... and in place of what was either at first mistaken or afterwards corrupted, to constitute that which is most conducing to ... justice and liberty.[67]

It is unnecessary, perhaps, to trace all Sidney's objections to Filmer's insistence that the King must be the sole author of law; the foregoing makes it clear what they will be. Since the primary matter for Sidney is not the origin of positive law but its rectitude, the argument runs that this rectitude is best established not by an individual, whose 'judgement is merely for himself', but by 'a popular assembly ... [where] no man judges for himself, otherwise, than as his good is comprehended in that of the public'. It hinges, in other words, like so much of the *Discourses* and the *Maxims*, and of *Patriarcha* itself, not on a description of reality so much as a return to basic (and rhetorical) assumptions; in this case the axioms of republican interest theory.

The further point, of which Sidney makes a very great deal, is that if it is the function of positive law to restrain human fallibility and wickedness, Filmer's proposal – by putting a fallible individual above the law – would have the opposite effect. If kings

come to the power by succession, which may be properly enough called by chance, it is reasonably to be feared they will be bad, and consequently it is necessary so to limit their power, that if they be so, the commonwealth may not be destroyed, which they were instituted to preserve ... Men are so subject to vices, and passions, that they stand in need of some restraint in every condition; but especially when they are in power. The rage of a private man may be pernicious to one or a few of his neighbours; but the fury of an unlimited prince would drive whole nations into ruin ... He is sometimes a child ... sometimes overburdened with years ... Some[times] weak, negligent, slothful, foolish, or vicious ... He always fluctuates, and every passion ... disorders him. The good of a people ought to be established upon a more solid foundation. For this reason the law is established, which no passion can disturb ... It is written reason retaining some measure of the divine perfection ... [It] commands that which is good, and punishes evil in all, whether rich or poor, high or low.[68]

Once again while much of this is directed against 'unlimited' princes, much of it is a criticism of monarchy in general, and hereditary monarchy in particular. This becomes particularly evident when Sidney returns to the topical theme – to which he devotes a whole chapter, with no basis in

[67] *Ibid.*, p. 405. [68] *Ibid.*, pp. 336, 346.

Filmer's text – of the uncertainty of royal succession. His eventual point – having 'observed five different manners of disposing crowns esteemed hereditary, besides an infinite number of collateral controversies arising from them, of which we have divers examples', is that any political system which exposes itself to such uncertainties is inherently unstable. 'While this remains undecided, it is impossible for me to know, to whom I owe ... obedience.'[69] And 'Contests will [always] in the like manner arise concerning successions to crowns, how exactly soever they be disposed by law. For though everyone will say, that the next ought to succeed, yet no man knows who is the next: which is too much verified by the bloody decisions of such disputes in many parts of the world.' Men who obstinately insist on only one candidate, one way, or one law (and Filmer is obviously the prime example) are in these situations a standing invitation to bloodshed, and 'go about to subvert all the governments of the world, and arm ... every man to the destruction of his neighbour'.[70] Sidney's eventual point is that it is not the question of who should succeed in such circumstances that is important – hypothetically speaking one king is much the same as another – but *who should decide* who should succeed. In England that is obviously the parliament.

> There must therefore be a judge of such disputes as may in these cases arise in every kingdom; and though it is not my business to determine who is that judge in all places, yet I may justly say, that in England it is the parliament ... No man can be thought to have a just title, till it be so adjudged by that power.[71]

This reminds us of the point referred to by the *Vindication* – and by his letters at the time – that as far as Sidney was concerned Charles II owed his title to the invitation of parliament in 1660. Now, in order to deny it the equally legitimate choice of his successor Charles was dispensing with parliament altogether. This was not only the usurpation of arbitrary powers, but 'injustice aggravated by perjury and ingratitude' – under these circumstances 'every man has recourse to force ... and that force is generally mortal to those who provoke it. No guards can preserve a hated prince from th[is] vengeance.'[72]

11.3 PART FOUR: RESISTANCE AND PARLIAMENT
(ch. 3, pp. 400–508)

The last hundred pages or so of the *Discourses* are characterised not so much by the introduction of new arguments as by the intensification, and the coming together, of certain established themes. What rules this process is the already quickening pace of external events. Thus here we find Sidney's

---

[69] *Ibid.*, pp. 363, 365.   [70] *Ibid.*, p. 365.
[71] *Ibid.*, pp. 377, 378.   [72] *Ibid.*, pp. 292, 257.

most powerful statement of three key arguments: for the necessity of political change; for the legitimacy of rebellion; and for the sovereignty of parliaments. All three come together in the practical scenario Sidney has in mind: of an armed rebellion that will force the re-summoning of a parliament with authority to alter and re-model the nation's constitution. Sidney clearly hoped that this last unhappy experience with the restored monarchy would encourage parliament to rescind the disastrous decision of 1660 once and for all. At the same time he continued the refutation of *Patriarcha*, giving rise to one of the best-known features of the *Discourses*: its history of the 'noble nation' of the Anglo-Saxons.

THE NECESSITY OF POLITICAL CHANGE

Many of the assumptions underlying this aspect of Sidney's thought have already been described above. Sidney's theory was progressive rather than static, and his belief in the legitimacy and necessity of change followed from his view of God's purposes for man. As God had given men reason to discriminate good from evil, so he gave them the liberty – and with it the moral responsibility – to use that reason to accumulate practical and moral knowledge. This was so certain that

whatever we enjoy, beyond the misery in which our barbarous ancestors lived, is due only to the liberty of correcting what was amiss in their practice, or inventing that which they did not know. And I doubt whether it be more brutish to say, we are obliged to continue in the idolatry of the druids ... [than that] we are forever bound to continue the government [our ancestors] ... established, whatever inconveniences might attend it.[73]

To affirm [otherwise] ... is no less than to ... render the understanding given to men utterly useless ... if it be lawful for us, by the use of that understanding, to build houses, ships, and forts, better than our ancestors ... to invent printing, with an infinite number of other arts beneficial to mankind, why have we not the same right in matters of government, upon which all others do most absolutely depend?[74]

We have seen accordingly how Sidney considered political science to be a form of architecture, charged with erecting the fabric for a progressive and ongoing self-improvement. This was not to say that Sidney over-estimated the capacity of reason in an imperfect world; indeed it was the imperfection of the world that made change necessary and inevitable. The only unchanging being was the perfect God. For 'there is a simple and a relative perfection. The first is only in God, the other in the things he has created ... if the perfection [of the world] were absolute, there could be no difference between an angel and a worm, and nothing could be subject to change or death; for that is imperfection.'[75]

---

[73] *Ibid.*, p. 404.   [74] *Ibid.*, pp. 304–5.   [75] *Ibid.*, p. 407.

It is because the world is an arena for 'relative' perfection only – relative to the 'simple' perfection of God – that Sidney is a relativist. Both of the dimensions within which this relativism must operate are mentioned by him here: time (change and death), and value (the difference between an angel and a worm). Since it is a condition of this world that absolute perfection in neither is possible (permanence; perfect good), the task of the 'political scientist' is to seek the relative perfection of both. This means that the only question which counts in politics is whether a state is more or less good – its relative perfection; its proximity to the perfection of God – and since absence of change is impossible this good must be sought and maintained on the basis of progressive improvement. It is precisely what Sidney cannot stand about Filmer that he is indifferent to these twin relativisms, of value and time, when in fact they are the keys to political conduct. It is precisely in this respect that Filmer's book denies 'all that in this life deserves to be cared for' – deserves to be cared for in this life, because it is relative to the perfection of the next.

[T]he wisdom of man is imperfect, and unable to forsee ... an infinite variety of accidents, which according to emergencies, necessarily require new constitutions, to prevent or cure the mischiefs arising from them, or to advance a good that at the first was not thought of. And as the noblest work in which the wit of man can be exercised, were (if it could be done) to constitute a government that should last forever, the next to that is to suit laws to present exigencies, and so much as is in the power of man to forsee. He that would resolve to persist obstinately in the way he first entered on, or to blame those who ... [seek change] when they find it necessary ... render[s] the worst of errors perpetual. Changes therefore are unavoidable, and the wit of man can go no farther than to institute such as in relation to the forces, manners, nature, religion, or interests of a people, and their neighbours, are suitable and adequate to what is seen, or apprehended to be seen. He, who would oblige all nations at all times to take the same course, would prove as foolish as a physician who should apply the same medicine to all distempers, or an architect that would build the same kind of house for all persons, without considering their estates, dignities ... number ... the time or climate in which they lived, and other circumstances; or ... a general who should obstinately resolve always to make war in the same way ... without examining the nature, number, and strength of his own and his enemies forces, or the advantages and disadvantages of the ground.[76]

This relativism again belongs to a tradition of political thought developed from Aristotle, through Bodin in the sixteenth century, Grotius and Sidney in the seventeenth, to Montesquieu in the eighteenth century. Its limits are clarified on the following page:

But as there may be some universal rules in physic, architecture, and military discipline, from which men ought never to depart, so there are some in politics also which ought always to be observed: and wise legislators, adhering to them only, will be ready to change all others, as occasion may require, in order to the public good. This

[76] *Ibid.*, p. 144.

we may learn from Moses, who laying the foundation of the law given to the Israelites in that justice, charity, and truth, which having its root in God is subject to no change, left them the liberty of [ordering all other things] ... as best pleased themselves; and the mischiefs they afterwards suffered proceeded not simply from changing, but changing for the worse ... The like having been proved by the examples of other kingdoms ... is in my opinion sufficient to manifest, that while the foundation and principle of government remains good, the superstructure may be changed according to occasions, without any prejudice.[77]

This passage contains a good deal of Henry Vane; and the last section reads like, and may very well be, a conscious criticism of Harrington.[78]

[N]o right judgement [then] can be given of human things, without a particular regard to the time in which they passed. We esteem Scipio, Hannibal, Pyrrhus, Alexander, Epaminondas, and Caesar, to have been admirable commanders in war ... and yet ... if the most skilful of them could be raised from the grave ... and placed upon the frontiers of France or Flanders, he would not know how to advance or retreat, nor by what means to take any of the places in those parts, as they are now fortified and defended; but would most certainly be beaten by any insignificant fellow with a small number of men ... Nay, the manner of fighting, is so much altered within the last threescore years [Sidney's lifetime] ... [that] if it be considered that political matters are subject to the same mutations (as certainly they are) ... government [will obviously require] ... the [same] ... changes.[79]

This is an interesting application of conclusions drawn from change in other areas of early modern life – and improvements in military technology were one of the most striking such areas – to the realm of seventeenth-century political theory. Here, as elsewhere, the *Discourses* has a distinctly Baconian ring. And if this passage in particular reads like a conscious correction, or update, of Machiavelli, the next is certainly so:

[S]uch is the condition of mankind, that nothing can be so perfectly framed as not to give some testimony of human imbecillity, and frequently to stand in need of reparations and amendments ... some men observing this, have proposed a necessity of reducing every state, once in an age or two, to the integrity of its first principle: but they ought to have examined, whether that principle be good or evil, or so good, that nothing can be added to it, which none ever was.[80]

Thus, as I have argued elsewhere,[81] both Harrington and Sidney made crucial amendments to Machiavelli, but they made them in opposite directions: the first to eliminate change, the second to advance it. Harrington sought to eliminate the need for such amendment forever, Sidney to amplify its scope, from cyclical repetition, to linear progress. English republican thought proved broad and rich enough to accommodate these diametrically

---

[77] *Ibid.*, p. 144.
[78] Scott, *Sidney and the English Republic*, pp. 32–3.
[79] Sidney, *Discourses*, p. 463.
[80] *Ibid.*, pp. 405–6.
[81] Scott, *Sidney and the English Republic*, pp. 30–5.

opposite conclusions to the heart of the seventeenth-century, and particularly republican, experience: the fact of instability and change. It was Sidney's conclusion that was to conquer the western world.

It is Sidney's principal object in the last section of the *Discourses* to apply this conclusion to the imperatives of the present situation.

A wise architect may show his skill, and deserve commendation for building a poor house of vile materials, when he can procure no better, but he no way ought to hinder others from creating more glorious fabrics, if they are furnished with the means required . . . And if a brave people, seeing the original defects of their government, or the corruption into which it may be fallen, do either correct, reform . . . or abolish that which was evil in the institution . . . men [like Filmer] impute it to sedition, and blame those actions, which, of all that can be performed by men, are the most glorious . . . Those who are of better understanding . . . often find reason to abrogate that which their fathers, according to the measure of the knowledge they had . . . had rightly instituted . . .[82]

To come more specifically to the point: 'The authority of custom as well as of law . . . consists only in its rectitude; and the same reason which may have induced one or more nations to create kings, when they knew no other form of government, may . . . induce them to set up another, if that be found more convenient to them . . .[83]

This is again a paraphrase of Vane, who said: 'no human . . . laws . . . must expect to be exempt from change . . . Ancient foundations, whence once [they] . . . prove hindrances, to the good and enjoyment of humane societies, are . . . upon the same reasons to be altered, for which they were first laid.'[84]

THE ANGLO-SAXONS

It is only having so lucidly mounted this argument for change that Sidney, in his determination to refute Filmer's every line, then engages in a species of ancient constitutionalism which it has just rendered intellectually redundant. This wouldn't matter much had it not laid the basis for a widespread mis-classification of Sidney's theory as a whole. Both Dickinson and Karsten saw Sidney as the proponent of a conservative ancient constitutionalism to be distinguished from the more radical natural law theory of Locke. This led Karsten to assume that the later radical use of Sidney by the Chartists to challenge the importance of political prescription was a misunderstanding of his theory. In fact however the Chartists were quoting (and understanding) Sidney perfectly correctly. In the *Discourses* Sidney

[82] Sidney, *Discourses*, pp. 404, 406.
[83] *Ibid.*, p. 403.
[84] M. Judson, *The Political Thought of Sir Henry Vane the Younger* (Philadelphia 1969), p. 30.

appended his ancient constitutionalism to a natural law argument notice-
ably similar to Locke's, though with rather fewer qualifications. It is thus
misleading to describe Sidney's theory as a whole by reference to a minor
(and ideologically inconsistent) part of it. Yet this misunderstanding has
underpinned a neglect of the most interesting aspects of the *Discourses*: its
arguments for rebellion, and for change. While Locke assumes the rectitude
of both, he does not argue the case for either, partly because he did not wish
to pay the price Sidney paid for doing so.

Coming, then, to Filmer's attack on ancient constitutionalism by way of
an assault on the antiquity of parliaments, Sidney pointed out that 'I do not
think myself obliged to insist upon the name or form of a parliament; for the
authority of a magistracy proceeds not from the number of years it has
continued, but the rectitude of the institution.' Yet the invitation of Filmer's
text is too much, and he cannot leave it at this:

> But if that liberty, in which God created man, can receive any strength from continu-
> ance, and the rights of Englishmen can be rendered more unquestionable by pre-
> scription, I say, that the nations, whose rights we inherit, have ever enjoyed the
> liberties we claim, and always exercised them in governing themselves . . . from the
> time they were first known in the world.[85]

Since these questions are begged rather than answered, the device here is
obviously not only to refute Filmer more completely, but to throw in as
complete a range of anti-absolutist arguments as possible. The resulting
(shall we say, intellectually cosmopolitan) jumble of content was not
unusual, particularly in a work of refutation. An obvious forerunner here,
as in many other respects, was Milton's reply to Salmasius, the equally
dogged attention of which to Salmasius' own text (which echoed many of
Filmer's arguments) resulted in just the same combination of natural law
theory and (therefore intellectually redundant) Anglo-Saxon history.

What has principally attracted attention to Sidney's history of the Anglo-
Saxons is not his assertion of their liberty (a mid-century commonplace) but
of their 'nobility', which is something new. Sidney's use of this term in this
context was of particular interest to Zera Fink, who took it to confirm an
aristocratic bias in Sidney's thought underlying his most common title – 'the
aristocratic republican' – and linking him with Fink's particular interest in
the aristocratic republic of Venice. As has been suggested however, and
unlike Harrington, Sidney downgraded the aristocratic republics of Venice
in particular and Sparta, as Machiavelli himself had, in favour of the popu-
list militarism of Rome and, in Sidney's case, Israel. This makes 'aristocratic
republicanism' a better description of Sidney's self-opinion and family background than of his political opinion. His use of the term 'noble' here indeed

---

[85] Sidney, *Discourses*, p. 421.

turns out to be, not aristocratic at all but military: the vehicle for another piece of Machiavellian militarism.

Sidney's Saxon 'nobility' are not an elite within civil society: they comprise the entire citizenry of the Anglo-Saxon nation. They have titles which 'were never made hereditary except by abuse'. Their sole claim to noble status is military: they are simply a numerous citizen army.

[T]he northern nations, who were perpetually in arms, put a high esteem on military valour; fought by conquest to aquire better countries than their own; valued themselves according to the numbers of men they could bring into the field, and to distinguish them from villains [sic], called those noblemen, who nobly defended and enlarged their dominions by war.[86]

This is a familiar enough concept, present in both Machiavelli and Harrington, that all citizens, all freemen of the state are by definition soldiers. What is peculiar to Sidney is that this qualification for citizenship is an equal qualification to nobility, because military service is a 'noble' activity. These nations were 'antiently divided only into freemen or noblemen (who were the same) and villains [who] were ... slaves'. That there is, or rather was and should be, nothing more to nobility than military service 'appears by the name of knights service; a knight being no more than a soldier, and a knight's fee no more than was sufficient to maintain one'.

The subversive purpose of this rhetorical device is to attack the modern English political state in general, and its 'effeminate titular nobility' in particular, for having lost the art of war. In the process they have lost all true claim to nobility, for as the *Court Maxims* earlier expressed what was a particular Sidney hobbyhorse: 'we examine not the reason why men are exalted, but why they should be exalted ... [in which respect] tis hard to see how riches or birth can enter into consideration'.[87] The implication of all this is that it is the modern commons of England, and in particular those who had taken up arms in the recent civil wars, who are the true 'nobility' of England. Sidney proceeds to make just this claim:

The antient nobility of England were composed of such men as had been ennobled by bearing arms in the defence or enlargement of the Commonwealth ... [by which] it cannot be denied, but that they were such gentlemen, and lords of manors, as we now call commoners together with freeholders, *and such as in war were found most able to be their leaders* ... [and] if the commoners are as free as the nobles, many of them in birth equal ... [and] in estate superior; and if they assist ... in wars with their persons and purses ... it must be confessed, that they are the true nobility of England.[88]

The effect of this section is not to recommend noble title so much as to

---

[86] *Ibid.*, pp. 420, 421.
[87] Sidney, *Court Maxims*, pp. 55–9.
[88] Sidney, *Discourses*, pp. 437–8.

undermine it by equating it with commonalty and replacing it with military title. On a personal level of course, what Sidney is doing is redefining the concept of 'true' nobility to include himself, one of those who 'in war, [was] found most able to be [a] leader'. On a political level on the other hand Sidney is not offering a redefinition of the modern concept of the nobility so much as a dilution which amounts to its abolition. For in modern England the Anglo-Saxon system of nobility has become as obsolete as the Gothic constitution by which it was sustained – 'and it is as impossible to restore it, as for most of those who at this day go under the name of noblemen, to perform the duties required from the antient nobility of England'.[89]

> It was not to be imagined, that through the weakness of some, and the malice of others, [noble] dignities should by degrees be turned into empty titles, and become the rewards of the greatest crimes, and the vilest services; or that the noblest of their descendants, for want of them, should be brought under the name of commoners, and deprived of all priviledges, except such as were common to them with their grooms ... By this means all things have been brought into the hands of the king, and the commoners; and there is nothing left to cement them, and to maintain the union ... [And if by destroying the nobility the monarchy has] by that means increased a party which never was, and, I think, never can be, united to the court, they are to answer for the consequences, and if they perish, their destruction is from themselves.[90]

In short while this whole argument is shot through with the aristocratic self-consciousness of a descendant of Hotspur and Sir Philip Sidney – both of whom died 'in the field' – its message is not in the end nostalgic but revolutionary. The nobility are gone forever, with the important consequence that the monarchy is about to follow them into the dustbin of history. By subverting the Gothic balance the modern monarchs of Europe have eliminated all alternatives to their absolutism but popularity; and in opposing his popular doctrines to Filmer's absolutism Sidney is counselling the only alternative – in particular the only militarily viable alternative – that there is. In the end Sidney's concerns are much the same as Machiavelli's, and his republicanism is no less popular or more aristocratic than Machiavelli's own. The touchstone of both is military strength.

THE ARGUMENT FOR REBELLION PART II: RESISTANCE AND PARLIAMENT

Finally we come, via these matters, back to Sidney's most immediate preoccupation: the justification of rebellion, this time intertwined with a series of claims for the political supremacy of parliament.

We have seen how a series of inflammatory gestures in this direction are a consistent feature of the second half of the *Discourses*. These had been

[89] *Ibid.*, p. 431: my emphasis.   [90] *Ibid.*, p. 464.

preceded by a theoretical argument for rebellion – which was discussed earlier under the sub-title *The argument for rebellion part I* – a domestic adaptation of the Grotian doctrine of just war. We can see here why Sidney named Grotius' *The Law of War and Peace* to Lantin in Paris as the most important early modern political text.[91]

Towards the end of the book we get the second instalment of this theory; one which builds on the last but is in its way even more striking. And as with the last, what is particularly intriguing about it is that, on the one hand, we find Locke advancing the same doctrine, up to a point; but that, on the other, there is an important difference in the way the argument is finally applied. Once again, one difference is that we find Sidney taking the point to its logical conclusion, regardless of the consequences. About the reason for the similarity itself we can only speculate.

We saw that the occasion for Sidney's last excursion in this direction was Filmer's denunciation of 'sedition, tumult and war'. Sidney's reply then was the rather startling assertion that – like all war – these things were not absolutely wrong but relative. They were right or wrong, justified or unjustified, according to their circumstances, manner, and cause. The second instalment of the same argument results from Filmer's equivalent denunciation of the most loaded word in the early modern political lexicon: 'rebellion'. This calls forth from Sidney exactly the same response.

[Filmer] endeavour[s] to persuade the people they ought not to defend their liberties, by giving the name of rebellion to the most just and honourable actions, that have been performed for the preservation of them ... [but] those who seek after truth will easily find, that [firstly] ... the general revolt of a nation cannot be called a rebellion ... and [furthermore] that *rebellion is not always evil* [my emphasis]. That this may appear, it will not be amiss to consider the word, as well as the thing commonly understood by it, as it is used in an evil sense.[92]

'[T]he word', Sidney explains, 'is taken from the Latin "rebellare", which signifies no more than to renew a war'. Unless, therefore, there had been some original state of war between the people and their magistrates, duly terminated, it makes no sense to use the term; otherwise the people 'having never been subdued, or brought to terms of peace with their magistrates, they cannot be said to revolt or rebel against them'. Secondly however, where these circumstances do apply, and so it is legitimate to use the word, 'rebellion is not always evil ... [for] the peace may be broken upon just grounds ... it ... be neither crime nor infamy to do it ... Rebellion, being nothing but a renewed war, can never be against a government that was not established by war, and of itself is neither good or evil, more than any other war; but is just or unjust, according to the cause or manner of it.'[93]

[91] Scott, *Sidney and the English Republic*, pp. 19–20.
[92] Sidney, *Discourses*, p. 457.   [93] *Ibid.*, pp. 457–60.

We come back again, therefore, not only to the relativity of the concept in general, but to the Grotian idea of just war, 'rebellare . . . being nothing but a renewed war'. As with 'sedition, tumult, and war', then, for 'rebellion' too this is the key concept. Just wars are fought 'for the protection of the innocent' against those whose will cannot be kept in check by 'judicial processes'; under such circumstances '*all . . . extrajudicial measures* [my emphasis] are justified'.

Sidney's mounting of this argument in connection with 'rebellion' is particularly noteworthy, on three counts. The first is that, as we saw in *Sidney and the English Republic* (p. 56), Sidney's father recorded exactly this explanation of the word 'rebellion' in his commonplace book in the 1650s, in the course of a Latin reading of Livy. Secondly – and of particular interest for this reason – at exactly this time, and in answer to this same part of Filmer's text, we find John Locke making exactly the same point: that the word 'rebellion' derives from the Latin 'rebellare – that is, [to] bring back again the state of war'.[94] We have already seen that this concern with war rests upon a similarly central use by both men of Grotius. Having made the point, however, Locke then uses it differently. If rebellion means to 'bring back again the state of war', then it is the monarch, whose absolutism dissolves the bonds of civil society, who is the true author of rebellion where it occurs. The effect of Locke's argument is thus not, actually, to justify rebellion, but to redirect the odium involved in it onto the monarch.

Finally then, the third reason Sidney's argument is noteworthy is that he is the only theorist of this period to actually *justify rebellion*. Alongside the intriguing parallel with Locke, this argument of his is, simply, original. Built upon the Grotian definition of just war, it liberated Sidney – and, he hoped, his readers – from any further qualms about this matter. Obviously well pleased, Sidney then backed this point up with a series of similar semantic investigations. The word 'Allegiance [for instance] signifies no more (as the words 'ad legem' declare) than such an obedience as the law requires. But as the law can require nothing from the whole people, who are masters of it, allegiance can only relate to particulars, and not to the whole nation.' Accordingly 'there can be no such thing in the world as the rebellion of a nation against its own magistrates'.[95]

And if 'the patience of a conquered people may have limits . . . it would be madness to think, that any nation can be obliged to bear whatever their own magistrates should see fit to do against them'. Once again

hands and swords are given to men, that they only may be slaves who have no courage . . . If it be said, that this may sometimes cause disorders, I acknowledge it; but no human condition being perfect, such a one is to be chosen, which carries with

[94] *Ibid.*, Locke, *Two Treatises*, ed. Laslett, p. 112.
[95] Sidney, *Discourses*, pp. 457–9.

it the most tolerable inconveniences ... it being much better, that the ... excesses of a prince should be restrained or suppressed, than that whole nations should perish by them ... no nation having been so happy, as not sometimes to produce such princes as Edward the second and Richard the second ... the rights and liberties of a nation must be utterly subverted and abolished, if the power of the whole may not be employed to assert them, or punish the violation of them.[96]

By this stage of the *Discourses*, as in the *Vindication*, Edward and Richard were becoming increasingly frequent guests in the text. The next time they are mentioned, however, Sidney adds more specifically 'and we know by what means the nation was preserved'. This remains, indeed, the only question still to be answered. How? It is in answer to this, as well as to Filmer's text, that Sidney turns his attention finally to the claims and powers of parliament. In doing so – although the text of the *Discourses* was not quite finished – he brings into focus both this crisis of parliaments and the political struggle of his life. This was the 'old cause'.

In these final chapters Sidney goes into some detail about the powers of the English parliament, the functions of the people's representatives in it, and the role of some of its continental equivalents. This was again a feature of the *Discourses* which particularly interested Montesquieu.[97] The general thrust of his message was, however, predictably enough, not so much about the nature of parliamentary power, as its extent. This had been a feature of the English constitution since Anglo-Saxon times, and faced with 'William the Norman',

the resolution of a brave people was invinceable. When their laws and liberties were in danger, they resolved to die, or to defend them; and made him see he could no otherwise preserve his crown and life, than by the performance of his oath, and accomplishing the ends of his election ... [this is again the language of the *Vindication*; and again an allusion to the contemporary situation, since Sidney considered Charles II to have been 'elected' by the parliament of 1660] And though perhaps they might want skill ... yet in general they maintained their rights so well, that the wisest princes seldom invaded them; and the success of those who were so foolish to attempt it was such, as may justly deter others from following their unprosperous examples. We have had no king since William the first more hardy than Henry the eighth, and yet he so entirely acknowledged the power of making, changing, and repealing laws, to be in the parliament, as never to attempt any extraordinary thing otherwise than by their authority. It was not he, but the parliament, that dissolved the abbies. He did not take their lands to himself, but received what the parliament thought fit to give him ... [and] a man of the acuteness and learning of Sir Thomas More [confirmed] ... that the parliament could do whatever lay within the reach of human power ... The parliament and people therefore have the power of making [or unmaking] kings.[98]

[96] *Ibid.*, pp. 458–9, 461–2.
[97] Montesquieu, *The Spirit of the Laws*, in Melvin Richter, *The Political Theory of Montesquieu* (Cambridge 1977), p. 248.
[98] *Ibid.*, pp. 416, 440, and see 499.

For this reason Bracton saith, that the King hath three superiors, to wit Deum, legem, et parliament; that is, the power originally in the people of England is delegated unto the parliament. He is subject unto the law of God, as he is a man; to the people that makes him a king, in as much as he is a king; the law sets a measure unto that subjection, and the parliament judges of the particular cases thereupon arising: he must be content to submit his interest unto theirs ... If he doth not like this condition, he may renounce the crown; but if he doth receive it upon that condition ... he must expect that the performance will be exacted, *or revenge taken by those he hath betrayed* [my emphasis].[99]

This matter settled, there remained only the practical problem of how, under present circumstances, to bring this august body into being. Thus, returning to the 'unprosperous examples' of 'Edward the second and Richard the second of England' we are told that 'The question [then] was not who had the right, or who ought to call parliaments, but how the commonwealth might be saved from ruin.'[100] 'The power of calling and dissolving parliaments is not simply in the king.'[101] In short

[Kings] may call parliaments, if there be occasion, at times when the law does not exact it; they are placed as sentinels, and ought vigilantly to observe the motions of the enemy ... but if the sentinel fall asleep, neglect his duty, or maliciously endeavour *to betray the city, those who are concerned may make use of all other means to know their danger, and to preserve themselves* ... if that magistrate had been drunk, mad, or gained by the enemy, no wise man can think, that formalities were to have been observed. In such cases *every man is a magistrate; and he who best knows the danger, and the means of preventing it, has a right of calling the senate or people to an assembly.* The people would, and certainly ought to follow him ... [for] nations ... would be guilty of the most extreme stupidity, if they should suffer themselves to be ruined for adhering to such ceremonies.[102]

We may therefore change or take away kings ... and in all the revolutions we have had in England, the people have been headed by the parliament, or the nobility and gentry that composed it, and, when kings failed of their duties, by their own authority called it.[103]

It was these final claims that were to attract the crown's most indignant attention at Sidney's trial.

---

[99] This part of the *Discourses* – ch. 2, section 32 – was quoted at Sidney's trial (see *Trial* in *Works*, pp. 24–5).
[100] Sidney, *Discourses*, p. 465.
[101] *Ibid.*, ch. 3, section 38.
[102] *Ibid.*, p. 466.
[103] Sidney, *Discourses*, ch. 2, section 32, read at Sidney's trial (see *Trial* in *Works*, pp. 24–5).

12

The self-defence of protestants

For God's sake have a strict eye to Mr S[ydney]. The Whigs have great Expectations of him. (Secretary Jenkins to Lawrence Hyde, 1 May 1682[1])

And when the Protestants of the Low-Countries were so grievously oppressed by the duke of Alva, why should they not make use of all the means that God had put into their hands for their deliverance? . . . by resisting they established a most glorious and happy Commonwealth, the strongest pillar of the Protestant Cause now in the world.[2]

Somme say the protestants of Holland, France, or . . . Piedmont were guilty of treason, in bearing arms against their princes, but [this] is ridiculous . . . when it is certaine, they sought noe more than the security of their own lives.[3]

Noblemen, Cittyes, Commonaltyes have often taken armes . . . to defend themselves, when they were prosecuted upon the account of religion.[4]

12.1 SIDNEY'S CAUSE

The beginning of the end of the Restoration crisis came, as we have seen, with a re-establishment both in the King's *Declaration* and in the minds of most people of the historical necessity of the Restoration. What followed, from 1681 to 1684, was a replay in miniature of many elements of that earlier event. One of these was the punishment of protestant dissent, and it was this which re-established for the *Discourses*, and the practical design underlying it, the same general context as for Sidney's *Court Maxims*.

The situations were far from identical of course, though it is worth noting the connectedness of the historical processes in operation. In Sidney's case

---

[1] PRO, State Papers 44, no. 68, p. 72; *CSPD* 1682, p. 190.
[2] Sidney, *Discourses*, ch. 2, section 32.
[3] East Sussex Record Office, Lewes, Glynde Place Archives no. 794, Sidney to John Hampden 6 October 1683.
[4] *Ibid.*

265

there was the major difference that this time he was inside the country. Moreover the historical context for his own perceptions was larger than this, for in their minds at least, Sidney, Essex, Hampden jnr and their friends were the direct political descendents of Pym, Bedford, Hampden and theirs. Their cause was the same, the cause of protestantism, and of parliaments, and the Restoration now required it to be refought. At this time there was neither a Scots rebellion, nor an English parliament in being. Yet as they prepared to supply these necessities, Sidney and his friends had one asset that their predecessors had had to make their way in the dark without. That was historical experience and 'example of the past'; example of the previous triumph over popery and arbitrary government.

Sidney and his colleagues were also now 'whigs'. This word appeared in 1681 as part of the nomenclature of the loyalist reaction. As such, it pointed precisely to the 'fanatic plot', with its roots in this 'example of the past', now assumed to be in existence. The 'whigs' were Scots, protestant extremists, steeped in the rebellious tenets of Knox and Buchanan. It was they who had brought the arbitrary government of Charles I down. The protestant zealots of 1681–3 were now (correctly) honoured by their opponents with this association.[5]

Such historical name-calling, significant though it is, was not, even now, enough to make a party. As from 1646 to 1666 (and as the *Discourses* has already suggested) it would be the same problem of 'divisions' which would cripple the latest design. There was no overall unity of political vision, of personal relationship, of organisation. These would be replaced, initially at least, and only up to a point, by a unity of desperation. That within fifteen years the name 'whig' would be accepted as a badge of honour, rather than infamy; that it would come to signify a publicly organised party rather than a band of rebels; and above all that it would denote a large proportion of the permanent political establishment, rather than the remnants of the civil wars whom they were hunting down – all of these were later transformations of the greatest magnitude, and importance.

As a 'whigg', therefore, and in the same loyalist terminology, Sidney was also a dangerous and insurrectionary 'fanatic'. He was one of 'the phanatiques' for whose cause – Scots, Dutch, French and English – he had earlier written the *Court Maxims*. Of the two key aspects of that cause – that it was in its basis, religious, and in its scope, European – the quotes at the head of this chapter serve to remind us.

For although, as we have seen, Sidney needed no further *theoretical* justification to take up arms against arbitrary government, in *practice* all of his treasons, his attempted insurrections, hinged upon religion. They were

---

[5] See chapter 2, last footnote. Also *The Whigs Lamentation* (1683); *A Pindarique Ode upon the late Horrid and Damnable Whiggish Plot* (1683).

all the justified effort of 'god's people' to protect themselves against persecution. In the Tower, he wrote to Hampden:

I . . . am very much comforted by that which you say of the prayers of good people. If I know my self at all, I doe love them, and never enterd into any publike action, upon any other motive than a desire of doing them good . . . if they are on my side towards god, I hope I shall not be much troubled whatsoever my lot be amongst men.[6]

This point is linked with another, equally evident in all the quotes: Sidney's religious cause was not the struggle for nonconformity within England, but for protestantism in Europe – the Protestant Cause – against persecution, and popery. This crisis, like the last, was the latest English chapter in the same European struggle: for protestant survival in the face of the Counter-Reformation. Everywhere, what protestant achievements there had been in this struggle had been effected, not by agreement, but by armed force – in France, in Holland, in England, in Ireland. Everywhere that armed force had failed – in Bohemia, in Magdeburg, in the Palatinate, perhaps now in France, protestantism had been wiped out. It was with this view of the troubles of his age that Sidney insisted, in both the *Maxims* and the *Discourses*, that it was grossly irresponsible to 'disallow the use of force, without which innocency cannot be protected, nor society maintained'.[7] It was with the same realities in mind that the practical enterprise underlying both of these works involved not simply England but the Netherlands, and France. As we have seen, what ultimately counted for Sidney in politics, as in religion, was not stability or peace, but the triumph of good (in a world full of evil). If the only way to advance or protect that good was armed force, then such force was, as the *Discourses* made it, the first essential in politics.

Similarly then, for Sidney the intrigue in which he now became involved was not the domestic 'Rye House Plot' of the historiography – with its pub talk, one-eyed maltsters, the Jolly Roger on the mainsail, and cutlasses at dawn.[8] It was the self-defence of protestants, the latest chapter in the European cause for which his father, his grandfather, and his grand-uncle had fought before him. His reference (above) to the glorious results of the Dutch resistance identifies this lineage, this perspective, and the cause for which Sir Philip Sidney gave his life. Now, a century later, Sidney announced himself ready to repeat the same sacrifice: 'that I may die glorifying thee for all thy mercies; and that at the last thou hast permitted me to be singled out as a witness of thy truth, and even by the confession of my

---

6 Sidney to Hampden, Letter 1, p. 3.
7 See Scott, *Sidney and the English Republic*, pp. 20, 199.
8 J.H.M. Salmon was, nevertheless, on the right track with his 'Algernon Sidney and the Rye House Plot', *History Today*, 4:10 (1954).

opposers, for that Old Cause in which I was from my youth engaged, and for which thou hast often and wonderfully declared thyself'.[9]

According to Sidney then, in the struggle between Reformation and Counter-Reformation, the use of arms in a 'just war' was the only instrument for the protection of their righteousness which protestants had. It was as the theorist of this situation that Sidney looked back on Grotius – the servant of Dutch republicanism, the protestant ambassador (with Algernon's father) in Paris during the Thirty Years War – as the greatest early modern political writer. For when the protestants had, accordingly, taken up arms in their just defence how 'wonderfully' God had declared for them. In the Low Countries (where they had broken the might of Spain), in England (where they had defeated the King, Scotland, Ireland and the Dutch), even in France, where protestant arms had established the faith in a legal enclave that was only now (with the active complicity of the English government) being destroyed. This was the lesson of Sidney's history, and of his family's history, and he now once again prepared to act upon it.

Needless to say, this view of Sidney's cause was not universally shared. It certainly didn't occur to the author of 'A Pindarique Ode' which accused Algernon of staining the family 'Name',

> In brave Sir Philip Known to Fame,
> For Perfect wit and Loyalty,
> Though now by Algernoon mark'd With so Black a Dye,
> As does almost Eclipse the Fame of his Good Ancestry.[10]

Not all contemporaries agreed that fighting for protestantism against a foreign prince and taking up arms against your own were the same thing. For Sidney, however, they were exactly so, as his whole life shows. As his political thought fixed itself on general principles, and insisted upon the relativism of particulars, so his loyalty was to a general (European) cause and his loyalty to particular governments relative to it. This general European and religious context at least was well understood by contemporaries. It now became a commonplace of loyalist literature that the 'bloody and fanatical' whig conspiracy in progress was the latest chapter in a history of European fanaticism – that is, religious warfare – stretching back to the French wars of religion of the sixteenth century. As with the popish plot, this was a loyalist inversion – or redirection – of the same (European) religious anxieties of the 1670s. Thus from 1681, in deference to protestant sensibilities, the 'whig cause' was associated by loyalists not with the protestant but with the catholic side of the French conflict. This was a tempting point, for not only did it create a streamlined enemy – 'religious

---

[9] Sidney, *Last Paper* in 'Memoirs of Algernon Sydney', *Works*, pp. 39–40.
[10] *A Pindarique Ode.*

fanaticism' in general – but it echoed Filmer, in drawing attention to the use
by 'the whigs', as by the Leaguers, huguenots and Scots rebels before them,
of Counter-Reformation natural law theory. Of the resulting formula,
Dryden's *Prologue to the Duke of Guise* (1682) is a pithy summary:

> Our Play's a Parallel: The Holy League
> Begot our Cov'nant: Guisards got the Whigg:
> Whate'er our hot-brain's Sheriffs did advance,
> Was, like our Fashions, first produc'd in France:
> And, when worn out, well scourg'd, and banish'd there,
> Sent over, like their godly Beggars here.
> Cou'd the same Trick, twice play'd, our Nation gull?[11]

Finally, therefore, Sidney's 'old cause' was much older than the English
civil wars. Though his frank declaration of allegiance on this score in 1683
did indeed cause a sensation, few realised what it was that made him such a
stout defender of it, in such hopeless circumstances. It was the fact that this
'cause', and this self-image, as (as Grotius' stoic sources put it) 'the
Christian soldier ... fighting on behalf of the safety of the innocent, on
behalf of justice',[12] didn't begin in 1643, but was anchored through his
ancestors much further back; and didn't belong only to England, but to
France, to the Netherlands, to Scandinavia, to Scotland, and elsewhere. One
problem for Sidney from 1681 to 1683 was that that age in England – 'an
age that makes truth pass for treason'[13] – had, apparently, among other
forms of corruption, begun to forget its own history. It had forgotten how
to value the priceless liberties that previous generations had won for it with
their own blood. It was in this sense that the Restoration – that act of
heedless youth – was the ultimate folly and ingratitude. This is the reason
for the constant stress in the *Discourses* on the value of liberties so precious
that 'our ancestors thought nothing too dear to be hazarded in defence of
them'.

There appear to be no grounds for doubting the reality of Sidney's
involvement in treasonous activities in 1683. Indeed throughout his vol-
uminous writings of this year one never gains the impression that he believes
himself 'innocent' of the charges. What infuriates him is that such activities
are called 'treason' at all, and it is this indignation that carries the burden of
his defence at the trial. Just as he was inclined, in one letter, to admit his
authorship of the *Discourses*, so the passages at the head of this chapter

[11] Dryden, *Prologue to the Duke of Guise* (1682), p. 1; see also *The Parallel: or, The New Specious Association an Old Rebellious Covenant* (1682). The general themes of these works, encapsulated in the word 'parallel', lie at the centre of hundreds of loyalist pamphlets of this period: see, for example, Cambridge University Library Sel. 2.118–Sel. 2.122.
[12] H. Grotius, *De Jure Belli ac Pacis Libri Tres* (Oxford, 1925), Book One, pp. 55–6, 75, 90; see Scott, *Sidney and the English Republic*, p. 20.
[13] Sidney, *Last Paper*, p. 37.

show that he wasn't inclined, even in prison, to deny the legitimacy of what he had been accused of either. In one part of his *Apology*, indeed, Sidney effectively let slip that the second meeting of the so-called 'Council of Six' did take place. Having ridiculed Howard for changing his testimony between Russell's trial and his own, Sidney attacked the court for 'making discourses at a private meeting, imperfectly variously and to their own knowledge falsely reported, by a man of most profligate life and reputation, to passe for a Conspiracy'.[14]

This is not to say that we can afford to be uncritical about such prosecution testimony, extracted under duress and/or in exchange for a pardon. As we will see, Howard appears to have embellished what he really knew into the 'Council of Six' formula deemed to be necessary to prove such a plot before a jury. On the whole, however, what it notable about the 'evidence' concerning Sidney's activities in 1683 is how consistent it is, both across a range of sources, and with what we know about him from other times.

None of this is surprising, since if the writer of the *Discourses* wasn't involved in such activities, 'the only question would be', as Blair Worden put it, 'why not?' In fact among all his colleagues Sidney's European insurrectionary credentials, in both theory and practice, were unrivalled. His whig admirers wanted a man of *espirit*, who believed what he wrote in the *Discourses* and his *Last Paper*; but they also wanted an innocent man to underwrite the *cause célèbre* of the most unjust of trials. Faced with the contradiction between these two, we will do Sidney the favour of believing that he meant what he said in the *Discourses*, and was prepared to act upon it. All of the evidence not only bears this out, but shows that in 1683, as in 1665–6, what distinguished Sidney among his colleagues was his forwardness.

Finally, a certain presumption of guilt allows us to treat Sidney's trial not as the judicial landmark it wasn't but as the brutal piece of political theatre it was, played as such by both sides, and by the rules of an age by now well accustomed to them.

12.2 1681–3

Between August 1681, following the completion of the *Vindication*, and January 1683, Sidney almost disappears from our view. His one public reappearance comes, as we will see, at the London shrievalty election of July 1682. In general he seems to have taken himself away from London to write the first three-quarters of the *Discourses*.

One possibility, mentioned in chapter 5, is that he moved back to Pens-

[14] Sidney, *Apology*, p. 22.

hurst, a suggestion supported, if not proved, by Howard's later testimony that during this time 'he was gone into the Countrey'.[15] What makes this likely is that Sidney had been required to surrender Leicester House in London to Philip in late 1681. Penshurst, however, remained under the control of the executors, and empty, since Henry was at the Hague. Penshurst would have been a fine place to write, not least because it may have still contained his father's library. It is also possible, however, that Sidney took up an offer of country accommodation with a friend – with Essex perhaps (whose country house John Locke visited in 1682),[16] or with the Earl of Clare.

Another strong possibility is that during this period he made a visit to France. He had asked Savile to forward a package into Gascony in February 1681;[17] and in 1683 he recorded in his *Apology*:

When a favourable decree, obtained in Chancery [in the second half of 1680], gave me hopes of being freed from such vexatious businesse I reassumed my former designe of returning into France; and to that end bought a small parcell of ground, in a friend's name, with an intention of going immediately unto it. This proceeded from the uneasiness of my life, when I found, that not only the reall discontents, that grew to be too common, were ascribed unto me, but sham plots fastened upon me, soe as I could never think my life a day in safety.[18]

Until now there has been no reason to believe that this purchase was completed in France by Sidney in person. But in 1683 the new English ambassador in Paris, Lord Preston, began to send bulletins back to the government relating disturbing connections between the English 'fanatics' and the huguenots. The reports focused on Sidney and his friend John Hampden jnr. In particular, one of Preston's informants related a conversation in Paris.

Upon the occasion of Mr Sidney's being in the Tower . . . One of the company, a Frenchman, said he wondered not at it, for he had particularly conversed with him when he was here, and had heard him often talking against the Royal prerogatives, and tacitly threatening the King with his father's fate for *dissolving Parliament in that manner* etc.[19] [my emphasis].

If Sidney hadn't been in France, either in 1679, or more probably in 1681–2, this report is difficult to explain.

It may be, then, that by August 1681 (the date of the last report on Sidney from Barillon) the *Vindication* was finished, and so, it appeared, were parliaments for the time being. Sidney had recently been involved with the tribulations of his friend Howard in the Tower. Leicester House was about

---

[15] *The Tryal and Conviction of John Hambden Esq* (6 Feb. 1684), pp. 11–12.
[16] Ashcraft, 'Revolutionary Politics', *Political Theory*, 8:4 (1980), pp. 444–50.
[17] Sidney, 'Letters to Savile' in *Works*, p. 3.
[18] Sidney, *Apology*, p. 4.
[19] HMC Rep no 7, Graham MSS p. 401.

to be surrendered. Sidney was now at the centre of a radical community in the City whose achievements were sufficiently noteworthy to make the new atmosphere of reaction worrying. He therefore returned to France, perhaps in late 1681, visiting friends both in Paris and Gascony, and putting the £2,000 paid by Philip for Leicester House towards a property in the latter place. This eventual bolt-hole established, he returned to England, settling at Penshurst, where he worked during 1682 on the *Discourses*, visiting London periodically, and keeping various Chancery cases, old and new, on the boil. This is a plausible though indefinite hypothesis.

All accounts of planned insurrection before 1683 centre on the Earl of Shaftesbury. Following his arrest and trial in 1681 Shaftesbury had, on the important issue of self-defence, undergone a conversion to radicalism. Even for Shaftesbury the problem now was not James, but Charles. By mid 1682, following the imposition of loyalist Sheriffs, his client Ferguson was at last composing papers with a much sharper eye for past and present than future reigns, detailing the crimes of 'K. James, K. Charles the first and his present Majesty . . . [their] Attempts . . . to introduce popery and Arbitrary Government'. He described York as just 'a skreen to shelter' Charles, who was 'the worse man', a 'papist' 'engag'd to establish popery . . . [and] Absolute power . . . in England'.[20] It became necessary, in short, even for Shaftesbury and those around him, to cover the nakedness left by exclusion with a fig leaf of the 'old cause'.

Inevitably, however, this process was neither smooth nor complete. More importantly, to the extent that it did occur it was the result less of long-term conviction than of short-term necessity. It was and is necessary to distinguish between the radicalism of settled belief, and that of political desperation, in a situation which threw together people of both categories, in fear for their lives. As both Shaftesbury and Sidney found in turn, this was thin ice upon which to organise a rebellion.

Consideration of this extreme course – armed self-defence – began in 1681 with the onset of religious and political persecution. This was the invasion of property – of 'lives, liberties and estates' – to which Locke's *Two Treatises* particularly addressed itself. But as long as there remained the radical fortress of London – as Shaftesbury's acquittal in 1681 had demonstrated – there remained hope of this defence by other means. What crystallised words into action, as all accounts, contemporary and historical, agree, was the successful loyalist assault on the shrievalty on 24 June 1682.[21]

---

[20] 'The Rye House Plot: Robert West's full Confession to the King'. BL Add. MS 38847, p. 7.
[21] See for instance, *ibid.*, pp. 2, 4: Ford Lord Grey, *The Secret History of The Rye House Plot* (1754), pp. 15–17; J. Walker, 'The Republican Party' (Manchester PhD 1930), p. 255; D. Milne, 'The Results of the Rye House Plot and Their Influence Upon the Revolution of 1688', *TRHS*, 5th ser., 1 (1951), 92.

This was a major public incident, and it became a political *cause célèbre*. It was a blatant abuse of the electoral procedures to which the City had been accustomed. It was almost certainly what Locke was referring to in the *Second Treatise* when he listed among the ways in which governments are dissolved from within: 'Thirdly, When by the Arbitrary Power of the Prince, the Electors or ways of Election are altered, without the consent and contrary to the common Interest of the People'.[22] When in 'the Great Hall . . . In which there were Assembled . . . Three or Four Thousand People . . . Papilion and Duboii [sic] were chose by the Majority abundantly but were put aside by the Lord Mayor',[23] there was a riot.

Given the centrality of the shrievalty to their previous political involvements, it should not surprise us that among those arrested for this affray were Bethel and Sidney. As Sidney's *Apology* later explained: 'when I only looked over a balcony to see what passed at the election of the Sheriffs of London I was indicted for a riot'. Bethel and a number of others were tried for this offence exactly a year later (on 26 June 1683) but Sidney could not appear. He had been arrested that very morning for treason.[24]

While predictably 'the earl of Shaftesbury had been for making use of the heat the city was in during the contest about the Sheriffs', even relative moderates like Russell considered this the specific event which released the King's subjects from their obedience and – as Essex put it – 'set them at liberty to look to themselves'.[25] What made it so crucial was, as has been explained, not only the defensive but the offensive capacities developed by the shrievalty between 1680 and 1682. There was now nothing for it but flight, or arms.

Throughout 1682, Shaftesbury's increasingly desperate attempts in the latter direction were a failure. For this the Earl was not entirely responsible. Undistinguished though his record of generalship was, his primary problem on this occasion seems to have been obsolete equipment. Heading this category were his two lieutenants, Monmouth and Russell.

Nothing that either is on record as saying throughout 1682 gives any indication that they had entered the real political world that Shaftesbury at least periodically inhabited. Both specialised in broad gestures devoid of any appreciation of the detailed requirements of an armed insurrection; both consequently drew back whenever talk gave way to the prospect of action. The insurrectionary capacities of Monmouth in particular, who even Lord

---

[22] Locke, *Second Treatise*, ch. 19, para. 216 (Laslett, 2nd edn., p. 427).

[23] *An Impartial Account of the Proceedings of the Common Hall of the City of London at Guildhal*, 24 June 1682, marginalia supplied by the tract's owner, Cambridge University Library Sel. 2.118.

[24] Sidney, *Apology*, p. 4; *Trial of . . . [those indicted] for the Riot at Guild-Hall on Midsommer-Day 1682* (1683).

[25] Burnet, *Own Time*, pp. 339, 346; Milne, 'Rye House Plot', p. 92.

Grey described as 'a formal timorous blockhead',[26] arrived at their logical conclusion in the debacle of 1685, at great cost to his supporters. Monmouth's aspirations were not, in the end, political at all. They were personal, and hinged on his power (versus York's) in his relationship with his father. His western progresses, like his plotting, were attempts to demonstrate power to influence that relationship, not to overthrow the government. Thus his plotting was dangerously and erratically punctuated by tearful reconciliations with Dad; and thus his 'rebellion' in 1685 became simply another western progress, leaving James to remind him painfully that he was now 'progressing' in front of the wrong monarch.[27] Monmouth was, in short, an insurrectionary disaster area, and his participation in any design against Charles was enough to deliver it the kiss of death. His wish, like Russell's, was to 'reform' the government, not overthrow it, and above all not to 'harm a hair on the King's head' (though a trim for James would not be off the agenda). Russell informed the incredulous Shaftesbury that he thought the English government 'the best in the world'. 'You must', Monmouth intoned, 'look on me as a son'.[28]

Thus when Shaftesbury finally delivered to Monmouth a frank report on his political capacities, when he turned on Russell and others in what Grey called 'the greatest passion I ever saw',[29] when he screeched at them that the 'patience' they had counselled once again 'would be their destruction', and when he fled, with Ferguson, to Holland and died shortly afterwards (possibly of sheer frustration), we must, for once, spare a kind thought for the Earl. And we must raise an apprehensive eyebrow for Algernon.

In the short term, Shaftesbury's departure left Russell, Monmouth and others relieved. Burnet's report that they looked on his 1682 plans as 'a mad exposing of themselves and their friends'[30] is echoed by Sidney's claim in 1683 that 'The Duke of Monmouth' and Howard both 'thought him to be mad'.[31] Essex too was on the receiving end of Shaftesbury's tongue and harboured 'thoughts of the same kind'.[32] The relief was temporary, however, for if the 'general discontent in the City on the Issue of the sheriffs' had resulted in 'unusual freedom and boldness of discourse',[33] it had also removed the judicial apparatus to protect those responsible from the consequences. The urgent problem remained, and in the absence of one political hothead, a *Situations Vacant* sign appears to have been posted for another.

[26] Grey, *Secret History*, p. 17.
[27] Scott, 'Radicalism and Restoration', p. 467.
[28] Grey, *Secret History*, p. 3.
[29] Burnet, *Own Time*, p. 339.
[30] Sidney, *Apology*, p. 15.
[31] *Ibid.*, p. 15.
[32] Confession of Robert West, BL, Add. MS 38847, p. 4.
[33] *The Tryal of John Hambden*, p. 12.

12.3 'THE WAR IN BOTH KINGDOMS' 1683

When once people come to believe that the raising of Tumults, and making seditions ... is a legal way to obtain their ends ... what will they not do under that pretence, That all they do is according to Law? They think it is lawful to resist and oppose the Government, and the Old Cause is a Good Cause to this day ... (George Jeffreys, *Tryal of John Hambden*, 6 February 1684[34])

Extrajudicial proceedings, by Sedition, tumult or war, must take place, when the persons concerned are of such power that they cannot be brought under the judicial. They who deny this deny all help against an usurping tyrant. (Sidney, *Discourses*, pp. 193–4)

it is not only the Law of the Land, but the eternall Law of nature, that permits such as are invaded to defend themselves. (Sidney to Hampden, 6 October 1683.[35])

ASSEMBLING THE TROOPS

If he can be believed, the man who brought this advertisement to Sidney's attention was Lord Howard. At Sidney's trial, Howard said simply that in January he, Sidney and Monmouth had been the first movers of the 'Council of Six'. At the later trial of Hampden, however, he was more specific. Having described the collapse of Shaftesbury's plans and his flight, Howard continued:

This was in November [1682]. After this there being frequent Conferences between Colonel Sidney and me; for Colonel Sidney by the way knew nothing of all this, and I was caution'd by My Lord Shaftesbury that I should not tell my Friend Sidney any thing of it, and asking him ... why I should not? Says he, I can't well tell; But you will wonder ... that his own Friend Major Wil[d]man has barred him and would not let him know it. The Gentleman [Sidney] is now dead; but I will assure you he did know nothing of this for a month after: For he was gone into the Countrey; but after my Lord Shaftsbury was dead, I told him the History of all these Transactions ... when I had aquainted him with what had been intended in London ... what Preparations had been made, and in what posture affairs then stood. We ... took up a Resolution to form a Council ... He undertook to speak to my Lord of Essex and Mr Hambden, and I was to bring the Duke of Monmouth to a right understanding with him in it.[36]

What this turns out to mean, is that (firstly) Howard told Sidney about Shaftesbury's designs, and (secondly) that he decided to trick Sidney and Monmouth into a meeting. Accordingly Howard

went to the Duke of Monmouth, and told him Col. Sidney did present his Service to him, and would willingly wait on him, but ... because he was a person of such Note,

---

[34] *Ibid.*, Lord Chief Justice's summing up, p. 48.
[35] East Sussex R O, Lewes, Glynde Place MSS no. 794, letter 4, p. 4.
[36] *The Tryal of John Hambden* (1684), Howard's testimony.

and thereupon so obnoxious . . . it might prejudice him to have him seen to come to him; and therefore if his Grace would please to appoint any third place, he should be very glad to kiss his Hand. Says the Duke, I do not know anywhere truly to appoint. Why then, said I . . . Let us e'en go to his House (having before prepared Colonel Sidney for it) and take him by surprise, and dine with him . . . But, said I, you must not expect to be treated as the Duke of Monmouth, because he does not expect you; but take him as a Philosopher, and dine with him as he uses to dine at his own Table.[37]

The reason for this elaborate arrangement was that Sidney hadn't issued an invitation to meet Monmouth at all. As he later put it: 'I had never spoken unto the duke of Monmouth until he brought the said duke to dine with me by a cheat put upon us both a few days before the pretended meetings.'[38] 'He told the duke I invited him, and he told me the duke invited himself; and neither of them was true.'[39] Burnet elaborated, explaining in the process why Howard saw fit to warn Monmouth 'not to expect to be treated' as a duke might:

Howard had made the duke of Monmouth enter into confidence with Sidney, who used to speak very slightly of him, and to say, it was all one to him whether James duke of York or James duke of Monmouth was to succeed . . . Lord Howard, by a trick put [on] both . . . brought them to be acquainted. He told Sidney that the duke . . . was resolved to come . . . and dine with him: and he made the duke . . . believe that Sidney desired this . . . and said that some regard was to be had to his temper and age.[40]

These accounts of Sidney's eccentricities – summed up by Jeffreys as that 'he was a Cynical man, and a Philosopher, and they were first to come to him, and to treat him in another manner than the rest'[41] – are intriguing references to the author of the *Discourses* in progress. Nor do they put one out of fear, on Monmouth's behalf, of a dinner of paragraphs.

We need not doubt Howard's information, however, that Sidney had not been concerned with Shaftesbury's designs. It corresponds with Sidney's own claim about the Earl that

beside the knowne dislikes which he had unto me, and I unto him and his wayes, I did not see his face in almost a yeare before he went out of England . . . and had no communication with him afterwards.[42]

There is good reason, on the other hand, as we will see, to doubt the taking up of a 'Resolution to form a council [of six]', that old chestnut of Restoration plotting politics. This was the 'put[ting the design] into some

---

[37] *Ibid.*
[38] Sidney, *Apology*, p. 11.
[39] *Trial* in Sidney, *Works*, p. 27.
[40] Burnet, *Own Time*, p. 343.
[41] *The Tryal of John Hambden*, Lord Chief Justices summing up p. 40.
[42] Sidney, *Apology*, p. 14.

[formal] Method' which it was necessary to demonstrate in a treason trial, and upon which Jeffreys accordingly laid particular emphasis.[43] It is clear, finally however, that the meeting with Monmouth did take place, and that this was followed by others, involving others.

Howard had thus established the link whereby Sidney and his friends (particularly Hampden and Essex) and the remnants of Shaftesbury's design (particularly Russell and Monmouth) came together to discuss some action. Sidney clearly decided to put his contempt for Monmouth to one side for present purposes, and it is not difficult to see why. Sidney argued at his trial that he was 'no popular man' and that he and Howard couldn't 'raise five men' each; the notoriously popular Monmouth, however, could.[44] Sidney's dim view of Monmouth's intellectual capacities gave him hopes of becoming the director of those that existed. Above all, Sidney's thinking hinged on Scotland, and Monmouth was the victor of Bothwell Bridge. The next Scots rebellion would feature the King's son *on the other side*. For this connection, through Howard, to Monmouth, was only one of two approaches to Sidney in January 1683, drawing him into the insurrectionary world vacated by Shaftesbury. The other was from the Netherlands, and it concerned Scotland. In 1685 William Carstares deposed (under torture in Edinburgh Castle):

That about ... December 1682 James Stuart [agent of the Earl of Argyle] ... wrote a letter to [me] ... from Holland, imparting, That if any considerable sum of Money could be procured from England, that something of importance might be done in Scotland.

Carstares sent a letter accordingly to Mr Shepherd, a London wine-merchant. By this time (probably January) Shaftesbury was gone. Shepherd reported that he had

communicat[ed] the Contents of the Letter ... to Colonel Sidney, and that Colonel Danvers [as we have seen, Sidney's election agent in Amersham] was present, and told the deponent that Colonel Sidney was averse from imploying the late Earl of Argile, or medling with him, judging him a man too Much affected to the Royal Family, and inclin'd to the present Church-Government.[45]

An informant of Lord Preston in Paris later confirmed this description of Sidney as the person in England 'to whom Argile's letters since Shaftesbury's death were directed'.[46]

As we have seen, Sidney was the last person to undervalue the Scots connection. His desire was to procure another Scots challenge, that would

[43] *The Tryal of John Hambden*, p. 41; and see pp. 322–4 below.
[44] *Trial*, in Sidney, *Works*, p. 31.
[45] *A True and Plain Account of the Discoveries Made in Scotland of the Late Conspiracies Against His Majesty and the Government* (1685), p. 50.
[46] Graham MSS, HMC Rep. no. 7, p. 364.

force another English parliament into being. And it is important to understand wherein, precisely, his hopes in this lay. They were not, above all, in the military power of the Scots, as the *Discourses*' treatment of 1637–40 makes clear. They hinged on Sidney's belief that under monarchy in general, and Charles II in particular, the military strength of the state was so rotten that it would crumble, as it had under Charles I, at the first challenge. It would do so all the more completely in the face of sympathy for the enemy. Every aspect of Charles II's military record bore this hope out, except Bothwell Bridge – and that general had just been recruited by the rebels. All that was necessary was to bring a credible challenge into being.

What Sidney would not do, however, was squander the Scots connection on Shaftesbury's terms. In particular, he would not engage in a rising that would expose the lives of the Scots nonconformists on behalf of a 'limited monarchy' solution (still favoured by Shaftesburians like Russell, Monmouth and Ferguson) that would neither justify nor protect it. The immediate upshot was that Carstares was forced to retire to Holland to meet Argyle without any commission from England, something which enraged 'Ferguson [who] blamed always Sidney, as driving designs of his own'. According to Carstares, Ferguson received his information from 'one Major Wildman, who is not of the Deponent his acquaintance'.[47] As we will see, when 'a Treaty' followed in London a few months later 'between the Scots, and our Persons of Quality here . . . Coll. Sidney and Major Wildman, had the management of it'.[48]

Those acquainted with Sidney's Dutch experience will recognise in this 'person of Quality', leading treasonous negotiations with a foreign power, Sidney's customary role. It was one of a number of respects in which the first half of 1683 returned him to the circumstances of 1665. According to Howard, the result of the Monmouth–Sidney meeting was that 'Monmouth undertook to engage my lord Russell and my lord Salisbury; and . . . Colonel Sidney, for my Lord Essex and Mr Hambden'.[49] Within a 'Fortnight . . . or Ten Days after, Colonel Sydney came to me, and told me, my Lord of Essex was very forward in it . . . and he himself did not doubt but Mr Hambden was very willing to be in it too'.[50]

It was at this time that Sidney and Essex had become so close that Burnet remorsefully imputed to this relationship the sudden radicalisation of his once-moderate friend. 'Sidney', he recorded, 'fataly subdued Essex so to him, that he turned him which way he pleased.'[51] The key to this relation-

[47] *True and Plain Account*, p. 51.
[48] See note 95 below.
[49] *Trial*, in Sidney, *Works*, p. 17.
[50] *The Tryal of John Hambden*, p. 12.
[51] Burnet, BL Add MS 63,057, vol. II, p. 138.

ship, Sidney and Essex's connection through the Percy family, has already been noted. The link was specifically through Elizabeth Percy, Jocelyn's sister, and the last surviving heir of the Percy family, whom Algernon had known since childhood. Essex and Elizabeth wed at Petworth in 1653, when Algernon was living there with the Northumberland family. Their eldest son was subsequently named Algernon. There is, for the biographer of Sidney, an automatic flavour of Northumberland about this whole political partner-ship, on the eve of the destruction of both men in the Tower, and on the scaffold. That this feeling is well founded is confirmed from several direc-tions. Burnet recorded:

Lord Essex had [in 1683] got into an odd set of some strange principles; and in particular, he thought a man was the master of his own life, and seemed to approve of what his wife's great grandfather, the Earl of Northumberland, did, who shot himself in the Tower after he was arraigned.[52]

This remains the most probable explanation for Essex's grisly suicide in the Tower following his arrest with Sidney in July – it was the only way for the family of a traitor to escape the forfeiture of his estate to the crown. 'Essex had apparently commend[ed] . . . the action of the [eighth] Earl of Northumberland, who prevented an attainder by killing himself in the tower, to save his honour and family estates.'[53]

At the very least this tells us that Essex was as mindful of his Percy heritage, and its bloody early modern history, as Sidney. A second report, however, may tell us more, and appears in an unpublished manuscript section of Burnet's *History*. It is worth quoting in full:

Essex came more than ordinary to me this winter [early 1683], and once he brought me Mariana's Book of a Prince . . . [I] read it . . . but told him I did not at all approve . . . his Maxims . . . he said yt as to ye Point of Assassinations he was of mind, but he thought Princes were but Ministers trusted by ye people and so might be restrained. He grew to have a strange aversation to ye Court, and spoke of publick affairs with a rage yt was contrary to his nature, he told me he knew the king intended to subdue his people as soon as he could, and yt he had said so himself, yt tho he would never bring things to the pass they were at in Turkey . . . yet he thought ye french Government was a much happier constitution than ye English, and yt he would have no body enquire into or question anything. He also told me many particulars concerning ye Massacres in Ireland, to prove yt ye Rebellion was both begun and carried on by ye Queen's [Henrietta Maria] direction; he said . . . ye Irish had undertaken to her to take possession of Ireland, and to drive ye English out of it, and then to bring over an Army to assist ye King in ye conquest of England . . . ye Marquess of Antrim, who was engaged very deep in ye blood that was shed, was all ye while in Correspondence with ye Queen, of which he told me this remarkable story.[54]

52 Quoted in W. Scott (ed.), *Somers Tracts*, vol. X, p. 66.
53 Capel, Arthur, Earl of Essex, *DNB*, vol. IX, pp. 16–17.
54 Burnet, BL Add. MS 63,057, vol. II, p. 139.

The 'remarkable story' Essex told Burnet – who had never heard this account of the Irish massacre before, though it can be read in Sidney's *Court Maxims*[55] – concerned a secret 'Committee of Councils' set up after the Restoration to 'examine ye orders upon which he [Antrim] pretended to have acted'. According to Essex, the Committee concluded to its deep embarrassment that the royal warrants for Antrim's conduct were indeed sufficient, and 'by ye Queen Mother's Interest' Ormonde was ordered to leave him unpunished. This whole proceeding was condemned by Clarendon as giving credence to the 'blackest of all ye Calumnies yt had been cast on ye late King'. The hero of the story however, and possibly its source, was Sidney's uncle and Essex's father-in-law the tenth Earl of Northumberland. For the Earl, a member of the committee, 'tho he did not deny but he had shewed orders for all he did, yet he said yt was no justification, since ye King's secret orders could not warrant a man to commit such crimes'.[56]

Given the centrality, to both Sidney's and Essex's careers, of Irish affairs, this story brought together both the political and the family links by which they were most closely tied. If, as seems likely, the story found its way from Algernon Percy and/or his family to Algernon Sidney, Sidney's transmission of the same to Essex seems to have had an electrifying effect. Burnet's account also adds yet more colour to that axiom of contemporary loyalism: that the 'fanatic' plot was merely the popish plot venturing abroad in presbyterian trousers; and most specifically that the 'fanatics' were king-killers actuated by jesuit natural law theory.[57] Here we find Essex wandering about with a copy of Mariana, a lethal weapon and the most notorious of all such texts, just as Sidney – the confessed admirer of Juan Marquez – was dismissing Filmer's accusation that his theory was that of Bellarmine and Suarez.

This family connection with Essex, Sidney's closest friend among the conspirators, helps to remind us of one crucial aspect of Sidney's insurrectionary psychology and its background. No less important, in a different way, was another aspect of the same psychology, shared with his other principal associate of this year, John Hampden jnr.

Hampden shared with Sidney his French huguenot experience, and contacts. He had spent most of the two years before September 1682 in France. What he took from this experience was not only practical, but intellectual. Burnet recorded:

[Hampden was] a young man of great parts, one of the learnedest gentlemen I ever Knew; for he was a critic both in Latin, Greek and Hebrew; he was a man of great

[55] Sidney, *Court Maxims*, pp. 180–2; Scott, *Sidney and the English Republic*, p. 205.
[56] See notes 54–55 above; and Lamont, *Richard Baxter and the Millenium*, Appendix.
[57] See Harris, *London Crowds*, pp. 140–4.

wit and vivacity, but too unequal in his temper; he had once great principles of religion, but he was corrupted by F. Simon's conversation at Paris.[58]

What Burnet meant by this is that in Paris Hampden had become 'greatly influenced' by exactly the same French sceptical theology that had made such an impact on Algernon on the eve of the civil war. Father Richard Simon's sceptical *Critical History of the Old Testament* (1678) was, to Hampden, just what Daillé's *Of the Right Use of the Fathers* (1651) had been to Sidney a generation before. Hampden had also met in Paris the historian Mezeray, who told him that France had once enjoyed the same free institutions as England, but lost them owing to the encroachments of its kings. 'Think nothing, he said, too dear to maintain these precious advantages; venture your life, your estates, and all you have rather than submit to the miserable condition to which you see us reduced.' 'These words', wrote Hampden, 'made an impression on me which nothing can efface.'[59] Mezeray was a major source for this same argument in Sidney's *Discourses*.[60]

What made Hampden's sojourn in France important alongside Sidney's own (earlier and/or more recent), was their shared contacts among protestant radicals. Here we catch glimpses of a French, alongside Dutch, department of the English design; and of a country where Sidney's fate appears to have caused as much concern as it did in England.

We have already encountered Preston's report from Paris on apparently recent conversations there between Sidney and French radicals. This was conveyed in the course of a general effort to gather intelligence on such Anglo-French contacts. We have also already seen (in chapter 6) that Hampden shared with Sidney both his links with Barillon, and his views on the Prince of Orange.[61] In late November 1682, Preston reported that one 'Charleton, an English gentleman who has lived 6 years in Monpellier', had been arrested on suspicion of 'a conspiracy against the King, and of holding correspondence prejudicial to his service with some of the Protestants of Languedoc ... and ... if Mr Hamden the younger had been here still he would also have been seized upon the same account.'[62] On 2 January 1683 he continued:

I have been endeavouring for some time to trace Mr Hampden the youngest in his travels through France, Switzerland, and Germany, in all which places he hath been extremely industrious to vilify and misrepresent our Governors and Government, both in Church and State, and here in particular he hath blown up the Protestants, and given them strange impressions of the King and his ministers. At this ... I should

---

[58] Quoted in *DNB*, John Hampden Jnr, vol. XXIV, pp. 262–3.
[59] *Ibid.*, taken from *A Collection of State Tracts published during the Reign of King William III* (1706), vol. II, p. 313.
[60] e.g. Sidney, *Discourses*, p. 253.
[61] See pp. 106–7, 121 above.   [62] HMC Rep. 7, Graham MSS, p. 275.

not have wondered much, because I know that it is the principle of his family to hate their Prince, and to endeavour to ruin our monarchy. But I must confess I am surprised at this . . . that he had a letter of recommendation from Monsr de Barillon to the Archbishop at Paris . . . and that he was at least for a short time with him during his stay here . . . I must, Sir, speak the truth to you . . . that the Phanatick party is highly countenanced from hence whatever may be pretended to the contrary . . . I [hope] . . . you will think it fit to have an eye upon the gentleman [in England].[63]

Later in the same year Preston reported (in October) 'Mr Algernon Sidney is much admired and spoken of by the French';[64] and (in November), more intriguingly still 'the French are much concerned for Mr Sidney, and fear he may blab something to their disadvantage. Those of the party here are in much consternation'.[65] By this time, as we will see, Sidney was corresponding with Hampden in the Tower and putting to him a plan for the two to retreat together to Gascony.

Sidney, with Hampden, thus apparently retained contacts with French radicals ('the party here'), as well as ambassadors. We should remember that this period (1680–3) saw the onset of religious persecution in France, as well as in England, and that Sidney had a huguenot refugee, Ducasse, living in his own household. We should, finally, given Preston's message that the 'Phanatiques' were 'highly countenanced' in France, remember Sidney's attempt to make the case to Barillon in 1680 for liberty of conscience for catholics under an English Republic. Discussion of such a scheme is certainly the most plausible explanation for Hampden's visit under Barillon's auspices to the 'Archbishop at Paris'. The overall design may have been religious toleration in all three countries: Britain, the Netherlands, and France.

Thus on the eve of Sidney's last practical effort for his cause, both of the companions he brought into the design remind us of crucial aspects of its (and his) background. Both the aristocratic insurrection of the Percies, and the protestant internationalism of the Sidneys, came together to unsheath the sword of war.

DIVIDED COUNSELS (JANUARY–JUNE 1683)

For an account of 'the first two meetings' of what he called the 'Council of Six' we are dependent on the testimony of Howard. Apart from its inherent unreliability, there is also the problem that Howard, alone of the six, disappeared into the country after the second meeting – to Essex and then 'the Bath'. This showed, at the least, as Sidney pointed out, a peculiarly relaxed

---

[63] *Ibid.*, p. 277.   [64] *Ibid.*, p. 343.   [65] *Ibid.*, p. 401.

attitude to 'the greatest businesse in the world'.[66] Howard was also a distinctly controversial member of the group: according to Burnet it was Sidney who 'prevailed on lord Essex to take Lord Howard into their secrets, though lord Essex had expressed such an ill opinion of him a little before to me, as to say he wondered how any man would trust himself alone with him'.[67] Essex in turn persuaded an equally disgruntled Russell. But, most importantly, Russell told Burnet a few days before his death that Lord Essex had forced him to admit Lord Howard to a meeting at his house; for when he saw Lord Howard, Sidney and Hampden coming in he said to Lord Essex, 'what have we to do with this rogue?' but Lord Essex forced him to stay'. Russell ascribed Essex's subsequent suicide to his 'regret for having introduced Lord Howard [who would betray them] to him . . .'[68]

What makes this important – apart from the fact that Russell is here, like Sidney previously, admitting that this meeting took place – is that the meeting at Russell's house (Southampton House) was the *second* reported by Howard, not the first. According to Howard, the same six – Essex, Russell, himself, Hampden, Monmouth, Sidney – had been at both. Yet the firm implication of Russell's account is that the occasion at his house was his first encounter with that 'rogue'. This introduces the possibility that Howard either missed the first meeting or invented it; the latter supported by the conspicuously vague nature of his testimony about it at the trial. It is only for the (second?) meeting at Russell's house – for his attendance at which we have Russell's corroboration – that Howard's testimony produces any significant detail.

The likely genuine scenario was therefore as follows. Howard did indeed, by a 'trick', bring Sidney and Monmouth to meet; and he did after that (despite protest), attend one meeting between the two of them and the others (Russell, Essex, and Hampden). Thereafter, for whatever reason, he left London and took no further part in the discussions. There was, in short, a nucleus of five at this stage rather than six, and probably one meeting rather than two. This meeting was, it turned out, enough for Howard to later betray them all; but a single gathering in a private house didn't sound like a sufficiently convincing proof of a settled design. Howard was therefore persuaded to massage his evidence into a more suitably formal structure: a 'Council of Six'; and a series of meetings of which he had attended the first two.

According to Howard then, in the second half of January, and less than two weeks after bringing Sidney and Monmouth together, Sidney told him 'they had appointed a Meeting at Mr Hambden's House, and he would

---

[66] Sidney, *Apology*, pp. 14–15.
[67] Burnet, *Own Time*, pp. 342–3.
[68] Berry, *Life and Letters of Lady Russell*, pp. 218, 221.

carry me thither to the House'.[69] At the meeting he claimed that Hampden (as host) had launched into vague and general account of the design as it had been under Shaftesbury; of the present situation; and of the importance of bringing things to a head now, and soon, under this revamped leadership. All the standard ingredients of a plot were discussed – plans, arms, money – but, remarkably, people were asked to think about them and nothing was concluded. All the meeting managed to agree on was that 'the first thing to be considered was, how to make a coalition of councils between Scotland and what we were doing here; and for that purpose we should bethink ourselves of some fit person to be sent thither to unite us into one sense and care'.[70] In short the one concrete particular produced by Howard from this meeting was an anticipation of his central testimony about the next.

For it was at the 'next' meeting – probably the first – that Sidney proposed the sending of Aaron Smith to Scotland. This was at Russell's house 'two or three weeks later', that is, early to mid February. That this 'private' meeting indeed took place we have seen effectively admitted by both Sidney and Russell. According to Howard, Hampden drew the attention of the meeting rather 'warmly' to the need to define ends: to 'put the properties and liberties of the people into such hands, as they should not be easily invaded ... and it was mentioned, to resolve all into the authority of a parliament. This was moved by him, and had a little harshness to some that were there [presumably Monmouth and Russell]; but yet upon the whole matter we generally consented ... it was ... [the] public good that we all intended'.[71] After this stunning beginning the group turned to 'that which we charged ourselves with at the first meeting, and that was sending into Scotland'.[72]

There is every reason to believe (as we will see) that Sidney was indeed the prime mover behind this Scots initiative, and the high priority it was accorded in the design, though it built on the correspondence already established by Shaftesbury with Argyll. This Scots project was Sidney's follow-up to the initial approach made to him through Carstares. After his refusal to uncritically bankroll Argyll, Sidney now sought to establish his own contact directly and see if a satisfactory agreement should be reached. It was a matter of replacing the remnants of Shaftesbury's design with the apparatus and aspirations of his own.

Thus although Howard initially testified that the sending into Scotland was for the purpose of 'settling an understanding with my lord of Argyll',[73] the people actually sent to were a wider group. The project was 'to send a messenger thither to [the] ... leading men of the interest in Scotland ... the

---

[69] *The Tryal of John Hambden*, Howard's testimony.
[70] *Trial*, in Sidney, *Works*, p. 18.
[71] *Ibid.*, pp. 18–19.   [72] *Ibid.*, p. 19.   [73] *Ibid.*, p. 19.

gentlemen named were my lord Melvin, Sir John Cockram, and the Campbells; I am sure it was some of the alliance of my lord of Argyll'. This contact with 'the leading men' in Scotland echoes Sidney's interest in the same in the Savile letters in 1679. And 'As soon as this was propounded, it was offered by . . . Colonel Sydney, that he would take care of the person; and he had a person in his thoughts . . . and he named Aaron Smith to be the man who was known to some of us, to others not.'

Smith – who we have already seen denouncing 'abhorrers' to the House of Commons in 1680–1 – was the first of several of Sidney's sub-aristocratic contacts to be brought in to manage various tasks. When the Scots came to London, Wildman was to be another. A third was Richard Nelthorp, who we have seen accompanying Sidney to his by-election in Amersham in December 1680. Both Nelthorp and Smith were republican lawyers in London and Nelthorp later claimed to have recommended Smith to Sidney for this mission.[74] There may have been a more direct link however: in the 1650s, during Sidney's sojourn with the Northumberland family at Petworth, 'Aaron Smith' (this Aaron's father?) had been one of Northumberland's chief tenants.[75]

Another republican lawyer, and friend of Nelthorp's, was Robert West. According to West's later testimony, he and Nelthorp were both involved in the real 'Rye House Plot' – the design to kill the King. This, said West, was proceeding simultaneously with, but separately from the aristocratic design, even indeed in some competition with it. What information West had and later reproduced about that latter design, he received through Nelthorp's connection with Sidney. Nelthorp subsequently fled the country with Nathaniel Wade, first to the Netherlands, and then to Vevey, Switzerland, where they tried to persuade Ludlow to lead an English rising. A conversation with Sidney about old times might have saved them the trouble: Ludlow was 'no wayes disposed to the thing, saying he had done his work he thought in the World and had resolved to leave it to others'.[76] Nelthorp eventually joined Monmouth's rising in 1685 and was captured, tortured, and executed.

Smith's mission, said Howard, was to 'carry a letter' to the Scots, in particular to Sir John Cockram 'under the disguise of carrying on some business of the plantation in Carolina. The letter, I suppose, was writ by my lord Russell . . . for [Cockram] was personally known to my lord Russell'. For his part 'the duke of Monmouth undertook to bring my lord Melvin hither, because he had a particular dependance upon him'. The purpose of

---

[74] 'Robert West's . . . Confession', Add. MS 38847, p. 21; T. Sprat, *A True Account of the Horrid Conspiracy* (1685), p. 64.
[75] Lord Leconfield, *Petworth Manor in the Seventeenth Century* (Oxford 1954), p. 5.
[76] *Nathaniel Wade's Confession* (1685), BL, Harleian MS 6845, 271.

the letter was, under the same disguise of the 'business . . . in Carolina', to bring the Scots to London,

to acquaint us how they found Scotland tempered . . . what opportunities . . . there were . . . of putting them into a commotion, and how men might be raised . . . and also to keep time and place with us. After this, I was with Colonel Sydney when he was going into London, and he did take out several guineas . . . about sixty . . . which he said were to give Aaron Smith . . . and after that he was sent.[77]

Smith completed his mission successfully, writing to Sidney from Newcastle (where his presence was noted and later reported to the government) on the way.

After this meeting, Howard's testimony ends, and we pick up the thread from a later participant in the design, Lord Grey. According to Grey, he was approached by Monmouth at Chichester in late February – that is, three weeks or so after the meeting at Russell's house. Monmouth told him that Essex, Sidney, Russell, Howard, Hampden and himself were planning simultaneous English and Scots risings. He told Grey that they had arranged to meet again on his return to London, but that he feared that the group might break up, since Essex, Sidney, and Hampden seemed to intend a Commonwealth, which would mean the destruction of the King, in which case he and Russell were determined to break away, and 'hazard all at the king's feet'.[78] Monmouth asked Grey to join himself and Russell for the group to balance the numbers against the three republicans. He said that the republicans would happily be rid of Russell 'were they able to act without him'. Grey promised to think about it.

In March, Grey met Monmouth again, with Russell this time. He was told there had now been four or five meetings in total. There would be a triple rising in England – in London, Chester, and the south-west – but in a support role: the plan was for Scotland to rise first. It had been agreed that Grey could join the group and Monmouth and Russell had deliberately avoided broaching the subject of ends – the 'heads of a Declaration' – until Grey had come in. They feared that Essex and Sidney were committed to a republic, and had thought they had won Hampden over, but were now not so sure of that. They told Grey that if they couldn't get agreement to a moderate declaration drawn up by Russell's (previously Shaftesbury's) lieutenant Ferguson, they were determined to break with Sidney and Essex. Ferguson's declaration adopted a time-honoured conservative formula: the rebellion was to preserve rather than change the government, and to rescue the King from evil advisers.[79]

In late April – at which point Grey still hadn't attended a meeting –

[77] *Trial*, in Sidney, *Works*, p. 19.
[78] Ford Lord Grey, *The Secret History of the Rye House Plot* (1754), p. 42.
[79] *Ibid.*, pp. 39–40, 43–6.

Russell informed Grey that the Scots had arrived in London. They included Lord Melvin, Sir John Cockram, and some relations of Argyll. Most interestingly however, Russell informed Grey that he had 'prepared' Cockram – who, we will remember, was his particular acquaintance – 'to give such an account of the inclinations of Scotland to monarchy, as should destroy all the hopes and provokes [sic] my lord of Essex and Colonel Sidney could have to a Commonwealth'.[80]

In this way the Scots connection became caught up, from the outset, with the internal rivalries of the English group. These rivalries were, in turn, an extension of the divisions we have seen throughout the crisis. These divisions were, like everything else about this crisis, both fluid and incomplete: we have seen individuals like Wildman, and Hampden, associating with Shaftesbury as well as Sidney. Yet they remained real, and fundamental.

Monmouth and Russell set to prepare Grey for the next meeting of the 'Council', crucial now that the Scots were in town. To this end Grey was taken to the house of Colonel Rumsey, to meet and talk to Ferguson. We can see how both factions within the group – the republicans and the Shaftesburians – had their own reservoir of sub-aristocratic assistants to call on. Sidney used his – Smith, Nelthorp and Wildman (described by Burnet as 'a commonwealthsman' and 'very active under Sidney's conduct') in the management of the Scots connection; Monmouth and Russell used theirs – mainly old Shaftesburians – to try to hold the design to its more moderate, pre-1683 aims.

At Rumsey's, Grey 'found the intention was, that I should be instructed by Mr Ferguson, and furnished with arguments to encounter my lord of Essex, and Colonel Sidney, at the next meeting. Accordingly Mr Ferguson did very learnedly teach me my lesson, as colonel Rumsey can inform your Majesty [James II] . . . for he was present at the time.'[81]

The next meeting, shortly afterwards (in early May), was at Russell's house. There Grey found 'Monmouth, my lord Russel, Colonel Sidney, and Mr Hambden; my lord of Essex was expected every moment, but did not come to town till so late that evening, that we were gone'. Grey's account of Sidney's behaviour is particularly true to form, and receives important corroboration from the *Discourses*.

Colonel Sidney addressing his discourse to me, began with a long prologue, of the necessity we were reduced to, of taking up of arms [compare Sidney to Hampden: 'Noblemen, Cittyes . . . have often taken armes . . . to defend themselves, when they were prosecuted upon the account of religion'], and of the lawfulness of it. ['It is not only the law of the land, but the eternall Law of nature, that permits such as are invaded to defend themselves.'][82]

[80] *Ibid.*, p. 47.   [81] *Ibid.*, p. 50.
[82] *Ibid.*, p. 51; see pp. 265, 275 above.

He summarised the group's earlier proceedings, and then 'went forward to this purpose'.[83]

That he looked upon a rising in Scotland to be of infinite advantage and security to us, both as it would give a diversion, and be a place of retreat for us if we met with ill success in England; that the oppressions there were so grievous, that (as he was inform'd) the hearts of all the common people were set upon an insurrection to shake off their yokes ... that if we did not assist them ... they would miscarry, as at Bothwell-bridge, which might be fatal to us also[;] that no men of quality or interest, who had common understanding [a very Sidney expression], would undertake such an affair, without a provision of arms ... which the gentry of Scotland, being poor, were not able to make, and therefore we must assist them with money ... that my lord Argyll ... had undertaken with ten thousand pounds to furnish himself in Holland with sufficient provision for the war; that they ... had sent into Scotland to some considerable men of that kingdom to come to London, that there might be a conjunction of counsels, in order to the ... carrying on the war in both kingdoms; and that those gentlemen were come to town ... and had given so good an account of their country, that the success of an insurrection was not to be doubted. That our preparations in England were in a great forwardness, my lord Russel having been industrious about the Western rising, and others for one in London; and ... for Cheshire, the duke of Monmouth had undertaken to engage my lord Macclesfield, lord Brandon, and Mr. Booth ... [only] the Scotch design moved slowly, because it required a sum of money, without which it would end in nothing but the destruction of those poor people ... therefore it was his opinion we take immediately into our consideration the manner of raising money ...[84]

This Grey called Sidney's 'history and his reasons upon the several heads of it (which I have cut as short as I can)'.[85] Both in content and style it is vintage Algernon, with its emphasis on (and sympathy with) Scotland, and its arguments for 'insurrection' and 'war'.

As counselled, Grey responded to this lecture by assuming Sidney 'had forgot to acquaint me with the heads of their Declaration, which I supposed was already drawn. He answered, No, there was none drawn that he knew of, but he thought we were of one mind.' Grey 'hoped so ... [but] desired, before we entered upon the thoughts of raising money, we might consider a Declaration'.[86] At this:

Colonel Sidney muttered to himself some time, and truly what he said I know not; all I could distinctly hear was, that my lord of Essex and my lord Howard not being there, it was not a proper time to talk of a Declaration; but if we would have his opinion of one; he thought we must tell the world how the King had broken the laws and his own oath, and secure the settlement of the kingdom to a parliament, which if we were successful would know how to provide for the safety of themselves and the people.[87]

Once again both the content of this passage – the argument of the *Dis-*

[83] Grey, *Secret History*, p. 51.
[84] *Ibid.*, pp. 51–3.   [85] *Ibid.*, p. 54.
[86] *Ibid.*, p. 54.   [87] *Ibid.*, p. 55.

courses – and Sidney's eccentric behaviour when confronted with a recalcitrant colleague – are notably true to life. His 'muttering to himself some time' reminds us of his confrontation with Montague in 1659 when he 'leaned in the window by himself apart, in a discontented manner' and then 'walked about the room with Mon Slingerland, alone discoursing'.[88]

Grey's response to all this seems, given the nature of the meeting, politically rather ludicrous, and his confession may have been adjusted at this point for James' benefit. Grey hoped Sidney 'was not out of Charity with the King and government, that he had not mentioned the preservation of either; and that tho' there had been that failure of justice in the administration of it . . . yet that was not the defect of the constitution, nor did it lie directly upon the King to answer for it'. Grey argued that it was the king's ministers only who were culpable, and that he 'thought the King a good and merciful prince ill advised, and the government the best in the world'; in short, the object of the rising should be 'a happy accommodation, between the King and his people'. At this point, recorded Grey, not only Russell and Monmouth, but Hampden too 'who had been silent all this while . . . declared they were all of my opinion'.[89]

At this level of provocation Sidney, who must have been rueing Essex's late arrival, displayed what for him was the patience of a saint. In 1659, much lesser provocation from Montague had produced the opinion that 'he . . . deserve[d] to lose his head'.[90] On this occasion he said only that '*he had heard, when wise men draw their swords against their King, they laid aside the thoughts of treating with him*; but he would talk no more of that matter since we were all of one mind'. This must be compared with the *Discourses*, at a point where Sidney was speaking of 'mischiefs . . . past all possibility of being cured by any other way than force. And such as are by necessity driven to use that remedy [compare Sidney's earlier speech: 'the necessity we are reduced to, of taking up arms'] know they must perfect their work or perish. *He that draws his sword against his prince, say the French, ought to throw away the scabbard.*'[91]

At this juncture, the discussion turned to the role and powers of a 'General'. Sidney argued (against Grey) that the Council, rather than any General, ought to retain direction of the overall design. But he also said 'he knew but of one General we could have, and that was the duke of Monmouth, whose conduct or integrity he did not doubt . . . but if he might advise him, he should go to Scotland . . . there he would get good footing, be

[88] Scott, *Sidney and the English Republic*, p. 134.
[89] Grey, *Secret History*, p. 56. This account of Hampden's relatively loyal political inclinations may owe more to his availability for punishment in this year (1685) than to historical reality. No such constraints applied in the case of Sidney and Essex.
[90] Scott, *Sidney and the English Republic*, p. 134.
[91] Sidney, *Discourses*, p. 186.

at the head of a conquering army, and then might treat with his father, for that was all he found us inclined to. I told him [said Grey] I would give the duke of Monmouth the same advice, if I desired never more to see him in England'.[92] Russell and Hampden then argued that Monmouth was needed for the western rising, 'so that put an end to colonel Sidney's proposals'. It had been a bad day.

Yet thereafter, added Grey, 'we had many discourses more tedious (if possible) than those I have related'. These seem, by sheer attrition, to have miraculously rescued some of Sidney's agenda. For the meeting finally concluded that 'we should chiefly apply ourselves to the affair of Scotland, till it was dispatched'; that the Declaration and way to raise money should be the business of the next meeting: 'that the ten thousand pounds should be lent to my lord Argyll with all speed, that, if possible, the Scotch rising might begin before the end of June'. The plan was then for a messenger to 'come from Scotland (as soon as ever they were in arms)' to trigger the English rising.[93]

In short, despite being quite outnumbered, and by displaying, on the surface, a quite uncharacteristic preparedness to back down, Sidney appears to have gained both of his principal points. It is clear that Sidney's priority was Scotland; his colleagues, on the other hand, were more interested in the English rising. Secondly, Sidney had succeeded in postponing the drafting of the Declaration until Essex at least should be present – though given the mathematics of the group he would probably have preferred to postpone it permanently. One must therefore deeply admire the way he subsequently handled this problem.

At the next meeting (ten days later) Grey could not be present – he received an account from Monmouth and Russell. They reported with the greatest satisfaction that the meeting had agreed on a Declaration 'which would be to our minds, and *that my lord Essex and colonel Sidney had undertaken to draw it*' (my emphasis). In short, outnumbered and impotent on this matter, Sidney and Essex had taken the brilliant rearguard action of offering no opposition, and thereby taking over the whole operation. This put both the timing and (to a lesser extent) the wording of the piece in their hands. In particular it gave them the capacity to delay it while practical measures continued.

Meanwhile the collection of money for Argyll went ahead, as far as possible through the group itself. Poor Monmouth gushed: 'he found my lord of Essex, colonel Sidney, and all of them, should agree in everything; and he was confident that when . . . the king saw how strong we were . . . there would be little blood.'[94]

[92] Grey, *Secret History*, pp. 57–8.   [94] *Ibid.*, pp. 59, 61.
[93] *Ibid.*, pp. 57–8.

This, in early to mid May, is the last 'Council' meeting of which we have information. But at the same time, the council's representatives were conducting the negotiations with the Scots in London. Once again we find 'Coll. Sidney' – this time assisted by 'Major Wildman', 'had the management of this business'. As we have seen Monmouth and Russell had already attempted to predetermine the outcome through Cockram. This was a mistake, and the result was disastrous. According to Robert West:

At last they came to . . . Terms . . . and came down at last to £5,000, and the Earl of Argyle was to Head them . . . but when Mr Ferguson paid me for the Arms, he told me, the Scots business was quite off, and Wildman and Sidney had done ill with the Scots; for after they had kept them, and treated with them Two or three Months, they broke off because the Scots would not declare a Commonwealth the first hour, and Extirpating of Monarchy, and the Family of the Stewarts, and that the Scots Answer was, That would be to Destroy all their Interest among the Lords; and Providence might order it so, as to bring it to a Commonwealth, but that was a business of time.[95]

Insofar as this account exhibits Ferguson's usual exaggeration, and rivalry with Sidney (inherited from Shaftesbury), it should not be taken for a balanced account of the proceedings. What it does illustrate is that the division between Sidneian and Shaftsburian factions of 'opposition' to the court was as wide in June 1683 as it had been in June 1680. It may be that it had already destroyed the design, just before its discovery in late June. For the negotiations with the Scots were broken off 'that [very] week the Plot was discovered'.[96] Sidney's last insurrectionary enterprise had perished from the same disease as its predecessors.

---

[95] Testimony of West at 'The Tryal of Captain Walcot', in *The Tryals of Thomas Walcot, William Hone, William Lord Russell, John Rous, and William Blagg for High-Treason* (1683), p. 16.
[96] 'The Trial of William Lord Russell' in *ibid.*, p. 38.

13

The Tower

I cannot have an assurance of my own constancy ... but I hope God will not abandon me. If he be with me, I shall not feare the face of man, and I doe from my hart desire and pray that I may be able so far to resigne my self unto his will, as not to retaine so much as an inclination of choosing [my fate] for myself. *This for me is the highest end I can observe.* [I]f I can attaine unto it, I shall be at rest, in Life, as in death. I wish the same for you, and desire that they whoe pray for us, may direct their prayers unto this end.   (Sidney to Hampden, 6 Oct. 1683)

13.1 DISCOVERY

'The Plot was discovered' in the second half of June, but the government had been closely monitoring the situation, and the potential for arrests, well before that. Sidney later said that 'In April last I was told by a person of eminent quality ... that I should infallibly be made a prisoner ... [that] somme [pretence] or other would be found; and that if I was once taken, it mattered not for what cause: it being impossible to avoide condemnation, before such judges and juryes as I should be tried by.'[1]

The 'person of eminent quality' may have been Gilbert Hollis, the Earl of Clare, a good friend of Sidney's at this time who was to be a defence witness at his trial. On 31 March Richard Stretton had written to a friend from London that the country was now full of government informers, and that any two witnesses would do to convict someone of treason. 'There is a villain, that was tenant to the Earl of Clare ... that the other week, with another such knave he had engaged, went down to Newmarket [where the king was] and swore high treason against the Earl of Clare and his steward, and Colonel Algernon Sydney and myself, and two more; and no less than killing the king and altering the government.'[2] According to Stretton the government had chosen not to act on this information immediately, but their 'keeping it so long on foot, shows they have no mind to part with it, but would fain lick it into some handsome form'.[3] The informant was

---

[1] Sidney, *Apology*, pp. 4–5.
[2] Ralph Thoresby, *Letters of Eminent Men*, vol. I, p. 23.
[3] *Ibid.*, p. 24.

292

Rejoice Fox, who deposed before Sunderland that the Earl of Clare's steward came to him 'in May or June last, and then hired him in the Earl's name and by his Order to kill the king ... Mr Alger[non] Sidney and another or two are touched upon in the evidence'.[4] Fox was driven to petition secretary Jenkins in April for protection 'against the Earl of Clare, Mr Cawthorne, Mr Stretton, Mr Smith [Aaron?], and Mr Sidney, against whom he made depositions at Newmarket', he having had a 'multitude raised against him' for being an 'Informing Dog against the Lord of Clare'.[5]

While all this is evidence that Sidney was a marked man, the informant who really set the ball rolling was Josiah Keeling, a minor conspirator and acquaintance of Rumsey and West, who visited Whitehall on 12 June.[6] On 20 June the King issued warrants for the arrest of West and Rumsey, who surrendered themselves on 23 and 25 June respectively.[7] These two in turn related not only their own activities but what they had heard second hand about the aristocratic council and its design. West's source of information was, as we have seen Nelthorp, and also Goodenough; Rumsey's was West; Keeling's was Goodenough.[8] These accounts gave a by now deeply insecure government what it needed; the occasion to arrest everybody in sight.

Unsurprisingly, the first person on that list was Sidney. Warrants of commitment to the Tower for treason were issued for Sidney on 25 June, Russell on 26 June, Wildman on 28 June, Aaron Smith on 5 July, Hampden on 9 July, Essex on 10 July.[9] Barillon reported Wildman's arrest on 12 July, describing him, like Burnet, as 'confident et intime amy du Colonel Sidney' and 'un republiquain declaré'.[10] By 9 July also Howard – who according to Russell, had 'change[d] colour' when West surrendered himself and 'confessed, he had been as free with him as with any man' – was taken in his house. After a long search, Burnet recorded, 'he was found standing up within a chimney. As soon as he was taken, he fell acrying: and at his first examination he told ... all that he knew'.[11] Monmouth went into hiding, and other more seasoned conspirators, including Ferguson, Armstrong, Nelthorp and Wade, succeeded in fleeing the country.[12]

According to Sidney

About the middell of June the towne was full of rumors of a plot sayd to be

[4] Dr Williams Library London. Roger Morrice'e Entering Book, vol. I, p. 362.
[5] *CSPD* 1683 Jan.–June, p. 220; PRO, State Papers 29/424, no. 17.
[6] Walker, 'The Republican Party', p. 282.
[7] Milne, 'The Rye House Plot', p. 122.
[8] *Trial* in Sidney, *Works*, pp. 13–16.
[9] *CSPD* 1683, Jan.–June, p. 385.
[10] PRO Baschet no. 155, p. 393.
[11] Burnet, *Own Time*, p. 361.
[12] Howard's Examination, PRO State Papers 29/428, p. 33.

discovered by Keeling, and not long after by West. Some persons fled . . . My name was in every coffee-house, and several informations were given me, that I should certainely be seased . . . but knowing no raison [sic] why I should absent myself, I resolved not to do it . . . though I was told, early in the morning on the 26th of June, that the duke of Monmouth was retired, and Colonel Rumsey had rendered himself. This concerned me so littell, that I spent that morning upon my usual studyes, or entertaining such friends as came to see me; and, whilest I was at diner, a messenger came and arrested me in the king's name.[13]

This is exactly the sort of stoic *sang-froid* Sidney earlier attributed to Vane.

For an account of the arrest we have both Sidney's *Apology* and the testimony of his servant Ducasse. It was Ducasse who safeguarded the *Apology* after Sidney's execution, reappearing with it in 1689.[14] Immediately after Sidney's arrest, which was 'about One of the Clock',[15] Sir Philip Lloyd came with an order to seize his papers. After searching the house he took, in the end, '[only] such as lay openly upon my table, or in a trunck that had not been shut in somme years'.[16] These included the manuscript of the *Discourses*, upon which work was possibly continuing 'upon my table' that day.

Although what became the extracts read at Sidney's trial were never to be reunited with the rest of the text, it does seem to have been the entire manuscript that Lloyd confiscated. It was later described by Serjeant Rotheram, defence counsel at Sidney's trial, as a 'Book . . . by Way of Questions, and merely about a Discourse of Government in general, as far as he could find, after several Hours reading in it, for he believes it consisted of about Seven or Eight Hundred Sheets'.[17] Lloyd asked Sidney to seal the trunk before its removal; a request which Sidney refused, an early sign of the non-cooperation that was to become a rule. Rather oddly Lloyd informed the government on 6 July that he had 'found amongst Col. Sydney's papers nothing but articles of an association',[18] though Barillon reported six days later: 'they found among the papers of Colonel Sidney some writings in his hand against monarchy in general and in favour of a republic'.[19]

From his house Sidney was taken before four lords of the privy council at Whitehall for examination. Their questions – put by Lord Keeper North – were based on the informations of Keeling, Goodenough and West; Sidney was therefore asked if he knew of any planned insurrection; if he knew Aaron Smith; if he had sent Smith to Scotland; if Smith's mission had been

---

[13] Sidney, *Apology*, p. 5.
[14] House of Lords MSS, Comm[itt]ee Book, vol. IV, 1688–90, p. 324.
[15] *Journals of the House of Lords*, Testimony of Ducasse, 1689, p. 390.
[16] Sidney, *Apology*, p. 5.
[17] *JHL*, 1688, 'testimony of Rotheram', p. 391.
[18] *CSPD* 1683, July–Sept., p. 57.
[19] PRO Baschet no. 155, p. 395.

to summon Cockrane, the Campbells and Monroe; and so on.[20] To these questions Sidney later claimed in his *Apology* 'I returned answeares with all the respect I could, without prejudice unto the truth ... [but] when I thought that I had given full satisfaction, was taken into the custody of a serjeant at armes ... [and] committed to the Tower for high-treason.'[21] In fact however 'the questions ... being distinctly read ... and his answer ... demanded ... [Sidney] excused himself with saying 'That he conceives that he ought not to answer to them untill He knows His charge and His accusers.'[22] In Burnet's account this became that Sidney 'said, he must make the best defence he could, if they had any proof against him: but he would not fortify their evidence by any thing he should say'.[23]

Sidney was later to complain – again echoed by Burnet – that (since Howard was not arrested until a week later) his committal at this time was without direct evidence and so against law. Yet the hearsay evidence from Keeling, Goodenough and West was all the government needed to determine that Sidney must be detained. Throughout his subsequent ordeal Sidney was to highlight the manifold injuries to 'justice' entailed by this political imperative. Yet such injuries had been characteristic of the crisis as a whole, and Sidney had not complained when the prosecuting agents had been his friends Waller and Jones. He had, however, drawn the line at the Irish informers used to destroy Oliver Plunket, Archbishop of Armagh, in 1681 – referring to them in the *Discourses* as 'rogues'.[24]

Technically speaking, not only was Sidney's committal against law, but his subsequent indictment arraigned him for a treason committed on 30 June, by which time he had already been in custody for four days. Such technicalities, however, were overridden from the beginning by a determination to bring Sidney to political, if not legal, 'justice'. York had always regarded him as dangerous; Charles, bitterly regretting his earlier clemency, now determined to rescind it. This fixity of royal purpose was something which Sidney, like Shaftesbury before him, underestimated. While the remorseful Russell's trial and execution followed quickly, however, for Sidney the government both lacked the requisite two witnesses, and faced a much more defiant defendant. They began a sustained effort to build a case against him, and Sidney began a sustained wait in the Tower.

On 5 July Henry Ingoldsby was examined. He said that he had seen 'Col. A. Sidney not long before he was taken, and dined with him. He took the air with him sometimes alone'. But he testified that he knew nothing of any design. On the same day one Samuel Starkey, 'late Clerk to Aaron Smith' testified that Smith had met with Dr Harrington, brother of Sir James

---

[20] PRO, State Papers 29/427, p. 118; *CSPD* 1683, Jan.–June, 364.
[21] Sidney, *Apology*, pp. 5–6.   [22] PRO, State Papers 29/427, p. 122.
[23] Burnet, *Own Time*, p. 356.   [24] Sidney, *Discourses*, p. 121.

Harrington the old republican MP, and Thomas Haselrig, 'kinsman of Sir Arthur'.[25] He said Smith had described the king's 'illimitable prerogatives' as an affront to English liberty: 'that the king and his cursed Councill were papists in their hearts, that they were resolved to destroy all Old English Liberty and totally extirpate ye Gospels of Christ. That it was high time to Arme themselves agt such horrid designes and regaine their Late Lost Rights and Priviledges'.[26] He said that 'the old King [Charles I] deserved his death' for associating with priests and jesuits, 'and that the king exactly followed his Father's steps and would assuredly receive his fate'.[27] Smith was arrested the same day, and was invited, to save himself, to 'discover what you know agst . . . this Rogue Sydney'. He declined, and was to remain in the Tower for some time.[28]

In addition to the crucial testimony of Howard, given on 9 July, the government received further hearsay evidence implicating Sidney from other sources: on 6 July Colonel Rumsey testified that Ferguson had told him about a 'project of Col. Sidneys, the counties to elect sheriffs, militia in the parliament etc'.[29] He claimed that Goodenough had been in correspondence with Sidney, 'about getting men in London' and other matters. On 8 July Thomas Walcott provided further second-hand testimony via the voluble Ferguson, mentioning both Sidney and Ludlow in connection with a design involving not only England and Scotland but Ireland as well. He testified that Wade, West, Nelthorp, Rumsey, Ferguson, and Colonel Norton – presumably the same Colonel Norton with whom Sidney had worked on naval administration under the Republic – used to meet together.[30] (Norton, along with Sidney's other friend Sir Charles Wolsely, had married one of Lord Saye and Sele's daughters.)[31]

On 9 July Hampden was also examined and brought to admit that in the past Monmouth and Russell had both been at his house together 'and that A Sydney might be there too',[32] and that he used to frequently visit Russell. He couldn't remember if Howard had been there. On 10 July Essex said that he knew nothing, but confessed that he did visit Russell when Monmouth was there; and that 'A Sydney might visit Lord Russell at the same time'.[33] He used, also, to visit Hampden.

In late August or early July secretary Jenkins ordered that 'Mr Sydney's

[25] *CSPD*, July–Sept., p. 42.
[26] PRO, State Papers 29/427, p. 99.
[27] *CSPD*, July–Sept., p. 42.
[28] House of Lords MSS, Comm. Book, vol. IV, 1688–9, pp. 329–30.
[29] *CSPD*, July–Sept., p. 56.
[30] *Ibid.*, p. 70; S.R. Gardiner and C.T. Atkinson (eds.), *Letters and Papers relating to the First Dutch War 1652–4*, vol. III (1906), p. 422.
[31] Ward, 'The English Peerage', p. 171, n.1.
[32] *CSPD*, July–Sept. 1683, p. 79.
[33] *Ibid.*, p. 90.

papers' be sent 'to Mr Attorney, that an indictment be framed on the passages. Mr Graham to see who can prove his hand'.[34] This was followed on 2 September by the note: 'Mr Shephard [the wine-merchant] to prove Col. Sydney's hand by himself and others'.[35] Meanwhile, Sidney's work had apparently become so current at court that when the 'libel of the Black box' (actually by Ferguson) was found in Shepherd's house the Duke of York, for whom its argument was a particularly sore point, opined that 'by the style and argument one might guess [it] to be [by] Algernon Sydney'.[36] Two weeks later, and still trying, the council ordered: 'The paper of Association to be found out and compared with Algernon Sydney's Book'.

Finally, and most ominously, the government began to assemble a dossier on Sidney's earlier treasons. Though he had been pardoned, in 1677, for all acts done before that date, that pardon was part of a contract which Sidney had not kept. A council note recorded, probably in September:

Things that may be proved. That Col Algernon Sidney with Gen Ludlow and Col. Ellison treated with the States General in John de Witte's time for mounting a rebellion in England, for which design they demanded . . . £200,000 and forty sailes of ships, saying they had 40,000 men ready to rise at their landing. This treaty was held at Ambassador Newport's house in a small island beyond Schiedam and young Herr Newport has but this last year showed Mr ____ the diamond ring Co. Sidney gave him for being their friend to the three deputies, the Pensioner de Witte . . . and old Newport, who was Ambassador at London in the time of the late rebellion. The reasons may likewise be proved on which the designs took no effect.[37]

This information was never used, but it may be taken as a reflection of the government's determination. The shadow of Sidney's past was beginning to close over him.

13.2 'MR SIDNEY HIS SELF-CONVICTION'[38]

We have seen that Sidney's activities in this year, like his writing, were in many ways a repetition of those of the mid 1660s. Now his incarceration in the Tower returned him to the experience of exile. If the exile on this occasion was internal rather than external; if the impassable barrier was stone rather than water; it nevertheless, over the next five months, reproduced a series of the same effects. From the same consequent feelings of loneliness, victimisation and deprivation there emerged, in time, the same self-righteousness, the same catalogue of the world's crimes against him, the same complaints. If Sidney was eventually to produce the consummate

---

[34] *Ibid.*, p. 233.
[35] *CSPD*, Oct.–April, pp. 83–4 (p. 49).
[36] *CSPD*, July–Sept., p. 366.
[37] *Ibid.*
[38] *Mr Sidney his Self-conviction, Or, his Dying Paper Condemned to Live* (1684).

martyrdom from this situation it was partly because he had spent so much of his life in training for it.

At the heart of this famous last act in Sidney's story there lies an essential irony. In the short term, and in their political context, Sidney's efforts (to free himself) were a failure. His performances in this period, both on paper and at his trial, were not his finest. He showed his age. He repeatedly sought refuge from his situation in labyrinths of largely irrelevant detail, and at his trial these became a forest in which he himself became lost. Semi-oblivious to the disaster by which they had been overtaken, Sidney repeated the same cases, claims and concerns with extravagant monotony between his letters to Hampden, trial, two petitions, *Apology*, and *Last Paper*. None of these efforts slowed his passage to the scaffold, though it is not clear that anything could have done so. The crown's determination to execute some species of 'justice' on Sidney never wavered, and Jeffreys showed himself determined to do whatever was necessary to this end. A considerable force had at last encountered its immovable object. Sidney was not a martyred innocent – he was locked here into a political (rather than judicial) battle in which he had met his match. Yet the crown's victory was exceedingly expensive, and perhaps pyrrhic.

This political defeat, terminally costly though it was for Algernon, is only part of the story of these months. Given the near legal *fait accompli*, what counted was less Sidney's practical effectiveness than his personal behaviour in the face of such overwhelming odds. This was a role in which he was uniquely qualified to triumph, and at an early stage he deliberately set out to do so. His victory was sufficient to considerably discomfit his tormentors at the time, and to damn them forever in the eyes of posterity. If Sidney's trial was, technically speaking, a piece of most 'enormous injustice', it was no different in this respect from any of the other (popish) plot trials, upon which it was modelled. What was different was that it was the first to be 'universally cryed out upon' as such, *at the time*. As Burnet put it 'The scandale of this Tryall was so gross yt I never met with a man yt offerd to defend it.'[39] This overwhelming victory in the field of public relations has remained largely unchallenged to this day.[40]

It occurred because this ordeal put Sidney back, for the last time, in the role for which he had received a lifetime's training. It was that of wronged and persecuted innocent, struggling (for liberty, for legality, for rights) in the face of an unjust world. This role had been framed by Sidney's birth, re-

---

[39] Burnet, BL, Add. MS 63,058, vol. II, p. 158.
[40] An exception is G.W. Keeton, *Lord Chancellor Jeffreys and the Stuart Cause* (1965), pp. 272–7. Keeton holds that by the legal conventions of the day Jeffreys has been unfairly maligned. Sidney is to be congratulated for doing something to change those conventions, prompting new legislation on the evidence required for treason trials after 1688.

imposed by his exile, and was now re-confirmed by his arrest. By the yardstick of merit, of virtue, of the rewards owing to natural (rather than artificial) inequality, Sidney had been born deprived. He had been re-deprived in 1660, and now again in 1683. After a lifetime of struggle to achieve an entangled personal as well as political justice, Sidney was not about to surrender his sense of that 'justice' to a mere public judicial tribunal. On the contrary, he would judge that 'tribunal' by it, and issue a series of publications in which the entire judicial apparatus of the state stood indicted for treason against Sidney's personal understanding of the law, and vision of justice. His *Apology* in particular is a counter-trial, written after, and approximately the same length as, the *Trial* itself. In it Jeffreys (a 'furious' drunk), his judicial assistants ('blemishes to the bar'), the jury ('meane inconsiderable fellows'), the political nation as a whole and eventually the entire 'age' are arraigned and condemned for hounding an innocent man to his death. What is extraordinary is that it was the verdict of this inversion – of Sidney's counter-trial, not of the trial itself – that was accepted by posterity. It was to this feat of inversion that Halifax referred when he said of Sidney's trial: 'Westminster Hall might be said to stand upon its head ... when the reason of him that pleads is visibly too strong for those who are to judge and give sentence.'[41]

For Sidney then, his ordeal was not about a particular (legal) innocence, about securing a particular (legal) justice, about avoiding a particular (legal) conviction. He was not, after all, innocent in these terms. It was about a larger innocence, a larger injustice, and a *self*-conviction that transcended these particular circumstances. It was this 'Mr Sidney his self-conviction' which proved deeply and securely enough rooted to triumph not only over these circumstances, but eventually (by 1689) over that conviction itself.[42] At no stage during this five-month period did Sidney's burning sense of this wider innocency falter in the face of his (actual) legal guilt. If the law of the land described his actions (the defence of the innocent; the defence of the oppressed) as treason then that law was an instrument of tyranny and to be disregarded. When positive law (the laws of man) so contradicted Truth and Justice (the laws of God) then it was not to be obeyed. 'We live in an age', as he said on the scaffold, 'that makes Truth pass for Treason.' No mere public conviction for treason would shake Sidney's private conviction in Truth. Accordingly, while Essex cut his own throat in the Tower, Sidney rehearsed to Hampden the essential justice of their actions; while Russell remorsefully

[41] Foxcroft, *Life and Letters of George Savile*, vol. II, pp. 285–6.
[42] Sidney's conviction was overturned by act of parliament (the Act for Annulling and Making Void the Attainder of Algernon Sidney esq.) on 11 May 1689. See HMC Rep. House of Lords MSS App. pt. 6, p. 96; and *Lords Journal* XIV, 189, 209. The Act was reprinted by G.W. Meadley in *Memoirs of Algernon Sidney* (1813), pp. 398–400.

confessed his sins on the scaffold, Sidney handed over a paper to the executioner justifying himself to the world. If the crown can be forgiven for deciding that the only thing to do with such a man was to execute him, Sidney has to be admired for causing them so much damage in the process.

It would be wrong to describe this conviction as simply personal, or 'autobiographical'. As the preceding chapters have attempted to make clear, Sidney was acting on the most fervently held political beliefs. Life had no meaning for Sidney if one couldn't, and shouldn't, distinguish between good and evil, between justice and injustice, and *fight* for the advancement of good. It was in this respect that he called God, in November 1683, to be 'the protector of my innocence'. He was sure that such behaviour was not only authorised by, but in some sense of God, 'the author of all that is good'. It was on these grounds also that he assured Hampden that they had done nothing unworthy of 'the Character of a gentleman, and a Christian'.[43] Experience had shown that in a wicked world such advancement could never be achieved by 'disallowing the use of force, without which justice cannot be protected, nor innocency maintained'.

Moreover if Sidney, having lived by the sword, now faced the prospect of dying by it, he faced it absolutely squarely. He did so because he had the courage of his convictions, and had not hesitated to put them into practice. His political beliefs thus lay at the centre of his predicament and achievement in 1683. What this biographical background helps to explain is their personal rootedness – their autobiographical grip – and so the particular and defiant resilience of those beliefs in the face of disaster. Behind 'Sidney's Cause', anchored in his ancestry, there was also 'Mr Sidney, his Self-Conviction'.

We have seen the teeth of this self-conviction bared to the world once before. This was at the beginning of his last exile, in 1660.[44] Now, as then, this defiance of the world (and law) of man could only locate itself in a deepening emotional relationship with God. Then Sidney had steadied himself with the thought that as God's (doubtless imperfect) creature he was nevertheless only answerable for his actions to God. Now he went further and set about resigning himself from 'the world of man' altogether. The quote at the head of this chapter gives some sense of the process, and of the power it gave him. While it was, of course, a way of rationalising, or coping with, the present situation, its effect was genuinely transforming. Thus it was in his darkest moment that Sidney finally achieved the certainty and calm, and with it the liberty, which had evaded him throughout his life. It

---

[43] East Sussex Record Office, Lewes; Glynde Place Archives no. 794, ten letters from Algernon Sidney (nine to John Hampden), hereafter referred to as the 'Hampden Letters', letter 4, 6 Oct., p. 6.

[44] Scott, *Sidney and the English Republic*, ch. 9.

was through this internal (and no external political) process that he at last attained an 'independency' from the human will – that of himself, and that of others. This was an independence from the blows of fortune, from 'so much as an inclination of choosing for myself'. It was in the Tower, and on the scaffold, that Sidney was finally able to free himself, and to rule himself – to achieve self-government. It was only when control of his life was lost that he was able to take control.

The story of the remaining chapters, then, is that of the triumph of this inner Sidney over his outer circumstances. In the process he achieved a transformation of temperament which 'amazed all that went to him'.[45] It is this process that makes Sidney's letters to Hampden so attractive, with their assurance, their strength, their generosity and warmth. It was this transformed Sidney who so impressed contemporaries and laid the foundation for the mythology to come.

Some of these saintly qualities were actual inversions of his own character – with its impatience, its petulance, its violence and its self-concern. But they emerged from a turbulent lifetime seen as a struggle between 'contraries'. They were a final victory in the struggle of a born tyrant to achieve liberty, and of an imperfect human being to find God. And the death which followed was a genuine sacrifice for the right to distinguish between good and evil in the world, and fight for that distinction. For all of these reasons the immortality it won him was a legitimate resolution (if not reflection) of his life, and it was appropriate that a self-conviction so impervious to place should prove equally impervious to time.

13.3 THE HAMPDEN LETTERS

'EXTREME RIGOUR'

I was kept with the most extreame rigour, to the great prejudice of my health, and almost destruction of my life, without any consolation from my friends, untill a few dayes before my trial.[46]

The first effect of Sidney's political indisposition was, as in 1660, that his goods and his beloved horses became a prey to others. In mid July he directed the first of several petitions to the King, complaining that

since his imprisonment persons pretending ... an order from his Majesty have seized several bills of exchange belonging to your petitioner in the hands of Thomas Shepheard, merchant, and also his horses with all the money and goods remaining in his house, and that none of his friends or domestics being suffered to come to him, he knows not what spoil they make, and therefore praying that his goods and bills be restored and his domestics suffered to come to him about his private affairs.[47]

[45] Burnet, *Own Time*, vol. II, p. 341.   [46] Sidney, *Apology*, p. 6.
[47] *CSPD*, July–Sept., p. 141.

A satisfactory response to this request Sidney owed to Halifax. Ducasse recorded that Sidney's

Goods both in Town and Country were seized, to his very Wearing Cloaths, that his servants had not the Liberty to carry him Linen to Change ... and I knowing that the Marquis of Hallifax was his kinsman, I applied myself to him, and by his Means obtained Relief from some of those Grievances; and had the Liberty to visit Colonel Sydney during his imprisonment.[48]

On 17 July the government ordered that 'Colonel Sydney ... name what servants he would have to look after his estate ... His estate and goods not to be meddled with'.[49] Ducasse was 'admitted to wait on his master as often as he shall desire at seasonable times in the presence of a warder'.[50] Later an investigation was made into whether money had been removed from Sidney's house. One source said £14,000 had been removed, but this wasn't followed up – if it were true, its purpose cannot have been legitimate, and Sidney made no attempt to pursue the matter.[51] Meanwhile, however, Sidney's horses were found, and Thomas Shepherd was ordered 'to deliver to Algernon Sydney ... all bills of exchange ... payable to the said Sydney'.[52] These are presumably the bills Sidney was to give in late November to a friend.

Throughout the remainder of his imprisonment, Sidney was visited regularly by Ducasse. He also received information, and by September some visits, from others. Meanwhile his house was put under guard by the bailiff of Westminster, and Ducasse had to seek access to it subject to this supervision. In August he complained that 'the guard ... becomes more insolent every day and today when I wished to take a horse for Mr Sydney's service ... one of the guard told me he had orders not to allow me to take anything. I asked to see this order, whereupon he gave me a great blow on the head saying, There's the order.'[53]

The first three months of Sidney's imprisonment must have been lonely, disturbed by Russell's execution and particularly by Essex's suicide. Yet he was furnished by Ducasse with the necessaries of life, and among these was pen and paper, for in September (at the latest) he began writing to his fellow prisoner John Hampden.

'A GENTLEMAN AND A CHRISTIAN' (LETTERS 1–2)

Wee are borne gentlemen: Professe to be Christians, and whether wee dye sooner or Later, together or asunder, I hope god will soe direct and uphold us that wee shall

---

[48] *Journal of the House of Lords* (1689), p. 390.
[49] *CSPD*, July–Sept., p. 147.
[50] *Ibid.*, p. 214.   [51] *Ibid.*, p. 191.
[52] *Ibid.*, p. 214.   [53] *Ibid.*, p. 343.

never doe anything, which doth not agree with the Character of gentleman and Christian. (Sidney to Hampden, 6 October[54])

Sidney's letters to Hampden interweave preparation for his trial with a range of revealing observations, both personal and political. They are among the most important and attractive of his letters to survive. They turned up recently in the East Sussex Record Office at Lewes, and were not known to his nineteenth-century biographers.

The letters reveal in detail Sidney's preparation for his trial. We find him reading previous treason trials (of Strafford, Vane, and Lilburne) to be clear about precedents; and examining the treason statutes, to be clear about what had to be proved to indict him on any one of them. The accent of these preparations was on a particularity which was, in the event, to be swept away. Sidney acknowledged this possibility; yet while dismissing the reality of his treason in a larger (moral) sense, he became determined to fight the crown doggedly on its own ground: that of the treason law. This was characteristic of Sidney the relativist: fighting his opponents with whatever weapons were to hand, their own in particular.

Equally noticeable is the realism, and consequent predictive powers, Sidney displayed about his own trial. Here we need only remember his own earlier role as patron to the sheriff (Bethel) and colleague of the Attorney General (Jones) under the politicised London judiciary of 1679–81.[55] But Sidney also had access to information about the trials of Russell and others. By the end of July these had resulted in four executions (of Russell, Walcot, Rouse and Hone). Sidney may have been owning this whole group – or perhaps only Russell and Essex – when he spoke to Hampden in September of 'us, and our friends that are dead'.[56]

In his first letter, written in mid-to-late September, Sidney congratulated Hampden for studying 'the Lawe', and assured him that he was too. 'I do already see enough' he continued,

to assure me of a good issue if wee could have Judges, that had understanding or honesty, but wee must expect, that all possible care will be taken, to give us such as have neither. You knowe what advances have bin of Late made towards that good work ... [We] may ... consider wheather ... the [crown's] Judgement against the Citty Charter doth not abolish the sheriffs chosen by it, and ... soe wheather wee may not plead against the validity of their new commission.[57]

Sidney discussed Strafford's trial at some length, observing particularly that 'thoes matters weare wholly layd aside that weare not exactly testified by tow witnesses'. These and other difficulties had eventually led to the replacement of the standard trial procedure with a Bill of Attainder, without which they could not be overcome. They had to expect, he predicted, 'all the

---

[54] See note 7 above.   [55] See chapter 8, pp. 172–3; and 63–4.
[56] Hampden Letters, letter 2, p. 3.   [57] *Ibid.*, letter 1, p. 1.

tricks' of 'bringing . . . severall witnesses testifying severall acts as to time and place, to be conducing to the same treason',[58] as well as confusing the two principal types of treason themselves, 'interpreting the raising of war, to be an imagining the King's death by reason of the consequences'. 'The point of the tow witnesses'[59] in particular seemed crucial:

This seemes to be written in the heart of man from the beginning, but first declared by Moses . . . *whoe soe killeth any person the murtherer shall be put to death, by the mouth of tow witnesses, but one witness shall not testify against any person to cause him to dye* Num:35:30 Deut:17:6 . . . This was not meerely a municipall law of the Jewes, but left by Christ as a perpetuall rule of Justice . . . Not but that there might be tow or three evil men as well as one, but because it was hard for tow or three to agree in a lye.[60]

The important thing in this respect, emphasised Sidney, was '*the necessity of concurring in [exactly] the same circumstances* [my emphasis]'; if witnesses could testify to different branches of the same crime such perjuries might never be discovered.

This is proved by Susanna's case. If [such testimony] . . . had bin enough . . . shee had perished in hir innocency, but they being brought both to testify the same act, one sayd she lay under one tree, the other under another, wheareupon she was freed, and they stoned. The same Lawe is in force whearsoever the authority of the Scripture is receaved . . . the Inquisition only excepted, wheare the same trick is found to destroy men under the name of heresy, as heare of treason, and witnesses are admitted though not agreeing in time and place, by which meanes they attaine this tow ends, that noe man, whome they have a minde to destroy, did ever escape, and . . . noe man was ever convicted of . . . perjury.[61]

Sidney's early focus on this point arose partly from the known difference between the evidence available for his own trial, and that of Russell's. At Russell's trial, Shepherd and Rumsey had testified to Russell's presence at a meeting with Shaftesbury in 1682; and Howard to the 'Council of Six' meetings in 1683.[62] In the case of the first two then, the crown clearly had the required two witnesses to the same time, act and place. In Sidney's case however, things would be different, for his rivalry with Shaftesbury had protected him from any involvement in the meetings of 1682. For his trial there was, and would remain, only one direct witness: Howard. This was the reason for the five-month delay in bringing him to trial, and accordingly Sidney remained optimistic about the prospects for his and Hampden's release on bail.

Throughout the year Sidney's friend Barillon had been reporting progress on this front. In early June he wrote to Louis:

[58] *Ibid.*, letter 1, pp. 1–2.   [59] *Ibid.*, letter 1, pp. 1–2.
[60] *Ibid.*, p. 5.   [61] *Ibid.*, pp. 5–6.
[62] 'The Tryal of William Lord Russell' in Howell (ed.), *Cobbett's Complete Collection of State Trials*, vol. IX (1811), pp. 597–9, 602–8.

The Colonel Algernon Signey [sic] (the one who lived for so long in France) is . . . in the Tower. It has not been proved that he was in the [murder] plot against the King . . . but it is claimed that he was more forward than anybody in the [other] project for an uprising and the design to establish a republic.[63]

A few days later Charles admitted to Barillon that neither Russell nor Sidney had been implicated in the murder plot, but that he failed to see any great difference between a plan to take away his authority, and one to take away his life.[64] Three days after, Barillon added: 'Men say that there is insufficient evidence for a conviction but that the sheriffs, entirely dependent upon his majesty, will be ready to do what he says.'[65]

Over the next three months Barillon reported (9 August): 'The court still intends to try Colonel Sidney and Mr Hampden but just at the moment there is insufficient evidence'; (26 August): 'It is believed that Colonel Sidney and Mr Hampden will be tried the next legal term; it doesn't seem that they will be pardoned if enough evidence can be found'; (6 September): 'The trial of Colonel Sidney and Mr Hampden has been put off to the next term and it is not yet clear that there will be enough evidence but if there is it doesn't appear that they will escape'; and lastly (7 October): 'Nothing more is said of the trial of Mr Sidney and Mr Hampden.'[66]

Thus Sidney's tone by September and early October was confident:

I heare the Lord Howard is used at court much according unto his merite, and is like to have a very ill issue in every respect, unlesse he finde wayes of gaining favour by enlarging his testimony, which he hath already sworne in court he cannot doe. To conclude wee must prepare for the worst, but according to the best informations I can get, it is not intended to bring us to a triall, unless Satan furnish them with such witnesses as they have not yet be[en] . . . able to finde . . . soe it will be hard to keep us beyond the end of the [legal] tearme. I presume your freinds think fit that an Habeas Corpus be demanded for the first day of it[?][67]

Sidney reassured them too with news of external support. Some of this was from France, where, as we have seen, his predicament was being followed with interest:

that which you heard of the gentleman [concerned is] . . . true, the words were *Ce[s] ne sont pas des actes de justice, ce[s] sont des Massacres*, and complaints weare thereupon made . . . the like opinion is in other places, and I heare it is as much believed in France, that the Ld Rus[sell] did cut of[f] his owne head, as that the E: of Essex cut his owne throat. I have examined my owne hart, and hope that without much reluctancy, I can resigne myself into the hands of God, to be disposed of, as to life or death as he pleaseth.[68]

He added:

I have sent word to such of my relations as seeme desirous to be usefull unto me, that

[63] PRO Baschet no. 155, p. 391 (my translation).
[64] *Ibid.*, p. 393. [65] *Ibid.*, p. 395. [66] *Ibid.*, no. 156, pp. 8, 35, 49.
[67] Hampden Letters, letter 1, p. 4. [68] *Ibid.*, pp. 2–3.

what soever they ... doe for me, they should doe ... for you ... this course, by the help of God, I shall hold, and hope never to doe anything so unworthy of a gentelman and a Christian, as to divide your concernements from my owne ...[69]

This French support apparently had its counter-weight in the hostility of the Spanish Ambassador. Sidney reported that while Barillon had irritated his Spanish opposite number by 'bragg[ing] that he would bring me out of this place',[70] the 'Spannish Ambr ... doth declare bravely against us, and our friends that are dead'.[71] His expression is *Il faut faire brusler tout cela, et jetter les cendres aut vent.*[72]

In the next letter Sidney's tone of optimism bordered on bravado. A 'young man' has 'receaved instructions', Sidney informs him:

in all the visites that he makes, to have just the same care of your concernements as of mine ... From the first day that I came hither, I thought my owne danger not great, and yours much lesse: Every day confirmes me in this opinion: The businesse is discountenanced: People generally murmure. The Ld Rus[sell's] triall is horribly condemned, the protestant plot scorned, all over Europe: the E: of Essex, generally believed to have bin murthered: And noe man can imagine how it is possible, that no proofe should be found of a plot, that the worthy Ld [Howard] sayth hath lasted above a yeare, and was then knowne to soe many that it could not be kept secret, of whome noe one can be produced to confirme his testimony of 10 000 brisk boyes or any thing else ... God of his goodnesse sanctify all troubles unto you, and bring you soone out of them.[73]

THE LAW OF SELF-DEFENCE (LETTERS 2–4)

Nevertheless, on the principle of preparing 'for the worst' the principal object of these letters was to develop a joint legal strategy. Sidney's reference to 'the points mentioned in your paper'[74] makes it clear that to this Hampden was an active contributor. The first task was to identify the statutes under which they could be tried. Sidney concluded (correctly) that the most likely was 25. Ed. III. The crucial point about this, according to Sir Edward Coke, who Sidney was reading on the subject, was that under this statute 'to make war, and to imagine the death of the King, are naturally distinct, and distinguished by the Stat[ute]; and that the one cannot be an evidence of the other'.

According to this interpretation, then, evidence of a conspiracy to levy war (which Howard could be expected to supply) was not evidence of imagining the death of the king, nor could he be indicted on the first branch of the statute (conspiracy to levy war) unless war were *actually levied*, and

---

[69] *Ibid.*, pp. 3–4.   [70] *Ibid.*   [71] *Ibid.*, letter 2, p. 3.

[72] *Ibid.* 'It is necessary to burn such, and throw their ashes to the wind'. This was an echo of the formal sentence at continental witchcraft trials: see R. Muchembled, *Popular culture and Elite culture in France 1400–1750* (1985), p. 245.

[73] *Ibid.*, pp. 3, 4.   [74] *Ibid.*, p. 1.

'open acts, shew it to be soe'.[75] The long contest at Sidney's arraignment revolved around the consequent need to see upon which statute, and which branch of it, he had been indicted. Yet whatever record of Russell's trial Sidney had, it wasn't a full one, for unfortunately he could have saved himself this trouble. Russell too had been tried on 25.Ed.III. He too had argued, on the same grounds, that mere conspiracy to levy war, even if proven, was no treason by that statute. The crown had to prove either, if indicted on the first branch, that war was actually levied (an 'overt act', not just meetings), or, if on the second, that they had conspired the death of the King (proven of the 'Rye House' conspirators but not of the 'Council of Six'). But in this Russell was overruled by the Solicitor General, who argued: 'this is [indeed] high treason within 25.Ed.3. To conspire to levy war, is an overt act to testify the design of the death of the king. And the error of my Lord Coke hath possibly led my Lord into this mistake . . .'[76] Both Russell and Sidney were indicted on the second branch of the statute (imagining the death of the King), of which conspiracy to levy war against him was taken to be a sufficient proof.

The final legal point upon which Sidney placed great emphasis, in addition to the two witnesses ('the lawes of god and man expressly requiring an exact concurrence in all')[77] and the two distinct branches of the statute (according to Coke), was what

> they call Pleading over, That is to say the accused person may deny the thing, or that there was a crime in it, if he had done it, wheare upon it commes to be argued, wheather an intention to levy war be treason. If it be not, he is discharged: If it be, the next work is to prove what is to be taken for an intention . . . This I take to be soe important, that if it can be obtained, neither of thoes tow points will be carryed against us, without such evident injustice, as will bring confusion upon every one concerned in it.[78]

In other words Sidney thought it might be possible, by 'Pleading over', to dispute the validity of the indictment even before pleading to the charge itself. Once again, if Sidney's final remarks do indeed point to a price he would extract from his tormentors, such optimism underestimated the offical resolve behind the trial when it came.

At this moment we come to the last, and one of the finest, in the catalogue of acts of unscrupulousness – the putting of ends before means – that we have seen characterise Sidney's political behaviour. It is a blessing that this letter, at least, was unknown to the generations of bibulous whigs who raised their cups to the sacrifice of Sidney and Russell 'on the scaffold' and

[75] *Ibid.*
[76] 'Tryal of William Lord Russell', *State Trials*, vol. IX, p. 629.
[77] Hampden Letters, letter 2, p. 2.
[78] *Ibid.*

Hampden 'in the field'. Even John Hampden jnr proved unprepared for the suggestion that they should secure as their defence attorney the 'murtherer' of Russell. Justice Pemberton, who had presided over Russell's trial, had just been replaced as Lord Chief Justice by Jeffreys, and this led Sidney to hope that he might now 'returne to [private] practice' for:

notwithstanding the villanyes he hath done, [I] think it not amisse to trye wheather he will be of Council unto you and me. He knowes, the bottome of all that is against us, and is probably put out, because he will not proceed against thoes in prison as he is directed. It might have bin believed, that after the steps he hath made, he would stick at nothing, but he hath a certaine capricious conscience, that gives him a strange latitude, and yet sometimes checks him ... I doe not think the new Chiefe Just: is troubled with any such scruples, but that he is preferred for such virtues as admit of none, and that wee, are the causes of his preferment.[79]

Hampden was taken aback by this proposition. This obliged Sidney to explain the literally Machiavellian thinking that lay behind it. In an imperfect world, and in politics above all, the most difficult and abstruse of all 'sciences', means had to be used appropriate to their ends.

My moralls doe not incline me easily to pardon ... [that] gentleman ... but for the same reason that one of the worthiest men, that ever I [knew – the Earl of Leicester?] ... having a great suit at Law, with a notorious raskall, refused an attorney recommended to him under the name of a very honest man, I desire to imploy him, for as he sayd, None but a knave, can prevent the tricks that will be put upon him by a knave, none can serve us but such as are like them, that pursue us ... [and Pemberton] hath a particular knowledge of that which may be of use. Your nearest friend is the most fit, to speak with him, but he hath scruples ... that I think are not seasonable.[80]

Hampden seems, in turn, to have been put out by this description of his friend, and Sidney was driven to explain further that 'your friend is a man of great virtue and understanding, but he hath naturally an unhappy and excessive cautiousness, that makes businesses miscarry in his hands, and occasions passe before he can take a resolution'.

The suggestion about Pemberton seems to have come to nothing. Nevertheless it is at this time (6 October) that we find Sidney's self confidence at its peak:

our businesse doth mend every day. Our adversaries seek witnesses, but finde none: The methode of putting men in prison, and after many moneths to search for such as shall tell why, is every day more and more discountenanced: I heare the last refuge is to keep us as long as the act of Habeas Corpus, will permit, and if none do by that time appeare ... I heare they expect [to] release us upon baile, or being bound to ... good behaviour, of which I think we cannot deny the first, but know not why wee should submit to the Latter.[81]

Subsequent letters expanded in detail on the legal points already opened,

---

[79] *Ibid.*, p. 3.   [80] *Ibid.*, letter 3, p. 5.   [81] *Ibid.*, p. 3; letter 4, p. 5.

partly in answer to Hampden's queries. Their considerable interest is less legal than biographical and intellectual. On the one hand they re-focus attention both on key themes of Sidney's past life and on the activities for which he was arrested. On the other they are, stylistically, very close to the *Discourses*, in all their historically and biblically supported detail. Deprived of one stimulus for this sort of monologue, Sidney secured another.

One of the letters centred on the trial of Sidney's republican mentor, Sir Henry Vane. Even someone like Vane, observed Sidney, deeply involved as he was in two civil wars, had been extremely difficult to convict under 25.Ed.III. He could not be tried for levying war in this period since although 'He did not deny but that he had bin in the Parlmt, Comttee of Safety, that of the Scotch and Irish Affairs, [and] the Admiralty and Councell of State, during the wars'[82] yet no testimony to any 'overt act' of war itself could be found. Nor could he be tried for conspiring to kill the King, 'he having absented himself from the parlmt, for the space of about six weeks, in which time it was contrived, soe as he could not be sayd to be an actor in it'. Consequently the government was forced to resort, for their 'overt act' of war, to testimonies that he had commanded a regiment in Southwark in 1659.[83]

Sidney's account of the subsequent trial drew on what one of Vane's defence witnesses, '[Col] Biscoe did afterwards tell me', in the Netherlands.[84] What the letter as a whole reinforces is the extent to which Vane's civil war involvements (beginning under Sidney's own patron, Northumberland) had set the pattern for Sidney's own. Sidney too had gone on, under the Republic, to work (with Vane) on the Committees for Irish Affairs, Anglo-Scots union, the Admiralty, and the Council of State. Sidney too had absented himself from Charles' execution; but had gone on to be Vane's envoy in the Baltic and a fellow conspirator with Bisco in 1665–6. This is a timely reminder, since Sidney was about to follow Vane's example through to its final chapter.

Another letter examined the statute in more detail. The key to identifying it (25.Ed.III, or 13.Car.II) was procuring a copy of the indictment: 'if they will not tell upon what stat: they indict us, the matter of their indictment must certainly doe it, and wee must thereupon order our defence'.[85] Since the probability was 25.Ed.III, it would be crucial to insist on distinguishing the branches of the statute. A design to levy war, even if proven, could not be assumed to be an imagining the death of the King, for

Nobleman, Cittyes, Commonaltyes have often taken armes, in the defence of their priviledges, upon quarrells with their neighbours, to defend themselves when they

[82] Hampden Letters, letter 3, p. 2.
[83] *Ibid.*, pp. 2–3.
[84] *Ibid.* See Scott, *Sidney and the English Republic*, p. 178.   [85] *Ibid.*, letter 4, p. 1.

weare prosecuted upon the account of religion (of which you know ... innumerable examples) and being satisfied in their demands ... have bin quiet; The princes against whome they took armes have ... [thereafter] found them as good or better than their other subjects ... it is ridiculous, to say ... the protestants of Holland, France, or ... Piedmont ... in bearing armes against their princes ... imagined their deaths, when ... they sought noe more than the security of their owne lives ... [Of course] It may soe fall out, [as in the 1640s] that thoes whoe rise against a king and doe not at the first imagine his death, being exasperated by long wars, and private injuryes, may change their minds, and kill him, [but others may not] ... David ... made war upon Saul ... but when Saul, fell into his hands, he would neither kill him, nor suffer [another] to doe it.[86]

On the other side,

Ther are also many conspiracyes against kings, that noe wayes tend to war: Many have bin taken away by their wives, sons, brothers, or strangers upon private hatred or revenge, which noe wayes tended to war. When Ravaillac killed Hen: the 4th, he did not intend ... to make war upon all France ... If therefore wars are often made that intend not the death of kings: And kings are often taken away without wars: Conspiracyes against kings, and the ... making of wars are naturally ... different ... and cannot be confounded ... the stat[ute] distinguishes them and they must forever be distinguished ...[87]

The similarity of all this to the *Discourses*, where both this subject matter (wars; and ways of 'taking away' kings) and the authorities (European and English history; and the Old Testament) are equally prominent, is clear. It is not diminished in the rest of the discussion, which concentrates rather more on English history, in particular the Anglo-Saxons and the 'Plantagenet Age'. It includes the interesting and entirely characteristic claim that 'in the Saxon time, the killing of [kings] ... was not punished with death, but the king's head was valewed at thirty thousand Thrinnes'; and elaborates at great length on the types of wars that occur which cannot be accounted treason. In particular, of course, there were justified wars of self defence:

If an army of Turks landed in England, I need not expect a Commission ... He that can be followed and hath skill to conduct such as will follow him, hath authority enough to oppose [them] .[88]

This should be compared with the *Discourses*, where

if the sentinel falls asleep ... or [be] gained by the enemy ... every man ... who best knows the danger, and the means of preventing it, has a right of calling the ... people to an assembly. The[y] ... would and certainly ought to follow him ...[89]

In general

it is not only the Law of the Land, but the eternall Law of nature, that permits such

---

[86] *Ibid.*, pp. 1–2.   [87] *Ibid.*, pp. 2–3.
[88] *Ibid.*, p. 4.   [89] Sidney, *Discourses*, p. 466.

as are invaded to defend themselves; and though both partyes make war, the Aggressor only is criminall. Such as defend themselves, doe not make war upon the king.[90]

Thereafter Sidney, having likened Howard to Judas, observed that even 'the Jewes in their corruption' refused to make use of him as a witness, he being ' "*participes crimines*" – but now this passeth for nothing'.[91]

HABEAS CORPUS (LETTERS 5–7)

On a happier note, Sidney passed on to Hampden the rash professions of a well-wisher, that 'if he weare obliged to passe his whole life with tow men, he would chose you and me'. This is the sort of sentiment which comes to people who are secured behind the walls of a maximum security institution, on a capital charge. Suitably fortified, Sidney conceived a new project: to precede their habeas corpus application with a petition to the King. This was 'to make our proceedings the more . . . respectfull even unto the king, wheare it may be done without prejudice unto our owne right and reputation . . . [in] that it is better for him to grant it upon petition. then to have our liberty extorted by law'.[92] Sidney promised, when it was framed ('with such arguments as the thing will beare'), to 'appoint a freind to know the opinion of him I most trust at court [Halifax?] thereupon'.

In the following letter (18 October) we find that Hampden has framed a petition which Sidney had approved and signed. Sidney signalled his intention to 'have it offered immediately; the tearme being very near, it is time to think of the Habeas Corpus, in case it should not be granted'.[93] The petition certainly was not granted, but there is also no record of its having been received. Instead the State Papers recorded, ominously (21 October) 'Memo. Mr Shepherd to prove Col. Sydney's hand by himself and others.'[94] At the same time a habeas corpus was filed by Sidney and Hampden, giving the crown a set time to release them, or bring them to trial.

In the meantime, Sidney explained to Hampden the procedure for 'pleading over'. 'The time of making the exception, is before Not guilty be pleaded for if the Indictment be voide, no man is obliged to answeare unto it.'[95] One 'authentike' example of particular force was at the trial of John Lilburne:

for Cromwell being then in the place of king . . . (whether justly or unjustly it concernes us not) . . . the more violent the government was, the greater was the power of the Law . . . [over those] whome he had a minde to destroy, and the Bench was then furnished with very able men, much devoted unto him . . . they would never have suffered the prisoner to escape, if they could have overruled his plea.[96]

Sidney was also interested in the case of Lilburne because 'a friend of

---

[90] Hampden Letters, letter 4, p. 4.   [91] *Ibid.*, p. 5.
[92] *Ibid.*, letter 5, p. 1.   [93] *Ibid.*, letter 6, p. 1.   [94] *CSPD* 1683–4, p. 49.
[95] Hampden Letters, letter 6, p. 2.   [96] *Ibid.*

mine drew that plea, and I will know of him, how far the like may be useful unto us, and how it should be put in'.[97] The other relevant case was again Vane's. At his trial, said Sidney, when Vane put in an exception to the indictment before pleading he was told:

> If he pleaded that [exception] . . . they would joine issue with him, but if it should be found against him it would be too Late to plead not guilty, But the court sayd in favour of life [i.e. in a capital case] a man [may] plead a double plea, and give in his exceptions, and plead over to the felony or treason not guilty . . . This you may [find] in his triall pg: 29, and if you have not the book I will send it to you.[98]

In another letter (18 October) we find that Sidney had changed his mind about a crucial aspect of European affairs:

> I am not able to make a judgement how far the rupture in Flanders may be of advantage or prejudice unto us . . . Nevertheless I confesse, That though I did (contrary unto the opinion of somme of your good friends, and mine) think that the peace of Nimueghen saved Europe and if the frensh [sic] had openly broken it the next yeare they would . . . have gained such advantages, as were not likely to be recovered in an age, since the defeat given to the Turks [at Vienna, 1683], and somme other things that have happened, I am not now of that mind, but to the contrary, hope, that a war . . . may be carried out against them with much more hope of good successe.[99]

This mention of France raised another subject:

> I did yesterday receive a letter from a freind in Guascony, who tells me that having . . . [heard that] I would goe into that country, as soone as I could . . . he had tow [spare] houses . . . which should be at my disposall: one . . . I know very well . . . a good one, about twelve leagues above Bordeaux, the other . . . much better, and in a better country, is eight or ten leagues higher. If you can for a while content yourself with a country life, and it please God to deliver us from hence, wee may probably expect as much peace, safety, and convenience ther as in any place I knowe.[100]

Until the end of October then, Sidney remained 'confident, that such rules being observed as the law requires, it is not possible to bring us into danger, though they could bring Jezabel's witnesses from hell to strengthen the Ld Ho[wa]rds testimony'.[101] But he was aware that this begged a large question: 'as you may see in the Ld Ru[ssell]s triall', instead of a precise charge[102] 'the indictment was a confused jumble of accusations . . . wee must expect the like measure if wee comme to a triall'.

On the whole

> I think . . . that wee shall succeed, but in this world wee must prepare ourselves against disappointments, in things that seeme to be much more assurd then theis . . . [and] wee are to expect . . . [all] manner of tricks will be used, if wee are brought to triall . . . If such [as] wee cannot foresee doe start up, wee must answeare as well as

---

97 *Ibid.*, p. 3.   98 *Ibid.*, letter 7, p. 3.
99 *Ibid.*, letter 6, p. 3.   100 *Ibid.*, pp. 3–4.
101 *Ibid.*, letter 7, p. 1.   102 *Ibid.*, p. 2.

wee can at present. I depend upon you, in this case much more than upon myself, for though I believe I could answeare, if I had time, it will be easy to surprise me, when I have not time to think ... you have heard me complaine of that decay which I found much growing upon me; But what soever wee doe before hand our trust must be in god: If he will bring us out of this streight, he will teach us what to say and doe: If he give us grace to relye upon him, he will not forsake us, but one way or other, will bring us unto the rest and happiness, for which we hope.[103]

Elsewhere this note was combined with a political defiance, which again does nothing to dispell the impression of a genuine (1683) design.

God direct us in that which is for our good, and prepare us well to defend our cause, or willingly to suffer for it, if he please to call us unto it.

What optimism existed was rather a confidence that the trial would not take place, than faith in the result of it did.

THE SECOND WITNESS (LETTERS 8–9)

Let my blood Lye, where god will Lay it, and I think it will be heavy.[104]

That is why shattering news lay around the corner. In the last week of October, pushed into action by the habeas corpus, the crown suddenly prepared to bring Sidney to trial. The Memo 'Mr Shepherd to prove Sidney's hand' (21 October) had been the ominous warning: the stratagem settled upon was to use Sidney's unfinished manuscript *Discourses* as the second witness to his treason. 'Mr Sidney' wrote a contemporary on 30 October, 'for certaine is comeing on his triall, and there is evidence enough against him.'[105]

This decision was to become, in the whig tradition, one of the greatest excesses of Stuart tyranny. Sidney was, claimed one pamphlet commenting on his trial,[106] the first man to be executed for writing something in relation to which there was no evidence of any intention to publish. Since there needed to be two witnesses to an 'overt act' of treason it required Jeffreys to rule, famously, that to write was an overt act: 'Scribere est agere' – and that such a writing would thereafter be a witness, in effect, to itself.[107] 'I could hardly believe he had said this' recorded Burnet, 'till I read it in ye Printed Tryall ... if it holds to be law and comes to be followed in practice England is ye miserablest Nation in ye world.'[108]

Sidney was stunned by this development, which he had not predicted. He

---

[103] *Ibid.*, letter 5, pp. 2–3.
[104] *Ibid.*, letter 8, (31 Oct.), p. 3.
[105] BL Add. MS 32, 500 f.75: G. Thornburgh to Mr Foley 30 Oct. 1683.
[106] Bodl. Library Rawl. C.710.263, *Remarks on Col. Sidneys Trial*, p. 266.
[107] *Trial* in Sidney, *Works*, pp. 46, 54.
[108] Burnet, BL Add. MS 63,057, II, p. 158.

was also depressed by it. Yet above all he was angry. Optimism was replaced by defiance.

On 29 October, Sidney 'petitioned his Majesty to have [his chosen] counsel permitted to come to him . . . to prepare himself for his trial'.[109] This was
granted, along with access to pen and paper, and, the next day, an order for
access to Sidney by his friends.[110] On 31 October he wrote to Hampden: 'I
make noe doubt but I shall be brought to a speedy triall, for . . . I believe
th[ese] indulgence[s] would not have bin granted, if it weare not resolved,
that it shall be for soe few days, as to be of littell help or consolation unto
me.'[111] Nevertheless he wrote five days later in a rather mixed vein 'somme
of my freinds being to appeare for me, and proceed in such a manner, as I
did noe wayes expect from them. I hope it is sincere, and if it should not be
soe the malice and barbarity of their dealings, would be without
example.'[112]

What proved especially depressing for Sidney, however, was the visit(s) of
his 'four Lawyers' (the names granted by the King were five: Thompson,
Polixfen, Bampfield, Williams, Rotheram).[113] For he found that according
to them, much of his detailed trial preparation would be useless. This was
particularly so with the 'plea to anull the indictment': Sidney recorded with
despair: '*I cannot put it into their heads.*'[114] In all

I finde I shall make nothing of it . . . They refer all to a dirty corrupt practice,
consisting only of a few new found tricks to elude and overthrowe the Law, and all
returnes unto what I told you of a Lawyer somme yeares since, whoe when I shewd
him, that reason, justice, and truth, weare one my side, answeard, That is nothing to
us.[115]

What is most interesting about Sidney's final two letters before the trial
(dated 31 October, and 5 November), is his response to the crown's decision
to use the *Discourses*. The most important eventual result, despite the need
for caution in these letters, is something his lawyers would not permit at the
trial, a frank (indeed defiant) admission of authorship.

I finde my prosecutors relye upon the papers sayd to be found in my house . . .
though the Inquisition, be the worst of all the tribunalls that have bin yet seene in the
world . . . noe Monk in Spaine could be questiond for papers of that nature . . . never
perfected, received, examind, or published, though they contained all the Heresyes in
the world, but they meane to make this an imagination of the king's death. I doe not
yet know how my councell will suffer me to proceed in this . . . but . . . I am much
inclined to owne them, and telling the utmost nature, meaning, and intention of
them, to put it upon a speciall Issue, that if such papers, soe written, are treason, I
am Guilty, if not not.[116]

[109] *CSPD* 1683–4, p. 64.   [110] *Ibid.*, p. 65.
[111] Hampden Letters, letter 8, p. 1.   [112] *Ibid.*, letter 9, p. 1.
[113] *CSPD* 1683–4, p. 64.   [114] *Ibid.*, letter 8, p. 1, my emphasis.
[115] *Ibid.*   [116] *Ibid.*, pp. 1–2.

When Sidney's counsel forbade such a proceeding his *Last Paper*, written too late to cause legal harm, was to act out this impulse. To this Sidney added some further extremely interesting and, from the standpoint of authenticity, reassuring information about his method of writing the work:

If I had written a book ready to be published (as is pretended) to stirre up a rebellion in prosecution of what they say wee designed, you must needs have seene it.[117] Besides the affection, and esteeme I have of you . . . the necessity of the businesse must have obliged . . . it . . . but I am sure you never saw a line of it, unlesse it weare a loose sheet, containing heads of Chap[ters] and Sections, to be treated, not knowing a word that was, or should be sayd upon them: never knew that it was finished, or like to be in a long time, or that I had any other thought concerning it, then when I had finnished, and examined it, if I was satisfied with it, to shew it to somme prudent freinds, and then either to publish, keep, or burne it, as they should advise. An eminent man speaking the other day of thoes papers, and the pretence of drawing them under the 25:Ed:III as imagining the king's death sayd *C'est pousser les affaires trop loin.*[118]

(These regular quotes in French all serve to reinforce the suggestion of a French context for Sidney and Hampden's relationship and activities.) The one piece of good news that Sidney could find in this situation was that the chances of finding a similar 'second witness' against Hampden seemed correspondingly remote.

I am now alltogether out of feare, that you can be brought to farther trouble, than the staying a week or two more in prison, and believe you are there rather that I may not call you to be a witnesse, then for any other reason.[119]

Hampden was indeed to be released on bail on 28 November, a week after Sidney's trial.[120] As for himself, Sidney prepared for the worst, but for that version of it that was to make him famous:

I shall have god to be the defender of my innocence. If he will, that I should perish . . . I hope he will give me grace to submit, and strenght [sic] to suffer, and having though with much frailty hitherto endeavourd to uphold the rights of mankinde and particularly of my owne country, doe not finde in my owne hart any great unwillingnesse, to be made a sacrifice of our expiring Liberty: Let my blood Lye, wheare god, will lay it, and I think it will be heavy. I hope it may in somme degree satiate the wrath and turne the judgments of god, from this nation, to the punnishment of thoes whoe are enemyes unto him and his people in it. That which I have now most need of is the prayers of good people, and I will rather apply my self unto god, then seeke wayes of contesting and cavilling before a court.[121]

This is a return to the sanguinary theory of the *Court Maxims* ('There will be, can be, no true peace, till by the blood of the wicked murderers a propitiation be made for the blood of the righteous'),[122] and of Sidney's

---

117 *Ibid.*, letter 9, p. 1. 118 *Ibid.*, p. 2. 'That's pushing matters too far.'
119 *Ibid.*, p. 1.
120 House of Lords MS, Committee Book vol. IV, 1688–90, Hampden's testimony, p. 273.
121 Hampden Letters, letter 8, p. 3. 122 Sidney, *Court Maxims*, p. 203.

inscription in Geneva ('Let there be revenge for the blood of the just'). And if this reminds us, once again, of Sidney's model in Vane, this was to be more appropriate and necessary than he imagined. On 4 December, after the trial, the government deposited in the state papers its 'Copy of ye pr[e]cepts or Rules of K[ing's] Bench in Sr Henry Vane's Case adapted to that of Algernoon Sidney'.[123]

[123] PRO, State Papers 44, no. 54, p. 228.

14

The reckoning

I did as farre as I could follow the directions of my councell ... but the impudent violence of the Ch: Just: overthrew all. (Sidney [to Henry Neville?] 22 November[1])

By these means I am brought to this place. The Lord forgive these practices, and avert the evils that threaten the nation from them. (Sidney, *Last Paper* (1683))

For my part, I can no way match this dying Gentleman, but in the Courage of some of the old King's Regicides Executed at Charing Cross ... this departing Enthusiast ... made his Exit like a perfect second Harrison.[2]

14.1 THE TRIAL

THE ARRAIGNMENT (7 NOVEMBER)

Sidney was arraigned – that is, required to plead to the indictment – two weeks before his trial. After the trial, he looked back on the arraignment as a crucial loss of the initiative. Denied the gambit of 'pleading over', upon which he had placed such reliance, 'by the violence and fraud of the chief justice'[3] 'I was forced to plead not guilty, and theareby lost the advantage, which was never to be recovered ... and they would never [thereafter] suffer me to get out of the snare in which they had caught me.'[4] 'Thus it came to pass' reported one contemporary '[that] he lost that point he hoped to have been relieved by in Law.'[5]

It was on 6 November, the day after his last letter to Hampden, that Sidney was suddenly informed by 'the lieutenant of the Tower, that an habeas corpus was brought unto him',[6] and that he would be brought to plead the next day. The following morning he was 'hurried to the bar', as he

---

[1] Hampden Letters, letter 10, p. 2.
[2] *Remarks on Algernon Sidney's Paper Delivered to the Sherriffs at his Execution* (1683), p. 4.
[3] Sidney, *Apology*, p. 7.
[4] *Ibid.*
[5] 'Roger Morrice's Entering Book', vol. I, pp. 385–6, Dr Williams Library, London.
[6] Sidney, *Apology*, p. 6.

put it, 'through a strong guard of soldiers, to be arraigned'.[7] He was 'sur-prised' and unsettled by the speed of this development and consequently later 'confesse[d] that, at the time of my arraignement, I was not fully provided with arguments and proofes ... [though] when I came to my tryall, had thoes which were abundantly sufficient'.[8]

At the bar the indictment was read: it was indeed long (as they all were), containing 'an heap of crimes put together'. Most importantly it entirely failed (deliberately) to allow Sidney to distinguish the statute upon which he was being tried. It accused Sidney of both 'contriving to stir up and move war and rebellion against ... the king'[9] and 'intending ... to bring and put the said lord the king to death',[10] thereby leaving open the possibility of either (13.Car.II, or 25.Ed.III) and either branch of the latter. Pointing to the nature of the crown's future evidence it specifically accused Sidney of two 'overt acts' of treason: sending Aaron Smith into Scotland[11] to which Howard would testify; and 'to fulfill ... those most wicked, horrid and devilish treasons ... compos[ing] ... and writ[ing] a certain false, seditious and traiterous libel ... to persuade the subjects of the said ... king ... that it is lawful to make and stir up an insurrection and rebellion'.[12] It closed with two quotations from the *Discourses*, subjecting the power of the king to that of 'the people of England ... delegated unto the parliament',[13] and arguing the lawfulness of rebellion.

Thereafter began the battle between Sidney and Jeffreys over the plea. Asked to plead guilty or not guilty, Sidney answered that the indictment contained 'an heap of crimes ... distinct in nature ... and distinguished by law ... [it] is thereupon void'.[14] Jeffreys replied that the court would not 'admit any discourses till you [plead]' and Sir Robert Sawyer, the Attorney General, added that he might demur to the indictment if he wished. In this case he would forgo any other plea, he would be assigned counsel to argue his 'causes' against the indictment, but that if this demurrer 'be not [found] good' that would be an end to the trial: 'your life is gone'.[15]

Sidney requested counsel to consider the matter, but this was refused. He argued that he did not wish to 'demur, it is only exceptions. I think in

[7] *Ibid.* The account of the arraignment which follows is taken from Sidney's *Trial* – other summaries exist in 'Roger Morrice's Entering Book', Dr Williams' Library, London, vol. I, pp. 385–6; Narcissus Luttrell's *A Briefe Historical Relation of State Affairs*, vol. I (Oxford 1857), p. 287; the testimony of Ducasse (largely based on Sidney's *Apology*) in the *Journal of the House of Lords 1689*, p. 390; and Sidney's own letter 10 (note 1, above), pp. 2–3; see also Sidney, *Apology*, pp. 6–8; and Petition to the King of 25 November, Bath MSS, Whitelocke Papers, vol. XX, f.176, (reproduced in Sidney's *Apology*, pp. 24–5).
[8] Sidney, *Apology*, p. 8.
[9] *Trial* in Sidney, *Works*, p. 3.
[10] *Ibid.*, p. 3.   [11] *Ibid.*, p. 4.
[12] *Ibid.*, p. 4.   [13] *Ibid.*, p. 5.
[14] *Ibid.*, p. 5.   [15] *Ibid.*, pp. 5, 7.

matters of life, a man may give in his exceptions to the bill and then [if necessary] plead not guilty afterwards. I am sure, in Sir Henry Vane's case the court said it, and offered him to do it; that which, under favour, I hope to do'.[16] Jeffreys simply ignored this and repeated: 'You must plead or demur'.[17]

Changing tack, Sidney attempted to see if he could identify the statute in question. He argued that the statute 13.Car.II 'is limited by time ... the indictment must be within three months'. Jeffreys refused to be taken in by this, and replied that such matters would be considered at the trial: now he must plead. This sparring continued for some time and the situation became tense. Sidney accused the Chief Justice of 'mak[ing] me run in dark and slippery places. I do not see my way.' He sought 'a day to consider it' which was denied: 'We must not introduce new methods or forms for any body. The same case that is with you, may be with other people.' Sidney produced a paper 'ready engrossed' of exceptions to the bill, and his lawyer Williams was 'reproved' for whispering to him about it.[18] He rehearsed all his objections to the indictment, and finally was cut short by Jeffreys: 'We are not to hear all this. You must plead as other people; or else, in plain English, we will pronounce sentence.'[19] Sidney had no choice: 'if you put me upon this inevitable necessity, it lies upon you; I must plead ... Not guilty'.

After this Jeffrey asked him if one week would be sufficient notice for his trial. Sidney requested two, and got them. He then requested a copy of his indictment, which was denied. This caused a further contest, at the end of which Jeffreys offered, as a consolation prize, the indictment to be read again to the court, this time in Latin. At the end of the reading Sidney asked 'What is that statute?' Jeffreys replied 'When you come to your trial, Mr Attorney will tell you what statute he goes upon.' This caused further altercation, in the course of which Sidney was asked again 'Sir, would you have a new indictment [just] for you?' The arraignment was over, and Sidney was returned to the tower.

At the arraignment, as at the subsequent trial, Sidney was treated as Russell, and before him the popish plotters of 1678–81 had been treated. They too had been refused counsel, a copy of the indictment, notice of the statute.[20] This was customary procedure in an age where treason trials were a political instrument. What Sidney had decided (hence the court's repeated references to this fact) was that such treatment was not good enough for him. His consequent accomplishment was to draw public attention to the manifest injustices of the whole procedure, as well as to those aspects of his trial that were strained, even by contemporary standards. By this he

---

[16] *Ibid.*, p. 5. [17] *Ibid.*, p. 6.
[18] *Ibid.*, p. 7. [19] *Ibid.*, p. 8.
[20] Kenyon, *The Popish Plot*, p. 116.

achieved not only widespread public sympathy at the time but, after 1689, changes in the law.

As for Jeffreys, although he had stoutly resisted Sidney's attempts to dictate the proceedings, he had not done so without effort. This was his first major trial as Chief Justice, and the arraignment left him unsettled, particularly by Sidney's use of the precedent of Vane's trial, for which he had been unprepared. At the time he had had no response but to ignore it. Thereafter, however, he re-examined Vane's case. Thus at the outset of Sidney's trial proper, he used it to defend himself in his refusal to allow Sidney a copy of his indictment: 'And because you did particuarly take notice of the case of Sir Henry Vane last time, I will shew you the court did indulge more to you, than was done to that person.'[21] Not only were both Vane and Russell refused copies of their indictments, but 'You had the indictment read to you in latin; which was denied in the case of Henry Vane.'[22] Jeffreys felt that he had been put on the defensive, that he had allowed the defendant to bully him into too much. He determined not to let this happen during the trial.

THE TRIAL (21 NOVEMBER)

Contemporary interest in Sidney's trial was high. Numerous English correspondents mention it. As one reported on its eve:

> There is great preparation to morrow for Mr Sydneys Tryall and the Court is neither to want Lords or Ladys for ... the prisoner has subpenad the D. of Bucks. D. of Norfolke, Dr Burnet, severall of ye Howards [and others] ... as is sayd to speake ther minds of my Lord [Howard of] Escrick. But tis sayd much will depend on ... his booke and how far yt will be found Treason, wch drives at ye Subvertion of Monarchy, and applauds an other forme of Govermt ... Tis sayd my Lady Portsmouth has curiosity to be in court, and son Neddy and I may be excused if we rise early to struggle for a little roome.[23]

Sidney's defence would involve raising (fruitlessly) a good number of the points we have already encountered, but it would rest principally on an attempt to discredit the crown's testimony. This involved, firstly, calling a procession of witnesses to challenge Howard; and, secondly, challenging the status of the *Discourses* as a witness to his treason in a variety of ways, particularly by denying that the crown could prove that he wrote it. A second line of defence had also been established, in that Sidney had, since the arraignment, already taken one further step back from 'the world of men'; to insulate and distance himself from the result he now feared. He was no longer relying on the trial to render him either satisfaction or justice. ('I

---

[21] *Trial* in Sidney, *Works*, p. 10.
[22] *Ibid.*, p. 10.
[23] Sir R. Southwell to Weymouth, Longleat, Thynne Papers, vol. XV, ff.8–9; see also *CSPD* 1683–4, p. 99.

will rather apply myself unto god, then seeke wayes of contesting and cavilling before a court.'[24])

He now concentrated on this self-transformation, which had the intended theatrical effect: Howard's Judas was now confronted by Sidney's Christ. 'The Prisoner' said one 'did carry himselfe with much temper, and mildness, offered to say ... many considerable things in his own defence ... raised many weighty points of Law grounded upon Coke and Hales opinion, but was over ruled I think in them all, and his Counsell might not be heard once in point of Law.'[25] Burnet reported that Sidney had always been a creature of 'passion, but he went through his whole Tryall with a temper yt surprized all yt knew him'.[26] Luttrell observed that during the trial 'he smiled several times, and was not in the least concerned even after his conviction'.[27]

Even a hostile account noted the curious fact that during the trial the defendant was 'often smileing as if he did not qu[e]stion to have a good delivery'. When the jury retired, by which time Sidney stood in no doubt about its verdict, he 'remain[ed] at the Bar, smileing and talking'.[28] This was partly a way of coping, but it was also a deliberate playing to the gallery, by someone who had always been at home 'upon the stage'. Despairing of acquittal, Sidney was making himself into a martyr, and the immediate effect was to cast enormous public odium upon Jeffreys and (particularly) Howard.

The trial lasted one full day, from ten in the morning until six in the evening.[29] Equipped with this double insurance policy (both the verdict and God's opinion already settled in his mind) Sidney went into bat early. Indeed he managed to provoke one argument (and score two runs) before the jury were even sworn. Taking up where the arraignment had left off Sidney reminded Jeffreys that he had requested a copy of his indictment and 'I thought the law allowed me a copy.'[30] In the course of this preamble he managed to rehearse again for the benefit of his audience the injustice of having been denied his 'special plea'. Now, however, he had brought a copy of the statute (46.Ed.III) 'wherin it is expressed, that ... all people, shall have a copy of every record'. He also had two recent precedents: 'My Lord Stafford had a copy, and my Lord Strafford'. And 'if it had bin pretended', said Sidney later, grandly[31] 'that such a priviledge was allowed only unto

[24] Hampden Letters, letter 8, p. 3.
[25] 'Roger Morrice's Entering Book', p. 389.
[26] Burnet, BL, Add. MS 63,057, vol. II, p. 158.
[27] Luttrell, *Briefe Relation.*, p. 291.
[28] *An Exact Account of the Tryal of Algernon Sidney Esq Who was Tryed at the Kings-Bench-Bar at Westminster* (1683), pp. 3, 4.
[29] Luttrell, *Briefe Relation*, p. 291.
[30] *Trial* in Sidney, *Works*, p. 9.
[31] Sidney, *Apology*, p. 8.

peeres, I was ready to say, that though I am not a peere, I am of the wood of which they are made, and doe not find, that our ancestors were less carefull of the lives of commoners, than of peeres, or that one law is made for them, and another for us'.

Sidney was not given an opportunity, however, to deliver this oration (it was part of the function of the *Apology* to include whatever Sidney was unable to say at the trial). Caught on the hop again, the Chief Justice evaded Sidney's ground ('We remember the law very well'), and instead had recourse to his previous discomfiting precedent now duly looked up, that of Henry Vane (and Russell). He concluded, irritably, 'arraign him ... we must not spend our time in discourses to captivate the People'.[32] Sidney responded by waving his copy of 46.Ed.III in the air and calling 'Is this a good law, my lord?' only to be reminded: 'You have the rule of the court.' It was going to be a long day.

Next came the swearing of the jury. Once again this produced a litany of complaints from Sidney; that some were not freeholders; that some were the King's servants; even that some had been 'concern'd in the personating the lord Russell's ghost'.[33] Once again these were all overruled as illegal challenges, backed by the precedent of Russell's trial. This led Sidney to protest in his haughtiest style 'if any person might be on a jury, he might be tried by his own groom ... [which] was very hard', an exclamation which produced the startled note from one contemporary 'this worthy to be thought on'. 'I thought', explained Sidney with fine imperiousness in his *Apology*,

> that my birth, education, and life, might have deserved a jury of the principal knights and gentlemen that were freeholders in Middlesex ... but I found that all rules of decency ... and humanity had bin neglected, as well as thoes of lawe; the bailifes had not bin suffered to summon such of the freeholders ... as seemed most fit for such a service; but receaved orders to summon by name such as Graham and Burton [the sheriffs] had, with the under-sheriff, agreed upon ... Upon examination I found, that they had not only put in a very many that were not freeholders, but picked up a rabble of men of the meanest callings, ruined fortunes, lost reputation, and hardly endowed with such understanding, as is required for a jury in a nisi prius court for a business of five pounds.[34]

The prosecution's case

The crown then re-read the indictment, and previewed its case. It said (following precisely the structure of the popish plot trials)[35] that first it would 'shew by many witnesses' what every 'Englishman ... does believe,

[32] *Trial* in Sidney, *Works*, p. 10.
[33] Sidney's objections to the jurors are omitted from the printed *Trial*; the fullest account is in Luttrell, *Briefe Relation*, p. 289.
[34] Sidney, *Apology*, p. 9.
[35] See Scott, 'England's Troubles', p. 11.

that for several years past a design was laid ... and [note] public libels spread abroad, to persuade the people that the king was introducing arbitrary power ... [and that] the king was a papist'. This became 'a design of raising and making a rebellion'. Some designed 'assassination of the king. Others ... thought it below persons of that great quality as the prisoner is, and therefore were for doing it by open force.'

It was only having 'given that general evidence, we shall then come to shew you what share and part the prisoner had in this design'.[36]

'For certainly', continued the Attorney-General [Sidney] ... was looked upon as a very eminent person, whose education abroad, and former practises at home, had rendered him fit to advise and proceed in such affairs.' The crown would then prove his involvement with the Council of Six, specifically the sending of Aaron Smith to Scotland; and then 'to demonstrate to the world that his head and heart was entire in this service [that] ... he was at this very time ... preparing a most seditious and traiterous libel ... to persuade the people of England, that it is lawful, nay, that they have a right, to set aside their prince, in case it appear to them that he hath broken the trust laid upon him by the people'.[37] Once again what appears to have particularly upset the crown is that this work not only used 'several arguments drawn from the most rebellious times that ever were in England, from the late rebellion', but also 'from other kingdoms where rebellion hath been prosperous against princes'.[38] Sidney was being tried partly as Dutch and French *agent provocateur*, as an importer of seditious 'education' and principles from abroad, and as a distributor of seditious libels back there again.

The 'witnesses' for the 'general' design were West, Rumsey, and Keeling. Since none of them could say anything first hand about Sidney in particular – only by hearsay – the function of this evidence was not to testify to the indictment but rather (as Sidney put it) to 'prepossess ... the jury'.[39] He was to protest bitterly against this proceeding too. But to this Jeffreys had a devastating reply:

Mr Sydney, you remember in all the trials about the late popish plot, how there was first a general account given of the plot in Coleman's trial, and so in Plunket's, and others; I do not doubt but you remember it. And Sir William Jones, against whose judgement, I believe, you will not object, was attorney at that time.[40]

This silenced Sidney for at least twenty minutes.

Between them the three witnesses reported a variety of aspects of the design with which they 'had heard' Sidney was acquainted. West had heard

---

[36] Scott, 'England's Troubles', p. 120; *The Tryal of William Viscount Stafford for High-Treason* (1681), p. 39.
[37] *Trial* in Sidney, *Works*, p. 21.
[38] *Ibid.*, p. 21. [39] *Ibid.*, p. 16. [40] *Ibid.*, pp. 12–16.

this from Nelthorp; Rumsey from West and Goodenough; Keeling from Goodenough. Then the crown 'came to the prisoner' directly, with the testimony of Howard, who began with the arresting introductory line: 'Truly my Lord, in the entering of the evidence I am about to give, I cannot but observe what a natural uniformity there is in truth.'[41]

We are already familiar with Howard's evidence, about the meetings at Hampden's and Russell's houses. What was notable here is that (as Sidney feared) some considerable embroidery had taken place since Russell's trial. Most strikingly Howard's whole account of Hampden's introductory discourse (as host) at the first meeting was added since Russell's trial, lending support to the thesis that that meeting was an invention.[42] As Sidney wrote in his final letter:

Ho[wa]rd gave a testimony altogether different from the former, whearein he had sworne he knew no more than what he sayd at the Ld Russells trial: He mentioned tow [new] points concerning Mr Hampden: At the first meeting that he had made (as it weare) an overture of the sessions, and at the second, that he had moved a point that seemed to be invidious, in relation into the end[s] of the design.[43]

In particular, and with the assistance of cross examination, Howard concentrated on describing Sidney's 'overt act' of sending Smith to Scotland. He was followed by two witnesses (Foster and Atterbury) to the resulting Scots presence in London.

The prosecution then turned to the other 'piece of our evidence', that at the same time 'the colonel (which will be another overt act of the treason) was writing a treasonable pamphlet'.[44] Here two things were done. First, witnesses were called to testify that the sheets concerned were in Sidney's handwriting, in particular Shepheard who had 'seen him write the indorsement on several bills of exchange'. This Sidney interrupted with the statement (repeated on numerous occasions thereafter) that 'similitude of hands can be no evidence',[45] but he was required to wait until his time for defence. Secondly, some large sections of the *Discourses* were read to the court (though Sidney interjected, entertainingly, 'I pray it may all be read').

The body of these extracts has been identified by Worden (locating them in relation to Filmer's text) as coming from the *Discourses*, chapter 2 section 32. Illustrating the crown's opinion of Sidney as an importer of foreign sedition, they included the superb passage about the armed resistance of the 'Protestants of the Low-Countries' laying the basis for 'a most glorious and happy commonwealth' and (pointedly) 'the strongest pillar of the Protestant

[41] *Ibid.*, p. 17.
[42] Russell's *Trial* in *State Trials*, vol. IX, p. 609; *Trial* in Sidney, *Works*, pp. 17–18.
[43] Hampden Letters, letter 10, pp. 3, 4.
[44] *Trial* in Sidney, *Works*, p. 21.
[45] *Ibid.*, p. 22.

cause now in the world'.[46] In line with the political context, what the prosecution particularly focused on were Sidney's arguments for rebellion: ('The general revolt of a nation from its own magistrates, can never be called rebellion'); and for the independent power of parliament. 'The power of calling and dissolving parliaments is not in the king.'[47]

There followed an attempt by Jeffreys to trick Sidney into admitting authorship ('Fix on any part you have a mind to have read'), which failed ('let him give an account of it that did it').[48] This was the end of the prosecution's case.

Sidney's Defence

Sidney began not by replying to the prosecution's case, but by challenging it in law, on familiar grounds. He began by demanding to know the statute upon which he was indicted, and was answered: 25.Ed.III.[49] He asked which branch and was told 'for conspiring and compassing the death of the king'. 'Then I conceive' he replied 'what does not come within that, does not touch me.' The response was unhelpful: 'Make what inferences you please, Colonel.'

This produced a torrential monologue – the first of several. In the course of it Sidney made all of his major legal points, some clearly and well, some rather garbled by the unburdening of months of preparation in one speech, and the deep frustration attending it. He argued that 'a paper found in my study of Caligula and Nero' was surely not intended as evidence, indeed testimony, of 'compassing the death of the king'. He repeated that 'similitude of hands' was no evidence, particularly 'in this age'.[50] Centrally however, he argued his main two points: that under 25.Ed.III 'the levying of war, and conspiring the death of the king, are two distinct things, distinct in nature and reason, and so distinguished in the statute' – evidence of the former, therefore, could not be used as testimony for an indictment on the latter. Secondly the law 'expressly' required two witnesses to any indictment *on the relevant branch of the statute*: this was confirmed not only by acts of parliament (1 E.6.12; 5 E.6.11), but 'The law of God and the law of men . . . Moses says so . . . and Christ says the same, that *every matter is to be established by two witnesses.*' Sidney spent some time ridiculing Howard's testimony but returned, in the end, to this point, that 'whatever my Lord

---

[46] *Ibid.*, pp. 24–5.
[47] *Ibid.*, p. 25. Concerning the authenticity of these extracts it is worth noting, however, that this last quote, which was taken from the section heading of chapter 3, section 38, actually reads in Sidney's text 'Simply in the king'. The qualification was presumably omitted in court to heighten the seditious effect.
[48] *Trial* in Sidney, *Works*, pp. 25–6.
[49] *Ibid.*, p. 26.   [50] *Ibid.*, p. 27.

Howard is, here is but one witness'. He explained that two witnesses to the same act was the only way of detecting perjury, and illustrated the point by 'the story of Susanna'.

To all of this the Lord Chief Justice responded simply by refusing to be drawn into debate about the status of the testimony. He agreed that there would need to be two witnesses, and 'I will tell the jury, if there be not two witnesses . . . they ought to acquit you.'[51] His arguments (and so the basis of his defence) effectively ignored, Sidney was flummoxed: 'You confound me, I cannot stir. You talk of a conspiracy . . . to kill the king . . . Is there any more witnesses than one for levying of war?' Once again Jeffreys replied: 'Pray do not deceive yourself. You must not think the court and you intend to enter into a dialogue. Answer to the fact.' Sidney made one last attempt to hold to his case: 'Then I say, There being but one witness, I am not to answer to it at all.'[52] Jeffreys' reply was brutally simple: 'If you rely upon that, we will direct the jury presently.'[53]

This exchange was the axis upon which the trial turned. Effectively rendered helpless, Sidney now lost the initiative permanently. Denied the opportunity to conduct (or end) the trial on his terms, Sidney found himself with no choice but to follow Jeffreys' direction: 'If you can give any testimony to disparage the witnesses, do it.' He was forced, in short, to conduct his defence on the prosecution's terms; to attempt (at length) to undermine testimony which he had just argued was, for an indictment on the specified branch of the statute, not testimony at all.

There followed another (longer) frustrated torrent of objections. Again he began with a further point of law with which we are familiar: that even by the other branch of the statute conspiracy to levy war was not treason, the war had actually to be levied to come within the statute.[54] To this Jeffreys replied again (while remarking 'you had as good . . . [tell] me . . . the first chapter in Littleton be [not] law'[55]) 'it is my duty to advertise you, that this is but mis-spending of your time. If you can answer the fact . . . do it, but do not ask us questions this way or the other.'[56] Sidney was accordingly driven to address 'the fact'.

There followed a long and rambling attack on both 'witnesses'. Howard, his motives in testifying, and his testimony itself were all assaulted at length.[57] A variety of inconsistencies were pointed up, particularly between what Howard had said at the trial and what he was on record as saying elsewhere. The whole idea of such a flimsy cabal, of such a conspiracy, was ridiculed at length: where were the guns for such a grand design, where were the men, the money? Sidney had complained similarly in the Hampden

[51] *Ibid.*, p. 29.   [52] *Ibid.*, p. 29.   [53] *Ibid.*, p. 29.
[54] *Ibid.*, p. 29.   [55] *Ibid.*, p. 34.   [56] *Ibid.*, p. 29.
[57] *Ibid.*, pp. 29–33.

letters about such deadly use of testimony of a design that clearly 'never went beyond words'. He had a point. It was bad enough to have spent six months trying against impossible odds to inject some real structure into a design, but then to be executed for it anyway was beyond a joke. Sidney then turned to the *Discourses*, attacking once again the 'similitude of hands' proof, invoking the precedent of 'my Lady Carr's case' where such proof had been ruled out. He claimed that the 'ink is so old' that the book (which 'is a polemical discourse, it seems to be in answer to Filmer') 'may be writ perhaps ... twenty years' ago. Finally he launched into a lengthy and entirely unwise defence of its contents, concluding that therefore 'first, it is not proved upon me: and secondly, it is not a crime if it be proved –'.[58]

There followed more jousting between Jeffreys and Sidney, Sidney attempting to re-open his legal case and Jeffreys continuing to stonewall:

LCJ: Take your own method, Mr Sydney; but I say, if you are a man of low spirits and weak body, it is a duty encumbent on the court, to exhort you not to spend your time upon things that are not material.

COL. SYDNEY: My Lord, I think it is very material that a whimsical imagination of a conspiracy ... [and] an ancient paper, intended as innocently as anything in the world ... should not pass for a real conspiracy of the death of the king ... [and] Then, my Lord, [there is another thing:] ... it is a right of mankind ... exercised by all studious men, that they write in their closets what they please ... and no man can be answerable for it, unless they publish it.

LCJ: ... I have been told, curse not the king, not in thy thoughts not in thy bed-chamber ... I took it to be the duty of mankind, to observe that.

COL. SYDNEY: I have lived under the inquisition, and there is no man in Spain can be tried for heresy –

MR J. WYTHINS: Draw no precedents from the inquisition, here, I beseech you, Sir.

Eventually Sidney returned to the straight and narrow, and called his witnesses (Lord Anglesey; Lord Clare; Mr Philip Howard; Gilbert Burnet; Joseph Ducasse; Lord Pagett; Mr Edward Howard; Mr Blake; Grace Tracy; Elizabeth Penwick) to second his attack on Howard's testimony.[59] All succeeded in doing what they had been coached to do, to agree between themselves and with Sidney's claim that Howard had been wandering around loudly taking God to witness that 'there was no plot'. With the exception of Ducasse, Tracy, and Penwick, Sidney's own servants, this impressive line-up had been selected with an eye to their 'eminent quality'. Several of these testimonies were conspicuously warm in their tone (one of Howard's own relations had to be reprimanded by Jeffreys for concluding: 'And I am sure from what I have said, if I had the honour to be of this gentleman's [Sidney's] jury, I would not believe him [Howard]')[60] and it is to be assumed that they made the intended public, even if no legal, impression.

[58] *Ibid.*, p. 33.   [59] *Ibid.*, pp. 35–42.   [60] *Ibid.*, p. 40.

Sidney's defence was now completed, and there remained only the summing up: by Sidney first, then the Solicitor-General, and finally the Chief Justice. It was not a structure calculated to impress upon the jury the case for the defence. Sidney's summary was what one would expect, and did not introduce anything new.[61] It began by restating the crucial points of law, particularly Sidney's interpretation of the 'distinct branches' of the statute; it ridiculed Howard's testimony and the evidence of 'similitude of hands' afresh; and it returned to the points of law. Clearly exhausted by this stage, Sidney stumbled in mid sentence and then appealed to Jeffreys: 'I should have somebody to speak for me, my Lord'[62] (Counsel was not permitted the defendant at treason trials). Jeffreys answered: 'We are of another opinion.' Sidney continued briefly, quoting lists of statutes, and then finished.

The Solicitor-General, at considerably greater length, then summed up for the prosecution.[63] The bulk of his summary was a repetition of the crown's evidence but he also tackled, as he had to, Sidney's points of law. He argued, first, as the prosecution had at Russell's trial, that 'it hath been adjudged over and over again, that an act which is in one part of the statute, may [indeed] be an overt act to prove a man guilty of another part of it'. Thus a conspiracy to levy war

is an overt-act to prove a man guilty of conspiring the death of the king; and this was adjudged in the case of Sir Henry Vane . . . And reason does plainly speak it to be so; for they that conspire to raise war against the king, cannot be presumed to stop anywhere till they have dethroned or murdered the king . . . [this] hath been settled lately by all the judges in England, in the case of my Lord Russel . . . therefore that point of law will be very plain against the prisoner.[64]

This brought an outburst from Sidney, who waved a copy of 'old Hale's . . . book' and quoted from it, insisting:

Mr Solicitor . . . [must] not think it his duty to take away men's lives any how . . . this matter of Sir Henry Vane is utterly misrepresented . . . Your lordship knows Coke and Hales were both against it . . .[65]

The Solicitor-General responded to this outburst by referring the matter to Jeffreys.

His other key legal point was against Sidney's insistence that there must be two witnesses to the same overt act. His reply was again that this was wrong: in fact, 'if we have one witness to one overt-act, and another to another, they will be two witnesses in law to convict the prisoner'. Once again Sidney's point 'hath been very often objected, and as often over-ruled: it was over-ruled solemnly in the case of my Lord Stafford'.[66]

---

[61] *Ibid.*, pp. 42–5.   [62] *Ibid.*, p. 45.
[63] *Ibid.*, pp. 45–53.   [64] *Ibid.*, p. 46.
[65] *Ibid.*, p. 53 (mistakenly called 35 in the 1772 edition of the *Works*).
[66] *Ibid.*, p. 46.

This claim about Stafford's trial was quite correct. His trial too had hinged upon this point, on which he had been similarly overruled by the then Solicitor-General, Sidney's friend Jones.[67] The truth is that whatever the Edwardian and Elizabethan statutes had envisaged, whatever Coke and Hales had argued, and whatever Moses and Christ had enjoined, Restoration judicial politics had for some time now been conducted by much harsher guidelines. It had been so because this was an age living in the aftermath, and still struggling with the aftershocks, of a civil war. It was understandable enough that the Restoration authorities above all should fail to grasp Coke's distinction between levying war and murdering a king. And now that 'the old civil war had ... as it were, transformed itself into a judicial war'[68] there was no escaping the consequences, 'unless' as Jeffreys put it, 'there be a law particular for Colonel Sidney'.[69]

There remained only Jeffreys' summing up. Its principal function was to re-trace the Solicitor-General's steps, firming up weak areas, confirming and in some cases adding to his refutations of Sidney's arguments, producing a more concise and forceful statement of the prosecution's case. Extracting the King's overdue revenge, Jeffreys drew particular attention to the precedent of Stafford's 'famous' trial, both for the structure of, and the construction of the statute in, Sidney's own. He drew particular attention to Sidney's book, remarking that it

contains all the malice and revenge and treason, that mankind can be guilty of ... [and] Gentlemen, I must tell you, I think I ought more than ordinarily to press this upon you, because, I know, the misfortune of the late unhappy rebellion, and the bringing the late blessed king to the scaffold, was first begun by such kind of principles.[70]

Finally, and most importantly, he delivered his famous ruling that 'Scribere est agere';[71] that to write a treasonable manuscript was an 'overt' treasonable act. Thus there were indeed two good witnesses to Sidney's treason; to his 'compassing and imagining the death of the king'.

Reassured on these matters the jury retired for a quarter of an hour, and returned with the verdict of guilty.[72] Even this Sidney challenged, 'and desired to have them particularly ask't, one after another, if they found him guilty, but the court said it must not be done'.[73]

Thus the prisoner 'Was remanded under a very strong guard to the

[67] See Kenyon, *The Popish Plot*, p. 117.
[68] Quoted in von Ranke, *History of England*, vol. IV, p. 159.
[69] *Trial* in Sidney, *Works*, p. 63.
[70] *Ibid.*, p. 58.
[71] *Ibid.*, p. 54.
[72] Luttrell (p. 291) and the author of *An Exact Account of the Tryal* (p. 4:) say 15 minutes; the printed trial says 30.
[73] Luttrell, *Briefe Relation*, p. 291.

Tower.'[74] Sidney had failed to save himself, but his persistent and heated self-defence had in fact made a major impression.

14.2 THE RECKONING

His execution was respited for three weeks, the trial being universally cried out on, as a piece of most enormous injustice.[75]

LAST LETTER; FIRST PETITION (22–25 NOVEMBER)

Over the next four days Sidney wrote his last letter. Although it has survived with the Hampden letters it was not written to Hampden, but to an unknown 'most deare friend and kinsman'. The two strongest possibilities, given the deaths of Jones and Essex, are Harry Savile, and Henry Neville.

At first sight Neville seems the less likely, simply because there is little hard evidence connecting him with Sidney at this time. On the other hand, Neville had, unlike Savile, been in London throughout this period. He was a republican, and he and Sidney had certainly been close as members of the mid-century Republic. Although he had apparently eschewed active plotting between 1680 and 1683, Neville had in that time written a republican work (*Plato Redivivus*) with obvious similarities to, as well as differences from, Sidney's own. It makes sense that, with his fellow conspirators imprisoned or destroyed, Sidney should direct such a letter to someone who had shared the political core of his life's experience, in both its practical and its ideological dimensions. But there are also two circumstantial pieces of evidence pointing to Neville. The first is that Sidney assumed the recipient had no status as a courtier. The second is that on 7 December, the day of Sidney's execution, Roger L'Estrange reported to Secretary Jenkins: 'This morning since Mr Sidney's execution H. Nevil, Mr Hampden [bailed on 28 November] and D. Cox went very frolic together into H. N[eville]s house.'[76] Neville was thus in contact with the (surviving) conspirators, and this meeting with Hampden suggests how this letter might have become collected together with those to Hampden. Since the letter was written between 22 and 25 November, and Hampden was released on 28 November, Sidney may well have entrusted it to Hampden for delivery to Neville. The letter itself (which mentions Hampden twice) also suggests its recipient knew him. If the letter was to Neville, then despite the significant differences in their republican ideology, Sidney's relationship with his cousin was obviously

[74] *Ibid.*
[75] Burnet, *Own Time*, p. 398.
[76] *CSPD* 1683–4, p. 136.

much more important over the long term than the total of other evidence has suggested.[77]

Sidney wrote:

My most dear friend and kinsman,

When I writ last unto you, I did believe my next would be a farewell, and not knowing how soone I may be hurried to judgement and execution, I lay hold of the first opportunity of giving it. When I grew first acquainted with you, I discovered thoes qualityes in you, that I had most loved in men, and by experience finding that I had judged rightly, grew to have more kindenesse unto you than ever I had to any man, and doe not think that anything could break it, but that which is now shortly to ensue. For want of a better way of expressing it, when I made my will in March last I gave you all I had ... That is now cut off and whatsoever is visible [?], can be saved only by one that is like to obtaine somme favour [at court]. I knowe none soe likely as my brother Harry and he having indeed behaved himself well unto me since I have been in prison, I have given it unto him,[78] and send you only as a token one bill for £1376 upon a very honest merchant in London, and tow bills of exchange from Holland for £507 ... If a few dayes of life remaine unto me, I may perhaps gather up a littell more. Pray doe not in this mistake me: I doe not think to endeare my memory unto you, though I could leave forty times as much, but such things as are usuall amongst men, must be sufferd to passe.[79]

Here Sidney broke off the letter to receive visitors. Finding that he was not, the next day, to 'be brought ... to receive judgement', he determined to finish it then. On 23 November he added an account of his trial, the first listing of the string of injustices that he was to repeat so often over the next two weeks.[80] He mentioned the 'overthrow' of his legal defence, the corrupt jury, Howard's changed testimony, the weakness of the crown's testimony about his book, the strength of his own testimony. At this point he was interrupted again by 'visits'.[81]

The letter was finished two days later on 25 November. This was the day Sidney submitted his first petition to the King, and the day before he was brought to receive judgement.

I cannot now it is Late say unto you the tenth part of what I would. Let this then suffice. Somme propositions have bin made unto me, for saving my life, but I doe not think them reasonable or decent. This night I have sent a petition to represent the irregularityes of the proceedings against me, and as an oppressed person, desiring reliefe, etc. ... The last night the D. of Monmouth went to Whitehall, and was for a long time under examination. Somme say he acts the Ld Ho[wa]rd's part. The king sayd that whosoever did not believe the plot, might be satisfied by him. What effect

---

[77] It would also support Blair Worden's instinct about the importance of the Sidney–Neville connection, a consistent feature of his interpretation of Sidney.

[78] The king received Henry's petition for Algernon's 'real and personal estate' (31 Dec. 1683) kindly, but referred it to the Treasury to report. The outcome is not known. *CSPD 1683–4*, p. 173.

[79] *Letters to Hampden*, letter 10, pp. 1, 2.

[80] *Ibid.*, pp. 2, 3–4.

[81] *Ibid.*, p. 4.

this may have upon others I cannot tell but if this be his temper it can hardly be good. Why he did not appeare before my triall I cannot tell . . . Though I doe what is rationall to bring my businesse to a new triall or to have an arrest of Judgement, I have littell expectation of it. My chiefe businesse is with god, and through his mercifull assistance, I neither finde that I did at my triall prejudice my reputation, or the cause of gods people, nor that the approaches of death doe terrify me, and I hope god will uphold me to the Last . . . remember that noe man had a more faithfull and affectionate friend. God of his goodnesse preserve and blesse you.[82]

The 'unreasonable' and 'indecent' suggestions made to Sidney for the saving of his life may have involved that old *bête noir*: confession of fault. As he insisted in 1660, 'contempt might procure safety; but I had rather be a vagabond all my life, than buy my being at so deare a rate'.[83] Once again, 'reputation' was all important; it was damage to that which was 'worse than ruine'.[84] Consequently, Sidney's view at this stage of what was 'rationall' (his first petition of 25 November) was somewhat less than supplicatory. Just like the letter he sent to Northumberland for the King in 1660, it conspicuously omitted to 'confess fault'. Consigned this time to Halifax to present, it was indeed 'a paper . . . not in the forme of a petition, but contained ye particulars, in which he thought he was unjustly used', and repeated 'the main points of his defence'.[85] It was, in short, a list of complaints, the flavour of which may be glimpsed from the later testimony of Ducasse about his master's preoccupations at this time:

He did much complain [to me] against the Lord Chief Justice, for interrupting him in his just Defence . . . He complained also against the Solicitor General, for misrepeating the Evidence on both sides . . . so he did much more of the Chief Justice, in misrepresenting the Evidence more than the Solicitor had done . . . He complained also of the Judges and Jury, for receiving such . . . Evidence as the Lord Howard['s and] some Scraps of Papers, written many Years before, in Answer to Filmer's book . . . Of these he did complain, and many other Particulars that would be too tedious to relate . . . [and so] applied himself to the king by his Petition . . . representing to His Majesty the Wrong he thought was done him; but could obtain no Relief, being referred to the same Judges of whom he complained.[86]

Sidney's petition[87] recorded in some detail every irregularity committed against the petitioner from his arrest through the arraignment and trial to the day of its composition. It then 'humbly pray[ed], the[se] premises considered, your majesty will be pleased to admit him into your presence; and if he does not shew that it is for your majestye's honour and interest to

[82] *Ibid.*, p. 5.
[83] Scott, *Sidney and the English Republic*, p. 150.
[84] *Ibid.*, p. 145.
[85] Burnet, BL, Add. MSS 63,057 vol. II, p. 158, and Burnet, *Own Time*, pp. 387–8.
[86] Testimony of Ducasse, *Journal of the House of Lords*, 1689, p. 391.
[87] There are copies in Sidney's *Apology*, pp. 24–6; PRO SP Dom Car II, 434, no. 96 (See *CSPD 1683–4*, p. 108); *State Trials*, vol. IX, col. 941; Longleat Bath MSS, Whitelocke Papers, vol. XX, f.176.

preserve him from the said oppression, he will not complaine, though left to be destroyed'.[88] According to Burnet, when 'Hallifax brought [the] ... paper yt Sidney sent him into the Cabinett Councell' Jeffreys was present. The Lord Chief Justice was 'highly provoked' and 'in his furious way said, either Sidney must die, or he must die'.[89] In this last anecdote, which found its way into Burnet's account at some point between the manuscript and published version, we have whig legend in the making. Whether or not it is true, it seems unlikely that Charles needed such an outburst to dissuade him from overturning the verdict of one of his own courts, or summoning Sidney to be the definer of his 'honour and interest'. The next day Sidney was brought to receive judgement.

SENTENCE (26 NOVEMBER)

This day Colonel Sidney received his sentence to be hanged, drawn, and quartered, and behaved himself very saucily in court, and said, after sentence; 'Now I am to suffer for the righteous cause ... My Lord [Chief Justice] told him that such language did not become the mouth of a dying man and that it was his misfortune to call that righteousness, which the law calls treason.[90]

Sidney, a man unused to 'suffering contradiction' under any circumstances, had now suffered a good deal of it, and in circumstances he could not readily amend. He accordingly came out to his judgement fighting. Jeffrey's misfortune was that it was part of the necessary form of this proceeding to ask the prisoner 'what can'st thou say for thyself, why judgement of death should not be given against thee, and execution awarded according to law?'[91] Sidney had a good deal to say, and, now somewhat rested, he conducted himself with energetic and aggressive theatricality. Once again this confrontation with the Chief Justice was reported widely[92] and it produced two famous incidents.

Sidney opened his reply on a wide front: 'I humbly conceive, I have had no trial.'[93] He then raised a series of particular objections, in support of this contention. The first, again, was that some of the jurymen were not freeholders. Jeffreys was required to repeat his ruling on this. Sidney then requested 'a day and counsel to argue it' and was refused. He then changed tack and requested that his indictment be re-read. After some further

[88] Sidney, *Apology*, p. 26.
[89] Burnet, Add. MSS 63,057, vol. II, p. 138; *Own Time*, p. 398.
[90] HMC Rep Dartmouth MSS 20.3, pp. 128–9.
[91] *Trial* in Sidney, *Works*, pp. 60–1.
[92] Apart from the accounts in Sidney's *Trial* (pp. 60–5) and Burnet (*Own Time*, p. 397; Add. MS 63,057, vol. II, p. 158) see both of those in HMC Rep Dartmouth MSS 20.3, p. 129; and that in 'Roger Morrice's Entering Book', p. 293.
[93] *Trial* in Sidney, *Works*, p. 61.

skirmishing Jeffreys wearily agreed. Following the reading Sidney claimed:
'My lord, there is one thing then that makes this absolutely void; it deprives
the king of his title, which is treason by law: *Defensor fidei* there is no such
thing there, if I heard it right.'[94]

Following the failure of this entirely characteristic attempt to convict his
prosecutors of treason, Sidney moved on. He reasserted that there was
nothing treasonable in 'those papers' – nothing that was not 'grounded in
... king James' speech ... to the parliament in 1603',[95] and that they were
not proven upon him anyway. This was successful in that it produced an
outburst from Jeffreys: 'That is the worst part of your case: when men are
[so] riveted in opinion that kings may be deposed ... that a general insurrection is no rebellion ... it is high time, upon my word, to call them to
account.' Towards the end of his long reply to this speech Sidney introduced
a further gambit: that there was someone who had been unavailable for his
trial 'but every body knows where to find him now': the Duke of
Monmouth. He requested a new trial with Monmouth as witness, offering
to stand or fall by his testimony. This, reported a contemporary, was 'so
wild, unprecedented a demand' that it was refused.[96] There followed a
verbal free for all, with Sidney reflecting on his trial ('If you will call it a
trial –') and demanding another ('I should be brought to a new trial'), and
four crown officials interjecting in an attempt to defend themselves ('*Mr
Just. Holloway*: I think it was a very fair trial'), and silence the prisoner
'*Clerk of the Crown*: Cryer, make an Oyes').[97] Eventually relative order was
restored by Jeffreys, who felt it necessary to defend his, and the court's
conduct:

It is a strange thing, you seem to appeal, as if you had some great hardship put upon
you. I am sure, I can appeal as well as you. I am sure you had all the favour shewed
you, that ever any prisoner had ... but if you begin to arraign the justice of the
nation, it concerns the justice of the nation to prevent you ... we act according to
our consciences, though we do not act according to your opinion.[98]

Unimpressed by this distinction, Sidney took the opportunity to reiterate
his grievances: the circumstances of his arraignment, the denial of a copy of
his indictment, the treatment of his special plea. Each of these was rede-
fended, but the last led to a (soon) famous encounter with Justice Wythins,
which was deleted from the official *Trial* record. Sidney was berating the
court for refusing to receive his special plea when Wythins replied that this
was 'false'.

[94] *Ibid.*, p. 61.   [95] *Ibid.*, p. 62.
[96] *Ibid.*, p. 62; Dartmouth MSS pp. 128–9.
[97] *Ibid.*, p. 62.   [98] *Ibid.*, pp. 62–3.

'False', said he [Sidney], 'I am now upwards of 60, and no man ever yet durst tell me I spoke a false thing.'[99]

This was vintage Sidney, and by the time Burnet reproduced the story it had acquired all the contours of martyrdom:

'He ... went over his objections to the evidence against him, in which judge Withins interrupted him, and by a strange indecency gave him the lie in open court. But he bore it patiently.'[100]

In fact the point Wythins was making was that he had not been denied a special plea, merely the liberty to 'plead over' (which was the court's to grant or deny). He would, in other words, be bound by that special plea if he made it.[101] The greater point, however, was that Sidney was deliberately provoking these responses and seizing upon them to wage the greater (public relations) war, in this his last public appearance before the scaffold.

This struggle accordingly continued for some time. Sidney raised further objections against the jury, the crown's testimony, and finally Jeffrey's crucial ruling that writing was *agere*, 'an act'.[102] At this point the court thought better of allowing this to continue, and called for silence. A last-minute interjection was made, on Sidney's behalf, by one of his counsel (Bamfield): 'I humbly suppose that your lordship will not give judgement, if there be a material defect in the indictment; as the clerk did read it, he left out *Defensor fidei* . . .'. 'We have heard of it already' responded Jeffreys, 'we thank you for your friendship, and are satisfied. Mr Sidney, there remains nothing for the court, but to discharge their duty, in pronouncing that judgement the law requires ... [for] high treason.'[103] This looked bad. Forced to push the judgement through against these objections Jeffreys returned to defend himself ('and ... though you seem to arraign the justice of the court, and the proceeding –') and Sidney interjected, again in vintage theatrical style: 'I must appeal to God and the world, I am not heard.'[104]

After this Jeffreys pronounced sentence. He preceded the sentence with a long preamble in its defence, re-emphasising the crimes for which the prisoner stood convicted, and the 'rankest treason' of his book, which

not only encourages, but justifies, all rebellion . . . Appeal to whom you will. I could wish with all my heart, instead of appealing to the world, as though you had received something extreme hard in your case, that you would . . . consider the guilt you have contracted by the great offence you have committed.[105]

---

[99] Dartmouth MSS, p. 128.
[100] Burnet, *Own Time*, p. 397.
[101] See *Trial* in Sidney, *Works*, p. 63; This distinction is correctly made by the well-informed 'Roger Morrice's Entering Book', p. 293.
[102] *Trial* in Sidney, *Works*, pp. 63–4.
[103] *Ibid.*, p. 65. [104] *Ibid.*, p. 65.
[105] *Ibid.*, p. 65.

The gruesome sentence for treason was then read out:

That . . . you shall be drawn upon an hurdle to the place of execution, where you shall be hanged by the neck, and being alive, cut down; your privy members shall be cut off, and burned before your face; your head severed from your body, and your body divided into four quarters . . . And the God of infinite mercy have mercy upon your soul!

But by the time it had finished Sidney, inverting matters to the last, had prepared a response of equal length, and sanguinary effect:

Then O God, O God, I beseech thee to sanctify these sufferings unto me, and impute not my blood to the country, nor the city through which I am to be drawn; let no inquisition be made for it, but if any, and the shedding of blood that is innocent must be revenged, let the weight of it fall upon those that maliciously persecute me for righteousness sake.[106]

Jeffreys, shocked by the tone of this outburst, and unprepared for the passing of judgement upon himself, called:

I pray God work in you a temper fit to go into the other world, for I see you are not fit for this.

Sidney replied

My Lord, feel my pulse [holding out his hand] and see if I am disordered. I bless God, I never was in better temper, than I am now.

APOLOGY

In the twelve days remaining of his life, Sidney had two matters to attend to. The first was his relationship with God, and the second his 'reputation among men'. An *Apology*, a testimony to posterity, was common for aristocrats facing the scaffold. Befitting the value he placed on the opinion of posterity, Sidney's *Apology* is long and must have employed a good proportion of this remaining time. For him it had a number of functions.

The immediate purpose was cathartic: Sidney had 'not [been] heard' in court, and had vowed to appeal to 'the world': this was that appeal. It was an opportunity to put the case for the defence without being interrupted by the 'violence of the Chief Justice', or by anyone else. The effect was to invert the proceedings: to put his prosecutors on trial.

Its second, wider purpose, was to extend this function back in time and chronicle the steady persecution of an innocent man from his youth to the grave. On this level it is not surprising that we find Sidney eventually directing his appeal less to 'the world' around him, than to God and to future ages. In line with his education and experience, Sidney pitched his appeal widely, in time and space. If his own country and generation had

[106] *Ibid.*, p. 65.

become so corrupt as to mistake truth for treason, the distinction would be understood in other places, and at other times.

The final purpose of the *Apology* – to be extended and built upon by the subsequent *Last Paper* – was to fearlessly identify the political principles upon which Sidney had acted. No longer required to 'cavil before a Court', this could be done with customary vigour. In all then, in addition to functioning as a counter-trial, the object of the *Apology* was to establish political value and fix it in time: both throughout Sidney's life and beyond it. Following his stoic *Character of Henry Vane*, and on the eve of his own execution, this was Sidney's stoic *Character* of himself.

'Being ready to dye', Sidney began,

I thought fit to leave this testimony unto the world, that, as I had from my youth endeavoured to uphold the Common rights of mankind, the lawes of this land, and the true Protestant religion, against corrupt principles, arbitrary power, and Popery, I doe now willingly lay down my life for the same; and having a sure witness within me, that God doth absolve me, and uphold me, in the utmost extremityes, am very littell sollicitous, though man doth condemne me.

There followed a brief and highly selective history, from 1642, of Sidney's steady adherence to these principles, and the steady malevolence of his enemies. This became much more detailed in the year 1683. This general chronicle of the persecution of an innocent man then gave way to an account, from Sidney's perspective, of the trial in particular – the case study of this persecution *par excellence*. This was very little less detailed than the trial itself, and culminated in a word-for-word account of the drama of the judgement, complete with the dramatic flourishes of the prisoner, and accusations of drunkenness against his adversaries (particularly Williams).[107] Sidney quoted in full his petition to the King, and acknowledged himself obliged to Jeffreys in nothing, save 'that he seemed to lay very much weight upon the Old Cause, and my engagement in it, with which I am so well satisfied as contentedly to dye for it'.[108] All of this ended in the indictment, trial, and condemnation of Jeffreys in particular, and the government in general, on a charge of carrying the exercise of corruption and arbitrary principles to a height never before seen in English history. Sidney finished by expressing the hope that

God ... will in his mercy speedily visit his afflicted people. I dye in the faith that he will doe it ... and am soe much the more confident ... [in] that his cause, and his people is more concerned now then it was in former [Charles I's?] time. The lust of one man and his favyrites was then only to be set up in the exercise of arbitrary power over persons and [e]states; but now, the tyranny over consciences is principally affected, and the civil powers are stretched into this exorbitant height, for the establishment of popery. I believe that the people of God in England have, in

---

[107] Sidney, *Apology*, p. 27.   [108] *Ibid.*, p. 29.

theis late yeares, generally growne faint ... But I think there are very many whoe have kept their garments unspotted; and hope that God will deliver them and the nation for their sakes. Gᵢd will not suffer this land, where the gospell hath of late flourished more than in any part of the world ... to be made a land of graven images: he will stir up witnesses of the truth, and, in his owne time, spirit his people to stand up for his cause, and deliver them. I lived in this belief, and am now about to dye in it ... I know my Redeemer lives; and, as he hath in [a] great measure upheld me in the day of my calamity, hope that he shall, giving me grace to glorify him in my death, receive me into the glory prepared for thoes that feare him, when my body shall be dissolved.[109]

LAST APPEALS

At the end of November or beginning of December, Sidney submitted a second petition to the King.[110] This contained no complaints but said, in effect, what Sidney would have said had he been granted the interview requested by the first. It argued that

your petitioner lying under sentence of death ... littell or noe advantage can be gained by the execution of it upon a man that by the course of nature is comme neare unto the last period of his life whereas an act of clemency ... will much redound to your glory [and] that thrones are better established by Mercy than Rigour.[111]

It prayed that 'your Majesty would be pleased to remit the said sentence against the prisoner and to suffer him to goe beyond the seas as he had long desired to doe giving security never to returne into Ingland without your Majesty's leave'.

Though a report on 4 December spoke of 'Col. Sidney, of whom there was some deliberation to banish'[112] there is no evidence that Charles was impressed by this last piece of political advice, or tempted to allow this last piece of biographical repetition. On 1 December Secretary Jenkins wrote to Jeffreys 'His Majesty being resolved that the judgement against Algernon Sidney be put in execution ... [he] will I assume ... in respect that [he] is the brother of a Peere ... dispense with all rigours except beheading of him and he is of opinion that Tower Hill is the fittest place.'[113]

At this time, as we have seen, Sidney's fellow conspirator Monmouth had made his peace with the court. When Monmouth told Sir James Forbes 'how kinde ye K had bin to him' Forbes 'desird him to save Col. Sidney'. Monmouth 'feard he could not, but he had told ye K[ing] how good a man ... L. Russell was'. At the same time Hampden, (just released on bail), 'desird to see ... [Monmouth] ... to try if he could save Col. Sidney's

109 *Ibid.*, pp. 30–2.
110 PRO State Papers 28/434 no. 116; (*CSPD* 1683–4, p. 125).
111 *Ibid.*
112 HMC Ormonde 36.10, vol. 1, 164.
113 *CSPD* 1683–4, pp. 127, 130.

life'.[114] Again however Monmouth replied that 'he thought it would be a very hard thing to doe'.[115] Finally Henry Sidney begged Monmouth to intercede with Charles but again 'The D. told . . . [him] that it was impossible to save him: he was such an enemy to the court.'[116]

As a part of the procedure of reconciliation the King had demanded from his son a signed confession of his involvement in the design. Monmouth obliged, confessing that:

Though I was not conscious of a design against your Majesty's life, yet I lament having had so great a share in the other part of the said conspiracy.[117]

This news became public, and Monmouth's friends, again particularly Hampden, reacted with alarm and persuaded the Duke that it would be used to destroy them (and Sidney).[118] Monmouth accordingly changed his mind and demanded the confession back. Charles flew into a violent passion, returned the letter, and banished Monmouth from court.

A number of contemporaries attributed the final decision to execute Sidney to one aspect or another of this drama. Hampden later testified that Monmouth's confession had cost Sidney his life: 'If Monmouth had not owned the plot, Sidney had not died. But [thereafter] it balanced with [Charles] to execute him. Wal[l]er the poet told him so';[119] 'the D of Monmouth's owning the Plott to ye K[ing] was the cause of cutting off Col. Sidneys head. The K[ing] ballanced before'.[120] Barillon, too, reported that Monmouth's confession had betrayed his friends, and admitted a plot which was hitherto insufficiently proven.[121] Yet Hampden's claim (before the Lords Committee investigating Sidney's death in 1689) was part of a vendetta against Halifax, who had been involved in extracting Monmouth's confession.[122] For his own part Halifax noted in his defence, 'Sidney executed sometime after this paper [of Monmouth's], ergo this paper hanged him, and ergo Ld Halifax got this paper on purpose to hang him. Note – the K. balanced till this was don, which is false.'[123]

To complicate matters further, another source, the Duke of Ormonde,

[114] *Journal of the House of Lords* 1689, pp. 276–8.
[115] *Ibid.*, p. 278.
[116] Foxcroft, *Halifax*, vol. 1, p. 380, no. 4, quoted in Milne 'Rye House Plot', p. 179.
[117] Von Ranke, *History of England*, vol. IV, p. 186.
[118] HMC Rep. 78.4, Hastings MSS p. 808; von Ranke, *History of England*, vol. IV, pp. 186–7.
[119] HMC Rep. 78.4 Hastings MSS, p. 808.
[120] House of Lords Committee Book, vol. IV (1688–9), p. 270; this (probably because of Barillon's supporting testimony) is accepted by von Ranke, *History of England*, vol. IV, p. 187.
[121] PRO, Baschet MSS no. 156, p. 84.
[122] HMC Hastings MSS 78.4, p. 309.
[123] Chatsworth, Devonshire MSS, Halifax papers vol. II, 97; quoted in Milne, 'Rye House Plot', p. 177, and Foxcroft, *Life and letters of Sir George Savile*, vol. II, p. 97.

attributed Sidney's execution not to Monmouth's confession, but to its successful retraction:

For the unseasonable expressions of joy by all the faction . . . as upon a victory gained, wrought a consternation and so visible a . . . dejection in the well affected, that it became necessary to mortify the one and raise the spirits of the other, and this happened in a conjuncture perhaps fatal to Mr Algernon Sidney, whose life could not then have been spared, but that the mercy would have been interpreted to proceed from the satisfaction the Duke of Monmouth [had] given the King that there was no real conspiracy.[124]

This may have been the meaning of Sidney's remark in his *Last Paper*, that 'I was long since told, that I must die or the plot must die.'[125] The fact is, however, that there is no evidence that the King ever wavered in his determination. On this score the testimony of Ormonde and Halifax, who both had frequent access to him, is more valuable than that of Hampden via Waller. It seems possible both to take Ormonde's point that Monmouth's antics left Charles even less room for manoeuvre than previously, while accepting Halifax's overall suggestion that in fact he never wavered.

It was well known what difficulty the crown had had procuring evidence against Sidney. Now, following the prisoner's combative performances in the dock, concern at what Burnet called the 'gross . . . scandal of this trial' had come to effect even the likes of the loyal John Evelyn. Evelyn noted Sidney's 'obstinate . . . avers[ion] to government by a Monarch' and yet that 'it was thought to be very hard measure . . . [to be] executed . . . upon the single wittnesse of that monster of a man the L: Howard . . . and some sheetes of paper taken in Mr Sidneys study, pretended to be written by him, but not fully proov'd nor the time when . . .'[126]

Even before his execution, Sidney's own version of the trial was doing a brisk trade in the marketplace of ideas. Roger Morrice reported that one of Sidney's jury [Mr Auger] had complained to the Court of Kings Bench of harassment: 'going through the Pallace Yard some dayes after Mr Sidney's Tryall, the company said there goes the Rogue that told his bretheren of Sidney's Jury, that they must finde the Prisoner Guilty, because the Chiefe Justice told them so who understood the Law better than they and good reason why he should dye etc'. Morrice added that three people were already in custody for other such instances of pro-Sidney harassment.[127] Barillon reported in early December that

all the party opposed to the court proclaim openly that it is without precedent in

[124] HMC Ormonde 36.10 p. 169, Ormonde to Arran 13 Dec. 1683.
[125] Sidney, *Last Paper*, p. 39; (cf D. Milne's helpful discussion of this whole question in 'The Rye House Plot', pp. 174–82).
[126] E.S. de Beer (ed.), *The Diary of John Evelyn* (Oxford 1955), vol. IV, p. 353.
[127] One of them was 'a joyner in [Sidney's property of] Licesterfields', 'Roger Morrice's Entering Book', p. 395.

England for someone to be condemned on the testimony of only one witness supported by a political book ...[128]

Another contemporary complained (3 December):

The Whigs pretend to get ground daily, and the Loyalists are damned with their very calumnies ... We stick not to say the King's friends ... are retrograded 15 degrees of what they were ten days ago [the time of Sidney's trial] ... nor did they scarce ever want a comforter as much as they do at this time: and this merely by the dapperness and insolency of the faction.[129]

In short the government had, in its determination to end the political danger Sidney represented, strained both its judicial and political resources to the limit. Milne attributes Hampden's subsequent escape from a similar fate to the public backlash caused by Sidney's trial. Indeed she argued (in line with Sidney's petition) that the decision to proceed with the execution was a mistake, which weakened rather than strengthened the government.[130] In fact, as we have seen, the evidence against Hampden was not the same; there was no manuscript to stand in as second witness. Nevertheless it is true that Sidney's trial and execution established, and slightly exceeded, the limits of public tolerance. Consequently, it was to be the last of this series. The protestant plot too had now run its course.

Since the government was well aware of the 'considerable outcry' which followed Sidney's trial,[131] the decision to proceed with the execution is another reflection of Charles' determination. Having proved his ability to damage and slander the government outside the country as well as in it, there was no longer anywhere to exile Sidney to. He was also executed partly, as Barillon reported,[132] because having been found guilty and sentenced, any other course would indicate weakness and might expose the government to retrospective questioning of the fates of Russell and others. But the whole judicially strained process reflected an official conviction, echoing that about Henry Vane, that Sidney was too dangerous to live[133] – one founded, perhaps, on that steadiness of purpose 'even by the confession of my opposers' which was his *Last Paper*'s proudest claim.[134]

The warrant for Sidney's execution was issued on 4 December, and Secretary Jenkins wrote to Peter Daniel, Sheriff of London:

I need not tell you it is a charity owing to a person in his circumstances to give him ... the timliest notice you can in order to his preparation for another world.[135]

[128] PRO Baschet no. 156, p. 92.
[129] HMC Dartmouth MSS, p. 128.
[130] Milne, 'Rye House Plot', p. 182.
[131] *Ibid.*, p. 174.
[132] PRO, Baschet MSS no. 156, p. 101.
[133] See A. Bryant (ed.), *Letters of Charles II* (1935), pp. 324–5.
[134] See Milne's 'Rye House Plot', pp. 176–8; and Sidney, *Last Paper*, p. 40.
[135] *CSPD* 1683–4, p. 30.

Given the centrality of the shrievalty to Sidney's own political conduct, and his present fate, his subsequent encounter with the two present incumbents was suitably poignant. When Daniel and his companion arrived at the Tower they found the prisoner with one limb in 'another world' already. The slimmest and soberest account of what transpired we have from Mr J. Jekyll, who went to take his 'leave of Col. Sidney before he died. He told me the Sheriffs had just been with them, and he told me he had locked them in and told them he laid his blood at their doors.'[136]

Eventually, and fairly rapidly however, this matured into the famous account of Burnet. The unfortunate Sheriffs, bearing their warrant, encountered a Christ-like Sidney who

was very little concerned in ye whole matter, and no change appeared in him [at the news], but that he was become so mild, yt those who saw him and knew his temper were amazed all at it ... he received it without any sort of disorder and desiring them to sit down by him, he told them yt he had no reason to blame them for what they now brought him ... [or] expostulate with them for all yt was past with him, but he desired them to consider how guilty they had made themselves of his blood, by returning a Jury yt had been packt by ye King's So[llicitor], whereas they ought to have returned a faire Jury, and ye doing otherwise was ye drawing innocent blood upon them, this he desired them to consider for their own sakes and not for his, and he pressed it so upon them, yt one if not both of them wept.[137]

By the published version of Burnet's *History of My Own time* this had become a firm 'One of the Sheriffs was struck with this, and wept', and Burnet recorded '[This Sherriff] told it to a person, from whom Tillotson had it, who told it me.'[138]

LAST PAPER

This Gentlemen, however, is an Original of his Kind; and if ... Candidness and not Inadvertency ... be to be thankt for 't, has dealt more plainly with the world than his Predecessor[s] ... for instead of Prayers for the King, and the prosperity of the Crown, and a Detestation of Anarchy, he very ingenuously avoids so poor a Disguise, and with a bar-fac'd openness, avows his Republican Principles and his utter aversion to Monarchy.[139]

In his last few days, Sidney 'had Ministers with him many times 2 or three hours together' and he spent the last day before his execution 'all [day in] ... a day of humiliation with some Ministers'.[140] He had also, however, one last piece of public relations to perform, and that was the composition of a *Last Paper* for delivery on the scaffold.

---

[136] HMC House of Lords MSS 13th Rep. 17.3, p. 51.
[137] Burnet Add MSS 63,057 vol. 2, pp. 157–8.
[138] Burnet, *Own Time*, p. 398: 'Admirable authority' noted Burnet's sarcastic editor, Swift.
[139] *Remarks on Algernon Sidney's Paper Delivered to the Sheriffs at his Execution* (1683), p. 1.
[140] 'Roger Morrice's Entering Book', p. 398.

Sidney had decided that he would not address the crowd personally on that day. He may, in this, have been influenced by the fate of Vane's speech, which was perpetually interrupted.[141] He was also conscious of the 'rigours of the season and the infirmities of my age', which he would give as the public reason for this decision. More importantly, perhaps, the scarcely concealed contempt he would show for the crowd and its opinion ('the ears of those that are about me will probably be found too tender to hear it')[142] was a much better way of registering his own. It was more effective to come to the scaffold, as he put it, 'not to talk, but die', and to confine his communications there to God: ('I have nothing to say to men').[143] Meanwhile, however, he had been careful to set down what he 'had to say to men', and to make sure it would be widely disseminated.

Sidney's *Last Paper* was a spectacular success. With it he took the opportunity, as one (hostile) commentator put it, to 'pull ... off the whole Vizard'.[144] This revealed, of course, not Bethel but Sidney underneath. Unrestrained any longer by his lawyers advice, Sidney wrote the *Last Paper* to do what he had first wished to do: to own the doctrines of the *Discourses*, and stand by them. Secondly he publicly owned and embraced the other thing that had so upset Jeffreys, the connection of those doctrines with the last rebellion, the much-maligned 'old cause'. This was the first time this had been done, and it caused a public sensation.

As a number of commentators pointed out, the *Last Paper* was consequently 'An Original of ... (its) Kind'. It contained none of the usual features of scaffold speeches, in particular prayers for the King, or an expression of remorse. It was a final and complete act of political defiance. In the wake of the *Apology*, Sidney produced an abstract of his sufferings less than two pages long.[145] This summarised 'the extravagance of my prosecutors' in a highly effective polemical style ('Lest the means of destroying the best protestants in England should fail, the bench must be filled with such as had been blemishes to the bar'). This provided a biographical frame for the paper's ideological centrepiece. Having repeated that the *Discourses* had not been legally proven his, he continued:[146]

But, if I had been seen to write them, the matter would not be much altered ... If [Filmer] might publish to the world his opinion, That all men are born under a necessity ... to submit to an absolute Kingly government ... restrained by no law

---

[141] Roger Morrice recorded: 'He did not offer to make any speech knowing it could not be without interruption', 'Entering Book', p. 398.
[142] Sidney, *Last Paper*, p. 37.
[143] *CSPD* 1683–4, p. 137: *Account by the Sheriffs of What Passed at Algernon Sidney's Execution*.
[144] [Anon] *Remarks on Algernon Sidneys Paper*, p. 4.
[145] Sidney, *Last Paper*, p. 38.
[146] *Ibid.*, p. 37.

... and none must oppose his will, but the persons and estates of his subjects must be indispensably subject to it; I know not why I might not ... publish my opinion to the contrary, without the breech of any law I have yet known ... I might as freely as he, publicly have declared my thoughts, and the reasons upon which they were grounded; and I am persuaded to believe, that God left nations to the liberty of setting up such governments as best pleased themselves ... That magistrates were set up for the good of nations; not nations for the honour and glory of magistrates ... That the right and power of magistrates in every country was that which the laws of that country made it to be ... That those laws ... and oaths ... having the force of a contract between Magistrate and people, could not be violated without danger of dissolving the whole fabric[147] ... This is the scope of the whole treatise; the writer gives such reasons, as at that time did occur to him, to prove it. This seems to agree with the doctrines of the most reverenced authors of all times, nations and religions. The best and wisest of kings have ever acknowledged it ... King James, in his speech to the Parliament anno 1603 doth in the highest degree assert it: the scripture seems to declare it ... [and even] If ... the writer was mistaken, he might have been refuted by law, reason and scripture; [rather than execution]. ... The Lord sanctify these my sufferings unto me! and though I fall as a sacrifice to idols, suffer not idolatory to be established in this land! Bless thy people, and save them. Defend thy own cause, and defend those that defend it. Stir up such as are faint; direct those that are willing; confirm those that waver ... Grant that I may die glorifying thee for all thy mercies; and that at the last thou hast permitted me to be singled out as a witness of thy truth, and even by the confession of my opposers, for that OLD CAUSE in which I was from my youth engaged, and for which though hast often and wonderfully declared thyself.[148]

Sidney had a copy made of the *Last Paper*, and gave it to a friend 'ordering him to spread it about, if ye Court suppressed ye other Copy'.[149] On the scaffold Sidney gave his copy 'into the sheriffs hand who said, was there nothing in it that was unfitt, or that reflected upon the Government, he replyed, if you doe not like it you may give it me again, for I have given a Duplicate of it to my friends. *Sher(iff)*: againe shall I give it to the King. [Sidney;] Yes if you please.'[150]

According to Anthony Wood, the Sheriffs thereupon delivered the speech 'to his majestie to be read: Whereupon as the report went a proclamation issued out to prohibit the printing thereof; but afterwards it came out by authority, otherwise it would have been printed beyond the seas'.[151]

In fact it came out overseas (in the United Provinces) almost instantly, and well before it was printed in England. Sidney's European background dogged the government to the end. This was doubly disturbing in that the day of

[147] *Ibid.*, p. 38.
[148] *Ibid.*, pp. 39, 40.
[149] Burnet, BL, Add. MSS 63,057 vol. II, pp. 158–9.
[150] 'Roger Morrice's Entering Book', p. 398; see also the slightly different accounts in *CSPD* 1683–4, p. 137; and *The Condemnation, Behaviour, Last Dying Words, and Execution of Algernon Sidney Esq* (1683), p. 2; Morrice (like many others) copied Sidney's paper out in full: 'Entering Book', pp. 404–6.
[151] A. Clark (ed.), *The Life and Times of Anthony Wood* (Oxford 1894), vol. III, p. 82.

Sidney's death the government received reports about gun-running between the English 'fanatics' and Holland.[152] The *Last Paper* was not actually printed until 'the Town was (so) full of written [manuscript] copys'[153] that the government prohibition no longer served any purpose. The case for printing it was put one week after Sidney's execution by Roger L'Estrange:

Great stress is laid on Mr Sidney's last paper and they say the *Haarlem Courant* has it at length. Abundance of manuscript copies of it are up and down the town and inferences drawn from the suppressing of the paper, as they call it, to the dishonour of the government, besides that it is more expressly an arraignment of the judicial proceedings, which, being false in matter of fact, may be easily answered. There is much discourse of the strength of Sidney's defence of the popular cause in his Essay on a reply to Patriarcha . . . I do not take it for a master piece and, if I had the sheets . . . I could lay the weakness of them very open.[154]

There is no record that L'Estrange carried through this intention: a discovery of the number of 'sheets' involved would presumably have been a disincentive. Yet it was not only among the (until recently disheartened) followers of the 'popular cause' that Sidney's *Last Paper* caused a sensation. Its publication was followed by a flood of (mainly loyalist) replies.[155] Though their precise tone varied a good deal, what struck them all was Sidney's open avowal of 'the OLD CAUSE'. 'Was ever villany so Patroniz'd as this OLD CAUSE in Capitals' demanded one?[156] 'How Capital was it' said another,

even during the Sessions of Three or four Parliaments, to pretend the least resemblence or tendency of Eighty and Eighty One to Forty, and Forty One . . . did not the very City it Self in their memorable Petition to his Majesty . . . renounce and abjure all Common-Wealth Principles . . . But this unpolitick Gentleman has very unfortunately pull'd off the whole Vizard . . . and made the present *true protestant* Zeal, as a Branch of the *Old Cause*, no less than a continued link of the old Chain of Rebellion.[157]

These replies were followed by ballads. 'View my Hack'd Limbs' said Sidney in one[158] 'each honourable wound The Pride and Glory of my numerous Scars in Hell's best Cause the old republic Wars'. 'How Roman-

[152] *CSPD* 1683–4 (8 Dec.), p. 138.
[153] Burnet, BL, Add. MSS 63,057, vol. II, pp. 158–9.
[154] *CSPD* 1683–4, pp. 150–1.
[155] See for instance: *Remarks on Algernon Sidneys Paper* (1683); *Some Animadversions on the Paper Delivered to the Sherriffs . . . by Algernon Sidney* (1683); *The Animadversions and Remarks upon Collonel Sidney's Paper Answered* (1684); *Reflections upon Coll. Sidney's Arcadia: The Old Cause* (1684); *Mr Sidney his Self-Conviction: Or, his Dying Paper Condemn'd to Live for a Conviction to the Present Faction* (1684); *A Defence of Sir Robert Filmer against the Misrepresentations of Algernon Sidney, Esq, in a paper Delivered by him to the Sherriffs etc.* (1684).
[156] *Some Animadversions*, pp. 3–4.
[157] *Remarks on Algernon Sidney's Paper*, p. 4.
[158] *Algernon Sidney's Farewel* [n.d.]

like' said another,[159] 'did our Old Rebel Dye, With his last breath profaning Majesty.'

LAST ACT (7 DECEMBER 1683)

(A) man of greate Courage, greate sense, greate parts, which he shew'd both at his trial and death; for when he came on the scaffold, in stead of a speech, he told them onely, that he had made his peace with God; that he came not thither to talk but to die ... sayed one prayer as short as a grace, laide downe his neck, and bid the Executioner do his office.[160]

By now entirely prepared, Sidney made his last public act brief and to the point. It impressed both his friends and his enemies. There was only a slight glimpse of the living (as opposed to dying) man when the headsman felt himself to have been underpaid.

On the freezing morning of 7 December, Sidney was taken from the Tower to the scaffold on Tower Hill, arriving at 10 o'clock. He was 'asked ... if he had any friends to accompany him on the scaffold. He said none but two servants of his brother's'. He was conducted 'on foot up to the scaffold. He said nothing in all his passage. As soon as he came up he said, I have made my peace with God and having nothing to say to men, but here is a paper.'[161]

Burnet claimed that Sidney had on the scaffold 'some Independent Preachers about him and expressed remorse for his sins, and great confidence in ye mercies of God'.[162] In this he is contradicted by both Barillon and Luttrell, the latter commenting that 'It (was) ... remarkable that he had no Minister with him, nor any of his relations, nor did he seem in the least concerned, and made no speech on the Scaffold.'[163] It would appear that Burnet, who had attended (and hounded) Russell to the scaffold, is at his least reliable when recording the clerical requirements of whig martyrs. In fact Sidney went out of the world as he insisted he had come into it: free of 'dependence upon any man'.

Once on the scaffold, Sidney 'bowed twice to the people', 'pulled off his hat and coat and doublet and gave them to his servants and said, I am ready to die'.[164] He 'gave three guineas to the executioner ... [who] seemed to grumble as if it were to[o] little, then he bid his man give him a guinea or two more, which he did'.[165]

---

[159] *The Reformation. A Satyr* [n.d.]
[160] *The Diary of John Evelyn*, vol. IV, p. 353.
[161] *CSPD* 1683–4, p. 137.
[162] Burnet, BL, Add. MS 63,057, vol. II, p. 158.
[163] Luttrell, *Briefe Relation*, vol. I, p. 293; Barillon recorded: 'Mr de Sidney did not wish at his death to be assisted by any protestant Minister, he had always been of the sect of independents.' PRO Baschet no. 156, p. 112.
[164] *The Execution of Algernon Sidney Esq*, p. 2; *CSPD* 1683–4, p. 137.
[165] *CSPD* 1983–4, p. 137.

'Traversing the Scaffold' Sidney 'kneeled on the South-Side, and Prayed to himself', 'Scarse 2 minuts', or 'while you might tell 20'.[166] Then, having 'Ordered the Executioner to take his time, without expecting any sign, he layd down his Head'.[167]

Sidney's head was 'struck off at one Blow, all but a small matter of flesh, which the Executioner sundred with his knife . . . the Body at the time of the stroak scarcely moving . . . and so [he] took up his head and showed it round the Scaffold, which was hung with mourning and the floor also covered with black and a black coffin'.[168]

Thereafter, Sidney's 'Body was carried thence by his friends to joyners Hall, and there continued a full day, and thence carryed to the sepulchar of his family [in the small parish church] at Penshurst in Kent.'[169] Permission for a private family burial had been granted that day to Henry Sidney by the King.[170]

A loyalist pamphleteer was quickly to wish, in vain, that 'the Dissenters would not, as sure those foolish people did, who made such haste after his Execution to get Hand-kerchiefs dip't in his Blood, look upon him as a Martyr'.[171] For the blow which had ended one life had indeed, thereby, begun another. This new Sidney would take what the old had given him, but he would be his own man. He would be moulded in the service of the living, not the dead. He would come to enjoy a success outside the experience, and perhaps the imagination, of Sidney himself. For the liberty he would seek, and enjoy, was of a different order. It was not the liberty of, but liberty from, the self-government of Sidney, and of history.

An Irishman among the souldiers that were on service at the execution of Mr Sidney . . . [who] left his rank and got his Handkerchif diped in his bloud, was examined by a Counsell of Warr and Casheared the Regiment, [and when] the weeke after enquiry was made why . . . he answered he had heard of a Popish Plott, and some Papists were executed for it, and he thought this Gentleman was a Catholick, and suffered martyrdome for the Catholicks and therefore he did it.'[172]

The wayward life of a martyr had begun.

---

[166] *The Execution of Algernon Sidney Esq*, p. 2; 'Roger Morrice's Entering Book', p. 398; *CSPD* 1683–4, p. 137.
[167] *The Execution*, p. 2.
[168] *The Execution*, p. 2; *CSPD* 1683–4, p. 139.
[169] 'Roger Morrice's Entering Book', p. 398.
[170] *CSPD* 1683–4, p. 138.
[171] *Reflections upon Coll Sidney's Arcadia*, p. 5.
[172] 'Roger Morrice's Entering Book', p. 402.

CONCLUSION

The Athens I love is not the one that is wronging me now, but that one in which I used to have secure enjoyment of my rights as a citizen. The country that I am attacking does not seem to me to be mine any longer; it is rather that I am trying to recover a country that has ceased to be mine. And the man who really loves his country is not the one who refuses to attack it when he has been unjustly driven from it, but the man whose desire for it is so strong that he will shrink from nothing in his efforts to get back there again.

Alcibiades, to the Spartans, 415 BC[1]

I

The remarkable career of Algernon Sidney the martyr has been recounted elsewhere.[2] Constructed, Frankenstein-like, from the remnants of a living person, Algernon the 'stern inflexible patriot' had a number of qualities true to his original. On the whole however that original was Sidney in death, rather than life. Reinforcing Sidney's stoicisation of himself was a perceptible rigormortis by which this inflexibility was maintained over continents, and centuries. Allied to it was an incorruptibility apparently superior to death itself. In the last decade of the eighteenth century, when public excitement could contain itself no longer, Algernon's grave was opened. 'Curiosity was excited – the body was very perfect.'[3] Sidney the patriot-hero was a triumph of the mortician's art.

Nevertheless, Algernon's posthumous admirers believed that they knew

---

[1] Thucydides, *History of the Peloponnesian War*, ed. M.I. Finley, translated by Rex Warner (1985), p. 469.

[2] Scott, *Algernon Sidney and the English Republic*, ch. 1; Worden, 'Commonwealth Kidney'; P. Karsten, *Patriot Heroes in England and America* (Wisconsin 1978); Caroline Robbins 'Algernon Sidney's *Discourses Concerning Government*', *William and Mary Quarterly*, 3rd series 4 (1947); *The Eighteenth Century Commonwealthsman* (1959). For Sidney's posthumous influence see also J.P. Kenyon, *Revolution Principles* (for England), Bernard Bailyn, *The Intellectual Origins of the American Revolution* (Cambridge, Mass. 1971) (for America` G.P. Gooch, *Germany and the French Revolution* (1920) (for Germany); A. Aulard, *The French Revolution 1789–1804* (1910) (for France).

[3] Karsten, *Patriot Heroes*, p. 114.

him well. This may even be true of the American who sternly invoked 'Alderman Sidney' in 1886.[4] And to the extent that this Sidney was their own creation they were quite correct. Deprived of contradiction, he was not difficult to understand. Relieved of imperfection he was not difficult to admire. Removed from his own time, all the darkness, the complexity and the signal violence of Sidney's actual life and thought faded away. In making these adjustments the hagiographic tradition was, of course, removing from Sidney's story the very things that are most important about it. The first work of the mortician, for preservative purposes, is to drain the blood from the body. Whatever Sidney achieved and has to teach us emerged from the great struggle in his life predicated upon just these characteristics. Without this struggle Sidney is not so much easier to know, as hardly worth knowing.

And yet the time has come to ask ourselves whether we now know him any better. Lacking Sidney's courage, as well as his education, the alert biographer rightly quails before this question. There is a natural inclination, at this point, to exchange knowledge for judgement. For most of its history in the public mind, Sidney's story has been a moral fable, culminating in the verdicts of hero, martyr or villain. My own view is that the real Sidney will not readily consent to be judged in this way. He fought hard against such judgement in his lifetime and it would be misguided to patronise him with it now. The Sidney of life, rather than death, was an altogether more complicated figure.

An attempt has been made to recover this living person. The author believed it would be a mistake in the process to attempt to become too comfortable with him, to domesticate him, let alone to take power over him. This was the one human failing of which he was least forgiving. Sidney is very able to take care of himself, he does not need to be excused or smoothed over. Taken as he was, his story has great power. But it has this precisely because of the element of struggle, of conflict within it, which defies our inclinations to passive judgement or resolution.

I believe Sidney asks for much more that this from us. He would like to goad us out of passivity, and into action. He is much less interested in resolving questions than in opening them up. The first step towards answering the difficult question above is, then, to recognise that Sidney invites us to struggle with him also. His whig admirers hoped to benefit from his achievement, for political purposes, without sharing in the conflict that created it. James Dalrymple succeeded in making this very difficult. As it is, conflict stands at the heart of Sidney's experience, whichever way we look at it. There are the conflicts within his family, within his personality, in his

---

[4] *Ibid.*, p. 72.

personal life, in his political conduct, and at the heart of his political thought. There are the over-arching conflicts between darkness and light, perfection and imperfection, self-government and slavery. Sidney distinguished himself from most of his contemporaries by his willingness to engage in these struggles – or his inability to disengage from them – in both thought and practice. Much of his power comes from the fact that he ended his life still thus engaged. It is as the unflinching defender of Machiavelli's tumults; of sedition, tumult and war, that we must come to know him.

Let us conclude, then, by leaving Sidney in possession of that power, and by meeting him on equal terms. If we are prepared to struggle with him he has a lot to teach us.

II

Not the least interesting thing about Sidney – yet another paradox – was his capacity to be both peculiarly of his time, and at war with it simultaneously. This makes him an exemplar of some aspects of our historical knowledge, and a challenger of others.

Sidney is an exemplar of some of the most important general forces at work in this period. He has something to teach us about the Renaissance, about the Reformation, about early modern Europe's wars of religion, about both the process of, and resistance to, European state centralisation, about the intellectual culture of the European elite. He invites us to think about the British civil wars and the interregnum, the republican experiment and the 'old cause', about the wholeness and the shape of the seventeenth-century English experience. At the same time, and perhaps as importantly, he reminds us that history is drama, that it is funny, suspenseful and sad, that it can incorporate the highest reaches of the human imagination and the greatest self-deception, the most exhilarating triumph and the completest tragedy.

In the same mode he reminds us of the complexity of the past, of how difficult it is to understand, and of the mental gulf that stands between our world and his. Despite, and because of, the peculiar richness of his writings, we can see that at the heart of Sidney's cause there is a test of the imagination that we may fail. To re-read the *Court Maxims* is to be aware of passionate hopes and hatreds central to the troubles in which he was involved which remain as mysterious as they are powerful. Of all his services to historians this one – to allow us to see so deeply into his time and our limitations – is the most touching.

Then there is Sidney the rebel, rather than the exemplar. This is the other aspect of his relationship with his time, and our history. By refusing to be straightforwardly summed up, by leaving writings so deeply revealing of himself and his situation, by operating on so many levels – personal, family, political, religious – by subsisting on controversy and paradox, Sidney does his level best to resist the historian's rather glib hunger for categorisation. In this role he is not the friend of historical generalisation but the questioner of it. Sidney was a troublemaker in his own time and it would be nice if he could remain one in ours. Indeed Sidney's difficult and combative relationship with his time may have given him an altogether rarer quality. It is that of the historiographic rebel – the refusal to answer the summons of historians to the bar of their preconceived categories and questions, and the ability to substitute some categories and questions of his own.

There are many examples of this quality but it works in more than one direction. There is Sidney refusing to fit his life into the professional categories of historians because they are perceived to be too narrow. And there is Sidney refusing the same thing because they are perceived to be too large. This is precisely the recalcitrance we have seen before Chief Justice Jeffreys and we should not expect to be exempt from it. There is, then, Sidney the bridge-builder, and Sidney the discriminator.

Our histories are still national histories but Sidney refused to live a national life. Our political crises are still perceived as national ones but Sidney's were not so. We divide seventeenth-century English (or British) history in half at 1660 but there is Sidney perplexed, frowning, telling us this misses the point. Nor will he settle for one century when it is clear that his cause, like his ancestry, is unimpressed by the division into centuries in general, and sixteenth and seventeenth centuries in particular. The influence of the *Discourses* carries the same cause over into the eighteenth and nineteenth centuries. We continue to study political and intellectual history as if they were distinct, but for Sidney this was not the case. Of course Sidney's mental universe was larger even than this since like most humanist scholars he saw his brief life against a backdrop of at least two and a half thousand years of European civilisation. In time, as in space, the modern biographer struggles ill-equipped, both linguistically and conceptually, to represent this world. He does so by employing the widest categories available to him: that Sidney was a product of the Renaissance, and of the Reformation.

Having done this he hastens to qualify this statement, to further categorise and subdivide. Throughout this process Sidney is wilfully obstructive. We may want to know which of these great movements held him more securely in its grasp. The longer we consider this question the more ill-conceived it seems to be. The mansion of the Renaissance, then, contains many houses – where can he be located? Sidney's habitation is sprawling, untidy, categorically disfiguring. Among ancients he will not prefer Greece or Rome: they are part of a process within which, he emphasises, the Greeks learnt from the Egyptians and Phoenicians, the Romans from their enemies the Carthaginians.[5] Thereafter his inspiration comes from Italy, France, Spain, the Low Countries, Scotland and England; from both protestant and catholic, medieval and modern. None of this displays a lack of commitment on his part since he is, as we know, fiercely committed and indeed partisan. But as he had, in Burnet's words, 'studied ye matter of Government and the History of power beyond any man yt ever I knew',[6] so he had done so with an impulse towards comprehension and connectedness, towards synthesis, which is at odds with the modern historian's impulse to categorise and subdivide. It is the pathway to understanding of a pre-modern whose ruling spirits – ironically enough – are unity, continuity, and harmony, rather than division and change.

All of this causes problems. Is Sidney a Platonist or Aristotelian? He is both. Is he a stoic or a sceptic? In an important sense he is both. Is he the believer in natural law universals, the most faithful English disciple of Grotius, or the believer in contingency and mutability, the most faithful English follower of Machiavelli? He is both.

At this point the intellectual historian points out that it is not possible, strictly speaking, to be a believer in universals and a sceptic.[7] This point is well made, but there is Sidney, leaning on his sword, and mumbling in a discontented manner. We should observe the sword, because it is very much the heart of the matter. He explains that to go down this road is to shut out half of his thought, and so deprive it of its meaning. It is precisely his appreciation of the mutability and variety of the world that underlies the search for universals, anchored beyond it. It is precisely the relationship between these two not intellectually compatible sets of beliefs, a relationship of tension, that lies at the heart of his thought. Without Thrasymacus there is no Plato, and no Sidney either.

We may, therefore, as historians, make our point. But in so doing we are bringing to Sidney's thought concerns for intellectual purity, and for categorical distinction, that are foreign to it. We are forced, in describing his thought, to employ categorical discriminators which are unsuitable to the task. This is partly because that thought was not, for Sidney, an end in itself but a means to something. Intellectually it was not knowledge, but a journey in search of knowledge, never to be completed. Politically, it was an accompaniment, and a means, to action. Consequently Sidney does not even have a straightforward relationship to Machiavelli. Is he Machiavelli's harshest critic or his greatest admirer? He is both.

What, then, of the Sidney of the Reformation? He is no more compliant.

---

[5] Sidney, *Discourses*, p. 59.
[6] Burnet, BL Add. MS 63,057, vol. II, p. 138.
[7] See Michael Mendle's interesting review in *Albion* (1989), pp. 496–7.

That his cause was the 'protestant cause' is clear enough. This does not stop him living for three years in the palaces of Roman cardinals, whose libraries were very fine. If we thought the Reformation and Counter-Reformation belonged only to the sixteenth century, Sidney reminds us that this was not so. But even as an (internationalist) protestant he is exceptionally difficult to pin down. On the one hand he insists that reason, the divine fragment in man, is the straightest link between God and his people. By this His creatures may know their Father's will – 'that which is good', both in general, and for them in particular – and construct a glorious political fabric to pursue it. On this subject Sidney's optimism becomes extravagant and it is this function of his Christianity which separates him finally from Machiavelli. On the other hand we find a range of other religious phenomena which do not sit easily with this platonic rationalism. There is the providentialism of the New Model Army, and the belief in blood-guilt by which it was accompanied, by which he was deeply affected.[8] There are the no less extravagant claims he makes for faith and spirituality as the keys to the relationship between God and man. There is his unwavering and emotional personal dedication to the Godly – 'those who live in and by faith' – around whom all his practical endeavours revolve. There is his insistence that the Old Testament and the Church Fathers are not politically prescriptive, except when they are.

At the same time there is Sidney in discriminating mode, requiring that we be more specific. This demand touches both republicanism and whiggism. It also invites us to think about the relationship between the two. Sidney reminds us that there was a relationship – or rather several – but that it was in no way straightforward. He shows us that the causes of 1678–83 had a long history, as his temper had a short fuse. When we equate these causes with exclusion we are being altogether too discriminating. When we talk about 'the first whigs' we are being insufficiently so. If Sidney mocked exclusion, while defending the Commons' right to demand it, perhaps we can understand its role in the crisis better for that. If his rudeness and bad manners have dissolved the first whigs then perhaps we can understand early whiggism, in all its complexity, better for that. Above all Sidney reminds us of the power of public memory, and of the multiplicity of its shapes, for a generation overshadowed by its past.

In Sidney's hands the 'old cause' looks a lot older. But within English republicanism, and classical republicanism, more discrimination may be

---

[8] This is most evident in the *Court Maxims*, and on the eve of Sidney's death, but we also see it elsewhere. There is, for instance, Lantin's remark that 'when the Prince of Orange was obliged to lift the seige of Maestrik, M. le Comte de Sidney whom I saw in Paris, said that the Event was an affect of the anger of God against the Prince. He attributed this to the blood of the [de] Wits – that this Prince had caused to be massacred, although he had great obligations to them. Bibliothèque Nationale, Fr. 23254, p. 101.

called for. When Felix Raab saw how un-Machiavellian Machiavelli had become in Harrington's *Oceana*, he wondered if there was any place for the real Machiavelli in mid-seventeenth-century England.[9] Sidney, with Nedham, reminds us that there was. And indeed the more we look at these two, the more the ideological centre of gravity within that republicanism shifts towards them, and the more idiosyncratic Harrington appears. This is no diminution of Harrington's status: he is the greater for it. But it does mean that we need to understand English republicanism less by reference to its oddest product than by the common stock upon which the whole range of republican thought drew. It looks very much as if, in the early hands of Milton and Nedham, this was as Livian and Machiavellian as Sidney's thought always remained.

Within that spectrum, of course, Sidney made his own contributions. The most important was his correction of Machiavelli in the direction of change, providing a counterpoint to Harrington's own in the pursuit of stasis. And with Milton and Vane, Sidney helps us remember the whole dimension of the republican experience, both practical and ideological, which was not classical but religious. This was where the natural law theory of Grotius, the law of God, came together with the classical republicanism of Machiavelli. Sidney the bridge-builder is at his most illuminating, as well as most perplexing, when he is the bridge between the classical Nedham and the religious Vane. Yet we know that in this role he sits, with Milton, at the centre of an extraordinary and crucial historical moment. A king has been beheaded, a government abolished, and all the mental resources and moral aspirations of both Renaissance and Reformation are pouring into the cavity of custom thus created. This was the grand and terrifying experiment which marked Sidney for life, and which has marked us partly through him.

III

Sidney was a figure of practical political importance in two phases of his life, both of them troubled and brief. The first was at the helm of the Republic, in 1652–3 and 1659–60. The second was during an attempt to restore some version of that battered fabric, between 1678 and 1683. These were small parts of a long and eventful journey, and yet the dialogue between them, both in Sidney's mind and outside it, has necessarily formed the core of this study.

In the course of this journey we have come across many sides of our central character. There is the solitary Sidney, who spent much of his life alone and in exile. There is the familial Sidney, who never produced a family

[9] Raab, *The English Face of Machiavelli*, ch. 6 in general, and pp. 214–17 in particular.

of his own to supplant that under whose troubled shadow he remained. There is the 'retired' Sidney, in Augsburg, Nerac and Rome. There is Sidney the scholar, and, never far behind him, the man of action. It is natural to wonder if there was a 'real' private person, behind the public posturing. It is unnecessary since, as we have seen, the relationship between Sidney's private and public selves, between the personal and the political struggles for liberty, was close and fundamental. Sidney was made angry, but he was also born so. Sidney complaining about partridges in Nerac sounds remarkably like Sidney complaining about corruption in the *Discourses*, or injustice in the Tower. If it was 'the broken limb of a shipwrecked faction' that limped, wounded, into retirement in 1660, so it was the same old seadog, a veritable seventeenth-century bluebeard, who repeatedly thereafter attempted to recover and rebuild that ship. All of those efforts were an attempt to reclaim Sidney's Republic, that self-governing community of which he had once been a citizen, a country forever lost. We have tried to understand its complicated topography, those elements of history and memory, of personal and political aspiration, of self-deception and hope.

In all of these endeavours, in practice as well as in theory, Sidney divided his own political world into two zones. There was the zone of mutability, variety, and change. These were effects of imperfection, 'perfection being in God only, not in the things he has created'. This was an echo of the Chaos from which the divine creation had come. This was the world in which Sidney lived, and operated. It is quite exceptional how deeply he saw into this darkness, and the lengths to which he was prepared to go to operate effectively within it. Sidney was, as we have seen, quite ferociously ends-directed. The presiding genius of this zone was Machiavelli, yet in his consideration of change, 'which is imperfection', Sidney took a step beyond his master. In a 'time of public calamity' he was even prepared to consider 'the harsh necessity of sinning against God'.

Then there was the zone of permanence, and perfection. This was the world to which Sidney aspired. Its inspiration lay beyond the reach of this life, in God. It was by the light of this beacon that Sidney attempted to navigate, 'though with much weakness and frailty', across the murky waters of the world. Its effects, 'those reflections of the divine rays', were the 'justice, virtue, and truth: in short, the good of mankind', with which Sidney identified his cause. The precondition for their recovery, and pursuit, was liberty, 'that liberty in which God created us', which amounted to the right to see Him clearly, and seek him out.

The tension inherent in this enterprise is obvious enough. But what distinguished Sidney was his refusal to shy from either aspect of this struggle. Thus he insisted to the end of his life on translating those ideals into action, in the ruthlessly observed conditions of an imperfect world. And he insisted upon directing his actions towards those ideals, when the imperfect world in fact made a mockery of them. For liberty was a double-edged property: the freedom to choose good, and virtue, entailed the freedom to choose wickedness, and vice. This was the harsh lesson of the 1650s. And yet for many reasons – biographical, familial, political – Sidney could not bring himself to abandon either side of the struggle for that dangerous and unstable substance which might at any moment blow up in his hands. Accordingly, what we will remember from Sidney's struggle for liberty are two sides of the same coin: exhilaration and despair. There is the exultation of the republican, and the bitterness of the Restoration experience. The people at the core of them are one, 'that stiffnecked people' of Israel who opted, willingly, for the restoration of monarchy. 'We could never be contented 'till we return'd againe into Egypt, the house of our bondage.'[10]

The great celebration of the republican experience is the *Discourses*. The effects of liberty in England have been as electrifying, and as glorious, as they were in Rome. Everything that was great in Rome, and worthy of imitation, 'grew up, flourished, and perished, with her liberty'. 'The same causes will ever have the same effects'. That

love to the public that the Romans had would have the same effect if it were now in being ... We need no other proof of this, than what we have seen in our own country, where, in a few years, good discipline, and a just encouragement given to those who did well, produced more examples of pure, complete, incorruptible virtue, than Rome or Greece could ever boast; or if more be wanting, they may be easily be found among the Switzers, Hollanders, and others: but it is not necessary to light a candle to the sun.[11]

But virtue was hard, and mankind frail. Sidney wrote a good deal about the frailty of man, both in himself and others. 'Man is not able to stand in his own strength. If he leave dependence on God he must become the servant of the Devil.'[12] And so there is the different tone of the *Court Maxims*, which anticipates much about the Restoration, including its author's death:

If we were as ripe for mercy as our enemies are for vengeance our desires would soon be accomplished. But God's time is best. They that depend upon Him fall not into impatience for the day of His coming, nor are affrighted at the boasting of His and their enemies. That Spirit that has planted faith in their hearts doth perpetually bring both fruits of hope and joy. They have resigned themselves and all they have and are into God's hands as willing sacrifices.[13]

These elements of faith and reason, of Christianity and Classicism, were never fundamentally reconciled in Sidney's thought. They simply co-existed.

---

[10] Sidney, *Court Maxims*, p. 203.   [11] Sidney, *Discourses*, p. 114.
[12] Sidney, *Court Maxims*, p. 102.   [13] *Ibid.*, p. 78.

in Sidney as in Milton. In the normal course of God's providence history operated according to certain laws, in England as in Rome. According to these the cause of liberty would 'ever produce the same effects'. And yet there were also times of particular providence, of God's special dispensations. Thus the great victories Sidney experienced, as an officer in the New Model Army, and a military administrator under the Republic, had not been simply the effects of 'mans valour and virtue'. They had also, unforgettably, been an effect of the particular intervention of God. And as God's presence could be vouchsafed to his people, so it could also be withdrawn. This occurred as a punishment for their sins, for their frailty – for that imperfection that was a condition of the world. At such times his people would suffer, and they had to be prepared to do so, as Sidney was.

IV

It was thus the coexistence of, and the relationship between, these two worlds – of perfection and imperfection, of God and man – which necessitated suffering and struggle in this life. The point where Sidney's classical and religious thinking came together securely was therefore appropriate. This was his commitment to the cutting edge of that struggle, to armed force. This is the thing about Sidney which, while reflecting his times, also distinguishes him most powerfully within them. In this also lies his most arresting contribution to political thought. No seventeenth-century hand ever held the sword of war more resolutely. All Sidney's major authorities – God, history, and experience – reinforced him in this. 'That state is best which is best constituted for making war.'

In considering Sidney's bellicosity we must remember his ancestry – both Percy and Sidney. We must remember the general context: that he, like Sir Philip, was a product of Europe's religious wars. We must remember his intellectual sources, above all in this respect Livy, Machiavelli, and Grotius. The decisive influence, however, was Sidney's personal experience, of the 1640s and the 1650s. It was this which gave this ancestry and these sources their luminous present meaning. In the 1640s arms taken, as Grotius had explained, in a just war of self-defence, had been recognised as such by the particular intervention of God. This had happened in the Netherlands as well as in England. The precious result, which was 'liberty, civil and spiritual', had thereafter become, as Livy and Machiavelli had explained it would, its own military reward. This was the good old cause, the cause of God, for which 'how often and wonderfully Thou hast declared thyself'. By 1653 England, Scotland and Ireland had been conquered, and 'we never bid fairer for being masters of the whole world'. This was a heady experience, and thereafter Sidney was condemned to live 'in the long shadow of a short republic'.[14]

This republican shadow was, as we have seen, but the most intense distillation of other, broader inheritances. They are encapsulated most completely by the figure of Sir Philip Sidney. He combined in his person those aspects of the Renaissance and the Reformation, of both internationalism and militarism, that made the greatest impact upon his grand-nephew. Above all he combined the public examples of life, and death in arms for that cause. By this he won himself 'immortall fame among the godly'[15] but his death had a deeper significance than this. To listen to William Byrd's peerless song for his funeral, 'Come to me griefe forever', is to catch the authentic early strains of what would be an approaching century of tragedy. The loss of Sir Philip Sidney was a first sign of what it would cost the protestant nation to endure the century of the European Counter-Reformation.

That century, and that struggle, were the contexts for Algernon Sidney's life and thought. So his story was, in the end, despite its dramatic high points, also one of tragedy. Little wonder that, in the process, in thought and practice, Sidney wielded the primary prerogative of arms. Thus it was that a defence, in the *Discourses*, of Machiavelli's tumults, became a defence of sedition and civil war. This turned into a justification of rebellion, which, 'being nothing but a renewed war, is either good or evil, just or unjust, according to the cause or manner of it'. It was the potency of this doctrine, in both theory and practice, which brought Sidney's story to a close.

In this way the struggles of Sidney's life, and the tensions of his thought, came together on the point of a sword. Here God and Livy, Grotius and Machiavelli could agree. The effect of their agreement was, in Sidney's hands, not concord, but conflict. It was both a justification and an explanation of its place in the world. Within that arena of imperfection there could be no pursuit of the ideal – no justice, no liberty, and no advancement of the public good – without a willingness to look conflict in the face. The ways of God were hard, and their progress necessitated a preparedness to take arms, both against the state, and for it.

This is a disturbing message, but Sidney has earned the right to put it to us. It is a product of disturbing times. But it is above all the result of Sidney's refusal to relinquish any aspect of his vision, or his circumstances. Peace would deserve praise 'if mankind were so framed, that a people intending hurt to none could preserve themselves. But the world being so far of another temper' this could not be so. Someone who would accept the

[14] Mark Goldie, *History* 1 (1990), pp. 131–2.
[15] Du Plessis Mornay, *A Worke Concerning the Trewnesse of the Christian Religion* (1587), Dedicatory Epistle.

imperfection of this world might have peace. Someone who would seek only the perfection of another, not considering how to translate its effects into the disturbing practical circumstances of this, they, too, might have peace. But Sidney could not take either of these roads. His struggle, and his achievement, resulted from his inability to accept anything less than the hard totality of his condition.

We end then, as we began, with Sidney the disturber of the public peace. What is important about him is not his realism, or his idealism, but his combination of the two. In this sense he is less notable for his superhuman consistency than for his human completeness. This is rare, and in him it took immense courage. We can, then, be as grateful to Sidney for his worldly imperfections as for his other-worldly aspirations. We can learn much from his willingness to see himself, and a complex and troubling world, as they were. And we can admire him for never giving up the struggle to understand that world, and to act in it.

I know people will say, I straine at knats, and swallow camels, that it is a strange conscience that lets a man runne violently on, till he is deepe in civil blood, and then stays at a few words and complements; that can earnestly endeavour to extirpate a long established monarchy, and then cannot be brought to see his error [and put] one finger towards the setting together the broken pieces of it. I have enough to answer this in my own mind; I cannot helpe if I judge amisse; I did not make myself, nor can I correct the defects of my own creation. I walk in the light God hath given me, if it be dimme or uncertaine, I must beare the penalty of my errors: I hope to do it with patience, and that noe burden shall be very grievous to me, except sinne and shame.[16]

[16] Blencowe, *Sidney Papers*, pp. 194–8.

BIBLIOGRAPHY

There follows (1) A bibliographic guide to Sidney's surviving writings, including correspondence: (2) A bibliography of sources cited in *Algernon Sidney and the English Republic 1623–77*, and *Algernon Sidney and the Restoration Crisis 1677–83*.

1 SIDNEY'S WRITINGS (in chronological order)

I write only today, that which I shall read the next week or month, and then burn. (Sidney, *Of Love*)

I . . . have burnt more of my own writings than a horse could carry. (Sidney, *Trial*)

LEGAL, POLITICAL AND OTHER WRITINGS

1. *Of Love* [1640–60], MS in Sidney's hand, BL Add. MS 34,100; published in *Tracts . . . of the late Lord Somers*, ed. W. Scott (1809–15), vol. VIII.
2. 'Statement in the handwriting of Algernon Sidney as to his transactions with Lord and Lady Strangford' [1660–64], MS in Sidney's hand, KAO, Maidstone, De Lisle MS U1475 E28/5.
3. *Court Maxims, Discussed and Refelled* [1665–6], MS in the hands of two copyists, Warwickshire Record Office MS CR1886 (publication is planned, edited by the present author, by Cambridge University Press).
4. *The Character of Henry Vane Jnr* [1662–70], MS in the hands of a copyist, Herefordshire Record Office D/EP F45; published in V. Rowe, *Sir Henry Vane the Younger* (1970) as Appendix F. The MS was 'recovered at Montpelier', where Sidney lived from 1666 to 1670–2, by Vane's son Christopher, Lord Barnard (HMC Rept 45.3, Buccleugh MS, vol. II, p. 756). Two other 'characters', of Charles Gustavus of Sweden and Oliver Cromwell, also recovered by Barnard, have been lost. Sidney's characters of the Roman Cardinals (1661) appear in a letter to his father, published by Collins (see Correspondence, below). The *Character* and *Court Maxims* are the only Sidney manuscripts to have survived in the hands of copyists, and it is possible that the *Maxims* was among the same batch of writings left by Sidney at Montpellier and subsequently returned to England from there.
5. *A Prophesy of St Thomas the Martyr* [1666], MS in Sidney's hand, Bodl. Lib. MS Engl. Letters C.200 fols. 24–5; published by Benjamin Furly in Dutch and English at Rotterdam, 1689 (see BL 1103.f.27, 15–18). *A Prophesy* was reprinted in P. Karsten, *Patriot-Heroes in England and America* (Madison 1978) as Appendix A.

6. 'The Case of Algernone and Henry Sydney referred to Sir William Jones, as it stands in reason, and commonsense, which is true equity and the ground of Lawe' [1680], MS in Sidney's hand, BL Egerton MS 1049.
7. (with Sir William Jones) *A Just and Modest Vindication of the Proceedings of the Two Last Parliaments* (1681), no MS, subsequently republished in *State Tracts of the Reign of Charles II* (1689), vol. IV, appendix XV.
8. *Discourses Concerning Government* [1681–3], no MS; published in London in 1698; republished in London 1702, 1704, 1751, 1763, 1772; in the Netherlands 1702, 1755; in Paris 1755, 1794; in Edinburgh 1750; in Germany 1705, 1793; in New York 1805. A modern reprint of the 1751 edition was produced by Gregg International Publishers, London 1968. A new American edition is due, edited by Tom West, for Liberty Classics. All references in this text are to the 1772 edition in: J. Robertson (ed.), *Sydney on Government: The Works of Algernon Sydney* (1772).
9. 'Notes concerning an action in Chancery: Algernon Sidney v. Philip, Earl of Leicester, Henry Sidney and Gilbert Spencer' [1682], MS in Sidney's hand, KAO, Maidstone, De Lisle MS U1475 L5.
10. *The Arraignment, Trial and Condemnation of Algernon Sydney* [1683]. References here are to the 1772 edition of Sidney's *Works*. Title abbreviated in text as *Trial*.
11. *The Apology of Algernon Sydney, in the Day of his Death* [1683], no MS, published in Hollis' edition of Sidney's *Works* (1763), and thereafter. References here are to the 1772 edition. A manuscript in Sidney's hand was presented by, and returned to, Joseph Ducasse before a Committee of the House of Lords in 1689 (*JHL* 1689, p. 390).
12. *The Very Copy of a Paper Delivered to the Sheriffs* (1683), no MS in Sidney's hand, numerous contemporary MS copies exist. Published in Haarlem and London in December 1683, and with Sidney's works thereafter. References here are to the copy in 'Memoir of Algernon Sydney', *Works*, 1772. Title abbreviated in text as *Last Paper*.

Postscript: Sidney's conversation is recorded:
a) with Bulstrode Whitelocke [1653], by Whitelocke, BL Add. MS 53727 pp. 53–7
b) with Edward Montague [1659], by Montague, *The Journal of Edward Montagu first earl of Sandwich* ed. R.C. Anderson (Navy Records Society 1928)
c) with Marshal Turenne [1670], by Turenne, transcript enclosed in a letter from Louis XIV to Colbert de Croissy, the French Ambassador in London. Paris, Ministre des Affaires Etrangères, Correspondence Politique Angleterre vol. 99, Du Roy à Colbert, 29 July 1970
d) with Jean Baptiste Lantin [1677], by Lantin, Paris BN Fr MS 23254, 'Lantiniana'
e) with Ford, Lord Grey [1683], by Grey, *Secret History of the Rye House Plot* [1685, published 1754]

LETTERS

1643 (1) to the Countess of Leicester, no MS, printed in J.T. Gilbert, *History of the Irish Confederation* 7 vols. (Dublin 1882–7), pp. xlviii–xlx
1645 (1) to Lord Fairfax, MS BL Sloane MS 1519 f.112

1648 (1) to William Aylesbury, no MS, printed in *State Papers Collected by Edward, earl of Clarendon* 3 vols. (Oxford 1767–86), vol. II, p. 421

1648 (1) to the Earl of Leicester, MS BL Add. MS 21,506, f.55, published in *Works*, 1772

1649 (1) to the Corporation of Sandwich, MS KAO, Maidstone, Sandwich MS Sa/ZB2/114

1649 (1) On behalf of the 'poore widdowe . . . [of] a gunner of this [Dover] Castle', MS reproduced in facsimile, E. Melling, *Kentish Sources* (Maidstone 1959), vol. II, pp. 32–3

1650 (1) to Bulstrode Whitlocke, MS Longleat, Bath MS, Whitelocke Papers XXVI, fol.250

1650 (1) to John Gay, MS BL Stowe MS 184, fol.269–72

1659 (5) to Bulstrode Whitelocke, MS Longleat, Bath MS, Whitelocke Papers vols. XIX, XX; two published by R. Blencowe (ed.), *Sydney Papers* (1825)

1659–60 (9) [with Robert Honewood and/or Thomas Boone] to the Council of State, printed in T. Birch (ed.), *A Collection of State Papers of John Thurloe* (7 vols., 1742), and *Works* (1772)

1658–63 (23) to the Earl of Leicester, MSS in KAO, Maidstone De Lisle MS U1475/C/84; published by A. Collins, *Letters and Memorials of State . . . from the Sydney Papers . . . at Penshurst* (2 vols., 1742), and in *Works* (1772)

1659–60 (9) to the Earl of Leicester, MSS in Sevenoaks Library, Kent, MS 1000/7 Z1, published by R. Blencowe (ed.), *Sydney Papers* (1825)

1663 (1) to the Earl of Leicester, published in HMC Rep. De Lisle MS vol. VI, pp. 520–3.

[1664–5] (1) to Benjamin Furly, no MS, published by R. Blencowe (ed.), *Sydney Papers* (1825)

1665–6 (4) Extracts of letters to Edmund Ludlow recorded by Ludlow, 'A Voyce from the Watchtower', Bodl. Lib., MS Eng Hist C.487, pp. 1056–1113 (see Scott, *Sidney and the English Republic*, pp. 175–83)

1677 (1) to Monsieur Bafoy, agent of the Duc de Bouillon, MS Paris, Archives Nationales R2/82 (see Scott, *Sidney and the English Republic*, pp. 240–2)

1677 (2) to Henry Coventry, MS Longleat, Bath MS, Coventry Papers, appendix vol. II, fols.134–5

1677–81 (22) to Henry Savile, MSS Chatsworth, Devonshire MS, Halifax Papers, twenty-one published in *Works* (1772) (one, 1677, mis-dated to 1682)

1679 (1) to George Savile, MS *ibid.*, published by H. Foxcroft, *Life and Letters of Sir George Savile* (2 vols, 1898), vol. I, p. 204

1678–80 (11) to Benjamin Furly, MSS in Bodl. Lib. Engl. Letters c.200, published by T. Forster (ed.), *Original Letters of Locke, Algernon Sidney, and Anthony Lord Shaftesbury* (1830)

1683 (10) nine to John Hampden jnr, one to an unknown 'deare freind and kinsman', possibly Henry Neville, MS East Sussex Record Office, Lewes, Glynde Place Archives no. 794

SUMMARY: 106 letters survive, of which 69 have been published. One outstanding collection remains unpublished – that of 1683.

POSTSCRIPT: Sidney's most famous 'letter', 'The Hon Algernon Sidney's Letter against Bribery and Arbitrary Government', printed in Rochester (ed.), *Familiar Letters* (1695), *Somers Tracts* (1809–15), vol. VIII, and Blencowe (ed.), *Sidney*

Papers, is a posthumous whig fabrication. (See Scott, *Sidney and the English Republic*, pp. 148–9.)

2 BIBLIOGRAPHY OF SOURCES CITED

PRIMARY SOURCES

MANUSCRIPTS

Public Record Office, Chancery Lane, London
a)   *Baschet Correspondence*, PRO 31/3, nos. 125 (1670), 140–56 (1678–83): correspondence of the French Ambassadors in London
b)   *Chancery Court Records*

Pleadings
C5 515/25; C6 4/193; C6 28/56; C6 81/75; C6 82/52–6, 60, 69; C6 124/78; C6 126/78, 82; C6 127/85; C6 128/110; C6 161/65; C6 205/51; C6 244/2; C7 317/62; C7 325/2; C7 327/50; C7 357/50; C7 419/39; C10 25/46; C10 70/104; C10 79/88; C10 132/119; C10 195/28; C10 469/235

Affidavits
C41/22 46, 116, 211, 367, 552; C41/23 158, 131, 209; C41/24 386, 1030

Decrees and orders (C33)
1677 Trinity p. 523
1678 Michaelmas pp. 41, 207, 223, 266, 276
1678 Easter pp. 307, 314, 315, 317
1678 Trinity pp. 431, 548
1679 Hilary pp. 258
1681 C33/258 pp. 208, 256, 288, 352
1682–3 C33/260 pp. 74, 115, 261, 293

Reports and certificates
C38/201 December (Mich.) 1678
C38/204 July 15 (Trinity) 1679

c)   *State papers*

Domestic: SP16/514; SP21/26; SP25/39–40, 68, 127, 132, 138; SP28/434; SP29/108, 171; SP44/68

France: SP78/101–11, 113, 129

Flanders: SP36/205

Archives de Lot-et-Garonne, Agen
Fonds Lagrange-Ferregues, Serie J, pp. 180–9; 'Notes Sur Nerac: Familles I', pp. 316–19.
Registre des Mariages bénie en l'eglise reformée de Nerac 4E 199/17

Archives Nationale, Paris
R2/82. Sidney to Monsieur Bafoy (1677)

Bibliothèque de Lille, Lille
Bullart MSS 682, no. 482

Bibliothèque Nationale, Paris
*E.994.H.a Sidney's *Discourses* (La Haye 1702), with inscription.
FM 2366
Fr MS 23254 'Lantiniana'

Bodleian Library, Oxford
MS Engl. Hist. C.487 Edmund Ludlow, 'A Voyce from the Watchtower'.
MS Engl. Letters C.200 Furly papers.
Rawlinson MSS A16, A65, A67.
Thurloe MSS vol. VII

British Library, London
Add MS 21,426 Baynes Correspondence
21,506 Sidney to Leicester 10 Jan. 1648
25,124 Coventry to Sidney 1677
32,500
32,680 Sidney Papers
33,058 Papers relating to Sussex
34,100 MS *Of Love*
38,847 'Robert West's full confession to the King'
44,729 Gladstone Papers
53,727 Bulstrode Whitelocke's diary.
63,057 Burnet transcript (2 vols.)
BL Casebook ref 105e.60(7) *The Case of Algernon Sidney* (1680)
Egerton MS 1049 'The Case of Algernone and Henry Sidney referred to Sir William Jones'
Northumberland MS Alnwick Micro Reel 286
Northumberland MS Syon House Micro Reel 291
Sloane MS 1519 Letters of State, Sidney to Fairfax 1645
Stowe MS 184 Papers Relating to Fee-Farm Rents

Buckinghamshire Record Office, Aylesbury
D/Dr/12/38 The Petition of Sir William Drake

Chatsworth, Devonshire MSS
a)   Halifax Papers, MS Sidney to Henry Savile
b)   Du Moulin Letters 21.9, 21.20

Dr Williams Library, London
Roger Morrice's Entering Book, vol. I

East Sussex Record Office, Lewes
Glynde Place Archives no. 794, Sidney to Hampden, and one other

Herefordshire Record Office
D/EP F45 MS *The Character of Henry Vane jnr*

Kent Archives Office, Maidstone
(a)   De Lisle MS [Sidney Family Papers]
(1)   U1475 (Main Collection)
Correspondence: C82/34; C83/18, 49, 53; C84/1–23; C85/7, 9, 15, 39; C87/4; C97/1; C114/26, 28; C113/1; C124/2–3; C125/2B; C126/1; C132/3, 76, 178; C133/31; C162/1; C164/2–5
Estate Papers; E28/4–8; E71/2, 7, 9; E99

Family Papers: F21/1–2; F30/10; F32/4–7
Legal Papers: L5
Official Papers: 089/11, 27; 092; 0101/1–6; 0142
Literary and Miscellaneous: Z1/1, 4–11; Z6; Z9; Z32–33; Z45/1–2

(2) U1500 (Additional Collection)
Correspondence: C2/4
Estate Papers: E48–51; E95/17

(b) *Sandwich MS*
Sa/ZB2/114

Longleat, Bath MSS
Coventry Papers appendix, vol. II
Portland Papers XVII fols. 65–6
Whitelocke Papers XXVI fol. 250, XIX fols. 66–7, 74–6, 94, 96–7, XX

Ministère des Affaires Etrangères, Paris
Correspondance Politique, Sous-série Angleterre vols. 99, 102

Warwickshire Record Office
MS CR 1886, *Court Maxims, Discussed and Refelled*

Westminster, House of Lords MSS
Committee Book HL vol. IV (1688–9)

PRINTED PRIMARY SOURCES (place of publication London,
unless otherwise specified)

BOOKS

A Collection of State Tracts published during the Reign of Charles II (1689), vol. IV

A Collection of State Tracts published during the Reign of William III (1706)

A Collection of Scarce and Valuable Tracts ... of the Late Lord Somers, 13 vols. (1809–15), vols. VIII–IX

Ailesbury, Thomas 3rd Earl of *Memoirs*, 2 vols. (1890)
Aristotle, *The Politics*, ed. T.A. Sinclair (Harmondsworth 1969)
  Ethics trans. J.A. Thomson (Harmondsworth 1984)
Aubrey, John *Brief Lives*, ed. O.L. Dick (1972)
Bacon, N. *Historical and Political Discourse of the Laws and Government of England* (1682, 1st published 1649)
Barbour, H. and Roberts, A. (eds.) *Early Quaker Writings 1650–1700* (Michigan 1973)
Berry, B.E. *The Life and Letters of Rachel Wriothesley, Lady Russell* (1819)
Bethel, S. *The Interest of Princes and States* (1680)
  The Present Interest of England Stated (1671)
  The World's Mistake in Oliver Cromwell (1668)
Blencowe, R. (ed.) *Diary of the Times of Charles II* (1843)
  Sydney Papers (1823)
Bodin, Jean *Six Bookes of a Commonweale* (1606), ed. K.D. McRae (Cambridge, Mass. 1962)
Borgeaud, C. *Histoire de L'Université de Genève: L'Académie de Calvin 1559–1798*, vol. I (Geneva 1900)

Brutus, Junius [Du Plessis Mornay] *Vindiciae Contra Tyrannos: A Defence of Liberty against Tyrants* (1689)
Bryant, A. (ed.) *Letters of Charles II* (1935)
Burnet, Gilbert *History of My Own Time*, 2 vols. (Oxford 1823)
   A Supplement to Burnet's History of My Own Time, ed. H. Foxcroft (Oxford 1902)
Burton, T. *Burtons Diary*, ed. J.T. Rutt, 4 vols. (1828)
Calendar of State Papers Domestic 1641–3; 1645–7; 1648–9; 1649–50; 1650; 1651; 1652–3; 1657–8; 1658–9; 1664–5; 1665; 1673; 1677–8; 1682; 1683; 1683–4
Calendar of State Papers Venetian 1659–61
Cameron, W.J. *New Light on Aphra Behn* (Auckland 1961)
Clarendon, Edward Hyde Earl of *History of The Great Rebellion*, ed. W.D. Macray, 6 vols. (Oxford 1887)
   State papers collected by Edward, Earl of Clarendon, 3 vols. (Oxford 1767–86), vol. II
Clarke, A. (ed.) *The Life and Times of Anthony Wood* (Oxford 1894)
Coleridge, S.T. *The Collected Letters of Samuel Taylor Coleridge*, ed. E.L. Criggs (Oxford 1959), Vol. III
Collins, A. (ed.) *Letters and Memorials of State in the reigns of Queen Mary, Queen Elizabeth, King James, King Charles I, part of the reign of King Charles II and Oliver's Usurpation ... from the Originals at Penshurst and from his majesty's Office of Papers*, 2 vols. (1742)
Daillé, J. *A Treatise Concerning the Right Use of The Fathers* (1651)
Dalrymple, J. *Memoirs of Great Britain and Ireland*, 2 vols. (1773), vol. II, appendix
D'Avaux, Count *The Negotiations of Count D'Avaux*, 4 vols. (1756), vols I–II
[De la Court, P. and De Witt, J.] *The True Interest and Political Maxims of The Republic of Holland* (1743)
D'Huart, S. *Inventaire des Archives Rohan-Bouillon* (Paris 1970)
Du Plessis Mornay, P. *A Woorke Concerning the Trewnesse of the Christian Religion* (1587), trans. Sir Philip Sidney.
Erskine-Hill, H. and Storey, G. (eds.) *Revolutionary Prose of the English Civil War* (Cambridge 1983)
Evelyn, J. *The Diary of John Evelyn*, ed. E.S. De Beer, vols. III–IV (Oxford 1955)
Falkland, Lucius Cary Viscount *Of the Infallibility of the Church of Rome, with Answer, and Reply* (1655)
Filmer, Sir Robert *The Anarchy of a Limited or Mixed Monarchy* (1648)
   Observations Upon Aristotles Politiques (1652)
   Observations Concerning the Originall of Government (1652)
   Patriarcha (1680)
   Patriarcha, ed. P. Laslett (1949)
Firth, C. and Rait (eds). *Acts and Ordinances of the Interregnum*, 3 vols. (1911), vols. I–II
Ford, Lord Grey *The Secret History of the Rye House Plot* (1754)
Forster, T. (ed.) *Original Letters of Locke, Algernon Sidney, and Anthony Lord Shaftesbury* (1830)
Gentillet, I. *Discours Contre Machiavel*, ed. A. Andrea and D. Stewart (Florence 1974)
Gilbert, J.T. *History of the Irish Confederation and the War in Ireland 1641–43*, 7 vols. (Dublin 1882–7)

Goodman, C. *How superior powers ought to be obeyed of their subjects and wherein they may lawfully by Gods word be disobeyed and resisted* (Geneva 1558; facsimile Amsterdam 1972)

Greville, Fulke *Life of Sir Philip Sidney* (Oxford 1907)

Grey, A. *Debates in the House of Commons 1667–94* (1763), vols. VI–X

Grotius, Hugo *De Jure Belli ac Pacis Libri Tres* (Oxford 1925), trans. F.W. Kelsey *Of the Law of Warre and Peace* (1655), trans. Clement Barksdale

Guizot, M. *Portraits Politiques* (Paris 1874)

Halifax (see Savile, George)

Hall, John *The Grounds and Reasons of Monarchy* (1651)

Hammond, Henry *Workes* (1674), ed. Fell
  A Defence of the Learned Hugo Grotius From the Accusations of Inward Socinianism and Outward Popery (1655)

Harrington, James *The Political Works of James Harrington*, ed. J.G.A. Pocock (Cambridge 1977)

Historical Manuscript Commission Reports:
  No. 7 Graham MSS
  77.1–77.6 De Lisle and Dudley MSS (6 vols.)
  No. 3 Northumberland MS
  No. 14 Ormonde MS vols. I–II
  No. 20 Dartmouth MS
  36.10 Ormonde MS
  63.2, 63.6 Egmont MS
  45.3, Buccleugh MS, Montague House Papers Vol. II
  78.4 Hastings MS

Hutchinson, L. *Memoirs of Colonel Hutchinson*, ed. J. Hutchinson (repr. 1965)

[Ireton, Henry] *The Humble Remonstrance of his Excellency the Lord General Fairfax* (16 Nov. 1648) in *The Parliamentary or Constitutional History of England from the earliest times to the restoration of Charles II*, 24 vols. (1751–62), vol. XVII

James II 'Life of James II 1660–98, written by Himself' in J. MacPherson (ed.), *Original Papers* (1775)

James, G.P.R. (ed.) *Letters Illustrative of the Reign of William III*, 3 vols. (1841), vol. I

Jefferson, Thomas *Writings* (New York 1984)

Journal of the House of Commons vols. III, V–VII (1679–81)

Journal of the House of Lords 1688, 1689

Jusserand, J.J. *Recueil des Instructions Données Aux Ambassadeurs et Ministres de France, vol. XXV: Angleterre* (Paris 1929)

Larkin, J.F. (ed.) *Stuart Royal Proclamations vol. 2: Proclamations of King Charles I 1625–1646* (Oxford 1983)

Locke, John *Second Treatise*, ed. J.W. Gough (Oxford 1966)
  Two Treatises of Government, ed. P. Laslett, 2nd edn (Cambridge 1967)

London Huguenot Society Publications Vol. XVI: Registers of the French Church, Threadneedle St, vol. III (1906)

Louis XIV *Mémoires pour les années 1661 et 1666*, ed. J. Longnon (Paris 1923)

Ludlow, Edmund *A Voyce From The Watchtower Pt 5 1660–62*, ed. A.B. Worden (1979) [For MS see Bodleian]
  Ludlows Memoirs, ed. C. Firth, 2 vols. (Oxford 1894)

Luttrell, N. *A Briefe Historical Relation of State Affairs* (Oxford 1857)

Machiavelli, N. *The Discourses*, ed. B. Crick (Harmondsworth 1985)

Milton, John   *Milton's Prose Works* vol. I, ed. J.A. St John (1848)
  Prose Works, vol. III (New York 1933)
  The Readie and Easye Way, 2nd edn (1659), ed. Erskine Hill and Storey (1983)
  The Tenure of Kings and Magistrates (1649)
Montagu, Edward   *The Journal of Edward Montagu first earl of Sandwich, admiral
  and general at sea 1659–1665*, ed. R.C. Anderson (Navy Records Society 1928)
Montesquieu   *The Spirit of the Laws* in M. Richter, *The Political Theory of Mon-
  tesquieu* (Cambridge 1977)
Nedham, M.   [see *Mercurius Politicus*, next section] *The Case of the Com-
  monwealth of England Stated*, ed. P.A. Knachel (Virginia 1968)
  The Excellency of a Free State (1656)
Neville, H.   *Plato Redivivus* (1st published 1680), in C. Robbins (ed.), *Two
  Republican Tracts* (Cambridge 1969)
Penn, W.   *The Works of William Penn*, 2 vols. (1756) [and see next section]
Pepys, S.   *The Diary of Samuel Pepys*, ed. Latham and Matthews, vols. II (1970)
  and IV (1971)
Plato   *Phaedrus; Phaedo; The Republic*; all in S. Buchanan (ed.), *The Portable
  Plato* (1982)
Ponet, John   *A shorte treatise of politike power and of the true obedience which
  subjectes owe to kinges and other civile governors* (Strasbourg 1556; facsimile
  Amsterdam 1972)
Puffendorf, Samuel von   *Histoire du Regne de Charles Gustave Roy de Suède*,
  2 vols. (Nuremberg 1697), vol. II.
Rousseau, J.J.   *The Social Contract and Discourses*, trans. and ed. G.D.H. Cole
  (1973)
  Political Writings, ed. C.E. Vaughan, 2 vols. (Oxford 1962)
Savile, George, Marquis of Halifax   *Complete Works*, ed. J.P. Kenyon (1969)
Scott, Sir W. (ed.)   *A Collection of Scarce and Valuable Tracts . . . of the late Lord
  Somers*, 13 vols. (1808–15), vols. VIII–IX
Sharp, A. (ed.)   *Political Ideas of the English Civil Wars 1641–1649* (1983)
Sidney, A.   *Sydney on Government: The Works of Algernon Sydney* (1772),
  J. Robertson (ed.) (and see section 1 'Sidney's writings' above)
St John, Henry, Viscount Bolingbroke   *The Works of Lord Bolingbroke*, vol. II
  (1967)
Sidney, Sir Philip   *The Complete Works of Sir Philip Sidney*, ed. A. Feiullerat
  (Cambridge 1923)
[State Trials]   *A Complete Collection of State Trials*, 33 vols. ed. T.B. Howell, vol.
  IX (1811)
Stubbe, Henry   *An Essay in Defence of the Good Old Cause . . . and A Vindication
  of the Hon Sir Henry Vane from the false aspersions of Mr. Baxter* (1659)
Temple, Sir John   *The Irish Rebellion: or An History of the Beginnings and first
  Progresse of the Generall Rebellion . . . 1641. Together With the Barbarous
  Cruelties and Bloody Massacres which ensued thereupon* (1646)
Temple, Sir William   *The Works of Sir William Temple*, 2 vols., ed. J. Swift (1950)
Thurloe, John   *A Collection of State Papers of John Thurloe esq*, ed. T. Birch, 7
  vols. (1742)
Toland, J. (ed.) James Harrington   *Oceana* (1771) (Toland's Preface)
Tyrrel, J.   *Bibliotheca Politica* (1718)
Vane, Sir Henry jnr.   *The Retired Mans Meditations* (1655)
White, Thomas   *Daillés Arts Discover'd*, (2nd edn, Paris 1654)

The Grounds of Obedience and Government (1655)
Whitelocke, Bulstrode   *Memorials of the English Affairs*, 4 vols. (Oxford 1853)

PAMPHLETS AND JOURNALS
A Brief History of the Succession (1681)
Account by the Sheriffs of What Passed at Algernon Sidney's Execution (1683)
A Dialogue at Oxford between a Tutor and a Gentleman, Formerly his Pupil, Concerning Government (1681)
A Dialogue between the Ghosts of the two Last Parliaments (1681)
Advice to the Men of Shaftesbury (1681)
A Letter from a Gentleman of Quality – Relating to the Succession (1679)
A Letter from Amsterdam to a Friend in England (1679)
A Letter on the Subject of the Succession (1679)
A Letter to a Noble Peer of the Realm about his late Speech and Petition to His Majesty (1681)
A Letter Written from the Tower by Mr Stephen Colledge (the Protestant Joyner) to Dick Janeway's Wife (1681)
Algernon Sidney's Farewell [n.d.]
Allen, Wm. [Sexby and Titus]   *Killing No Murder* (1657, repr. 1689)
Animadversions on the late Vindication of Slingsby Bethel esq. (1681)
An Account of the bloody massacre in Ireland (1678)
An Account of the Reasons which induced Charles II . . . to declare War against the States General . . . in 1672 (1689)
An Answer to the Second Letter from Legorn (1679/80)
An Answer to a Letter from a Gentleman of Quality (1681)
An Essay upon the Change of Manners, Being a second Part of the true Protestants Appeal to the City and Country (1681)
An Exact Account of the Tryal of Algernon Sidney esq. Who was Tryed at the Kings-Bench-Bar at Westminster (1683)
An Examination of the Impartial State of the Case of the Earl of Danby (1680)
An Explanation of the Lord Treasurers Letter to Mr. Montague . . . March 25th (1679)
An Impartial Account of the Arraignment, Trial and Condemnation of Thomas Late Earl of Strafford 1641 (1679)
An Impartial Account of the Proceedings at the Common Hall of the City of London at Guildhal June 24 1682 (1682)
An Impartial Survey of Such as are, and Such as are Not, Justly Qualified to sit in this Present Parliament (1679)
A Perfect Diurnall of some Passages in Parliament no. 303
A Pindarique Ode upon the late Horrid and Damnable Whiggish Plot (1683)
A Seasonable Address to both Houses of Parliament concerning the Succession, the Fears of Popery, and Arbitrary Government (1682)
A Seasonable Address to the . . . City of London upon their Present Electing of Sheriffs (1680)
A Seasonable Answer to a Late Pamphlet entitled The Vindication of Slingsby Bethel esq. (1681)
A Sober Vindication of the Reverend Dr and the Harmless Board (1682)
A Speech Made by a True Protestant Gentleman to Incourage the City of London to Petition for the Sitting of Parliament (1679/80)
A True and Exact History of the Succession (1681)

A True and Just Account of the Most Horrid and Bloody Plot Conspired against his Most Sacred Majesty (1683)

A True and Plain Account of the Discoveries Made in Scotland of the Late Conspiracies Against His Majesty and the Government (1685)

A Word Within Doors Concerning the Bill for Succession (1679)

A Word Without Doors, Concerning the Bill for Succession (1679)

Bedloe, W. *A Narrative and Impartial Discovery of the Horrid Popish Plot* (1678)

Bethel, S. *The Vindication of Slingsby Bethel esq From the Several Slanders Cast upon Him* (1681) [and see previous section]

Bohun, E. *A Defence of Sir Robert Filmer against the Mistakes and Misrepresentations of Algernon Sidney, Esq, in a Paper Delivered by him to the Sheriffs* (1684)

Burroughes, J. *A Briefe answer to Doctor Ferne's Book* (1643)

Cooke, E. *Memorabilia; Or the Most Remarkable Passages and Counsels Collected out of the Several Declarations and Speeches ... Made by the King* (1681)

Danvers, J. *Certain Queries Concerning Liberty of Conscience* (1648)

Diggs, T. *England's Defense. A Treatise Concerning Invasion* (1681)

Dryden, John *Prologue to the Duke of Guise* (1682)

England's Concern in the Case of H R H James Duke of York (1680)

Fair Warning, or the Burnt Child Dreads the Fire (1680)

Great and Weighty Considerations Relating to the ... Successor to the Crown (1680)

Goodman Country: To His Worship the City of London (1680)

His Majesties Declaration Defended, in a Letter to a friend (1681)

His Majesties Declaration ... touching the Causes and Reasons That Moved Him to Dissolve the Two Last Parliaments (1681)

His Majesties Most Gracious Speech ... to parliament (21 Oct. 1678)

Lettre de Felicitation de Milord Sidney aux Parisiens et a la Nation Francoise, ou ressurection de Milord Sidney (Paris, 1789)

Malice Defeated: A Vindication of Elizabeth Cellier (1680)

Marvell, A. *The Growth of Popery and Arbitrary Government* (Amsterdam 1677; repr. 1971)

Matchiavel Junior: or the Secret Arts of the Jesuites (1683)

Mercurius Politicus nos. 31–114 (Jan. 1650–Aug. 1652)

Modesty Triumphing over Impudence, or some notes upon a late Romance published by Elizabeth Cellier (1680)

More last Words ... of the True Protestant Elm-Board (1682)

Mr. Sidney his Self-Conviction: Or, his Dying Paper Condemn'd to Live for a Conviction to the Present Faction (1684)

Nedham, M. *Interest Will Not Lie* (1659) [and see previous section]

Notes Conferred, or a Dialogue Betwixt the Groaning Board, and a Jesuite (1682)

Penn, W. *England's Present Interest Considered* (1675)

    The Great Case of Liberty of Conscience once more Briefly Debated and Defended (1671)

    ('Philanglus') *Englands Great Interest in the Choice of this New Parliament* (1678) [and see previous section]

    Pereat Papa; or Reasons why a Popish Successor should not inherit (1679)

    Perfect Occurrences nos. 94 (1648), 145 (1649)

    'Philanglus', *The Protestant's Remonstrance against Pope and Presbyter* (1681)

'Philolaus', J.   *A Character of Popery and Arbitrary Government . . . [and] how [to] prevent the same, by Choosing Good Members to serve in this New Parliament* (1679)

Reasons offered by a Well-Wisher to the King and Kingdom against Addressing to the King with a petition for the Sitting of the Parliament (1681)

Reflections upon Colonel Sidney's Arcadia: The Old Cause (1684)

R.G.   *A Copy of a Letter from An Officer in the Army in Ireland* (1656; Exeter repr. 1974)

Settle, E.   *Remarks on Algernon Sidney's Paper Delivered to the Sheriffs at his Executio* (1684)

   The Character of a Popish Successor, and what we may expect from such a One (1681)

Shaftesbury, Anthony Ashley Cooper, Earl of, *A Letter from a Person of Quality to His Friend in the Country* (1675)

A Speech Made by a Noble Peer of the Realm (1681)

Sprat, T.   *A True Account of the Horrid Conspiracy* (1685)

Some Animadversions on the Paper Delivered to the Sheriffs by Algernon Sidney (1683)

The Act of Parliament of the 27th of Queen Elizabeth, To Preserve the Queens Person and Protestant Religion and Government, from the Attempts of the Papists (1679)

The Animadversions and Remarks upon Colonel Sydney's Paper Answered (1684)

The Case of Thomas Dangerfield, with some Remarkable Passages [from] the Tryal of Elizabeth Cellier (1680)

The Character of a Good Man, neither Whig nor Tory (1681)

The Character of a Modern Whig (1681)

The Character of a Rebellion and what England may Expect from One (1681)

The Character of a Tory (1681)

The Complaint of Liberty and Property against Arbitrary Government (1681)

The Condemnation, Behaviour, last Dying Words, and Execution of Algernon Sidney Esq (1683)

The Declaration of the Rebels Now in Arms in the West of Scotland (1679)

The French Intrigues Discovered. With the Methods and Arts to Retrench the Potency of France by Land and Sea (1681)

The Ghost of the Late House of Commons to the New One appointed to meet at Oxford (1681)

The Great and Weighty Considerations, Relating to the Duke of York . . . Considered (1680)

The History of Whiggism, or the Whiggish Plots . . . in the Reign of King Charles the First (1682)

The Humble Address of the Commons in Parliament Assembled. Presented to his Majesty Monday 28th day of November 1680

The Humble Representation and Petition of the Lords and the Commons Concerning the Romish Pries and Jesuits (1663)

The Last Will and Testament of Anthony King of Poland (1682)

The Last Words and Sayings of the True Protestant Elm-Board (1682)

The Loyal Protestants Vindication . . . By a Queen Elizabeth Protestant (1681)

The Parallel: or The New Specious Association an Old Rebellions Covenant (1682)

The Plot Reviv'd: or a Memorial of the late and present Popish Plots (1680)

The Popish Plot, Taken out of Several Depositions Made and Sworn before the Parliament (1678)
The Power of Kings Learnedly Asserted by Sir Robert Filmer, Kt. With a Preface of a Friend: Giving an Account of the Author and his Works (1680)
The Present Great Interest both of King and People (1680)
The Whigs Lamentation (1683)
The Proceedings of the Guild-Hall in London on Thursday July 29th 1680 (1680)
The Reformation. A Satyr [n.d.]
The Right Saddle upon the Right Mare (1681)
The Speech of Hodge the Clown from the top of the Mountain (1679)
The Speech of Sir Edmund Turner Knt, Speaker of the House of Commons, to the Kings most Excellent Majesty (1666)
The Speech of the Hon William Williams . . . upon the Electing of him Speaker (1680)
The Trial of . . . [those indicted] for the Riot at Guild-Hall on Midsummer-Day 1682 (1683)
The True Protestants Appeal to the City and Country (1681)
Tryal of Elizabeth Cellier (1680)
Tryal and Defence of Elizabeth Cellier for Writing a Scandalous Libel called Malice Defeated (1680)
The Tryal and Conviction of John Hampden Esq (1684)
The Tryal of William, Viscount Stafford, for High Treason (1681)
The Tryals and Condemnation of Thomas White, William Harcourt . . . John Fenwick [etc.] . . . all Jesuits and Priests (1679)
The Tryals of Thommas Walcot, William Hone, William Lord Russell, John Rous, and William Blagg for High Treason (1683)
The Tryals of William Ireland, Thomas Pickering, and John Grove (1678)
The Two Associations, One Subscribed by CLVI members of the House of Commons in the Year 1643, The other seized in the closet of the Earl of Shaftesbury (1681)
The White Rose; Vindicating the Right of Succession [n.d.]
To the Praise of Mrs. Cellier . . . on her Incomparable Book (1680)
Vox Populi, or The People's Claim to their Parliaments Sitting (1681)
Wolesly, Sir Charles   *Liberty of Conscience the Magistrates Interest* (1668)

SECONDARY SOURCES
BOOKS

Annas, J.   *Plato's Republic* (Oxford 1981)
Ashcraft, R. and Pocock, J.G.A. (eds.)   *John Locke* (Los Angeles 1980)
Ashcraft, R.   *Revolutionary Politics and John Locke's Two Treatises of Government* (Princeton 1986)
Ashley, M.   *John Wildman: Plotter and Postmaster* (1947)
Aulard, A.   *The French Revolution 1789–1804* (1910) vol. I
Aylmer, G. (ed.)   *The Interregnum* (1972)
Bailyn, B.   *The Ideological Origins of the American Revolution* (Cambridge, Mass. 1971)
Barker, E.   *The Political Thought of Plato and Aristotle* (New York 1959)
Beatty, E.C.O.   *William Penn as Social Philosopher* (New York 1939)

Bevan, E.   *Stoics and Sceptics* (Oxford 1913)

Bishop, M.   *The Life and Adventures of La Rochefoucauld* (Ithaca 1951)

Blackburne, G.M.   *Algernon Sidney: A Review* (1885)

Browning, A.   *Thomas Osborne, First Earl of Danby* 3 vols. (1951)

Buell, A.C.   *William Penn* (New York 1904)

Butler, M.   *Theatre and Crisis* (Cambridge 1984)

Cartwright, Julia   *Sacharissa* (1901)

Chandaman, C.H.   *The English Public Revenue 1660–88* (Oxford 1975)

Chase, Sidney R.   *Brief Memoirs of Algernon Sidney* (1835)

Church, W.,   *Richelieu and Reason of State* (Princeton 1972)

Clarke, J.   *The Life of James II* (1816) vol. I

Condren, C. and Cousins, A.D.   *The Political Identity of Andrew Marvell*
  (forthcoming)

Cornford, F.M.   *Before and After Socrates* (Cambridge 1932)

Coveney, P.J.   *France in Crisis 1620–75* (1977)

Cranston, M.   *John Locke* (New York 1979)

Cruikshanks, E.   *Ideology and Conspiracy: Aspects of Jacobitism* (Edinburgh
  1982)

Cust, R.   *The Forced Loan* (Oxford 1987)

Cust, R. and Hughes, A. (eds.)   *Conflict in Early Stuart England: Studies in Religion and Politics 1603–42* (1989)

Daly, J.   *Sir Robert Filmer and English Political Thought* (Toronto 1979)

Davis, J.C.   *Utopia and the Ideal Society* (Cambridge 1981)

De Sola Pinto, V.   *Peter Sterry, Platonist and Puritan* (Cambridge 1984)

Dickinson, H.T.   *Liberty and Property* (1977)

Dictionary of National Biography vols. XX, XIIV, X

Du Boulay, F.R. and Barron, C.M. (eds.)   *The Reign of Richard II* (1971)

Dunn, J.   *The Political Thought of John Locke* (Cambridge 1968)

Dunn, M.M. and R.S.   *The Papers of William Penn* 2 vols. (1981–2)

Dunn, M.M.   *William Penn: Politics and Conscience* (Princeton 1967)

Elliott, J.H.   *Richelieu and Olivares* (Cambridge 1984)

Everitt, A.   *The Community of Kent in the Great Rebellion* (Leicester 1973)

Ewald, A.C.   *The Life and Times of Algernon Sidney* 2 vols. (1873)

Feiling, K.   *A History of the Tory Party 1640–1914* (Oxford 1924)

Ferguson, J.   *Robert Ferguson the Plotter* (1877)

Fink, Zera   *The Classical Republicans* (Evanston 1945)

Finlayson, M.   *Historians, Puritanism and the English Revolution* (Toronto 1984)

Fletcher, A.   *Sussex 1600–1660* (1975)

Foxcroft, H.C.   *The Life and Letters of Sir George Savile* 2 vols. (1898; repr. 1986)

Franklin, J.H.   *Constitutionalism and Resistance in the Sixteenth Century* (New
  York 1969)

Gardiner, S.R.   *History of the Great Civil War 1642–9* 4 vols. (1893)
  History of the Commonwealth and Protectorate 3 vols. (1894–1901)

Geyl, P.   *The Netherlands in the Seventeenth Century Part Two 1648–1715* (1964)
  Orange and Stuart (1969)

Goldie, M., Harris, T. and Seaward, P. (eds.)   *The Politics of Religion in Restoration England* (Oxford 1990)

Gooch, G.P.   *Germany and the French Revolution* (1920)
  English Political Thought in England from Bacon to Halifax (Oxford 1946)

Goubert, P.   *Louis XIV and Twenty Million Frenchmen* (1970)

Greaves, R.   *Deliver Us from Evil: The Radical Underground 1660–63* (1987)
Greaves, R. and Zaller, R.   *Biographical Dictionary of British Radicals in the Seventeenth Century* 3 vols. (Brighton 1982–4)
Gunn, J.A.W.   *Politics and the Public Interest in the Seventeenth Century* (1969)
Haley, K.H.D.   *The First Earl of Shaftesbury* (Oxford 1968)
   William of Orange and the English Opposition 1672–4 (1953)
Haigh, C.   *Elizabeth I* (1988)
Haitsma Mulier Eco, O.G.   *The Myth of Venice and Dutch Republican Thought in the Seventeenth Century* (Assen 1980)
Harris, R.W.   *Clarendon and the English Revolution* (1983)
Harris, T.   *London Crowds in the Reign of Charles II* (Cambridge 1987)
Hamilton, A.C.   *Sir Philip Sidney* (Cambridge 1977)
Henning, D. (ed.)   *The House of Commons 1660–90* (1983)
Hibbard, C.   *Charles I and the Popish Plot* (North Carolina 1983)
Hill, C.   *Milton and the English Revolution* (1977)
   The Experience of Defeat (1984)
   The Intellectual Origins of the English Revolution (Oxford 1965)
Hirschman, O.W.   *The Passions and the Interests* (Princeton 1977)
Hirst, D.   *The Representative of the People?* (1975)
   Authority and Conflict: England 1603–58 (1986)
Holmes, G.   *British Politics in the Age of Anne* (revised edn 1987)
Hopkins, P.   *Glencoe and the End of the Highland Wars* (Edinburgh 1986)
Hull, W.   *Benjamin Furly and Quakerism in Rotterdam* (Swarthmore, Penn., 1941)
   William Penn (New York 1937)
Hutton, Ronald   *The Restoration* (Oxford 1986)
Israel, J. (ed.)   *The Anglo-Dutch Moment* (Cambridge 1991)
Jenkins, P.   *The Making of a Ruling Class* (Cambridge 1983)
Jones, J.R.   *The First Whigs* (1961)
   Country and Court: England 1658–1714 (1978)
Judson, M.   *The Political Thought of Henry Vane the Younger* (Philadelphia 1969)
Karsten, P.   *Patriot Heroes in England and America* (Wisconsin 1978)
Keeton, G.W.   *Lord Chancellor Jeffreys and the Stuart Cause* (1965)
Kenyon, J.P.   *Robert Spencer, Earl of Sunderland 1641–1703* (Cambridge 1958)
   Revolution Principles (Cambridge 1977)
   The Popish Plot (1974)
Keohane, N.O.   *Philosophy and the State in France: From the Renaissance To The Enlightenment* (Princeton 1980)
Kishlansky, M.   *The Rise of The New Model Army* (Cambridge 1979)
   Parliamentary Selection (Cambridge 1986)
Knowles, W.E. (ed.)   *Lorenzo Magalotti at the Court of Charles II* (Ontario 1980)
Lamont, W.   *Richard Baxter and the Millenium* (1979)
Larkin, J.F. (ed.)   *Stuart Royal Proclamations* vol. III *Proclamations of King Charles I 1625–1646* (Oxford 1983)
Leconfield, Lord   *Petworth Manor in the Seventeenth Century* (1954)
Lenman, B.   *The Jacobite Risings in Britain 1689–1746* (1980)
Levine, M.   *The Early Elizabethan Succession Question 1558–1568* (Stanford 1966)
Lichtenstein, A.   *Henry More* (Cambridge 1962)
Lough, J.   *An Introduction to Seventeenth Century France* (1954)
   (ed.)   *Locke's Travels in France* (1953)

Macaulay, T.B.   *The History of England during the Reigns of King William, Queen Anne, and King George I, with an introductory review of the reigns of the Royal brothers Charles and James* 2 vols. (1844–6)
Maier, P.   *From Resistance to Revolution* (1973)
Maravall, J.A.   *La philosophie politique espagnole au XVII siècle* (Paris 1955)
Maycock, A.   *Chronicles of Little Gidding* (1954)
McPherson, J.   *A History of Great Britain from the Restoration to the Accession of the House of Hanover* (1775)
Meadley, G.W.   *Memoirs of Algernon Sidney* (1813)
Mettam, F. (ed.) *Government and Society in Louis XIV's France* (1977)
Miller, J.   *Popery and Politics in England 1660–1688* (Cambridge 1973)
   Restoration England: The Reign of Charles II (1985)
Morrall, J.B.   *Aristotle* (1977)
Morrill, J.S.   *The Revolt of the Provinces* (1980)
   (ed.)   *Oliver Cromwell and the English Revolution* (1990)
Mousnier, R.   *The Institutions of France under the Absolute Monarchy 1598–1789* (Chicago 1974)
Oestrich, G.   *Neostoicism and the Early Modern State* (Cambridge 1982)
Ogg, D.   *England in the Reign of Charles II* 2 vols. (Oxford 1955)
Packer, J.W.   *The Transformation of Anglicanism 1643–60 With Special Reference to Henry Hammond* (1969)
Parker, G.   *Europe in Crisis 1598–1648* (1979)
Parker, H.T.   *The Cult of Antiquity and the French Revolutionaries* (Chicago 1937)
Parker, W.   *John Milton* (Oxford 1968)
Plumb, J.   *The Growth of Political Stability in England 1675–1725* (1967)
Pocock, J.G.A.   *The Ancient Constitution and the Feudal Law: A Reissue with Retrospect* (Cambridge 1987)
   (ed.)   *The Political Works of James Harrington* (Cambridge 1977)
   The Machiavellian Moment (Princeton 1975)
   Virtue, Commerce and History (Cambridge 1985)
Pontalis, A.L.   *John De Witt* 2 vols. (1885)
Powicke, F.J.   *The Cambridge Platonists* (1926)
Prendergast, J.P.   *The Cromwellian Settlement in Ireland* (Dublin 1922)
Raab, F.   *The English Face of Machiavelli* (1964)
Ralph, J.   *The History of England* 2 vols. (1744)
Ranke, L. von   *The History of the Popes* (1908)
   The History of England vol. IV (Oxford 1875)
Robbins, C.   *The Eighteenth Century Commonwealthsman* (Cambridge, Mass. 1959)
   (ed.)   *Two English Republican Tracts* (Cambridge 1969)
Robinson, F.G.   *The Shape of Things Known* (Cambridge, Mass. 1922)
Ronalds, F.S.   *The Attempted Whig Revolution of 1678–81* (Urbana 1937)
Rothkrug, L.   *Opposition to Louis XIV* (Princeton 1965)
Rowe, V.A.   *Sir Henry Vane the Younger* (1970)
Rowen, H.   *John De Witt* (Princeton 1978)
   The Low Countries in Early Modern Times (1972)
Russell, B.   *The History of Western Philosophy* (1946)
Russell, C.S.R.   *The Crisis of Parliaments: English History 1509–1660* (Oxford 1971)
Sabine, G.H.   *A History of Political Theory* (1938)

Salmon, J.H.M.   *The French Religious Wars in English Political Thought* (Oxford 1959)
Sanford and Townsend   *The Great Governing Families of England* (1865)
Schochet, G.   *Patriarchalism in Political Thought* (Oxford 1975)
Scott, J.   *Algernon Sidney and the English Republic 1623–1677* (Cambridge 1988)
Seaward, P.   *The Cavalier Parliament and the Reconstruction of the Old Regime 1661–1667* (Cambridge 1989)
Sensabaugh, G.F.   *That Grand Whig Milton* (Stanford 1952)
Shackleton, R.   *Montesquieu: A Critical Biography* (Oxford 1961)
Sharpe, K. (ed.)   *Faction and Parliament* (Oxford 1978)
Skinner, Q.   *The Foundations of Modern Political Thought* 2 vols. (Cambridge 1978)
Sommerville, J.   *Politics and Ideology 1603–40* (Cambridge 1986)
Spalding, R.   *The Improbable Puritan* (1975)
Speck, W.   *Reluctant Revolutionaries* (1988)
Stone, L.   *The Causes of the English Revolution* (1972)
Sutherland, James   *English Literature of the Late Seventeenth Century* (Oxford 1969)
Thomas, K.   *Religion and the Decline of Magic* (London 1971)
Thomas-Stanford   *Sussex in the English Civil War* (1910)
Trevelyan, G.M.   *The English Revolution 1688–9* (1939)
Trevor-Roper, H.   *Princes and Artists* (1976)
Tuck, R.   *Natural Rights Theories* (Cambridge 1979)
Underdown, D.   *Prides Purge* (Oxford 1971)
Van Santvoord, G.   *A Life of Algernon Sidney with Sketches of Some of his Contemporaries* (New York 1851)
Van Someren, L.   *Umpire to the Nations* (1965)
Veall, D.   *The Popular Movement for Law Reform 1640–60* (Oxford 1970)
Walcott, R.   *Eighteenth Century British Politics* (1959)
Wallace, J.M.   *Destiny His Choice: The Loyalism of Andrew Marvell* (Cambridge 1968)
Watkins, W.N.   *Hobbes System of Ideas* (1965)
Western, J.R.   *Monarchy and Revolution* (1972)
Whiting, C.   *Studies in English Puritanism 1660–1688* (1968)
Wildes, H.E.   *William Penn* (New York 1975)
Wilson, C.   *Profit and Power* (1957)
Winthrop, R.C.   *Addresses and Speeches 1852–1867* (Boston 1867)
Wittreich, J.A.   *The Romantics on Milton* (1970)
Woolrych, A.   *Commonwealth to Protectorate* (Oxford 1982)
Worden, A.B.   *The Rump Parliament 1648–53* (Cambridge 1974)
Young, R.B. and Madson, W.G.   *Three Studies in the Renaissance: Sidney, Jonson, Milton* (Yale 1958)
Yule, G.   *The Independents in the English Civil War* (Cambridge 1958)
Zagorin, P.   *A History of Political Thought in the English Revolution* (1954)

ARTICLES

Adamson, J.S.A. 'Oliver Cromwell and the Long Parliament' in J.S. Morrill (ed.), *Oliver Cromwell and the English Revolution* (1990)
Anthony, H.S. 'Mercurius Politicus under Milton', *Journal of the History of Ideas* 27 (1966)

Ashcraft, R. 'Revolutionary Politics and Locke's *Two Treatises of Government: Radicalism and Lockean Political Thought*', *Political Theory* 8:4 (1980)

Behrens, B. 'The Whig Theory of the Constitution in the Reign of Charles II', *Cambridge Historical Journal* 7:1 (1941)

Browning, A. 'Parties and Party Organisation in the Reign of Charles II', *Transactions of the Royal Historical Society*, 4th series, 30 (1948)

Burke, P. 'Tacitism' in T.A. Dorey (ed.), *Tacitus* (1969)

Butler, M. ' "Mercurius Brittanicus": A Case Study in Caroline Theatre', *Historical Journal* 27:4 (1984)

Cant, R. 'The Earl of Leicester's Embassy to Denmark 1632', *English Historical Review* 54 (1949)

Colie, R. 'John Locke in the Republic of Letters' in E.H. Kossman (ed.), *Britain and The Netherlands I* (1960)

Connif, J. 'Reason and History in Early Whig Thought; The Case of Algernon Sidney', *Journal of the History of Ideas* 43:3 (1982)

Cust, R. 'News and Politics in Early Seventeenth Century England', *Past and Present* 112 (1986)

Dahlgren, S. 'Charles X and the Constitution' in M. Roberts (ed.), *Sweden's Age of Greatness* (1973)

Davis, J.C. 'Pocock's Harrington: Grace, Nature and Art in the Classical Republicanism of James Harrington', *Historical Journal* 24:3 (1981)

Figgis, J.N. 'On Some Political Theories of the Early Jesuits', *Transactions of the Royal Historical Society*, new series 11 (1897)

Furley, O.W. 'The Whig Exclusionists: Pamphlet Literature in the Exclusion Campaign 1979–81', *Cambridge Historical Journal* 13:1 (1957)

Goldie, M.A. 'The Roots of True Whiggism 1688–94', *History of Political Thought* 1 (1980)

Haydon, B. 'Algernon Sidney 1623–83', *Archaeologia Cantiana* 76 (1961)

Kishlansky, M. 'Ideology and Politics in the Parliamentary Armies 1645–9' in John Morrill (ed.), *Reactions to the English Civil War 1642–49* (1982)

Kossman, E.H. 'The Development of Dutch Political Theory in the Seventeenth Century' in Kossman (ed.), *Britain and the Netherlands I* (1960)

Lipson, E. 'The Elections to the Exclusion Parliaments 1678–81', *English Historical Review* 28 (1913)

MacInnes, A. 'When was the English Revolution?', *History* 63:221 (1982)

Miller, J. 'The Potential for Absolutism in Later Stuart England', *History* 69 (1984)

Milne, D. 'The Results of the Rye House Plot and their Influence upon the Revolution of 1688', *Transactions of the Royal Historical Society*, 5th series, 1 (1951)

Nash, G.B. 'The Framing of Government; Pennsylvania', *William and Mary Quarterly* 23 (1966)

Pearl, V. 'Royal Independents in the English Civil War', *Transactions of the Royal Historical Society*, 5th series, 18 (1968)

Pocock, J.G.A. 'The Onely Politician', *Historical Studies: Australia and New Zealand* 12 (1965–7)

'The History of British Political Thought: The Creation of a Center', *Journal of British Studies* 24:3 (1985)

Reay, B. 'The Quakers, 1659 and The Restoration of Monarchy', *History* 63 (1978)

Robbins, C. 'Algernon Sidney's *Discourses Concerning Government:* Textbook of Revolution', *William and Mary Quarterly* 3rd series, 4 (1947)

378   *Bibliography*

Roorda, D.J. 'The Ruling Classes in Holland in the Seventeenth Century', *Britain and The Netherlands II* (Utrecht 1964)

Rowe, K.T. 'Romantic Love and Parental Authority in Sidney's Arcadia' in *Contributions in Moderr. Philology* no. 4 (Michigan, April 1947)

Russell, C.S.R. 'The British Context of the English Civil War', *History* 42 (1987)

Salmon, J.H.M 'Algernon Sidney and the Rye House Plot', *History Today* 4:10 (1954)

Scott, J. 'England's Troubles: Exhuming the Popish Plot' in M. Goldie, T. Harris and P. Seaward (eds.), *The Politics of Religion in Restoration England* (Oxford 1990)

  'Radicalism and Restoration: The Shape of the Stuart Experience', *Historical Journal* 31:2 (1988)

Shackleton, R. 'Montesquieu and Machiavelli: A Reappraisal', *Comparative Literature Studies* 1:1 (1964)

Smit, J.W. 'The Netherlands and Europe in the Seventeenth and Eighteenth Centuries' in E.H. Kossman and J.S. Bromley (eds.), *Britain and the Netherlands in Europe and Asia* (1968)

Sommerville, J. 'From Suarez to Filmer: A Reappraisal', *Historical Journal* 25 (1982)

Tawney, R.H. 'Harrington's Interpretation of His Age', *Proceedings of the British Academy* 28 (1941)

Thirsk, J. 'Younger sons in the Seventeenth Century', *History* 54 (1969)

Trevor-Roper, H. 'Cromwell and His Parliaments' in *Religion, The Reformation and Social Change* (1967)

Tuck, R. 'The Ancient Law of Freedom: John Selden and the Civil War' in John Morrill (ed.), *Reactions to the English Civil War 1642–49* (1982)

  'A New Date for Filmer's *Patriarcha*', *Historical Journal* 29:1 (1986)

Worden, A.B. 'Classical Republicanism and the Puritan Revolution' in A.B. Worden, V. Pearl and H. Lloyd-Jones (eds.), *History and Imagination: Essays in Honour of H.R. Trevor-Roper* (1981)

  'The Commonwealth Kidney of Algernon Sidney', *Journal of British Studies* 24 (Jan. 1985)

UNPUBLISHED THESES

Dzelzainis, M. 'The Ideological Context of John Milton's *History of Britain*', Cambridge PhD 1983

Furley, O.W. 'The Origins and Early Development of the Whig Party, with special reference to Shaftesbury and Locke', Oxford BLitt 1953

Hopkins, P. 'Aspects of Jacobite Conspiracy in England in the Reign of William III', Cambridge PhD 1981

Houlbrooke, M.E. 'Paul Barillon's Embassy in England 1677–88', Oxford MPhil 1971

Knights, Mark 'Politics and Opinion during the Exclusion Crisis 1678–81', Oxford DPhil 1989

Milne, D. 'The Rye House Plot and its Consequences until 1685', London PhD 1948

Sommerville, M.R. 'Independent Thought 1603–49', Cambridge PhD 1982

Walker, J. 'The Republican Party in England from the Restoration to the Revolution', Manchester PhD 1930

Ward, I. 'The English Peerage 1648–60: Government, Authority and Estate', Cambridge PhD 1989

Willey, F.R. 'The Independent Coalition and Changing Parliamentary Alignments December 1646–January 1648', Cambridge PhD 1971

INDEX

Cambridge Studies in Early Modern British History